Barry E. Cushing

University of Utah

Accounting Information Systems and Business Organizations

Third Edition

 ADDISON-WESLEY PUBLISHING COMPANY
Reading, Massachusetts   Menlo Park, California
London   Amsterdam   Don Mills, Ontario   Sydney

Library of Congress Cataloging in Publication Data

Cushing, Barry E.
 Accounting information systems and business
organizations.

 1. Accounting—Data processing.   2. Management
information systems.   3. Information storage and
retrieval systems—Accounting.   I. Title.
HF5679.C84   1982   657'.028'54   81-2411
ISBN 0-201-10111-4   AACR2

ISBN 0-201-10111-4
BCDEFGHIJ-HA-89876543

Preface

Today's professional accountant performs in a world that is dynamic and complex. Progress in information technology is being made at an increasing rate. Patterns of organizational behavior are evolving rapidly. Economic and legal considerations are having a much greater impact upon the work of accountants. All of these environmental trends require the accounting student of today to be better prepared than ever before to enter the accounting profession.

A central feature of accounting work in today's business world is the interaction of accounting professionals with information systems. As the major users of information systems in organizations, accountants must participate in their design and understand their operation. Accounting managers must measure and evaluate the performance of information systems. Internal and external auditors must assess the quality of information processing and evaluate the accuracy of information output. The major share of the work of accounting consultants is in the design, implementation, and evaluation of information systems.

To be prepared adequately for a career in the accounting profession, today's accounting student must acquire a basic knowledge of information systems and their role in the performance of the accounting function in contemporary business organizations. Fundamental to this basic knowledge are (1) an understanding of the patterns of flow of accounting data and information in business, (2) a familiarity with the tools of accounting systems work, such as flowcharting, (3) an understanding of the use of computer technology in information processing, and (4) a thorough knowledge of the principle of internal control and its application in various organizational contexts. The objective of this book is to provide students with these essential elements of preparation for an accounting career. The goal is to provide a foundation for the development of today's accounting students into tomorrow's users, auditors, and managers of information systems.

This book is intended for use in a one-semester course in accounting information systems for advanced undergraduate accounting majors and for others interested in business applications of computers. Introductory financial and managerial accounting courses are necessary prerequisites, and an introductory course in data processing that covers a computer language is helpful. The book should also serve as a useful supplement either to graduate or advanced undergraduate courses in management information systems.

Organization

The third edition has the same basic structure as the first two editions. The book is divided into four parts. Part I, consisting of four chapters, reviews several underlying concepts that are basic to an understanding of any kind of accounting information system—regardless of the technology employed. These include principles and practices of business organizations, responsibility accounting, records management, information coding, file processing, and internal control concepts and techniques.

Part II, which contains five chapters, examines contemporary information technology from an accounting perspective. The first three of these chapters introduce basic hardware and software concepts. The important techniques of systems and program flowcharting are introduced here. The last two chapters of Part II review the more advanced topics of data base management systems and real-time systems.

Part III, which encompasses six chapters, explores a variety of issues relating to the management of information technology, including systems planning, management involvement in systems, and systems selection and acquisition. Also covered in Part III are numerous techniques of systems work, including work measurement, document flowcharting, reliability analysis, feasibility studies, point scoring, PERT, and various control and auditing techniques.

Part IV, which consists of five chapters, integrates the first three parts by providing a detailed look at applications of accounting information systems in a typical business organization. This section discusses the information needs of the marketing, logistics, personnel, and finance functions in business and explains the accounting processes and data bases that help to fulfill those needs. Within each application area, manual, computerized batch processing, and real-time systems are described and contrasted.

Changes in the Third Edition

One new chapter has been added to this edition, and significant changes have been made to several of the other nineteen chapters. Many new photographs and illustrations have been incorporated. Furthermore, several new problems and cases have been added, and many others have been revised to reflect changes made in the text.

The following list summarizes by chapter the major changes that have been made in the text.

1. Chapter 1 opens with a discussion entitled "Why Study Accounting Information Systems?" in order to provide students with an initial motivation for studying the subject.

2. Chapter 2 compares and contrasts functional and divisional forms of organization structure.

3. Chapter 3 contains a new section dealing with Principles of Forms Design.

4. Chapter 4 treats the impact of the Foreign Corrupt Practices Act.

5. Chapters 5 and 6 have been completely restructured. Coverage of punched card systems has been dropped. Chapter 5 contains an expanded section on Basic Computer Concepts, and a new section on Computer Data Entry that expands upon and replaces the treatment of input devices and media formerly contained in Chapter 6. Chapter 6 contains a new section on Computer Hardware Configurations that encompasses the material on minicomputers formerly found in Chapter 5. Chapter 6 also includes coverage of microcomputers and larger computer systems. The material on systems flowcharting formerly found in both Chapters 5 and 6 has been combined and placed in Chapter 6.

6. Chapter 8 has been modified in order to make the subject of data base management more understandable to undergraduate students. A section on Putting Data Base Concepts to Work has been added that introduces the concepts of the data dictionary and the relational data base.

7. Chapter 9 contains expanded coverage of distributed processing and data communications networks.

8. Chapter 10 introduces Nolan's "Stage Hypothesis" of data processing evolution in organizations.

9. Chapter 11 includes coverage of decision support systems and computer graphics.

10. Chapter 13 describes Gantt charts as a means of planning and scheduling systems projects.

11. Chapter 14 contains an expanded treatment of controls in online systems.

12. Chapter 15 is the new chapter, entitled "Auditing of Computer-Based Information Systems." Its two largest sections deal with the review and evaluation of internal control in EDP systems and with computer-assisted auditing techniques.

13. Chapters 16–20 (formerly 15–19) now incorporate a description of the data base structure (schema) associated with each of the functional areas. Furthermore, the computerized batch processing system descriptions in each chapter have been modified to incorporate magnetic disk, rather than magnetic tape, as the primary file storage medium.

Teaching Aids

From the very beginning, my guiding objective in preparing this book has been to simplify the teaching of accounting information systems by freeing the instructor from the burden of locating, assembling, and distributing materials and enabling him or her to concentrate on classroom presentation and discussion. I view this book and the related materials available from Addison-Wesley as not just a textbook but as a teaching system. The major elements of this teaching system follow.

1. Over 200 figures containing photographs and diagrams illustrating major concepts are contained in the book.

2. Over 250 discussion questions and problems and cases suitable for assignment to students appear at the end of each chapter. These include selected items from professional examinations, such as the CPA, CIA, and CMA examinations, for those instructors who wish to expose their students to them.

3. An Instructor's Resource Guide is available to instructors who consider adoption of the book. For each chapter the guide contains (a) a one-page outline of major topics, suitable for reproduction in transparency form, (b) a brief discussion of the content and objectives of each problem, (c) guidelines for leading a discussion of each discussion question, (d) suggested solutions for each of the problems and cases, and (e) ten or more multiple-choice questions suitable for use in quizzes covering the material in the chapter. Furthermore, the solutions to the problems and cases have been paginated in a modular fashion in order to facilitate the preparation of transparencies of the solutions.

4. A bibliography is included at the back of each chapter, and footnotes have been used liberally within the text. This should help those instructors who wish to locate background material or additional readings for assignment to their students.

5. The book, *Accounting Information Systems: A Book of Readings with Cases,* by James R. Davis and me (Addison-Wesley, 1980) was prepared with the idea of supplementing this book with outside readings organized according to the same topical outline, and with more complex and comprehensive cases.

By incorporating these features, I have attempted to develop a comprehensive teaching package that will render the teaching of accounting systems courses an enjoyable experience rather than an unwelcome burden.

Acknowledgments

I am indebted to numerous faculty members throughout the country who have adopted the earlier editions and who have been generous with their suggestions for improvements. Among those who have been most helpful are Professors Myles Stern of Wayne State University, Fred Davis of North Texas State University, Marshall Romney of Brigham Young University, Robert Baker of the University of South Carolina, John Wragge of the University of Florida, Howard Shapiro of Eastern Washington University, Norman Tooby of Notre-Dame de Grâce, and Norman Pendegraft of California State University, Chico.

Special thanks are extended to Jim Coaklay and David Denton, Ph.D. candidates at the University of Utah, for their assistance in preparing illustrations and problem solutions, and for other helpful suggestions.

Suggestions and comments on the text and the related materials are welcome.

Salt Lake City, Utah   Barry E. Cushing
January 1982

Contents

Part 2
The Technology of Information Systems

Part **3**

Systems Management

Part **4**
Accounting Information Systems Applications

Part 1

Conceptual Foundation of Accounting Information Systems

Chapter 1

Accounting Information Systems: An Overview

Accounting information is essential to the efficient management of economic affairs. Within a business organization, accounting information is produced by a system. Most readers are probably familiar with many of the elements of such systems. These elements include journals, ledgers, and other records, as well as the people who carry out the procedures necessary to the operation of the system. And increasingly they include machines designed to relieve people of the burden of routine and repetitive tasks. The purpose of this book is to develop an understanding of these accounting information systems—the elements they contain, the ways in which they are designed, and the role they play in supplying information to those requiring it, both within the business organization and outside of it.

Why Study Accounting Information Systems?

Accounting students often ask why a course in accounting information systems is a necessary part of the accounting curriculum. Such a course is quite different in structure and content from other accounting courses, which leads students to question its relevance. However, there are several reasons why the student's knowledge of accounting is not complete without an understanding of accounting information systems.

In most other accounting courses, the student is placed in the role of an information user. It is assumed that certain information is available to the student, who will address such questions as (1) how to account for the information, (2) how to re-

2

port the information to managers, stockholders, taxing authorities, or other government bodies, or (3) how to audit the information. These questions are certainly relevant, but by focusing only on these, most accounting courses virtually ignore another very relevant question—Where did the information come from?

The answer is, of course, that the information used by accountants, managers, auditors, etc. is produced by an information system. This raises a number of other questions: (1) Who decides what information is relevant for a particular purpose? (2) How do they make that decision? (3) What steps are required in order to obtain the relevant information and make it available? (4) What resources (people, machines, money, etc.) are consumed in obtaining the information and making it available? (5) What is the most cost-effective way of coordinating the necessary resources to perform the required steps? (6) Is the value of the information worth the cost of producing it? (7) How can it be ensured that the information is available on a timely basis? (8) How can it be ensured that the information is accurate and reliable? These are the kinds of questions that are addressed by a course in accounting information systems. Virtually all organizations must find answers to these questions —and in most organizations the accountant plays a central role (often a dominant role) in finding these answers.

The accounting student of today may tomorrow become an auditor, accountant, manager, or management consultant. Each of these positions requires a close involvement with the information system. For example, one of the auditor's main objectives is to evaluate the accuracy of information, and one of the most common approaches used by auditors for this purpose is a detailed assessment of the reliability of the information system. The accountant—whether in industry, government, or nonprofit organizations—is likely to have a major responsibility for the evaluation of existing information systems and the design of new ones. Accountants at the managerial level are often directly responsible for the management of the information systems department. Finally, many accountants become management consultants because of the opportunity to employ more effectively their expertise in the design, evaluation, and management of information systems.

Within the past several years an ongoing revolution in information technology has continued to exert a profound effect on accounting information systems (as well as all other types of information systems). The driving force behind this revolution is, of course, the computer. In virtually all large organizations, and in many smaller ones as well, the computer is responsible for processing accounting transactions and preparing accounting reports. As computers become smaller, faster, more reliable, easier to use, and less expensive, this trend toward the computerization of accounting work will continue. This development makes it even more essential for the accounting student to understand accounting information systems, and especially the role of the computer in these systems. The organization of the future that does not use a computer to do its accounting work will be a rare exception. Therefore a course in accounting information systems that emphasizes the role of the computer is an essential element of a student's preparation for a career in accounting.

This belief is widely shared by accounting educators as well as professional accountants. For example, the following statement was issued by a joint task force of the American Accounting Association (representing accounting educators) and the American Institute of CPAs.

> *The accounting graduate will very likely be involved in the use of the computer. Corporations are expanding their data processing applications, and CPA firms are also increasingly using computer systems in-house. (The availability of lower cost and easier to use computing equipment has accelerated this trend.)*
>
> *The accounting graduate should not start a career in awe—or fear—of a computerized accounting system. Rather, the graduate should have a good appreciation of the benefits and drawbacks of a computer system as well as a general understanding of its operation.* [1]

It is true that most undergraduate accounting and business curricula have incorporated computer education for many years. However, many prominent practicing accountants feel that the emphasis in such education has been misplaced. For example, one describes educational deficiencies of newly hired staff auditors as follows.

> *The first [deficiency] involves computer applications in business. Their [students] experience with computers has been in a problem-solving mode, using canned packages or programming rather simple mathematical problems. They seem to have very little feel for accounting transaction processing: the concepts of files, transaction updates, editing, reporting, and so forth. The second common deficiency was in flowcharting analysis and documentation, not strictly limited to computers, but emphasizing computers.* [2]

Although general coursework dealing with computers and electronic data processing is important and useful, many accounting students are still left with a gap in their knowledge of how modern information technology relates to accounting. This book is written with the intention of closing this gap and providing a more solid foundation of knowledge for future accounting graduates who will participate in the evaluation, design, audit, and management of accounting information systems.

The Role of the Accounting Information System

Virtually all organizations—from businesses and government agencies to hospitals, educational institutions, and churches—have an accounting information system. Among these groups, the accounting information systems of business organizations tend to be the most highly developed and innovative, and for this reason will be the primary focus of this book. However, many of the same concepts, techniques, and principles are equally applicable to accounting information systems in other kinds of organizations.

[1] *Committee on Accounting Education, American Accounting Association, and Computer Education Subcommittee, American Institute of Certified Public Accountants. "Inclusion of EDP in an Undergraduate Auditing Curriculum: Some Possible Approaches,"* The Accounting Review *49 (October 1971), p. 863.*

[2] *Michael R. Moore, "Undergraduate Computer Curriculum Requirements for Entering Staff in Accounting and Auditing," in* Education for Expanding Computer Curriculums, *edited by Daniel L. Sweeney (New York: American Institute of Certified Public Accountants, Inc., 1976), p. 7.*

The modern business organization served by the accounting information system is a very complex institution. Such an organization may employ thousands of people in tasks ranging from the development and engineering of new products to the management of a large sales force. The activities of prominent companies generate interest in many segments of society—customers, suppliers, employees, lenders, stockholders, and the various governments under whose jurisdiction it operates.

How can the modern business organization plan, coordinate, and control the multitude of activities that it undertakes? How can it supply information to the many people and institutions that are interested in its activities? The accounting information system plays a vital role in accomplishing these tasks. Figure 1.1 exhibits the relationship of the accounting information system to the business organization and to the environment (indicated by the large E-shaped structure to the left) of which the business organization is a part. Several aspects of this diagram will be referred to at various points in this section.

It is useful to examine accounting information systems from the viewpoint of users who utilize accounting information as a basis for making decisions. There are two basic categories of such users—those external to the business organization, and those internal (management). External users are many and varied. Their needs are met to some extent by the publication of general purpose financial statements, such as the income statement and balance sheet. The subset of accounting that is concerned with the information needs of external users is known as *financial accounting*.

Internal users are also many and varied, but their needs for information do reflect a common objective—to maximize the economic well-being of the business organization in society. *Management accounting* is the subset of accounting concerned with internal information needs and how such information should be put to use. The accounting information system serves both external and internal users of information.

External information requirements   The six major external interest groups that receive information from the business organization are indicated in Fig. 1.1. The information each group receives includes both information for decision making and routine data concerning the execution of transactions. The six groups and some examples of their information needs are as follows.

Customers   In this era of market orientation, the customers of a business organization are perhaps the most important of the external interest groups. The requirements of customers include information regarding the products of the business: prices, features, where and how they can be purchased, and guarantees and related servicing arrangements. These requirements are met through a combination of advertising, publication of catalogs and price lists, and communications by sales repre-

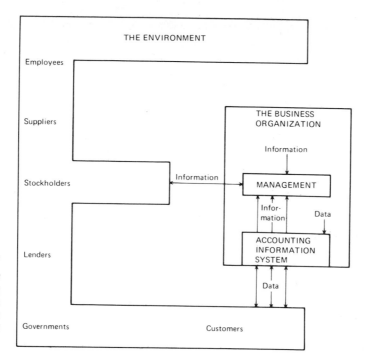

*Fig. 1.1
Relationship of the
accounting
information system
to the business
organization and
its environment.*

sentatives. Customers may often obtain some product information, such as the reputation of the product for reliability and quality performance, from sources external to the business itself.

Routine information required by the customers of a business organization includes billing data, which is typically included on the document of sale prepared as a record of the transaction. Credit customers also require periodic information concerning the status of their accounts, including the amount owed, the discount available, and the date payment is due. These routine information requirements are met by the accounting information system.

Suppliers   The typical business entity purchases its inventories of raw materials or salable goods from a large variety of sources. If the business entity makes its purchases on credit (and most do), its suppliers require information concerning its reliability, credit standing, and ability to pay. A supplier typically obtains such information partly from external sources, such as credit rating agencies, and partly from the accounting information system of the business entity itself.

In the exchange between a business entity and its supplier, the supplier also requires certain routine transaction documents. One of these is the purchase order, which indicates the items, quantities, and special features required by the business placing the order. If the goods are not acceptable to the business entity, information must be exchanged concerning possible adjustments in sale terms or the return of the goods. When the business entity pays for the goods, its payment will be accompanied by supporting transaction documents. Much of this routine transaction data is furnished by the accounting information system.

Stockholders   A company's stockholders are vitally interested in all phases of its operations. They wish to evaluate past and predict future performance. The publication of annual financial statements is perhaps the single most important means of meeting these requirements. Quarterly financial reports are also becoming an increasingly important form of management reporting to stockholders. Providing such reports to stockholders is often referred to as the *stewardship function* and has traditionally been the responsibility of the accounting information system. Stockholders often obtain additional information regarding the business entity from external sources, such as securities analysts and financial publications. Also required by stockholders is certain routine information concerning the execution of their stock transactions and the receipt of dividend payments. These routine information requirements are often met by the accounting information system.

Employees   As a group, employees are interested in certain general information regarding the business entity. This includes financial information, such as average wage levels, fringe benefit costs, and profits, as well as nonfinancial information such as levels of employment and productivity. Labor unions often represent the employee group in obtaining this information. Much of this information is provided by the accounting information system.

As individuals, employees expect periodic receipt of wages and salaries, accompanied by detailed information concerning deductions for income taxes, social security, insurance, union dues, etc. In the day-to-day performance of their job, employees often must refer to manuals to obtain information on company policy in a particular situation or on how a certain aspect of their job should be performed. The accounting information system is usually responsible for providing much of this routine information.

Lenders   Financial institutions that supply the business entity with capital for investment or expansion are very much interested in such factors as the reputation and ability of the company's management, its ability to meet its financial obligations, and its prospects for future success. A company's financial statements are an important source of information in this regard. Perhaps more so than other groups, lenders will also rely on outside sources for their information. The need of lenders for routine information concerning lending transactions requires an interchange of information with the accounting information system of the borrowing entity.

Governments   Many agencies of federal, state, and local governments require information concerning the business entity. The Internal Revenue Service requires information concerning the company's profits and the amount of taxes that the company owes to the government. The I.R.S. also requires information about the amount of employee taxes withheld. The Social Security Administration requires information concerning the amount of wages earned and social security taxes withheld. If the company is in a regulated industry, such as railroads or insurance, one or more federal or state agencies is likely to desire information about its operations. If the company has international operations, many foreign governments may desire information about its activities in their countries. The requirements of governments are perhaps the most varied of all external reporting requirements faced by the business organization. The accounting information system plays an important role in satisfying such requirements.

Many other groups also desire information about the business entity. These may include (1) credit agencies, such as Dun & Bradstreet, which publish information about a company's credit standing; (2) industry and trade associations, which publish information about a particular industry; (3) competitors, interested, of course, in a company's pricing policies, marketing strategies, product development plans, and profitability; (4) the community of which the business organization is a part; (5) financial analysts, who advise clients interested in making investments; or (6) private citizens, who are simply interested in some aspect of the company's activities.

For the most part, the information supplied to external users is either "mandatory" or "essential." Examples of mandatory information include reports to governments on taxable income and tax withholdings, and financial statements, which must be issued to stockholders by all publicly traded corporations. Examples of essential information include product information and billings to customers, and credit capacity information to lenders. The necessity for reporting information of this type places certain constraints upon accounting information systems, which will be discussed later in this chapter.

As shown in Fig. 1.1, much of the routine data provided to external parties by the business organization is channeled through the accounting information system. In turn, the accounting information system also receives much routine data from these exchanges. However, note that the information for decision making that is provided to external parties is shown to be provided directly by management rather than by the accounting information system. This reflects the fact that the ultimate responsibility for the fairness and accuracy of any information reported by the business upon which external parties base their decisions rests with management. This is true even though the accounting information system may serve as the actual channel for reporting this information.

Internal information requirements

In sharp contrast to external information is internal, or "discretionary," information. This means that choices must be made regarding information: what should be made available, to whom, how frequently, and so forth. Primarily because of this fact the area of internal information presents a much greater challenge to those who design accounting information systems than the external reporting area. In meeting mandatory and essential information requirements, the primary consideration is to minimize costs while meeting minimum standards of reliability and usefulness. When the reporting of information is discretionary, the primary consideration is that the benefit obtained from each report exceed the cost of supplying it. Much of the challenge in designing an information system is due to the fact that it is often very difficult to measure the benefit derived from reporting a given set of information.

All of the various levels of management in a business organization—from the executive management responsible for achieving overall company goals to the operating management responsible for achieving the specific objectives of a single department—require information in the performance of their duties. As indicated in Fig. 1.1, the accounting information system is a major, but not the only, source of information to management. The general business environment provides information on such matters as economic conditions, new technologies, legal constraints, and market standing. Other sources within the organization provide information on the success of research and development projects, the morale of employees, the level of worker productivity, and other company matters.

Although the accounting information system is the primary "formal" information system in most organizations, there are many other formal, as well as "informal," channels of information. A formal information system is one to which an explicit responsibility for information production has been assigned. In contrast, an informal information system is one that simply arises out of a need unsatisfied by a formal channel and operates without a formal assignment of responsibility. The "grapevine" is a familiar example of an informal channel of information common to all organizations. As organizations grow in size, it is natural for some informal channels to become formalized.

As shown in Fig. 1.1, the accounting information system receives data not only from sources outside the business but also from internal sources. For example, product cost information in a manufacturing firm is generated from data on materials usage, labor usage, etc., that are collected within the factory. The accounting information system prepares information for management by performing certain operations on all of the source data it receives. The management of the business organization receives this information and utilizes it as a basis for decision making. Management decisions in turn affect the internal operation of the business organization, including the accounting information system, and also affect the relationship of the business organization with its environment.

Two major roles of accounting information in management decision making can be identified. First, accounting information often provides a stimulus for management decision making by indicating the existence of a situation requiring management action. For example, a cost report that indicates a large variance of actual costs over budgeted costs might stimulate management to take corrective action. Second, accounting information often provides a basis for choice among possible alternative actions. For example, accounting information is often used as a basis for setting prices or for choosing which capital assets to purchase. The importance of accounting information in this latter role is due to its contribution to the reduction of uncertainty regarding the merits of various alternatives.

Designers of accounting information systems must determine what the information requirements of management are and must respond quickly to changes in those requirements. The accounting system must be designed to meet these needs effectively. If management does not receive enough information, or receives poor information, its performance will not be as effective as it potentially could be. This could have an adverse effect on the entire organization. Thus the accounting information system plays an important role in contributing to the effectiveness of the business organization.

Analysis of the Accounting Information System

Thus far the accounting information system has been examined as a "black box"—that is, its role in the business organization has been discussed, but the way in which it operates internally to perform that role has not. In this section the lid of the black box is lifted in order that its contents and the operations performed within it may be analyzed. The objective is to formulate a precise definition of what is meant by the term accounting information system.

Many readers may already be more or less familiar with the concept of the management information system. Accounting information systems are closely related to management information systems, both conceptually and in the real world. It is worthwhile to define and explore the concept of management information systems as a prelude to developing an understanding of accounting information systems.

Management information systems

The term *management information system* has been defined in many different ways.[3] However, for our purposes, it will be defined as the set of human and capital resources within an organization, which is responsible for the collection and processing of data to produce information that is useful to all levels of management in planning and controlling the activities of the organization. To many people, the term implies a computer-based system, but the term encompasses noncomputer systems as well. All business organizations have a management information system, but such systems vary greatly in their level of sophistication.

A fuller understanding of the concept of a management information system can be obtained from a careful analysis of the definition above. Several of the concepts referred to in the definition will now be examined in greater depth.

Management planning and control The major purpose of management information systems is to facilitate the management of an organization. As used here, the term management encompasses all levels of administration in an organization, from

---

[3] *For example, seventeen different definitions are listed in Raymond J. Coleman and M. J. Riley,* MIS: Management Dimensions *(San Francisco: Holden-Day, Inc., 1973), pp. 4–7.*

top management responsible for the overall success or failure of the organization, to operating management responsible for the day-to-day operation of a single department. Depending on the size of the organization, there may be one to several layers of management between these two extremes.

The basic functions of management are planning and control. Planning includes such activities as setting objectives, establishing policies, choosing subordinate managers, deciding on capital expenditures, and making decisions on products and their promotion. Control involves implementing policies, evaluating the performance of subordinates, and taking action to correct substandard performance. Information of various kinds is required in the performance of all of these functions.

Data vs. information   As implied in the definition, a distinction is generally drawn between data and information. *Data* can be thought of as comprising any set of characters that is accepted as input to an information system and is stored and processed. *Information* refers to an output of data processing that is organized and meaningful to the person who receives it. For example, data concerning a sale may indicate who the salesperson was. When a large number of such data elements is organized and analyzed, it may provide important information to marketing directors attempting to evaluate their sales forces. The term "data processing system" is often used interchangeably with "information system."

The major categories of information that can be distinguished in a business organization are (1) financial information, which concerns the flow of financial resources through the organization; (2) logistics information, which concerns the physical flow of inventories and resources within and through the organization; (3) personnel information, which concerns the people who work for the organization; and (4) marketing information, which concerns the markets for the organization's product and the means of serving those markets. Much information within a business organization overlaps into more than one of these categories.

The data processing cycle   Much of the study of information systems involves the operations that are performed on data in order to generate meaningful and relevant information. A useful method of classifying these operations is the concept of the data processing cycle. As shown in Fig. 1.2, the data processing cycle may be perceived as having five stages: collection, refinement, processing, maintenance, and output.

The collection stage includes two fundamental activities. The first is *observation* of the data generating environment, usually by a human observer, though sometimes a machine may perform this function. The second is the *recording* of data, generally in the form of written source documents, though again it is possible that data may be recorded in a nonwritten, machine-readable form.

The data refinement stage includes a number of operations performed on data in order to facilitate subsequent processing steps: (1) *classifying* of data, which involves the assignment of identification codes (account number, department number, etc.) to data records based on a predetermined system of classification, such as a

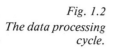

Fig. 1.2
The data processing
cycle.

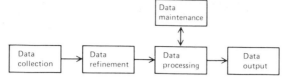

chart of accounts; (2) *batching* of data, which involves the accumulation of similar input records to be processed as a group; (3) *verification* of data, which involves a variety of procedures for checking the accuracy of data prior to submitting it for processing; (4) *sorting* of data, which involves the arrangement of a batch of input records into ·some desired numerical or alphabetical sequence; (5) *transmission* of data from one location to another; and (6) *transcription* of data from one form to another, such as from handwriting to typing or from documents to punched cards. Data refinement activities of some kind are performed in virtually all types of information systems, but they generally take on greater significance in more automated systems.

The processing stage of the cycle also includes a variety of activities. *Calculating* encompasses any form of mathematical manipulation. *Comparing* involves the simultaneous examination of two or more items of data, such as an "inventory balance on hand" and "reorder point," as a basis for subsequent action. *Summarizing* is a very important processing activity involving the aggregation of bits of data into meaningful totals or condensations. A related activity is *filtration,* which is the screening out of extraneous data from subsequent processing. Still another processing activity is *retrieval,* which is the fetching of data items from storage for use in processing or for output purposes.

There are several activities in the data maintenance stage, the most prominent being the *storage* of data for future reference. Other maintenance activities include the *updating* of stored data to reflect more recent events; the *indexing* of data, which involves cataloging of reference information pertaining to a body of stored data (such as in a library card catalog) in order to facilitate retrieval of specific items of data upon request; and the *protection* of stored data, which encompasses a variety of procedures and techniques for preventing its destruction or unauthorized disclosure.

The output stage represents the ultimate objective of the data processing cycle. Data output may be in one of two general forms—documents or reports. The term *issuance* may be used to refer to the preparation of output documents, such as checks, invoices, and purchase orders. Such documents may be returned to the information system for use in other data processing activities, or they may be provided to external users. The other major output activity is *reporting,* which is the formal presentation and distribution of processed data (information), usually in summary form.

It is important to note that most data do not have all of these activities performed upon them, and some data may not even pass through all five stages. For example, data from a transaction may be simply recorded and stored, perhaps never reaching the output stage. On the other hand, data on the plans of competitors may be collected and immediately reported to management without passing through any processing steps. Since such cases are generally the exception rather than the rule, the study of information systems must focus on all stages of the data processing cycle.

Information system resources A management information system utilizes both human and capital resources, the latter consisting primarily of data processing equipment. With reference to the relative utilization of these two types of resources, two basic categories of data processing systems can be distinguished: (1) manual data processing systems, in which the major share of the data processing load is carried by people; and (2) automated data processing (ADP) systems, in which the major share of the data processing load is carried by machines. Several levels of sophistication are possible within these two categories.

The lowest level of sophistication in data processing systems is a completely manual system in which people perform all data processing functions. Such systems are common in small, local businesses, in which the data processing functions may be a secondary part of the responsibilities of several persons rather than the primary responsibility of a single individual. The major advantages of people as data processors are their flexibility, or ability to perform all of the various functions of a data processing system, and their judgment, or ability to adapt to unfamiliar situations. The major disadvantages are their lack of reliability and speed.

Most manual data processing systems utilize one or more forms of special purpose business machines. The most common types of these machines include (1) typewriters, which increase recording speed and legibility; (2) calculating machines, which increase speed and accuracy of calculation; (3) cash registers, which record, classify, and provide control over cash receipts; (4) duplicators, which conserve time in the making of duplicate copies of documents or reports; and (5) cassette tape recorders, that record, store, and play back voice data. This is by no means a complete list of available types of business machines. In general, machines of this sort increase the speed and reliability of data processing in manual systems. They require constant interaction with people, and so do not undermine the advantages of people as data processors, but neither do they completely eliminate the disadvantages of people.

Historically, the earliest form of automated data processing system was the *punched card system*. Such a system, which has been made obsolete in recent years by the computer, consisted of several different machines. Using the punched card as a data medium, each machine was capable of performing one or a limited number of data processing functions that included recording (punching), sorting, collating, calculating, duplicating, and printing. Human intervention was required at the beginning and end of each processing step, but was minimal in between. For many years prior to the advent of computer systems, punched card systems represented the highest level of automation in office equipment. At the present time, some organizations still use one or more punched card machines as auxiliary equipment within a computer system.

A vastly more sophisticated level than the punched card system is *electronic data processing* (EDP), or computer systems. Because of their ability to store and execute a set of instructions (called a *program*), computers can perform many processing steps in a series with no human intervention. Computer systems are much faster and more accurate than punched card systems because of their use of electronic, rather then electromechanical, components. However, computer systems also tend to be less flexible and adaptable than manual systems, and the extent of the initial design effort is often enormous. Available computer facilities have a wide range of capabilities and features, including differences in speed and storage capacity. The pace of change in this area has been very fast in recent years, making this one of the most challenging aspects of the entire field of information systems.

The degree of mechanization required by an information system increases in direct proportion to the volume of data processing that the system must accomplish. It is useful to compare data processing systems conceptually in terms of the relationship between processing cost and the volume of data items processed. In a manual system, most data processing costs are variable relative to volume. Therefore, as processing volume increases, total processing costs increase proportionately and cost per item processed stays relatively constant.

On the other hand, fixed costs of facilities represent a very significant portion of the cost in an automated data processing system. Therefore, as processing volume increases, total processing costs in an automated system do not increase in the same proportion, and cost per item processed actually declines. These concepts are illustrated graphically in Fig. 1.3. The curves shown represent relative values rather than actual figures. These graphs help to explain why manual systems are suited to low-volume operations, and automated systems to high-volume operations. In a growing organization, the increasing volume of data processing work represents one of the major pressures toward converting from a manual to an automated system. The line connecting the two graphs represents a break-even point between the two modes of processing.

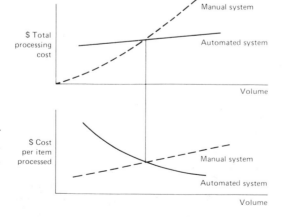

Fig. 1.3
Relationship of processing costs to processing volume in manual and automated data processing systems.

System The final aspect of the definition of management information system to be discussed here is the concept of *system,* a word having many diverse meanings and implications. In its broadest and most abstract sense, a system is an entity consisting of two or more components or subsystems that interact to achieve a goal. Used in this sense, the term could be applied to a community, a family unit, or a business organization. In a more specific sense, the term is used by specialists in the computer field to refer to either the equipment and programs making up a complete computer installation, or a set of programs and related procedures for performing a single task or set of related tasks on a computer.

Closely related to this notion is the process known as *systems analysis,* which also has both abstract and specific meanings. In its most abstract sense, systems analysis refers to a rigorous and systematic approach to decision making, characterized by a comprehensive definition of available alternatives and an exhaustive analysis of the merits of each alternative as a basis for choice. The approach often involves attempts to quantify factors that would otherwise be considered on an intuitive basis and also frequently makes use of computers. The central theoretical principle of systems analysis is referred to as the *systems concept.* According to this principle, choices among alternative courses of action within a system must be evaluated from the standpoint of the system as a whole rather than any single subsystem or set of subsystems.

When applied to information systems in complex organizations, one major effect of the systems concept has been to encourage *integration,* which refers to the combining of previously separated subsystems. Integration has made data processing more efficient by eliminating duplication of recording, storage, reporting, and other processing activities within an organization. For example, where it was formerly common in many businesses for the preparation of bills and maintenance of accounts receivable records to be performed separately, these functions are often combined in a single operation in modern business organizations. Integration has been facilitated by the increased utilization of computers, which have tended to replace specialized clerks and thereby reduce the need for separate specialized subsystems.

In a more specific sense, the term systems analysis is used by computer professionals to refer to the process of designing computer applications. It is the step that immediately precedes the preparation of computer programs. A meaning of the term dating back to precomputer times is that systems analysis is the process of designing procedures and selecting equipment for performing data processing functions in manual or punched card systems.

Accounting information systems—A definition Accounting information systems possess all of the characteristics of management information systems. They utilize the same kinds of resources and have a data processing cycle that produces information for management planning and control. The major difference is one of scope. The management information system encompasses all data entering the organization, all processing activities within the organization, and all information used by persons in the organization. The accounting information system is concerned only with certain types of data and information. Thus the accounting information system is a subsystem of the management information system within an organization.

It is possible to identify two types of management information with which accounting information systems are primarily involved: (1) financial information, and (2) information generated from the processing of transaction data. Although much management information actually falls into both of these categories, there is also much that fits only one or the other description. For example, unit inventory or unit sales information is not financial but is often produced from transaction processing. Similarly, budgets and capital investment analyses are representative of the kinds of financial information that are not generated directly from transaction processing. Figure 1.4 illustrates that these two types of information are subsets of management information, that they do overlap, but that neither is a complete subset of the other.

The accounting information system is the most pervasive and often the largest of the information subsystems in business organizations. It is pervasive in the sense that all members of the organization participate in some way in the generation of transaction data, and all managers utilize financial information to some extent. In many organizations, the accounting information system is the only formally designated information system and is thus in effect the management information system. In most organizations that do have a formally designated management information system, accountants play a key role in its administration and operation. Thus an understanding of accounting information systems is essential to the study of management information systems, and vice versa.

To summarize, the term *accounting information system* is defined as the set of human and capital resources within an organization, which is responsible for the preparation of financial information and also of the information obtained from the collection and processing of transaction data. This information is then made available for use by all levels of management in planning and controlling the activities of the organization. The functions of transaction processing and financial information preparation will now be examined in greater detail.

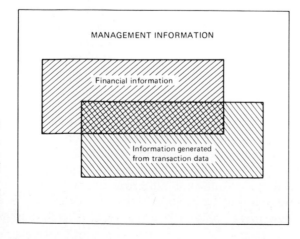

Fig. 1.4
Relationship of management information, financial information, and information generated from transaction data.

Transaction processing

The processing of transaction data in accounting utilizes its own version of the data processing cycle, illustrated in Fig. 1.5. The portion of this process that begins with source documents and ends with financial statements is often called the double entry accounting process. Many other reports and analyses containing both financial and nonfinancial information may be generated as a by-product of the double entry accounting process.

It is helpful to use the terminology of the data processing cycle when examining the accounting process. Input data are observed and recorded on source documents, such as sales invoices or time cards. These data may then be verified for accuracy, classified and batched by type of transaction, sorted into sequence by document number or account number, transcribed from source documents to journals, and perhaps at some point transmitted to a different location, such as a central accounting or data processing office.

Steps in the data processing stage of the accounting cycle include calculation of payrolls, invoice totals, taxes, and numerous other totals and percentages. Various comparisons of these figures to each other and to stored data may be made as a matter of routine during processing. The preparation of the trial balance is an important summarizing step, while the balancing of the trial balance is a useful means of verifying the accuracy of the entire accounting cycle. Retrieval of accounting information in response to inquiries from customers or management occurs frequently. Filtration is represented by ignoring data irrelevant to the accounting process, such as a customer's telephone number or an employee's height and weight (though such data may be relevant for other purposes).

The storage activity is represented by the saving of accounting data in ledgers and other files. A *file* is defined as a set of logically related records, such as the payroll records of all employees. A *record* is defined as a set of logically related data items, such as all payroll data relating to a single employee. The updating activity is represented by the posting of transactions from journals and source documents to ledgers and files. Indexing occurs when each record is assigned one or more identifying codes, such as account number, product stock number, or department number,

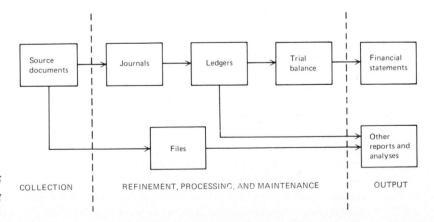

Fig. 1.5
The data processing cycle in accounting.

COLLECTION   REFINEMENT, PROCESSING, AND MAINTENANCE   OUTPUT

for reference purposes. Protection of stored data may involve such simple techniques as locking of filing cabinets.

The reporting step in the output phase of the double entry process is exemplified by the financial statements of the organization, which are perhaps the most important single summary of the organization's activities. Numerous other reports may also be prepared as a by-product of accounting data processing. In addition, documents such as customer statements and employee paychecks are issued by the accounting system.

A typical business entity will engage in a large volume of transactions, which may also be greatly varied. However, designers of accounting information systems can be thankful that a great majority of transactions fall into one of a few basic categories. This fact allows the system to achieve a greater degree of efficiency in processing. At this point, a few basic categories of business transactions will be reviewed.

Purchasing of assets and services   The purchase of inventories, fixed assets, services, and supplies is one of the most basic business transactions of all business entities. This transaction could be considered the starting point of the entire business process. The transaction is represented by the following journal entry.

Purchases	XXX	
Fixed assets	XXX	
Expenses (various accounts)	XXX	
Accounts payable		XXX

The purchases account represents either the raw material inventory of a manufacturing concern, or the merchandise inventory of a retail or wholesale firm. The accounts involved in this transaction are summary accounts, so such an entry usually represents a large volume of transactions. Individual inventory purchases may be recorded in a detailed inventory ledger by item number, individual fixed asset purchases may be recorded in a fixed asset ledger, and expenses may be recorded in various expense ledgers. Each accounts payable entry would be posted to the appropriate vendor record in an accounts payable ledger. These detailed ledgers and transaction data may be used to generate many useful reports and analyses of expenses, inventories, vendor activity, and so forth.

Payroll   The payment of wages and salaries is another type of transaction that is very basic in most business entities. It is represented by the following journal entry.

Payroll	XXX	
Taxes payable (various accounts)		XXX
Other deductions		XXX
Cash		XXX

This entry is a summarization of tens, hundreds, or perhaps thousands of individual transactions with employees. Detailed records must be kept for each employee, primarily to fulfill tax requirements. The amount in the payroll account is distributed to various expenses and inventory accounts. The payroll account is also frequently analyzed to prepare various detailed cost reports used for decision-making purposes.

Sale of products   The sale of a product is perhaps the most essential of the basic business transactions. It is represented by the following journal entry.

Accounts receivable	XXX	
Cost of goods sold	XXX	
Sales		XXX
Finished goods inventory		XXX

Once again, this entry represents several detailed sets of records. A detailed accounts receivable ledger contains a record of the account of each individual customer. Cost of goods sold may be analyzed in detail by inventory categories as a basis for planning the composition of future inventories. Sales may be analyzed according to salesperson or territory as a basis for evaluating the effectiveness of marketing effort.

Cash receipt and disbursement   Transactions involving the receipt and disbursement of cash are very important to all business entities. Receipt of cash usually initiates the following journal entry.

Cash	XXX	
Accounts receivable		XXX

Disbursement of cash is reflected by the follow entry.

Accounts payable	XXX	
Cash		XXX

Such entries affect the detailed accounts receivable and accounts payable ledger records as well as the cash account. These detailed ledgers, and the transaction details underlying these entries, may be used to generate many different reports, including cash flow analysis and projections, and cash budgets.

Flow of inventory through production   This process is represented by two basic transactions, the first of which reflects the accumulation of all production costs.

Work in process inventory	XXX	
Raw materials inventory		XXX
Payroll		XXX
Manufacturing overhead		XXX

The second reflects the completion of production.

Finished goods inventory	XXX	
Work in process inventory		XXX

These transactions are, of course, peculiar to a special type of business organization—one which is engaged in manufacturing. They are also distinguished from those mentioned previously in that they are "internal" rather than "external" transactions, meaning that there is no outside party involved. These transactions reflect several detailed sets of inventory and production records and the data underlying the entries are used in the preparation of a large number of various "cost accounting" reports.

The transactions outlined above represent the vast majority of all business transactions in terms of volume. Each of the entries summarizes hundreds, or perhaps thousands, of typical, individual transactions. Of course, there are many other types of transactions with which an accounting system must cope, but none which are as basic in terms of volume. A major concern in the study of accounting information systems is the design of systems to perform these high-volume tasks efficiently and reliably.

Preparation of financial information

The design of accounting information systems must also concern itself with the preparation of financial information for management. As mentioned previously, much financial information is generated directly as a by-product of transaction processing. However, it is dangerous for management to rely solely on by-product information. In most businesses of medium to large size, management's needs for financial information go well beyond that which is generated from transaction processing.

For example, consider the planning function. Since transaction-generated information necessarily involves only the past, it is not by itself relevant in planning for the future. The budget is an important financial planning tool, as is capital expenditure analysis. Both of these techniques use transaction data to some extent but must also rely upon financial forecasts. Financial information relating to the environment of the business firm is also important for planning purposes. Examples include price level and national income information as well as information on the prices and profitability of the products of competitors.

As business organizations grow in size, the number and variety of financial reports necessary also multiply. This is confirmed by considering the number of ways in which reports may be categorized. For example, reports may be categorized according to scope (from firmwide to departmental), time horizon (from historical summaries to long-range forecasts), format (narrative, numeric, tabular, graphical, oral), user (operating employees, managers, governmental agencies), timing (issued weekly or monthly, or by request only, or according to circumstances), and purpose (stewardship, planning, control, motivation).[4] These and other factors are important considerations in the design of effective financial reports.

An example of an accounting information system

At this point it may be helpful to illustrate the concepts discussed thus far by describing briefly the main components of an accounting information system for a typical small business. Let us consider a retail home-appliance dealer whose product line includes refrigerators, freezers, electric ranges, washers, dryers, television sets, radios, stereo and hi-fi equipment, air conditioners, vacuum cleaners, and other household appliances. Such a dealer would probably employ from ten to fifteen persons—two or three office personnel, two or three in delivery, two or three in service and repair, and four to six in sales.

---

[4] *For further elaboration on such categorizations, see Joseph W. Wilkinson, "Effective Reporting Structures,"* Journal of Systems Management *(November 1976), pp. 38–42.*

Our dealer's most important management decisions relate to inventories—determining what is on hand, what should be purchased and when, what prices should be charged, what trade-in allowances should be provided, and so forth. The dealer also needs to be able to assess the relative profitability of the various product lines. Other significant management concerns include advertising and promotion, credit and collection of receivables, and supervising of personnel. The accounting system should provide information useful for making many of these decisions.

It is helpful to consider the most significant categories of accounting transactions engaged in by the dealer: (1) sales, including cash sales, credit card sales, installment sales, sales of trade-ins, and sales of parts and service, (2) purchases of inventory, (3) payroll, (4) expenses such as utilities, advertising, supplies, insurance, taxes, (5) cash receipts on account, and (6) cash disbursements.

As is the case in most retail business, the typical home-appliance dealer uses a manual data processing system, augmented by a few small business machines such as a cash register, typewriter, and calculator. Accounting personnel might include a bookkeeper, credit manger, and secretary. The owner is very likely to be involved in numerous procedures and activities related directly to the accounting function.

An important component of any accounting system consists of the documents used to record input data. In a retail home-appliance store, two of the more important of these are the sale document and the service work order. The sale document is filled out at the point of sale and includes data pertaining to the customer, terms of sale, items and quantities sold, prices and total charges, and delivery information. The multiple copies that are prepared include one for the customer, one for delivery, and one for accounting. The service work order, which is also prepared in multiple copies, contains data relating to the customer, product, work performed, parts sold, and amount collected.

The files and records maintained by the store's accounting system reflect the information requirements of its owner–manager. The two most important files are the inventory ledger and the accounts receivable ledger. The inventory ledger contains one record for each type of inventory item carried. This record contains data on the cost, list price, quantity on hand, quantity on order, and pattern of past sales of an inventory item. It must be updated when sales are made and when purchase orders are placed or delivered. The accounts receivable ledger includes one record for each installment sale containing data on the amount due and payments received. New installment sales and customer payments are posted to these records. Other significant accounting files include an accounts payable file, a payroll file, and the general ledger, whose records are the balance sheet and income statement accounts.

A significant part of any accounting system consists of the procedures followed in processing accounting data. One procedure is a daily comparison of the cash in the register against the cash register tape and the sales documents. A similar comparison is made of cash received for parts and service against the service work orders. Service workers and delivery people are required to have the customer sign one copy of a work order to acknowledge receipt of goods or services. To provide control over customer payments on account, the owner opens all mail and totals all checks received. The owner also signs all outgoing checks and prepares a monthly bank reconciliation. A periodic review of accounts receivable records is made in order to detect customers who are behind in their payments; these customers are sent letters encouraging them to keep their accounts current. Inventory stocks and ledger records are also reveiwed periodically to determine what items should be ordered. At the end of each month various procedures are performed: journal entries are posted from the general journal to the general ledger; detailed ledgers are totaled and reconciled to their general ledger control account balance; accrual and adjusting entries are made, a trial balance is prepared and balanced; closing entries are made; and finally a balance sheet and income statement for the month are prepared.

This has been only a very brief description of a small business accounting information system, the main components of which are summarized in Fig. 1.6. This example is intended to give a preliminary idea of the nature of accounting informa-

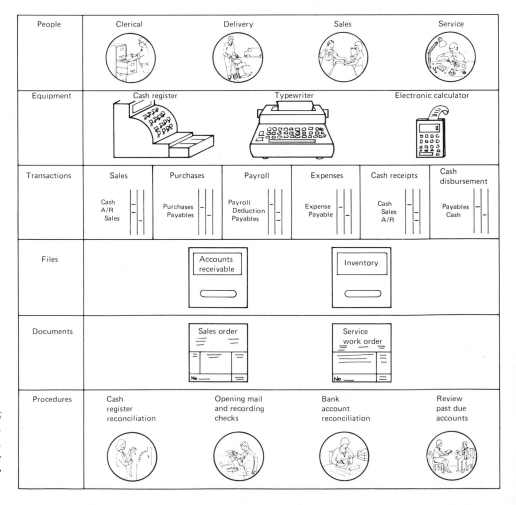

Fig. 1.6
Components of an accounting information system for a home appliance dealer.

tion systems. Later, the book provides many other examples of accounting information systems in greater detail. However, all such systems contain the same basic set of components—people, equipment, transactions, files and records, documents, and procedures.

The Evolution of Accounting Information Systems

The system life cycle

In a growing business organization, an information system undergoes a limited life cycle, from the point at which it is born to meet needs not satisfied by its predecessor system, to the point at which it is replaced because it fails to meet the new needs of the business. Two factors have tended to shorten the life cycles of business and accounting systems in recent years: the rapid growth of business organizations, and rapid changes in information processing technology. The life cycle of information systems is examined here in three separate stages, (1) analysis and design, (2) implementation, and (3) operation.

Analysis and design   The analysis and design stage is equivalent to the gestation period of an information system. It begins with the recognition that the continuing growth of the organization is raising problems with which the old system may be unable to cope. This initiates an extensive survey of the existing system, and of current and future information processing needs. An analysis of the information obtained in the survey may delineate the major problem areas in the existing system. If the old system is a manual one, the feasibility of automation may be considered.

One of the most important steps in this phase is the survey of information requirements. In accounting information systems, much of the data processing and information preparation is either mandatory or essential, particularly that done for external users. These mandatory and essential requirements are thus fixed and given to the designer of an accounting information system. The designer faces the problem of determining the remaining information needs, primarily internal, which the system should fulfill. The next step is to determine the extent to which these internal information needs may be satisfied by information prepared as a by-product of the processing of mandatory and essential information. Any remaining information needs must be met with discretionary information, which will involve the systems designer in comparing the value of the information with the cost of enlarging the accounting information system to enable the information to be prepared.

Following the survey and analysis is a period of *synthesis,* in which a program of corrective action is developed. Such a program may entail only minor modification of the existing system, or it may entail complete replacement of the system. Throughout this period each alternative is rigorously evaluated in terms of its costs and benefits to the organization. If the program recommended in the synthesis is approved by management, work proceeds on the detailed systems design.

All aspects of the new system are considered in the detailed systems design, including personnel, hardware, procedures, and data flows. Almost any major systems project will involve some personnel problems—such as employee displacement, relocation, hiring, and retraining—which must be planned for. Also common are problems associated with equipment acquisition, such as selection of desired features, arranging for maintenance service, and financing the purchase. Procedures must be designed to ensure efficiency and reliability of processing. In EDP systems, many procedures must be programmed. Data flow problems include deciding on the content and arrangement of data on source documents, designing record layouts, establishing the content and organization of files, and determining the appropriate content, format, and distribution of reports.

Implementation   Once the detailed systems design is completed, the new system must be successfully implemented. If the new system is a major revision or replacement of the old, the first important step in this stage will be to plan and coordinate properly the various implementation activities. Another step in implementation is to hire and train new employees, and to relocate existing employees if necessary. In addition, new processing procedures must be tested and perhaps modified. New equipment must be installed and tested. Standards and controls for the new system must be established. Complete system *documentation,* consisting of descriptions of procedures, charts, instructions for employees, and other descriptive material, must be developed. When the new system is ready to begin functioning, it may be operated simultaneously with the old system for a brief period, with the output of the two systems being compared to ensure that the new system has no major defects. The final step in this phase is the dismantling of the old system and complete conversion to the new.

Operation   After the new system has been operating on its own for a short while, follow-up studies are usually conducted to detect and correct the inevitable minor, and sometimes major, design deficiencies that were not apparent at the point of conversion. Throughout its lifetime the system will be subject to periodic review. Minor modifications may be made as problems arise or as new needs become evident. Eventually the reviews will indicate that major modification or replacement should be considered and the process will begin all over again.

The accountant's role in systems change

In most business organizations, accountants will play a key role in this process of systems change. As mentioned previously, the accounting and information systems functions are one and the same in some firms, and accountants are thus directly responsible for performing systems work. In other firms, accountants are at least one of the primary users of the information system, and so are vitally interested in how the system operates. It is always important for the users of an information system to become involved in its design.

In many smaller companies, the expertise necessary to analyze and design information systems may not be present within the company and, as a result, reliance may have to be placed upon outside consultants. One of the main sources of such consultants is the public accounting profession. Many public accounting firms, particularly the larger ones, employ specialists in systems work in their "management advisory services'' departments. Other major sources of consulting in the systems area are business machine manufacturers and management consultants not associated with public accounting.

Future Challenges to Accounting Information Systems

Change is inevitable in society, and the pace of change in today's society seems to be accelerating. Such change will bring new problems and new challenges to designers of accounting information systems. It is possible to predict some of the major challenges of the future by looking at the trends visible in society today.

Social responsibility in business

A major trend of the present era is the demand by society that business organizations become more socially responsible. This trend is evident in several respects, including the consumer protection movement, legislation encouraging the hiring and training of members of socially disadvantaged groups, and perhaps more dramatically in the movement to save the environment. The business world is beginning to respond to these demands. Accounting information systems have a definite contribution to make here. They can estimate the costs and benefits of proposed projects designed to improve the well-being of society and thus assist business management in deciding which projects are worthwhile. While such projects are in operation, there is a need for information systems to process data on them and to provide business management with information that is useful in evaluating existing projects and planning future ones. Business organizations are increasingly required to report to government agencies on their compliance with social or environmental goals established by regulation or legislation—and business executives look to their accounting information systems to meet these demands.

Accounting for human assets

Another major trend is the growing importance of human knowledge and skill as a valuable economic resource. The initial development of modern accounting information systems took place early in the twentieth century. During this period, the most important assets were physical assets, such as cash, inventories, buildings, and machinery. The vast majority of the labor force was unskilled. Physical assets were thus the primary concern of accounting information systems.

In modern business organizations, human knowledge and skill are usually primary factors in their success or failure. Yet the accounting information systems of the present day do not reflect this fact. They continue to treat physical assets as being of primary importance, and all but ignore human assets.

The effective management of human assets requires information. The function of accounting information systems is to provide such information. Management must develop new methods of recording, classifying, and processing data concerning human resources. Systems designers must revise methods of reporting information to management to incorporate the human factor and give it adequate consideration in management decisions. Systems of internal control for human assets are needed. These needs clearly call for innovative thinking and action on the part of designers of accounting information systems.

Scientific approaches to management

Another major trend is the movement toward more scientific approaches to management. The last three decades have seen the development of an entirely new discipline, commonly referred to as *management science* or *operations research*. This discipline approaches management decision making by attempting to construct mathematical models of real decision problems. Solutions to such models are then used in making the actual decisions. Practitioners of this discipline make liberal use of computers in building and solving mathematical models. The field is often considered to be a branch of systems analysis.

Among the most important variables that operations researchers require in building models of business decision problems are measures of cost and benefit. However, when they attempt to obtain such measures from accounting information systems, they are often frustrated to find that the information is not in the form they require because accounting systems have never before had to provide inputs to operations research models.

The operations research approach has tremendous potential for generating better management decisions. The full realization of this potential requires that accounting information systems be structured to provide relevant and reliable inputs to operations research models. Designers of accounting information systems must study the common forms of operations research models in order to develop an understanding of the type of information that is needed. Changes in patterns of recording, classifying, and processing will be required.

Inflation accounting

In recent years price inflation has become an increasingly significant phenomenon of modern industrial society. Inflation causes a significant distortion of accounting information, which affects financial statements and other accounting system outputs. This has been recognized by those organizations that regulate financial reporting, including the Financial Accounting Standards Board and the Securities and Exchange Commission in this country and their counterparts in numerous other countries. These groups have issued proposals and requirements for financial reporting that reflects the impact of inflation. The most recent of these is Statement 33 of the Financial Accounting Standards Board, issued in September of 1979, that requires all public companies meeting certain criteria of size to prepare inflation accounting information and disclose it in their annual reports to stockholders.[5]

Inflation accounting has a significant impact upon accounting information systems. There is a need to collect, process, and maintain data on price levels, replace-

---

[5] *For further information on this development, see Robert W. Berliner and Dale L. Gerboth, "FASB Statement No. 33 'The Great Experiment',"* The Journal of Accountancy *(May 1980), pp. 48-54.*

ment costs, current values, and so forth. Systems of accounting for inventories, fixed assets, and other financial items must be revised. Systems of reporting to stockholders and other external parties must be modified to meet the requirements imposed by regulatory groups. Perhaps even more important is the need to revise internal management reports to eliminate inflationary distortions that might lead to bad management decisions. Implementation of the systems required for these purposes is presently underway in many large companies. If the experience obtained from Statement 33 is successful, then inflation accounting may be required for all public companies in the near future.

A look ahead

The problems discussed in this chapter represent only a few of the major challenges in the field of accounting information systems today. Before students can fully appreciate and respond to these future challenges, they must first develop an understanding of the present state of the art in accounting information systems. This book will help them to achieve this end. Part 2 discusses the processing equipment and systems available to designers of accounting information systems, with particular emphasis on computer systems. Part 3 covers the major issues involved in the analysis, design, implementation, management, and control of information systems. Part 4 develops an understanding of the primary uses to which accounting information is put in the management of the marketing, logistics, personnel, and finance functions in the modern business organization.

As has been discussed, accounting information systems may be completely manual, partially mechanized, or fully automated. However, there are certain concepts, principles, and techniques common to all of them regardless of their degree of mechanization or other differences. One example is the concept of the accounting cycle discussed in this chapter. In the remainder of Part 1, several other fundamental topics are covered. The topic of business organization is examined in Chapter 2, which focuses on the impact of business organization upon the collection and processing of accounting data and the reporting of accounting information, and on the internal organization of accounting function. In Chapter 3, the general concepts of file processing and records management are introduced and explained. In Chapter 4, the basic concepts and principles of control in a business organization are discussed. Note that these topics are closely interrelated. Together they provide a strong general understanding of accounting information systems useful in exploring the more specific topics of information technology, systems management, and business applications of systems.

Review Questions

1. Define the following terms.

financial accounting

management accounting

stewardship function

systems analysis (three meanings)

systems concept

integration

management information system	accounting information system
data	file
information	record
punched card system	synthesis
electronic data processing	documentation
program	management science
system (three meanings)	operations research

2. Explain why the study of accounting information systems is important for today's accounting students.

3. What are two major categories of users of accounting information? What are the major user groups within each category, and what is the nature of their information needs?

4. From what sources other than the accounting information system does management receive information?

5. Distinguish between "mandatory," "essential," and "discretionary" reporting of information and give an example of each.

6. Distinguish between "formal" and "informal" information systems and give an example of each.

7. Identify two major roles of accounting information in management decision making.

8. The two basic management functions are assumed to be planning and control. What are some of the specific activities involved in each of these functions?

9. Identify and describe four major categories of information in a business organization.

10. Identify the five major stages of the data processing cycle, and indicate the major activities in each stage. Relate the data processing cycle to the double entry accounting process.

11. Identify two basic categories of data processing systems. Within each category describe the various levels of sophistication in data processing facilities that are available to the information systems designer.

12. What are the advantages and disadvantages of people as data processors? As a data processing system becomes more automated, what effect is there on these factors?

13. What are some of the common types of special purpose business machines?

14. Compare manual and automated data processing systems in terms of the relationship between processing costs and the volume of data items processed? What are the implications of this comparison for an accounting system in which processing volume is growing?

15. What are the advantages of integration of accounting systems? Describe an example of integration.

16. How are accounting information systems distinguished from management information systems?

17. What are some of the basic transactions of a business organization? Can you give the journal entries for these transactions?

18. Why is it dangerous for management to rely solely on information generated as a by-product of transaction processing in meeting its needs for financial information? What are some examples of financial information that is not generated from transaction processing?

19. Describe some of the ways in which financial reports may be classified.

20. Describe the components—people, equipment, transactions, files and records, documents, procedures, etc.—that you might expect to find in the accounting information system of a typical retail home-appliance store.

21. What are the three major stages in the life cycle of an information system? What activities are performed in each stage?

22. What are four contemporary social trends that present challenges to the designers of accounting information systems?

Discussion Questions

23. Should an accounting information system be structured to meet the needs of external or internal users? To what extent are these two categories of needs similar, and to what extent do they differ?

24. How do the information systems of nonprofit organizations or governments differ from those of business organizations? In what ways are they similar?

25. How do general-purpose financial statements meet the needs for information about the business organization of (a) customers, (b) suppliers, (c) stockholders, (d) employees, (e) lenders, (f) governments?

26. When a business undertakes projects to improve the well-being of society, how can it measure the benefits of such projects in order to evaluate their relative worth?

27. Suppose a business wished to record its human assets on its balance sheet. How could it assign asset values to them?

Problems and Cases

28. In this chapter, several of the highest volume transactions of a typical manufacturing company were discussed, and corresponding accounting journal entries were illustrated.
    a) List several of the highest volume transactions of a typical life insurance company and give the corresponding journal entries.
    b) List several of the highest volume transactions of a typical banking institution and give the corresponding journal entries.
    c) List several of the highest volume transactions of a typical management consulting or similar service organization and give the corresponding journal entries.

29. You are a payroll clerk responsible for the manual preparation of the weekly employee payroll for a small firm having about 150 employees. Every Monday you receive from all department heads or supervisors a list of the hours worked by each employee in their departments for the previous week. You must determine the gross pay, net pay, and payroll deductions for each employee. You utilize a series of tax withholding tables to help determine the amount of social

security and income tax withholding. You also utilize, and update each week, a payroll master file containing for each employee such data as identification number, pay rate, the number of tax exemptions claimed, and year-to-date totals of gross pay, net pay, and all deductions. You must prepare all pay-checks, and also a report listing for each employee the hours worked, gross pay, net pay, and deductions for the week. Consider the activities in the data processing cycle described in this chapter. For each of these activities, give an example from the process described above.

30. List in the appropriate order the journal entries reflecting the movement of inventory through a manufacturing firm.

    a) Which of these entries represent internal transactions and which represent external transactions?

    b) Which of the accounts included in your journal entries would normally be summary accounts representing a large number of subsidiary ledger records?

31. Katie Kimball has decided to go into the florist business under the name of Katie's Flower Shop. She has made arrangements to lease a downtown store and to purchase a delivery truck. One full-time employee has been hired to help Katie prepare floral arrangements, wait on customers, keep records, and so forth. Katie expects to hire two part-time delivery boys.

    There are three wholesale florists in the area that Katie expects to use as a source of supply. In the florist business, a wide variety of flowers and plants must be kept in stock, but the product is perishable. Intelligent buying and inventory control is a major factor in the success of a florist. Knowledge of seasonal trends is very important.

    Katie expects that a good majority of her sales will be made over the telephone, and will be on account rather than for cash. Collection of accounts is thus likely to be a significant problem.

    Katie has come to you for assistance in designing an accounting information system for her business.

    Required

    a) Design a document for the recording of sale transactions. How many copies of this document should be prepared, and for what purposes?

    b) Design a set of records, procedures, and reports to enable Katie to obtain up-to-date information on unpaid customer accounts.

    c) Design a set of records, procedures, and reports to provide Katie with the information she needs to manage her inventories properly.

    d) Design a set of records and procedures to enable Katie to maintain control of cash receipts and disbursements and to prepare monthly financial statements.

32. The McCann brothers have decided to open an auto repair shop. John will be in charge of machine work, stocking of parts and supplies, and accounting. Ted will be the head mechanic and supervise the auto repair work. Arrangements have been made to lease a suitable building, and three other qualified auto mechanics have been hired.

The shop will maintain an inventory of the most commonly used parts and accessories. Other parts and accessories can be obtained as needed from local parts wholesalers. A separate room within the shop has been equipped with shelving to serve as a parts storeroom. The McCanns wish to minimize their investment in inventories as much as possible but also hope to avoid the need for frequent trips to buy unstocked parts.

As customers bring their autos into the shop for repairs, a service work order detailing the work to be done will be prepared. At this time, many customers will ask for an estimate of the repair cost and when the work will be completed. As the work is performed, the cost of parts and labor will be recorded on the service work order. When the customer returns to pick up the repaired vehicle, a copy of the service work order will serve as a bill. Customers may pay their bill by cash, check, or credit card. The McCanns intend to guarantee their work for thirty days.

The McCanns have asked you for assistance in designing an accounting information system for their business.

Required

a) Design a format for the service work order document. How many copies of this document should be prepared, and for what purposes?

b) What type of records and procedures should the McCanns utilize to help them make inventory decisions?

c) What type of records and procedures should the McCanns utilize to help in making estimates of repair costs?

d) What type of records and procedures should the McCanns utilize to control cash receipts and disbursements and enable the preparation of monthly financial statements?

References   Berliner, Robert W., and Dale L. Gerboth. "FASB Statement No. 33 'The Great Experiment'." *The Journal of Accountancy* (May 1980): 48–54.

Churchman, C. West. *The Systems Approach*. New York: Dell, 1968.

Coleman, Raymond H., and M. J. Riley. *MIS: Management Dimensions*. San Francisco: Holden-Day, 1973.

Committee on Accounting Education, American Accounting Association, and Computer Education Subcommittee, American Institute of Certified Public Accountants. "Inclusion of EDP in an Undergraduate Auditing Curriculum: Some Possible Approaches." *The Accounting Review* **49** (October 1974): 859–864.

Committee on Management Information Systems, American Accounting Association. "Report of the Committee." *The Accounting Review,* Supplement to Vol. 49 (1974): 140–155.

Davidson, H. Justin, and Robert M. Trueblood. "Accounting for Decision-Making." *The Accounting Review* **36** (October 1961): 577–582.

Davis, Gordon B. "Computer Curriculum for Accountants and Auditors—Present and Prospective." *Education for Expanding Computer Curriculums.* Daniel L. Sweeney (ed.). New York: American Institute of Certified Public Accountants, 1976: 12–21.

Emery, James C. *Organizational Planning and Control Systems.* New York: Macmillan, 1969.

Feltham, Gerald A. *Information Evaluation.* Studies in Accounting Research, No. 5. Sarasota, Florida: American Accounting Association, 1972.

Firmin, Peter A. "The Potential of Accounting as a Management Information System." *Management International Review* (February 1966): 45–55.

Johnstone, Anthony Gordon. "The Systems Accountant: How? Where? When? Who?" *The Internal Auditor* (February 1979): 23–28.

MacVeagh, Charles. "MIS: Building a Structure That Works." *Price Waterhouse Review* **22** (2) (1977): 42–49.

Moore, Michael R. "Undergraduate Computer Curriculum Requirements for Entering Staff in Accounting and Auditing." *Education for Expanding Computer Curriculums.* Daniel L. Sweeney (ed.). New York: American Institute of Certified Public Accountants, 1976.

Murdick, Robert G., and Joel E. Ross. *Introduction to Management Information Systems.* Englewood Cliffs, N.J.: Prentice-Hall, 1977.

Wilkinson, Joseph W. "Effective Reporting Structures." *Journal of Systems Management* (November 1976): 38–42.

Chapter 2

Organization and Accounting Information Systems

The distribution of authority and responsibility within an entity is indicated by its organizational structure. An understanding of the patterns of authority and responsibility distribution is essential to the assessment of information needs within an organization. In turn, information needs define the required structure of data collection and processing activities within the accounting information system. Therefore, the structure of data collection, processing, and reporting activities within an accounting information system must closely parallel the organizational structure of the entity it serves. An understanding of the concepts of organization thus provides part of the foundation for the study of accounting information systems.

Introduction to Concepts of Organization

Organization may be defined as the way in which the activities of people are coordinated to achieve a goal. In large complex organizations, the goal is usually divided into several subgoals, each of which is assigned to various subunits of the organization. Each subgoal may be further subdivided into still smaller subgoals, and so on down to the lowest levels of the organizational structure. This pattern of subdividing organizational goals and tasks into a graded series of lower level goals and tasks is called a *hierarchical* structure of organization.

A simple example of an organizational hierarchy is illustrated in Fig. 2.1. Each circle represents an organizational unit having a goal or subgoal and a manager responsible for achieving the goal or subgoal, and the lines between the circles repre-

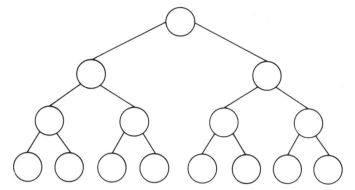

Fig. 2.1
A hierarchical
structure.

sent relationships between subordinate managers and their superiors. These relationships reflect the assignment of subgoals to subordinates by their superiors. The authority of the superiors must be delegated to the subordinates to direct the operations of lower level units toward the accomplishment of assigned subgoals. Acceptance of this authority creates for the subordinates a responsibility to manage operations in a manner that will result in the achievement of assigned subgoals. This is accompanied by a responsibility to report results to superiors. Subordinates may divide assigned subgoals into still smaller subgoals, and delegate the authority for achieving these to other persons, who become responsible to them. However, managers cannot delegate their responsibility—that is, they do not escape responsibility for achievement of assigned subgoals, even though they may delegate a portion of their authority.

An organization is partially described by its number of *levels of supervision* and average *span of control.* The number of levels of supervision is simply the number of ranks between the highest and lowest level units of the organization. Span of control refers to the number of subordinates reporting to a superior. For example, in Fig. 2.1 there are four levels of supervision, and the average span of control of each manager is two.

An organization can also be described in terms of the degree of centralization or decentralization of authority among its management levels. In a highly centralized organization, authority is concentrated at the higher management levels, with lower levels possessing a minimum of decision-making power. In a highly decentralized organization, a significant amount of decision-making authority may be delegated to lower levels. The concept is relative, and most organizations fall well within the two extremes. Even within the same organization, authority may be highly centralized in one functional area, such as production, and highly decentralized in other functional areas.

In Chapter 1, the two basic functions of management in an organization are defined as planning and control. These two functions are performed through the medium of organizational structure. An overall plan for the business organization is subdivided into more specific plans for lower level organizational units. At each level, plans are subdivided into lower level plans with the objective of providing effective coordination among all organizational units at that level. Control in the sense of implementing plans is carried out within organizational units at the lowest levels, under the supervision of managers acting in accordance with plans. Middle-level and higher-level managers reinforce this control by monitoring the performance of the organizational units whose managers report to them relative to the plan. When actual performance does not compare favorably with the plan, control action is initiated by the managers responsible for the organizational unit in which the deviation took place. Organizational structure is therefore clearly essential to the effective performance of the management functions of planning and control in large organizations.

Problems of modern organizations

According to Whisler,[1] the four most prominent problems of modern organizations that have implications for information systems are (1) rigidity, (2) information failures, (3) suboptimization, and (4) individual motivation.

Rigidity refers to a tendency within organizations to resist change. This problem has definite implications for information systems in particular. In the past several years improvements in information technology have accelerated. Organizations have been and continue to be faced with the problems of adopting these new technologies in a manner that obtains the maximum advantage from their expanded capabilities. Rigidity has tended to aggravate the organizational problems of transition to new information technologies.

The second problem refers to failures in communication between organizational units because of their physical separation and specialization of functions. Messages may be lost in transit, inaccurate or distorted, or vague or unclear. Information channels may become overloaded, causing delay or loss of information. This set of related problems has direct implications for the design of information systems. As organizations grow and functions become more separated and specialized, systems designers must identify problems of information failure as they arise and must design information systems in a manner that minimizes these problems.

The problem of *suboptimization* occurs when an organizational subunit, by attempting to optimize in the accomplishment of its assigned subgoal, makes it more difficult for the organization as a whole to optimally achieve its collective goals. This situation may be caused by the ineffective decompositon of goals into subgoals, but it is primarily a problem of coordination of operations among the various units within an organization. Because the accurate and timely reporting of information is essential to coordination, it is obvious that the problem of suboptimization also has direct implications for designers of information systems. Modern computer systems, if properly implemented, have great potential for improving the degree of coordination within large organizations, thus reducing the magnitude of the problem of suboptimization.

---

[1] *Thomas L. Whisler,* Information Technology and Organizational Change *(Belmont, California: Wadsworth, 1970), pp. 20–23.*

The problem of individual motivation refers to the areas of conflict between individual goals and organizational goals. This problem is often aggravated by attempts to implement new information technologies. Designers of information systems may be able to relieve this problem to some extent by incorporating motivational factors into their designs.

Business organization

Thus far the discussion of organizational concepts has been general, applying to all types of organizations. We will now turn to business entities and attempt to relate general organizational concepts to the specific problems and practices of business organizations.

Most business organizations define their primary goal as the maximization of long-run profits. There are two commonly used patterns of division of this overall goal into subgoals through organization. The first is the *functional organization structure,* under which employees with the same or similar occupational specialties, such as marketing, production, and accounting, are grouped together within organizational subunits of the business. The second pattern is the *divisional organization structure,* under which the organization consists of several divisions, each of which is relatively independent of the others and operates almost as a separate smaller company.

For example, in a manufacturing business organized along functional lines, the overall goal of profit maximization may be divided into subgoals through the use of the following organizational subunits: (1) marketing, with the goal of maximizing sales revenue; (2) production, with the goal of minimizing the production cost per unit; (3) finance, with the goal of providing the resources required for operation of the business at a minimum of expense; and (4) accounting, with the goal of measuring the success of the organization in achieving its goals. These goals may be broken down still further into additional sets of subgoals, assigned to lower level units, and so on. For example, the finance function could be further divided into the subunits of (a) investor relations, with the goal of maintaining good relations with the firm's sources of long-term debt and equity funds; (b) credit and collections, with the goal of establishing and enforcing credit policies that will maximize the excess of sales revenue over bad debt losses; and perhaps (c) insurance, with the goal of optimum management of the risk of loss of resources by the firm. This is an example of how the efficiencies of specialization may be achieved by means of the hierarchical structure of organizations.

A familiar means of illustrating patterns of authority delegation is the organization chart. A partial organization chart for a typical, single-plant manufacturing company organized along functional lines appears in Fig. 2.2.[2] Many of the general concepts discussed thus far are reflected in this chart. Each box represents an organizational unit supervised by a manager. Each line connecting a manager to a

[2] *This figure is adapted with some revision from John A. Higgins, "Responsibility Accounting," The Arthur Andersen Chronicle 12, (2) (April 1952), pp. 1–17.*

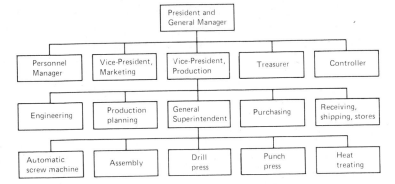

Fig. 2.2
*Sample organization
chart for a company
organized along func-
tional lines.*

lower-level manager represents the delegation of authority to a subordinate and the corresponding responsibility of the subordinate to report to the superior. A manager is responsible for all the activities that appear under that manager's span of control on the chart; that is, for the performance of all managers to whom a portion of that manager's authority has been delegated. The hierarchical structure of the organization is clearly apparent.

The chart illustrates organizational relationships within the production department in detail, but provides no detail with regard to the other major functional areas. A more detailed breakdown of the controllership function is provided in the next section of this chapter, while the other major functions are discussed in greater detail in later chapters. The chart omits reference to the information systems function, but it must be pointed out that in many modern organizations this function has achieved status as a major department of the same level as production, marketing, and accounting. The information systems function is also discussed in greater detail in subsequent chapters.

The functional organization structure provides the advantages of greater functional effectiveness due to specialization, centralized control, and economies of scale. However, as a business organization grows by adding new product lines, new plants, or even by diversifying into other lines of business, the pure functional organization structure may prove ineffective in coordinating and motivating employees to achieve the overall goal. Under the divisional organization structure, each division has virtually the same primary goal—that is, maximization of long-run profits—as the organization as a whole. An example of a business organization using a divisional structure appears in Fig. 2.3. Note that even when the divisional structure is used at the higher levels of the organization, the functional structure is still likely to be used at the lower levels, as shown in the figure. Furthermore, some vestiges of the functional structure may also appear at the top of the organization in the office of the Executive Vice-President for Administrative Services, which coordinates such functions as personnel, accounting, finance, and systems.

If an organization can divide its overall goal into subgoals in such a way that all employees working to achieve their assigned subgoals are also contributing to the optimal achievement of the overall goal, the situation is referred to as one of *goal*

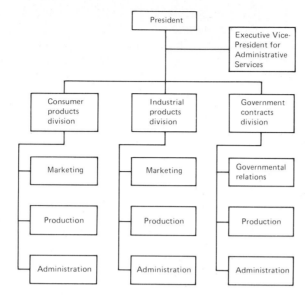

Fig. 2.3
Sample organization chart for a company organized along divisional lines.

congruence. The larger the organization becomes, the more difficult it is to achieve goal congruence, and the more likely it is that situations of *goal conflict* will arise in which a decision or action consistent with one subgoal is at variance with a decision or action dictated by another subgoal. This is true regardless of the form of organization chosen. For example, in a business organized along functional lines, the marketing subgoal of maximizing sales revenue may suggest offering a highly diverse product line, whereas the production subgoal of minimizing per unit production costs suggests offering a limited product line. In a divisionalized company, goal conflict may be present when two divisions compete with each other in the same market. Goal conflict also occurs frequently in divisionalized companies when a raw material or component produced by one division is used as input by another division. The producing division may maximize its profits by selling to the consuming division at a specified price, whereas the consuming division may be able to maximize its profits by buying the input from another source at a lower price.

Variations of the functional and divisional forms of organization include the use of project groups, the use of product line groups, and the matrix organization structure. Project groups are temporary organizational units consisting of employees drawn from several functional specialties and assigned to a particular task, such as building a new plant, introducing a new product line, or implementing a new information system. Product line groups also consist of employees from different functional specialties, but their assignment involves a somewhat more permanent responsibility for all aspects of a particular product line. In a *matrix organization structure,* both functional departments and project or product groups are present, and many employees have a dual responsibility to both a functional department and a particular project or product line.

A business organization's choice of its organization structure has significant implications for its accounting information system. A major responsibility of the accounting information system is to provide financial information to each organizational unit to assist in planning and controlling its operations. Thus the information required by any particular organizational unit is a function of its assigned subgoal. Planning information must assist the unit's manager in making decisions and taking actions to achieve its subgoals. This becomes especially difficult when the manager's span of control encompasses several departments among which a goal conflict exists. Control information includes measures of financial performance relative to goals. In order to provide the most relevant set of financial information for planning and control purposes, the designer of the accounting information system must understand (1) the structure of the organization, (2) the way in which the overall goal has been divided into subgoals, (3) the kinds of decisions and actions necessary to achieve the various subgoals, and (4) the information that is most useful in making those decisions and taking those actions.

Another relevant organizational issue in large businesses is the problem of establishing the degree of centralization of decision-making authority within the organization as a whole. If decision making is highly centralized, an organization will, theoretically, be better able to coordinate and control its activities in order to achieve optimal results with respect to its overall goal. However, it is generally believed that decentralization of decision-making authority to the divisional level results in divisional managers being more highly motivated to achieve maximum levels of performance. Furthermore, information failures may occur in the reporting of information from the divisions to a central location, and these failures could cause centralized decision makers to receive bad information and make poor decisions. Modern information technology permits accounting information systems to minimize the problem of information failures, and therefore encourages a strategy of centralization. However, the motivational factor continues to be a strong influence in favor of a strategy of decentralization. Whichever of these strategies is adopted by a business organization, the accounting information system must be designed to provide the necessary planning and control information to the appropriate managers on a timely basis.

According to a prominent organizational concept known as the *contingency theory,* the best way for a particular business enterprise to structure its organization is contingent upon a number of factors, including its size, the diversity and complexity of its products and production processes, and the degree of variability of its environment. For each business enterprise, some ways of organizing are likely to be better than others. However, there is no general method of organization that is superior for all types of businesses. A corollary of this theory must be that there is no general design for an accounting information system that is superior for all types of businesses. Thus the accounting information system must be designed to match the unique needs and characteristics of the business organization of which it is a part.

Organization of the accounting department

The way in which the accounting and information processing functions are organized may have a significant influence on the effectiveness of an accounting information system. Therefore, recommendations concerning the organization of these particular functions are a legitimate concern of the accounting systems designer. Figure 2.4 provides one example of how the accounting function in a typical manufacturing company might be organized. It should be understood that the illustration does not represent a prescription for all organizations but merely serves as an example reflecting patterns of organization that are somewhat common in practice.

The chief accounting executive is commonly referred to as the *controller,* a top-level executive in most business organizations, ranked on the same level with or one level below the executive vice-presidents. As such, the controller is a participant in top-level decision making affecting the entire organization.

Reporting to the controller are the staff functions of budgeting, records management, tax planning, and internal audit. The budgeting function involves the preparation of operating budgets, capital expenditure budgets, and related forecasts and analyses to assist management in planning and controlling the operations of the organization. Records management involves the design of business forms and the establishment of policies and procedures governing the retention and retrieval of business records. The tax planning function involves the administration of tax-reporting activities and the planning of transactions having significant tax effects in order to minimize the total long-run tax liability of the organization. The internal audit function is described more fully in the paragraph below. In large business organizations there are likely to be several additional staff departments reporting to the controller, whereas in small- or medium-sized companies the controller alone, or together with a single assistant, may perform all of these functions. Also reporting to the controller are a general accounting manager, whose responsibility is to supervise the routine operating functions of the accounting department, and a cost accounting manager, who supervises those accounting activities directly relating to factory operations.

An active internal audit department plays an important role in a well-managed business. The responsibilities of this function typically include (1) independent appraisal of the performance of various levels of management with regard to efficiency and adherence to company policies; (2) continuous review and recommendation of improvements in the system of internal checks and protective measures in the organization; (3) periodic assessment of the reliability of financial records and the effectiveness of processing methods; and (4) the execution of certain miscellaneous control functions that must be performed independently of other operating units. Examples of the last function include the preparation of bank reconciliations and the control of cash register tapes. Because of the necessity for independence and objectivity in this function, many companies require that the internal audit executive report to the president or board of directors instead of, or in addition to, the controller.

The distribution of general accounting functions shown in Fig. 2.4 is in accordance with major transaction account categories and is fairly typical. The payroll function maintains employee payroll records and prepares paychecks. The accounts payable department authorizes and disburses payments to short-term

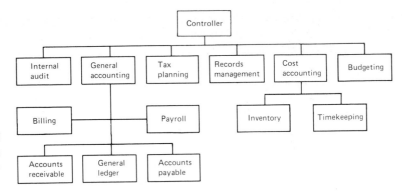

Fig. 2.4
Internal organization of a typical accounting department.

creditors for goods and services, and maintains records of these accounts. The general ledger department maintains the ledger of all balance sheet and income statement accounts. The billing function is distinguished from accounts receivable in that billing is responsible for sending out invoices at the time of sales, whereas accounts receivable is responsible for the records of customer accounts and for sending out periodic statements of account.

The relative significance of the cost accounting function depends on the type of company and its industry. In a manufacturing company, the cost function is an important one and includes the keeping of inventory records for raw materials, work in process, and finished goods, and perhaps the timekeeping function for factory employees whose wages are charged to work in process.

Two functions closely related to accounting—cashier, and credit and collections—are not shown in Fig. 2.4 because in most organizations they are the responsibility of the treasurer. The cashier is responsible for maintaining a record of cash receipts, endorsing and depositing checks, and reviewing and/or signing checks disbursing company funds. The credit-and-collections function involves the establishment of credit policies, the granting of credit to customers, and in some cases the administration of mailroom procedures relative to the receipt of customer payments through the mail. In some companies, either function, or both, may be performed within the accounting department itself.

In the sample organization chart, the clerical functions within the accounting department have been detailed to a considerable degree. In all but very large single-plant operations, each clerical function shown reporting to the accounting manager would probably be performed by one or two persons, rather than by completely separate departments. Furthermore, in organizations using a computer system, some of these clerical functions—particularly billing, payroll, and inventory—might well be replaced completely by the computer. Note that the primary purpose of the sample chart is to illustrate common patterns of distribution of functions within accounting departments. It bears repeating that the chart is *not* intended to be a model of how manufacturing companies *should* be organized, and that each company must adopt that structure best suited to its own particular needs and characteristics.

Responsibility Accounting

Responsibility accounting is a term describing the reporting of financial results in accordance with the assignment of managerial responsibilities within an organization. There are three major factors in a responsibility accounting system: (1) initial assignment of managerial responsibilities, which is reflected in the organization chart, (2) translation of these responsibilities into a formal set of goals, expressed in financial terms, and (3) reports showing how actual performance compares with the established goals. Responsibility accounting, particularly as it relates to the second and third of these factors, is one of the more vital functions of the accounting information system.

It can be said that a responsibility accounting system mirrors the organization structure, a point that is stressed throughout this section, which focuses on formal goal setting and performance reporting.

When a formal statement of the goals or plans of an organization is expressed in financial terms, it is called a *budget*. Business organizations commonly use several types of budgets, including operating budgets, capital budgets, and cash budgets. An *operating budget* is an estimate of an organizations' revenues and expenses for normal operations; it generally covers a period of either one month or one year. A *capital budget* represents an appropriation of funds for acquisition of major capital assets and investment in significant long-term projects. A *cash budget* is simply a forecast of cash inflows and outflows for the short-term future. Because operating budgets are the ones most commonly associated with responsibility accounting, the remainder of this section will be limited to them.

The preparation of budgets for a business organization is a function of the controller's staff, but this process also requires the participation of personnel from production, marketing, and other operating departments. The budget of a business organization has a structure that corresponds to the organization structure; that is, the overall budget of the entity is made up of a hierarchy of smaller budgets, each representing the financial plan of a division, department, or other unit of the organization structure.

The process of preparing the annual budget for a business organization begins with the sales forecast. Detailed predictions of the quantities of each individual product to be sold during the budget period are prepared at the lowest level of the marketing organization. These predictions are aggregated, adjusted, and approved by each field manager, who then submits them to an immediate superior for approval. The process is continued until a complete sales budget for the organization is developed. This budget not only summarizes total predicted sales for each of the products in the organization as a whole but also provides a breakdown of these totals for every organizational unit within the sales organization.

The sales budget must then be disaggregated to provide an estimate of the level of activity for every organizational unit in the firm during the budgeted period. For example, if the sales budget estimates total sales of 45,000 units of product X, this total may be disaggregated by assigning Plant A to produce 25,000 units and Plant B to produce 20,000 units. These production goals in turn provide a basis for estimating the level of activity required within individual departments of the two plants. A forecast of the expenditures required for each department is prepared from this.

These expenditures may be categorized according to the important types of activities engaged in by the department. The result is the department budget—an explicit statement in financial terms of the subgoals for which the department is responsible.

Whereas the budget is the primary vehicle of financial planning in a business organization, the *performance report* is the primary vehicle of financial control. A performance report is a summary of actual, as opposed to planned, results achieved by a particular manager. Of primary concern here is the financial performance report, which typically includes an itemized list of budgeted revenues, costs or expenses, the corresponding actual dollar amounts, and the *variances,* which are the differences between budgeted and actual dollar amounts for each item.

Note that the budget is not simply an exercise in estimating the future; it is in addition an important instrument of management control. The budget represents a standard of performance established by management for the achievement of the organization's goals. All managers, aware that their job performance will be evaluated relative to the budget, are motivated to attain and perhaps exceed the budgeted results. To the extent that the budget accurately reflects the organization's goals, managers are motivated to direct their activities toward the achievement of those goals. Therefore the budget and the financial performance report, which are the cornerstones of a responsibility accounting system, are also vital elements of management control within the business organization.

The effective responsibility accounting system incorporates two additional concepts, flexible budgeting and controllability of performance criteria. *Flexible budgeting* involves adjusting the budgeted elements of the performance report for differences between the forecasted level of activity and the actual level of activity. This means that all cost and expense items must be classified either as fixed or variable. *Fixed costs* remain constant as the level of activity (sales or production volume) increases or decreases, while *variable costs* rise or fall in proportion to increases or decreases in the level of activity. If the actual level of activity varies from the forecast level of activity upon which the budget was based, then flexible budgeting requires that the variable cost elements of the budget be adjusted to reflect the actual level of activity. This places the budgeted costs and actual costs in the performance report on a comparable basis, which makes the report a more equitable measure of performance.

To illustrate the concept of flexible budgeting, suppose that the monthly cost of repair and rework in an assembly department (see Fig. 2.2) is deemed to be partially fixed and partially variable, with the fixed portion estimated as $300 and the variable portion as $5 per unit on the average. If the budget for a particular month is based upon *estimated* production of 100 units, then the amount budgeted for repair and rework will be $300 + $5(100) = $800. However, if the *actual* production volume is 120 units, then $800 is no longer an equitable performance standard. A flexible budgeting system would adjust the budgeted amount on the performance report to $300 + $5(120) = $900.

The concept of controllability means that a manager's performance should be evaluated in terms of only those factors for which that manager has responsibility and authority. Thus *controllable costs* are those over which managers, through the exercise of their delegated authority, have some influence. To the foreman of a production department who has no influence over the purchase of assets, depreciation on that department's machinery is not controllable. To the same foreman, however, materials usage and labor usage represent controllable costs. A performance report should focus on controllable costs in its comparison of budgeted and actual costs.

Since the performance report is essentially an extension of the budget, the performance reporting system within a business organization will, like the budgeting system, possess a hierarchical structure. This point is illustrated in Fig. 2.5,[3] which shows performance reports for managers at each of the four levels of Fig. 2.2. Note that each report shows actual costs and variances (the amount budgeted is not shown) for the current month and the year to date, but only for those items which are controllable at that level. The hierarchical nature of performance reporting is evident in that the total cost of each department below the top level becomes a single line item on the performance report of the manager at the next higher level. Thus the hierarchy of cost aggregation and reporting in a responsibility accounting system corresponds almost exactly to the hierarchy of authority delegation as reflected in the organization chart. This is an important example of how the accounting information system is influenced by organization structure.

In a responsibility accounting system, each organizational unit may be designated as either a cost center, a profit center, or an investment center. A *cost center* is an organizational unit whose assigned objective is to achieve its operational function at a minimum cost. Reports on a cost center thus focus on variances from actual costs that are controllable with the center. The reports in Fig. 2.5 are illustrative of this type of reporting. The organizational units most commonly treated as cost centers are operating departments and project groups. A *profit center* is a department or division whose assigned objective is to maximize net profit. Reports on a profit center must therefore include both the costs and revenues assignable to it. Product line groups within a division are often treated as profit centers. An *investment center* is a department or division whose assigned objective is to maximize return on investment (net profit divided by total assets). Investment center performance reports thus include costs, revenues, and assets identifiable with its operation. Business organizations using the divisional form of organization structure generally treat their divisions as investment centers.

Another important concept closely related to responsibility accounting is the principle of *management by exception*. If the performance report shows actual costs of less than, or only slightly greater than, budgeted figures, a manager can assume that the item is under control. On the other hand, if actual costs are significantly higher than budgeted costs, management is made aware of an item of cost that may be out of control. The exception triggers a study of the situation and, where needed, action to correct the problem.

In general terms, the position and responsibilities of managers in a business organization provide useful insight into their needs for information. Knowledge of

---

[3] *Ibid.*

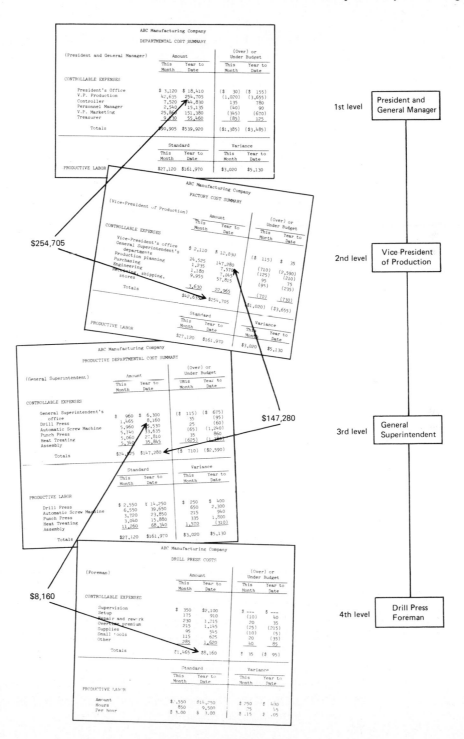

$254,705

$147,280

$8,160

1st level — President and General Manager

2nd level — Vice President of Production

3rd level — General Superintendent

4th level — Drill Press Foreman

*Fig. 2.5
The hierarchy of per-
formance reports.*

the organizational structure and the division of authority and responsibility within an entity is thus essential to a designer of accounting information systems. Once the nature of the desired output of the system is known, the system designer can concentrate upon structuring the system to produce that output most effectively.

Review Questions

1. Define the following terms.

organization	operating budget
hierarchical	capital budget
levels of supervision	cash budget
span of control	performance report
suboptimization	variance
functional organization structure	flexible budgeting
divisional organization structure	fixed costs
goal congruence	variable costs
goal conflict	controllable costs
matrix organization structure	cost center
contingency theory	profit center
controller	investment center
responsibility accounting	management by exception
budget	

2. Why is an understanding of concepts and practices of organization important to the study of accounting information systems?

3. Can responsibility be delegated? What is the relationship of responsibility to authority delegation?

4. Explain the concepts of centralization and decentralization of authority.

5. Explain how organizational structure contributes to the effective performance of the management functions of planning and control.

6. Identify and briefly explain four prominent problems of modern organizations and their implications for information systems.

7. What is the commonly accepted goal of business organizations? In what way does organizational structure contribute to the achievement of that goal?

8. What are the relative advantages and disadvantages of the functional and divisional forms of organization structure? Which form is best?

9. Describe some examples of goal conflict in a business organization.

10. Describe three forms of organization structure other than the functional and divisional forms.

11. How does the organization structure of a business affect the design of its accounting information system?

12. What are the relative merits of centralization and decentralization of authority within a business organization?

13. What are some examples of staff functions reporting to the controller in a typical business organization?

14. What are the responsibilities of the internal audit function in business? What are the issues in the question of to whom the internal audit executive should report?

15. What distinction is there between the billing function and the accounts receivable function in a business?

16. Explain the three major factors in a responsibility accounting system.

17. Explain how the responsibility accounting system mirrors the organization structure.

18. Identify three different kinds of budgets commonly used in business organizations.

19. Describe the steps in the process of preparing the annual operating budget in a business organization.

20. Explain the relationship of a performance report to a budget.

21. How does management by exception enter into the process of budgetary control?

Discussion Questions

22. What contribution can the accounting information system make to the resolution of goal conflict within a business organization? (It may be useful to refer to the examples of goal conflict presented in the chapter.)

23. It is stated in this chapter that ''Business organizations generally interpret their primary goal to be the maximization of long-run profits.'' Is this goal in conflict with social goals such as a clean environment and a lasting world peace? How can the accounting profession contribute to the resolution of such conflicts of business and social goals?

24. Discuss the similarities and differences between the organization structure of a business and of a university. What is the nature of the role played by an accounting information system within a university?

Problems and Cases

25. Prepare a simple illustration of an organizational hierarchy. Using a set of descriptive labels, identify one example within your illustration of each of the following.
    a) a manager
    b) an organizational unit
    c) the goal of the organization
    d) a subgoal
    e) delegation of authority
    f) reporting responsibility
    g) span of control

26. Mr. John Newman is President of the New Manufacturing Company. His three sons are Vice-Presidents: Robert is in charge of the Production Department, David is responsible for the Marketing Department, and Steven heads the Accounting Department.

Within the Production Department are four departments, each headed by a supervisor who reports to Robert Newman. These are Personnel (with two employees in addition to the supervisor), Purchasing (with four additional employees), Engineering (with two additional employees), and the Factory. There are three departments within the Factory, each with a boss who reports to the factory supervisor. These are Shipping and Receiving (with three employees in addition to the boss), Assembly (with six additional employees), and Finishing (with six additional employees).

Within the Marketing Department are three departments, each headed by a manager who reports to David Newman. These are Advertising (with two additional employees), Credit (with two additional employees), and the Sales Manager (who supervises six field salespersons).

Within the Accounting Department are three departments, each headed by a manager who reports to Steven Newman. These are General Accounting (with four additional employees), Data Processing (with three additional employees), and the Treasurer (with two additional employees).

Required

a) Prepare an organization chart for the New Manufacturing Company.
b) How many levels of supervision are there within the company?
c) What is the average span of control within the company?
d) Identify the major differences in allocation of responsibilities between the New Manufacturing Company and the company whose chart is shown in Fig. 2.2. Do these differences imply that the New Manufacturing Company has a problem with its organization structure? Comment.

27. Bill Werner is the boss of a factory department in a small manufacturing company. The company recently began to prepare financial performance reports to assist in evaluating its bosses. However, Bill feels that his performance report for the most recent month was an unfair measure of his managerial performance.

There are two principles of performance reporting that, if not followed, could have caused the problem in evaluating Bill's performance. Identify these two principles, and explain how they should be incorporated into a performance reporting system.

28. Several years ago, Dr. Grey formed the Grey Corporation to perform research in the energy field. The company has grown dramatically but continues to operate as it was originally organized. Grey still tries personally to supervise all major projects and support functions, although he now finds it virtually impossible to do so. Nevertheless, he hesitates to relinquish operating control, fearing that quality might deteriorate. The present staff of 70 researchers requires the support of three financial, ten technical, twelve clerical and two custodial employees. Grey Corporation may have as many as 25 research projects underway at any given time.

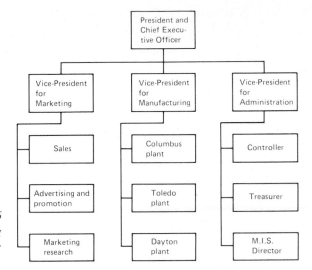

Fig. 2.6
Ohio Manufacturing
Company organiza-
tion chart.

Required

a) State an important organizational principle that Grey is violating.

b) Give three recommendations that would improve Grey Corporation's current organizational structure.[4]

29. A partial organization chart for the Ohio Manufacturing Company is shown in Fig. 2.6.

Draw another chart showing how the organization might be structured if it were to adopt a divisional rather than a functional organization structure.

30. General Hardware Industries (GHI) is a large manufacturer of hardware for home and industrial use. GHI is organized along divisional lines, each of its three major plants being a separate division. These are the Power Tools Division (St. Louis), the Hand Tools Division (Omaha), and the Specialty Tools Division (Kansas City). A partial organization chart for GHI is shown in Fig. 2.7.

GHI has recently completed the acquisition of Kimball's Lawn Management, Inc. (KLM), a manufacturer of lawn and garden equipment and chemical sprays and fertilizers. KLM has five major plants located in the midwest and specializing in the following product lines.

Chicago plant (company headquarters)—fertilizers

Springfield plant—weed and bug sprays

St. Paul plant—garden tools (hoes, rakes, shovels, etc.)

Sioux Falls plant—sprinkler systems

Milwaukee plant—power mowers, tillers, spreaders, etc.

KLM is organized along functional lines, as shown in the chart in Fig. 2.8.

[4] *Question 18, Part III (Principles of Management). From the Certified Internal Auditor Examination, 1978. Copyright 1978 by the Institute of Internal Auditors, Inc. Reprinted by permission of the Institute of Internal Auditors, Inc., 249 Maitland Ave., Altamonte Springs, Florida 32701.*

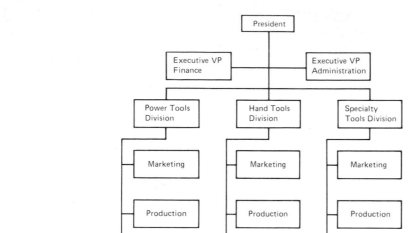

Fig. 2.7
GHI organization
chart.

Required

a) Discuss whether the newly merged company should be organized along functional or divisional lines.

b) If the new organization structure is to be functional, draw an organization chart indicating how it might be formed.

c) If the new organization structure is to be divisional, draw an organization chart indicating how it might be formed.

d) Assuming that the company will use the divisional form of organization, identify some organizational units that could be treated as investment centers, profit centers, and cost centers.

e) If the company changes its name to GHIJKLM, Inc., what will the "J" stand for?

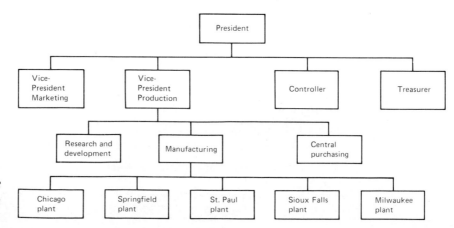

Fig. 2.8
KLM organization
chart.

31. In the Carlton Manufacturing Company, the supervisors of three production departments (Machining, Assembly, Finishing) and one service department (Maintenance) report to the plant manager. Among the plant manager's other responsibilities are the making of recommendations concerning salary increments for these subordinates as well as his own staff and the making of recommendations concerning equipment purchases for the departments under his span of control.

The following summary of costs for the Assembly Department for the month of May, 1981, was compiled for use in inventory costing:

Cost	Budget	Actual
Direct labor	$3,500	$4,000
Materials spoilage	200	210
Overtime premium	500	580
Reassembly	400	390
Supplies and small tools	300	310
Supervisor's salary	650	650
Allocation of depreciation on building	100	100
Allocation of depreciation on equipment	100	120
Allocation of plant manager's salary	200	200
Allocation of salaries of plant manager's staff	250	260
Allocation of maintenance department costs	1,200	1,290
Total	$7,400	$8,110

Additional information

- Budgeted costs are based upon budgeted activity of 1000 units of production. Actual number of units of production was equal to 1100.
- All other departments also exceeded their budgeted activity level by exactly 10 percent.
- Maintenance Department Costs are allocated in three equal amounts to the three production departments.
- All other allocations are made in four equal amounts to the four departments under the plant manager.
- Budgeted and actual salaries for the four department supervisors total $2,500, including $650 for the maintenance supervisor.
- Depreciation is computed on a straight-line basis. Equipment has been purchased during 1981 that was not included in the initial budget for the year.

Required

a) Categorize each cost in the above list according to whether it is (1) controllable by Assembly Department supervisor, (2) controllable by plant manager, or (3) controllable by neither.

b) Categorize each cost in the above list according to whether it is (1) fixed, or (2) variable with the level of activity.

c) Prepare a performance report for the month of May for the Assembly Department supervisor. Use a three-column format, with the first column listing budget amounts, the second listing actual amounts, and the third listing variances. Assume that it is company policy for performance reports to include only controllable costs and to use the principle of flexible budgeting.

d) The total actual cost from the performance reports for the Machining and Finishing departments, and the total budgeted cost for these departments according to the budgeted (rather than the actual) activity level are as follows.

Department	Budget	Actual
Machining	$2,500	$2,800
Finishing	2,000	2,100

Using the same format and company policies described in part (c), prepare a performance report for the plant manager.

References

Anstine, Patricia A., and Michael E. Scott. "ARCO Establishes Responsibility Accounting at Prudhoe Bay." *Management Accounting* (March 1980): 13–20.

Bridge, Ronald E. "The Plant Controller—A Member of the Management Team." *Financial Executive* (September 1979): 26–30.

Clancy, Donald K. "The Management Control Problems of Responsibility Accounting." *Management Accounting* (March 1978): 35–39.

Emery, James C. *Organizational Planning and Control Systems.* New York: Macmillan, 1969.

Galbraith, Jay. *Designing Complex Organizations.* Reading, Mass.: Addison-Wesley, 1973.

Hernandez, William H. "Is the Controller an Endangered Species?" *Management Accounting* (August 1978): 48–52.

Higgins, John A. "Responsibility Accounting." *The Arthur Andersen Chronicle* **12**(April 1952): 1–17.

Horngren, Charles T. *Cost Accounting, A Managerial Emphasis.* (4th ed.) Englewood Cliffs, N.J.: Prentice-Hall, 1977.

Jackson, John H. and Cyril P. Morgan. *Organization Theory: A Macro Perspective for Management.* Englewood Cliffs, N.J.: Prentice-Hall, 1978.

Krueger, Donald A. "Responsibility Accounting in Perspective." *The Arthur Andersen Chronicle* (December 1966): 1–14.

March, James G., and Herbert A. Simon. *Organizations.* New York: Wiley, 1958.

Osborn, Richard N.; James G. Hunt; and Lawrence R. Jauch. *Organization Theory: An Integrated Approach.* New York: Wiley, 1980.

Porter, Grover L. "Organization for Third Generation Controllership." *Financial Executive* **37**(April 1969): 41–45.

Reece, James S., and William R. Cool. "Measuring Investment Center Performance." *Harvard Business Review* (May/June 1978): 28–46, 174–176.

Simon, Herbert A. "On the Concept of Organizational Goal." *Administrative Science Quarterly* (June 1964): 1–22.

Toy, James H. "Responsibility Accounting: A Practical Application." *Management Accounting* (January 1978): 23–26.

Vancil, Richard F. "Managing the Decentralized Firm." *Financial Executive* (March 1980): 34–43.

Whisler, Thomas L. *Information Technology and Organizational Change.* Belmont, Calif.: Wadsworth, 1970.

Chapter 3

Records Management and File Processing

Records management involves a systematic approach to all phases of the life cycle of business records, including (1) the creation of business forms to serve as a medium for the collection and storage of record data; (2) the period of active processing, storing, and retrieving of the records themselves; (3) the period of retention of inactive records; and (4) the point of discarding obsolete records. In many business organizations the significance of the records management function is indicated by its existence as a separate department, as previously illustrated in Chapter 2. (See Fig. 2.4.)

Some of the functions that are commonly the responsibility of a records management department include the analysis and design of forms, the selection of filing systems and equipment, the administration of a printing and copy center, the establishment and staffing of a record retention center for bulk storage of inactive records, and the administration of mail handling and distribution services. Other related functions include typing and secretarial services, telecommunications services, and the design of office work methods and procedures. In some companies many or all of these functions are grouped together organizationally in a department of "office services" or "office administration."

Because records play such an important role in the accounting information system, this chapter focuses on certain key aspects of the record life cycle. The first section of the chapter discusses the principles involved in the design of business forms; the second section discusses the closely related topic of coding of business data and records; and the third section discusses the concepts and techniques of file processing.

The principles and techniques discussed in this chapter are applicable both to manual and automated data processing systems, to the accounting function as well as the marketing, personnel and production functions in a business organization, and to governmental agencies, educational institutions, charitable organizations, and many other types of nonbusiness organizations. The material in this chapter thus provides an important foundation for later chapters dealing with automated data processing and applications of accounting information systems to various functional areas of modern organizations.

Principles of Forms Design

A *form* is a document preprinted with headings and spaces for the insertion of data. The preprinted data on a form are referred to as *constant data,* while the items to be filled in are referred to as *variable data.* Once the variable data have been filled in, the form becomes a record. Figure 3.1, a sample credit memorandum form, illustrates many of the principles of forms design discussed in this section.

Most forms consist of four major elements: (1) the introduction, (2) instructions, (3) the main body, and (4) the conclusion. The introduction generally should appear at the top of the form and should contain the title of the form, the form number, and, if the form is to be distributed to outside parties, the name and address of the organization sending the form. Each of these elements is present in the sample form in Fig. 3.1.

Instructions are generally of two types: (1) how to fill out the form, and (2) what to do with the form after filling it out. In simple forms such as the sample credit memo, the preprinted data that indicate what information is to be recorded on the form usually serve as the instructions on how to complete the form. Specialized forms that are infrequently used or that deal with technical information may require more specific written instructions on the body of the form or occasionally on the reverse side. Instructions on what to do with the form should indicate, when applicable, the sequence of departments to which the form is to be routed, or the appropriate distribution of completed copies of the form, as illustrated in the sample credit memo.

In the main body of the form, the primary design objective is to make the form as simple as possible to use. Logically related information should be grouped together on the form, with box and columnar arrangements used as much as possible to set off spaces for recording data. Care should be taken to provide ample room for recording the data required by each space. In addition, the sequence in which the data item spaces appear on the form should be consistent with the sequence in which the data itself will be initially recorded on the form, and/or the sequence in which the data items will be transcribed from the form to some other medium. The latter point is especially critical when the form is to be used as a source document for keying the data into an automated data processing system. Each of these principles is evident in the design of the form in Fig. 3.1.

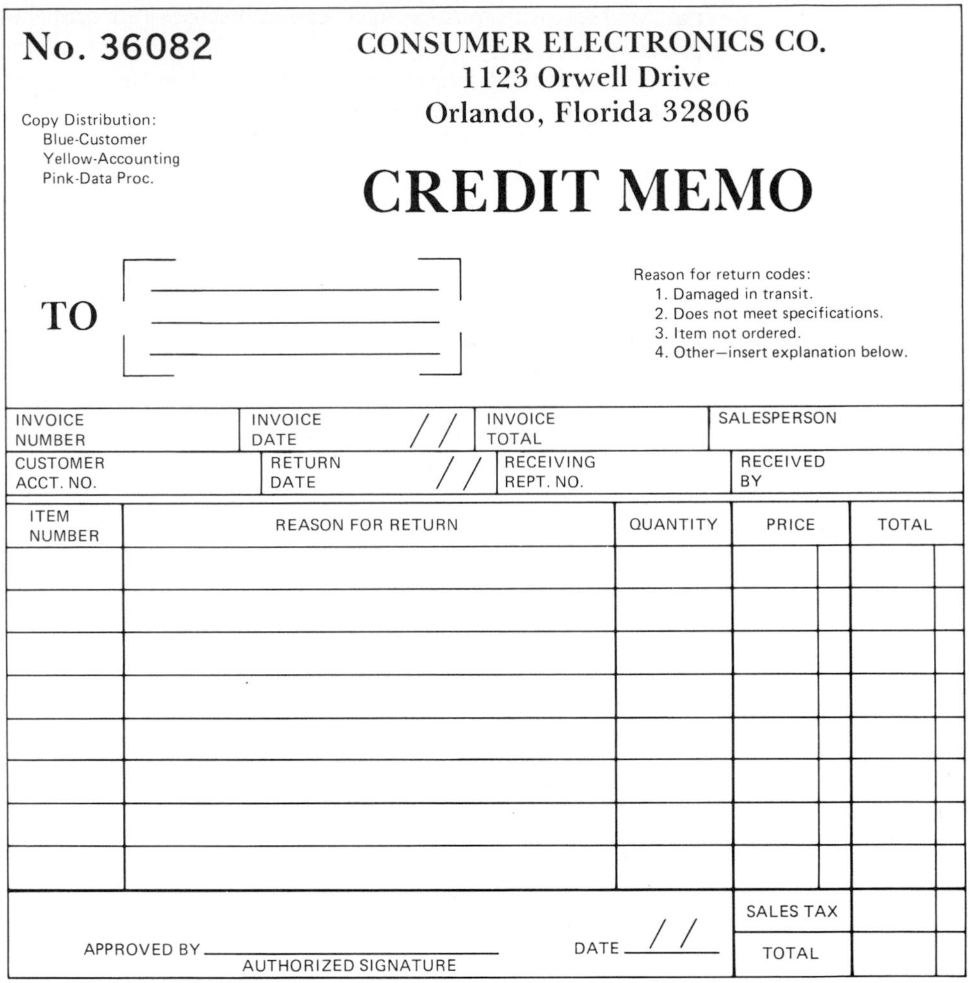

No. 36082	CONSUMER ELECTRONICS CO.

CONSUMER ELECTRONICS CO.
1123 Orwell Drive
Orlando, Florida 32806

Copy Distribution:
Blue-Customer
Yellow-Accounting
Pink-Data Proc.

CREDIT MEMO

TO

Reason for return codes:
1. Damaged in transit.
2. Does not meet specifications.
3. Item not ordered.
4. Other—insert explanation below.

INVOICE NUMBER	INVOICE DATE / /	INVOICE TOTAL	SALESPERSON
CUSTOMER ACCT. NO.	RETURN DATE / /	RECEIVING REPT. NO.	RECEIVED BY

ITEM NUMBER	REASON FOR RETURN	QUANTITY	PRICE		TOTAL	
					SALES TAX	
APPROVED BY _____ AUTHORIZED SIGNATURE		DATE __ / / __			TOTAL	

Fig. 3.1
Sample credit
memorandum form.

A useful technique that minimizes the extent to which users are required to write explanations or other lengthy statements on a form is to preprint the most commonly used of such explanations or statements on the face of the form. The user then decides which of the preprinted items is applicable and simply records the code number associated with it, or checks off a box next to it. To provide for unusual cases not encompassed by the preprinted list, an "other" category may be provided, along with sufficient space to record a written explanation. The application of this technique is illustrated by the "reason for return codes" in the sample credit memo. It is clear that this technique will significantly reduce the time required to fill out a form.

The concluding portion invariably appears at the bottom of the form. This portion should allow space to record information concerning the final disposition and/or final approval of the transaction recorded on the form, including an approval signature and date. If the form concerns a financial transaction, a dollar total will also appear here. Once again, these elements are illustrated in the sample credit memo in Fig. 3.1.

There are also certain principles that apply to the form itself. For example, the weight and grade of paper used in the form should be appropriate to its usage and retention requirements. Boldface type, extra thick rulings, varying colors, and shaded areas should be used liberally to highlight key aspects of the form, to separate distinct parts, or to otherwise facilitate user comprehension and utilization. The size of a form should be consistent with whatever standardized sizes are used throughout the organization. The size chosen for a particular form must of course provide sufficient room to record all required data, but should also take into account requirements for filing, binding, or mailing the form. If the form is to be mailed, the name and address of the addressee should be located in a position that will correspond with the opening in a window envelope, as exemplified by the sample credit memo in Fig. 3.1.

The various principles discussed above are summarized in the forms design checklist appearing in Fig. 3.2. This checklist serves as a useful tool for both the evaluation of existing forms and the design of new ones.

FORMS DESIGN CHECKLIST

General Considerations
1. Are preprinted data used to the maximum extent feasible?
2. Is the weight and grade of paper appropriate for planned usage?
3. Are bold type, double-thick rulings, varying colors, and shaded areas appropriately used?
4. Is the form of a standard size?
5. Is the form large enough for its intended purpose?
6. Is the size of the form consistent with requirements for filing, binding, or mailing?
7. Does the design of the form enable its use in a window envelope?

Introductory Section
8. Does the name of the form appear in bold type?
9. Are copies of the form consecutively prenumbered?
10. If the form is externally distributed, is the company's name and address preprinted on it?
11. Do all introductory data appear at the top of the form?

Instructions
12. Is it clear how the form is to be filled out?
13. Is the routing of the form indicated?
14. Is the distribution of completed copies indicated?

Main Body
15. Is logically related information grouped together?
16. Are box and columnar arrangements appropriately used?
17. Is there sufficient room to record each data item?
18. Is the ordering of the data items consistent with the sequence in which they are recorded or transcribed?
19. Are standardized explanations preprinted to enable codes or checkoffs to replace written user entries?

Conclusion
20. Is space provided to record data concerning final disposition of the form?
21. Is space provided for a signature or signatures indicating final approval?
22. Is space provided to record the date of final disposition or approval?
23. Is space provided for a dollar or other numeric total?
24. Do all concluding data appear at the bottom of the form?

Fig. 3.2
Forms design
checklist.

**Coding
Techniques**

Coding techniques are an essential aspect of the design and control of business records. Virtually all data processing systems, whether manual or automated, use codes—a fact that is especially true of accounting information systems. *Coding* has been defined as

> *the assignment of numbers, letters, or other symbols according to a systematic plan for distinguishing the classifications to which each item belongs and for distinguishing items within a given classification from each other.* [1]

Codes are essential to such data processing activities as sorting, summarizing, storage, reporting, and retrieval. This section describes and illustrates some of the basic types of codes used in an accounting information system.

**Basic coding
concepts**

Most business and accounting codes use either alphabetic or numeric symbols, or some combination thereof. Alphabetic symbols have two primary advantages over numeric symbols. First, an alphabetic code can be mnemonic, or suggestive of the name of the item it represents. For example, in the three-letter code used by airline companies to identify airports, DFW represents Dallas–Fort Worth, and JFK stands for New York's Kennedy airport. The second advantage is that a single position in an alphabetic code can represent up to twenty-six different possible categories, as opposed to only ten for a numeric code. Thus alphabetical codes are potentially more economical in terms of the number of code positions used.

Despite these factors, numeric codes have long been more common in business and accounting. It has been found that numeric codes are less error prone and more easily remembered when the length of the code is more than just a few positions. Furthermore, numeric codes are more amenable to machine processing.

Perhaps the most common application of coding in data processing is the assignment of a unique identification number to each data record within the system. This number is referred to as a *key* or, more specifically, a *primary key*. Figure 3.3 lists some of the common types of data records in a business organization and identifies the key most commonly used for each. The basic purpose of the key is to fix the location of each record within a large file of similar records. The key is therefore essential to such data processing activities as retrieval of specific records from a file, storing of records, and updating of records to reflect the occurrence of transactions.

Many of the codes used in business and accounting applications are *sequence codes*. In this coding system, items are numbered consecutively, and each new item is assigned a number one higher than the last to ensure that there will be no gaps in the sequence. The basic advantage of this technique is that it enables the user to account for all of the items because any missing items will cause a gap in the numerical sequence. Applications of this technique in business and accounting systems include the numbering of checks, invoices, purchase orders, job orders, and many other

---

[1] *National Association of Accountants. Classification and Coding Techniques to Facilitate Accounting Operations,* Research Report 34 (New York: National Association of Accountants, 1959), page 3.

Fig. 3.3
Examples of record keys for typical business records.

Record Type	Primary Key
Payroll	Employee Number
Customer	Account Number
Parts Inventory	Stock Number
Work in Process	Job Number
Finished Goods	Product Code
General Ledger	Account Code
Fixed Assets	Asset Number
Accounts Payable	Vendor Code

documents. In most cases these documents are prenumbered to further facilitate control.

Another commonly used coding technique is the *block code.* This involves reserving blocks of numbers within a numerical sequence, with each block corresponding to a category having meaning to the user. For example, consider a manufacturer of home appliances with four basic product lines—electric ranges, refrigerators, washers, and dryers. Within each product line, there may be a wide variety of models, varying in size, style, color, year of manufacture, and so forth. If a seven-digit product code is used, block coding can be applied by reserving a specific range of code numbers for each of the four major product categories, as illustrated in the following example.

Product code	Product type
1000000-2999999	Electric range
3000000-5999999	Refrigerator
6000000-7999999	Washer
8000000-9999999	Dryer

Under this scheme, a user familiar with the code can readily identify the type of item by code number alone. In addition to product code numbers, this technique can be applied to ledger account numbers (blocked by account type), employee numbers (blocked by department), customer numbers (blocked by region), and several other codes used in business and accounting.

Still another technique, often used in conjunction with the block code, is the *group code.* Under this scheme, there are two or more subgroups of digits within the code number, and each subgroup is used to code the item. If the seven-digit product code number is used as an example, the group-coding technique may be applied as follows.

Digit position	Meaning
1–2	Product line, size, style
3	Color
4–5	Year of manufacture
6–7	Optional features

Thus there are four subcodes within the product code, with a different meaning conveyed by each subcode. Given the actual code number of a particular product, a user who decodes the number can learn a significant amount about the item itself. Furthermore, this type of code enables sorting, summarizing, and retrieval of information based upon one or more of the subcodes. This technique is often applied to general ledger account numbers, and has several other possible applications in business data processing.

The chart of accounts

The *chart of accounts* is a list of codes for all balance sheet and income statement accounts of a business. The codes are account numbers, and they represent the key field for the general ledger records. There are few other areas in which coding techniques are more highly developed or widely applied than in the development of a chart of accounts. This fact reflects the importance of the chart of accounts in the processing and reporting of information by the accounting information system.

Most charts of accounts use numeric codes with a combination of group coding and block coding techniques. An example of a group coding scheme for account numbers is the following.

Digit position	Classification
1–2	Division, plant, or office
3–4	Department
5–7	Major account
8–9	Subaccount

The first two digits indicate the division, plant, or office location to which the transaction relates, and the second two digits indicate the specific department within that division, plant, or office. The major account code identifies broad account classifications, such as cash or selling expenses. Finally, the subaccount code identifies the account according to more detailed categories, such as cash in bank or sales commissions.

Block coding is usually applied to the major account codes, and often to the divisional and departmental codes as well. One possible block coding scheme for a chart of accounts appears at the top of page 61.

A simplified chart of balance sheet accounts consistent with this block coding scheme appears in Fig. 3.4. A corresponding chart of income statement accounts appears in Fig. 3.5. These charts are "simplified" in that many of the accounts represent general categories that can include a number of more-detailed accounts. For example, categories within the cash account may include cash on hand, petty cash funds, demand deposits, savings accounts, and certificates of deposit. The degree of

Major account code	Major account type
100–199	Current assets
200–299	Noncurrent assets
300–399	Liabilities
400–499	Capital
500–599	Revenue
600–699	Cost of goods sold
700–799	Selling expenses
800–899	General and administrative expenses
900–999	Nonoperating income and expenses

Fig. 3.4 Simplified balance sheet chart of accounts.

Account Code	Account Name	Account Code	Account Name
100–199	Current Assets	300–399	Liabilities
100	Cash	300	Accounts Payable
110	Marketable Securities	310	Accrued Wages and Salaries
120	Accounts Receivable	320	Accrued Taxes
125	Allowance for Doubtful Accounts	330	Accrued Interest
130	Notes Receivable	340	Dividends Payable
140	Inventory—Raw Materials	350	Notes Payable
150	Inventory—Work in Process	360	Bonds Payable
160	Inventory—Finished Goods	370	Other Liabilities
170	Prepaid Expenses		
		400–499	Capital Accounts
200–299	Noncurrent Assets	400	Capital Stock
200	Land	410	Preferred Stock
210	Buildings	420	Paid-in-Surplus
215	Allowance for Depreciation—Buildings	430	Retained Earnings
220	Equipment		
225	Allowance for Depreciation—Equipment		
230	Office Fixtures		
235	Allowance for Depreciation—Office Fixtures		
240	Long-Term Investments		
250	Intangible Assets		
260	Other Assets		

Fig. 3.5 Simplified income statement chart of accounts.

Account Code	Account Name	Account Code	Account Name
500–599	Operating Revenues	700–799	Selling Expenses
500	Sales Revenue	700	Sales Commissions
510	Sales Discounts	710	Advertising
520	Sales Returns and Allowances	720	Entertainment
530	Miscellaneous Revenue	730	Delivery
		740	Warrantee
		750	Other Selling Expenses
600–699	Cost of Goods Sold		
600	Cost of Goods Sold		
610	Direct Materials	800–899	General and Administrative Expenses
620	Direct Labor	800	Payroll Control
630	Factory Overhead Control	810	Wages and Salaries
631	Indirect Labor	820	Legal and Consulting
632	Supplies and Small Tools	830	Travel
633	Supervision	840	Depreciation—Office Fixtures
634	Depreciation—Plant	850	Stationery and Supplies
635	Depreciation—Equipment	860	Postage
636	Heat, Light, and Power	870	Communications
637	Taxes and Insurance	880	Interest
640	Applied Factory Overhead	890	Taxes
		895	Other Administrative

detail required will vary with the size of the organization and its needs. For example, the level of detail shown in the figures might be adequate for a very small company, while a large company might require hundreds of separate accounts.

The chart of accounts is an extremely useful tool for processing of accounting data in organizations of all types and sizes. It facilitates the recording and posting of transactions, and it simplifies the preparation of financial statements and a variety of other summary reports. The account codes are suitably concise to be used for cross-referencing purposes. A well-designed chart of accounts is easily adapted to automated methods of data processing. Even a very small single-location business can obtain substantial benefits from the use of a chart of accounts.

Organizational codes

In a medium-size to large company, it is generally very useful for the chart of accounts to incorporate subcodes indicating the division or branch responsible for the transaction, and also the department within that division or branch. In the group coding scheme for accounts shown earlier, the first two digits represent the division, and the third and fourth digits represent the department. The importance of these codes is quite simple: they greatly facilitate the accumulation, analysis, summarization, and reporting of accounting information according to responsibilities. In other words, such codes are an essential part of a responsibility accounting system as described in Chapter 2.

An example of a two-digit departmental coding scheme is shown in Fig. 3.6. The organization structure reflected in this illustration is consistent with, but somewhat more detailed than, the organization chart shown in Fig. 2.2.

The following sample transactions illustrate how these departmental codes might be used in conjunction with the account codes in recording accounting data: an expenditure for indirect labor within the Drill Press Department; a requisition of raw materials from Stores by the Assembly Department; a sale on account within Sales District 43; the purchase of office fixtures for use in the Controller's Office; and a consultant's fee incurred by the Marketing Department.

The indirect labor expenditure would be debited to account number 23–631, where "23" refers to the Drill Press Department, and "631" refers to the Indirect Labor account. The account credited would be 00–800, where "800" refers to the Payroll Control account. The "00" is used as the departmental code to indicate that the Payroll account is a general account not applicable to any particular organizational unit.

The materials requisition would result in a debit to an account coded 22–610, where "22" indicates that the Assembly Department accepted responsibility for the materials, and "610" represents the account code for Direct Materials (alternatively, the debit might be made directly to "150," the Work-in-Process Inventory account). The credit for this transaction would be made to an account coded 14–140, where "14" indicates that the Stores Department relinquished its responsibility for the materials, and "140" indicates the account code for Raw Materials Inventory.

Code	Department	Code	Department
00	General Accounts	50-59	Finance Department
01	President's Office	50	Treasurer
10-29	Production Department	51	Credit and Collections
10	Vice-President, Production	52	Cashier
11	Engineering	53	Insurance
12	Production Planning	60-69	Accounting Department
13	Purchasing	60	Controller
14	Receiving, Shipping, Stores	61	Budgeting
20	General Superintendent	62	Tax Planning
21	Automatic Screw Machine	63	Internal Audit
22	Assembly	64	Cost Accounting
23	Drill Press	70	Accounting Manager
24	Punch Press	71	Billing
25	Heat Treating	72	Accounts Receivable
30-49	Marketing Department	73	Accounts Payable
30	Vice-President, Marketing	74	General Ledger
31	Advertising and Promotion	75	Payroll
32	Product Planning	80-89	Personnel Department
33	Customer Service	80	Personnel Manager
34	Marketing Research	81	Employment Office
40	Sales Manager	82	Education and Training
41-49	District Sales Managers	83	Welfare and Safety

Fig. 3.6
Sample departmental codes for chart of accounts.

The sale transaction would be debited to account 00–120 (General-Accounts Receivable) and credited to account 43–500 (District 43 Sales Revenue). Note that only the sales district is reflected by the account number. An indication of the salesperson, the product, and the customer would have to be obtained from codes other than those in the chart of accounts.

The purchase of office fixtures for the Controller's office would be debited to account 60–230 (Controller-Office Fixtures). The credit would normally be to account 00–300 (General-Accounts Payable).

The account code used to charge the consultant's fee would depend upon which manager within the Marketing Department had received the consulting services. For example, if the services had been performed for the Marketing Research Department, the correct departmental code for the debit portion of the entry would be "34." If the services had been performed for the Vice-President of Marketing, "30" would be the appropriate departmental code. The journal account code for the debit portion would in either case be "820," Legal and Consulting Expenses. The credit portion of the entry would be made to account 00–300 (General-Accounts Payable).

In general, all costs and expenses incurred by the organization should be charged to an account coded to indicate the department for which the cost or expense is controllable. All sales should be coded to reflect the regional department that generated the sale. Asset accounts such as Inventories or Fixed Assets may be coded to indicate the department having custodial responsibility for the asset. Most other accounts are general or control accounts, such as Cash, Accounts Payable, or Payroll, and need not contain any specific departmental code.

The organizational codes facilitate several data processing activities related to responsibility accounting. For example, cost and expense data may be sorted by department code and then summarized for each department to generate reports of controllable costs for all departments. Budgeted data would be similarly coded and processed to enable the preparation of performance reports indicating budget variances. The codes are used to perform the function of filtration in preparing these reports, meaning that for each department uncontrollable costs are filtered out and not included in the performance summary. The organizational codes serve as a partial index to store cost and expense data, thus simplifying the retrieval of such data for purposes of comparing and analyzing past trends within and among departments.

Other examples of coding

The coding concepts discussed above may be applied within a business organization to a wide variety of items in addition to accounts—items such as raw materials and parts, customers, employees, vendors, job orders, fixed assets, sales transactions, and salespeople. This section contains a brief description of two such coding systems, one for employees and the other for sales transactions.

Employee number serves as a key field for the payroll and personnel files. An example of a group code for employee numbers is as follows.

Digit position	Meaning
1–2	Division
3–4	Department
5	Pay code (salaries, wages, etc.)
6–10	Unique employee number

Numerous data processing activities can make use of this code. For example, pay records would likely be batched by pay code, and perhaps also by department number, prior to preparation of paychecks. Since payroll processing is generally sequential, pay records would be sorted by employee number prior to processing. The employee code could serve as a basis for summarizing, reporting, retrieval, and analysis of personnel or payroll information by division, by department, and/or by pay code for numerous purposes.

The analysis of sales transactions is an important management activity that is facilitated by a good coding system for sales transactions. An example of such a code is as follows.

Digit position	Meaning
1–2	Geographical area
3–5	Type of product
6–10	Salesperson number
11	Type of customer
12	Customer's credit rating
13–17	Customer's identification number

In this type of coding system, sales may be sorted, summarized, and reported in a variety of ways useful to management. For example, a summary report of sales by geographic area indicates which regions are making the best contributions to sales and provides a guide to future allocation of marketing resources among regions. A summary report by type of product is useful for making product-line decisions. A summary report by salesperson would be useful in evaluating the performance of salespeople. Finally, summary reports by type of customer and customer number are useful in assessing the significance of various classes of customers and identifying the most important individual customers.

Coding design considerations

The most obvious consideration in the design of a coding system is that the codes be chosen in a manner consistent with their intended usage. This implies that the code designer must determine the types of system outputs desired by users prior to selecting the code. For example, a responsibility accounting system certainly requires that accounting transactions be coded by organizational unit. Similarly, if sales analyses according to salesperson are important to the evaluation of sales performance, then sales transactions should include the salesperson code.

There are numerous other considerations in code design. One is that the designer should allow sufficient latitude in the code for likely growth in the number of items to be coded. For example, a three-digit employee code is probably inadequate for an organization with 950 employees. Another consideration is that the coding system be as simple as possible in order to minimize costs, facilitate memorization and interpretation of coding categories, and ensure employee acceptance. The likely use of mechanized processing should also be taken into account, even though the data processing system may not yet be mechanized. Finally, it is important that the coding systems selected in different areas of an organization be consistent in order to facilitate subsequent integration of data processing activities across functional lines. For example, the group coding system given earlier for account numbers is consistent across the first four positions with the employee number codes given in the previous section. Also, the appearance of the salesperson number in positions 6–10 of the sales transaction code shown above is consistent with the corresponding digit positions of the employee number code.

File Processing

As defined in Chapter 1, a file is a set of logically related records, and a record is a set of logically related data items. Examples related to accounting include employee records in a payroll file, customer records in an accounts receivable file, vendor records in an accounts payable file, and ledger account records in a general ledger file. Forms are the most common medium upon which file records are contained, but records also frequently exist on microfilm, punched cards, magnetic tape, and other machine-readable media.

File processing encompasses all of the methods and procedures that can be applied to records in a file. As such, it encompasses virtually all of the activities in the data processing cycle, as described in Chapter 1, including but not limited to recording, sorting, transcription, calculating, storage, updating, and retrieval. Virtually all business data are at one time or another stored in a file. Therefore file processing is probably the single most pervasive of all data processing functions. Because of this fact, file processing considerations are the dominant factor in the design and marketing of computers and other data processing equipment.

Speaking in very general terms, we may say that file records contain data concerning the attributes of various entities. We may define an *entity* as an item about which information is stored in a record. Examples would thus include employees, inventory items, and customer accounts. An *attribute* is a property of an entity, such as the pay rate of an employee or the address of a customer. Generally all entities of the same type possess the same set of attributes. For example, all employees possess an employee number, a pay rate, a home address, and so on. However, the specific data values for those attributes will differ among entities—for example, one employee's pay rate might be $4.00, while another's is $4.25. Using this terminology, we may say that a record is a collection of data values for the attributes of an entity, and that a file is a group of records for all entities of a particular type.

Within a particular file, each record will have a format similar or identical to the format of every other record. This format will generally consist of a series of *fields,* with each field designated to contain a data value for a particular attribute. For example, the first field in all employee records may be reserved for the employee number, the second field for employee name, and so on.

The relationship between these concepts and terms is illustrated in Fig. 3.7. Whereas entity group, entity, attribute, and attribute value are very general terms, file, record, field, and data value represent their specific counterparts in data processing. A specific example is given by the general ledger file, which contains various account records, such as cash or prepaid expenses. Each account contains several fields, one of which is the account balance. The data value $150.00 is one that could occur within the account balance field.

Types of files   Four major categories of files are the master file, the transaction file, the table file, and the index file. A *master file* is a permanent file of records containing current or nearly current data that is regularly updated. Examples would include the employee payroll file, the parts inventory file, and the accounts receivable file. Such files are permanent in that they exist indefinitely, even though individual records may be frequently inserted, deleted, or changed.

Fig. 3.7
Relationship between
processing concepts.

General Terminology	Specific Terminology	Specific Example
Entity group	File	General ledger
Entity	Record	Account
Attribute	Field	Balance
Attribute value	Data value	$150.00

A *transaction file* is a file of records that reflects current activity in an organization and is used to update a master file. Examples include a file of employee time-keeping records, a file of inventory issue and receipt transactions, or a file of sales transaction data. A transaction file may or may not be permanent, depending on whether it is to be discarded once the updating process is complete.

Transactions may be classified into four general types according to their impact upon the master file—record additions, record deletions, updates, and changes. Additions refer to insertions of entire new records into the file, while deletions refer to extracting entire records from the file. Updates involve revising a current master file balance, generally by adding or subtracting an amount from a transaction record. Changes involve such things as corrections of balances, revisions to credit ratings, or changes of address.

The periodic processing of transaction files against master files to make current the master file records is referred to as *file maintenance*. In accounting, this process is frequently referred to as *posting*. File maintenance is the most common processing task performed in accounting information systems. The posting of accounting journal entries from journals to the general ledger is a classic example. Others include maintenance of the accounts receivable file for cash receipts, credit sales, returns and allowances, and bad debt write-off transactions; the maintenance of inventory files for purchases, receipts, issues or sales, spoilage and scrap transactions; and the maintenance of accounts payable records for payment authorization and cash payment transactions. However, file maintenance is obviously performed not only in accounting systems but in virtually all kinds of data processing systems. A diagram of the file maintenance process appears in Fig. 3.8.

A *table file* is a master file of reference data, generally numeric, that is retrieved during data processing to facilitate calculations or other tasks. An example would be a payroll tax withholding table, which is entered according to marital status, number of deductions, and gross pay, and provides the correct amount of income tax withholdings. Other examples include sales tax tables, freight rate tables, and statistical tables.

An *index file* is a master file of record identifiers and corresponding storage locations. A familiar example is the card catalog in a library. An index file generally

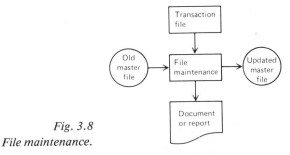

Fig. 3.8
File maintenance.

uses a record identifier such as name or account number as the key field. Such files are commonly used in data processing, particularly in advanced systems.

Other file characteristics

Files have numerous other characteristics that are relevant from the standpoint of data processing. One is the medium upon which the file data are stored. The most common and well known of such media is the paper used in documents and forms. However, advances in information technology have brought forth a variety of other data media. Among these are magnetic tape, magnetic disk, punched cards, and microfilm. On magnetic media such as tape and disk, data are represented by means of patterns of magnetization, or demagnetization, of magnetic bits, which can be interpreted by computer input devices. On punched cards, data are represented by patterns of hole punches, also interpretable by computer input equipment. With microfilm, document records are simply reduced drastically in size by photographic means, but can be enlarged by microfilm equipment for visual display. Subsequent chapters provide more extensive discussion of these and other file storage media and their related equipment.

Other concepts relevant to the design of files and file processing procedures include the activity ratio, volatility, and accessibility. The *activity ratio* is a measure applied to the file maintenance process to indicate the proportion of master file records referenced by transaction records during the process.

$$\text{Activity ratio} = \frac{\begin{array}{c}\text{Number of master file records}\\ \text{referenced during file maintenance}\end{array}}{\text{Total number of master file records}}$$

Volatility is a measure of the relative frequency of additions, deletions, and other transactions requiring reference to a particular master file during a specified time period.

$$\text{File volatility} = \frac{\begin{array}{c}\text{Total number of transactions}\\ \text{relating to the file}\end{array}}{\text{Standard unit of time (day, week, etc.)}}$$

A payroll file has a high activity ratio, while an airline reservations file has high volatility. These measures are useful in establishing file content, selecting file storage media and equipment, designing file processing procedures, and making other similar file design choices.

Accessibility refers to the ease with which records can be retrieved, and is a function of the storage medium and equipment used, the coding system used, the availability of indexes, and the extent of cross-referencing between records. Accessibility is an important factor in holding down the costs of file processing. Its importance increases in proportion to the degree of volatility of the file. Therefore records in the most highly volatile files should be provided maximum accessibility. The need for accessibility is a key factor in the establishment of record retention policies, which are discussed later in this chapter.

Sequential file processing

Sequential file processing refers to the performance of file maintenance or other file processing activities on records that are in consecutive order. The three most common sequences are alphabetic (usually involving a name), chronological (by date), and numeric (involving a numeric coding system).

Records are generally maintained in sequence according to their primary key. However, records may at times be sorted into sequence on a different key field for some other purpose. For example, payroll records may normally be sequenced by employee code number, but may be sorted by social security number prior to preparation of tax reports. The term *secondary key* refers to such fields. At times a secondary key is used as a secondary determinant of file sequence when many records have the same primary key. For example, a bank that maintains its customer transactions file in sequence according to the primary key of account number may also use the secondary key of date processed to order transactions within each customer account. Secondary keys are also useful for indexing purposes.

In sequential file maintenance, both the master file and the transaction file must be ordered in the same sequence. This generally requires sorting of the transaction file according to the primary key field of the master file. Subsequent processing involves the matching of each transaction file record with its master file counterpart according to the primary key value. Matches result in the posting of the transaction to the master file record. Unmatched master records imply no activity relating to that entity, and are therefore skipped over in processing. Unmatched transaction records may have an incorrect primary key value, or may be additions for insertion into the file.

When the activity ratio for a particular file maintenance procedure is high, it is generally advantageous to sort the transactions file prior to the file maintenance process. However, when the activity ratio is low, it may be advantageous to leave the transactions in random or other nonsequential order for processing, rather than to take the extra time to sort them.

Sequential files are virtually mandatory in manual data processing systems. However, modern information technology often permits a choice between sequential file organization and random file organization, in which records are stored not according to any particular sequence. This technology and its implications for file processing will be discussed in subsequent chapters.

Record retention policies

Virtually all business records experience a relatively short period of active use followed by a much longer period of inactivity. Retention of records during this inactive period may be important—the records may be needed for occasional reference, or they may be used to satisfy legal and tax requirements. Eventually, most records reach a point when they are no longer needed for any purpose and can be destroyed.

A systematic approach to the management of business records requires the establishment of a record retention schedule. Such a schedule identifies all of the types of records stored throughout the organization, and indicates (1) the period of time after which each type of record can be transferred from active to inactive status, and

(2) the period of time after which each type of record can be safely destroyed. Inactive records should be stored in inexpensive bulk storage equipment located in a record storage center, out of the way of regular data processing activity but nonetheless accessible when needed.

Organizations that have established a formal record retention program of this kind have generally experienced substantial cost savings by significantly reducing the volume of records stored in active files. The need for expensive filing equipment is reduced, which also brings about a savings in office space. Furthermore, office employees can work more efficiently with smaller files that are not clogged with inactive records.

Review Questions

1. Define the following terms.

form	attribute
constant data	field
variable data	master file
coding	transaction file
key	file maintenance
primary key	posting
sequence code	table file
block code	index file
group code	activity ratio
chart of accounts	volatility
entity	secondary key

2. What are the phases in the life cycle of business records that are encompassed by records management?

3. List several functions commonly performed by a records management department.

4. When does a form become a record?

5. List the four major elements of a form, and describe what each of these should contain.

6. What is the primary design objective in the main body of a form? Describe several principles that can help to achieve this objective.

7. Which activities in the data processing cycle rely heavily on the use of codes?

8. Describe the advantages and disadvantages of alphabetic codes relative to numeric codes in data processing.

9. Identify the likely primary key for several types of business records.

10. What is the basic advantage of the sequence code? Give some examples of the use of this type of code.

11. Give some business examples of the use of block codes.

12. Give some business examples of the use of group codes.

13. Describe and illustrate the use of both block codes and group codes in the chart of accounts.

14. Explain some of the benefits of using a chart of accounts in processing accounting data.

15. Describe the use of organizational codes in accounting data processing. Explain the advantages of using these codes.

16. Explain several considerations relevant to the design of a coding system.

17. Give several examples of the types of records and files typically found in accounting systems.

18. True or false.

    a) File processing is common in accounting, but it is not a major activity in other areas of data processing.

    b) File processing capabilities have had a significant impact upon the design and marketing of computer systems.

19. Explain the relationships between the concepts of entities and attributes on one hand, and the concepts of files, records, fields, and data on the other.

20. Identify, describe, and give examples of four major categories of files.

21. Identify and describe the four major categories of transactions.

22. Identify some examples of file maintenance within an accounting information system.

23. Identify several media upon which file records may be stored.

24. Give an example of (a) a file that has high volatility, and (b) a file that has a high activity ratio.

25. Explain the concept of record accessibility. How is this concept related to file volatility?

26. What is sequential file processing? Identify three common record sequences used in this procedure.

27. Explain three ways in which secondary keys may be used.

28. Explain the steps involved in sequential file maintenance.

29. When might it not be advantageous to sort transactions prior to file maintenance on a sequential file?

30. Give some examples of file maintenance in an accounting system.

31. Explain the purpose of a record retention schedule.

32. How can cost savings be achieved by a formal record retention program?

Discussion Questions

33. Examples of files and file processing given in this chapter related primarily to retail or manufacturing companies. Identify some of the types of files and file processing procedures you would be likely to encounter in the following organizations:

    a) a university
    b) a hospital
    c) a bank
    d) an insurance company
    e) a stockbrokerage
    f) an advertising agency

34. For each type of organization listed in the previous question, select one of the major files, and discuss the type of coding system that would be appropriate for records in that file.

35. In theory, a business organization should not use any procedure or technique unless its benefits exceed its costs. Discuss the benefits and costs of a chart of accounts.

36. The BMI Manufacturing Company has recently merged with another company and substantially expanded its product line. As a result, marketing executives have decided to redesign the company's coding system for products. Discuss the role which the accounting department should (or should not) play in this redesign process.

Problems and Cases

37. Consider the sales document form you designed for Katie's Flower Shop (Chapter 1, Problem 31). Evaluate your form using the forms design checklist in Fig. 3.2.

38. Consider the service work order form you designed for McCann's Auto Repair Shop (Chapter 1, Problem 32). Evaluate your form using the forms design checklist in Fig. 3.2.

39. The Wong-Lee Restaurant uses customer checks with prenumbered sequence codes. Waitresses prepare the customer's check, which the customer then presents to the cashier. Waitresses are told not to destroy any checks and, if a mistake is made, to void the check and prepare another. All voided checks are given to the manager daily.

   Required   Explain the role of sequence codes in controlling cash receipts in this situation.

40. Refer to the discussion in Chapter 1 of the accounting information system of a retail home appliance dealer. Design a form to be used as a sales document by a company of this type.

41. As an accountant for Radiotronics Corporation, a manufacturer and distributor of radios, you have been asked to design a sales analysis code. Some facts relevant to this task follow.

   ■ The company has four major product lines: portable radios, table radios, digital clock radios, and citizen's band radios. The number of styles available within each product line are 12, 4, 10, and 5, respectively.

   ■ The company has divided its sales area (that covers most of the United States and part of Canada) into nine regions. Each region is divided into six to twelve districts, each of which is assigned to a salesperson.

   ■ The company sells to seven major categories of customers and has approximately 1500 separate customer accounts.

   Required   Design a group coding system for assignment of sales analysis codes to sales transactions. Indicate the meaning and usefulness of each digit position or group of digit positions within the code.

42. Using the codes from the sample charts of accounts in Figs. 3.4 and 3.5 and the organizational codes in Fig. 3.6, assign a five-digit transaction code

to both the debit and credit entries for the following accounting transactions.

a) sale of a used punch press for cash equal to its book value
b) authorization to pay a bill for a national advertising campaign
c) accrual of salary and sales commission for a salesperson in District 48
d) approval of an allowance for damaged merchandise requested by a customer in District 46
e) authorization to pay a bill for travel expenses incurred by the President

43. Prepare a diagram representing file maintenance of an accounts receivable file.
Use a format similar to Fig. 3.8, except label each of the peripheral symbols
according to their specific content (i.e., specific to accounts receivable processing).

44. In five recently completed file maintenance jobs, the Dalton Department Store
processed the following numbers and types of transactions.

- three fixed asset acquisitions
- two fixed asset retirements
- 150 credit journal entries
- 5400 credit sales on account
- 650 debit journal entries
- 18,000 items of merchandise sold
- 300 payment authorizations
- 270 payments on account to suppliers
- 30 purchase returns
- 1800 receipts of payment on account
- 870 receipts of merchandise from suppliers
- 100 sales returns

The five master files being maintained, together with the number of records
within each file, are

- accounts payable, 2000 records
- accounts receivable, 8800 records
- fixed asset ledger, 250 records
- general ledger, 100 accounts
- inventory, 7600 records

During file maintenance, some of the master file records updated will have only
one related transaction, while others may have several transactions posted to
them at once. For each of the master files mentioned above, the average number of transactions pertaining to each master file record referenced (i.e., excluding those master records having no transactions) is

- accounts payable, 1.5
- accounts receivable, 2
- fixed asset ledger, 1
- general ledger, 8
- inventory, 5

Required

Compute the activity ratio for each of the five files given above. [**Hint:** First compute the total number of master file records referenced during the file maintenance for each file.]

45. Prepare a diagram representing file maintenance of a raw materials and parts inventory file, using a format similar to that shown in Fig. 3.6. Label each of the peripheral symbols according to their specific content (i.e., content specific to inventory processing).

46. As controller of the Easy Insurance Company, you have recently authorized a study by a records management consultant on the feasibility of establishing a formal record retention program that would include the installation of a bulk record storage center. The consultant has prepared the following estimates.

- There are approximately 500,000 documents now stored in Easy's office files.
- If a formal record retention program is established, three-fourths of Easy's documents can be moved out of active storage. Of these, two-thirds can be destroyed, and the remaining one-third can be stored in the record storage center.
- The cost per year of storing a document in the active office files will be $0.02, which includes the cost of equipment, labor, supplies, and overhead.
- The cost per year of storing a document in the record storage center will be $0.002.
- Retrieval of a document from the record storage center will cost an additional $3.00. There will be an estimated 200 such retrievals per year.
- The initial cost of starting up the program and establishing the record storage center will be $10,000.

Required

a) Compute the estimated annual cost savings if the proposed record retention program is established.

b) Should you authorize establishment of the record retention program? Discuss.

References

Caldwell, Don L. "Managing Information Resources." *Information and Records Management* (April 1980): 14–22.

Clark, Frank J.; Ronald Gale; and Robert Gray. *Business Systems and Data Processing Procedures.* Englewood Cliffs, N.J.: Prentice-Hall, 1972.

Gildersleeve, Thomas R. *Design of Sequential File Systems.* New York: Wiley-Interscience, 1971.

Hatfield, Jack D. "How to Establish an Effective Records Retention Program." *Management Accounting* (March 1980): 55–57.

National Association of Accountants. *Classification and Coding Techniques to Facilitate Accounting Operations.* Research Report 34. New York: National Association of Accountants, 1959.

Martin, James. *Computer Data-Base Organization* (2nd ed.). Englewood Cliffs, N.J.: Prentice-Hall, 1977.

Place, Irene, and Estelle L. Popham. *Filing and Records Management.* Englewood Cliffs, N.J.: Prentice-Hall, 1966.

Raymond, Morton M. "Records Management in the 1980s . . . Where Will You Be?" *Information and Records Management* (January 1979): 8, 57, 60.

Terry, George R. *Office Management and Control* (7th ed.). Homewood, Ill.: Irwin, 1975.

Chapter 4

Control and Accounting Information Systems

In an abstract sense, control is the process of exercising a restraining or directive influence over the activities of an object, organism, or system. Assisting management in the control of business organizations is one of the primary functions of accounting information systems.

Accountants often use the term *internal control* as a synonym for control within business organizations. A brief history of the concept of internal control is of interest. The term was first defined in 1949 by a committee of the American Institute of Accountants (now named the American Institute of Certified Public Accountants, or AICPA) as follows.

> *Internal control comprises the plan of organization and all of the coordinate methods and measures adopted within a business to safeguard its assets, check the accuracy and reliability of its accounting data, promote operational efficiency, and encourage adherence to prescribed managerial policies.* [1]

This definition still appears in AICPA professional literature, although they have several times published extensions or clarifications of it. For example, a 1958 pronouncement drew the following distinction between *accounting controls* and *administrative controls*.

> *Accounting controls comprise the plan of organization and all methods and procedures that are concerned mainly with, and relate directly to, the safe-*

---

[1] *Committee on Auditing Procedure, American Institute of Accountants,* Internal Control *(New York: American Institute of Certified Public Accountants, 1949), p. 6. Copyright © 1949 by the American Institute of Certified Public Accountants, Inc., and reprinted with permission.*

76

guarding of assets and the reliability of the financial records . . . . Administrative controls comprise the plan of organization and all methods and procedures that are concerned mainly with operational efficiency and adherence to managerial policies . . . . [2]

In 1972, an AICPA pronouncement provided the following clarifications of these definitions.

Administrative control includes, but is not limited to, the plan of organization and the procedures and records that are concerned with the decision processes leading to management's authorization of transactions. Such authorization is a management function directly associated with the responsibility for achieving the objectives of the organization and is the starting point for establishing accounting control of transactions.

Accounting control *comprises the plan of organization and the procedures and records that are concerned with the safeguarding of assets and the reliability of financial records and consequently are designed to provide reasonable assurance that*

a) *Transactions are executed in accordance with management's general or specific authorization.*

b) *Transactions are recorded as necessary (1) to permit preparation of financial statements in conformity with generally accepted accounting principles or any other criteria applicable to such statements and (2) to maintain accountability for assets.*

c) *Access to assets is permitted only in accordance with management's authorization.*

d) *The recorded accountability for assets is compared with the existing assets at reasonable intervals and appropriate action is taken with respect to any differences.* [3]

According to AICPA, the primary concern of the independent auditor is accounting controls. However, the internal accountant responsible for the design of accounting information systems is concerned with all aspects of internal control.

In 1977, shock waves were sent through the accounting profession when the United States Congress incorporated certain language from AICPA's 1972 pronouncement into the Foreign Corrupt Practices Act. Specifically, all publicly owned corporations subject to the Securities Exchange Act of 1934 are now legally required to

[2] *Committee on Auditing Procedure, American Institute of Certified Public Accountants,* Statement on Auditing Procedures No. 29 *(New York: American Institute of Certified Public Accountants, 1958), pp. 36–37. Copyright © 1958 by the American Institute of Certified Public Accountants, Inc., and reprinted with permission.*

[3] *Committee on Auditing Procedure, American Institute of Certified Public Accountants,* Statement on Auditing Procedure No. 54. *(New York: American Institute of Certified Public Accountants, 1972), pp. 239–240. Copyright © 1972 by the American Institute of Certified Public Accountants, Inc., and reprinted with permission.*

(A) make and keep books, records, and accounts, which, in reasonable detail, accurately and fairly reflect the transactions and dispositions of the assets of the issuer; and (B) devise and maintain a system of internal accounting controls sufficient to provide reasonable assurances that—

> *(i) transactions are executed in accordance with management's general or specific authorization;*
>
> *(ii) transactions are recorded as necessary (I) to permit preparation of financial statements in conformity with generally accepted accounting principles or any other criteria applicable to such statements, and (II) to maintain accountability for assets;*
>
> *(iii) access to assets is permitted only in accordance with management's general or specific authorization; and*
>
> *(iv) the recorded accountability for assets is compared with the existing assets at reasonable intervals and appropriate action is taken with respect to any differences.*[4]

In essence, corporations are now required by law to maintain good systems of internal accounting control! Needless to say this requirement has in recent years generated tremendous interest among managements, accountants, and auditors in the design and evaluation of internal control systems.

Another way to view control concepts in business organizations is from the standpoint of management theory. From this perspective, control systems may be classified into three general types—feedback control systems, feedforward control systems, and preventive control systems. *Feedback* is defined as the informational output of a process that returns as input to the process, in the sense that it initiates the action necessary for process control. Feedback control systems operate by measuring some aspect of the process being controlled and adjusting the process when the measure indicates that the process is deviating from plan.

In contrast to this detection and correction mode of operation, both feedforward and preventive controls attempt to stop errors and deviations from occurring. However, they approach this task in quite different ways. Feedforward controls monitor both process operations and inputs in an attempt to predict potential deviations, in order that adjustments can be made to avert problems before they occur. Preventive controls operate from within the process by placing restrictions on and requiring documentation of employee activities in such a way that the occurrence of errors and deviations is retarded. Because preventive controls operate from "within" the process being controlled, they are perhaps the type of control most consistent with the original meaning of the term "internal" control.

One way to reconcile these theoretical control concepts with the regulatory definitions is to assume that preventive controls correspond to what AICPA labeled accounting controls, while feedback and feedforward controls correspond to AICPA's administrative controls. Because the Foreign Corrupt Practices Act refers only to "internal accounting controls," its focus is seen to be primarily on preven-

---

[4] Foreign Corrupt Practices Act of 1977, U.S. Code, *1976 edition, Supplement II, Volume One. Washington: United States Government Printing Office, 1979, p. 862.*

tive controls. This interpretation is consistent with the primary intent of the act, which was to "prevent" bribes and other corrupt practices.

Regardless of what the law requires, all three forms of control are important to business organizations. Furthermore, the accounting information system plays a central role in implementing each form of control. Therefore this chapter provides a general description of each of the three major types of control systems, and describes numerous examples of each from business and accounting information systems.

Feedback Control Systems

Fundamental characteristics

A feedback control system contains five fundamental components. In general terms, these are (1) an operating process, which converts an input into an output; (2) a characteristic of the process, which is the subject of control; (3) a measurement system, which assesses the state of the characteristic; (4) a set of standards or criteria against which the measured state of the process is evaluated; and (5) a regulator, whose functions are to compare measures of the process characteristic to the standards, and to take action to adjust the process if the comparison reveals that the process is deviating from plan. The relationships of these components are illustrated graphically in Fig. 4.1.

Incorporating feedback control into a process creates a dynamic, self-regulating system. In such a system, the process is expected to deviate from equilibrium occasionally. However, the ability both to restore the process to equilibrium and to know when such restoration is needed is built into the system itself. Thus it can operate for long periods of time, performing its necessary functions and correcting itself when necessary, without the need for external direction. The theoretical study of feedback control systems is referred to as *cybernetics*.

A commonly cited example of a feedback control system is the thermostat. This control system operates by measuring the temperature of an object or process, and triggering a heating (or cooling) device when the temperature deviates from a specified level of coldness (or warmth).

Feedback control systems are common within business organizations. The production of goods or the operation of a department are processes requiring control. Characteristics of such processes which are controlled might be quality of output, cost of operation, or speed of operation. Measurement systems are frequently component parts of the accounting information system. Standards or criteria for evaluating the process are established by management policy. Finally, the regulator is a manager, or person responsible for the satisfactory operation of the process.

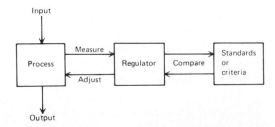

*Fig. 4.1
A feedback control
system.*

Though it is instructive to apply the concept of a feedback control system to various processes within business organizations, it should be noted that business organizations cannot operate as precisely and automatically as, say, a thermostat. This is true because of the complexity of business operations and because of the limitations in perception and memory of people generally. However, the concept is useful as a theoretical ideal for control systems in business.

Essentials of proper functioning

The successful application of feedback control systems in a business organization requires that certain general principles be observed. First, it is essential that a control have a benefit value at least as great as the cost of administering it. Deciding whether a given control meets this criterion will usually be a matter of subjective judgment. The cost of a control may not be too difficult to estimate, but its benefit might be expressed only in vague terms, such as "increased efficiency" or "better customer service." Ability to make this judgment with a fair degree of success is one factor that separates good managers from inferior ones. Satisfaction of this principle is essential not only to feedback control systems but also to preventive control and to all activities of a business.

A second essential principle in a feedback control system is that its measurement component report deviations from standards on a timely basis, so that corrective action can restore the process to its desired state as quickly as possible. This principle has direct implications for accounting information systems, which, as noted, often provide the measurement function in a feedback control system. A common criticism of accounting reports is that they are not timely, which indicates that perhaps more attention should be given to this factor by designers of accounting information systems.

The third basic principle is that feedback reports be simple and easy to understand and that they highlight important relationships or factors requiring the attention of the manager to whom the report is directed. This principle also has implications for accounting systems design. Accounting reports are sometimes criticized for not containing enough information, or for not emphasizing the most important aspects of the process upon which they are reporting. On the other hand, some accounting systems, particularly those that are computerized, may be criticized for providing too much information. Managers who receive a 40- or 50-page report or printout may have difficulty in determining exactly what has been communicated to them. It is thus important that control reports be easy to comprehend and be tailored to the purpose of the control system.

The fourth basic principle is that feedback control systems be integrated with the organizational structure of which they are part. The boundaries of each process subject to control must be within the span of control of a single manager. That manager must be the one who receives control reports on the process and who has the authority to direct the operations of, and implement necessary changes in, the process. Being the one who perhaps best understands the process, that manager should participate in the formation of the standards against which its performance will be evaluated.

The functions of a feedback control system in business correspond roughly to the internal control objectives of promoting operational efficiency and encouraging adherence to prescribed managerial policies. These functions are effectively accomplished by means of a reporting system adhering to the general principles outlined above. Feedback reports promote operational efficiency by highlighting inefficient operations requiring management's attention. Furthermore, such reports encourage adherence to managerial policies through the knowledge that deviations from such policies and standards are promptly reported.

Feedback control systems in business

Discussion of the principles of feedback control systems underscores the importance to accounting information systems of the concepts of organization and control. To further clarify these relationships, some examples of feedback control systems in business will be presented.

Responsibility accounting systems   As discussed in Chapter 2, an information system that reports financial results in accordance with the assignment of responsibilities within an organization is called a responsibility accounting system. This is a prime example of a feedback control system.

Each of the five components of a feedback control system is exemplified in a responsibility accounting system. The process being controlled is the operation of the department or other organizational unit. The characteristic being controlled may be either cost, profit, or return on investment. The measurement system is the accounting information system, which collects and processes data and reports information in accordance with the organizational considerations discussed in Chapter 2. The regulator of the system is the manager under whose authority the department operates. Finally, the set of standards is represented by the budgets, quotas, and/or prior performance levels against which actual performance is compared.

Standard cost systems   Standard cost systems are a close relative of responsibility accounting systems. According to its most common usage, the term *standard cost* refers to the cost that should be incurred in producing a unit of product under efficient operating conditions. The total standard cost per unit of product may be broken down into costs of material components, labor and overhead elements, and by departments or other cost centers. In the latter case, standard costs may serve as the basis for budgeted amounts on performance reports in a responsibility accounting system.

In a standard cost system, actual costs are compiled on a per unit basis and compared with standards to obtain standard cost variances. Two general types of standard cost variances are rate variances and usage variances. A *rate variance* indicates that portion of a total variance attributable to a deviation from a standard rate or price, such as a labor rate or a material price. A *usage variance* indicates that portion of a total variance attributable to a deviation from some standard amount of usage of, for example, labor hours or material quantities.[5] Standard cost variances of this sort provide a good indication of the corrective action necessary to restore the production process to a satisfactory state.

Credit control   The credit control system governs the relationship between a business organization and customers who have purchased from it on credit. The characteristic of this process that is the subject of control is the loss from bad debts. The accounting information system can provide two measures of success for this process. The first of these is an aging of accounts receivable balances, which indicates those customers who have become delinquent in paying their accounts. When such delinquencies reach a prescribed level, the credit manager can act to refuse additional credit to the customer and perhaps initiate special procedures to collect the amount of the existing past due balance. The second measure provided by the accounting system is the total of bad debts written off as uncollectable during a given period. If this total rises beyond an acceptable level, the credit manager may act to tighten policies governing the initial extension of credit.

Internal audit   The internal audit function was discussed in Chapter 2. Two aspects of this function provide feedback for management control. First, the function of independent appraisal of the performance of various levels of management provides feedback to top management on the effectiveness of subordinate managers. Second, the function of reviewing and assessing the system of preventive controls within an organization provides feedback to accounting executives on the effectiveness of that system. In both cases there are no precise standards or measures of effectiveness, no formula or sum that can easily be determined. Therefore, this type of feedback control system is perhaps more difficult to administer successfully than those described previously.

Examples of the kinds of control problems that the internal audit function is often able to uncover include failure to pay on account in time to earn discounts, excess overtime, underused assets, obsolete inventory, conservative budgets and quotas, failure to adhere to prescribed policies and procedures, poorly justified capital expenditures, and production bottlenecks. Feedback on the existence and nature of such problems is very useful to management in maintaining effective control of an organization.

Production control   The production control process is concerned primarily with maintaining efficiency and avoiding delays in the production process. Thus the characteristic being controlled is time, and the standard used is the production schedule.

---

[5] *For a detailed treatment of standard cost accounting, see Charles T. Horngren,* Cost Accounting, A Managerial Emphasis, *(4th ed.). (Englewood Cliffs, N.J.: Prentice-Hall, 1977), Chapters 7 and 9.*

The regulator consists of the production planning or production control department and the expeditors it employs to monitor production in the factory.

Feedforward Control Systems

Feedback control systems are essential in many areas of management control. However, their basic disadvantage is that they do not signal a deviation until after it has become significant. As a result, costly deviations may persist or worsen before corrective action becomes effective. Feedforward control systems aim directly at this problem by attempting to prevent such deviations before they occur.

Fundamental characteristics

The components of a feedforward control system are similar to those of a feedback system. They include (1) an operating process, which converts input into output; (2) a characteristic of the process, which is the subject of control; (3) a measurement and prediction system, which assesses the state of the process and its inputs and attempts to predict its outputs; (4) a set of standards or criteria against which the predicted state of the process is evaluated; and (5) a regulator, which compares predictions of process output to the standards and takes corrective action when this comparison indicates a likely future deviation. The relationship of these components is diagramed in Fig. 4.2.

As indicated by this description and the diagram, a distinguishing feature of feedforward control systems is the monitoring of process inputs. Therefore in order for a feedforward control system to be effective, there must be a reasonably predictable relationship between process inputs and process outputs. As in the case of feedback systems, business applications of the feedforward control concept should not be expected to operate as precisely and automatically as their engineering counterparts. Nevertheless there are some business systems whose essential features parallel the basic feedforward model.

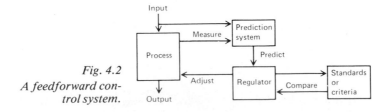

Fig. 4.2
A feedforward control system.

**Feedforward
control systems in
business**

Koontz and Bradspies describe three examples of feedforward systems in a business context.[6] Each of these is described briefly here.

Cash planning   The objective of a cash planning system is to maintain the organization's cash balance at some desired level. The process being controlled encompasses all aspects of the organization's activities and decisions that impact upon the level of cash. Among the input variables that must be monitored in a typical business organization are the level of sales, receipts on account, purchases and payments on account, wages and salaries, selling, administrative and other expenses, tax payments, capital expenditures, borrowing and loan repayments, investments, and dividends.

The process characteristic subject to control in a cash planning system is simply the cash balance. The control standard is generally a desired range within which the cash balance should fall, which in turn may be based upon a desired relationship between the cash balance and the balance of other current asset or current liability accounts. The measurement and prediction system is the accounting information system, which measures cash flows via the traditional accounting process and predicts future cash flows and cash balances via a budgeting system.

The regulator in the cash planning process is the executive responsible for cash management, who may be the treasurer or financial vice-president. Actions available to this person to adjust or correct the cash balance include investing excess funds, short-term borrowing, and delaying capital expenditures.

Note the inadequacies of feedback control in the cash planning situation. If feedback indicates that the cash balance is higher than the desired level, then the investment of the excess cash in interest-bearing securities has already been delayed. Similarly, if feedback indicates an abnormally low cash balance, the opportunity to avoid costly borrowing by delaying expenditures or making other adjustments may be lost. Thus the application of the feedforward concept provides an important contribution to the efficiency of cash management.

Inventory control   The process being controlled by an inventory control system is the operation of ordering, storing, and making available when needed within the organization various items of raw materials, parts and supplies, and finished goods inventories. The characteristic being controlled is the balance of each item of inventory. The measurement system is the set of inventory records maintained by the accounting information system. The regulator may be either an inventory clerk or a computer.

The most significant input variable to an inventory feedforward control system is either the expected rate of sales (for a retail or wholesale company) or the planned usage requirements (for a manufacturing company). Other input variables include the amount of inventory purchases, purchase returns, sales returns, spoilage, and

6   Harold Koontz and Robert W. Bradspies, "Managing through Feedforward Control," Business Horizons 15 (June 1972), pp. 25–36.

shrinkage. Order and shipping times are also important considerations. These variables are used to predict the future inventory level in order to determine the best time at which to reorder. In many systems, the criterion established to decide when to reorder is the *reorder point,* or the level to which the inventory balance of an item must fall before an order to replenish the stock is initiated. The reorder point for each inventory item is established to minimize the sum of holding costs and costs of being out of stock. Thus placing an order to replenish the stock of inventory represents the corrective or regulative action in the system.

In another sense, the characteristic being controlled in an inventory system is the sum of the costs of holding and ordering inventory and of stockouts. The input variables that must be measured in order to achieve this objective include the expected demand or usage of each inventory item, the *lead time* (the time between order and receipt for each item), the holding cost rate of each item, the cost of placing an order for a batch of each item, and the cost of a stockout of each item. The standards that must be established should include not only the optimal reorder point for each item but also the *economic order quantity,* which is the order quantity of an item that minimizes the sum of holding costs and ordering costs for that item. A simple formula for economic order quantity is

$$EOQ = \frac{(2)(C_2)(D)}{C_1}$$

where C_1 is the carrying cost per unit per year, C_2 is the cost of placing a single order, and D is the demand per year.

New product development The goal of a new product development program is to introduce a successful new product while making efficient use of time, cost, and other resources. Such a project requires close coordination among a variety of activities including product research and development, market research, production engineering, capital expenditure planning, sales and distribution planning, packaging design, and advertising and promotion. Such coordination of multiple activities may be provided by a management control plan based upon the feedforward concept.

In this process, the primary characteristics subject to control are the timing of related activities and the quality of the results. The standard against which success is measured is the product development plan. The measurement system consists of periodic progress reports and meetings between project staff. Input variables to be monitored include the activities, findings, and conclusions of those people playing a key role in the process. The regulator is represented by the project manager, marketing vice-president, or other executive in charge.

The importance of the feedforward concept in this process is related to the future-oriented nature of project control. Results obtained and conclusions reached are evaluated primarily in terms of their impact upon the ultimate success of the project, rather than in terms of past expectations. For example, if the engineering department concludes that the product cost will be substantially higher than previ-

ous estimates, or if the marketing research department estimates that product demand will be lower than expected, an attempt is made to predict the resulting impact upon the product's success and to adjust plans for subsequent stages of the development process accordingly. It is entirely possible that this process will result in the termination of the product development process in many cases. The feedforward concept therefore plays a very important role in the success or failure of new product development.

Preventive Control Systems

Both feedback and feedforward controls function externally to the process being controlled, monitoring its operations and intervening to make corrective adjustments where necessary. In contrast, preventive controls are policies and procedures that are actually a part of the process itself. As such, they are often more effective than either feedback or feedforward controls, but they are more costly. In this section, the generally accepted principles and practices of preventive control systems are explained, and several examples from the field of accounting are described.

Functions of a preventive control system

The AICPA definition of internal control cited previously provides a useful way of classifying the functions of a preventive control system. Of the four functions cited in that definition, the first two—safeguarding of assets, and checking the accuracy and reliability of its accounting data—are most consistent with the concept of preventive control. This section elaborates on the nature of these two functions.

Safeguarding assets According to AICPA, safeguarding of assets refers to their "protection against loss arising from intentional and unintensional errors in processing transactions and handling the related assets."[7] Examples of unintentional errors include such things as "understatement of sales through failure to prepare invoices or through incorrect pricing or computation; overpayments to vendors or employees arising from inaccuracies in quantities of materials or services, prices or rates, or computations; and physical loss of assets such as cash, securities, or inventory."[8] "Intentional errors" is a reference to *embezzlement,* which is the fraudulent appropriation of business property by an employee to whom it has been entrusted, often accompanied by falsification of records. Safeguarding of assets also encompasses protection against theft of assets by shoplifters, burglars, etc.

Embezzlement results in substantial loss to business firms each year. The United States Fidelity and Guaranty Co., a major bonding company, cites estimates that place the annual loss in the neighborhood of $4 billion. In addition, they estimate that more than 30 percent of all bankruptcies are caused by employee dishon-

[7] *Committee on Auditing Procedure, American Institute of Certified Public Accountants,* Statement on Auditing Standards No. 1 *(New York: American Institute of Certified Public Accountants, 1973), p. 17.*
[8] *Ibid.*

esty.[9] Such losses are costly not only in financial terms but also in terms of the loss of a productive human resource to the firm and to society. Many embezzlers would never commit a crime if it were not for the weak control system that encourages the act.

Embezzlement is committed in a large variety of ways. The study cited above describes 40 different cases of embezzlement.[10] An article by Elmer I. Ellentuck describes 20 methods of employee fraud, and presents a checklist containing a large number of suggested control procedures for preventing such frauds.[11] An article by E. J. Gurry lists 18 methods of embezzlement and describes internal control remedies for each of them.[12]

The accounting information system contributes quite effectively to the safeguarding of assets by means of keeping a record of the assets. Discrepancies between the records and the actual quantity on hand can be investigated to discover their source. With respect to cash, the accounting records and the quantity on hand may be compared and brought into agreement weekly or monthly by means of a bank reconciliation. Each individual discrepancy is resolved in this process. In the case of inventories, such a reconciliation typically takes place once annually, when a physical inventory is taken. In most cases, tracing of individual differences between inventory records and quantities on hand is impossible, and so trends in the total discrepancy may be used as the basis for relaxing or tightening overall control policies.

Safeguarding of assets is also accomplished by close supervision of asset-handling operations and physical protective measures such as plant security forces and limited access to storage areas. These are not strictly accounting functions, although they may be under the authority of the accounting executive in some businesses. However, the accounting system provides information that is useful in evaluating the effectiveness of such controls. The accounting information system thus plays a central role in safeguarding assets in business as well as nonbusiness organizations.

Internal check   The function of checking the accuracy and reliability of accounting data in a system is referred to as *internal check*. This function is obviously compatible with the functions of recording and processing data. Internal check is a form of verification and is often accomplished through utilization of the maxim of the double entry accounting system that debits must equal credits. Payroll processing provides a good example of this form of internal check. Debits in a payroll entry are allocated to numerous inventory and/or expense accounts. Credits are allocated to several liability accounts for taxes, insurance, union dues as well as the liability to employees. At the end of this complex operation, the comparison of total debits to

[9] *United States Fidelity and Guaranty Co.,* The Forty Thieves *(Baltimore: USF&G, 1970), pp. 2–3.*

[10] *Ibid., pp. 9–50.*

[11] *Elmer I. Ellentuck, "How to Minimize Employee Fraud: A Checklist."* The Practical Accountant *5 (March/April 1972), pp. 30–37.*

[12] *E. J. Gurry, "Locating Potential Irregularities,"* The Journal of Accountancy *140 (September 1975), pp. 111–114.*

total credits provides a powerful check on the accuracy of the process. Any error will create a discrepancy, which will initiate action to discover and correct the error.

In the processing of data in batches, internal check is accomplished by means of *batch totals,* or *control totals,* which are sums of a numerical item accumulated from all documents in a batch. Batch totals are typically established at the point of initial formation of a batch, and then checked at various stages in processing to control against loss of records or errors in data transcription.

Errors in accounting data can have harmful effects upon the relationship of a business to all of the major external parties with which it deals. Such errors may also damage the effectiveness of internal management, which relies upon accounting information as a basis for decision making. Finally, errors in the accounting records of a publicly held corporation could indicate a lack of compliance with the Foreign Corrupt Practices Act. In many respects the maintenance of accurate and reliable records is closely related to the safeguarding of assets, because the former will contribute significantly to the latter. The remainder of this section discusses the essential elements of preventive control systems and describes some common examples, and then explains the steps corporate managers can take to demonstrate compliance with the Foreign Corrupt Practices Act.

Essential elements of preventive control systems

Sound organizational practices   Reference to the ''plan of organization'' in the definition of internal control underscores the importance of sound organizational practices. Of particular importance is the separation of assigned duties and responsibilities in such a way that no single employee can both perpetrate and conceal errors or irregularities. This separation of functions is often referred to as *organizational independence.*

Three general categories of functions must be separated in order to maintain effective organizational independence. These are (1) functions involving custody of assets, such as writing checks or handling cash or other assets; (2) recording functions, such as maintaining the disbursements journal or preparing the bank reconciliation; and (3) performance of line operating functions, especially those involving the authorization of transactions. Separation of custodial and recording functions prevents an employee from falsifying records in order to conceal the theft of assets entrusted to that employee's custody. Separation of custodial and operating functions prevents an employee from authorizing a fictitious or inaccurate transaction as a means of concealing theft. Finally, separation of recording and operating functions prevents operating employees or managers from falsifying records in order to conceal substandard operating performance. Figure 4.3 illustrates some of the primary examples of custodial, recording, and operating functions that should be separated.

In a system that incorporates an effective separation of duties among employees, it should be almost impossible for any single employee to successfully commit embezzlement. In such a system *collusion,* or conspiracy of two or more persons to

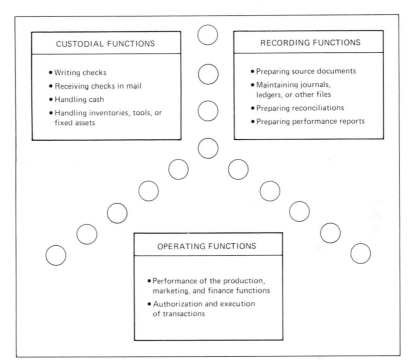

Fig. 4.3
Separation of cus-
todial, recording,
and operating
functions.

commit fraud, may still be possible, but a well-designed system can minimize the chances of successful collusion.

Sound personnel practices   The safety of assets and the reliability of accounting records are both affected by an organization's personnel policies. The qualifications established for each job designation in a company should reflect the degree of responsibility associated with the position. Qualifications for responsible positions may include a level of experience, intelligence, character, dedication, and capacity for leadership. Training programs should be planned carefully to familiarize new employees with their responsibilities. Policies with respect to working conditions, raises in salary, and promotion are very important, and can be a powerful force in encouraging efficiency and loyal service. For employees in positions involving direct access to property, fidelity bond coverage is important. A *fidelity bond* is a contract with an insurance company that provides a financial guarantee of the honesty of a named individual.

Another very important personnel practice is that all employees holding key positions with respect to recording or custody of assets should be required to take an annual vacation, during which time their functions are performed by someone else. Many of the employee frauds that have been discovered were revealed when the embezzler was suddenly forced by illness or accident to take time off. Periodic rotation of duties among key employees is another policy that may achieve the same results.

Written guides to policies and procedures   Closely related to sound organizational and personnel practices is the need for manuals of policies and procedures. Such manuals should describe in detail the responsibilities of each individual position in the organization, a feature that makes the manuals useful in training new employees. The manuals should also give an overview of the functioning of the system with respect to each type of transaction, so that the relationship of one employee function to another is clear. The manuals should also contain a detailed listing of the chart of accounts, in order to facilitate the accurate initial recording of transactions. Other instructions for filling out forms used in processing are also important.

Systems and procedures manuals encourage uniformity in data processing and financial operations, thereby preventing the confusion and inefficiency that would result from unnecessary inconsistencies. For example, automated data processing systems require input whose form and content are rigidly specified. If a manual describing the required form and content is available to the various individuals who provide a particular type of input to the system (perhaps the sales force or production workers), the problems of jumbled or incomplete input can be minimized. Using the manuals in employee training programs also contributes to consistency of practices within the organization.

Physical protection of assets   An important factor in the safeguarding of assets is an adequate program of physical protection. Access to cash should be limited to responsible employees. Important documents or records should be stored in limited-access file cabinets or perhaps a safe. Access to inventory storage areas should be limited. Plant facilities should be protected during nonoperating hours by means of security police, burglar alarms, and other safeguards.

An important factor in the physical protection of cash in retail businesses is the cash register and its numerous control features. For example, the bell that sounds when a cash sale is rung up and the totals that appear in the display window facilitate supervision of sales clerks. The display window total and customer receipt provide the opportunity for the customer to notice a discrepancy between the amount paid and the amount recorded, which discourages any deliberate errors. Once a sale is recorded, a record of it is printed on a paper tape locked inside the register to prevent subsequent alteration. At the end of a day this internally accumulated total should check with the amount of cash accumulated in the cash drawer. Other available features of cash registers that provide increased control are multiple cash drawers, so that each sales clerk can be made responsible for an individual cash drawer, and an attachment that dispenses the exact amount of coin change due to a customer.

Well-designed documents   Documents that are designed carefully and used effectively can contribute greatly both to the safeguarding of assets and to the accuracy of records. Source transaction documents should be designed to facilitate the collection of all necessary information with respect to the transaction. Documents that initiate a transaction should contain a space for the authorization of the person or persons charged with that responsibility. Transfer of responsibility for assets from one department to another should be recorded in order to enable the pinpointing of responsibility for any subsequent shortages. Document design should also be simple so that processing can be as efficient as possible. The document format should facilitate review and verification.

An important practice with respect to the design of any document used for control purposes is the sequential prenumbering of all documents. This practice makes it possible to account for and review every document used in a process. Any missing documents would create a missing number in the sequence. This practice reduces the likelihood of fraudulent use of documents by dishonest employees.

The record-keeping system throughout a business organization should be well coordinated in order to facilitate the tracing of individual transactions through the system. The path that a transaction traces through a data processing system, from source document to summary reports, is referred to as the *audit trail*. The audit trail consists of such things as reference numbers, dates, and names that are recorded in files, ledgers, and journals to facilitate the tracing of these records to source documents or to records in other files. Good audit trails facilitate the correction of errors and the verification of output information in a system.

Supervision   The availability of supervisory assistance contributes to accuracy of records by reducing the possibility that employees engaged in data processing activities will err in recording situations with which they are unfamiliar. Surveillance of employees who have direct access to assets provides an additional safeguard over such assets. Supervision is especially important as a means of safeguarding assets in businesses that are too small to fully achieve organizational independence.

Examples of preventive control systems   Preventive control systems in business generally are integrated with transaction processing subsystems, each of which is concerned with processing a particular class of accounting transactions. These subsystems are often referred to as transaction processing cycles. An example of the partitioning of the accounting information system into transaction processing cycles is provided by the delineation in Chapter 1 of five basic categories of business transactions—purchasing, production, payroll, sales, and cash receipts and disbursements. In this section some of the most important control features within these cycles are reviewed. The emphasis here is on manual rather than automated systems, but the basic control concepts in both systems are similar. Each of the processing and control systems discussed in this section is described in greater detail in Part 4 of this text.

Purchasing of inventory   The basic function of controls in the purchasing function is to ensure purchase of all needed inventory items while preventing losses of inventory. To ensure that only items that are needed are actually purchased, initiation of a purchase order should result from the preparation of a formal requisition by a responsible employee in the stores-keeping or production departments. Copies of the purchase order should be furnished by the purchasing department to both the accounts payable department and the receiving department. The receiving department should be responsible for preparing a report listing the quantity of each item received. This report should be signed by an employee of stores to acknowledge the transfer of goods from receiving to stores.

The accounts payable department performs the most significant control function in a purchasing system through its procedure for authorizing payment of vendor invoices. Such authorization is granted only after a review of the purchase order, to ensure that the goods were actually ordered, and of the receiving report, to ensure that they were received and have been properly transferred to the stores-keeping department. Organizational independence in this process is achieved by separation of the operating functions (purchasing and authorization of accounts payable) from the custodial functions (the receiving and stores-keeping departments) and from the recording functions (record keeping for accounts payable and inventories).

Flow of inventory through production   The primary functions of controls in a production accounting system are to ensure production of only those items that are needed and to prevent loss of inventories. The production planning department decides what items will be produced. A reliable system of reporting on sales trends and finished goods inventory balances is essential to this function.

Control over goods in production begins with the transfer of raw materials from stores-keeping to the factory. This is controlled by documents initiated by the production planning department authorizing the transfer. The production planning or cost accounting department must keep strict documentary control over each batch of work in process as it moves through the factory. Maintaining a record of quantities involved in each transfer of goods from one department to another enables the tracing of any shortage to a single department. The final step in the production process is the transfer of goods to the finished goods storeroom, which is evidenced by a document signed by the finished goods custodian acknowledging receipt of the goods.

Organizational independence with respect to production work in process is achieved by separation of the custodial functions (raw material stores, factory departments, and finished goods stores) from the recording function (cost accounting), and from the authorization function (production planning). Although the factory departments are operating departments that also perform custodial and recording functions, their operating activities in this case do not extend to the authorization of transactions, and their recording functions are effectively controlled by the signed acknowledgment required for every transfer of goods from one department to another. In addition control over production is also provided by effective supervision on the part of factory supervisors and by a program to maintain the physical security of the factory premises.

Payroll   The primary purpose of controls in a payroll processing system is to ensure that wages and salaries are paid in appropriate amounts for services properly rendered. In a typical manufacturing company, a record of hours worked for each factory employee is obtained both in the form of clock cards, showing when employees punch in and out, and in the form of job tickets, which are verified by supervisors and show the time an employee spent at a particular job. These two input records should be reconciled as an initial step in payroll processing. Job time tickets form the basis for distribution of labor costs to the various inventory accounts representing work in process. Clock cards are used as a basis for the calculation of gross pay, net pay, and various deductions, and for the preparation of paychecks. When these two processes are completed, the total amount of payroll computed in one should be compared with the other as a check upon the accuracy of both.

In processing payrolls for office employees or in a nonmanufacturing company, the supervisor's function is even more significant in providing input to payroll processing. Often the only such input will be a written form prepared by a supervisor listing time worked for each employee, though time clocks may also be used in some cases. For salaried employees, the weekly or monthly salary is constant, and so control over input data is not needed unless extra pay is provided for overtime work.

Records of employment, rates, and authorized deductions for each employee should be maintained by the personnel department as well as the department responsible for preparing checks. All changes in these records, including hirings and terminations as well as rate changes, should be authorized through the personnel department. Organizational independence in payroll processing is achieved by separation of the operating function (the personnel department) from the custodial functions (preparation and distribution of paychecks) and from the recording functions (timekeeping, payroll record keeping, and cost accounting). A separate bank account for payroll only is also a desirable control feature because it facilitates the subsequent preparation of bank reconciliations.

Sale of products   Nearly all transactions between companies are on account, and so problems of handling cash do not arise. The primary functions of controls in a sales order processing, billing, and accounts receivable system are to ensure that all sales of finished goods are properly recorded, to prevent loss of finished goods inventories, and to facilitate the collection of accounts. Toward these ends, shipments of goods are not approved until the credit of the customer has been approved. Transfer of goods from the finished goods storeroom to the shipping department must be authorized by documents evidencing a sale. The shipping department must acknowledge receipt of the goods and notify the billing department once the shipment is made. The billing department then prepares the invoice from the original sales order and the documentation supplied by the shipping department. After the invoices are prepared and copies are mailed to the customer, they are posted in batches to the accounts receivable ledger, with batch totals being used to control the accuracy of posting. The accounts receivable department may prepare and send to each customer a periodic statement of his or her account.

Cash receipt and disbursement   The basic purpose of controls in systems for processing cash receipts and disbursements is to prevent loss of cash. With respect to sales of merchandise for cash by a retail store, the primary controls are good supervision and the proper use of a cash register. Another control is the use of prenumbered sales slips, which enables each department to account for all sales slips. At the end of each day, an internal check on cash sales may be performed by comparing the total of all cash sales slips with the total recorded on the cash register tape.

With respect to receipt of payments on account, it has been noted that nearly all such payments are made by check. Control over these receipts typically begins in the mail room where they are opened, recorded, and batched. If customers are requested to return a copy of the invoice or other document indicating the amount of the payment enclosed, an independently prepared record of each payment is obtained. Close supervision provides additional control over the mail opening function.

The cashier's department is responsible for endorsing and depositing checks. The accounts receivable department posts the records of payment to individual accounts. The batch total established in the mail room provides a control over both of these processes. Additional control is provided by the preparation of a bank reconciliation by the internal audit department. Organizational independence is achieved by separation of the functions of opening incoming mail, posting to customer accounts, endorsing and depositing checks in the bank, and preparing a bank reconciliation.

One form of embezzlement involving cash receipts is called *lapping*. In order to do this, an employee would have to be responsible for both depositing checks and maintaining the record of accounts receivable. Lapping involves concealing a cash shortage by means of a series of delays in posting collections of accounts. The employee would cash a check received from a customer and keep the cash, neglecting to make the entry debiting cash and crediting accounts receivable. Since the customer's account balance cannot be left in error for too long, the employee credits the balance of the first customer upon receiving a check from a second customer. This corrects the first customer's balance, but leaves the second in error. This process of falsifying one customer's account to correct that of another must be continued indefinitely if the shortage is to be concealed.

In companies that are too small to establish a separation of functions, lapping can be prevented by an agreement with the bank that all checks made out to the company will be deposited directly into the company's account. A bank can also help to provide control over a company's cash receipts in other ways. For example, many firms use a "lockbox" collection system in which customers are requested to mail payments on account to a post-office box. The bank empties the post-office box daily, deposits the payments received in the customer's account, and provides the customer with a record of the receipts. Though not appropriate for all firms because of its cost, such a system not only provides a good control over receipts but also provides faster deposit of collections and faster notification of checks drawn on insufficient funds.

With respect to cash disbursements, it is essential that the function of authorizing payment and recording accounts payable be separated from the function of writing checks. Many firms use a system in which the assembly of documents supporting a disbursement is followed by the preparation of a *voucher,* which summarizes the data relating to the disbursement and represents final authorization of payment. The person writing checks should examine the voucher and other supporting documents provided by the payables clerk prior to making the check, and should stamp "paid" or some other notation on the supporting documents to prevent them from being used more than once. Further control is provided by having a second person examine the supporting documents and sign the checks. The function of preparing the bank reconciliation should also be performed independently of authorizing payment and signing checks.

In many organizations it is convenient to be able to make some small disbursements in cash in order to avoid the delay and inconvenience of the voucher and check preparation procedure. In such cases it is often appropriate to establish a petty cash fund from which small disbursements of cash may be made. For control purposes it is best to limit the size of disbursements that may be made from the fund, and to require its custodian to obtain a receipt for every disbursement made. The total amount of the fund should be maintained at a constant sum in order that the total of all receipts and cash on hand is equal to the fund total at all times. Responsibility for the fund should be assigned to one person only and not separated. Checks to replenish the fund should pass through the regular voucher procedure, and supporting documentation in the form of all petty cash receipts should be required for such checks.

Compliance with the foreign corrupt practices act

As mentioned previously, the Foreign Corrupt Practices Act of 1977 requires all publicly held corporations to maintain good systems of internal accounting control. However, most if not all companies would contend that their systems of internal accounting control were already good prior to the Act. Despite such contentions, wise executives should take positive steps to demonstrate that their companies are complying with the Act.

The first step in a compliance program is to document the company's existing internal control systems. This requires the development of narrative descriptions of control objectives and procedures, flowcharts of data and information flows, and organization charts and other descriptions of assigned responsibilities. Many authorities suggest that this process can be facilitated by considering the internal accounting control system as a series of transaction processing cycles, as described in the previous section.[13] Each cycle then becomes the focal point of a separate analysis and documentation effort.

[13] *See for example Arthur Andersen and Co.,* A Guide for Studying and Evaluating Internal Accounting Controls *(Chicago: Arthur Andersen, 1978); or American Institute of Certified Public Accountants,* Report of the Special Advisory Committee on Internal Accounting Control *(New York: American Institute of Certified Public Accountants, 1979).*

The second step in a compliance program is to evaluate the quality of the internal accounting control system. To do this requires an understanding of the risks to which a company is exposed in the absence of good control, such as loss of assets, inaccurate records, poor management decisions, fraud and embezzlement, and excessive operating costs. The control system is then evaluated in terms of the degree to which it minimizes these risks. Any risks that are not effectively minimized by the control system represent potential weaknesses that should be further evaluated.

The third step is to take action to correct any significant weaknesses in the internal control system. In deciding which of the potential weaknesses are significant enough to require correction, a company should rely on cost-benefit considerations. That is, the anticipated cost savings from minimizing a potential risk should be compared with the cost of the required controls. If the cost of a control procedure is less than the estimated cost savings from adopting it, then that control procedure should be implemented.

Compliance with the internal control requirements of the Foreign Corrupt Practices Act is a continuous process—not simply a one-year project—of reviewing and evaluating control systems. The primary responsibility for this process rests with management, who in turn rely upon the assistance of accounting systems designers and internal and external auditors. The corporation's board of directors and its audit committee are also responsible for ensuring that management is adopting the necessary policies and processes involved in compliance. Many corporations have discovered that, regardless of the legal requirements, a compliance program that continuously monitors the effectiveness of internal accounting controls also makes good business sense.

A Perspective on Control Concepts

Each of the three types of control systems discussed in this chapter has its advantages and disadvantages. Feedback systems are generally less costly and easier to implement, and are effective in restoring a process that goes out of control. Their basic disadvantage is that they may permit costly errors or deviations from plan to persist for too long before they are detected and corrected. Feedforward systems may overcome this deficiency, but they are generally the least effective and most difficult (or even impossible) to implement due to uncertainty in predicting future process outputs.

Preventive systems are also quite effective in avoiding costly errors and deviations. They are generally easy to implement, but tend to be more costly because of the necessity for separation of functions, additional documentation, and other requirements. In addition, preventive controls are not self-regulatory; that is, once an error or irregularity occurs and avoids detection by preventive controls, there is no mechanism that will ensure subsequent review, discovery, and correction of the problem. In contrast, both feedback and feedforward systems have regulatory mechanisms in the form of periodic reviews that activate an automatic corrective action when problems are disclosed.

Control system advantages	Characteristic of:		
	Feedback	Feedforward	Preventive
Low cost	√		
Ease of implementation	√		√
Effectiveness	√		√
Minimal time delays		√	√
Self-regulation	√	√	

Fig. 4.4
Comparative summary of advantages of the three primary types of control system.

Figure 4.4 summarizes this discussion by indicating in tabular form the most significant advantages of each type of control system relative to the others.

As this discussion suggests, these control concepts are most effective when they are used to complement one another. Few if any processes can operate efficiently for long periods of time using only one type of control. In some processes, all three types of control may be useful. For example, credit control makes use of feedback concerning bad debt losses and customer payment records, as discussed earlier. However, feedforward control in the form of analysis of the financial statements and credit ratings of potential customers is also an important policy of credit control. In addition, the requirement that the shipping department obtain shipment authorizations from the credit department is a form of preventive control over this process. Therefore, credit control policies often integrate all three of the control concepts discussed in this chapter. There are probably several other business processes for which this is true.

All three types of control systems bear a close relationship to the accounting information system. Preventive controls are an integral part of virtually all accounting data processing, and much of the information generated by the accounting system is used for preventive control purposes; examples of the latter include control totals, the bank reconciliation, and the trial balance. In feedback control systems, accounting often performs the functions of standard setting, measurement of performance, and reporting on results of process operations. In feedforward control systems, accounting may also be involved in standard setting, as well as in the monitoring of process inputs and operations and in the prediction of process outputs. Thus it is true that control and accounting are inexorably intertwined. Indeed it might be said that control is the central concept and purpose of accounting, and that accounting is the primary vehicle of control in business organizations.

Review Questions

1. Define the following terms.

   internal control   embezzlement
   accounting controls   internal check
   administrative controls   batch totals
   feedback   control totals
   cybernetics   organizational independence

standard cost   collusion
rate variance   fidelity bond
usage variance   audit trail
reorder point   lapping
lead time   voucher
economic order quantity

2. Describe the legal requirements of the Foreign Corrupt Practices Act with respect to internal controls. To what type of company does this law apply?

3. Identity three general types of control systems. What are their distinguishing features?

4. Relate the distinction between feedback, feedforward, and preventive control systems to AICPA's distinction between accounting and administrative controls.

5. What are the five fundamental components of a feedback control system and how are they related?

6. In what respect is a feedback control system a self-regulating system?

7. How do feedback control systems in business operations differ from mechanical feedback control systems such as the thermostat?

8. What are four essential factors in the successful operation of feedback control systems in business? Which of these have direct implications for accounting systems?

9. How do feedback control systems in business operate to promote operational efficiency and encourage adherence to managerial policies?

10. What are five examples of feedback control systems in business? Describe the operation of each.

11. List several examples of control problems that the internal audit function should discover.

12. Describe the five fundamental components of a feedforward control system and explain the relationships between them.

13. What condition must exist in order for a feedforward control system to be effective?

14. Identify three examples of feedforward control systems in business, and explain the operation of each.

15. Explain in general terms how an accounting system uses preventive controls to contribute to the safeguarding of assets.

16. The loss to society from embezzlement may be looked at in different ways. Describe some of them.

17. Describe two examples of preventive control through internal check.

18. Describe six essential elements of preventive control systems in accounting processes.

19. Identify three general classes of functions that should be separated in order to maintain effective organizational independence. Give some examples of each.

20. Explain why it may be important for an organization to have a policy requiring certain key employees to take annual vacations.

21. Explain several ways in which the cash register contributes to the physical control of cash receipts in a retail enterprise.

22. Explain how sequential prenumbering of documents adds to control.

23. Describe the nature of preventive control systems in business relating to the following functions.

    a) purchasing of inventory   b) flow of inventory through production
    c) payroll   d) sale of products
    e) cash receipts   f) cash disbursements

    Indicate the basic purpose or purposes of the control system in each case and, where relevant, describe applications of the principles of organizational independence, control by recorded documentation, batching, physical protection, and supervision.

24. Describe the steps that a corporation might take in order to effectively demonstrate compliance with the Foreign Corrupt Practices Act.

25. Describe the relative advantages and disadvantages of preventive, feedback, and feedforward control systems.

26. Explain how preventive, feedback, and feedforward control systems are related to accounting information systems.

Discussion Questions

27. Organizational independence is sometimes difficult to achieve in small companies. What other elements of control take on more importance in such situations?

28. Some people feel that controls in business organizations are dysfunctional in that they create resentment and loss of morale without producing much benefit. Discuss this position.

29. For each of the control activities listed below, discuss whether the activity contains elements of a preventive control, a feedback control, and/or a feedforward control. (Note: Some may contain elements of two or all three.)

    a) Audit of a governmental agency by the General Accounting Office
    b) Tabulation and review of customer complaints by a manager
    c) Review of sales statistics indicating the impact of various advertising techniques on consumer buying behavior
    d) Review of trends in number of passengers on various routes by an airline
    e) Analysis of resumes of potential employees by a manager responsible for hiring
    f) Reporting of student grades in a university
    g) Analysis of accident statistics in a factory

30. You are an executive with a corporation that has in recent years received from its external auditors clean opinions on its financial statements and favorable evaluations of its internal control systems. Discuss whether it is necessary for your corporation to take any further action to comply with the Foreign Corrupt Practices Act.

Problems and Cases

31. You are employed as the Internal Auditor for the Easy Manufacturing Corporation. Prior to your recent appointment, the company had not employed anyone in this position. To familiarize yourself with the company, you have investigated several clerical operations, and have discovered the following:

    a) The person who opens incoming mail prepares a list of receipts of payments on account, which is then supplied to the accounts receivable clerk. The mail opener is also responsible for endorsing checks and preparing the bank deposit.

    b) A third individual receives invoices from suppliers, files them by due date, and writes checks to pay the invoices on the due date.

    c) A fourth employee is responsible for the timekeeping function, and each week supplies a record of hours worked by each factory employee to a fifth employee, who prepares paychecks. The former is also responsible for maintaining personnel records and for distributing paychecks to employees.

    d) Only one bank account is used and no bank reconciliation is prepared.

    Which of the above employees could possibly embezzle company funds and how? What changes would you recommend to strengthen the system of accounting controls?

32. Prudence Honeyfeather is responsible for maintaining the accounts receivable ledger for the Perfect Controls Corporation. Twice daily she receives a batch of invoices from billing and posts them as debits to customer accounts. One day she mistakenly posted the amount of $1,007.67 to a customer account, when the proper amount was actually 1,070.67. At the next step in processing, the existence of an error was discovered, and a comparison of invoices with amounts posted quickly revealed the account in which the error occurred, and it was corrected.

    What procedure or control probably resulted in the discovery that an error existed?

33. The Y Company, a client of your firm, has come to you with the following problem: It has three clerical employees who must perform the following functions:

    a) Maintain general ledger
    b) Maintain accounts payable ledger
    c) Maintain accounts receivable ledger
    d) Prepare checks for signature
    e) Maintain disbursements journal

    f) Issue credits on returns and allowances

    g) Reconcile the bank account

    h) Handle and deposit cash receipts

Assuming that there is no problem as to the ability of any of the employees, the company requests that you assign the above functions to the three employees in such a manner as to achieve the highest degree of internal control. It may be assumed that these employees will perform no other accounting functions than the ones listed and that any accounting functions not listed will be performed by persons other than these three employees.

    a) State how you would distribute the above functions among the three employees. Assume that, with the exception of the nominal jobs of the bank reconciliation and the issuance of credits on returns and allowances, all functions require an equal amount of time.

    b) List four possible unsatisfactory pairings of the functions listed above.[14]

34. The Wise Wholesale Company wishes to establish an inventory control system for Widgets, its best-selling item. The demand rate for Widgets is a constant 10 units per day, or 3600 per year. The cost of placing an order for Widgets is $50. The lead time is a constant two days, and the holding cost rate is $1.00 per unit per year.

Required

    a) Determine the appropriate standards for an inventory control system which will minimize the sum of the costs of holding and ordering inventories and of stockouts.

    b) Identify the five fundamental components of a feedforward control system in the above situation.

    c) If demand and lead time were variable instead of constant, what additional problems would exist in the system?

35. McClain's lumberyard uses the following procedures in selling lumber to customers:

    a) The customer informs a clerk in the office of the sizes and quantities of lumber to be purchased.

    b) The clerk records the items on a sales document, calculates the total cost, and collects payment from the customer.

    c) A yard worker obtains the lumber from the yard and assists in loading it onto the customer's car or truck; or if the purchase is large and the customer wishes, McClain's will deliver the order.

Required

Explain several aspects of the design and usage of the sales document that will facilitate control of cash receipts and inventories by McClain's.

36. The following is a list of duties performed by Ms. C. Nation for the Quick and Easy Corporation.

---

[14] *Question 2, Auditing Section, American Institute of Certified Public Accountants Examination. November 1956, Copyright 1956 by the American Institute of Certified Public Accountants and reprinted with permission.*

a) Credit sales for the day are totaled and reported to the general bookkeeper.

b) Collections on accounts receivable for the day are totaled. The checks and an adding machine tape of receipts are turned over to the cashier.

c) Sales and cash collections are posted daily to the accounts receivable ledger.

d) A trial balance of the receivable ledger is prepared monthly and the total is compared with the total shown by the general control account.

e) Statements are prepared and mailed on each account monthly. Accounts not paid by the tenth of the month are followed up with a series of collection notices and letters.

f) Accounts determined to be uncollectible are reported to the general bookkeeper for write-off of the amount included in the control account.

The company is considering hiring another person to help Ms. Nation with her numerous duties. Cite at least two forms of manipulation that could possibly be accomplished by Ms. Nation as her duties are presently defined. What division of duties between Ms. Nation and a new employee would you recommend to prevent such manipulation?

37. The cashier of the Easy Company intercepted Customer A's check payable to the company in the amount of $500 and deposited it in a bank account which was part of the company petty cash fund, of which he was custodian. He then drew a $500 check on the petty cash fund bank account payable to himself, signed it, and cashed it. At the end of the month while processing the monthly statements to customers, he was able to change the statement to Customer A so as to show that A had received credit for the $500 check that had been intercepted. Ten days later he made an entry in the cash received book which purported to record receipt of a remittance of $500 from Customer A, thus restoring A's account to its proper balance, but overstating the cash in bank. He covered the overstatement by omitting from the list of outstanding checks in the bank reconcilement, two checks, the aggregate amount of which was $500.

List what you regard as five important deficiencies in the system of internal control in the above situation, and state the proper remedy for each deficiency.[15]

38. In the XYZ Company, when supplier invoices are received they go to the cashier, who reviews supporting documentation and prepares a payment voucher authorizing a disbursement. The vouchers, with the invoices attached, are then provided to the assistant controller, who records them in a vouchers payable ledger and files them by due date. Each day the batch of vouchers due for payment is provided to the cashier, who prepares and signs checks and stamps the vouchers "PAID." The assistant controller then records all disbursements in the cash disbursements journal, and files all the paid vouchers. The checks go to the treasurer for mailing to the suppliers.

[15] Question 4, Auditing Section, American Institute of Certified Public Accountants Examination. May 1958. Copyright 1958 by the American Institute of Certified Public Accountants and reprinted with permission.

Required   Identify (a) a form of embezzlement that could be perpetrated by one of these persons, and (b) the deficiencies in the internal control system that make this possible.

39. What principle of feedback control systems is probably being violated in each of the following cases?

a) A monthly report to the credit manager of the Morgan Company indicated that one of the firm's customers, Shylock Corporation, owed Morgan a large sum of money on account, which was over 90 days past due. Morgan's policy is to refuse to sell on account to customers whose account is 90 days or more past due. However, on the day before the monthly report was received, a large order by Shylock was approved by the credit manager.

b) Each month the Morgan Company provides its factory supervisors with a performance report indicating budgeted and actual costs for each supervisor's department. Each report contains an analysis of material, labor, and overhead costs. Among the overhead costs are proportionate allocations of the salary of the plant manager and staff and of depreciation for the plant and equipment. The performance reports are considered to be the single most important tool for evaluating the performance of factory supervisors.

c) A special study indicated that lax control over office supplies in the Morgan Company had resulted in waste totaling from $100 to $300 per month. As a result a room was set aside to be a supplies storeroom, a clerk was hired to manage the storeroom, and a control system designed around a supplies requisition document was implemented.

d) Each week the purchasing agent of the Morgan Company is provided with a computer listing of the parts inventory ledger. The purchasing agent determines which parts must be ordered by comparing the quantity on hand with the reorder point on the report for each item. For those items that must be reordered, the agent refers to catalogs listing which vendors sell the part, selects a vendor, and then prepares the purchase order. Delays in this process have often resulted in stockouts of parts needed in production.

40. Explain how the principle of organizational independence is being violated in each of the following situations.

a) A payroll employee recorded a 40-hour workweek for an employee who had quit the previous week. He then prepared a paycheck for this employee, cashed it by forging the signature, and kept the cash.

b) While opening the mail, the cashier set aside two checks payable to the company on account, and later cashed these checks and pocketed the cash.

c) The cashier prepared a fictitious invoice from a company having the name of his brother-in-law, and wrote a check in payment of the invoice, which the brother-in-law later cashed.

d) An employee of the finishing department walked off with several parts from the storeroom, and recorded the items as being issued to the assembly department in the inventory ledger.

e) The cashier cashed a check from a customer in payment of an account receivable, pocketed the cash, and concealed the theft by properly posting the receipt to the customer's account in the accounts receivable ledger.

41. It has been said that internal auditors are not responsible for detecting defalcation, embezzlement, or fraud. Yet, when a fraud is uncovered, the question is usually asked, "Where were the auditors?"

    While it is obvious that an internal auditor cannot be expected to guarantee that there is no fraud, there are a number of indicators which an alert auditor might spot and investigate, as a deterrent to fraud or as an early disclosure of possible fraud.

Required   Discuss the following six indicators or danger signs including the potential fraud which could be involved, and the initial approach you would take in each case.

a) Employees living beyond their apparent means

b) Reluctance by a key employee to take a vacation

c) Unreasonable association with supplier's personnel by members of the Purchasing Department

d) Erasures, changes, or manually inserted times on time cards

e) Date of deposits per cash book significantly different from date of deposits on bank statements

f) Lack of cooperation in relinquishing records for audit.[16]

References   American Institute of Certified Public Accountants. *Report of the Special Advisory Committee on Internal Accounting Control.* New York: American Institute of Certified Public Accountants, 1979.

Arthur Andersen and Co. *A Guide for Studying and Evaluating Internal Accounting Controls.* Chicago: Arthur Andersen, 1978.

Benjamin, James J.; Paul E. Dascher; and Robert G. Morgan. "How Corporate Controllers View the Foreign Corrupt Practices Act." *Management Accounting* (June 1979): 43–45.

Committee on Auditing Procedure, American Institute of Certified Public Accountants. *Statement on Auditing Standards No. 1.* New York: American Institute of Certified Public Accountants, 1973. (Note: This statement codifies and incorporates all of the material contained in *Statements on Auditing Procedure* referred to in this chapter.)

Cook, J. Michael, and Thomas P. Kelley. "Internal Accounting Control: A Matter of Law." *Journal of Accountancy* (January 1979): 56–64.

Cushing, Barry E. "A Further Note on the Mathematical Approach to Internal Control." *The Accounting Review* **50** (January 1975): 151–155.

Ellentuck, Elmer I. "How to Minimize Employee Fraud: A Checklist." *The Practical Accountant* **5** (March-April 1972): 30–37.

---

[16] *Question 13, Part I (Principles of Internal Auditing). From The Certified Internal Auditor Examination, August 1974. Copyright 1974 by The Institute of Internal Auditors, Inc. Reprinted with permission of the Institute of Internal Auditors, Inc., 249 Maitland Ave., Altamonte Springs, Fla. 32701.*

Elliott, Robert K., and John J. Willingham. *Management Fraud: Detection and Deterrance.* United States: Petrocelli Books, 1980.

Foreign Corrupt Practices Act of 1977. U.S. Code, 1976 edition, Supplement II, Title 15, Selection 78. Washington: United States Government Printing Office, 1979.

Grollman, William K., and Robert W. Colby. "Internal Control for Small Businesses." *The Journal of Accountancy* (December 1978): 64–67.

Gurry, E. J. "Locating Potential Irregularities." *The Journal of Accountancy* **140** (September 1975): 111–114.

Horngren, Charles T. *Cost Accounting, A Managerial Emphasis.* (4th ed.). Englewood Cliffs, N.J.: Prentice-Hall, 1977.

Koontz, Harold, and Robert W. Bradspies. "Managing through Feedforward Control." *Business Horizons* **15** (June 1972): 25–36.

Loebbecke, James K., and George R. Zuber. "Evaluating Internal Control." *The Journal of Accountancy* (February 1980): 49–56.

MacKay, A. E. "Management Control in a Changing Environment." *Financial Executive* (March 1979): 25–36.

McQueary, Glenn M., II., and Michael P. Risdon. "How We Comply with the Foreign Corrupt Practices Act." *Management Accounting* (November 1979): 39–43.

Mautz, Robert K.; Walter G. Kell; Michael W. Maher; Alan G. Merten; Raymond R. Reilly; Dennis G. Severance; and Bernard J. White. *Internal Control in U.S. Corporations: The State of the Art.* New York: Financial Executives Research Foundation, 1980.

Mautz, Robert K., and Bernard J. White. "Internal Control—A Management View." *Financial Executive* (June 1979): 12–18.

Passage, Howard D., and Donald A. Fleming. "An Integrated Approach to Internal Control Review." *Management Accounting* (February 1980): 29–35.

Romney, Marshall B.; W. Steve Albrecht; and David J. Cherrington. "Red-flagging the White-Collar Criminal." *Management Accounting* (March 1980): 51–54, 57.

Sawyer, Lawrence B.; Albert A. Murphy; and Michael Crossley. "Management Fraud: The Insidious Specter." *The Internal Auditor* (April 1979): 11–25.

Sherwin, Douglas S. "The Meaning of Control." *Dun's Review* (January 1956): 45–46, 83–84.

Touche Ross and Co. *The New Management Imperative: Compliance with the Accounting Requirements of the Foreign Corrupt Practices Act.* New York: Touche Ross, 1978.

United States Fidelity and Guaranty Co. *The Forty Thieves.* Baltimore: USF&G, 1970.

Part 2

The Technology of Information Systems

Chapter 5

Introduction to Business Data Processing

The variety of business machines that assist business organizations in collecting and processing data and generating information is enormous. A partial list includes computer systems, cash registers, adding machines and calculators, typewriters, microfilm systems, duplicating machines, mail preparation devices, postage meters, word processing equipment, and communications equipment. Each of these categories contains several subcategories and/or a wide assortment of optional features. To attempt to describe all of these various categories, subcategories, and optional features would be impractical. Part 2 of this book (Chapters 5 through 9) reviews the basic features of those business machines that have direct applications in accounting. Except for one section of this chapter, the coverage in Part 2 is devoted entirely to computer systems, which provide the most advanced form of data processing capability available to modern organizations today.

Basic Computer Concepts

A *computer* is a high-speed electronic device capable of performing arithmetic and logical operations; it can also store and execute a set of instructions, which enable it to perform a series of these operations without human intervention. The impetus for the early development of high-speed computing machines was provided by the Second World War. In the late 1940s and early 1950s several such machines were developed and used in scientific applications at various government and university sites around the country. Computers were first made commercially available in the early 1950s, and their application to high-volume data processing tasks on a large scale dates from that point.

A major development in computer technology occurred in the late 1950s when transistors and printed circuitry replaced the vacuum tubes upon which early computers had been based. This led to computers that were not only much smaller in size but also much faster and more reliable. This development was considered so significant that from this point the early computers were referred to as "first generation," and the new ones as "second generation."

In 1963 and 1964, computers with microelectronic circuitry, much smaller and faster than anything that preceded them, were introduced. These computers provided a greatly improved capability for handling data communication from remote locations and for executing several different jobs at the same time. So significant were these improvements that a "third generation" of computers was hailed. Though many further advances in computer technology have occurred since 1964, none has been as momentous as the introduction of the third generation of computers. Therefore, many experts feel that the computer industry has not yet truly entered the "fourth generation" even though several new waves of advanced computers have been introduced since 1964.

The essential elements of a computer system can be divided into two basic categories, *hardware* and *software.* Computer hardware comprises all of the physical equipment necessary for computer processing. Software includes all of the nonhardware elements of a computer system, including programs, programming languages, and documentation. This distinction is useful for purposes of studying computer concepts. Accordingly, this chapter and Chapters 6 and 9 focus primarily on computer hardware, while Chapters 7 and 8 concentrate on computer software.

Overview of computer hardware

Computer hardware consists of a number of different input, output, and storage devices in addition to the central computer. These devices may be classified according to the functions they perform. The concept of the data processing cycle, discussed in Chapter 1, provides a useful means of classification. Recall that the five stages of the data processing cycle are data collection, data refinement, data processing, data maintenance, and data output (see Fig. 1.2). With respect to the functions they perform, most computer hardware devices fall within one of these five categories.

The functions of observation and recording are included within the data collection stage. Most computer data are originally observed and recorded manually. However, there are some devices that collect source data in machine-readable form at the time and place of origination of the data. This technique, which is called *source data automation* (SDA), is gradually becoming more prevalent. Among the more familiar devices for this purpose are embossed-card imprinters (used for credit card sales in many retail stores and gas stations), factory data collection devices, bank teller machines, and point-of-sale (POS) recorders (used as cash registers in many grocery and other retail stores).

Most manually recorded data must be transcribed onto some type of machine-readable medium prior to being processed on the computer. Such transcription is a major function within the data refinement stage. Among the more common machine-readable media are punched cards, magnetic tape, documents printed in special characters that are readable by optical scanning devices, and diskettes. Among the more common devices for performing this transcribing function are key-punches, key-to-tape encoders, and key-to-diskette encoders.

Other functions within the data refinement stage include verification, sorting, and transmission of data, all of which are performed by hardware devices. For example, the keyverifier is a manually operated device used in the verification of data on punched cards. The card sorter is a device that sorts punched cards into numerical or alphabetic sequence. Data transmission is performed by a combination of teleprocessing equipment and data communications lines.

The last stage in data refinement (or perhaps the first stage in data processing) is the input of data on machine-readable media to the computer. Hardware devices that perform this function include punched card readers, magnetic tape readers, diskette readers, and optical scanners.

The primary hardware device in the entire computer system is the central processing unit (CPU), which performs processing functions under the control of computer programs. In essence, the CPU is the actual "computer" element of a computer system. It has three main components: (1) the control unit, which interprets and initiates execution of program instructions; (2) the arithmetic and logic unit, which performs calculations and logical operations on data; and (3) memory, which stores program instructions and data until they are needed.[1] The relationship of these components to each other, and to computer input and output, is illustrated in Fig. 5.1. Note that memory is much larger than the other two components within the CPU, and that all other components, both internal and external to the CPU, interact with and through the memory component.

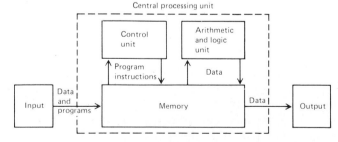

Fig. 5.1
Interaction of main
components of a
computer.

---

[1] *According to some authorities, the technically correct definition of CPU includes only the control unit and the arithmetic and logic unit. Practically speaking, however, all three of these components are physically located in the same piece of equipment, which is customarily referred to as the CPU.*

In addition to the full range of processing functions—calculating, comparing, summarizing, filtration, and retrieval—the CPU is capable of performing many other data processing functions under the control of a stored program. These include verification, sorting, transcription, updating, and indexing. Thus while most other computer hardware devices specialize in performing one, or sometimes a few, functions, the CPU is flexible enough to perform virtually all functions in the data processing cycle.

The data maintenance stage of the data processing cycle utilizes secondary storage devices and media in a computer system. The term "secondary" storage is used to refer to data storage that is external to the CPU, in contrast to CPU memory that is sometimes referred to as "primary" storage. Examples of computer secondary storage hardware include magnetic disks and magnetic drums. Examples of secondary storage media include punched cards and magnetic tape. Secondary storage is used to store programs when they are not being executed, and files when they are not being updated or referenced.

Several computer hardware devices are available to perform the data output functions of issuing documents and reporting. These include printers, magnetic tape drives, computer-output-microfilm (COM) units, card punches, and data terminals.

This discussion of the relationship of computer hardware to the data processing cycle is summarized in Fig. 5.2, in which each device mentioned in this section is placed in the appropriate segment of the cycle. Figure 5.3 shows a modern computer system that includes several of the most commonly used items of computer hardware.

This section has provided a very brief overview of some of the primary hardware components of computer systems. The nature and operation of these and other computer hardware devices are explored in greater depth in subsequent sections of the text.

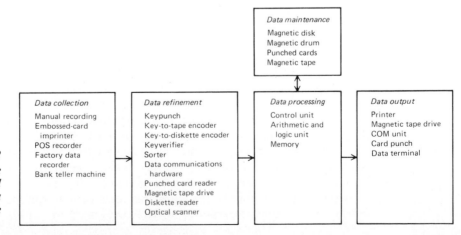

Fig. 5.2
Computer hardware elements and corresponding data processing cycle functions.

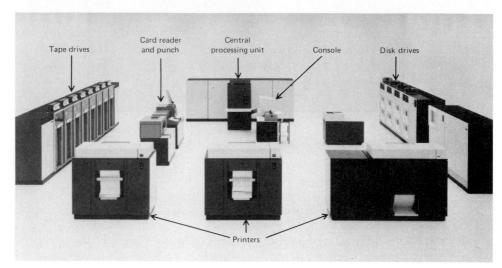

Card reader and punch — Central processing unit — Console — Tape drives — Disk drives — Printers

Fig. 5.3
A computer system.
(Courtesy of IBM
corporation.)

The central processing unit

We shall now take a closer look at the CPU and its operations. In addition to interpreting program instructions and to performing arithmetic and logical operations, the CPU controls the operation of all computer input, output, and storage devices in the system. Thus if a computer system were to be viewed as an organization, the CPU would represent the chief executive officer. The *mainframe* is another name frequently used for the CPU.

To understand how the CPU works, refer to Fig. 5.1. Note that as a data processing job is being performed by the CPU, both the program instructions to be performed, and the data values upon which those instructions are to be performed, are transferred from an input device into the CPU's memory. Each instruction and each data value is stored in a separate location in this memory. The CPU can keep track of the location of any particular instruction or data value because each storage location in the CPU's memory has an *address*—a number or other label that uniquely identifies a specific memory location.

As a computer program is being executed, its instructions are transferred one at a time to the control unit for interpretation. Each make of computer has a specific set of instructions that it can perform. When the control unit receives an instruction from memory, it must analyze the instruction code to determine which one of its instructions it is to perform. Once this determination has been made, the control unit initiates the detailed set of electronic operations corresponding to that instruction.

There are two distinct ways in which a CPU control unit may be designed. Under one approach, the series of operations necessary to implement each instruction exists in the form of hardwired electronic circuits. The other, more modern, approach replaces most of the hardwired logic with *microcode,* which is a series of elementary computer operations stored in program form within a special location of the computer. Microcode is generally stored in *read-only memory* (ROM)—a storage area whose contents may be read but may not be altered by other program instructions. Whichever approach to control unit design is used, when the control unit encounters a particular instruction, it will access the hardwired logic or the microcode corresponding to that instruction and initiate the appropriate sequence of elementary computer operations.

If the instruction involves input or output, the operations initiated by the control unit will activate an input or output device, which will cause data either to be read from an input device into the CPU's memory or to be written from the CPU's memory to an output device. If the instruction involves a logical operation (such as comparing the values of two data items or testing the sign of a numeric value) or an arithmetic calculation, the control unit will cause the appropriate data values to be transferred to the arithmetic and logic unit, which will perform the necessary operations and return the result.

As instructions and data are transferred from memory to the control unit or to the arithmetic and logic unit, they must be stored in a place where they are quickly accessible. The devices used for this purpose are called *registers*—high-speed temporary storage locations containing those instructions and data that are currently being processed by the control unit and the arithmetic and logic unit. Register storage is temporary in the sense that after one instruction is executed the instruction codes and data pertaining to the next instruction are loaded into the registers to replace those of the previous instruction. There are several different types of registers, each classified according to its function. For example, an *instruction register* holds an instruction code, an *address register* holds a memory address of another instruction or data value, and an *accumulator* holds the results of an arithmetic operation.

Although hundreds, or even thousands, of instructions and data values may be stored in the CPU's memory, the control and the arithmetic and logic units can operate on only one instruction at a time. After the control unit finishes with one instruction, it checks the appropriate address register to determine the location in memory of the next instruction, and then causes that instruction to be read into an instruction register for interpretation and execution.

The operator of a computer system exercises control over its operations by means of the control console of the CPU. In the system illustrated in Fig. 5.3, the console consists of a panel containing various lights and switches, and a keyboard and printer. The console panel enables the operator to monitor certain aspects of the CPU's operations, while the console keyboard and printer provide limited input-output capability.

The hardware components most commonly used for data representation within the CPU are magnetic cores and semiconductors. A magnetic core is a very tiny, doughnut-shaped ferrite ring, which can be magnetized in either a clockwise or counterclockwise direction by electric current conducted through wires running through the center of each core. A semiconductor consists of a tiny chip of silicon upon which is inscribed a number of miniature circuits, each of which may be either closed (conducting electricity) or open (not conducting). These two forms of data representation are contrasted in Fig. 5.4, which shows a closeup of a semiconductor

Fig. 5.4
Semiconductor
memory chip with
magnetic core plane
in background.
(Courtesy of IBM
Corporation.)

memory chip against a magnetic core plane background. Note that both forms of data storage use a binary form of data representation; that is, the storage element may assume one of only two possible states. More is said about data representation in the next section.

Magnetic cores were the predominant form of primary storage in the CPU throughout the 1960s and early 1970s. Integrated circuitry, of which the semiconductor memory is an advanced form, was used only in control and arithmetic and logic units until 1971. Semiconductor memory is smaller and faster than magnetic core memory. However, until the mid-1970s magnetic core memory was much less expensive. This factor prevented semiconductors from being used in CPU memories, which are typically very large. Since the first computers with semiconductor memories were installed in 1971, this form of primary memory has declined substantially in cost, and is expected to ultimately replace magnetic cores.

When comparing one computer with another, some of the more important measures of CPU performance include access time and execution time. *Access time* refers to the time required to retrieve data from memory. Access time for data in core memory averages around one to two *microseconds* (millionths of a second) in modern computers. Semiconductor memories offer faster access times of from 10 to 400 *nanoseconds* (billionths of a second). *Execution time* refers to the time required to perform a computer instruction, such as add, multiply, or compare. Execution times vary widely according to the instruction and the make of computer, but they generally range from one to several hundred microseconds. The reason that such speeds are possible is that the internal operation of the CPU is entirely electronic. In contrast, computer input, output, and secondary storage devices operate electromechanically, and their speeds are generally measured in *milliseconds* (thousandths of a second).

Data representation At this point the reader may wonder just how the computer can understand the instructions and data that it works with; that is, how can instructions and data be represented in such a way that an electronic machine can interpret them? This section attempts to answer this question by examining the subject of data representation.

In the preceding section, brief mention was made of the fact that magnetic core and semiconductor memories made use of the binary form of data representation. Actually, all computer data storage media and equipment represent data in binary form. Thus the basic unit of data in a computer system is the *bit* (short for "binary digit"), which is a single storage location capable of assuming one of only two possible states. These can be referred to as "on" and "off" states, or "yes" and "no" states, but in a computer environment it is logical to refer to them as the "0" state and the "1" state. Figure 5.5 illustrates the way in which both states are represented on a variety of computer storage media.

Given that we can communicate a 0 or a 1 to the computer, the reader may next wonder how it is possible to communicate complex instructions and large data values. We need a coding system capable of communicating more than just two possible characters. At a minimum, we would want a coding system capable of representing each of the 26 letters of the alphabet, the ten decimal digits, and several other symbols and arithmetic operators such as "$" and " + ". Obviously, a single bit is not capable of representing all of these possibilities.

The answer to this dilemma lies in using a different combination of bits to represent each of the possible characters in our desired character set. For example, if we use two bits to represent a character, then there are four possible combinations of the two bits—00, 01, 10, and 11—which means that a maximum of four different characters can be represented. In general, if there are n bits per character, then the maximum number of characters that can be represented is equal to 2^n. Thus a coding system that uses six bits per character is capable of representing up to $2^6 = 64$ different characters. One prominent computer coding system that uses a six-bit code is called the *Binary Coded Decimal* (BCD) notation.

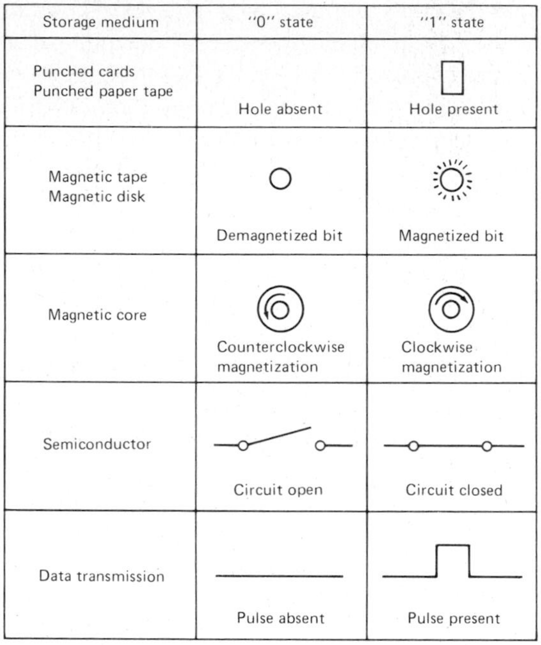

Storage medium	"0" state	"1" state
Punched cards Punched paper tape	Hole absent	Hole present
Magnetic tape Magnetic disk	Demagnetized bit	Magnetized bit
Magnetic core	Counterclockwise magnetization	Clockwise magnetization
Semiconductor	Circuit open	Circuit closed
Data transmission	Pulse absent	Pulse present

Fig. 5.5
Examples of binary data representation on various computer data media.

The familiar punched card utilizes twelve bits per column, which provides for a total of $2^{12} = 4096$ different characters that could possibly be represented in each column. The coding system used on the punched card is called the *Hollerith code*. It was named after Herman Hollerith, a Census Bureau statistician who in the 1880s invented the punched card and related equipment to assist in tabulating the United States census. Since the character sets commonly used in data processing contain many fewer than 4096 characters, the Hollerith code has a larger number of bit positions than is required for computer equipment.

Probably the most commonly used coding system in modern computers is *EBCDIC* (pronounced eb-see-dik), an acronym for Extended Binary-Coded Decimal Interchange Code, which is an eight-bit code providing for 256 possible characters. Figure 5.6 illustrates the EBCDIC bit pattern for selected characters. In contrast to Binary-Coded Decimal notation, EBCDIC enables both uppercase and lowercase letters of the alphabet to be represented, and it has the capacity to represent an even larger variety of special symbols.

Another advantage of an eight-bit code is *packing*—which means that since only four bits are required at a minimum to store one decimal digit, it is possible to store two decimal digits within one group of eight bits. In order to store data in packed form, special symbols must be inserted into the data stream to tell the computer when the storage format is switched from regular to packed or from packed to regular. Since a large proportion of the data used in a business computer system is numeric data, packing can provide a considerable savings in storage requirements.

A group of *n* bits, where *n* is the number of bits used in the computer's coding system, is called a *byte*. Thus in a computer that uses the EBCDIC coding system, a byte consists of eight adjacent bits. Generally, one byte stores one character of data, the exception to this being numeric data stored in packed form, in which case one byte can store two characters of (numeric) data.

As the computer moves data values, address values, and instructions between its storage locations and registers, it will virtually always need to move more than one character at a time. Therefore most computers use a unit of information called a *word*—a group of adjacent bits larger than one byte, which is treated by the computer as a single entity. Generally, a computer moves one word at a time to and from its storage locations. Although word sizes vary from one model of computer to another, the most common word size among standard computers is 32 bits.

In a typical computer system, different coding systems are used on different storage media; therefore the central processor and its input and output devices must be capable of translating from one coding system to another. For example, consider a computer that uses EBCDIC for its internal code. When a punched card is read into this computer, all of the characters on the card must be converted from the Hollerith code to EBCDIC. Furthermore, when data are transmitted to this computer over telecommunications facilities, a conversion must be performed from the code used for data transmission purposes to the EBCDIC code.

Symbol	Bit configuration		Symbol	Bit configuration	
A	1100	0001	0	1111	0000
B	1100	0010	1	1111	0001
C	1100	0011	2	1111	0010
D	1100	0100	3	1111	0011
E	1100	0101	4	1111	0100
F	1100	0110	5	1111	0101
G	1100	0111	6	1111	0110
H	1100	1000	7	1111	0111
I	1100	1001	8	1111	1000
J	1101	0001	9	1111	1001
K	1101	0010	.	0100	1011
L	1101	0011	<	0100	1100
M	1101	0100	(	0100	1101
N	1101	0101	+	0100	1110
O	1101	0110	&	0101	0000
P	1101	0111	$	0101	1011
Q	1101	1000	*	0101	1100
R	1101	1001	)	0101	1101
S	1110	0010	/	0110	0001
T	1110	0011	,	0110	1011
U	1110	0100	%	0110	1100
V	1110	0101	–	0110	1101
W	1110	0110	>	0110	1110
X	1110	0111	?	0110	1111
Y	1110	1000	:	0111	1010
Z	1110	1001	=	0111	1110

Fig. 5.6
Selected character codes in EBCDIC.

Computer Data Entry

The subject of computer data entry encompasses all of the ways in which data may be converted from their raw form into a machine-readable form for entry into the computer. In terms of the data processing cycle, it includes the first two stages—the data collection stage, and the data refinement stage.

In a business data processing environment, computer data entry is concerned almost exclusively with the preparation of transaction files for processing against master files. In Chapter 3, four general types of transaction records were presented: additions to the master file, deletions, updates, and master file changes. Of the four, updates account for the vast majority of all transaction records because they include the standard business transactions—sales orders, billings, collections, purchases, disbursements, etc.

In a business data processing facility, the cost of data entry is often a major portion of the cost of data processing. The hardware, personnel, and supplies required for data entry may consume up to 40 percent of the total data processing budget. This is true because data entry is the only major function in an automated system which makes extensive use of human labor, with its limitations in speed and reliability. Once data have been successfully entered into a computer system, subsequent processing steps may proceed rapidly and accurately with a minimum of human intervention.

For discussion purposes, the various methods of computer data entry may be divided into two basic categories: (1) general-purpose data entry, which includes devices that may be used by virtually all organizations for virtually all types of applications, and (2) special-purpose data entry, which includes devices and techniques whose application is limited to specific kinds of transactions and/or specific types of organizations. This section describes a wide variety of data entry methods in both categories. Note that no organization is likely to use just one form of data entry for all of its input transactions. Indeed most organizations utilize several different forms of data entry, which enables them to choose the method best suited to each of their data entry applications.

With respect to each method of data entry discussed in this section, the reader should be alert to the distinction between (1) the medium upon which the data are recorded, (2) the device for originally recording the data on this medium, and (3) the device for reading the data from the recording medium into the computer.

General-purpose data entry

There are essentially four forms of general-purpose computer data entry—(1) punched cards, (2) magnetic tape, (3) diskettes, and (4) data terminals. Each of these is discussed in this section.

Punched cards   The processing of data on punched cards is based on the *unit record concept,* whereby all data regarding a particular subject or transaction are recorded on a single document—the punched card—which then serves both as an input record and as a reference document. Figure 5.7 illustrates the standard

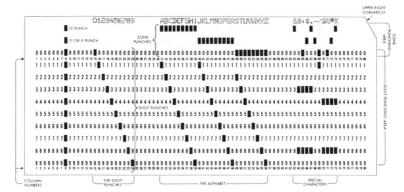

*Fig. 5.7
Standard 80-column
punched card.
(Courtesy of IBM
Corporation.)*

80-column punched card, showing the hole pattern for numeric, alphabetic, and selected special characters according to the Hollerith code. A smaller card having 96 columns and utilizing a different coding system is also widely used, but it is much less common than the 80-column card.

Whereas the commercial use of computers in data processing dates only from the mid-1950s, automatic data processing systems based on the punched card have actually been around since the late nineteenth century. These systems utilized a series of electromechanical devices, each of which specialized in performing a particular function—such as sorting, collating, interpreting, reproducing, and printing—using punched cards as input. Although these machines are now obsolete and have not been manufactured for many years, a working specimen may still occasionally be encountered in a modern data processing facility.

Herman Hollerith, the inventor of the punched card and of punched card data processing equipment, founded a company called the Tabulating Machine Company to market his inventions. In 1924, after several mergers, this company became the International Business Machines Corporation. Commonly known as IBM, it soon grew to dominate the data processing industry. In the early 1950s, when it became evident that the new technology of automatic computers might be applied successfully to business data processing, IBM responded by developing computer equipment that utilized punched cards as a data input and storage medium. This facilitated the move from punched card equipment to computers for many of IBM's customers. As a result, IBM has long been the dominant company in the computer industry, and the punched card has also enjoyed a long period of popularity.

The machine used to record data on punched cards is called the *keypunch*. This machine, illustrated in Fig. 5.8, uses a typewriter keyboard to initiate both the punching of holes in cards and the printing of data across the top of the cards. It has a small electronic memory in which data entered by the operator are stored temporarily until all the data for one card have been keyed. In this way if a keying error is made, the operator may backspace and enter the correct character, instead of having to repunch the entire card. Modern keypunch machines may also be "programmed"

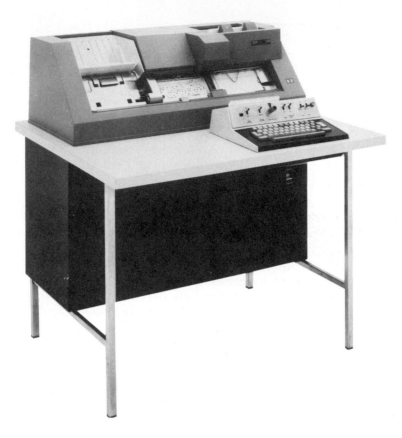

Fig. 5.8
The keypunch.
(Courtesy of IBM
Corporation.)

to perform certain functions automatically, such as automatic punching of data common to all cards in a batch, and skipping of blank spaces within fields such as name and description when the data do not fill up all of the allotted spaces.

Another function modern keypunches can perform is *keyverification*. When the machine is in the verify mode, cards that have already been punched are loaded into its input hopper, and the operator keys source data from the same source documents that were originally used in keypunching the cards. The machine checks the holes in each card for agreement with the keys being punched. If there is a discrepancy, the machine signals the operator, who then checks the card for a possible error. This is an expensive form of data checking because every field that is to be keyverified must be keyed in twice. As a result, keyverification is generally only applied to the most critical data input fields. Names, addresses, inventory item descriptions, and other nonnumeric data are often not keyverified.

Once data have been entered into punched cards, they are read into the computer by a device called a card reader. This machine senses the pattern of holes in each card, converts the pattern into electronic impulses, and transmits these impulses via a cable to the central processor. The speed with which punched card reading can be performed by available card readers ranges from 300 to 1200 cards per minute, which is slow relative to other forms of computer input.

Under the control of the central processor, output data may be punched into cards by an automatic card punch device. These devices operate at speeds ranging from 100 to 500 cards per minute. This form of output is quite common in business and accounting systems because punched cards are often used as turnaround documents. A *turnaround document* is produced in machine-readable form as output from an automated system, used as a record in an external process, and then returned to the system as an input record relating to the external process. An example is the punched card which many utility companies send out as a bill with the request that the card be returned with the payment. Since turnaround documents are originally produced automatically, their use reduces the volume of input preparation work and also reduces the possibility of errors in the input data.

The multifunction card machine is a device very commonly found in computer systems of all types. It combines in one unit the functional capability of the card reader, automatic card punch, and collator, and it can also interpret the data values that have been punched into a card and then print those values on the face of the card. This last capability is useful to the preparation of turnaround documents. An example of the multifunction card machine appears in Fig. 5.9. This machine has two input hoppers and five output hoppers. Cards from both input hoppers may be read, punched, and/or printed, and then distributed to any of the output hoppers.

*Fig. 5.9
Multifunction
card machine.
(Courtesy of IBM
Corporation.)*

Magnetic tape   Data are represented on magnetic tape by means of magnetic bits rather than holes. The magnetization of a bit is analogous to the presence of a hole in a punched card. A reel of magnetic tape is typically one-half inch in width and up to 2400 feet long. Tape cassettes, similar to those used in audio recording, may also be used for magnetic data recording. Magnetic tape generally has seven or nine horizontal rows, called tracks, into which data are recorded. Figure 5.10 illustrates the standard character pattern of seven-track magnetic tape.

The illustration shows that each character in the character set is represented by some combination of magnetization of the seven bits in a single column. However, the coding system shown actually uses only six bits to represent each character—the two zone bits and the four numerical bits. The seventh bit, which is called a *check bit* or a *parity bit,* is not part of the character code, but rather is used on magnetic tape as a means of checking the accuracy of each recorded character when the tape is read. The check bit will be magnetized only if the number of the other six bits that is magnetized is an odd number; in this way the total number of bits in any column should always be even. If a bit is lost, the check would be violated and the erroneous data would be discovered. (The system described is an *even parity* system. It is also possible to have *odd parity,* where every column contains an odd number of magnetized bits.)

The original recording of source data on magnetic tape may be done in one of several ways. One means of direct recording of data on magnetic tape is the keyboard-to-tape encoder. This device is similar to the keypunch, with the data being recorded on tape instead of punched cards. Data may also be recorded on tape by a shared-processor key-to-disk-to-tape system.[2] In this type of system, several keying stations are linked to a small computer that has an attached disk memory. Data may be entered simultaneously from each of the several keystations and pooled on the disk file. The small computer performs such functions as formatting, skipping blank spaces, testing the data for consistency, accumulating and reporting batch totals, and sorting. Once all of the records on a transaction file have been entered, they are written from the disk file onto a magnetic tape file for subsequent processing on the main computer.

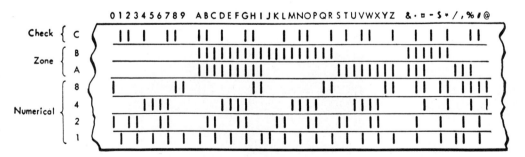

*Fig. 5.10
Standard character
pattern for seven-
track magnetic tape.
(Courtesy of IBM
Corporation.)*

[2] *Despite the fact that the purpose of these systems is to record data on magnetic tape, they are commonly referred to in the computer industry as "key-to-disk" systems.*

Another commonly used method of recording data on magnetic tape is to first record them on another medium, such as punched cards, and then to transcribe them onto magnetic tape. The transcription process may be performed by the main computer, by an auxiliary computer, or by an offline device not connected to the computer. The advantage of this approach is that, while it is often more efficient to record data initially on a medium other than magnetic tape, magnetic tape is generally a much faster form of input to the computer than any of the alternatives.

Data on magnetic tape is read into the central processing unit by means of magnetic tape drive units, an example of which is illustrated in Fig. 5.11. A tape drive

Fig. 5.11
Magnetic tape drive
unit. (Courtesy of
IBM Corporation.)

also is used to write data from the central processor onto magnetic tape. Typical
peak operating speeds of available tape drive units range from 60,000 to 1,250,000
characters per second. Magnetic tape is by far the fastest of the commonly used
forms of input as well as output. This factor represents its greatest advantage as a
form of computer data entry.

Diskettes   A diskette (also called a flexible disk or a "floppy disk") is a round piece
of flexible magnetic film, about eight inches in diameter with a large hole in the center. Enclosed in its permanent plastic envelope for protection, it resembles a 45 rpm
record in its jacket (see Fig. 5.12). Data may be recorded magnetically on one or
both sides of the diskette in several tiny concentric circular tracks on its surface. The
plastic envelope has an oval-shaped opening that permits contact between the diskette and a read/write mechanism when it is inserted into a diskette input-output
unit.

A single diskette can hold up to 1.6 million bytes of data. Initial recording of
data on a diskette is performed using a manually operated keyboard device with a
small screen that displays the data being entered. Once data are recorded on the diskette, they are read into the computer by a diskettee input-output unit, which is also
capable of writing computer output onto the diskette if desired. Effective reading
speeds range from 15,000 to 60,000 characters per second.

Since its introduction in the early 1970s the diskette has become popular as a
medium for both input and storage of data. As an input medium it has been employed by many firms to replace punched cards or punched paper tape. As a storage
medium, its relatively modest storage capacity makes it most popular among small
organizations whose file sizes are more compatible with its limitations. Its greatest
advantages are its compactness as a storage medium and its relatively low cost.

Data terminals   The data terminal does not use any form of physical input medium,
but instead enables input data to be entered directly into the computer via an online

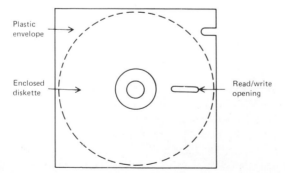

Fig. 5.12
Diskette in protective
envelope.

keyboard. The two major forms of data terminal are the teleprinter, illustrated in Fig. 5.13, and the cathode ray tube, or CRT, terminal, illustrated in Fig. 5.14. Input is originated with these devices by means of a keyboard similar to that of a typewriter. On a teleprinter, input is typed onto a paper copy as it is entered, and output from the computer is also typed onto the paper copy. Input and output on a CRT terminal appear on a screen similar to a television screen. With many CRTs a hardcopy unit may be attached to the terminal to produce a paper copy of the data on the screen when desired. A third type of data terminal is the push-button telephone, which sometimes incorporates the picture phone screen as a device for displaying input and output.

The use of online terminals as a means of data entry has at least two significant advantages. First, the checking of transaction data for accuracy is greatly facilitated because (1) the computer can perform various logic tests on each data item, (2) the computer can check the reasonableness of the data on each transaction record by comparing them to data on the corresponding master file record stored in the system, and (3) the computer can notify the terminal operator of any definite or suspected errors, thereby enabling the operator to correct such errors before they are

Fig. 5.14
CRT terminal.
(Courtesy of IBM
Corporation.)

posted to the master files. Second, terminals can be placed in several locations remote from the central processor, which enables transaction data to be entered into the system from their place of origin as they occur. This arrangement requires the use of telephone lines or special cables to transmit data and messages between the terminal and the central processor. The use of terminals and data transmission facilities for this purpose is discussed further in Chapter 9.

**Special-purpose
data entry**

There is a wide variety of special-purpose devices and techniques. Each device and technique is designed to best serve the needs of a particular class of data entry applications. It would not be feasible to review all of these devices and techniques here, so we will focus on a few of the more popular of them. These include (1) magnetic ink character recognition (MICR), (2) optical character recognition (OCR), (3) optical mark readers (OMR), (4) point-of-sale (POS) recorders and systems, including bar code readers and tag readers, (5) industrial data collection devices, (6) bank teller terminals, (7) punched paper tape, (8) light pens, and (9) portable data recorders.

Magnetic ink character recognition   MICR involves the use of special stylized characters encoded on documents in a special magnetic ink. The only significant application of this data entry technology is in the United States banking industry in which it is the national standard for encoding accounts numbers and amounts on customers' checks and deposit tickets. If you examine a blank check, you will see the bank number and account number encoded on the lower left portion. If you examine a processed check that has been returned by the bank, you will notice that the check amount has also been inscribed on it in the lower right portion.

The original encoding of magnetic ink characters on a document is performed by special inscribers. Other necessary equipment in an MICR installation, often combined in one machine, includes a reader and an electromechanical sorter. MICR readers have speeds ranging from 700 to 1600 characters per second. In a bank, the sorter is required to sort all checks received by bank number for mailing to other banks, and then to sort the bank's own checks and deposit tickets by customer number for return to its customers.

Optical character recognition   OCR is a technique for reading documents containing typewritten, computer-printed or, in some cases, hand-printed characters. OCR differs from MICR in that the former does not require characters printed in a special magnetized ink. However, each model OCR reader can read only a limited number of type fonts. A *font* is a complete character set (digits, letters, and special symbols) in which the size, style, and shape of each character is rigidly specified. OCR is commonly used on turnaround documents, such as oil company statements, bank credit card statements, insurance company premium notices, and utility company billings. If you inspect the bills you have received from organizations of this type, you will notice that many of them are printed in a stylized font. These documents have been automatically printed by a computer printer and, when returned to the company, they may be automatically read by an OCR reader. Thus significant human participation in the data entry process is necessary only when a customer does not pay the full amount of the bill, or when the reader rejects a document as unreadable.

Another device used to imprint characters readable by OCR onto documents is the embossed-card imprinter. This device, which should be familiar to anyone who uses a credit card, is used in retail outlets to imprint raised characters from plastic cards or metal plates onto paper forms. A carbon process is commonly used to accomplish the imprinting, with pressure applied by a manually operated bar or lever. Some of these devices permit the entry of variable data, such as the sale amount, in addition to the fixed customer data on the cards and the fixed store data on the imprinter's metal plate. The embossed-card imprinter provides a quick, inexpensive, and reliable method of preparing machine-readable source data.

Reading speeds of typical OCR readers range from 500 to 1500 characters per second. Because the equipment required to utilize OCR entails a relatively high fixed cost, it is best suited for high-volume applications in which turnaround documents may be used to minimize the need for manual data preparation.

Optical mark readers   OMR, also known as "mark sensing," involves the automatic reading of pencil marks made in specific locations on preprinted cards or forms. An application of this technique, which should be familiar to all students, is the machine grading of multiple-choice and true-false exam questions.

Mark readers may be classified into two categories—card readers and page readers. Card readers utilize the standard 80-column card, and frequently are equipped to read both punches and marks. A common application of these devices involves turnaround documents in a factory environment. A card may be prepunched with the part number, operation number, and department number for a particular factory operation, and the worker will mark the quantity completed, time required, and employee number at designated locations on the card. The cards then become input to a computerized production cost accounting system.

Page readers can read marks from one or both sides of a page that has been preprinted to indicate the appropriate mark locations. A common application of this method involves accounting for customer purchases along a delivery route. For example, a milkvendor may be furnished with a preprinted form for each customer on the route indicating the customer's name, address and account number, and designated locations for marking the quantity of milk and other dairy products delivered. The vendor then simply marks the quantity of each product delivered to each customer on the appropriate form for that customer, and delivers the completed forms to the data processing department at the completion of the route.

Point-of-sale equipment   Application of the concept of source data automation in the retail environment has led to the development of point-of-sale (POS) recorders and related equipment. A POS recorder is an electronic cash register which is capable of being used as a data terminal online to a computer system. These devices are designed to facilitate the collection of sales data in retail stores. Functionally, they consist of a keyboard for entering transaction data, a display window in which transaction data are displayed as they are entered, a printer for printing customer receipts, and a communications link to a small central computer that controls all terminals in a store. A typical POS recorder is pictured in Fig. 5.15.

Many POS recorders utilize devices attached to them by a cable to read price or product code data from products. One example is the OCR tag reader, pictured in Fig. 5.16, that reads these data from price tags printed in an OCR font. Other examples include the bar code wand commonly used in grocery stores and pharmacies to read characters encoded in the Universal Product Code (UPC), and the automatic tag reader often found in clothing and department stores for reading characters from prepunched product tags.

Fig. 5.15
Point-of-sale record-
er. (Courtesy of NCR
Corporation.)

The attachment of a POS recorder to a central computer enables it to perform several functions that are beyond the capability of the conventional cash register. For example, it can make price times quantity calculations, sales tax calculations, or discount calculations. If the product code has been read automatically, it can access a product file to retrieve the current price and to update the quantity sold and inventory balance data stored in the file. For credit sales, it is also possible to enter the customer's account number and have the system check the customer's credit. The automatic performance of these and similar functions greatly enhances the productivity of retail sales clerks.

Industrial data collection devices Application of the concept of source data automation to the factory environment has led to the development of industrial data col-

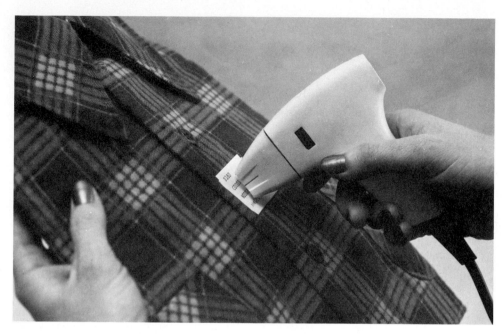

Fig. 5.16
OCR tag reader.
(Courtesy of NCR
Corporation.)

lection devices. This category encompasses a wide variety of devices designed to collect data relating to manufacturing operations and inventory control. Generally they are equipped to record both constant data and variable data. Employee numbers read from badges issued to each employee are a common example of the entry of constant data into such devices. The date, time, and device location can be supplied automatically by the device. Variable data pertaining to operations performed and quantities completed are generally entered using a keyboard or a series of dials or switches. These devices may be directly connected to a central computer to enable online data entry, or they may record the data on punched cards or magnetic tape cassettes for subsequent processing.

In view of the environment in which they are used, industrial data collection devices must be designed to be durable and easy to operate. Their primary advantages are the speed with which input data may be captured in machine-readable form, and the greater accuracy of the input data. Improvements in input data accuracy result from limiting the amount of variable data that the operator has to enter to one or two items, making it as simple as possible to enter those data, and then performing all subsequent processing steps automatically with limited human intervention.

Bank teller terminals   Source data automation is manifested in the banking environment in the form of bank teller terminals. These are specialized data terminals designed to meet the unique requirements of bank tellers with respect to checking and savings account transactions. Typically they consist of a keyboard, a printer for customer receipts and passbook entries, and a display. They are normally connected directly to the bank's central computer system so that if a customer wishes to cash a check or make a savings account withdrawal, the teller can use the terminal to access the customer's file to determine if the current balance is sufficient. Like point-of-sale terminals, bank teller terminals have greatly enhanced the productivity of bank tellers.

A variation of the bank teller terminals used by bank employees are the self-serve teller terminals that may be used directly by customers. These include a series of buttons that the customer uses to indicate the type of transaction (deposit, withdrawal, payment, or account transfer) and type of account (checking, savings, or credit card), and a numeric keyboard for entering the amount and account number. A plastic card carried by the customer may also be used to enter the customer's account number. These devices may be online to the bank's central computer twenty-four hours a day, and thus can check customer balances and execute standard banking transactions at any time.

Punched paper tape   Machine-readable characters may be recorded in a strip of paper tape by means of holes punched across its width according to a standardized coding system. Punched paper tape was one of the earliest forms of general-purpose computer data input and storage. More recently, its use has been limited to the preparation of machine-readable input as a by-product of transaction recording on a typewriter or other manually operated device, and to the recording and storage of data transmitted over data communications lines. At present, paper tape is virtually obsolete. Its demise may be attributed to several factors, including its relatively slow input speed, difficulty in correcting errors, and lack of reusability.

The light pen   The light pen is a photosensitive device, resembling a wand, that is used in conjunction with a CRT terminal. When the user places the light pen on the CRT screen, the computer can sense and make note of its location. The light pen may be used for data entry by programming the system to display on the CRT screen a series of data requests to which the operator may respond by placing the light pen at one of a limited number of locations. Though not commonly used for accounting data entry, the light pen is very useful in computer-assisted product design and other engineering applications.

Portable data recorders   This category includes a variety of source data automation devices that are small and lightweight and therefore easily carried to the point of origin of source data. Such devices are useful for applications in which the points of origin of source data are widely separated and the volume of source data from any single location is not sufficient to justify a stationary device. Portable data recorders may be used to collect meter readings and to take physical inventories.

Portable data recorders may be characterized by their data entry mechanism and by their data recording medium. Two commonly used data entry mechanisms

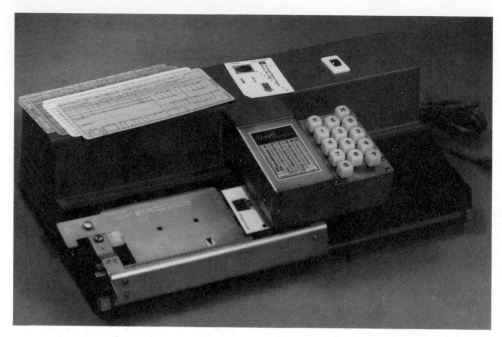

*Fig. 5.17
Portable data
recorder. (Courtesy
of Wright Line.)*

are keyboards and optical wands for reading bar codes. Among the most common data recording media are punched cards, magnetic tape cassettes, and semiconductor memories. Some of these devices, particularly those that use semiconductor memories, are designed to store batches of data temporarily and subsequently to transmit those data to the computer over data communications lines. One example of a portable data recorder which records data on punched cards appears in Fig. 5.17.

**Computer
data entry
and accounting**

Accountants within an organization must be concerned about computer data entry for at least two reasons. First, in most organizations a large volume of accounting data are entered into the computer for processing, and the accountant is concerned about the accuracy, timeliness, and security of this operation. Second, in many organizations, accountants in their roles of controller or internal auditor are responsible for evaluating the efficiency and effectiveness of data entry personnel and operations. In this section, each of these two concerns is briefly discussed.

Accounting applications of the computer are typified by high volumes of input; a need for documentation of activity for purposes of reference, control, and audit; an emphasis on reliability and accuracy; and often by a need for timely data entry in order to keep the master files current. Of course, cost considerations are also very important to the choice among data entry alternatives. However, accounting applications differ to such an extent that no single method of data entry is likely to be appropriate for all accounting uses.

Computer applications that have extremely large volumes of input require a method of data entry that (1) minimizes the amount of manual keying or other data preparation work, (2) utilizes a compact recording medium, and (3) utilizes a high-speed computer input device. Unfortunately, no single approach meets all of these criteria. The use of turnaround documents, such as punched cards, OCR forms, or OMR forms, is ideal from the standpoint of minimal data preparation, but computer input devices for all of these media are relatively slow. Magnetic tape and diskette input devices are very fast, but extensive keying operations are required to initially record the data on these media. A good compromise for high volume applications is to use turnaround documents but to transcribe the input data from the documents to magnetic tape prior to inputting the transaction data to update the master files. However, not all accounting applications are by nature suitable for the use of turnaround documents.

The use of data terminals is indicated for those accounting applications in which timeliness in entering transaction data is important in order that master files are as current as possible. If special-purpose terminals are available to match the task, then they should be considered in preference to general-purpose teleprinters and display terminals because their user-oriented design generally facilitates the data entry process. In other cases, general-purpose data terminals may be a very satisfactory choice.

The importance of good documentation of accounting transactions favors data entry media that are readable by people. This criterion would tend to favor punched cards, OCR, or OMR in preference to magnetic tape, diskettes, or industrial data collection devices. POS recorders and bank teller terminals generally produce a written record as a by-product of their use. With respect to online data terminals, a computer may be programmed to prepare a record of all transactions entered from them.

The need for accuracy and reliability exists both at the point of initial preparation of input data and at the point of entry of the data into the computer. Turnaround documents may be prepared with a high measure of accuracy because they are prepared automatically as an output from the computer. However, cards or documents may be easily lost or mutilated, and the accuracy of card readers, mark readers, and OCR readers is relatively low. Magnetic tape, especially if prepared on a shared processor key-to-disk system, measures high in both data preparation accuracy and reading accuracy. Online data terminals provide even greater accuracy because they reduce the number of steps in the data entry process to one, and because the computer can be programmed to detect many data entry errors and request immediate reentry of the suspect data.

It is difficult to generalize about the cost of data entry alternatives because cost is a function of volume. For low-volume data entry, punched cards, diskettes, data terminals, and magnetic tape prepared by stand-alone key-to-tape encoders are most economical. For high-volume applications, cost factors tend to favor special-purpose data terminals, OCR, or magnetic tape prepared by shared processor key-to-disk systems.

The second major concern of the accountant with respect to computer data entry involves the efficient and effective performance of the data entry function. One useful approach to this problem is performance measurement and evaluation. This involves setting a standard performance rate for all personnel employed in a centralized data entry operation. One standard unit of measure for such work is "keystrokes per hour." Initially, records of operator performance in keystrokes per hour must be collected and analyzed in order to establish performance standards. Once appropriate standards have been obtained, a schedule of data entry work can be established, with each application scheduled to consume a total time estimated on the basis of the standard. The performance of the data preparation department may then be evaluated in terms of whether it meets its schedule. The performance of individual operators may also be measured and evaluated in terms of the standard, with raises and promotions being based on superior performance.

Data preparation efficiency may also be improved by proper design of the formats of source documents and input transaction records. Transaction record formats should correspond to source document formats in terms of the sequencing of data to ensure that data entry personnel can read the source document easily while keying, without having to shift their eyes from side to side or top to bottom and back again. Another method of improving data entry efficiency is for constant data, such as batch number, date, or transaction code, to be entered into all records automatically rather than manually.

This concludes our discussion of computer data entry. The elements of computer hardware that have not yet been discussed—output and secondary storage—are covered in the next chapter. In the remaining section of this chapter several types of business machines other than computers are described and illustrated.

Other Business Machines

There are enormous numbers of business machines (other than computers) that are commonly used in large organizations that also use computers. Many of them are also used in small organizations that do not use computers. In this section we will review several types of noncomputer business machines that are commonly used in accounting and related business data processing applications.

Adding machines and calculators

These devices have long been favorites of accountants in the performance of calculating, verification, and summarizing functions. Most of these machines consist of a keyboard and a screen or roll of paper for displaying or printing results. The adding machine is capable only of addition and subtraction. A common use of the adding machine is to accumulate and/or verify the accuracy of the sums of columns of figures in a ledger or journal. Another common use is to accumulate control totals as batches of documents are processed. The adding machine tape produced in these operations serves as a useful record for purposes of internal check and audit. An illustration of the ten-key adding machine, a very popular device among accountants, is provided in Fig. 5.18.

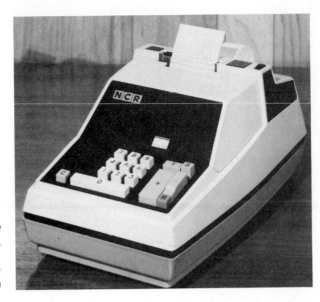

Fig. 5.18
Ten-key adding
machine.
(Courtesy of NCR
Corporation.)

Electromechanical adding machines and calculators are fast being superseded by small, inexpensive, and powerful electronic calculators. All college students in business and accounting should be familiar with these devices. They typically consist of a keyboard and small display screen in a pocket-sized plastic container. The simplest ones perform only the four basic arithmetic functions, but versions that are more advanced can store intermediate results, determine logarithms, raise numbers to powers or find roots, and perform a variety of other mathematical operations. Prices for typical electronic calculators range from $5 to $50. The primary disadvantage of these devices from the standpoint of accounting work is that most do not provide printed output for visual inspection and permanent reference. However, their computational power is still quite useful in numerous accounting jobs.

The most advanced form of the electronic calculator is the "programmable" calculator. These devices have a small internal memory that enables them to learn a sequence of operations entered on their keyboard. They can then repeat that sequence of operations on different sets of data values entered via the keyboard. These devices can be purchased for as little as $100. Many of them provide optional attachments that may be used to prepare printed output, thus satisfying the accountant's demand for documentation. These devices are easy to use and can be extremely useful to accountants for such applications as financial forecasting, present value analysis, depreciation calculations, and inflation adjustments.

Cash registers   The cash register, illustrated in Fig. 5.19, is indispensable to virtually all types of retail business. The main functional elements of a typical cash register are the keyboard, cash drawers, a display window or screen, and a receipt imprinter. The cash

*Fig. 5.19
Cash register.
(Courtesy of NCR
Corporation.)*

register performs several data processing functions, including recording, classifying, calculating, and summarizing.

Electromechanical versions of the cash register are rapidly being displaced by electronic versions. Electronic cash registers can store sales tax tables, perform tax or discount calculations, and perform numerous other functions not within the capabilities of their electromechanical ancestors. Some electronic cash registers are designed to be operated in a stand-alone mode, while others may be linked to a computer system. The latter, called POS recorders, are discussed and illustrated (see Fig. 5.15) in the previous section.

A major factor in the usefulness of cash registers is the control they provide over the recording of cash sales transactions. The noise made by the machine as it is being operated, and the totals that are displayed, facilitate supervision of sales clerks. The display window total and customer receipt provide the opportunity for the customer to notice a discrepancy between the amount paid and the amount recorded. This discourages any deliberate errors. Once a sale is recorded, a record of it is printed on a paper tape locked inside the register to prevent subsequent alteration. At the end of a day this internally accumulated total should check with the amount of cash accumulated in the cash drawer. Other available features of cash registers that provide increased control are multiple cash drawers, so that each sales clerk can be made responsible for an individual cash drawer, and an attachment that dispenses the exact amount of coin change due to a customer.

Some cash registers have a separate set of keys whereby an indication of type of merchandise or department can be made on the tape for each item sold. This feature facilitates the data processing function of classification, providing a basis for subsequent analyses of sales and inventory for planning and control purposes.

Word processing   *Word processing* is a specialized form of data processing in which the equipment is designed to facilitate the manipulation of a particular class of data: words and text. Word processing equipment may be viewed as an electronic extension of the conventional typewriter. The primary data processing functions performed by word processing equipment are storage, transcription, issuance, and reporting.

A basic word processing installation consists of a typewriter keyboard, a printer, an internal memory, a small internal processor that can perform editing functions such as insertion or deletion of text, and an input–output device for recording data on a magnetic medium. The most commonly used magnetic media are magnetic cards, magnetic tape cassettes, and magnetic diskettes. A configuration of this type costs between $5,000 and $10,000. Many word processors also include a video display screen on which is displayed the text currently being worked on by the operator.

In a typical business organization, there is a wide variety of potential applications for word processing. The applications include the typing of letters, memos, proposals, reports, manuals, product catalogs and price lists, brochures and sales literature, newsletters, billings, and financial statements. The magnetic recording media may be used to store form letters, manuals, name and address lists, and product catalogs and price lists. The basic advantage of word processing is that it minimizes the need for duplicate typing operations by storing text internally or on a readily accessible medium so that it can be easily corrected or modified, and then printed automatically as needed. This greatly enhances secretarial productivity, increases the speed with which printed output can be obtained, and generally provides printed output of superior quality.

There is a wide variety of optional features that may be incorporated into a basic word processing configuration. For example, some word processors can be equipped to operate as terminals online to a central computer system. Some have a data communications capability that enables them to be linked by telecommunications lines to other word processors located in other parts of the country; this enables a multilocation organization to send its internal mail by means of a word processing network rather than by means of the post office. Some word processors can be equipped with an OCR wand that can read text typed in specified type fonts into the processor's memory. For larger offices it is possible to obtain a shared-processor word processing system in which several word processing stations share the processing capabilities, memory, and input-output capabilities of a small central computer.

Microfilm systems The use of microfilm in business data processing is becoming increasingly popular. Whereas microfilm was formerly considered to be a method of storing inactive records for legal and tax purposes, it is now commonly used to maintain current records as well.

The equipment in a typical microfilm system includes (1) a microfilm camera that photographs documents or reports and develops the film; (2) a processor that organizes the film in one of several forms; (3) a reader-printer that reads and displays on a screen the images on microfilm and produces paper copies if desired; and (4) a system of storage and retrieval of the microfilm. In addition, many systems include equipment for preparing microfilm as computer output (see Chapter 6).

A microfilm camera includes a mechanism for automatic feeding of documents to be filmed (see Fig. 5.20). Operating speeds of these devices range up to six hundred documents per minute. They produce a roll of film 16 or 35 millimeters in width, containing up to three thousand 8½″ by 11″ documents. Microfilm may be stored in roll form, or it may be converted by special processors to one of several other forms, including cartridges, special punched cards called aperture cards, or microfiche or jackets, in which a set of related documents are included on a single sheet of film. Each of these various forms of microfilm storage is illustrated in Fig. 5.21.

Fig. 5.20
Microfilmer (right)
and microfilm
processor (left).
(Courtesy of
Eastman Kodak
Company.)

Fig. 5.21
Some alternative
forms of microfilm
storage: (1) micro-
fiche, (2) roll, (3)
aperture card, and (4)
cartridge. (Courtesy
of Minnesota Mining
and Manufacturing
Company.)

Fig. 5.22
Microfilm reader-
printer. (Courtesy of
Minnesota Mining
and Manufacturing
Company.)

A microfilm reader-printer is illustrated in Fig. 5.22. It consists of a device for inserting and reading microfilm in one or more of the forms described above, a display screen, and a unit that produces a paper copy of the screen image at the push of a button.

A microfilm storage and retrieval system may consist simply of specially designed filing cabinets for manual retrieval, or it may consist of special equipment that enables immediate access to selected records in large files. Systems of the latter type include a keyboard and screen for request and display of the records desired, and a file storage unit with the capability of automatic retrieval of records on microfiche or aperture cards. Many systems also incorporate a printer that can be used to prepare a hard copy of any desired record. These systems enable access to a single record within a file of thousands in a period of only a few seconds.

The most obvious advantage of microfilm systems is that they reduce space requirements for records storage from 95 to 99 percent or more. In addition, they provide savings in handling and distribution of records. Microfilm itself is less expensive as a storage medium than paper. Records on microfilm can be retrieved faster than those on paper documents stored in filing cabinets, particularly if automatic retrieval systems are used.

The primary disadvantage of microfilm systems is the cost of the required equipment, which limits its application primarily to high-volume situations. In addition, microfilm is not an appropriate storage medium for records which must be frequently updated. Examples of common applications of microfilm systems in accounting and related areas include the retention of charge sale documents or invoices by retail or industrial firms, retention of documentation supporting cash disbursements, and the retention of copies of depositors' checks by banks.

Review Questions

1. Define the following terms.

computer	bit
hardware	Binary Coded Decimal
software	Hollerith code
source data automation	EBCDIC
mainframe	packing
address	byte
microcode	word
read-only memory	unit record concept
register	keyverification
instruction register	turnaround document
address register	check bit
accumulator	parity bit
access time	even parity
microsecond	odd parity
nanosecond	font
execution time	word processing
millisecond	

2. What periods of history correspond to the first, second, and third generations of computers? What major developments in computer technology separate the second from the first generation, and the third from the second?

3. For each of the five stages of the data processing cycle, identify some elements of computer hardware which may be classified, on the basis of functional capabilities, into each stage.

4. Identify the three basic components of a central processing unit and explain how they interact with each other and with computer input and output.

5. What is the difference between "primary" and "secondary" storage in a computer system? Identify some examples of secondary storage media and hardware.

6. Explain how the operator of a computer communicates with the computer system.

7. Describe and compare the two most commonly used forms of CPU primary storage.

8. Identify and explain two measures of CPU performance.

9. Identify several of the ways in which a bit is represented on various computer data media.

10. How many bits are used to represent one character in some of the more common data processing coding systems?

11. Why is data preparation often such a significant portion of the cost of business data processing?

12. Identify several general-purpose methods of computer data entry. In each case, if possible, describe the data recording medium, the device or devices used to initially record data on the medium, and the device used for reading data from the medium into the computer.

13. Explain the advantages of turnaround documents and give an example of their use.

14. Identify and explain the operation of several special-purpose methods of computer data entry. Indicate one example of the kinds of business applications for which each is commonly used.

15. What are two reasons why accountants within an organization must be concerned about computer data entry?

16. What are four characteristics of accounting applications that might influence the selection of data entry devices and media for a computerized accounting system? Use these characteristics as a basis for comparing the various methods of computer data entry described in this chapter.

17. Explain how cost considerations and data entry volume influence the choice among data entry alternatives.

18. Explain how performance measurement and evaluation techniques may be applied to the data entry operation.

19. Explain how data preparation efficiency may be improved by proper design of record formats.

20. Describe briefly the features and capabilities of adding machines and calculators.

21. Describe the data processing functions performed by the cash register.

22. Give several examples of how the cash register contributes to control of cash sales in a retail business.

23. Describe some advantages that electronic cash registers possess relative to electromechanical cash registers.

24. What does a basic word processing installation consist of? What are some typical applications of word processing in a business environment?

25. Explain the advantages of word processing.

26. Describe and explain the functions of the primary items of equipment in a microfilm system.

27. Identify and describe the four primary forms of microfilm storage.

28. Explain the advantages and disadvantages of microfilm systems.

29. What are some common applications of microfilm systems?

Discussion Questions

30. In many modern information systems, processing and output functions are automated while input functions are performed manually. Discuss the potential of source data automation. What do you feel are its primary advantages and/or disadvantages?

31. It is stated in Chapter 1 that machines are generally faster and more reliable than people, but also less flexible and adaptable. Of the machines discussed in this chapter, are there any exceptions to these general statements? If so, explain.

32. A major computer manufacturer uses the motto, "Machines should work. People should think." in advertising its products. However, isn't a computer a "thinking machine"? Explain what is meant by the motto.

33. Review the steps in the data processing cycle as described in Chapter 1. Which of the steps can be performed better by a computer system than by a person?

Problems and Cases

34. Prepare a list of all of the activities in the data processing cycle described in Chapter 1. For each individual activity, if possible, list two devices described in this chapter which can perform that activity.

35. Moose Mursatz operates a small clothing store in Moscow, Idaho. He employs three sales clerks and utilizes a cash register for recording sales. Due to his other business and personal interests, Moose is present at the clothing store during only 50 percent of its hours of business.

    You may assume that Moose's cash register has any or all of the optional features described in this chapter except that it is not a data terminal hooked up to a computer system. What procedures would you recommend to Moose to take maximum advantage of the control features of the cash register?

36. Callison Manufacturing Company wishes to estimate the cost of data preparation for its information system. This cost includes (a) rent of keypunch ma-

chines, (b) salaries of keypunch and keyverification personnel, and (c) cost of punched cards. Determine the number of keypunch machines required (assuming only one shift is worked by the keypunch operators) and then calculate the total monthly cost of data preparation for the system, using the following information.

- monthly keypunching volume, 9,000,000 characters
- monthly rent of each keypunch, $80
- of all characters keypunched, 40 percent are keyverified
- rate of operation of keypunch and verifier, 6000 keystrokes per hour
- productive hours per month of keypunch and keyverification personnel, 150
- monthly salary of keypunch and keyverification personnel, $800
- number of characters punched on each card, 60
- cost per thousand cards, $2.40
- keypunch department supervisor's salary, $1000 per month

37. Using the Hollerith code as illustrated in Fig. 5.7, determine the pattern of hole punches required to represent each character in the following set: "BALANCE—$1,076.42." For example, the letter "Z" is represented by a combination "0–9" punch.

38. Using the EBCDIC code as illustrated in Fig. 5.6, determine the bit configuration required to represent each character in the set, "BALANCE—$1,076.42."

39. Suppose that a company's accounts receivable records contain 200 characters each, 75 percent of which are numeric.

Required

a) If a 6-bit code such as BCD is used to store the records, how many bits are required for each record?

b) If an 8-bit code such as EBCDIC is used to store the records, but all numeric characters are stored in packed form, how many bits are required for each record?

40. When the Sunnydale Electronics Company receives invoices from its suppliers requesting payment for merchandise purchased, it provides them in batches of 50 to data entry personnel for keying onto 100-character magnetic tape records. These are subsequently entered into its computerized accounts payable system. When the due date for each invoice arrives, the computer automatically issues a check to the vendor for the net invoice amount. Characteristics of the data items on each vendor invoice record are as follows.

- Batch number, two characters
- Discount rate code, one character
- Gross invoice amount, never exceeds $20,000
- Invoice due date, six characters
- Purchase order number, six characters
- Transaction-type code, one character
- Vendor invoice number, eight characters
- Vendor code number, six characters

- Vendor name, 21 characters
- Vendor street address, 21 characters
- Vendor city, state, and zip code, 21 characters

Required
a) Assuming that the data entry device may be programmed to automatically enter constant data values into each record, which of the data items listed above could be entered in this way?

b) Design a format for the magnetic tape input record that indicates the sequence in which these items are to be keyed. Explain the reasons for your choice of format.

c) Assume that keyverification is the only available means of checking the accuracy of the keyed data before it is entered into the main computer system. Which of the data items listed above should be keyverified, and which should not? Explain.

d) Assuming a volume of 500 invoices per day, and a keying rate of 6000 keystrokes per hour, how many hours of keying are required to complete the entry and verification of these records each day?

e) Which of the data items listed above could generally be stored within the computer system so that they would not have to be re-keyed for each and every invoice? Assuming that this is done, determine the effect that it would have on your answer to part (d).

41. Able and Baker are employees in the Data Preparation Department. During a recent six-hour period, Able keyed 455 80-character records, and Baker keyed 1368 25-character records. When these records were entered into the computer, several keying errors were discovered in each batch. The errors in Able's batch required an additional 30 minutes to correct, while the errors in Baker's batch required 20 minutes for correction. You are concerned with measuring the relative performance of these two data entry employees.

Required
a) Compute a measure of net keystrokes per hour for each employee that takes into account the additional time required for correcting the errors.

b) Identify any factors other than "net keystrokes per hour" that should be considered in evaluating the performance of these or other data entry personnel.

42. Hatu University has just established a Graduate Business Research Center (GBRC). One of the functions of GBRC will be to provide manuscript typing services. Two equipment options are being considered—a conventional electric typewriter costing $600 and a word processing system costing $7500.

GBRC can hire manuscript typists at an hourly rate of $4.50. These employees would work eight hours a day, of which approximately seven hours would be devoted to typing. Their average typing speed would be 30 words per minute. GBRC expects to receive an average of 16 new manuscripts per week from its very productive faculty. These manuscripts will average 5,000 words apiece. In addition to its original version, each manuscript will undergo two revisions. If conventional typewriters are employed, each revised manuscript must be completely retyped. If a word processor is used, the first revision would require re-typing only 40 percent of the manuscript, while the second revision would require retyping only 10 percent.

a) What is the typing capacity of one manuscript typist measured in words per week?

b) If conventional electric typewriters are used, what will be the average number of words per week which must be typed in order to complete all new and revised manuscripts? How many typewriters and manuscript typists will be required?

c) If a word processor is used, what will be the average number of words per week that must be typed in order to complete all new and revised manuscripts? How many word processors and manuscript typists will be required?

d) From an economic standpoint, which of the two options appears to be most desirable? Show computations.

43. The Western Oil Company began issuing credit cards several years ago. The volume of its credit card business has increased rapidly in recent years. At present the company's data processing center must process an average of 10,000 charge sales documents per business day. This has resulted in a decision to replace the company's keypunch machines, which are presently used for entry of data from charge sales documents. The two alternatives being considered are an Optical Character Recognition (OCR) system and a shared-processor key/disk system.

The OCR system rents for $3000 per month. It would require an operator who would receive a monthly salary of $1000. It could be expected to read successfully between 95 percent and 98 percent of all charge sales documents. For those documents it rejects, the operator would manually enter the correct data from a console. Even considering the time required to deal with rejected documents, this system would have more than enough capacity to handle Western's current and projected volume of charge sales.

If the key/disk system is acquired, the shared processor would rent for $1000 per month, and each keystation required would rent for $500 per month. Each keystation would be operated by a data entry clerk who would receive a monthly salary of $800. These operators could be expected to achieve a net productivity rate of 7500 keystrokes per hour. During each eight-hour day they would spend approximately six hours and 40 minutes working at the keyboard. Each charge sale document has 15 characters that must be keyed.

a) If the key/disk system is acquired, how many keystations and operators will be required, assuming that all work is to be done during the day shift?

b) From an economic standpoint, which of the two alternatives is most attractive? Show computations.

c) Can you identify any additional factors that should be considered in making this choice?

References   Bergeron, Lionel L. "The Word Processing Survey." *Journal of Systems Management* (March 1975): 20–24.

Bohl, Marilyn. *Information Processing* (3rd ed.). Chicago: Science Research Associates, Inc., 1980.

Caswell, Stephen A. "Computer Peripherals: A Revolution Is Coming." *Datamation* (May 25, 1979): 83–87.

Datapro Research Corporation. "All about Data Collection Equipment." In *Datapro 70: The EDP Buyer's Bible.* Delran, N.J.: Datapro Research Corporation, 1980.

_____. "All about Optical Readers." in *Datapro 70: The EDP Buyer's Bible.* Delran, N.J.: Datapro Research Corporation, 1980.

_____. "How to Select and Use Data Entry Devices." In *Datapro 70: The EDP Buyer's Bible.* Delran, N.J.: Datapro Research Corporation, 1980.

Feingold, Carl. *Introduction to Data Processing* (3rd ed.). Dubuque: Wm. C. Brown, 1980.

Feist, Edward F. "Measuring Productivity of Data-Entry Operators." *The Office* (April 1977): 18–26.

Greene, Richard Jay. "How to Use Word Processing Equipment in Your Accounting Work." *The Practical Accountant* (March 1979): 27–40.

Kelley, Neil D. "Micrographics: A Role in the Paperless Office." *Infosystems* (February 1980): 52–56.

_____. "Point of Sale Systems: More Than Meets the Eye." *Infosystems* (March 1980): 72–80.

Krasan, Victor J. "Enter the Electronic Editor." *Management Focus* (November–December 1980): 2–8.

MacCormack, Robert D. "Evaluating Data Entry Systems." *Data Management* (October 1976): 16–21.

Neary, Dennis R. "The Future of Micrographics." *Information and Records Management* (April 1978): 27–29.

Oman, Ray C. "Comparing the Benefits and the Costs of Electric Typewriters and Word Processors." *The Office* (June 1977): 77–79.

Steifel, Mal. "Floppy Disk Systems." *Mini–Micro Systems* (November 1978): 38–51.

Wooldridge, Susan. *Computer Input Design.* New York: Petrocelli, 1974.

Chapter 6

Computer Systems and Data Processing

The previous chapter presents a brief overview of the elements of computer hardware, and then takes a closer look at the central processing unit and at computer data entry equipment. The first two sections of this chapter extend this discussion by examining the two remaining elements of computer hardware—output devices and secondary storage devices. The third section of this chapter integrates these separate discussions of the elements of computer hardware by describing a variety of computer system configurations that include hardware components from each of the four major categories. The fourth and final section of this chapter discusses several aspects of the use of computer systems in the performance of data processing work in business and accounting.

Computer Output Devices

To a large extent the choice of output devices in a computer system is determined by the choice of data entry devices and media. Many devices used for entering data into the computer also prepare output for computer users. Among these devices are the multifunction card machine (see Fig. 5.9), the teleprinter (see Fig. 5.13), the CRT display terminal (see Fig. 5.14), and the bank teller terminal. Some devices used for reading data into the computer also prepare computer output for data storage purposes. Among these are the magnetic tape drive (see Fig. 5.11) and the diskette input-output unit, which is also called the diskette drive. Since all of these devices are discussed in the previous chapter, they are not discussed further here.

This section describes four forms of computer output which are not directly related to any specific form of computer data entry: printers, plotters, voice response units, and computer-output microfilm.

The printer   The *printer* is the most common of all the devices that prepare computer output for human use. A typical computer printer appears in Fig. 6.1. The printer is connected to the central processing unit by means of a cable, over which it receives signals which it must interpret to determine which characters to print. Printer output speeds generally range between 50 and 2000 lines per minute, although for high-volume applications there are models available that can print over 10,000 lines per minute.

In addition to printing reports on regular computer printout paper, computer printers may be used to print variable data on accounting documents such as invoices, purchase orders, and paychecks. For this purpose, special forms are used

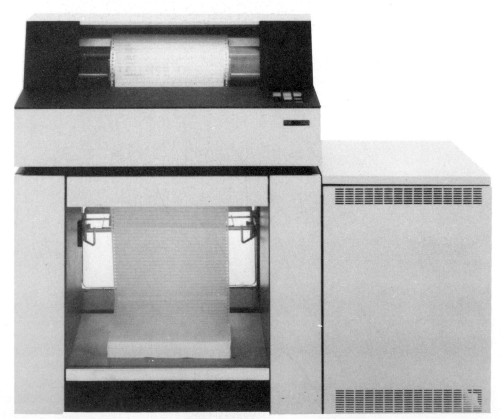

Fig. 6.1
Printer. (Courtesy of
IBM Corporation.)

which have been preprinted with constant data, a document format, and a sequential document number. Blank printout paper or forms are fed into the printer in a continuous stack, with each page or form separated from the preceding page or form by means of a folded perforation. After a complete report or set of forms has been printed, the individual pages or forms may be automatically separated from each other along the perforations by means of an offline device called a burster.

Two basic categories of printers are impact printers and nonimpact printers. Impact printers, which are the most common, print by striking an embossed character against an inked ribbon positioned next to the paper. Conventional impact printers use raised characters that have been preshaped in metal on a drum, belt, or other base; these operate in a manner similar to typewriters. Impact matrix printers form a printed symbol by using various combinations of dots, each of which is printed by striking a needle-shaped hammer against the inked ribbon.

Nonimpact printers use a variety of technologies, including xerography, ink jets, thermal printing on heat-sensitized paper, and electrostatic printing. Thermal and electrostatic printers require special paper, whereas xerographic and ink jet printers use regular paper. Some ink jet printers also use the matrix concept to form characters. The major advantage of nonimpact printing is speed, which ranges up to 18,000 lines per minute as compared to 2500 lines per minute with the fastest impact printers. However, impact printers have two primary advantages over nonimpact printers: (1) impact printers are generally much less expensive; (2) impact printers can produce multiple printed copies of reports or documents using carbons or similar duplication methods, whereas nonimpact printers can produce only a single version of each printed output.

The plotter

The *plotter* is a computer output device that prepares graphical output on paper. Plotters operate by moving a writing arm across a paper surface. Modern plotters can produce three-dimensional drawings and multicolored drawings. Plotters are used primarily in architectural and engineering design applications. However, the growing interest in computer graphics as a tool for management decision making has led to an increasing use of plotters for preparing management reports.

Voice response units

Voice response units are used to provide computer response by "voice" to telephone inquiries. They are most useful when the desired response is relatively small in content and when no documentation is necessary. Examples related to accounting include the checking of a customer's credit by a sales clerk and the inquiry to determine the size of a customer's account balance by a bank teller. An application of voice response with which most people should be familiar is its use by telephone companies to respond to calls to telephone numbers that have been changed or disconnected.

A typical voice response unit contains a collection of recorded words and phrases representing its vocabulary. Each word or phrase has an address. The computer determines the sequence of addresses necessary to respond to an inquiry, and accesses these addresses to generate the necessary recorded sounds. These sounds are then transmitted over the telephone to the user.

Computer output microfilm devices

Computer output microfilm (COM) devices use a photographic process to produce computer output in the form of microfiche. In addition to providing the advantages of microfilm generally (see Chapter 5), this approach is an extremely fast output technique, with output speeds ranging from 20,000 to 50,000 lines per minute. COM recorders may be operated either online to the computer or offline with input from magnetic tape. Figure 6.2 illustrates a system that may be operated either offline, using magnetic tape input, or online. The primary disadvantage of this form of output is the cost of the COM recorder and other necessary microfilm equipment.

Fig. 6.2 Computer Output Microfilm system. (Courtesy of 3M Micrographic Products Division.)

Secondary Storage Devices and Media

Two basic categories of secondary storage are *sequential access* storage and *direct access* (sometimes called *random access*) storage. A sequential access storage medium is one in which any single record stored on the medium may be accessed only after first reading all other records that precede it. The two basic forms of sequential access media are magnetic tape and punched cards. Sequential access files are generally stored offline when they are not being processed. All records in a file stored on a sequential access medium must be maintained in sequential order, numerically or alphabetically, according to an identifying number or name that is stored in the same field within each record. As discussed in Chapter 3, this identifying number or name is called the primary key of the record.

A direct access storage device is one in which any single record stored in the device may be accessed directly without reading any other records. This is possible because each storage location has an address (just like storage locations within the central processor), and once the computer determines the address of the desired record it can access and read the data content of that address directly. A file stored on a direct access device must have a primary key, and may also have one or more secondary key fields. Such a file may or may not be ordered sequentially according to one of its key fields. Direct access files are often maintained online to the computer at all times, or they may be stored offline at times other than while they are being processed. There are a variety of forms of direct access storage, but magnetic disk is by far the most common.

Sequential access storage media

Though the punched card is a common medium for source data entry into a computer system, its use as a secondary storage medium is much less common. However, punched cards do have some advantages over magnetic tape as a secondary storage medium. If the use of punched card storage makes it possible to avoid any use of magnetic tape in a system, then the cost of acquiring and maintaining several magnetic tape drives may be avoided. Punched cards themselves are in some ways more flexible than magnetic tape as a storage medium. Cards can be read by visual inspection, whereas magnetic tape cannot be. It is thus easier with punched card storage to change or extract for reference purposes a single record or small number of records. Furthermore, a tape reel is not divisible in accordance with the size of a file. Some small files may consume only five to ten percent of the capacity of a tape reel.

Magnetic tape possesses several significant advantages over punched cards as a secondary storage medium. Each punched card has a fixed record capacity of 80 or 96 characters, but magnetic tape has no such constraint—in fact, different records on the same magnetic tape file may be of varying lengths. Data recorded on magnetic tape may be erased and written over with new data, so that each reel of tape may be reused many times. But the primary advantages of tape over cards are reading speed and storage capacity. To understand these factors more fully, it is necessary to have some knowledge of the way in which data records are stored on magnetic tape.

Data may be very tightly packed on magnetic tape. The most common recording density is 1600 bytes per inch, but densities as high as 6250 bytes per inch are also in use. A typical reel of magnetic tape might hold as many as 40 million characters. At 80 characters per card, 500,000 punched cards would be required to hold the same amount of data.

Records are stored on magnetic tape in *blocks* of several records, with a gap called the *interblock gap* between each consecutive pair of blocks. Figure 6.3 illustrates a section of magnetic tape upon which records are stored in blocks of four. The interblock gaps provide room for the tape drive to slow down and stop after reading one block of data, and start up again and reach peak speed prior to encountering the next block of data. Depending on the speed with which the computer is actually processing the data, this space for stopping and starting may be required at some times, while at other times the tape drive is able to pass the interblock gap at peak speed without stopping and starting.

Blocking of records obviously reduces the effective data storage capacity of magnetic tape because no data are stored in the interblock gaps. For example, suppose that records of 320 characters each are being stored on a magnetic tape having a density of 1600 bytes per inch. Assume that one byte is used to store one character. If there were no blocking, then the tape capacity would be 1600 characters per inch ÷ 320 characters per record, or five records per inch. To determine the effect of blocking, it is necessary to know the size of the interblock gaps and the number of records per block. Assume that the interblock gaps are each 0.6 inch in width (a common size) and that seven records are to be stored in one block. Then the number of characters per block is equal to 320 characters per record × 7 records per block, or 2240. The number of inches required for these seven records is therefore equal to 2240 characters per block ÷ 1600 characters per inch, or 1.4. However, for each and every block of seven records there is also an interblock gap 0.6 inch in width, so that effectively 1.4 + 0.6 = 2 inches are required for every seven records. Blocking thus reduces the tape capacity from five records per inch to three and a half records per inch in this case.

Blocking also reduces the effective reading speed of records stored on magnetic tape. For example, assume that tape records are being read on a tape drive that operates at 60,000 bytes per second. It is useful to convert this into inches per second by dividing by the tape recording density: 60,000 bytes per second ÷ 1600 bytes per inch = 37½ inches per second. In the case above, if there were no blocking, the reading speed would be 37½ inches per second × 5 records per inch = 187½ records per second. Blocking reduces the effective reading speed to 37½ inches per second × 3½ records per inch = 131¼ records per second. The actual reading speed may be even less than this if the tape drive is required to stop and start between blocks.

This example may be extended to provide a comparison of the effective reading speeds of punched cards and magnetic tape. Suppose that a file of 63,000 records is to be read. At the rate of 131¼ records per second, 480 seconds or eight minutes would be required to accomplish this task. If this file were on punched cards, four 80-column cards would be required to hold each 320 character record. Thus a total of 252,000 cards would be needed for the 63,000 records. Using a relatively fast card

Fig. 6.3
Blocking of records.

| Interblock gap | Record #21 | Record #22 | Record #23 | Record #24 | Interblock gap | Record #25 | Record #26 | Record #27 | Record #28 | Interblock gap |

reader operating at 1200 cards per minute, 210 minutes or 3½ hours would be required to read all of this data into the computer. Thus the input speed for tape records is roughly 25 times as fast as for card records in this case.

Direct access storage devices

In addition to magnetic disks, direct access secondary storage devices include magnetic drums, magnetic strips (also called data cells), magnetic cards, diskettes, magnetic cores, magnetic bubbles, and charge-coupled devices. At present only magnetic disks and their smaller relatives, diskettes, enjoy widespread usage. Magnetic drums were popular in the early 1960s, but are much less common now. Magnetic strips and magnetic cards never achieved widespread usage and are rarely seen today. Magnetic cores, though used mainly for primary memory within the CPU, may also be used as a high-speed form of secondary storage for applications requiring extremely fast access.

Magnetic bubbles and charge-coupled devices are newer forms of direct access memory introduced in the mid-1970s. Magnetic bubbles are tiny cylindrical magnetic domains that form in a thin magnetic film in the presence of an external magnetic field. Data are represented by means of the presence or absence of bubbles. Charge-coupled devices are a variation of semiconductor memory, and represent bits of data through the presence of either a positive or negative electric charge. Both of these forms of direct access storage are faster but more expensive than magnetic disks, and slower but less expensive than magnetic cores or semiconductor chips. They are roughly comparable to each other in terms of cost, but charge-coupled devices generally provide faster access times than magnetic bubbles. Offsetting this advantage is the fact that, unlike magnetic forms of memory, charge-coupled devices are *volatile,* which means that the data stored in them is lost whenever the power supply is cut off. The earliest commercial applications of both of these forms of memory have been to small computers, programmable calculators, electronic cash registers, and data terminals.

Magnetic disks have long dominated the market for direct access computer data storage. They seem to provide the optimum trade-off among such factors as cost, access time, storage capacity, and flexibility. Therefore, the remainder of this section is devoted to a detailed discussion of magnetic disk storage devices.

A magnetic disk storage unit is a device that contains a set of magnetic disks and a mechanism for reading and writing data on the disks. Figure 6.4 illustrates several characteristics of a typical disk unit. Note that the set of disks has the appearance of a stack of phonograph records. There is space between each adjoining pair of disks, and data are recorded on both the upper and lower surfaces of each disk. The unit shown has one read/write head for each surface. Data are stored in each of several concentric circular *tracks* (somewhat analogous to the grooves on a

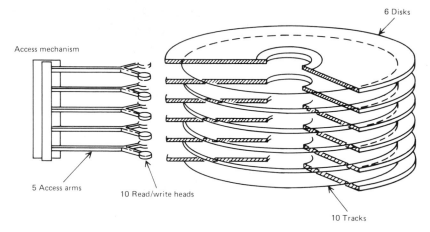

Fig. 6.4
Magnetic disk
storage features.

phonograph record) on each recording surface. Data are accessed by moving the head in or out to the appropriate track while the disk revolves to the appropriate segment of the track. Data are stored in each track in the form of a serial string of bits, each of which may be in either a magnetized or demagnetized state.

Magnetic disk storage units may be classified in several ways. For example, a *fixed disk* is one in which the disks themselves are permanently attached to their disk drive unit and cannot be removed, while a *removable disk* is one in which the set of disks, called a *disk pack,* may be physically removed from the disk drive unit and replaced by another disk pack. Also, a *fixed-head disk* is a unit in which there is a separate read/write head for each track, which enables data to be accessed without the in-and-out movement of the read/write heads. In contrast, *moving-head disks* have one or a few heads per surface, so that the in-and-out movement of the heads is required in order to access the appropriate track. The unit shown in Fig. 6.4 is a moving-head disk.

The time required to read a record from a disk file is the sum of the access time and the data transfer time. Access time is the sum of the time required for the access arm to move the read/write head to the appropriate track and the time required for the disk to rotate to the necessary location within the track. Both of these times will vary depending on the initial location of the read/write head relative to the location of the desired record, so it is only possible to speak in terms of average times. The data transfer time is determined by dividing the number of characters in the record by the device's transfer rate. For example, consider the average time required to read a 156-character record stored in a disk file that has an average head movement time of 60 milliseconds, a rotation speed of 2400 revolutions per minute, and a transfer rate of 312,000 bytes per second. First convert the rotation speed into revolutions per second (2400 revolutions per minute ÷ 60 seconds per minute = 40 revolutions per second), and then the rotation time required for one revolution may be determined (1 second ÷ 40 revolutions = .025 seconds per revolution, or 25 milliseconds per revolution). The average rotational delay is one-half of the rotation time, 25 milliseconds ÷ 2, or 12.5 milliseconds. The average access time is the sum of the average-head movement time of 60 milliseconds and the average rotational delay of 12.5 milliseconds, or 72.5 milliseconds. Next, assuming no packing, 156 bytes will be required to store 156 characters, and the data transfer time may be computed as 156 bytes ÷ 312,000 bytes per second = .0005 seconds, or 0.5 milliseconds. Finally the average read time is the sum of the average access time of 72.5 milliseconds and the data transfer time of 0.5 milliseconds, or a total of 73 milliseconds.

Note that if records on a disk file are being accessed sequentially, then the access time will be zero. This is true because when they are finished reading one record, the read/write heads are already positioned to read the next one, thus eliminating both the head movement time and the rotation time. Also note that if records are being accessed randomly on a fixed-head disk, the head movement time is zero because the existence of one read/write head for each track eliminates the need for head movement.

Disk units vary widely in storage capacity and cost. The capacity of a disk pack depends on the number of bytes per track, the number of tracks per surface, and the number of surfaces. A typical small disk has 7294 bytes per track, 200 tracks per surface, and 20 surfaces, for a total capacity of about 29 million bytes. A typical large disk has 13,030 bytes per track, 808 tracks per surface, and 19 surfaces for data storage, providing a total capacity of 200 million bytes. Monthly rentals vary from $500 to over $1000.

Diskettes use the same data storage techniques and access methods as magnetic disks. The most significant physical difference is that each diskette is a separate unit unlike a regular disk that is attached to a spindle containing several other disks in a disk pack. In terms of its use as a data storage medium, the major difference between the diskette and the magnetic disk pack is that the diskette has a much smaller storage capacity. In addition, the access time to records on a diskette is generally much slower than for ordinary magnetic disks. As a result the diskette is commonly used for secondary storage only in smaller computer systems, and otherwise is primarily used as a data entry medium.

In some smaller computer systems that have limited file storage requirements, disk storage has completely replaced magnetic tape as the secondary storage medium. The smaller disk units cost less than a set of magnetic tape drive units, and the direct access feature of disk storage is also a desirable feature. Larger systems commonly utilize both magnetic tape and disk storage, using disk for storage for which the direct access feature is necessary, and tape for all other data.

Some accounting applications are well suited to the utilization of direct access storage devices such as magnetic disk, while others do not require it. A multiproduct firm in a competitive industry finds it very useful to have immediate access to up-to-date information regarding the availability and location of an assortment of products in various price ranges and styles. A large manufacturing company may require immediate access to data on parts inventories. Banks and retail stores often require immediate access to data on customer accounts. Generally most business organizations find sequential access storage acceptable for such accounting applications as payroll and accounts payable.

**Computer
Hardware
Configurations**

In this and the previous chapter, separate sections have described each of the four major hardware elements of a computer system, (1) the central processing unit, (2) data entry devices, (3) output devices, and (4) secondary storage devices. This section discusses how various examples of each of these types of hardware may be combined to form a computer hardware *configuration*—a set of computer equipment that is operated as a unit to perform data processing work. Although computer hardware configurations vary widely in size and cost, all of them have at least one component belonging to each of the four major hardware categories.

It is difficult to classify the wide variety of systems available in today's computer marketplace. Nevertheless, some type of classification scheme is essential for discussion purposes. In this section we treat computer system hardware configurations as falling into one of four categories, (1) microcomputers, (2) minicomputer systems, (3) medium-scale computer systems, and (4) large-scale computer systems. Examples of basic configurations and equipment options in each of these categories are described.

Microcomputers

Modern technology has made it possible to place the circuitry of a computer control unit and arithmetic and logic unit onto a single tiny chip of silicon. These "one-chip computers," which are called *microprocessors,* are now being produced for less than ten dollars. When they are combined with other chips and circuits that provide memory, timing, and input/output interfaces, a *microcomputer* is formed. Technically, a microcomputer is simply a computer that incorporates a microprocessor as its major component.

Following their development in the early 1970s, microcomputers have been used to incorporate computer capabilities into airplanes, automobiles, industrial machinery, communications equipment, electronic control devices, office copiers, pocket calculators, electronic games, household appliances, television sets, and a wide variety of other electronic devices. The number of existing applications is enormous, and the number of potential applications appears limitless. For purposes of our discussion, however, the one specific application of the microcomputer that is most significant is the development of very small, inexpensive, and user-oriented computer systems. These are called *personal computers* or *desktop computers.*

A typical desktop computer consists of a keyboard for input, a microcomputer for processing, 16,000 to 64,000 bytes of primary storage, a video display screen for output, and a flexible disk drive or cassette tape drive for secondary storage. The distinguishing feature of the desktop computer is that all of these components are contained in a single unit only slightly larger than a typewriter. This basic configuration can be purchased for as little as $1000. A typical desktop computer is pictured in Fig. 6.5. Computers of this type have been commercially available since the mid-1970s, and their prices have declined significantly since that time.

For business applications, additional peripheral equipment must be obtained for a desktop computer. The first necessity is a printer for preparing invoices, checks, and other business documents. A second cassette tape drive or flexible disk drive is also useful to provide for backup storage of critical files. Additional primary

Fig. 6.5
Desktop computer.
(Courtesy of Apple
Computer Inc.)

memory may also be obtaincd to increase the processing capability of the desktop computer. These additional features may increase the cost of a desktop computer by several thousand dollars.

Desktop computers generally use very simple programming languages, and their suppliers also offer a wide variety of optional application programs. These are intended to make them as simple as possible to use in order that they will appeal to businesspeople, professionals, and others who are not expert in computer use. Though designed to be primarily stand-alone computers for individual use, many are also capable of being used as data terminals connected to larger computer systems.

Desktop computers may be used in a wide variety of applications. Many are used as "home computers" to maintain checking accounts and other household records, play electronic games, and control home appliances. Many are used for educational purposes to provide computer-assisted instruction. Many are used by scientists and engineers for process control, data analysis, mathematical problem solving, and similar applications.

In a small business, a desktop computer equipped with appropriate software may be useful for both file processing and word processing applications. Though the capacity of a cassette tape or floppy disk may be inadequate for file storage in larger business organizations, it may be just right for the customer files, payroll files, inventory files, and general ledger filcs of a small business. Possible word processing applications include correspondence, mailing lists, price lists, and promotional literature.

In both small and large businesses, desktop computers are proving very useful as problem-solving tools. Examples of problem-solving applications relating to business and accounting include forecasting, risk analysis, depreciation calculations, tax analyses, present value and interest computations, financial planning, statistical analyses for cost control and audit sampling, inventory planning and control, actuarial calculations, and operations research models of various kinds. Indeed the widening availability of low-cost computing power is likely to increase the use of such analytical techniques among accountants and businesspeople.

Minicomputers   Whereas the origin and initial development of microcomputers took place during the 1970s, the history of minicomputers dates back to the mid-1960s. In the early 1960s, all computer systems were very large and very expensive collections of equipment housed in a centralized facility especially built to provide raised floors, air conditioning, and other environmental controls. Available software was generally complex and designed to be used by computer specialists rather than by inexperienced users. In this environment, those in the organization who proposed to use the computer in their area had to deal with programmers, systems analysts, and a centralized administrative staff. At that time, the computer marketplace was ready for any technological development that could make the power of the computer more accessible to its potential users.

Into this environment the first minicomputer was introduced in 1965, and the computer industry will never be the same again. *Minicomputers* are distinguished from their larger ancestors by their smaller word sizes, smaller memories, and more limited instruction processing capabilities; in turn, these features enabled them to be much smaller in physical size and cost. Furthermore, minicomputers were designed to require little or no special environmental controls, enabling them to be housed in laboratories, factories, offices, and warehouses, rather than in a special centralized facility.

Technologically speaking, minicomputers were not a particularly significant development. They were simply scaled-down versions of larger computers. The subsequent development of the microprocessor, or computer-on-a-chip, was a much more impressive step from a technological point of view. However, from a conceptual point of view, the minicomputer was much more significant because it changed the way that people thought about the use of computer systems in organizations. It brought the concept of "power to the people" into the realm of computer applications by enabling computer power to be more easily distributed to its end users. From this perspective, microprocessors and microcomputers were just additional steps (although very significant ones) along a path originally charted by the minicomputer.

The first minicomputers were oriented toward scientific and engineering applications, such as industrial process control, laboratory research, and data communications. They typically had very limited input/output capability, and so were not well suited to the high-volume data processing jobs common in business and accounting information systems. However, it was not long before the concept of small, inexpensive, special-purpose computer systems was extended into the realm of business and accounting.

Today the variety of minicomputer systems available for business applications is enormous. It is difficult to classify the systems into a few homogeneous categories. This section will discuss two major categories of minicomputers—(1) small accounting computers and (2) small business computers.

Small accounting computers   The small accounting computer is designed primarily for standard accounting applications, including payroll, accounts receivable and billing, accounts payable, and general ledger. This class of business machines evolved during the early 1970s from the electromechanical bookkeeping machines that were very common in business organizations during the 1950s and 1960s. This evolutionary process was accomplished by adding stored program capability and computer input/output peripherals to the older machines, while retaining many of the functional characteristics which had for many years provided an inexpensive and efficient form of mechanized data processing.

The typical small accounting computer has an operator-controlled keyboard with numeric, alphabetic, and special-function keys; a display terminal; a printer; and a device for file and program storage such as a disk, diskette, or tape cassette drive (see Fig. 6.6). Many small accounting computers also include special forms handling devices that permit simultaneous processing of multiple forms such as ledger cards, journals, checks, and invoices. The forms handler illustrated in Fig. 6.6 automatically positions forms at the proper line for recording data, automatically feeds subsequent copies of continuous forms, and uses a bar code reader to read document numbers from the documents being processed.

The heart of a small accounting computer system is the central processing unit that, though relatively small, includes arithmetic, logic, control, and memory capabilities, just as do large computer systems. The CPU holds program logic for system functions, and also stores data relating to applications in process. In the system shown in Fig. 6.6, the CPU is incorporated into the CRT display unit.

Some small accounting computers incorporate the feature of magnetic stripe ledger records (see Fig. 6.7). The magnetic stripes on the reverse side of these records can be encoded with file data such as account numbers and balances or employee payroll data. When the ledger card is inserted into the machine, the data are read automatically from the magnetic stripes. As the operator keys in transaction data to be posted to the ledger, the system computes updated balances and records them on the magnetic stripe at the same time that it is printing data on the front of the card. Thus the magnetic stripe ledger card represents an efficient combination of human and machine-readable data storage.

Small accounting computers can be used effectively as "stand-alone" systems for small businesses, or alternatively may be used as components of a large configuration that includes one or more big general-purpose computers. For example, many small accounting computers can be operated as data terminals, connected to large

Display   Printer

Flexible
disk units

Forms handler   Keyboard

Fig. 6.6
Small accounting
computer system.
(Courtesy of NCR
Corporation.)

computers by data transmission lines. Alternatively, a small accounting computer can be operated on a stand-alone basis at a branch location of a large company, but also be designed to produce machine-readable input for a large central computer as a by-product of its operations. In the latter case, commonly used media are magnetic tape cassettes or diskettes. This is another form of source data automation.

An example of the use of a small accounting computer in a typical accounting operation is provided by an accounts payable application. The functions to be performed include posting vendor invoices to an accounts payable master file, generating checks, preparing a list of disbursements, and accumulating total debits and credits for subsequent posting to the general ledger.

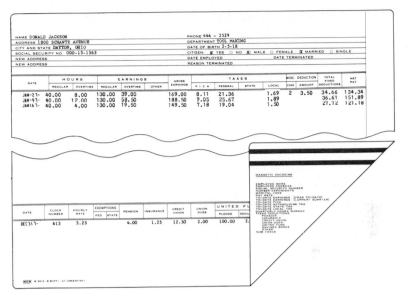

*Fig. 6.7
Magnetic stripe
ledger record.
(Courtesy of NCR
Corporation.)*

In the small accounting computer system, the accounts payable master file data are stored either on a magnetic stripe ledger record or in a disk file. Each such record contains a vendor's account number, name and address, amounts, due dates and discount rates for all outstanding invoices, and a total balance due. The operator enters data for new invoices using the keyboard, and these data are recorded in the proper master file records by the system. Each vendor master record is reviewed to select those outstanding amounts that are due for payment, and the system accumulates the amount due, deducts any applicable discount, and prepares a check. The system reads the old account balance from each master record, adds the amount of any new invoices to the balance, and subtracts for payments to obtain a new balance, which is then written back onto the master record. At the same time the system is accumulating summary debits and credits for subsequent posting to general ledger accounts such as cash, purchase discounts, accounts payable, inventory, and various expenses. The system also prepares a printed listing of all checks prepared, which serves as a reference report and audit trail.

The major characteristic distinguishing the small accounting computer from other minicomputers or from larger computer systems is its greater dependence on the operator for entry of transaction data and monitoring of application processing. Essentially the operator and the system work as a unit in processing an application, with some functions performed manually by the operator and others automatically by the system. In terms of the activities in the data processing cycle, the small accounting computer system emphasizes the activities of calculating, summarizing, transcribing, updating, storage, issuance, and reporting. Prices for such systems generally range from $15,000 to $60,000 depending on which optional features and peripherals are acquired.

Small business computers   A small business computer system is a minicomputer-based system that includes general-purpose peripheral equipment and software designed and configured specifically for business applications. In essence, a typical small business computer system resembles a medium-scale, general-purpose business computer system, with the major differences being size, price, and number of attached peripheral devices.

The typical base hardware configuration for a small business computer includes a central processing unit with 32,000 to 64,000 bytes of primary storage, a video display terminal for direct data entry and inquiry response, a disk file for online storage, a diskette drive for offline and backup storage, and a printer. The cost of this base configuration would range between $30,000 and $50,000. Optional extensions of this system would include additional primary storage, tape drives, a card reader and punch, additional disk storage units, and additional terminals. The price of a small business computer system incorporating selected options of this kind may range up to $100,000, a figure that represents the generally accepted dividing line between minicomputer systems and medium-scale, general-purpose computer systems.

One factor that distinguishes small business computer systems from both small accounting computers and desktop computers is that the former operate with less human intervention. Once the appropriate input records and files have been properly loaded, a small-business computer system can complete an entire file processing application without significant interaction with its operator. In contrast, desktop computers and small accounting computers are operator-oriented machines designed to interact regularly with their human operators. In addition, many CPUs in small business computer systems are capable of controlling several different processing applications concurrently, whereas the CPU in a desktop computer or a small accounting computer is dedicated to the specific application that its operator is running at any one time.

Because small business computer users tend to be less knowledgeable than other computer users about computer systems and applications, many suppliers of these computer systems have developed packages of hardware, software, and maintenance services that can be acquired and implemented by users with little or no computer expertise. Systems of this kind have been labeled *turnkey systems* because theoretically all that the user has to do is turn the system on and let it do the rest. While no system is quite that easy to use, turnkey systems are nonetheless very popular among small business users who wish to automate their data processing without having to hire a specialized staff of computer experts. However, it is very important that the small-business user who is considering the acquisition of a turnkey system obtain assurances that the vendor is a stable and reliable company that will still be around to help when something goes wrong with the system.

The primary applications of small business computer systems are transaction processing, file maintenance, and management reporting. Files maintained on such systems typically include accounts receivable, inventories, employee payroll records, accounts payable, and general ledger records. Transactions processed include sales orders, shipments, cash receipts, inventory purchases, and cash disbursements. Documents generated typically include invoices, customer statements, purchase orders, payroll statements, and checks. Management reports include accounts receivable aging schedules, inventory turnover analyses, sales analyses, cash flow summaries, and conventional financial statements.

Like small accounting computers, small business computers are capable of being linked to larger computer systems and operated as terminals or satellite processors. Thus many large organizations that have a large centralized computer facility have also chosen to acquire small business computer systems to be located in warehouses, branch offices, or subsidiary plants, and linked to the central facility through data communications lines.

Medium-scale and large-scale computer systems

A medium-scale computer system is distinguished from a small business computer system by the following characteristics. It has (1) a purchase price of $100,000 or more, (2) a general-purpose orientation, which means that the system is designed and configured for a wide variety of uses from scientific and engineering applications to business file processing, (3) a central processing unit having larger word sizes, more primary storage, and a larger instruction set, (4) the ability to perform a larger number of independent data processing jobs concurrently, (5) a larger number and variety of peripheral devices, and (6) the ability to utilize specialized forms of input or output such as OCR, MICR, OMR, special-function terminals, plotters, COM, or voice response equipment.

The CPU in a typical medium-scale computer system includes from one-half to four megabytes of primary storage. A *megabyte* is approximately one million bytes, or exactly $2^{20} = 1,048,576$ bytes. The remainder of the hardware configuration probably includes a multifunction card machine, several tape drives, several disk drives, one or two high-speed printers, and a variety of terminals located both within the computer center and at separate plant or branch locations. In addition, the configuration might include data preparation equipment for handling large volumes of data entry, such as a shared processor key-to-disk-to-tape system or OCR equipment. Except for remote terminals, all of this equipment is likely to be located at a specially designed central facility staffed by a specialized group of operators, programmers, systems analysts, and managers. The system pictured in Fig. 5.3 represents a typical system in this category.

A medium-scale computer system may be used for virtually any application in an organization that is capable of being automated. In all cases the standard accounting-oriented business data processing applications described in our earlier discussion of small business computers would be included. Additional applications in a typical manufacturing company might include production planning and control, research and development, engineering design, quality control, personnel administration, marketing research, financial planning, and numerous others.

It is difficult to know where to draw the line between medium-scale and large-scale computer systems. Essentially, a large-scale system will include most or all of the features of a medium-scale system, and more. A large-scale system will include a CPU that is larger and faster, and will include input, output and storage devices having higher speeds or greater capacities. A large-scale system is more likely to incorporate specialized forms of input, output, or storage such as OCR, specialized terminals, COM, magnetic drum storage units, or magnetic core secondary storage. A large-scale system is also more likely to perform specialized applications incorporating advanced technology, such as data base management systems (see Chapter 8), real-time systems (see Chapter 9), or distributed processing (also covered in Chapter 9). The total cost of the hardware for large-scale computer systems may run to several million dollars, but this cost is nonetheless likely to be exceeded by the costs of software and personnel to operate and manage these systems.

Computer Data Processing in Business and Accounting

Computer applications are generally divided into two basic and distinct categories—(1) business data processing, and (2) scientific applications. The use of a computer system for business data processing typically involves a high volume of input and output, and computations that are routine and simple. Business data processing is typified by such accounting applications as updating an accounts receivable master file for sales and cash receipts transactions, or processing employee time cards to update a payroll master file and print paychecks.

In sharp contrast to business data processing, scientific applications often involve limited input and output, but require a great deal of computation. Of course computers may be used in the application of a scientific technique such as statistical analysis or operations research to a business problem, but such an application would still be categorized as scientific rather than as a business data processing application. Though the computer system in a business organization may be used for some scientific applications, the vast majority of its volume of work is likely to be for business data processing applications.

The requirements of business data processing have had a significant influence on the design of computer systems. In the first part of this section, several aspects of this influence are described in order to provide a more complete understanding of business data processing. Next the techniques of systems flowcharting are explained, and then used as a vehicle for illustrating typical processing operations and equipment configurations employed in business data processing. Finally, the two primary modes of business data processing, batch processing and online processing, are described and contrasted.

Systems design considerations for business data processing

Computer systems for business data processing face a unique design problem. As mentioned above, business systems are characterized by high volumes of input and output and relatively simple computations. However, the speeds of available computer input and output devices are much less than those of central processors. Recall that central processor operating speeds are measured in microseconds or nanoseconds. In contrast, the operating speeds of input and output devices are stated in terms of such measures as cards per minute or lines per minute. This creates a basic mismatch of CPU speeds and input/output speeds, which is more severe in business systems because of their high volume of input and output. Business systems are often referred to as *input/output bound* because the speed of completion of business data processing applications is limited by the speed of input and output devices. In contrast, scientific applications are much better suited to currently available hardware because they typically involve limited input and output and a great deal of computation.

Throughput is a word used to indicate the total amount of useful work performed by a computer system during a given period of time. This concept encompasses input and output as well as computation. Approaches to increasing throughput in business systems must focus upon circumventing the basic mismatch of CPU speeds and input/output speeds. Several approaches to this problem are discussed here.

One capability which greatly increases the throughput of modern computer systems is that of *overlap*. This is the capability of the computer system to perform one or more input/output operations and CPU processing simultaneously. Actually a CPU can execute only one instruction at a time. In first- and second-generation computers, after the CPU executed an input or output instruction, it would remain idle until the input or output device completed the task. However, in a third-generation computer system the CPU does not execute input/output instructions. Instead, input and output functions are performed by *channels,* which are the communication interfaces between the CPU and all input/output devices. The CPU can instruct a channel to perform an input or output task, and while the channel is carrying out this instruction, the CPU may continue processing. CPU processing is thus carried out simultaneously with input and output operations.

The number of input and output operations that may be overlapped with CPU processing is a function of the number of channels in the system. A channel is like a tiny computer that specializes strictly in input and output functions. Once a channel has completed its assigned input or output function, it signals the CPU that the input data have been read into the electronic memory of the channel or that the output data have been written. The CPU may then instruct the channel to transfer its input data into primary memory and perform another input operation, or to accept additional output data from primary memory and perform another output operation. Meanwhile, the CPU continues its processing operations. The overlap capability does not eliminate the basic mismatch of CPU speeds and input/output speeds, but it at least assures that the CPU does not remain idle while waiting for input and output operations to be performed.

Third-generation computers also permit *multiprogramming,* which is the simultaneous execution of two or more programs on the same computer system. Recall that the CPU cannot execute more than one instruction at one time, and therefore can work on only one program at a time. However, modern CPUs are so fast that they can switch back and forth among a number of different programs fast enough to keep the input and output devices for all of the programs working at peak speed. Though the CPU is working on only one program at any one instant, the computer system as a whole is executing several programs at the same time. For example, one program might be reading a deck of cards and transferring their contents to tape while simultaneously a second program is reading a second tape and writing its contents on a printer and a third program is handling terminal inquiries relating to a disk file. Needless to say, this capability greatly increases the throughput potential of a computer system.

While overlap and multiprogramming are capabilities that come with the system itself, several avenues to increased throughput are available to the systems designer. One example relevant to accounting information systems is the application of the principle of exception reporting. This principle indicates that the output reports from a system should include only that information that might affect a user's decision or cause him or her to take action. Complete listings of all data in a file are not necessary if only a fraction of the information is to be used. For example, a report concerning credit customers should perhaps include data on only those customers whose accounts are past due, rather than contain data on all customers. This approach could not only improve throughput in an information system, but could increase the usefulness of system output as well.

Other approaches to increasing throughput in business data processing systems involve the substitution of fast input or output devices for slow ones. For example, magnetic tape drives, flexible disk drives, COM units, and CRT display terminals are faster by one or two orders of magnitude than are punched card readers, printers, and teleprinter terminals. If these faster devices can be substituted for their slower counterparts, more efficient use is made of the CPU's time, and throughput may be increased as a result. This helps to explain why so many organizations have switched from keypunching of source data onto punched cards to the use of a key-to-tape encoder, a key-to-disk-to-tape system, or a key-to-diskette encoder. Furthermore, even organizations that still keypunch source data onto cards, or that use punched cards or OCR forms as turnaround documents, often transfer these source data onto magnetic tape prior to processing them against the master files. On the output side, the data content of printed reports or documents prepared as a by-product of file processing may first be written onto magnetic tape for later conversion to printed form on the printer. Also, many organizations with extremely large volumes of output have substituted COM for printed reports. Similarly, CRT displays are much faster than teleprinters for online output.

The conversion of records from punched cards to magnetic tape or from magnetic tape to printed form may be done by offline converters, by small peripheral computers used primarily for this purpose or, most frequently, by the main computer itself as one of several jobs being processed in a multiprogramming mode. In the latter case, the conversion program takes up relatively little primary storage, and each conversion operation performed by the program consumes very little CPU time, so that this process represents a very efficient use of CPU resources. An alternative to the use of magnetic tape in this way is the use of magnetic disk; that is, card records being read into the system are transferred to magnetic disk storage prior to being processed against the master file, or records to be printed are first written onto magnetic disk storage prior to being transmitted to the printer. When tape or disk files are used in this way simultaneously with the execution of the job that requires the card input or printed output, the operation is called *spooling* (SPOOL is an acronym for Simultaneous Peripheral Operations On-Line).

Storage of master file records on a direct access storage medium such as magnetic disk also enables throughput to be increased. For one thing, it permits integrated processing of transactions that must be posted to more than one master file; these can be posted to all such files by one program using the direct access feature. This eliminates the need to utilize a separate posting program for each master file being updated, and also eliminates the need for intermediate sorting steps to resequence the transactions according to the primary key of each successive master file. Furthermore, master file records stored on magnetic disk files may be updated from online terminals, which eliminates time-consuming data preparation, record transcription, and record sorting processes.

One other factor which affects throughput in a business data processing system is the size of primary storage in the CPU. Generally, a larger primary storage area provides a greater multiprogramming capability, which permits more jobs to be processed concurrently. Also, the number of records that may be contained in a block of records is limited by the size of the memory area available for holding blocks of records. This factor is significant because the more records there are in a block, the fewer are the number of interblock gaps, which enables faster tape processing speeds. Therefore an increase in CPU memory size could potentially increase throughput in a business data processing system.

This section has touched upon just a few of the factors that affect the efficiency of a computer system used for business data processing. Factors such as these are of interest to the accountant for a number of possible reasons. For example, the information systems department is located within the controller's office in many business organizations, in which case the accountant has direct management responsibility for the computer function. Even in organizations in which this arrangement does not exist, management accountants and internal auditors are responsible for reviewing and reporting on the performance of other managers, including the manager of the computer facility. Further, the accounting department is often the primary consumer of computer services within an organization, and is therefore especially concerned that such services are provided efficiently and effectively.

Systems flowcharting   A *flowchart* is a diagrammatical representation of the flow of information and/or the sequence of operations in a process or system. There are several different types of flowcharts and each has its own specialized set of symbols. A *systems flowchart* presents the flow of data through a series of operations in an automated data processing system. Many of the topics covered in this and the previous chapter may be further explained and illustrated through the use of systems flowcharting. The flowcharting symbols shown in Fig. 6.8 are widely used in systems practice and form the basis for our presentation. The reader may wish to note at this time that systems flowcharts employing these symbols are used as a tool to explain and illustrate data processing systems and operations throughout the remainder of this book, and also must be used to complete many of the problems and cases appearing at the back of

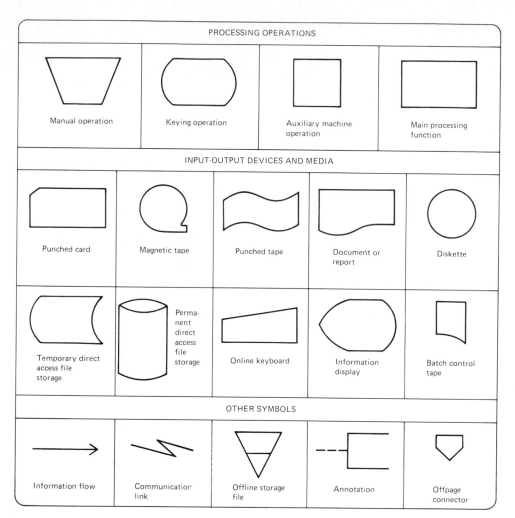

Fig. 6.8
Symbols for systems
flowcharting.

this and subsequent chapters. For this reason the reader may wish to obtain a flow-charting *template*—a rectangular sheet of clear plastic, out of which the shapes of these symbols are cut, used for tracing of the symbols.

As shown in Fig. 6.8, systems flowcharting symbols may be divided into three major categories, (1) processing symbols, (2) input/output symbols, and (3) other symbols not fitting into the first two categories. There are four processing symbols, each corresponding to one of the four major operations performed in a data processing system. These are (1) manual operations performed with no machine assistance, (2) keying operations performed manually at a keyboard not connected to the main computer, such as a keypunch, key-to-diskette, or typewriter keyboard, (3) auxiliary machine operations performed automatically by a machine not connected to the main computer, such as a card sorter or offline converter, and (4) main processing functions, which encompass any operations performed by the central computer. Input/output symbols represent either devices or media which provide input to, or record output from, processing operations. Note that the use of these symbols in a flowchart will be indicative of (1) the operations performed, (2) the hardware devices used, and (3) the input, output, and storage media employed.

When a systems flowchart is prepared, a label is inserted into each symbol describing the data or operations represented by that symbol. If there is insufficient room for the necessary label, the annotation symbol may be used to provide a more complete explanation. Straight lines with arrows attached indicate the flow of information and the sequence of operations. If there is insufficient room on one page for a complete flowchart, the offpage connector is used to show the links between separate pages.

One common feature of all systems flowcharts is that they consist of a sequence of processing steps, each having one or more related input and output symbols. According to the "sandwich theory" of flowcharting, processing symbols are the meat, and input/output symbols are the bread! In larger flowcharts, the output of one processing step becomes the input to a subsequent processing step. This may be likened to a "Dagwood special"! The reader may observe this pattern in all of the sample flowcharts presented in the remainder of this section.

Our first sample flowchart, in Fig. 6.9, shows the use of a shared processor key-to-disk-to-tape system for source data preparation. Source data are read by the ma-

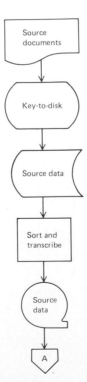

Fig. 6.9
Key-to-disk-to-tape
processing of
source data.

chine operator from source documents and keyed into the system to be recorded on a temporary disk file. Once a complete set of transaction records has been entered, the processor sorts the records into sequential order and transfers their contents onto magnetic tape. The records are then ready to be entered into the main computer for processing, but the offpage connector indicates that this step appears on a separate page.

Figures 6.10 and 6.11 illustrate the preparation of source data using two different media—punched cards and punched paper tape. In Fig. 6.10 the keypunching and keyverification of source data on cards is followed by the reading of the cards into the central computer to transfer their contents to magnetic tape for subsequent processing. In Fig. 6.11 retail transaction data are recorded on punched paper tape as a by-product of the operation of a point-of-sale keyboard by a sales clerk. The paper tape records are also subsequently converted to magnetic tape by the main computer.

Figure 6.12 illustrates a manual batching and filing procedure. In this case the source documents are vendor invoices that have been approved for payment. The manual operation symbol is used to represent the sorting of these invoices by hand according to their payment due date. Batch totals of amount due by due date are prepared as part of this process. The chronologically sorted invoices are then filed in separate batches. The annotation symbol is used to provide an extended description

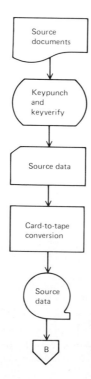

Fig. 6.10
Source data preparation using punched cards.

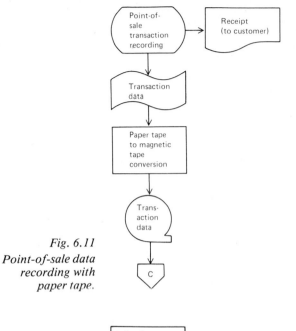

Fig. 6.11
Point-of-sale data
recording with
paper tape.

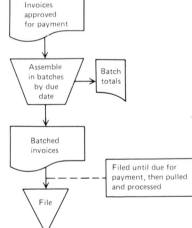

Fig. 6.12
Manual batching
and filing
procedure.

of the procedure followed at certain points in the flowcharted process—in this case at the point of filing the invoices.

Figure 6.13 illustrates both source data preparation and file processing using a diskette as the data entry medium. A key-to-diskette encoder is used to enter transaction data from source documents onto the diskette, and then a diskette drive is used to enter the data into the main computer for processing against the master file, which is stored on a magnetic disk unit. Because there is no sort step shown, the master file record pertaining to each transaction is apparently accessed randomly

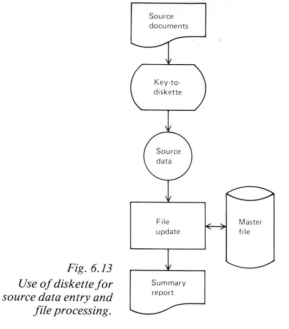

Fig. 6.13
Use of diskette for
source data entry and
file processing.

using the direct access feature of the disk. A summary report is generated as a by-product of the file updating process.

Figure 6.14 utilizes the offpage connector to represent the continuation of the processing steps shown in Fig. 6.10. The first process shown is the use of the central computer to sort the magnetic tape records into sequence according to the primary key of the master file. This is followed by sequential processing of the magnetic tape records to update the master file and generate a summary report. Note that the line connecting the magnetic disk master file to the CPU shows arrows going both ways. This is necessary because the updating of disk records consists of reading the old record from the disk into the CPU, updating it, and then writing the new record back onto the disk unit into the same location from which the old record was read.

Flowcharting symbols may be used to represent an equipment configuration as well as a data processing operation. For example, Fig. 6.15 illustrates a small configuration consisting of a teleprinter terminal, a remote CRT terminal, a CPU, and a magnetic disk file. Note that the communication link symbol is used to indicate that the CRT is geographically remote from the central processor, connected to it through a telephone hookup. In contrast, the ordinary line connecting the teleprinter to the central processor indicates that the teleprinter is located on the same site as the processor. A second factor of note in this illustration is the use of combinations of symbols to represent the terminals. There is no single flowcharting symbol with which to represent either a teleprinter terminal or a CRT display terminal. However, because a teleprinter consists of a keyboard and printer, it can be repre-

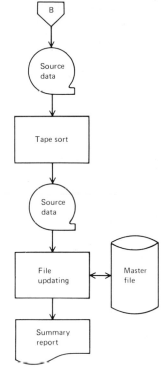

Fig. 6.14
Processing of source
data on magnetic tape
to update a master file
on magnetic disk.

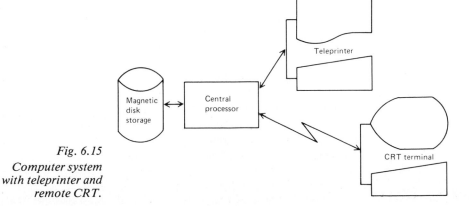

Fig. 6.15
Computer system
with teleprinter and
remote CRT.

sented by a combination of the online keyboard and document or report symbols. Similarly, a CRT terminal can be represented by a combination of the online keyboard and information display symbols.

A more typical business data processing equipment configuration is shown in Fig. 6.16. This illustrates a computer system that includes four tape drives, two disk

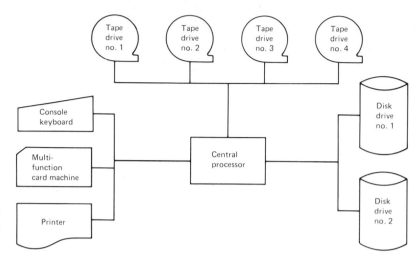

*Fig. 6.16
Business-oriented
computer system.*

drives, a multifunction card machine for punched card input and output, a printer, and a CPU with an online console keyboard. Note that the four tape drives are connected to the CPU through a single line; this line may be interpreted as representing the channel which is shared among all of the tape drives. The console keyboard, card machine, and printer share a second channel, and the two disk drives share a third channel.

Although our primary purpose here is to use systems flowcharting to illustrate data processing concepts, it should be pointed out that systems flowcharts are a very important tool of systems analysis. They play a key role in the evaluation of existing systems, the design of new systems, and the documentation of systems. Using a template makes them relatively easy to prepare. They are universally employed in systems work, and therefore provide a ready form of communication among systems personnel.

The eight sample flowcharts presented in this section have included at least one example of each of the 19 symbols included in Fig. 6.8. Additional systems flowcharts using these symbols are included in subsequent chapters. In addition, two other types of flowcharting are described and illustrated in subsequent chapters. These are program flowcharting, which is covered in the next chapter, and document flowcharting, covered in Chapter 11.

Batch processing   As mentioned previously, many data processing applications in business and accounting consist of the updating of master files for the occurence of transactions or other file activity, which is called file maintenance. Due to the high volume of input which is typical of many business data processing applications, it is common in business systems for transactions to be accumulated in batches that are processed at given time intervals or after the batch reaches a certain size. This method of data processing is referred to as *batch processing*.

If a batch of records to be processed is particularly large, one of the first steps in batch processing is often to manually assemble the source documents into smaller groups. Batch totals of dollar amounts and other important data items are then prepared for each group using an adding machine. The computation of separate batch totals for each group of records in this manner facilitates subsequent tracing and correcting of errors. The next step is to convert the input data from source documents to a machine-readable medium such as punched cards or magnetic tape. This is typically done using a keyboard-operated device such as a keypunch, key-to-tape encoder, key-to-diskette unit, or key-to-disk-to-tape system.

In updating a file using batch processing, the transactions are typically processed sequentially. If so, then the next step must be to sort the transaction records into sequential order according to the primary key of the master file. Sorting is accomplished most efficiently when the records to be sorted are on a magnetic tape file or a magnetic disk file. Therefore, records that are originally entered onto cards or diskettes will generally be read into the computer to be transferred onto a magnetic tape or disk prior to sorting. The sorting operation is controlled by the CPU. At the conclusion of the sorting operation, the records are still on the magnetic tape or disk file, but they have been rearranged into sequential order.

An alternative means of assembling transactions for batch processing is called *remote batch processing*. This approach involves accumulating transaction data for batch processing at one or more locations geographically separated from the central computer. The data may be accumulated on cards, magnetic tape, or paper tape. When a batch of transactions is ready to be processed, it is read into a special terminal and transmitted to the central computer by telephone lines or special cables. At the central computer site, the data may be written onto tape or disk and then sorted in preparation for processing.

Once the transactions have been sorted, the next step in batch processing is to process them on the computer together with the master file. The master file itself is most likely stored on either magnetic tape or disk. The central processor executes a file maintenance program, which results in the reading of the transactions and master file records, matching them according to their respective primary key values, computing the updated values of appropriate fields in the master file record, and then writing an updated version of the master file record onto tape or disk. At the same time, a document or report might be printed out. Another possible output is an error report and summary, which lists any erroneous transactions detected by the system together with batch totals, journal entries, and other summary information.

For master files stored on magnetic tape, sequential batch processing is the only practical means of file updating because of the sequential access nature of the file storage medium. For master files stored on magnetic disk, sequential batch processing is still a commonly used form of file updating. However, if the batch of transaction input is small, it may be practical to skip the sorting operation and process it nonsequentially, using the direct access feature of the disk file. Still another possibility is to process the transactions one by one as they occur instead of letting them accumulate in batches; this mode of processing is discussed further in the next section.

There is one significant difference between updating a master file stored on magnetic tape and updating one stored on magnetic disk. When a magnetic tape file is updated, there are two versions of the master file—the old version that is read into the computer, and the new version that is written onto a second reel of tape by a second tape drive. When processing is completed, the old version of the master still exists in the same form as it existed prior to processing. This is not true when a magnetic disk file is updated. Instead, each old magnetic disk record is read into the CPU, updated, and then written back onto the same disk unit, into the same location as the old record, thereby erasing the old version of the record. When processing is completed, only the new version of the file exists on the magnetic disk.

An example of a generalized batch processing operation similar to that described in this section is flowcharted in Fig. 6.17. This chart could represent any number of specific accounting applications, such as the updating of an accounts receivable file for sales and cash receipt transactions, or the updating of an inventory file for issues and receipts. The process shown could be completed using the configuration represented in Fig. 6.16. The processing steps shown in Fig. 6.17 are very similar to those described earlier in this section.

To further clarify the concepts of computerized batch processing, suppose that the process illustrated in Fig. 6.17 involves accounts receivable. Then the source documents are probably sales orders and/or cash receipt tickets. Batch totals would

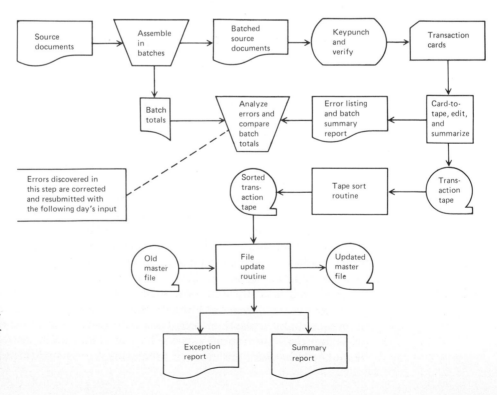

Fig. 6.17
Systems flowchart of a generalized batch processing system for file maintenance.

be accumulated for such data items as the gross dollar amount ordered, the net dollar value of shipments, and the amount of cash received on account. The data to be keypunched would include items such as the customer account number, transaction date, and dollar amount. Transactions would be sorted by account number, which would be the primary key of the accounts receivable master file. The exception report generated during the file updating process would probably be a listing of past due accounts. The summary report would include aggregate journal entries to the cash, accounts receivable, and sales revenue accounts.

Online processing

The term *online processing* refers to the processing of individual transactions through a system as they occur and from their point of origin as opposed to accumulating them in batches. Online processing generally requires that data files be maintained on a direct access storage device. The means of input is typically a network of data terminals, many of which may be geographically remote from the location of the central computer system. Thus the minimum equipment configuration for online processing is similar to that illustrated in Fig. 6.15.

Two major categories of online processing are online updating and inquiry processing. *Online updating* is a form of file maintenance in which individual transactions are processed to update a master file immediately as they occur. In *inquiry processing* the computer system responds to queries from users about information in the file.

In online updating the keying of a transaction into the system initiates the direct accessing of the record in storage to which that transaction pertains. That record is read into the central processor, updated, and then written back onto the online storage device. At the same time a record of the transaction itself may be written on tape or some other medium. The process may also result in the printing of a document relating to the transaction, such as an invoice if the transaction is a sale.

In inquiry processing the nature of an inquiry may be very simple or very complex. The simplest form of inquiry is a request to examine the contents of a particular record in a file. Examples of more complex inquiries would be a request to list all customers whose accounts are more than 60 days past due, or to list the five salespeople in the state of Texas whose total dollar volume of sales was highest for the month of May. To process such inquiries, special programs and advanced file organization techniques are required. These are described in Chapter 8 of this book.

In most business data processing systems that use online processing, there will be some applications for which processing is done in the batch mode, and others for which processing is done in the online mode. As a result, several online users may desire to access the computer at the same time, and that may also be the time during which a batch job is being run. This requires that the system use multiprogramming. However, in a conventional multiprogramming environment, the system continues processing a particular user program until that program issues an input or output command; the system then forwards this command to the appropriate channel and proceeds to the next user program. If one or more of the programs in the system at a particular time involve complex calculations and limited input and output, they may tie up the CPU for long periods of time, causing the other programs to wait. This may be fine if all of the programs in the system are batch processing jobs. However, if some of the programs in the system are online processing jobs, this form of multiprogramming will frequently cause online users to wait long periods of time for the system to respond, and this represents a very significant problem. To avoid this problem, an alternative form of multiprogramming called *time-sharing* is used in online systems. In time-sharing a tiny fraction of time is allocated to the current program, and if this is used up the system will place that program at the end of its queue and transfer its attention to the next program. As a result, no single program can tie up the system for a period of time longer than the prespecified time fraction. The system is always able to work its way rapidly through its queue of programs, with the objective of making each online user perceive that the system has devoted its full attention to his or her job.

Online updating of files provides the advantage that all records are up to date at all times. Any user can therefore obtain up-to-date information in response to a request. Such a capability is very useful in decision making or in dealing with customers. In contrast, with batch processing, files are up to date only immediately after the processing of a batch is completed, which may be once a day, once a week, or even once a month. Another advantage of online updating is that it minimizes or eliminates the need for record transcription, sorting, and similar batching operations.

Online processing also has some disadvantages relative to batch processing. The software required for online processing is generally much more expensive. If transactions originate in a large number of scattered locations, the cost of data terminals and data communications facilities could be extremely high. Online processing is also less efficient than batch processing in terms of machine utilization; that is, it takes more machine time to process a set of transactions individually than sequentially in a batch.

The decision of whether online or batch processing is appropriate for a particular application must be made on an individual basis. Among accounting applications, those best suited to online processing relate to the information necessary to provide high levels of service to customers. For example, if data pertaining to finished goods inventories are maintained by online processing, a salesperson utilizing a data terminal can provide up-to-date information to a customer regarding the availability of any number of inventory items. If the customer decides to purchase, the salesperson can enter the necessary transaction data on the terminal, resulting in the reduction of inventory balances for the items purchased and the preparation of documents authorizing shipment. The customer can be told on the spot the day upon which to expect delivery. If batch processing were used for an application of this sort, a salesperson would not always be certain whether particular items were available, there could easily be a delay in delivery due to the time required to process the transaction, and the salesperson would be less reliable in estimating a delivery date. Thus an online processing system oriented toward customer service can provide a company with a competitive advantage. The crucial question is whether the benefit from such a competitive advantage is great enough to offset the extra cost of the system.

**Review
Questions**

1. Define the following terms.

plotter	turnkey system
sequential access	megabyte
direct access	input/output bound
block	throughput
interblock gap	overlap
volatile	channel
track	multiprogramming
fixed disk	spooling
removable disk	flowchart
disk pack	systems flowchart
fixed-head disk	template
moving-head disk	batch processing
configuration	remote batch processing
microprocessor	online processing
microcomputer	online updating
personal computer	inquiry processing
desktop computer	time-sharing
minicomputer	

2. Identify and describe several forms of computer output devices and media. If possible, indicate for each a range of output speed.

3. What are the basic advantages and disadvantages of impact printers relative to nonimpact printers?

4. Identify the two basic categories of secondary storage and explain their essential differences.

5. What are the relative advantages and disadvantages of punched cards and magnetic tape as secondary storage media?

6. Explain how the blocking of records affects the reading speed and data storage capacity of magnetic tape.

7. Identify several types of direct access secondary storage devices. Which are the most commonly used today?

8. Explain how data are stored on a magnetic disk. How are stored data read from a magnetic disk? Explain some of the ways in which magnetic disk units may be classified.

9. What is the general range of storage capacities for currently available magnetic disk storage units?

10. What is the major difference between the ordinary magnetic disk and the diskette as a secondary storage medium?

11. Give some examples of accounting applications for which direct access file storage may be useful.

12. Identify four general categories of computer system hardware configurations. List several items of computer hardware that you might expect to find in a busi-

ness-oriented system within each of the four categories. What would be a typical price for each of these systems?

13. Identify several possible applications of desktop computers in accounting and business.

14. What significant impact did the development of the minicomputer have on the use of computer systems in organizations?

15. Describe the nature and use of small accounting computers. Explain how magnetic stripe ledger records are used with some small accounting computers.

16. Give a detailed example of how a small accounting computer might be used in performing a data processing task.

17. Identify several factors which distinguish a medium-scale computer system from a small business computer system.

18. Compare and contrast the typical business data processing application with the typical scientific application. Into which category would the solution of an operations research model of a business problem using a computer fall?

19. Will the creation of faster central processing units necessarily increase throughput in business data processing? Explain. What recent developments have helped to increase throughput in business data processing?

20. What approaches to systems design can help to maximize throughput in a business data processing system?

21. Explain why a knowledge of computer system efficiency considerations may be relevant to an accountant.

22. What are three major categories of systems flowcharting symbols? Identify the specific symbols within each category, and explain the meaning of each.

23. Explain the ''sandwich theory'' of systems flowcharting, and give two examples.

24. Explain why systems flowcharts are useful in the study of information systems and in the practice of systems design.

25. Describe the steps in a file maintenance procedure using batch processing in a computer system.

26. Is a sequential access storage medium the only appropriate kind for batch processing applications? Explain.

27. What significant difference exists between the way a magnetic tape file is updated and the way a magnetic disk file is updated?

28. In online processing what means of input and what type of file storage are generally used?

29. What are some examples of the kinds of inquiries to which an inquiry processing system must be designed to respond?

30. What are the relative advantages and disadvantages of online processing and batch processing? How does a systems analyst decide which is more appropriate in a given case?

31. What kinds of accounting applications are best suited to online processing? Describe an example.

Discussion Questions

32. Volume of processing is an important consideration in the design of a data processing system. Explain how volume of processing would be taken into consideration in selecting the best equipment configuration for a computer system.

33. Computers are highly reliable. Would you expect that a computer system would therefore have little need for accounting controls to check the accuracy of processing and to safeguard assets? Discuss.

34. Do you believe that it is necessary for an accountant to have an understanding of computer data processing as covered in this and the prior chapter? Discuss.

Problems and Cases

35. You wish to compare the input speeds of several devices. The devices and speeds as given by producers of each device are as follows.

- card reader, 600 cards per minute
- tape drive, 30,000 characters per second
- punched tape reader, 400 characters per second
- terminal, 6000 keystrokes per hour
- OCR, 800 characters per second

Your problem is that the device speeds are not all stated in terms of a common measure. Convert all of these speeds to "records per minute" where it is assumed that each input record contains 80 characters. For magnetic tape assume that records are blocked in sets of six, that the tape recording density is 800 bytes per inch, and that the width of each interblock gap is 0.6 inch.

36. You wish to store employee payroll records on a reel of magnetic tape 2400 feet long with a density of 800 bytes per inch, and with interblock gaps measuring 0.6 inch. Each record contains 400 characters, and there are 800 byte storage positions available in the central processor for storing a block of input records.

   a) How many employee payroll records may be stored on one reel of magnetic tape?

   b) Assume that the magnetic tape has nine tracks and that, by storing data in packed form, the equivalent of 80 percent of the data in each record can be stored at two characters per byte. Compute the effect of this change in assumptions on your answer to (a).

37. Prepare systems flowcharting segments for each of the operations described below.

   a) processing of transactions on punched cards on the computer to update a master file stored on magnetic tape,

   b) processing of transactions on punched cards on the computer to update a master file stored on a magnetic disk unit,

   c) conversion of source data from OCR documents to magnetic tape using an offline OCR reader/converter,

   d) online processing of OCR documents to update a master file on magnetic tape,

    e) reading of data on paper tape into the computer to be listed on a printed report,

    f) keying of data from source documents to magnetic tape using an offline key-to-tape encoder,

    g) manual sorting and filing of invoices,

    h) online processing of source data using a CRT terminal from a remote location to a central computer system for updating a magnetic disk master file and also for recording the source data on a magnetic tape file.

38. Suppose that a payroll record having 538 characters is stored in unpacked form on a disk file. The disk unit has a head movement time of 30 milliseconds, a rotation speed of 3600 revolutions per minute, and a transfer rate of 806,000 bytes per second. The record is to be accessed randomly in response to a management inquiry.

Required

    a) How much time is required for the disk unit to read the record?

    b) Consider each of the following changes in assumptions independently of the others, and compute a revised answer to (a).

      i) The disk unit is a fixed-head disk.

      ii) The record is accessed sequentially as part of a batch processing run.

      iii) The bit storage density is doubled, which doubles the transfer rate.

      iv) The rotation speed is only 3125 revolutions per minute.

      v) Of the 538 characters, 324 are numeric and are stored in packed form.

39. The Dewey Construction Company processes its payroll transactions to update both its payroll master file and work-in-process master file in the same computer run. The payroll master file is maintained on magnetic tape and accessed sequentially, while the work-in-process master is maintained on disk and accessed randomly.

Input to this system is keypunched and verified from job time tickets. The cards are then read into the computer to transfer their contents to magnetic tape. The tape is then processed by a tape sorting routine on the computer to sort the records into sequence by employee number. The sorted tape is then processed to update the files. This run also produces a payroll register on magnetic tape, employee paychecks and earnings statements, and a printed report listing error transactions and summary information.

Required

Prepare a systems flowchart of the process described above.

40. You are a systems analyst employed by the New Acme Manufacturing Company. You have been asked to design a computer system application that will control the company's raw materials and parts inventories. A master file will be maintained and updated twice weekly for purchases, production usage, and other transactions. The average size of each master record will be 400 characters, and there will be about 20,000 records in the master file.

Required

    a) Assume that you have a choice of designing this system so that the master file is stored on either magnetic disk or magnetic tape. All of the equipment required for either approach is available. Explain the arguments which could be advanced in favor of *both* approaches.

b) Consider each of the following items of additional information independently, and explain whether or not it would affect the choice between tape and disk, and if so, how.

   i) The activity ratio for each update run will be close to 100 percent.

   ii) The activity ratio for each update run will be close to 1 percent.

   iii) Production planners will require frequent access to the information in the file.

   iv) The size of the file is expected to double within five years.

41. The Happy Valley Utility Company uses turnaround documents in its computerized customer accounting system. Meter readers are provided with pre-printed forms prepared by the computer, each containing the account number, name, address, and previous meter readings of a customer. Each of these forms also contains a formatted area in which the customer's current meter reading may be marked in pencil. After making their rounds, meter readers turn in batches of these documents to the computer data preparation department, where they are processed by a mark-sense document reader that transfers their contents to magnetic tape.

The magnetic tape file containing the customer meter readings is then sent to the computer center where it becomes input to two computer runs. The first run sorts the transactions records on the tape into sequential order by customer account number. On the second run, the sorted transaction tape is processed against the customer master file, which is stored on a magnetic disk unit. Outputs of this second run are (1) a printed report listing summary information and any erroneous transactions detected by the computer, and (2) customer bills printed in a special OCR-readable font. The bills are mailed to the customers, with the request that the stub portion be returned with the customer's payment.

Customer payments are received in the mail room, where they are checked for agreement with the returned stubs. Customer checks are then sent to the cashier's office. The mail room provides the data preparation department with three sets of records, (1) stubs for which the amount received agrees with the stub amount, (2) stubs for which the amount received differs from the stub amount, and (3) a list of amounts received from customers who did not return their stubs. For the latter two types of records, data preparation personnel use a special typewriter to prepare corrected stubs. All of the stubs are then processed by an OCR document reader which transfers their contents onto magnetic tape.

The magnetic tape containing the payment records is then sent to the computer center where it is (1) sorted on the computer into sequential order by customer account number, and (2) processed against the customer master file to post the payment amounts. Two printed outputs from this second process are (1) a report listing erroneous transactions and summary information, and (2) a report listing past due customer balances.

Required   a) Draw a systems flowchart of the billing operations, commencing with the computer preparation of the meter reading forms, and ending with the mailing of bills to customers.

b) Draw a systems flowchart of the processing of customer payments, starting with the mail room operations and ending with the computer run that posts the payment amounts to the customer master file.

c) Prepare a list of the equipment in the company's hardware configuration that is required at a minimum to accomplish all of the operations described.

42. You are involved in design of a systems application in which a group of records are to be sorted and processed to update a disk file. The records are originally keypunched onto cards. The hardware that might be used includes a card sorter, a small computer system, and a large computer system. The card sorter operates at 2000 cards per minute and all costs relating to its operation total $3 per hour. The small computer system has a 1000-cards-per-minute card reader and tape drives whose operation may be overlapped with the card reader. All costs relating to the operation of the small computer system total $48 per hour. The large computer system also has a 1000-cards-per-minute card reader, and tape drives that process at 30,000 characters per second. All costs relating to operation of the large system total $120 per hour.

There are 13,500 records of 80 characters each, with a numeric control field of eight characters. They may be stored on tape in blocks of nine records. The magnetic tape has a density of 800 bytes per inch and an interblock gap of 0.6 inch. Assume that every machine operation requires a set-up time of three minutes. Further assume that a tape sort on the small computer would require ten minutes (not including set-up) and on the large computer would require three minutes (not including set-up). Finally, note that if cards are sorted on the card sorter, one pass is required for each digit in the sort field, although the set-up time is incurred only once.

The disk file is part of the large computer system, and its operation may be overlapped either with card or tape input operations. You must determine the fastest and most economical way of sorting and processing the transaction records. Your design choices are (1) sort the cards using the card sorter, after which either (a) the cards could be processed directly on the large computer, or (b) the data on cards could be transferred to tape on the small computer and the tape processed on the large computer; or (2) transfer the unsorted card data to tape on the small computer, after which a tape sort would be performed either by (a) the small computer or (b) the large computer, after which the tape would be processed on the large computer.

Required   Determine the time required and cost incurred by each of the four approaches outlined above. Assume that the cost rates provided for each machine apply to set-up times as well as operating times. Also assume that processing operations on the large computer are bound by the speed of tape processing.

43. The Cain Company uses a card-oriented computer system in its billing operation. As part of this operation, a file of 13,000 prepunched cards is maintained, each of which contains the account number, name, and address of one of the company's 13,000 customers. This file is maintained in sequence by customer account number, a six-digit field. Also maintained are batches of commodity cards, each of which is prepunched with the item number, description, and price of an inventory item.

When a sale is made to a customer, clerks manually obtain one commodity card for each item type purchased by the customer. The cards and corresponding sale documents are provided to keypunch operators for keying the customer account number, date, and quantity sold onto each commodity card. On the average there are 1000 sales orders processed daily.

In the next processing step, the commodity cards are sorted by account number on a card sorter. Then both the commodity cards and name and address cards are processed on the computer and multifunction card machine to compute and punch extensions (price $\times$ quantity) into the commodity cards and to merge the two decks into one. During this process, unmatched commodity cards are selected out for manual error correction and subsequent resubmission.

The next step is to process the matched deck together with a deck of blank cards on both the computer and multifunction card machine. During this step the system prints customer invoices and punches and prints summary invoice cards. It also separates the name and address cards from the commodity cards. The name and address cards are saved for the next day's processing, while the commodity cards are also saved for use in subsequent processing. The summary invoice cards are then merged into a permanent file of summary invoice cards.

Required

a) Prepare a systems flowchart of the processing steps described.

b) Assume that the company has just acquired magnetic tape drives and magnetic disk storage equipment for its computer, in addition to its punched card equipment. Describe how the billing system could be redesigned to use the tape and/or disk equipment.

c) Prepare a systems flowchart illustrating the redesigned system which you described in response to part (b).

44. The Central Purchasing Office of the Sunnydale Electronics Company uses a card-oriented computer system to maintain accounts payable records and prepare checks in payment of accounts. Input to this process consists of vendor invoices that have been approved for payment. Each invoice contains, among other things, the vendor's name and address, the quantity and price of each item purchased, the gross invoice total, the due date of payment, and the discount rate. In addition to approval of payment, the purchasing department also writes the vendor's code number on the invoice.

The data processing section maintains a master file in which the data for each unpaid vendor invoice is on a punched card. This file is sequenced by vendor code number, and augmented each day by new invoices approved that day. Each day the newly approved invoices are keypunched, keyverified, sorted by vendor code number on a card sorter, and processed on both the computer and multifunction card machine together with the invoice master file. This last step merges the two decks together, while simultaneously selecting out all invoice cards due for payment on that day. A listing of all of the newly approved invoices is printed during this step.

The next step is to process the invoice cards due for payment, together with pre-printed blank check cards, on both the multifunction card machine and the computer. During this step, the vendor name, date, and amount are printed on each check, and a printed listing of disbursements is prepared.

Required

a) Prepare a systems flowchart of the processing steps described.

b) Assume that the company has acquired magnetic tape drives and magnetic disk storage equipment for its computer system, in addition to its punched card equipment. Describe how the accounts payable system could be redesigned to use the tape and/or disk equipment.

c) Prepare a systems flowchart illustrating your solution to (b).

45. The independent auditor must evaluate a client's system of internal control to determine the extent to which various auditing procedures must be employed. A client who uses a computer should provide the CPA with a flowchart of the information processing system so the CPA can evaluate the control features in the system. Shown in Fig. 6.18 is a simplified flowchart, such as a client might provide. Unfortunately the client had only partially completed the flowchart when it was requested by you.

Required

a) Complete the flowchart shown in Fig. 6.18.

b) Describe what each item in the flowchart indicates. When complete, your description should provide an explanation of the processing of the data involved. Your description should be in the following order.

  i) "Orders from Salesman" to "Run No. 5."

  ii) "From Mailroom" to "Run No. 5."

  iii) "Run No. 5" through the remainder of the chart.

c) Name each of the flowchart symbols shown below and describe what each represents.[1]

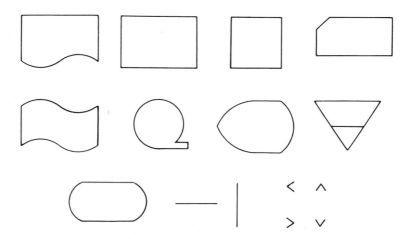

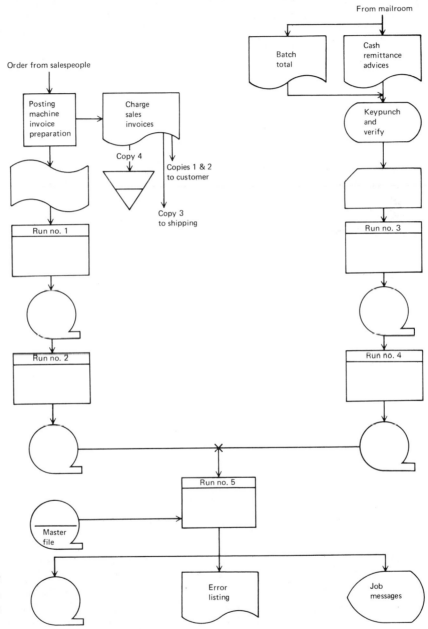

*Fig. 6.18
Partially com-
pleted system
flowchart.*

References   Bhandarkar, D. P.; J. B. Barton; and A. F. Tasch, Jr. "Charge-Coupled Device Memories: A Perspective." *Computer* (January 1979): 16–24.

Bohl, Marilyn. *Information Processing* (3rd ed.). Chicago: Science Research Associates, 1980.

Bromberg, Howard. "The Consequences of Minicomputers." *Datamation* (November 15, 1978): 98–103.

Chapin, Ned. *Flowcharts.* Princeton: Auerbach, 1971.

Datapro Research Corporation. "All about Small Business Computers." In *Datapro 70: The EDP Buyer's Bible.* Delran, N.J.: Datapro Research Corporation, 1980.

_____. "IBM 4300 Series." In *Datapro 70: The EDP Buyer's Bible.* Delran, N.J.: Datapro Research Corporation, 1980.

Davis, William S. *Information Processing Systems.* Reading, Mass.: Addison-Wesley, 1978.

Dock, V. Thomas, and Edward L. Essick. *Principles of Business Data Processing with MIS.....including BASIC.* (4th ed.). Chicago: Science Research Associates, 1981.

Dowell, J. Richard. "So, You Want to Buy a Minicomputer?" *Price Waterhouse and Co. Review,* Vol. 22, No. 3 (1977): 18–25.

Hoagland, A. S. "Storage Technology: Capabilities and Limitations." *Computer* (May 1979): 12–18.

Honickman, Howard W. "Minicomputers—A Big Risk?" *CA Magazine* (August 1979): 42–52.

Howson, Hugh R. "The Microcomputer Challenge." *CA Magazine* (August 1977): 50–53.

Juliessen, J. Egil. "Where Bubble Memory Will Find a Niche." *Mini-Micro Systems* (July 1979): 48–61.

Kapur, Gopal K. "Minicomputers: The Future Is Now." *Journal of Applied Management* (July/August 1979): 13–18.

Lines, M. Vardell, and Boeing Computer Services Company. *Minicomputer Systems.* Cambridge, Mass.: Winthrop, 1980.

Lusa, John M. "The COM Peripheral: An Idea Whose Time Has Come." *Infosystems* (March 1979): 60–64.

Pittis, Alan R. "The Future of Large Computer Systems." *CA Magazine* (March 1979): 70–74.

Ross, Edward A., and Lewis I. Solomon. "Technology Trends in Desktop Computers." *Mini-Micro Systems* (December 1978): 46–57.

Schwartz, Donald A. "Microcomputers Take Aim on Small Business Clients." *The Journal of Accountancy* (December 1979): 57–62.

Solomon, Leslie. "A New Approach to Data Storage: Bubble Memories." *Popular Electronics* (February 1979): 74–76.

Stiefel, Malcolm L. "Small Business Computers." *Mini–Micro Systems* (March 1978): 60–74.

White, Robert M. "Disk-Storage Technology." *Scientific American* (August 1980): 138–148.

Wieselman, Irving L. "Product Profile: Printers." *Mini–Micro Systems* (January 1978): 52–70.

_____. "Technology Profile: Non-Impact Printing in the 1980s." *Mini–Micro Systems* (January 1980): 93–100.

Withington, Frederick G. "Beyond 1984: A Technology Forecast." *Datamation* (January 1975): 54–73.

Wooldridge, Susan. *Computer Output Design.* New York: Petrocelli/Charter, 1975.

Chapter 7

Computer Software and Programming

The term software refers primarily to computer programs but also encompasses related nonhardware elements of computer systems. These include operating manuals, program documentation, and the standards and techniques used in systems analysis and program development. Software is certainly as essential a part of a computer system as its hardware. It has been mentioned that one of the features of a computer that sets it apart from less sophisticated data processing devices is its ability to store and execute a program of instructions without human intervention. For a majority of computer users, the costs relating to software, including the personnel costs of systems analysis and programming, exceed those relating to hardware. The purpose of this chapter is to build a foundation of understanding of computer software and its development.

Software development is the objective of *programming*, which might be defined as the process of preparing a set of computer instructions for accomplishing a data processing task or solving a problem. Computer programming has become a significant occupational skill in our society. It is estimated that over 200,000 persons are presently employed as computer programmers. A continuing problem for those organizations which use computers is that the demand for qualified programmers far exceeds the supply.

A Survey of Software Concepts

Several major categories of software are reviewed in this section. These include programming languages, application programs, utility routines, operating systems, and nonprogram software. The section concludes with a discussion of the software used in accounting systems.

Programming languages

A programming language is the basic tool that a computer programmer uses to instruct a computer. There are many different programming languages. Each make of computer has its own *machine language,* in which each instruction is written in a binary code that may be interpreted by the internal circuitry of that computer. Each machine language instruction is simply a string of zeroes and ones. A typical machine language instruction might consist of (1) an operation code, (2) the address of one or two *operands,* which are the data items upon which the operation is performed, (3) an address in which the result of the operation is to be stored, and/or (4) the address of the next instruction to be performed. Programming in machine language is very difficult not only because of the inherent complexity of the binary instruction codes but also because the programmer must keep track of the storage addresses of each instruction and data item used in the program. Because of these difficulties, programming in machine language is no longer common. Most programming in business organizations is done using either of two basic types of programming languages: a *symbolic language* or a *procedure-oriented language.*

In a symbolic language each machine instruction is represented by a mnemonic symbol that bears some relation to the instruction. For example, the symbols "A," "CP," "GET," and "MV" might represent "Add," "Compare," "Read," and "Move" instructions, respectively. Furthermore, each data item used in the program is given a name, and the computer keeps track of the storage address where each named item of data is stored. These improvements greatly simplify the programming process.

Because instructions in its own machine language are the only commands that a computer can directly understand and execute, a symbolic language program must be converted to machine language before it can be used on the computer. This conversion is accomplished by a special program called an *assembler.* In this conversion process, the symbolic language program, called the *source program,* and the assembler are input to the central processing unit, and the machine language program, called the *object program,* is the output. Upon completion of this conversion, the object program is ready to be processed.

Procedure-oriented languages, examples of which are FORTRAN and COBOL, are designed to simplify the programming process even further. One simplification is the use of *macroinstructions,* which are instructions that translate into two or more machine language instructions. For example, the macroinstruction "ADD A TO B GIVING C" would be translated into a series of machine language instructions involving moving the values of A and B from storage addresses in primary memory to registers in the arithmetic and logic unit, summing the contents of those registers, reserving a new address labeled ''C'' in primary memory, and moving the sum to this new address. Because macroinstructions in a procedure-oriented language consist of mathematical formulas or even English language expressions, they are much more easier to use and interpret than are the codes of symbolic and machine languages.

In contrast to symbolic languages, a procedure-oriented language is *machine independent,* which means that the same language can be used on any make of computer, although some minor differences may exist between different machines. As with symbolic language programs, it is necessary for programs written in a procedure-oriented language to be converted to machine language. Programs that perform this conversion are called *compilers.* The terms source program and object program have the same meaning with respect to compiler programs as they do with respect to assembler programs.

A systems flowchart showing the process of compiling and executing a program written in procedure-oriented language appears in Fig. 7.1. As the chart shows, in order to translate a program written in a particular procedure-oriented language, the computer must first read in the compiler program for that particular language. The compiler program accepts the source program statements as input, translates them into a machine language object program[1] that is written onto a temporary disk file, and also prints a report listing the source program. If there are any programming errors, this compilation report will include *diagnostics,* which are codes or messages indicating the location and nature of each error. The presence of significant programming errors will abort the program before it is executed. If there are no significant programming errors, the machine language object program is then read into the computer from its temporary disk file. This program is then executed (processed), which causes input data and/or file records to be read into the computer, and results (printed reports and/or updated files) to be written out.

In an online environment where several users working at terminals are each writing their own programs in a procedure-oriented language, the use of compilers is inefficient because a separate copy of the compiler program is required for each user. To overcome this problem, an alternative type of translation program called an *interpreter* is used for procedure-oriented languages such as BASIC that are generally used in an online mode. An interpreter translates each programming instruction into machine language immediately as it is entered by the user, and when necessary immediately prints appropriate error messages on the user's terminal. Only one copy of the interpreter program needs to be maintained on the computer, and this program simply directs its attention back and forth among users as each user enters program statements to be interpreted.

The use of procedure-oriented languages in writing computer programs offers several advantages over the use of symbolic languages. Procedure-oriented languages are generally much easier to learn than symbolic languages. They enable pro-

---

[1] *A variation of this procedure is for the compiler to translate the instructions into symbolic language, after which an assembler is used to translate them from symbolic to machine language.*

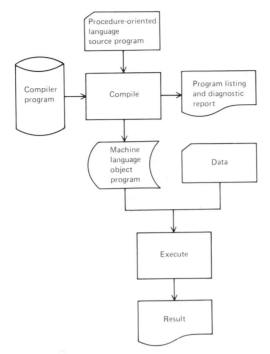

Fig. 7.1
Compiling and executing a procedure-oriented language program.

grammers to write programs much faster. Because the language instructions are fairly simple to interpret, a procedure-oriented language program offers better documentation than a symbolic language program, which also makes it easier to revise existing programs. The feature of machine independence also provides significant advantages for procedure-oriented languages. Programs do not become obsolete when a new computer is installed. Programs can be shared with other users. General programs for particular applications can be purchased.

There are significant disadvantages of procedure-oriented languages relative to symbolic languages. Perhaps the major disadvantage is that a program written in symbolic language by an expert programmer is likely to be much more efficient than one compiled from a procedure-oriented language. Because there is a one-to-one correspondence between symbolic language instructions and machine language instructions, a programmer writing in symbolic language can take maximum advantage of his or her expertise in designing an efficient program. It is difficult to design a compiler program that is as skillful as an expert programmer. Thus a machine language program produced by a compiler is likely to be slower and consume more core storage than if the same program were originally written in symbolic language. The difference in computer run time becomes quite significant if the program is one which must be used on a regular basis.

Another disadvantage of procedure-oriented languages is that their regular use may consume significant quantities of computer time in the process of compilation.

In contrast, the conversion of symbolic language programs to machine language consumes relatively less time. Still another disadvantage is that a compiler program itself may be quite large, and could require more primary storage than is available on smaller computers.

The question of whether procedure-oriented languages or symbolic languages are "better" for business data processing applications has no clear-cut answer. Some computer users may utilize both, choosing between them on the basis of each individual application. Thus a program to be run only once would probably be written in a procedure-oriented language, whereas a program to be used regularly over a long period of time might be written in symbolic language. Some installations may use only procedure-oriented languages because most of the programmers are not familiar with the symbolic language. Other installations may use only symbolic language because of limited availability of primary storage. Installations which do primarily batch processing may not be making full use of available central processor time, and so would probably be less concerned about the reduced efficiency of procedure-oriented language programs. Generally if there is any trend taking place, it is probably in the direction of greater use of procedure-oriented languages.

Application programs

Application programs include those which are used for the specific computer applications of the user. A computer user may purchase standard application programs from manufacturers or software vendors, or may prepare original application programs. In a business data processing system, many different types of application programs are used. Some of the major categories include file maintenance, report generation, information retrieval, and problem solving. Each of these application categories is examined in turn in this section.

File maintenance   The most common form of utilization of business data processing programs is for file maintenance, which has previously been defined as the updating of a master file for the occurrence of transactions. Examples of files whose maintenance is an accounting function include payroll files, accounts payable and receivable files, and inventory files. File maintenance may be performed in a batch processing or online processing mode. File maintenance programs also generally perform certain other functions, such as the editing of input data for errors and the preparation of reports and documents.

File maintenance applications generally involve the processing of a wide range of file activity. On the one hand are regularly recurring transactions, such as sale of goods on account or purchase of inventory. On the other hand, there are many different types of nonrecurring transactions, such as the addition or deletion of a record, a change in an employee's pay rate or in the price of an inventory item, or the correction of an erroneous record. Generally it is more efficient to update a master file for all of the different types of transactions that affect it in a single processing run, using a single program. When the number of different kinds of transactions affecting a given file is large, as is commonly the case in many business applications, one can see that the file maintenance program can be very complex.

Report generation   As the name implies, these programs prepare management reports. In business systems, report generation programs generally utilize updated master files as input. The functions which they perform on this data include summarization and highlighting of exception conditions. Examples of summarization by report generation programs include reports analyzing total unit and dollar sales by product line, or reports classifying total accounts receivable into totals of current accounts and past due accounts. The latter can be further classified according to the number of days past due. Examples of highlighting of exception conditions by report generation programs are reports listing the ten best-selling and ten worst-selling products or salespeople, or reports listing all accounts that are more than 60 days past due. Report generation programs may be used in either a batch processing or online processing mode.

Information retrieval   Programs of this type are utilized in online systems to provide quick responses to user inquiries concerning the contents of data files. The functions which they perform include the retrieval and display of any record specified by the user, or the selection and display of records from a file having one or more characteristics specified by the user. An example of the latter function is the selection from an accounts receivable file of all accounts that are both 60 or more days past due and in excess of $1000. Information retrieval in this sense is synonymous with inquiry processing.

Problem solving   The category of problem-solving applications in business data processing encompasses a wide variety of mathematical analysis techniques used to facilitate management decision making. Of importance are statistical applications involving correlation and regression, analysis of variance, statistical sampling, or time-series analysis. Also significant are applications utilizing operations research models, such as linear programming, inventory models, queueing models, PERT and critical path analysis, and simulation. Other examples include cash flow discounting, forecasting, and cost-volume-profit analysis. The input to such application programs may be in the form of regular business files, but more often than not the required input must be extracted from several different files and specially formatted to meet the requirements of the problem solving technique. The output of a problem solving program generally consists of a short printed report.

System software   Whereas application programs are written by a specific programmer to solve a problem for a specific user, *system software* consists of programs that perform general data processing functions useful to most or to all system users. Language translators such as assemblers, compilers, and interpreters represent one major category of system software. Two other major categories of system software discussed in this section are operating systems and utility routines.

Operating systems   An *operating system* is a group of related programs that manage the processing operations of a computer. Each make of computer has an operating system written for it by the computer manufacturer. The operating system resides in main memory, or in an offline storage device readily accessible to main memory, at all times.

The operating system performs administrative functions such as scheduling of jobs, allocation of primary memory space to the programs and data needed for those jobs, maintenance of logs and operating statistics relating to each job, communication with equipment operators, and coordination of operations for the variety of input and output devices found in modern computer systems. Prior to the advent of multiprogramming, operating systems were relatively simple. However, in a multiprogrammed system several jobs are being processed on the computer at the same time, and the operating system must be very sophisticated in order to successfully manage all of the programs, data, and peripheral devices that are simultaneously under its control.

Some of the primary component programs of an operating system include the job control program, the scheduling program, the library manager, the memory manager, the peripherals manager, and the supervisor. The job control program reads and interprets instructions written in *job-control language* (JCL), which is the language used to instruct the operating system. The scheduling program establishes priorities for all jobs being processed or waiting to be processed on the system. The library manager keeps track of the storage locations of all language translators, application programs, utility routines, and other system programs in order that these programs may be retrieved and read into primary memory when they are called upon. The memory manager assigns primary memory space to programs and data, maintains a record of the status of all available areas of primary memory, and protects the areas reserved for one program from being used by other programs. The peripherals manager controls the assignment of input and output devices to jobs in process. Finally, the supervisor may be viewed as the "chief executive officer" among all of the programs in the system; it directs the operations of all the other programs and is called upon to resolve any conflicts in job scheduling or resource management in the manner that is most efficient from the standpoint of the system as a whole.

Utility routines   Programs designed to perform common data processing functions that are a necessary part of many applications are called *utility routines.* Common examples include programs to sort and merge files on tape or disk, programs to transfer data from one medium to another (cards to tape, tape to disk, etc.), and programs to translate data from one coding system into another. Other examples include program debugging aids such as a memory dump program that prints out the contents of computer memory to assist a programmer in locating program errors, or a trace routine that prints out data values and diagnostic information after the execution of each program instruction. A *text editor,* which is a program that enables a user to modify the contents of a program or data file from an online terminal, is another example. Routines which perform spooling (see Chapter 6) are still another example. Perhaps the most complex example of a utility routine is a file management system, which coordinates updating and retrieval of data on master files. Data base management systems, which are the most sophisticated form of file management systems, are discussed at length in the next chapter.

An overview of program software

Numerous examples and categories of program software have been discussed thus far in this section. Figure 7.2 illustrates how all of these various forms of program software fit together in a typical data processing system. As the form of the illustration suggests, program software within a data processing system has an organization structure similar to that of a business. The supervisor program serves as the chief

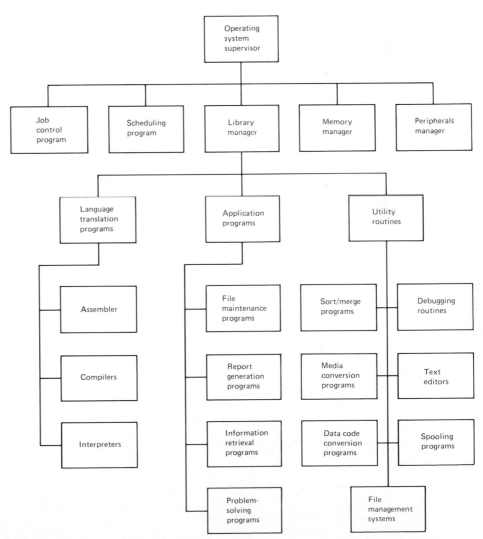

Fig. 7.2
The computer software hierarchy.

executive, the other components of the operating system represent executives at a vice-presidential level, the application programs represent the line organization, and the language translators and utility routines perform staff support functions. While this analogy is not a perfect one, it does serve to clarify the respective roles of these various categories of program software.

Nonprogram software

An important part of the nonprogram software used in a computer installation is the various services offered by hardware and software vendors. These include maintenance services, training, documentation of system software, and assistance in implementation and development of initial application programs. For many years computer manufacturers provided service software of this type, and program software as well, to their hardware customers free of charge. In 1969 International Business Machines (IBM) Corporation, the industry's leading firm, under antitrust pressure from several competitors and from the government, announced an "unbundling," or separation of pricing, for software and hardware. Most other manufacturers in the industry quickly followed IBM's lead. This has tended to stimulate competition in the software field, and has probably resulted in an improvement in the quality of available software products and services.

The various tools and techniques used in systems analysis and programming constitute another category of nonprogram software. Some examples are publications, such as language manuals and trade journals, design checklists, and flow-charting and related design techniques.

A third category of nonprogram software is the documentation of computer applications. For each system application, this documentation should include a narrative description of the objectives, functions, and cost justification of the application; systems flowcharts; an indication of the equipment configuration used; *record layouts,* which illustrate the arrangement of items of data in input, output, and file records; program flowcharts, and decision tables (as described subsequently in this chapter); program listings; program change descriptions and authorizations; instructions to the operator for running the programs; a list of the recipients of each output report; and a summary of the control features used in the system. Good applications documentation of this type is essential to program development and system control.

Software and accounting applications

Many of the early applications of computers in business were to the processing of accounting data. This specialization has been reflected in the development of computer software, particularly in the areas of programming languages and commercially designed application programs. Several programming languages have been created to accommodate the characteristics of data processing applications in accounting, such as complex input and output data structures and a need for control. Some of the major accounting firms have developed their own higher-level languages to assist them in auditing work. Such languages utilize commands which are peculiar to audit work, and programs written using these commands must first be translated into a procedure-oriented language. For example, the command to FOOT must be translated into a procedure-oriented language routine which will accumulate the total of a column of figures.[2]

Many commercially developed application programs are used in accounting operations. Programs for processing payrolls, billing and maintaining customer accounts, keeping inventory records, and so forth are available from manufacturers as well as from firms specializing in software development. For most companies using computers in data processing, there is no need to "reinvent the wheel" by writing such standard programs from scratch when they can be purchased commercially. Even when a company's requirements differ from those assumed in the standard application programs, such programs can often be appropriately modified.

Because more and more accounting work is being performed by computer systems, there is a need for accountants to understand software concepts and functions. This does not mean that accountants should have a detailed knowledge of programming; however some familiarity with at least one programming languages does provide a useful perspective. Of greater importance is the need for accountants to understand system documentation as a basis for understanding and controlling computer applications in accounting.

The Life Cycle of a Data Processing Program

A student obtaining an initial exposure to programming is likely to conceive of a computer program as a device prepared to solve a single problem, after which it is discarded. With regard to programs for business data processing, this is a misconception. A program written for a business data processing application may be used every day for several years. It will be useful to examine the life cycle of a data processing program in two separate stages, preparation and utilization.

Program preparation

The time required for program preparation may range from a few days to over a year, depending upon the complexity of the program. This section describes the several steps in the preparation process.

Preliminary steps   The first step in the preparation of a computer program for business data processing is to gain authorization for the project. This requires a statement of objectives and an analysis of costs and benefits as justification for the program. Output requirements and input sources must be determined, and the contents of files must be specified. A systems flowchart is prepared to illustrate the preliminary design of data flows relative to the program.

[2] *The nature of this "computer audit software" is explained in detail in Chapter 15.*

Program flowcharts   Once approval of the project has been obtained, the next step is the detailed design of the program. This begins with the drafting of a *program flowchart,* or *block diagram,* that illustrates the sequence of logical operations performed by a computer in executing a program. The program flowchart might be said to represent the detailed steps performed within the central processor symbol of the systems flowchart. Like the systems flowchart, the program flowchart uses a set of symbols with specialized meanings. These symbols and their meanings are identified in Fig. 7.3. The symbols shown are from the standard flowchart symbols adopted by the American National Standards Institute (ANSI).[3]

The flow direction line is used to connect the other symbols, and indicates the sequence in which logical operations are performed. In the absence of the arrowhead or other directional indicator, the sequence of operations is assumed to proceed from the top and/or from the left of a page to the bottom and/or to the right. The input/output symbol represents either the reading of input or the writing of output. The decision symbol represents a check or comparison of one or more variables and the transfer of flow to one of two or more alternative locations depending on the results of the comparison. The processing symbol represents a data movement or arithmetic operation, such as the assignment of a value to a variable or the performance of a calculation. All points in a program flowchart at which the flow begins, ends, or is interrupted are represented by the terminal symbol. The entry or exit connector is not a logic symbol, but merely provides a convenient means of representing the continuation of the logic flow at a different location on the chart. Each connector in a flowchart is labeled with a digit or capital letter. When the logic flow reaches an exit connector, it continues from that point at the entry connector having the same label. Whereas several exit connectors may have the same label, there can be only one entry connector with a given label.

A simple illustration of a program flowchart appears in Fig. 7.4. After starting, the program reads a record, which results in a value being assigned to one or more program variables. The next step compares one of the values read to a number which is known to occur on the last record only, such that if the record *is* the last record, the program branches to print a total and stop. If the record is *not* the last record, the next step accumulates a total based upon the data read from the record. The connector following this step indicates that flow control transfers back to the point where another record is read. The program continues through this loop of reading a record and accumulating a total until the last record is recognized.

A more complex example of a program flowchart illustrating a generalized file maintenance program appears in Fig. 7.5. It is assumed that there are two sets of inputs to this program, a master file and an activity file, which are ordered in the same sequence. Each master file record contains an identifying number and a balance, and each activity record contains an identifying number and a positive or

[3] American National Standard Flowchart Symbols and Their Use in Information Processing, *X3.5. American National Standards Institute, 1971.*

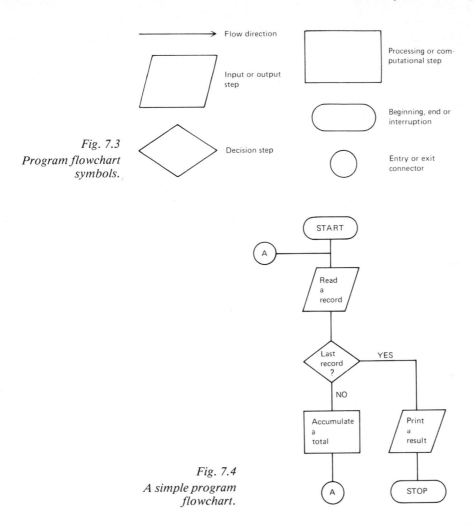

Fig. 7.3
*Program flowchart
symbols.*

Flow direction

Input or output
step

Decision step

Processing or com-
putational step

Beginning, end or
interruption

Entry or exit
connector

Fig. 7.4
*A simple program
flowchart.*

negative amount to be entered to its corresponding master record. There may be several activity records pertaining to a single master record, or there may be none for some master records. Output produced by the program consists of an updated master file and a printout of errors and summary data.

After reading both a master record and an activity record (Steps 1 and 2), the file maintenance program compares their identifying numbers (Step 4). If these are equal, a match exists and the program posts the activity amount to the master balance (Step 6) and reads another record (Step 2). This loop is continued until an activity record with a higher number is read. At that point program control is shifted by the identifying number comparison to the sequence headed by connector C, which writes the new master record (Step 7). The fact that the identifying number of the activity is greater than the identifying number of the

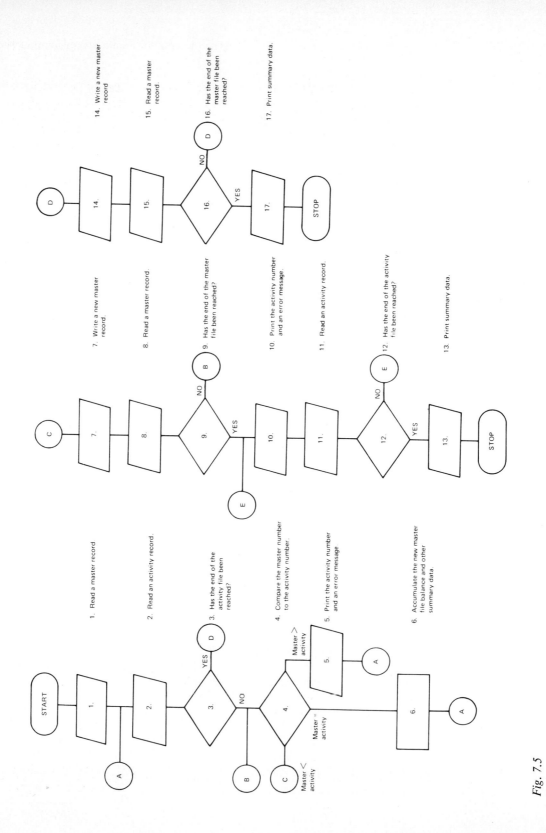

Fig. 7.5

A generalized file maintenance program flowchart.

master indicates that there is no more activity pertaining to that master, which is why the new master record is written at this point. The next step is to read the next master record (Step 8) and then compare its identifying number with that of the previously read activity record (Step 4).

If a comparison of identifying numbers reveals that the master number is greater than the activty number, this indicates that the activity record was not matched with a master record. This is an error condition, because a master record should be present for every activity record.[4] If this condition arises, the program prints an appropriate error message identifying the number of the activity record (Step 5) and proceeds to read another activity record (Step 2).

When the end of the activity file is reached (Step 3) the program writes the previously read or updated master record (Step 14). Then, since there may be one or more master records that have not yet been processed, the program reads another master record (Step 15) and checks for the end of the master file (Step 16). If the record is a regular master record and not the end-of-file indicator, the program writes the record on the new master file (Step 14) and reads another master (Step 15). This loop is continued until the end-of-file indicator is reached, at which point the program prints whatever summary data it may have accumulated as part of Step 6 and stops execution. Note that the reading and writing of master records in this loop can continue without the need to check for activity because it is known before this loop is entered that there are no remaining activity records.

It is also significant that the program execution as described above made no use of Steps 10 through 13 in the flowchart. These steps will in fact not be executed in most runs of the program, but they are necessary in the unlikely event that the end of the master file is reached prior to the end of the activity file. In such an instance the activity record being processed and all subsequent activity records are in error, because they cannot match with a master record. Thus if the end of the master file is reached prior to the end of the activity file (Step 9), an error message is printed indicating that there is no master record for the activity record in process (Step 10) and another activity record is read (Step 11). If the end-of-file check (Step 12) indicates that this next record is not the end-of-file indicator, the program loops back to again print the error message (Step 10) and read another activity record (Step 11). When the end-of-file indicator is read, the program prints out the summary data for the run (Step 13) and stops execution.

Decision tables   A *decision table* is a tabular representation of program logic that indicates the possible combinations of alternative logic conditions in the program and the corresponding courses of action taken by the program for each condition. A decision table may be prepared as an alternative or supplement to a program flowchart. They differ in that the program flowchart emphasizes the sequence of logical

---

[4] *One other possibility (not provided for in this program) is that instead of being a regular transaction this could be a new master record to be added to the master file. An additional set of program steps would be required to deal with this possibility.*

operations, while the decision table emphasizes alternative logic relationships among the data being processed.

The general form of the decision table is illustrated in Fig. 7.6. The upper half of the decision table is concerned with the various logic conditions tested for in the input data, while the lower half is concerned with the actions taken by the program for each set of conditions. The condition portion of the table consists of a number of horizontal rows, each of which represents one condition test within the program. The action portion of the table also consists of a number of horizontal rows, each representing an action taken within the program. The conditions or actions are written out in the left half, or stub portion, of the table. The right half, or entry portion, of the table consists of a set of vertical columns, each representing one possible combination of logical relationships. Each such column is called a decision rule. Each entry in a cell of the upper right quarter, or condition entry portion, of the table indicates the result of the condition test in that row within the decision rule of that column. Each entry in a cell of the lower right quarter, or action entry portion, of the table indicates whether or not the action in that row is executed if the decision rule in that column is met. These concepts are illustrated in the sample decision table of Fig. 7.7, which represents the file maintenance program flowcharted in Fig. 7.5.

The condition entries in a decision table may be in one of two forms. In the "limited entry" form, the condition test result may be either yes or no, as, for example, with the condition test for end of activity in the illustration. In the "extended entry" form, more than two condition test results are possible, and the exact specifications of each result are indicated in the entry. If the illustration is taken as an example, in the comparison of master record and activity record account numbers, three results are possible: the master record account number may be (1) less than, (2) equal to, or (3) greater than the activity record account number.

The remaining condition entry illustrated in the table is the dash, or "don't care" entry. This indicates that the result of the condition test in that row makes no difference with respect to the decision rule of that column. For example, when the end of the activity file or the master file is reached in the sample program, a comparison of account numbers is no longer relevant. The don't care entry may appear in either an extended entry row or a limited entry row.

The entry in each cell of the action entry portion of the table may be either an "X" or a blank. An X indicates that the action described in that row is performed if the input data meet all of the condition test results specified in that column. A blank indicates that the action is not performed. Using the first column of the sample table as an illustration, we see that if the input data represent the end of neither the activity file nor the master file, and if the account number of the master record is less than that of the activity record, the program writes a new master record, reads a master record, and repeats the condition tests.

Several observations regarding the construction of decision tables are relevant. First, note that the decision rules in a table must be mutually exclusive, which means that no decision rule should be repeated in the table. Second, the set of decision rules should be logically complete, which means that there should be one decision rule for

Fig. 7.6
General form of a
decision table.

Condition stub	Condition entry
Action stub	Action entry

Fig. 7.7
Sample decision
table for generalized
file maintenance
program.

End of activity	No	No	No	Yes	No	Yes
End of master	No	No	No	No	Yes	Yes
Compare account number: Master vs. activity	M<A	M=A	M>A	——	——	——
Print activity number and error message			X		X	
Update new master and summary data		X				
Write new master record	X			X		
Read an activity record		X	X		X	
Read a master record	X			X		
Print summary data						X
Stop processing						X
Repeat this table	X	X	X	X	X	

every possible combination of logical relationships among the input data. Third, to the extent possible, the conditions listed in the condition stub portion of the table should be sequenced in the order in which the conditions are to be tested in the program, and the actions listed in the action stub should be sequenced in the order in which the actions are to be performed following the condition tests. This rule was followed in the table of Fig. 7.7, but cannot always be followed precisely. Finally, note that, for completeness, a decision table should include the action "repeat this table" if the program is designed to operate on more than one input record.

Decision tables provide some advantages and some disadvantages relative to program flowcharts as a tool in program planning. The primary advantage is that a decision table indicates clearly all of the possible logical relationships existing among the input data. As a result, the program can be prepared to recognize and respond properly to each possible decision rule. The primary disadvantage of decision tables relative to program flowcharts is that decision tables do not reflect the sequence in which operations are to be performed within the program. Another disadvantage of decision tables is that they may become unmanageably large if the program is quite complex. Program flowcharts are a more popular tool of program design than decision tables, but decision tables in many cases provide a useful supplement to program flowcharts.

Implementation   After the design of a computer program by means of a program flowchart and/or a decision table, the next step in program preparation is the actual writing of the program instructions in a computer language. This is referred to as *coding*. Coding is distinguished from programming in that the latter encompasses all the steps involved in program preparation, whereas the former is only a single step. The program can usually be coded relatively easily by using the program flowchart or decision table as a reference.

Once the coding is completed, the source program is keyed onto an input medium such as punched cards, magnetic tape, or diskette. The computer may then be used to prepare a printed listing of the source program. The next step in the process is *desk-checking,* which is a visual review of the source program listing for the purpose of discovering keying or programming errors. Desk-checking is generally more effective if performed by someone other than the original programmer. After correcting any errors discovered during desk-checking, the program is compiled (see Fig. 7.1), and any errors identified by the diagnostic report are investigated and corrected.

Once the program has been successfully compiled, the next step is to test the program by devising a series of test input data that simulates all varieties of real processing situations or input data combinations to which the program may be exposed. The response of the program to each test case is observed, and an improper response indicates that the program contains some flaw, or ''bug.'' *Debugging* is the process of discovering and eliminating an error in a program once its existence is known. Once all of its bugs have been removed, the program is ready for final compilation and utilization.

Another important step in program preparation is preparation of program documentation. The need for this step should be given attention throughout the program preparation process. For example, during the program coding, descriptive remarks should be inserted into the program where appropriate. System flowcharts, record layouts, program flowcharts, decision tables, and related items used in program preparation should be prepared according to prescribed standards and retained as part of the program documentation. At the completion of program preparation, the program documentation should also be complete and ready to be organized into a meaningful documentation manual.

Program utilization   The pattern of utilization of a business data processing program over its life cycle depends on the nature of the program. File maintenance and report generation programs are typically used on a regular schedule—once a day, once a week, or once a month. Information retrieval and online updating programs must be maintained online for utilization at any time, and the pattern of their utilization is often quite irregular. A problem-solving program is also likely to experience an irregular pattern of usage, and is commonly used less frequently than other kinds of programs because of its specialized nature.

During the period of years in which a program is utilized, any of a number of factors may at times require the revision of the program. This process is referred to as *program maintenance*. Examples of factors which may necessitate a specific change include requests from managers for new reports, or for revisions in old reports; changes in program input or file content; change in some constant values, such as tax rates, which are part of the program; correction of a previously undiscovered bug; or modification to convert to new system hardware.

The period of utilization of a business data processing program varies widely, but will probably be no longer than six or seven years. A program may be made obsolete by the growth of a business or a change in information needs within the business, or perhaps by changes in system hardware or software. At this point its life cycle has come to an end and the program is discarded, replaced, or substantially revised.

Program design considerations

Now that the reader has gained some perspective on the development and use of computer programs in business and accounting applications, a brief discussion of the principles of program design is appropriate. The fact that a single program may be used for several years underscores the importance of careful program design. Three basic principles of program design will be discussed here.

The first and most important principle of program design is the principle of modularity. This principle dictates that programs be composed of *modules,* which are separate segments or subroutines within a program, each of which performs a separate logical function. For example, in a file maintenance program that processes several different types of transactions, there would be a separate module for each type of transaction. Each module should have only one entry point and one exit point to facilitate testing and changing of individual modules. Generally these modules should have no interaction with each other, interacting primarily if not exclusively with the program's "control module" or central logic section. In a file maintenance program the control module would be responsible for determining the type of each transaction and directing program control to the appropriate module. This modular approach to programming is generally referred to as *structured programming*.

Application of the principle of modularity begins in the flowcharting process. The proper approach to designing a complex program begins with the preparation of a *macroflowchart,* in which each symbol represents either a set of related program steps—a module—or a key control module step. Once a macroflowchart has been designed, preparation of the *microflowchart* showing each program step in detail can proceed more effectively. This process of designing a program from the top level down to the detail level is often referred to as "hierarchical program design."

Successful application of the principle of modularity facilitates program design and utilization in several respects. Program preparation is made easier in many ways: flowcharting is simplified; coding is made easier and may even be split, with different programmers working on different modules; documentation is made easier; and debugging is facilitated because errors requiring correction of one module should not affect any other modules. Modularity also makes a program easier to review and understand because the control module provides a capsule summary of the entire program. Program maintenance is also easier to accomplish with modular programs.

The second basic principle of program design is the principle of generality. This principle requires that programs not be designed for only a single specific task or set of requirements, but for the general case. This means that a program must be able to accommodate different sets of circumstances and changes in requirements. A general program will not generate unexpected errors, and therefore is likely to require less program maintenance.

The key to applying the principle of generality is thorough program planning and testing. Use of decision tables in program planning helps to ensure program generality, for a decision table may reveal unusual logical relationships that would not otherwise be planned for. A simple example of program steps that are necessary to provide a general program is furnished by Steps 10 through 13 in the file maintenance program flowchart of Fig. 7.5. These steps are necessary for the program to cope with unlikely and unexpected—but possible—characteristics of the input data.

The third basic principle of program design is that of maintainability. According to this principle, extra care in program design is justified if the program is made easier to maintain, because program maintenance will be necessary over a period of several years. As mentioned above, program maintenance is simplified with programs which are modular and general. Good documentation is also an essential factor in easily maintained programs.

Examples of Programming Languages

In this section, a brief overview of three of the most common procedure-oriented languages, FORTRAN, COBOL, and BASIC, will be presented. This section is not intended to develop a working knowledge of those languages, but instead to provide a general knowledge of their basic characteristics. The primary purposes are to develop a perspective on the nature of procedure-oriented languages and to establish a basis for discussion of the relative merits of these languages, particularly FORTRAN and COBOL.

The FORTRAN language

FORTRAN was the first procedure-oriented language to be widely used and accepted. The name FORTRAN is an acronym for FORmula TRANslator. Development of the language was begun in 1955, and it has evolved through a number of versions, including FORTRAN II and FORTRAN IV, the most recent version.

The FORTRAN language is oriented toward scientific data processing problems which can be expressed in terms of mathematical formulas. It can also be applied to other kinds of problems, including business data processing. It is still the most popular computer language, and most computers have available a FORTRAN compiler.

This brief overview of the characteristics of the FORTRAN language will employ the sample program shown in Fig. 7.8. The tasks which the program performs are (1) reading the records of utility customers, each of which contains the customer number, previous utility meter reading, and current reading; (2) calculating the amount of each customer's utility bill; and (3) printing out a report containing this information. A FORTRAN program consists of a series of statements, some of which are numbered because they are referred to elsewhere in the program. The statements in a FORTRAN program can be classified into three basic types—input-output, control, and arithmetic.

Input and output operations in FORTRAN both must utilize the FORMAT statement which specifies the format in which the input data and output reports will appear. The READ statement, labeled number 23, performs the input operation in conjunction with the FORMAT statement labeled number 1. Output is accomplished by the use of the WRITE statement in conjunction with the FORMAT statement. The first three WRITE statements in the program result in the printing of headings for the output report, which are specified in FORMAT statements, numbers 3, 4, and 5. The WRITE statement near the bottom of the program, together with FORMAT statement number 2, performs the printing of output data for each customer.

Control statements regulate the sequence in which FORTRAN statements are executed. In the absence of control statements, the FORTRAN statements would be executed one at a time from top to bottom (except for FORMAT statements, which are not executed separately). The IF statement is one of the control statements in FORTRAN. An IF statement is executed by evaluating the expression which appears in parenthesis following the IF. If the value of the expression is negative, control is transferred to the first statement number appearing after the parenthesis; if the value is zero, control transfers to the second statement number; and if the value is positive, to the third statement number. The GO TO statement directly transfers program control to the statement number indicated. Another common FORTRAN control statement which does not appear in the illustration is the DO statement, which establishes a loop in which a set of statements is executed over and over for a specified number of times. Another control statement is the STOP statement, which terminates the execution of the program.

Arithmetic statements accomplish the calculations in a FORTRAN program. All arithmetic statements appear in the form of an equation, with a single variable name to the left of the equal sign and one or more variables or numbers appearing on the right together with an indication of the operations (addition, multiplication, etc.) to be performed. The statement is executed by performing the operations on the right side, and setting the left side variable equal to the resulting value.

```
        PROGRAM UTILITY
1       FORMAT(I4,2F6.0)
2       FORMAT(1X,I4,5X,F4.0,8X,F6.2,5X,F6.2,8X,F6.2)
3       FORMAT(1H1,13X,23HCUSTOMER BILLING REPORT)
4       FORMAT(2X,49HCUST      UTILITY    AMOUNT     AMOUNT      TOT AMT)
5       FORMAT(2X,49HNO        USAGE      RATE-1     RATE-2      CHARGED)
        OPEN (UNIT=6,ACCESS='SEQINOUT',DEVICE='PTR')
        OPEN (UNIT=5,ACCESS='SEQINOUT',DEVICE='RDR')
15      NTCR=0
        WRITE(6,3)
        WRITE(6,4)
        WRITE(6,5)
23      READ(5,1)NO,RD1,RD2
        IF(NO-9999)27,70,27
27      USE=RD2-RD1
        IF (USE-500.)31,31,35
31      AMT1=USE*.025
        AMT2=0.
        GO TO 40
35      AMT1=500.*.025
        AMT2=(USE-500.)*.03
40      TOT=AMT1+AMT2
        WRITE(6,2)NO,USE,AMT1,AMT2,TOT
        NTCR=NTCR+1
        IF (NTCR-30)23,15,15
70      STOP
        END
```

Fig. 7.8
Sample FORTRAN language program.

The COBOL language

COBOL is an acronym for COmmon Business Oriented Language. As the acronym suggests, the language was designed specifically for business applications involving records processing and file updating. The language was developed in 1960 and 1961 by a committee containing representatives of computer manufacturers and large users, including the federal government. This development group was called CODASYL, an acronym for COnference on DAta SYstems Languages. COBOL is now the most common procedure-oriented language used for business data processing.

A sample COBOL program appears in Fig. 7.9. This program is designed to accomplish exactly the same task as the FORTRAN program in Fig. 7.8. Every COBOL program consists of four major divisions—the Identification, Environment, Data, and Procedure divisions, which must always appear in that order. The Identification division is used only for documentation purposes, and may contain only a program name. The Environment division describes the equipment configuration on which the program will be run, including the computer which will compile the program (the source computer), the computer which will execute the program (the object computer), and the devices which will be responsible for each input and output file.

The Data division specifies the format of each input and output file, and of each variable used in the program. In the sample program, the four lines under 01 USAGE-CARD describe the content of an input record to the program. The several lines under 01 PRINT-LINE describe the format of the output report. The lines under WORKING-STORAGE SECTION indicate the specifications for all variables used in the program but not contained in either an input or output file.

```
IDENTIFICATION DIVISION.
PROGRAM-ID.  UTILITY BILLING
REMARKS.  PROGRAM COMPUTES A MONTHLY UTILITY BILL AND FORMATS A
          CUSTOMER BILLING REPORT.
ENVIRONMENT DIVISION.

CONFIGURATION SECTION.
SOURCE-COMPUTER.  DECSYSTEM-20.
OBJECT-COMPUTER.  DECSYSTEM-20.
SPECIAL-NAMES. PRINTER  IS PRTR.

INPUT-OUTPUT SECTION.
FILE-CONTROL.  SELECT USAGE-FILE ASSIGN TO CARD-READER.
               SELECT PRINT-FILE ASSIGN TO PRINTER.

DATA DIVISION.
FILE SECTION.
FD USAGE-FILE
       LABEL RECORD IS OMITTED
       RECORD CONTAINS 80 CHARACTERS.
01 USAGE-CARD.
       02 CUST-NO            PICTURE X(4).
       02 READ-1             PICTURE 9(6).
       02 READ-2             PICTURE 9(6).
       02 FILLER             PICTURE X(64).
FD PRINT-FILE
       LABEL RECORD IS OMITTED
       RECORD CONTAINS 136 CHARACTERS.
01 PRINT-LINE.
       02 FILLER             PICTURE X.
       02 CUST-NO-OUT        PICTURE X(4).
       02 FILLER             PICTURE X(5).
       02 USAGE-OUT          PICTURE 9(4).
       02 FILLER             PICTURE X(5).
       02 AMT-RATE-1         PICTURE ZZZ9.99.
       02 FILLER             PICTURE X(5).
       02 AMT-RATE-2         PICTURE ZZZ9.99.
       02 FILLER             PICTURE X(5).
       02 TOT-AMT-OUT        PICTURE ZZZ9.99.
       02 FILLER             PICTURE X(86).

WORKING-STORAGE SECTION.
       77 CTR                PICTURE 99.
       77 NET                PICTURE 9(6).
       77 AMT-R1             PICTURE 9999V99.
       77 AMT-R2             PICTURE 9999V99.
       77 NET-USAGE          PICTURE 9(6).
       77 TOT-AMT            PICTURE 9999V99.

PROCEDURE DIVISION.
START.  OPEN INPUT USAGE-FILE, OUTPUT PRINT-FILE.
HEAD-PROCEDURE.  MOVE 0 TO CTR.
       DISPLAY "1             CUSTOMER BILLING REPORT" UPON PRTR.
       DISPLAY " CUST      UTILITY     AMOUNT       AMOUNT      TOT AMT"
          UPON PRTR.
       DISPLAY " NO        USAGE       RATE-1       RATE-2     CHARGED"
          UPON PRTR.

READ-USAGE.  READ USAGE-FILE INTO USAGE-CARD AT END GO TO FINISHED.

COMPUTE-LOGIC.
       SUBTRACT READ-1 FROM READ-2 GIVING NET-USAGE.
       IF NET-USAGE IS GREATER THAN 500 PERFORM DISCOUNT
          ELSE PERFORM REG.
       ADD AMT-R1, AMT-R2 GIVING TOT-AMT, GO TO PRINTT.

DISCOUNT.
       MULTIPLY 500 BY .025 GIVING AMT-R1.
       SUBTRACT 500 FROM NET-USAGE GIVING NET.
       MULTIPLY NET BY .03 GIVING AMT-R2.

REG.
       MULTIPLY NET-USAGE BY .025 GIVING AMT-R1.
       MOVE 0 TO AMT-R2.

PRINTT.
       MOVE SPACES TO PRINT-LINE, MOVE NET-USAGE TO USAGE-OUT.
       MOVE TOT-AMT TO TOT-AMT-OUT.  MOVE AMT-R1 TO AMT-RATE-1.
       MOVE AMT-R2 TO AMT-RATE-2, MOVE CUST-NO TO CUST-NO-OUT.
       WRITE PRINT-LINE  ADD 1 TO CTR.
       IF CTR EQUALS 30 GO TO HEAD-PROCEDURE ELSE GO TO READ-USAGE.

FINISHED.  CLOSE USAGE-FILE, PRINT-FILE.  STOP RUN.
```

Fig. 7.9
Sample COBOL
language program.

The Procedure division contains the actual instructions for processing. In the COBOL language these instructions are in the form of English language words, so that one can understand what the program does fairly well by reading the Procedure division. COBOL Procedure division statements perform the same set of functions as do FORTRAN statements. Input is accomplished in COBOL through the READ statement, and output through either the WRITE or DISPLAY statement. Control statements in COBOL include the IF and GO TO statements, which execute in a manner quite similar to their counterparts in FORTRAN. Arithmetic operations in COBOL are performed by statements such as those beginning ADD, SUBTRACT, or MULTIPLY.

A comparison of FORTRAN and COBOL

A comparison of these two procedure-oriented languages should take into account the fact they were designed for different purposes. FORTRAN was designed for application to scientific problems. The use of mathematical notations, subscripts, formulas, and so forth is done more easily in FORTRAN than in COBOL. However, FORTRAN lacks many of the features that are desirable in a computer language for business and accounting applications, especially those involving the maintenance of files and the processing of complex data structures.

Despite its lack of orientation to business data processing, FORTRAN should not be completely ruled out for all business applications. FORTRAN would be most appropriate for the application of mathematical modeling techniques to the solution of business problems, or to any situation in which the amount of computation is significant while the input and output are simple in structure. For installations that have only limited requirements for file processing, the lack of availability of a COBOL compiler, or of programmers skilled in COBOL, may make it more appropriate to use FORTRAN even for file maintenance programs. For small installations making an initial decision to obtain a procedure-oriented language compiler, the fact that a working knowledge of FORTRAN is easier to develop may be significant. For most business organizations with a medium- to large-scale computer system, frequent usage of both languages would be likely.

There are several reasons why COBOL is a superior language for writing file maintenance and related programs. One of the major factors is the self-documenting nature of the language. Instruction verbs and related syntax in COBOL are very descriptive of the items they represent. This makes it much easier for a person other than the original programmer to understand what a given program is intended to accomplish.

As will be explained in more depth in a later chapter, the additional documentation provided by COBOL is also a significant factor in the accounting control of a computer system. Such audit functions as program review, monitoring of program changes, tracing of audit trails, and the preparation of test decks are facilitated by good documentation.

Some additional features of COBOL that serve to protect files from unintentional destruction include the provisions for assigning files to equipment in the

Environment division and for automatic checking of file labels to guard against loading the wrong file for a job.

Because the processing of input and output is a major factor in business and accounting applications, the advanced features of the COBOL Data division are a significant advantage of COBOL relative to FORTRAN for this type of application. The Data division enables the establishment of a complex hierarchical file structure in which each record contains several fields, each field may contain several smaller fields, and so forth. Data editing provisions in COBOL facilitate the design of output reports having a very neat appearance, with dollar signs, debit and credit notation, commas, and so forth inserted where appropriate. Such provisions are not available in FORTRAN, which makes programming for input and output more difficult.

Although the writing of programs to accomplish simple tasks is easier with FORTRAN, the writing of complex file maintenance programs is easier and less time consuming with COBOL because of its self-documentation and because it enables separation of the programming effort between the writing of procedures and the description of input and output. The superior documentation provided by COBOL also (1) facilitates communication among several programmers working on a single large project; (2) contributes to easier program testing and debugging; and (3) simplifies program maintenance over the life cycle of a program.

The BASIC language

BASIC is an acronym for Beginner's All-purpose Symbolic Instruction Code. As the acronym implies, the language was designed to be very simple to learn so that non-programmers could easily use it. It bears a close resemblance to FORTRAN, although it is simpler and easier to learn than FORTRAN. BASIC is the language most commonly used both by small personal computer systems and by online time-sharing services.

A sample BASIC program appears in Fig. 7.10. Once again, this is a program written to accomplish the same task as those in Figs. 7.8 and 7.9. Note that all statements in BASIC must be numbered, and they are arranged in numerical order, which is not true of FORTRAN. READ statements together with DATA statements are one primary means of data input, and the PRINT statement is used for output. The IF and GO TO statements perform control functions as in FORTRAN. Mathematical expressions are prefaced with LET. Very few conventions have to be learned to obtain a working knowledge of BASIC, but the language is lacking in some of the advanced features of FORTRAN.

One of the special characteristics of BASIC is the INPUT verb (not shown in Fig. 7.10) that enables *conversational programs* to be written. Such programs interact with a user at a remote terminal by printing questions for him or her to type in answers to, or printing requests for specific data. After the user responds, the program continues its execution in accordance with the responses, and may subsequently print output and/or ask for more input from the user. The INPUT verb performs the functions of stopping program execution while the user responds and of reading the user's responses.

```
00100 LET N=0
00110 PRINT '             CUSTOMER BILLING REPORT'
00120 PRINT
00130 PRINT 'CUSTOMER ','UTILITY','AMOUNT','AMOUNT','TOT AMT'
00140 PRINT ' NUMBER',' USAGE'.'RATE-1','RATE-2','CHARGED'
00150 READ N1,R1,R2
00160 IF N1=9999 THEN 290
00170 LET U =R2-R1
00180 IF U>500 THEN 220
00190 LET A1=U*0.025
00200 LET A2=0
00210 GO TO 240
00220 LET A1=500*.025
00230 LET A2=(U-500)*0.03
00240 LET T=A1+A2
00250 PRINT N1,U,'$';A1,'$';A2,'$';T
00260 LET N=N+1
00270 IF N=30 THEN 100
00280 GO TO 150
00290 STOP
00300 DATA 123,4700,5500,124,6300,6650,9999,0,0
00310 END
```

Fig. 7.10 Sample BASIC language program.

Most online versions of BASIC are implemented using an interpreter rather than a compiler. This means that if the programmer makes an error in entering a line of BASIC code, the system will immediately respond with an error message. As a result, many kinds of programming errors can be detected and corrected prior to actually running the program.

Although the BASIC language, like FORTRAN, is inappropriate relative to COBOL for file maintenance applications, it has many potential applications to mathematical problem solving in accounting. In fact, its simplicity gives it a significant advantage over FORTRAN for this purpose, since most accountants will not use such a language enough to justify an extensive learning effort. A common use of BASIC in accounting involves the programming of financial planning models, which simulate the financial aspects of a firm's operations for one or more years into the future. The interactive capability of the language enables such programs to be easily used by nontechnical persons, such as top management executives. Other areas of accounting in which BASIC is useful include tax planning and cost analysis.

Other languages

The total number of procedure-oriented languages is well over one hundred. To give some idea of the variety of such languages that is available, a few of them will be briefly mentioned here.

One very popular scientific language is ALGOL (ALGOrithmic Language). An increasingly popular language that offers powerful data structuring and data manipulation features is Pascal. A language that is common in small installations with business applications is RPG (Report Program Generator). A language designed by IBM to incorporate features of both COBOL and FORTRAN is PL/I (Programming Language I). A language offered by IBM for time sharing is APL (A

Programming Language). Several languages designed specifically for simulation problems include SIMSCRIPT, DYNAMO, and GPSS (General-Purpose Systems Simulator).

Generally, each computer language is designed to perform certain tasks well. This inevitably means that there are other tasks that the language does not perform well. It is probably not possible to design a universal language that will do a good job of satisfying the needs of all users. Therefore, the present situation in which different languages are appropriate for different purposes may be expected to continue for the foreseeable future.

Review Questions

1. Define the following terms.

programming	utility routines
machine language	text editor
operand	record layout
symbolic language	program flowchart
procedure-oriented language	block diagram
assembler	decision table
source program	coding
object program	desk-checking
macroinstruction	debugging
machine independent	program maintenance
compiler	module
diagnostic	structured programming
interpreter	macroflowchart
system software	microflowchart
operating system	conversational program
job control language	

2. List and describe several major categories of computer software. Explain how these various types of software fit together within a data processing system.

3. What are the component parts of a typical machine language instruction?

4. Why is it uncommon for a programmer to use machine language in writing a program?

5. Can a computer directly execute a symbolic language program? Explain.

6. What are the advantages and disadvantages of procedure-oriented languages relative to symbolic languages?

7. What are some of the characteristics of a data processing installation that would influence the decision of whether to program in symbolic language or in a procedure-oriented language?

8. List, describe, and give examples of four types of application programs common in business data processing.

9. What are some examples of the different types of file activity processed in file maintenance programs?

10. Identify and briefly describe the functions of some of the primary component programs within an operating system.
11. Identify and briefly describe some examples of utility routines.
12. What does "unbundling" mean, and what is its significance to computer software?
13. What are the essential elements of documentation for computer system applications?
14. Describe two ways in which the application of computers in accounting has influenced the development of computer software.
15. Describe the steps in the preparation of a computer program.
16. Identify the symbols used in program flowcharting, indicate the meaning of each, and describe or give an example of the usage of each.
17. In all batch processing file maintenance programs, one essential step is a comparison of the identifying number of the master record with that of the activity record. What are the three possible outcomes of this comparison? Explain one possible meaning of each outcome.
18. Describe the format of a decision table.
19. Distinguish between the "limited entry" and "extended entry" form of a decision table.
20. Describe the primary advantages and disadvantages of decision tables relative to program flowcharts as a tool of program preparation.
21. Distinguish between file maintenance and program maintenance and give an example of each.
22. Explain three basic principles of program design.
23. What are the phrases for which FORTRAN, COBOL, and BASIC are acronyms?
24. What are three basic types of statements in the FORTRAN language? Give an example of each.
25. What are the four divisions of a COBOL program and what is the purpose of each?
26. What years mark the beginning of development of the FORTRAN and COBOL languages?
27. Describe the advantages of FORTRAN relative to COBOL for programming of mathematical and scientific problems.
28. For what kind of business situations would FORTRAN be more appropriate than COBOL?
29. Describe the advantages of COBOL relative to FORTRAN for writing file maintenance programs.
30. How can the use of COBOL contribute to the internal control of a computer system?
31. Identify two environments in which BASIC is commonly used? Give some specific examples of applications for this language in accounting.
32. Name six procedure-oriented languages in addition to COBOL, FORTRAN, and BASIC.

33. Which language should the student of business be taught first? FORTRAN? BASIC? COBOL? Discuss.

34. If the definition of computer software were to be restricted to programs, would you consider programming languages to be a form of software? Why or why not?

35. Is it necessary for an accountant in a firm which uses computers extensively in data processing to have either (a) some knowledge of, or (b) an expert's knowledge of, programming in a language such as COBOL? Discuss.

36. Is it necessary for an auditor working for a public accounting firm to have either (a) some knowledge of, or (b) an expert's knowledge of, programming in a language such as COBOL? Discuss.

**Problems and
Cases**

37. Prepare a program flowchart of the illustrative program of this chapter (see Fig. 7.8, 7.9, or 7.10).

38. The Hi-Lo Manufacturing Company utilizes a medium-sized computer system for data processing. Compilers for both the FORTRAN and COBOL languages are available, as are programmers who specialize in each language.

    The Company has decided to write a computer program to analyze its monthly financial statements. Input to the program would consist of detailed balance sheets and income statements for the current and preceding months. The program would calculate various ratios, percentages, growth rates, etc., and print out an analysis in the form of several schedules. The program would, of course, be run once monthly.

    Required   What arguments could be made favoring the use of COBOL in writing this program? of FORTRAN? Explain.

39. This exercise involves tracing the operations performed on a hypothetical set of master and activity records through the program flowchart of Fig. 7.5. Assume that the master file and activity file are composed of the record numbers shown below in the sequence given.

    Master: 011, 013, 014, 015, 016, 017, 018, 019, EOF
    Activity: 011, 012, 014, 014, 016, 018, EOF

    Required   a) Construct a table containing five columns with headings as follows: Read Master, Read Activity, Match, Write Master, Write Error. Begin tracing the records above through the program. Each time a record is read, a match is found between a master and activity record, or a record is written, write down the identifying number of the record in the appropriate column of the table. Number each item that you write in the table in sequence beginning with one. Continue until you have traced all records through the program.

    b) Assume that there had been an activity record with the number 020 after record number 018 and in front of the end-of-file record. Beginning at the point at which this change would first have made a difference, trace the records through the program to the finish, recording in your table as described above.

40. You are to modify the generalized file maintenance program flowchart (Fig. 7.5) and the related decision table (Fig. 7.7) to provide for the possibility that some of the activity records may be newly created master records that are to be added to the file. To simplify this problem, you may assume that there should not be any regular activity records that update the newly created master records.

Required

   a) Prepare the revised decision table.

   b) Prepare the revised program flowchart. Note that the rightmost module of the flowchart (Steps 14–17) is not affected by the required modification, and need not be redrawn.

   c) Suppose that we drop the simplifying assumption and allow regular activity records that update the newly created master records. Briefly discuss the additional complexities that this would introduce into the program.

41. Prepare a program flowchart and a decision table for the following program.

   Input to the program consists of an accounts receivable file containing (among other things) the amount due, due date, and credit limit for each customer. The program checks the due date of each customer record against the current date, and prepares an aging schedule. Each customer's record is listed on a separate line of the aging schedule, with the amount due printed in one of three columns: (1) less than 60 days past due, (2) 61–180 days past due, and (3) over 180 days past due.

   The program next compares the amount due to the customer's credit limit. Customer records that are both over 180 days past due and have an amount due in excess of the credit limit are printed on a "Bad Debts Report" for possible writeoff by the Credit Manager. Other accounts that have an amount due in excess of the credit limit are printed on a "Credit Review Report" that goes to the Treasurer.

   After the last record in the accounts receivable file is processed, the program is halted.

42. Prepare a program flowchart and a decision table for the program described below.

   Input to the program consists of records in an inventory file, each of which contains the item number, quantity on hand, price, and total cost of an inventory item. At the beginning of processing, and after every 50 lines of output, the program prints a set of report headings.

   For each input record, the program calculates the product of price and quantity on hand and then compares this product with the total cost. If the product and total cost do not agree, the item number and an error message are printed out on one line. If the product and total cost do agree, the four items of data in each record are printed out, along with a message, on one line of the report. The message field contains blank spaces if the total cost of the item is less than $1000; otherwise, the message is used to place the label "high-value item" beside the item.

   When the end of the inventory file is reached, processing is halted.

43. From the description below of the processing of casualty claims by an insurance company, prepare (1) a system flowchart, (2) a program flowchart of the file maintenance program, and (3) a decision table of the file maintenance program.

The data processing section maintains on magnetic tape a master file of all outstanding claims in sequence by claim number which it updates daily. Input to this computer run, in addition to the master file, consists of two types of transactions-records of newly filed claims, and authorizations to pay existing claims. These transactions are keypunched and verified from source documents provided by the claims department. The resulting punched cards are converted to tape on the computer. The conversion run generates a printed report of batch totals which is compared to batch totals provided by the claims department on an adding machine tape.

The transaction tape is sorted and processed against the claims master by the file maintenance program. Output of this run consists of (1) the updated claims master, which contains only unpaid claims; (2) checks in payment of all claims as authorized; and (3) an error list and financial summary report. Among the errors listed on the latter report are invalid transactions, including payment authorizations for which no claim exists on the file, and new claims having the same claim number as claims already on the file.

After the file maintenance run is completed, the claims master file is processed by a report generation program to prepare a report of outstanding claims for the claims department.

44. From the description below of the processing of patient charges by a hospital, prepare a block diagram.

The data processing section maintains on magnetic tape a master file of charges for all patients. This file is updated daily in a computer run, the input to which consists of punched cards sorted into sequence by social security number of the patient. (The master file is also in this sequence.) Punched cards relating to an individual patient may be a record of admittance, a charge, or a notice of release, in that order. To simplify matters, you may assume that an admittance and release for the same patient are never processed together in the same run. The computer run generates an updated master file containing a record of each in-patient and all of that patient's accumulated charges to date and also a printed report listing error transactions and summary information. When a notice of release is included, the program prints a report of all accumulated charges for the patient, and does not include this patient's record in the updated master file.

45. Prepare a program flowchart for the inventory file updating process described below.

The master inventory file is on magnetic tape, and contains the inventory part number, a description, and the quantity on hand. The file is in part number sequence. Inventory transactions are on punched cards, and include (1) new inventory items for which a record is to be created in the file; (2) receipts; and (3) issues. Prior to processing, the transaction cards are sorted into part number sequence. In the event that more than one transaction type exists for a particular inventory item, the transaction types are sequenced in the order given above. During processing, receipts are added to the inventory balance of each item and issues are deducted, and a new updated master file is generated on magnetic tape. Two printed reports are also prepared, which are a stock status report listing the contents of the updated master file and a listing of error transactions and summary information.

References

Aron, Joel D. *The Program Development Process.* Reading, Mass.: Addison-Wesley, 1974.

Bohl, Marilyn. *Information Processing* (3rd ed.). Chicago: Science Research Associates, 1980.

Boillot, Michel H.; Gary M. Gleason; and L. Wayne Horn. *Essentials of Flow-charting.* Dubuque: Wm. C. Brown, 1975.

Chapin, Ned. *Flowcharts.* Princeton: Auerbach, 1971.

Davis, William S. *Information Processing Systems.* Reading, Mass.: Addison-Wesley, 1978.

Feingold, Carl. *Fundamentals of Structured COBOL Programming* (3rd ed.). Dubuque: Wm. C. Brown, 1978.

Holton, John B., and Bill Bryan. "Structured Top-Down Flowcharting." *Datamation* (May 1975): 80–84.

McGowan, Clement L., and John R. Kelly. *Top-Down Structured Programming Techniques.* New York: Petrocelli/Charter, 1975.

Maes, R. "On the Representation of Program Structures by Decision Tables: A Critical Assessment." *The Computer Journal* (November 1978): 290–295.

Morris, Robert A. "Comparison of Some High-Level Languages." *BYTE* (February 1980): 128–139.

Murach, Mike. *Structured COBOL.* Chicago: Science Research Associates, 1980.

Myers, Ware. "The Need for Software Engineering." *Computer* (February 1978): 12–26.

Ogdin, Carol Anne. "The Many Choices in Development Languages." *Mini–Micro Systems* (August 1980): 81–84.

Reifer, Donald J., and Stephen Trattner. "A Glossary of Software Tools and Techniques." *Computer* (July 1977): 52–60.

Shneiderman, Ben. *Software Psychology.* Cambridge, Mass.: Winthrop, 1980.

Weinberg, G. M. *The Psychology of Computer Programming.* New York: Van Nostrand Reinhold, 1971.

Yourdon, Edward. "A Brief Look at Structured Programming and Top-Down Program Design." *Modern Data* (June 1974): 30–35.

Zelkowitz, Marvin V. "Perspectives on Software Engineering." *Computing Surveys* (June 1978): 197–216.

Chapter 8

Data Base Systems

Organizations which have used computers in data processing for several years have typically experienced a proliferation of computer applications. Often this has led to growing problems concerning the management of data. For example, the same item of data, such as an inventory balance on hand, might be needed in several different computer applications. Under the traditional approach, separate files would be maintained for each application. This leads to *data redundancy,* where the same item of data is stored in several different places within an information system. In addition to requiring greater amounts of file storage space, data redundancy can result in inconsistencies between data items which should agree. For example, one record may indicate that the balance on hand of a particular inventory item is 200 units, while another shows 120 units. The confusion which may result from this problem tends to negate the advantages of computerized data processing.

In the mid-1960s the need for a more coordinated approach to the management of data was identified. This has led to the data base approach. A *data base* might be defined as a set of interrelated data files which are stored with as little data redundancy as possible and which may be accessed by one or more application programs. The specialized computer program which manages the data and interfaces between the data and the application programs is referred to as a *data base management system* (DBMS). The combination of the data base, the DBMS, and the application programs which access the data base through the DBMS is referred to as a *data*

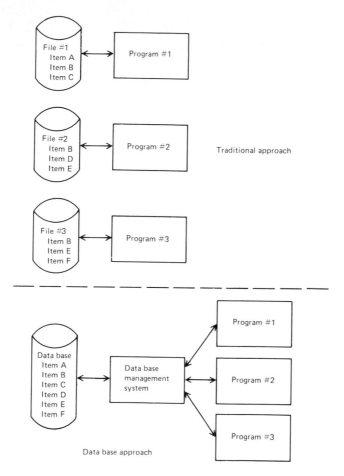

Fig. 8.1
Traditional approach
vs. data base
approach.

base system. This chapter discusses some of the basic concepts and techniques used in data base systems, and illustrates their application to typical accounting and business data processing examples.

Figure 8.1 illustrates the basic differences outlined above between the traditional approach to data processing and the data base approach. Note that the redundancy of data items B and E shown under the traditional approach does not exist under the data base approach. Further note that the data base approach provides *data independence,* which is not present under the traditional approach. By this is meant that under the traditional approach each program has its own fixed data file, whereas under the data base approach the data exist separately from the programs.

Some Fundamental Data Base Concepts

Several concepts introduced in prior chapters are relevant to the study of data base systems—the concepts of records, files, fields, entities, attributes, primary keys, and secondary keys. For convenience these concepts are briefly reviewed.

An entity is an item about which data are stored in a system, while an attribute is a property or characteristic which a particular entity may possess. For example, the entity "car" possesses the property "color." Entities and attributes exist in the physical world of tangible things, and would continue to do so even if there were no information systems. In contrast, records, files, fields, and keys exist only in the context of an information system.

Individual data items are stored in fields within a record. Each field contains a data value for a particular attribute, and each record is a collection of data values, organized by fields, for a particular entity. A file is a group of records for all entities of a particular type. For example, in the information system of a retail car dealer, data on cars are stored within an inventory file having one record for each car; each record in this file contains fields such as "model name," "color," etc., in which data values such as "Buick" and "red" are stored. The structure of each record in a file, in terms of the fields it contains, is similar to all other records in the same file.

Within each file, one field is designated to contain a data item which represents a unique identifier of the items in the file. The identifier itself is called the primary key, and the field which contains it is the primary key field. The primary key of a car inventory file would be the auto serial number. Other fields within the records of a file may be designated as secondary key fields. Secondary keys do not uniquely identify a file record, but they do identify specific attributes within the record that facilitate its storage, processing, and retrieval. In a car inventory file, a good candidate for a secondary key would be the car's model name (Electra, Skylark, etc.). A particular file may have several secondary key fields, but need have only one primary key field.

In addition to its designation as a primary key, secondary key, or nonkey item, a field may also be characterized by the type of data which may be stored in it. Five commonly used field designations are numeric, alphabetic, alphanumeric, monetary, and date. A numeric field is one such as social security number or telephone number that can contain only numeric data. Fields that can contain only alphabetic data, such as name or city and state, are alphabetic fields. Alphanumeric fields are those that can contain both alphabetic and numeric characters, such as street address or inventory item description. Wage rate, price, and account balance are examples of fields that always contain monetary data. The characters within a date field are always interpreted by the system to represent a specific month, day, and year.

A description of the overall logical organization of a data base is referred to as a *schema* (plural: schemata). A subset of the schema that includes only those data items used in a particular application program is referred to as a *subschema*. From a given schema there may be derived several subschemata—in fact, one subschema for each of the programs which accesses the data base. For example, the schema for a customer data base might include account number, balance due, detail of current transactions, credit history, name and address, product lines sold to, and salespersons' call reports. However, an accounting program might define a subschema consisting only of account number, balance due, and detail of current transactions. On the other hand, a marketing program might use a subschema which includes account number, name and address, product lines sold to, and salespersons' call reports. Several other subschemata might also be derived from this schema.

An important distinction in the study of data base systems is that between physical data organization and logical data organization. *Physical data organization* refers to the manner in which data are physically arranged and stored on data storage media. *Logical data organization* is concerned with the way in which data users view the relationships among data items, as reflected by the schemata and subschemata that they design. In some cases the physical data organization that optimizes data storage factors such as access time and capacity utilization may differ from the logical data organization best suited to the needs of data users. As a result, data items such as customer account balance, name and address, and credit history may be stored in separate locations or devices even though users perceive a close logical relationship among them. It is the responsibility of the data base management system to manage the data base in such a way that a user may work effectively with a logical set of data items, without being aware of the possible complexities involved in the physical organization of that set of data items.

An interesting issue in the application of data base technology to data processing in modern organizations is whether all of an organization's data should be organized into a single comprehensive data base. Most companies presently using data base systems have several different data bases for different areas of the organization—for example, a customer data base, an inventory data base, an employee data base, etc. This situation will likely continue to hold true. However, in some data base systems it is possible to define relationships among data items which are part of different logical data bases. To some extent these systems function as though there were only one comprehensive data base.

Logical Data Structures

If we were to study in detail the general content of files within a typical business organiztion, and the logical relationships that users perceive among individual data elements within those various files, we would find three basic types of logical data structures. These are called flat file structures, tree structures, and network structures. Each of these structures is discussed in turn in this section.

Flat file structures

A file structure in which each record is identical to every other record in terms of attributes and field lengths may be termed a *flat file*. A simple example of a flat inventory file appears in Fig. 8.2. Note that each and every record maintains data on an identical set of attributes—stock number, description, color, vendor, on hand

Stock Number	Description	Color	Vendor	On Hand	Price
1Q36	Refrigerator	White	Gibman	12	$349.99
1038	Refrigerator	Yellow	Gibman	07	$359.99
1039	Refrigerator	Copper	Gibman	05	$379.99
2061	Range	White	Hotspot	06	$489.99
2063	Range	Copper	Hotspot	05	$499.99
3541	Washer	White	Whirlaway	15	$349.99
3544	Washer	Yellow	Whirlaway	10	$359.99
3785	Dryer	White	Whirlaway	12	$249.99
3787	Dryer	Yellow	Whirlaway	08	$259.99

Fig. 8.2
A flat file.

quantity, and price. Further, the field size available for each attribute is identical for each record. These characteristics are typical of many accounting files. Most data files stored on punched cards are, of necessity, structured as flat files. However, the use of tape and disk files and more sophisticated software enables more complex file structures to be adopted.

Tree structures

A *tree* is a data structure in which relationships among data items may be expressed in the form of an hierarchical structure (see Fig. 2.1). A schema for a customer accounting file in which data relationships are represented in the form of a tree structure appears in Fig. 8.3. This tree consists of four *nodes,* which are the record types customer data, credit transactions, invoices, and invoice line items. The uppermost record type, which in this case contains the customer data, is referred to as the *root* of the tree. One characteristic of a tree is that each node other than the root is related to one and only one other node at a higher level, which is called its *parent.* However, each node may have one or more nodes related to it at a lower level, and these are called its *children.*

The arrows shown in Fig. 8.3 have important implications for the data relationships. In the diagram each line between a parent and child has one arrow pointing to the parent and two arrows pointing to the child. This indicates that each is a *one-to-many* relationship. This means that for any data record which is a physical occurrence of the parent-child relationship, each child has only one parent, but each parent may have several children. For example, each invoice is associated with only one customer, but each customer may have several invoices. Also, each line-item belongs to a single invoice, but a given invoice may have several line-items. In a one-to-many relationship, the child record type is often referred to as a *repeating group.* Such relationships are very common in accounting records.

Any tree or segment of a tree involving data relationships at only two levels may be referred to as a *set.* In a set there may be only one record type at the upper level, which is referred to as the *owner.* There may be one or more record types at the lower level, and these are called *members* of the set. The data structure shown in Fig. 8.3 could be said to involve two sets. In the first set the customer data is the owner and the credit transactions and invoices are the members. In the second set the invoice is the owner and the line-item is the member. Thus a record type that is a member in one set may be an owner in another set.

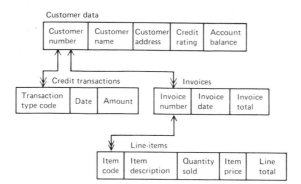

Fig. 8.3
Customer accounts
data in a tree
structure.

Network structures

In traditional business systems, virtually all files are either flat files or trees. For example, in a manual data processing system in which customer records are maintained in filing cabinets, it would not be uncommon for there to be a separate file folder for each customer containing an account ledger card and copies of invoices, remittance advices, and credit memos. The content and structure of such records are identical to that of the tree illustrated in Fig. 8.3. If such records were to be converted from file folders to magnetic tape as part of the computerization of customer accounting, they would undoubtedly continue to be structured in the form of a tree.

However, even in a business organization in which all records are structured as trees or flat files, relationships exist among data items or groups of items in separate files. Refer again to the sample data structure in Fig. 8.3. This company probably also maintains a separate file of general ledger accounts in which invoices sent to customers and credits to customers are entered as transactions. Furthermore, the organization may also have an inventory file in which sales to customers are recorded as reductions in the quantity on hand. In conventional data processing systems, such relationships among data in separate files are not recognized explicitly. However, when such files are converted from file folders or magnetic tape storage to a direct access medium such as magnetic disk, it becomes possible to explicitly recognize data relationships across files. This results in the type of data structure known as a network.

A *network* may be defined as a data structure involving relationships among multiple record types such that (1) each parent may have more than one child record type (as in a tree), *and* (2) each child may have more than one parent record type (not possible in a tree). For example, if we add the record types "general ledger account" and "inventory records" to the data structure of Fig. 8.3, and incorporate the relationships mentioned in the preceding paragraph, we obtain the network data structure illustrated in Fig. 8.4. In this figure the names of the individual data elements have been omitted to enable us to focus upon the relationships among record types. Note that, in accordance with the definition of a network, the child record type "credit transactions" has more than one parent record type—both "general ledger

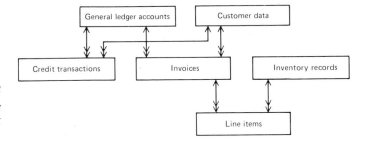

Fig. 8.4
Accounting data files
in a network
structure.

accounts'' and ''customer data.'' The record type ''invoices'' has the same two parents. Also, both ''invoices'' and ''inventory records'' are parents of ''line items.''

A fundamental characteristic of business records is that records in one file tend to be related to records in one or more other files. For example, all financial records in a business are fundamentally related because each is associated with two or more accounts within the double entry accounting system. What this means is that in a fundamental sense virtually all business records are part of a network structure. However, traditional file storage approaches involve filing cabinets, punched cards, magnetic tape, and related methods that can handle only flat files or simple tree structures. In contrast, direct access file storage devices and data base management software permit network structures to be explicitly recognized and processed. This is done by allowing the data base user to define schemata that have a network structure. Fig. 8.4 is one example of such a schema. Separate users may then define separate subschemata in either a flat file, tree, or network structure. The tree structure in Fig. 8.3 is an example of one subschema that could be derived from the schema in Fig. 8.4.

Each of the data relationships represented in Fig. 8.4 is a one-to-many relationship. One additional characteristic distinguishing network structures from tree structures is that a network structure may contain one or more *many-to-many* relationships. These are distinguished from one-to-many relationships in that a particular occurrence of a child record type may be owned by one or more occurrences of its parent record type. For example, consider the relationship between production parts, subassemblies, and finished products as diagrammed in Fig. 8.5. A subassembly may consist of several parts, and a product may consist of several subassemblies and parts, which is consistent with a one-to-many relationship. In addition, however, a given part may be included in several different subassemblies or products, and a particular subassembly may also be a component in several different products. Therefore each of the three relationships shown in the schema is a many-to-many relationship; this is represented in the diagram by the double arrows going in both directions for each relationship.

A network in which all of the data relationships are one-to-many, as in Fig. 8.4, is referred to as a *simple network*. One in which some or all of the relationships are many-to-many, as in Fig. 8.5, is referred to as a *complex network*.

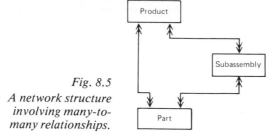

Fig. 8.5
A network structure
involving many-to-
many relationships.

Physical Data Base Organization

While each data user within a business organization may have his or her own separate logical view of the data, the system stores the data in only one way. Data base management software provides the link between the actual organization of the data on file storage media and the various logical views of the data in the minds of the users. Ideally, the system should appear to each user to behave *as if* the data were physically stored in exactly the way in which that user logically views them.

Whereas the previous section dealt with how users logically view data and data relationships within a data base, this section is concerned with how the data are physically stored, organized, and retrieved. It is assumed throughout the discussion that direct access storage devices such as magnetic disks are used to store the data base. The section begins with a look at several techniques of record addressing, and then explores the concepts of pointers, chains, and inverted files. Armed with an understanding of these concepts, the reader should better comprehend how data base management systems can minimize data redundancy while at the same time provide support for multiple user views of the data in the data base.

Methods of record addressing

As explained in Chapter 5, an address identifies a location in storage at which data are stored. In order to access a data record, its address must be obtained. Usually a key is available from which the address may be derived. This section is concerned with some of the more important methods of determining the physical address of a record based upon a key.

Sequential files   Records in sequential files are stored in numerical or alphabetical order according to the key. Given the key of the desired record, its location is obtained by reading through all the records in the file, one at a time, until the desired record is reached. For purposes of data base systems, this is a rather inefficient means of accessing a record. Therefore, sequential files are not generally used in data base systems.

Indexed-sequential files   In this method of file organization, the records are in key sequence and may be processed sequentially if desired. However, individual records may also be accessed directly by referring to a separate table of addresses called an *index* or *directory*. Each entry in the index contains a key and a corresponding address. Each storage address contains a block of records. Therefore, the index contains one entry for every nth key, where n is the number of records in a block.

An example of a file segment stored under the indexed-sequential access method appears in Fig. 8.6. In this example, 25 customer records numbered from 1478 to 1711 are stored in blocks of five in five storage addresses numbered from 4061 to 4065. The index contains five entries—one for each address. Each entry in the index contains the key of the last customer record in a block, and the address of that block.

To access a record in an indexed-sequential file, the system must perform several steps. First, the index itself must be accessed and read into primary memory. Then the index must be searched to find the key corresponding to the one desired. This search may be time-consuming, especially if the index is large. To shorten these search times, an index to the index is sometimes used to help zero in on the key being sought. Once the key is located in the index and the corresponding address is obtained, the block of records comprising the contents of that address are read into primary memory. Finally, the records in that block are searched to find the specific record desired.

The indexed-sequential file is the most common type of direct access file. Its basic advantage is that it enables efficient processing in both the sequential and online mode. For batch processing applications which need to be processed sequentially, the indexed-sequential file is treated essentially as a sequential file, whereas for online processing applications requiring direct access to specific records, the index provides for such access in a relatively efficient manner.

Indexes may also be used to facilitate access to a file which is not in sequential order on the indexed key. For example, indices based upon secondary keys are common in data base systems, and files are rarely maintained in sequential order on a secondary key.

Direct addressing   For some records it may be possible to establish an equivalence between record keys and machine addresses. For example, if invoices are numbered sequentially from 0001 to 9999 with no gaps, then it may be possible to store the invoice records sequentially at machine addresses 0001 to 9999. Then, when the system obtains a record key, it interprets the key value as a machine address and reads the record directly. This method, called *direct addressing,* is the fastest form of record addressing. A variation of direct addressing involves the application of a computational formula to convert the key into the machine address. For example, suppose the invoice records mentioned above are to be stored sequentially in blocks of four at machine addresses 7000 through 9500. Then the address of each record may be found by dividing its key by 4 and adding 7000 to the quotient.

Though direct addressing is a very fast method of record access, it is not feasible for the coding systems upon which many sets of record keys are based. For example, in many coding systems, not all of the numbers that could possibly be assigned as keys are used. Changing such keys to correspond to machine addresses may not be feasible because the key values may have some intrinsic meaning that

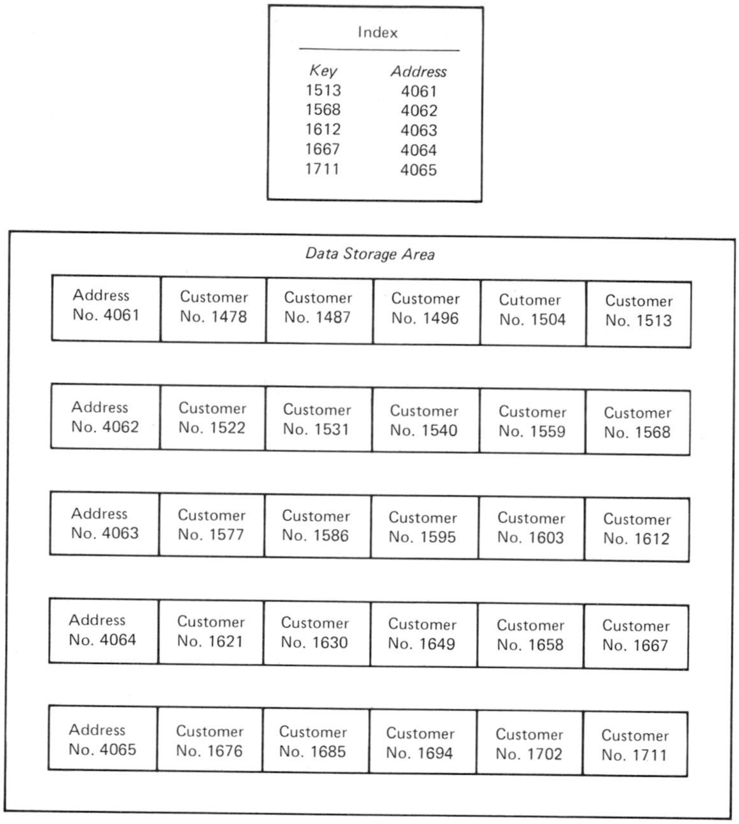

Index

Key	Address
1513	4061
1568	4062
1612	4063
1667	4064
1711	4065

Data Storage Area

Address No. 4061	Customer No. 1478	Customer No. 1487	Customer No. 1496	Cutomer No. 1504	Customer No. 1513
Address No. 4062	Customer No. 1522	Customer No. 1531	Customer No. 1540	Customer No. 1559	Customer No. 1568
Address No. 4063	Customer No. 1577	Customer No. 1586	Customer No. 1595	Customer No. 1603	Customer No. 1612
Address No. 4064	Customer No. 1621	Customer No. 1630	Customer No. 1649	Customer No. 1658	Customer No. 1667
Address No. 4065	Customer No. 1676	Customer No. 1685	Customer No. 1694	Customer No. 1702	Customer No. 1711

Fig. 8.6
An indexed-sequential file.

would be lost in such a conversion. Account numbers in a chart of accounts based upon a block coding design provide one example. Another problem involves volatile files in which the total set of record keys is constantly changing as records are added to and deleted from the file. In this situation, some of the available storage locations may be left empty because their addresses do not correspond to any of those generated by the key transformation formula, while other storage locations may overflow because several different record keys transform to the same address. In view of these kinds of problems, direct addressing is generally used only in a limited number of cases in which it is compatible with the characteristics of the file and the key coding system.

Randomizing   A technique of record addressing called *randomizing* involves the performance of a computation on the record key to convert it into a near-random number, which in turn is converted into the address of the record or of a block of records containing the one sought. In contrast to direct addressing, this technique may be applied to virtually any coding system, because the use of the random number ameliorates the problems of a keying system in which many keys are not used, or in which the keys are constantly changing due to record additions and deletions. This advantage, together with its relative speed, makes randomizing an increasingly popular method of record addressing.

One commonly used form of randomizing is the division remainder method. Under this method the address for each key is found by dividing the key value by a prime number approximately equal to the total number of storage addresses required for the file.[1] The quotient resulting from this calculation is discarded, and the remainder is used as (or converted into) the record address. For example, suppose 2400 employee records having social security number for a key are to be stored in blocks of five at 500 available storage addresses numbering from 000 to 499. When a social security number is divided by 499, the prime number closest to 500, a remainder ranging from 0 to 498 may result. Ideally, each of the 499 possible remainders will be obtained approximately five times, thereby minimizing the amount of overflow and the number of unused storage locations. Though randomizing will generally reduce the amount of overflow and unused storage capacity in comparison to direct addressing, it is almost never possible to achieve the ideal result of 100 percent storage utilization and no overflow.

To summarize, the use of sequential files is appropriate where applications involve only batch processing with no need for direct access. The use of indexed-sequential files is appropriate when both batch processing and direct access applications are significant. Where there is little or no batch processing, and direct access is significant, direct addressing should be used in those infrequent situations in which it may be readily adopted to the keying system, and randomizing should be used where direct addressing is not appropriate.

Pointers   A data item in one record which indicates (or "points to") the location in storage of another related record is called a *pointer*. The use of pointers is a very common method of delineating data relationships in a data base system. The pointer may consist of the actual machine address of the record pointed to, or it could consist of a key value for the record pointed to. In the latter case, the key value would have to be converted to a machine address by means of a record addressing technique, as discussed in the prior section.

A pointer may be contained within a data record, or it may be contained in an index. A pointer contained in a data record is called an *embedded pointer*. The term *directory pointer* is used to refer to a pointer that is stored within an index.

Pointers may be used to link records whose logical structure is in the form of a tree or network but which are not physically stored in adjoining locations. For example, consider the hypothetical set of record occurrences illustrated in Fig. 8.7. As shown, the general relationship among these records is in the form of a tree structure. However, even if the seventeen separate records shown are stored in the same disk unit, they are unlikely to be stored in adjoining storage locations. Nonetheless, the linkages represented in the figure can be established by including within each

---

[1] *A prime number is a number that is evenly divisible only by itself and by 1.*

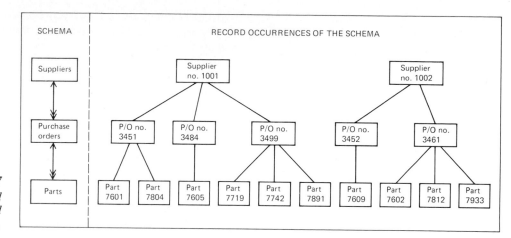

Fig. 8.7
*Schema and related
set of record
occurrences.*

Fig. 8.8
*Use of pointers to
link records stored in
separate locations.*

Supplier record storage area	Record content	Purchase order pointers			
	Supplier no. 1001	3451	3484	3499	———
	Supplier no. 1002	3452	3461	———	———

Purchase order record storage area	Record content	Parts pointers			
	P/O no. 3451	7601	7804	———	———
	P/O no. 3452	7609	———	———	———
	P/O no. 3461	7602	7812	7933	———
	P/O no. 3484	7605	———	———	———
	P/O no. 3499	7719	7742	7891	———

Inventory parts record storage area	Record content	Record content
	Part no. 7601	Part no. 7602
	Part no. 7605	Part no. 7609
	Part no. 7719	Part no. 7742
	Part no. 7804	Part no. 7812
	Part no. 7891	Part no. 7933

parent record a series of pointers to each of its children. This approach is illustrated, using this same set of records, in Fig. 8.8. For example, the link between supplier 1001 and purchase orders 3451, 3484, and 3499 is established by the pointers within the supplier 1001 record that contain the key values of those three purchase orders.

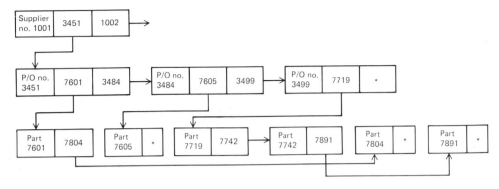

*Fig. 8.9
Child and twin
pointers.*

Under the arrangement illustrated in Fig. 8.8, each parent record has one pointer to each of its children. One problem with this approach is that the number of pointers per record varies depending on the number of children. Such "variable length pointer lists" increase the complexity of processing the records. In order to avoid this problem, an approach involving "child and twin pointers" is often used. Under this method each record contains only two pointers—one to its first child, if any, and one to its next twin, if any. Figure 8.9 illustrates this technique using the supplier 1001 record from Fig. 8.7. Note that parts records have no children, and therefore need contain only twin pointers. Also note that if a particular record has no first child or next twin, an (*) or another symbol may be substituted for the pointer value in the field reserved for the pointer.

Chains A series of data records, which may be physically dispersed throughout the files, but which are interconnected by means of a succession of pointers, is referred to as a *chain* or *list*. An illustration of a chain is provided in Fig. 8.10. The grid shown is assumed to represent a physical storage layout, with each cell containing one record. The records to be chained are the letters of the alphabet, which are physically scattered throughout the grid, but which are logically related in their proper alphabetical sequence by means of the chain. The pointers are embedded within the records, and are assumed to contain the machine address of the subsequent record. The arrows merely symbolize that each pointer "points to" the physical storage location of the next record.

There are many applications of chains in data base systems. One example commonly found in accounting systems is the association of a set of detail records with a master record. A general ledger record or a customer accounts receivable record may have associated with it a number of transaction detail records, which could be connected to it by means of chaining. Similarly, an invoice or purchase order record could have a chain of line-item records connected to it.

Another application of chains involves dealing with the overflow of data storage locations that, as previously mentioned, can arise under certain methods of record addressing. For example, if six records are assigned to a storage location that

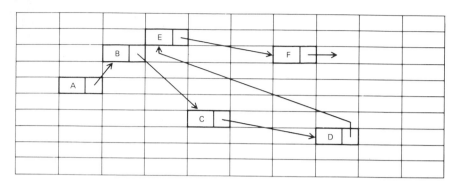

Fig. 8.10
A chain.

can hold only four records, then the two excess records must be stored in other locations. However, the two excess records can be linked to their originally assigned
storage location using a chain. All that is required is that the last of the four records
in the assigned storage location contain a pointer indicating the actual machine
address of the first excess record, and that the first excess record contain a pointer to
the machine address of the second excess record. This approach will be effective
(though not always efficient) regardless of the extent of overflow in a file.

Another example of the use of chains is to link together all records in a file that
meet a particular criterion, such as all accounts past due or all salespeople whose
total dollar sales exceed a particular amount. Chains may also be used to link together all records in a file which have the same secondary key, such as all employees
who work in the same department, or all products which are part of the same
product line.

Figure 8.11 illustrates the use of embedded pointers to chain together parts
records having the same secondary keys. Each record includes only a limited version
of the data that would normally be contained in a parts file—the part number,
supplier of the part, and product in which the part is used. Each record is assumed to
reside in a storage location coded with a two-digit machine address. For each of the
secondary keys, supplier and product line, there are four different chains—one for
each of the four possible values that each secondary key might assume. The links in
each chain are embedded pointers contained in the fields labeled ''Next S'' and
''Next PL,'' each of which ''points to'' the machine address of the next record
having the same value for supplier and product line respectively. For example, the
chain for all parts supplied by ABC Co. may be traced through the records at machine addresses 11, 16, 17, 21, and 30.

The last item in a chain may or may not point back to the beginning of the
chain. When the pointer in the last record of the chain points back to the first
record, the chain is referred to as a *ring*. When a chain is not a ring, the pointer in
the last record must contain an end-of-chain indicator, such as the asterisk used in
Figs. 8.9 and 8.11.

A chain may be connected by means of only one pointer per record, starting
with the first record, or *head* of the chain, and proceeding to the end of the chain. In

Address	Part No.	Supplier	Next S	Product Line	Next PL
11	125	ABC Co.	16	Widget	17
12	164	XYZ Inc.	14	Doodad	16
13	189	GHI Corp.	18	Clavet	15
14	205	XYZ Inc.	24	Lodix	18
15	271	RST Mfg.	19	Clavet	22
16	293	ABC Co.	17	Doodad	20
17	316	ABC Co.	21	Widget	23
18	348	GHI Corp.	20	Lodix	19
19	377	RST Mfg.	22	Lodix	21
20	383	GHI Corp.	23	Doodad	24
21	451	ABC Co.	30	Lodix	25
22	465	RST Mfg.	25	Clavet	27
23	498	GHI Corp.	26	Widget	*
24	521	XYZ Inc.	28	Doodad	26
25	572	RST Mfg.	*	Lodix	28
26	586	GHI Corp.	27	Doodad	29
27	603	GHI Corp.	29	Clavet	*
28	647	XYZ Inc.	*	Lodix	30
29	653	GHI Corp.	*	Doodad	*
30	719	ABC Co.	*	Lodix	*

Fig. 8.11
Parts records chained on two secondary keys using embedded pointers.

this case the pointers are referred to as *forward pointers*. Records in a chain may also include *backward pointers,* which point to the prior record in the chain, and *parent pointers,* which point to the head of the chain. Figure 8.12 illustrates a chain with forward, backward, and parent pointers. Within each record the first pointer (moving from left to right) is a forward pointer, the second is a backward pointer, and the third is a parent pointer.

The use of backward and/or parent pointers in addition to forward pointers, though more costly in terms of the additional storage space required, does have some advantages. One such advantage relates to the frequent need to delete records from a chain. Suppose for example that we have entered the chain in Fig. 8.10 at record C, which is to be deleted. This would require that the pointer in record B be changed so that it points to record D. However, there is presently no way to get from record C to record B unless the chain is a ring, and even then it would be necessary to travel all the way around the ring. A backward pointer would make it possible to access the prior record in one step. If there were parent and forward pointers, but no backward pointers, the system could go directly from record C to the head of the chain, and then follow the chain until it came to record B.

The use of both forward and backward pointers also facilitates recovery from damage or loss of pointers due to a system malfunction of some kind. Consider again the chain in Fig. 8.10. If the pointer in record C were damaged, there would be no way to access any of the subsequent records, and they could be permanently lost. However, suppose all of the pointers in record 3 of Fig. 8.12 are damaged. Because this chain has both forward and backward pointers, all records would still be accessible from the head, and the pointers in record 3 could be reconstructed in a few simple steps.

Chaining of records has several advantages. A major advantage is that it enables considerable reduction of record redundancy, because a record that is physically stored only once may be a member of several chains. Chaining may also be used to reduce the need for sorting, which is a very time-consuming operation in

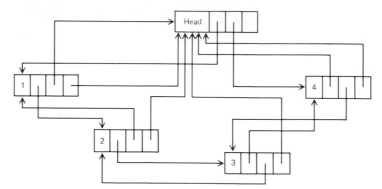

Fig. 8.12
A ring with forward,
backward, and par-
ent pointers.

many systems. If the records are chained together in a particular sequence, then it may not be necessary to perform a sort operation when they must be processed in that sequence. Chaining also facilitates the retrieval of records whenever their physical sequence does not correspond to the logical sequence according to which the user wishes to retrieve. For example, customer accounts may be in sequence by account number, but a user may wish to retrieve only those that are past due. Similarly, employee records may be in sequence by employee number, but a user may wish to retrieve only those for a particular department.

Chaining does have some significant disadvantages. First, additional storage space is required for the pointers. Second, and more significant, chains must be updated as new records are added, old records are deleted, and chained data within current records are modified. The necessity to update chains adds considerably to the complexity of the file updating process.

Inverted lists   The chains discussed and illustrated in the prior sections involved embedded pointers. Chains may also be maintained using indices of directory pointers. A chain which consists of a series of key values or machine addresses stored together in an index is referred to as an *inverted list*. An *inverted file* is one in which inverted lists are maintained for some of the attributes. Such a file is *fully inverted* if there are inverted lists for every one of its attributes. Fully inverted files are unnecessary for most business applications. A *partially inverted file* is one for which inverted lists are maintained for some but not all attributes.

Using the sample data records from Fig. 8.11, inverted lists for the secondary keys supplier and product line are shown in Fig. 8.13. There is one list for each value of each attribute, and each list contains the machine addresses of all records having that value for that attribute. In some cases inverted lists might contain the key values of the records rather than their machine addresses.

The basic advantage of inverted files is that they facilitate the retrieval of information from a data base. This point is further explained in the next section. The dis-

Fig. 8.13
Inverted lists for the
secondary keys of
Fig. 8.11.

Supplier	Addresses		Product Line	Addresses
ABC Co.	11, 16, 17, 21, 30		Clavet	13, 15, 22, 27
GHI Corp.	13, 18, 20, 23, 26, 27, 29		Doodad	12, 16, 20, 24, 26, 29
RST Mfg.	15, 19, 22, 25		Lodix	14, 18, 19, 21, 25, 28, 30
XYZ Inc.	12, 14, 24, 28		Widget	11, 17, 23

advantages of inverted files are that the indices may require a substantial amount of storage space and that the indices must be continually updated as the data records are updated.

Information Retrieval

Thus far the discussion of the merits of data base systems has mentioned only their operational advantages to an organization, such as the minimization of data redundancy and inconsistency. Data base systems also offer significant advantages in the form of enhanced capabilities to retrieve useful managerial information from the data base.

In traditional data processing systems, the ability of managers to obtain information from the data files is often constrained by the limitations of the system. The identification of which entities in a file possessed certain attributes would require a costly scan of the entire file. The modification of report formats would require a costly reprogramming effort. And the generation of any special purpose report involving data from two or more separate applications could require substantial amounts of money and manpower, and might end up taking so long to complete that the final report is not timely enough to be useful.

The use of data base systems can substantially reduce these limitations, particularly if these systems include a query language that can be easily learned and applied by managers at an online terminal. Consider for example questions of the form "Which entities in the file possess attribute X?" Answers to such questions are frequently needed by managers in the course of their work. On short notice a manager may need to know "Which employees can speak Spanish?" or "Which parts are supplied by GHI Corp.?" or "Which deliveries are past due?" Using a data base system in which inverted lists are maintained for the appropriate fields, answers to such questions may be quickly obtained. For example, to answer the question "Which parts are supplied by GHI Corp.?" the system would reference a supplier index, such as the one in Fig. 8.13, to obtain the machine addresses or keys of all such parts, and then access the records of those parts to provide the answer to the question.

In some cases managers may wish to identify entities possessing more than one specified attribute. Questions such as, "Which employees in the Engineering Department speak Spanish?" or "Which parts used in the Clavet product line are supplied by GHI Corp.?" fall into this category. The term *multiple key retrieval* is used to refer to the process of answering questions of this kind. If the data base system maintains an inverted list for both of the attributes involved, then this type of question is readily answered. Again using the parts question as an example, the system would retrieve from the supplier index the machine addresses of all parts supplied by GHI Corp, and would obtain from the product line index (see also Fig. 8.13) the machine addresses of all parts used in the Clavet product line. These two lists of parts would then be compared to find those machine addresses common to both, which in this case are 13 and 27. These addresses would then be accessed to retrieve the parts information, thereby satisfying the original question. Note that in the absence of the inverted file capability, the only way to answer this question would be to use a special program which examined every record in the file.

The reporting capabilities of a data processing system are substantially enhanced by data base capabilities. Report formats can be easily revised in a data base system in response to managerial needs. Reports may be generated on an "as needed" basis instead of, or in addition to, using a regular weekly or monthly schedule. By using the interactive capability of a data base system with a query language, a manager can "browse" through the data base to search for causes underlying the problems highlighted on an exception report, or to obtain detailed information underlying a summary report. The interactive feature of the system enables the manager to formulate new questions based upon the system's response to previous questions.

Data base systems support "cross-functional" data analysis much more readily than do traditional systems. This term refers to the analysis of data relating to different functional areas of the business, such as marketing and accounting. Many data relationships exist which are cross-functional in nature, such as the association between dollar sales and marketing regions, or between selling costs and promotional campaigns. A traditional data processing system is typically capable of recognizing only a few such relationships among data elements. In a data base system, most or all such relationships may be explicitly defined and utilized in the preparation of management reports. A greater variety of reports in terms of content and format is thus possible. Further, the system is more capable of responding to managerial requests of an unusual nature that arise on short notice and may not have been foreseen.

Data Base Management Systems

Within the past few years many software packages offering data base management capabilities have become commercially available. All of the major computer manufacturers and some independent software companies offer such products. This section briefly reviews the general nature of these data base management systems (DBMS).

DBMS functions

The functions of DBMS may be divided into three broad categories: creation of the data base, processing of the data base, and retrieval of information from the data base. Creation of the data base involves (1) defining the data structure and relationships and (2) loading the data values into the physical data base facility. In defining the data base, most DBMS use a format resembling an expanded version of the COBOL Data Division (see Fig. 7.9). Each data item is listed, its size and type are given, its status as a primary or secondary key (necessitating a separate index) is indicated, and its relationship to other data items is designated. To assist in loading data values into the data base, some DBMSs provide special programs that are run with the data after the data structure has been defined.

Processing of the data base involves normal file maintenance activities such as addition of new records, deletion of old records, and updating of existing records to reflect transactions. In addition to updating the data records themselves, indices maintained by the system must also be updated during processing. Modification of the data structure as necessary could also be encompassed under processing. Also important are a variety of procedures relating to the protection of the data base from exposure to unauthorized persons or from either accidental destruction or modification by inaccurate transaction input.

One of the most significant differences between the processing of traditional files and the processing of data bases is that traditional files are processed only by a small number of programs each doing its work at a separate time, while data bases are processed by several programs, some of which may be working on the same data base concurrently. In this situation there is a danger that errors may be introduced into the data base when different programs attempt to modify the same data items simultaneously. Data base management systems must include specialized capabilities for dealing with these multiple concurrent updates.

A DBMS also provides an output capability in the form of report generation programs, inquiry processing languages, or both. Report generation programs are usually quite simple, and enable the user to specify input data, operations performed, and output format. Although available inquiry languages are generally simple and user-oriented, considerably more work is necessary in the development of a simple but effective inquiry language.

CODASYL DBTG report

The CODASYL Data Base Task Group (DBTG) is a group consisting of systems vendors and users that has been working since 1969 on the development of specifications for DBMS. You may recall from the prior chapter that CODASYL also developed the COBOL programming language. In April of 1971 the DBTG issued a report that was published and has had considerable impact upon the development of DBMS. This report contributed the concepts of set, schema, and subschema that have been previously discussed. It proposed specifications for a data base description language to be used in defining the structure of a data base during its creation, and for a data base manipulation language to be used to enhance the capabilities of other "host" languages, such as COBOL, in processing the data base.

While the DBTG provided some impetus to the development of DBMS, it also invoked some criticism. Some in the industry felt that it was too COBOL-oriented. Also, it virtually ignored inquiry languages, which are very valuable in many applications of DBMS. Finally, many felt that the report was simply not adequate as a standard that could guide all subsequent development of DBMS.

Since the DBTG report was issued, several DBMS software packages have been developed and made commercially available. Figure 8.14 lists some of the more im-

Package	Vendor	Consistent with DBTG	Remarks
ADABAS	Software AG	No	A unique system with many special features. Based on the inverted file approach. Has a good query language.
DMS–1100	Univac	Yes	Available free to users of UNIVAC equipment. Not compatible with other vendors' equipment.
IDMS	Cullinane Corp.	Yes	A widely used system which ranks high in user satisfaction.
IDS	Honeywell	Yes	One of the first systems developed and implemented. Was forerunner of the DBTG approach.
IMS	IBM Corp.	No	A relatively complex system, but widely used.
SYSTEM 2000	MRI Systems Corp.	No	Easy-to-use system based on the inverted file approach. Has an excellent query language.
TOTAL	Cincom Systems, Inc.	Yes	A relatively simple system. Is the most widely used of all DBMS packages.

*Fig. 8.14
Commonly used
DBMS software
packages.*

portant of these and their vendors. Some of these are consistent with the DBTG specifications, but others are not. Present trends seem to indicate that there will continue to be a wide variety of packages available offering different features and capabilities, as opposed to a set of similar packages based upon an industrywide standard.

Putting Data Base Concepts to Work

To summarize the advantages of data base systems that have been mentioned at various points throughout this chapter, they are (1) the minimization of redundancy of data stored within a system, and of the related inconsistency among stored data elements that may result from data redundancy, (2) the establishment of data independence, which facilitates the development and maintenance of computer application programs, (3) the explicit recognition of data relationships in a way that makes possible the integration of file updating procedures which are traditionally separated, and (4) the enhancement of information availability to managers which is provided by query languages, simple report generation capabilities, and support for cross-functional data analysis.

When an organization decides that it will attempt to realize these advantages by acquiring a data base capability, there are numerous steps it must take. Among the most significant of these are (1) taking an inventory of data elements used throughout the organization, (2) designing schemata for initial data base applications, (3) surveying available DBMS software and selecting a package that best meets its requirements, (4) defining subschemata for specific applications, (5) writing new application programs, or modifying existing ones, (6) loading the data into the data base, (7) processing of transaction data to update the contents of the data base, and (8) maintenance of schemata, subschemata, and application programs.

To treat properly the subject of implementing data base systems within an organization would require a separate chapter, or perhaps an entire book. Accordingly, this section examines only two of the steps listed above—the taking of a data inventory and the design of a data base schema. These two issues have been selected for discussion because they represent areas in which the accountant should be able to make a significant contribution to the implementation process. The section concludes with a discussion of the general implications of data base systems for accounting.

The data dictionary

A data base system cannot be successfully implemented in an organization unless the implementers have a thorough understanding of the data elements used within the organization, where they come from, and how and by whom they are used. This is why the taking of an inventory of data elements is one of the very first steps in the process of implementing a data base system. The information collected during the inventory is recorded in a special file called a *data dictionary*.

The data dictionary is essentially a centralized source of data about data. For each data element used in the organization, there is a record in the data dictionary that contains data about that data element. For example, each record might contain the name of the data element, the name of the file in which it is stored, the name of the source document from which it originates, its size, its field class (numeric, alphanumeric, etc.), the names of all programs in which it is used, the names of all output reports in which it is used, the names of people (programmers, managers, etc.) who use it, and any synonyms (other data names applied to the same data element within other files or systems) which it may have.

The maintenance of the data dictionary is usually automated. In fact, this is often one of the first applications of a newly implemented data base system. Inputs to the data dictionary may include records of any new data elements, as well as changes in names, descriptions, or usages of existing data elements. Outputs from the data dictionary include a variety of reports useful to programmers, data base designers, and users of the information system. Sample reports include a list of all programs in which a data item is used, a list of all synonyms for the data elements in a particular file, a list of all data elements used by a particular user, or a list of all output reports in which a data element is used. One can easily imagine how reports of this type are extremely useful to the design and implementation of a data base system.

Within a business organization, the accountant probably has a better understanding than almost anyone else of the data elements that exist in the organization, where they originate, and where they are used. This knowledge is a result of the accountant's traditional role in the design of information systems and in the processing of financial data. Therefore, an experienced accountant should play a key role in the development of the data dictionary.

The design of data base schemata

Another critical early step in the implementation of a data base system is the design of data base schemata. As mentioned earlier in the chapter, most organizations will utilize separate data bases for major functional areas, rather than a single comprehensive data base for the entire organization. Thus the first step in schema design is the determination of which data elements to include in which schema. To resolve this problem, it will be necessary to identify "clusters" consisting of files and programs closely related to each other in terms of processing and usage, but not closely related to files and programs in other clusters.

Once the data elements to be included within a particular schema have been identified, it is necessary to specify the relationships that exist between them. Those data elements having a one-to-one relationship with each other are candidates to be included within the same record. Each record within a schema may be related to one or more other records, and each such relationship may be either a one-to-many or many-to-many relationship. All relationships that are relevant, either to the integrated processing of update transactions against the data base, or to the retrieval of related information from the data base in response to user needs, should be explicitly recognized in the data base schema.

Another important aspect of data base schema design is the designation of those data elements that will serve as keys. The appropriate primary key for each record is generally obvious. However, the choice of secondary keys is also significant because secondary keys can enhance the efficiency of processing of the data base and facilitate the retrieval of information from it. The data elements most appropriate for selection as a secondary key generally are those that identify certain properties held in common by groups of records. Examples include invoice due date, employee department number, and inventory location code.

An important objective in the design of a data base schema is the simplification of the data structure. The reason for this is that complicated data structures such as networks (especially complex networks) are more difficult for DBMS software packages to work with than are simpler data structures such as trees and flat files. In fact, the schema definition techniques used by some DBMS software packages do not allow network data structures to be specified explicitly. For example, each CODASYL set must be a two-level tree containing only one-to-many relationships.

By introducing a limited amount of redundancy into a data base schema, it is possible to represent a network data structure as a series of tree structures. For example, consider the network data structure shown in Fig. 8.5. As illustrated in Fig. 8.15, this complex network can be represented by a series of four CODASYL sets. Though there is redundancy in the record types appearing in this schema, this does not necessarily mean that there will be redundancy in the physical data stored in this data base because the links shown in Fig. 8.15 can be represented by pointers without having to store redundant data records.

Many data base specialists feel that it is desirable to go even further toward simplified schemata by reducing all files in a data base to flat files. Under this approach, each relationship that exists between data records in a pair of flat files is represented by storing the primary keys for the two files together. In essence each relationship between data records in the data base is established by means of embedded key pointers that appear to be simply additional data elements but that in fact provide the data linkages necessary to represent any form of tree or network structure. This type of data base is called a *relational data base*. Figure 8.16 illustrates the tree data

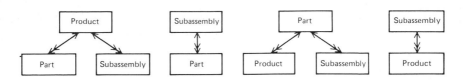

Fig. 8.15
Representation of a
network data struc-
ture by means of a
series of tree
structures.

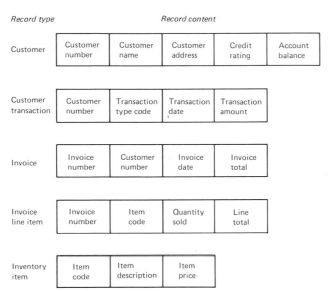

Record type   *Record content*

Customer

Customer number	Customer name	Customer address	Credit rating	Account balance

Customer transaction

Customer number	Transaction type code	Transaction date	Transaction amount

Invoice

Invoice number	Customer number	Invoice date	Invoice total

Invoice line item

Invoice number	Item code	Quantity sold	Line total

Inventory item

Item code	Item description	Item price

Fig. 8.16
A relational data
base.

structure from Fig. 8.3 converted to relational form.[2] Note that each of the three relations represented by arrows in Fig. 8.3 is represented in Fig. 8.16 by pairs of data elements which are contained within the same record. For example, the link between customer and invoice records is established in Fig. 8.16 by the inclusion of both the customer number and the invoice number within the invoice record.

Any type of data base structure can be reduced to a relational form. Again note that the relational schema contains redundant data elements, but this does not necessarily mean that there will be any more physical data redundancy than would otherwise be necessary. Advocates of the relational approach to data base design believe that this approach provides data bases that are easier to work with, more flexible, and more easily modified than any other type of data base.

As with the development of a data dictionary, the accountant should play a key role in the design of data base schemata. The accountant's basic familiarity with

[2] *The process of converting a conventional data base to relational form, which is called "normalization," is beyond the scope of this book. A good treatment of this topic may be found in James Martin,* Computer Data Base Organization *(2nd ed.). Englewood Cliffs, N.J.: Prentice-Hall, 1977, Chapters 13 and 14.*

record content and data relationships endows him or her with the perspective necessary to ensure that schema designs adequately satisfy all user requirements. It is also important that other management personnel be involved in the design of those schemata that relate specifically to their areas of responsibility.

Implications of data base systems for accounting

Within a few years most or all accounting data within many large organizations may be stored in data base systems. This has some interesting implications for accounting. One of these—the need for accountants to be involved in the process of implementing data base systems—has already been examined. At the organizational level, another significant issue involves the impact of data base systems on internal control. The centralization of data storage and the integration of data processing brought about by data base systems require that greater emphasis be placed upon matters such as the accuracy of input data, the preservation of audit trails, the control of access to the data, and the maintenance of backup copies of data files. In essence, the organization's data base is an asset that must be safeguarded just like cash, inventories, and equipment.

At a more general level, data base technology may have a profound impact upon the fundamental nature of accounting. For example, the accounting process traditionally begins with the recording of transactions from source documents onto journals, which is followed by posting from the journals to ledgers, balancing of ledger accounts, and ultimately the generation of financial statements. If the accounting system is converted to a data base, all that the accountant needs to do is enter the source document data into the data base. Because of predefined data linkages within the accounting data base, the posting and balancing steps are accomplished automatically and immediately as the source data are entered. Financial statements or other accounting reports may then be generated at any time in response to a user request.

At an even more fundamental level, data base technology could conceivably lead to the abandonment of the double entry accounting model. The basic philosophy of the double entry model is the utilization of redundancy to provide a check on the accuracy of data processing. Every transaction generates equal debit and credit entries, and the equality of debits and credits is checked and rechecked at numerous points in the accounting process. However, as we have seen, data redundancy is the antithesis of the data base concept. If the amounts associated with a transaction are correctly entered into a data base system, it is necessary to store them only once, not twice. Computer data processing is sufficiently accurate to ensure that the elaborate system of checks and double checks, which characterizes the double entry accounting model, is unnecessary. Thus data base technology could conceivably do away with the need for the double entry model. This has not happened yet because data base technology is not yet widely implemented in accounting systems, and because nobody has yet developed an alternative accounting model that is more consistent with data base concepts. Furthermore, the double entry model is so firmly entrenched in accounting that it may never change—rather, it may just be implemented on data base systems with little or no modification, in spite of the apparent inconsistencies. Whatever happens, the increasing application of data base systems in accounting promises to make the next several years very interesting for the accounting profession.

Review Questions

1. Define the following terms.

data redundancy	complex network
data base	index
data base management system	directory
data base system	direct addressing
data independence	randomizing
schema	pointer
subschema	embedded pointer
physical data organization	directory pointer
logical data organization	chain
flat file	list
tree	ring
node	head
root	forward pointer
parent	backward pointer
children	parent pointer
one-to-many relationship	inverted list
repeating group	inverted file
set	fully inverted file
owner	partially inverted file
member	multiple key retrieval
network	data dictionary
many-to-many relationship	relational data base
simple network	

2. Explain some of the differences between the traditional approach to data processing and the data base approach.

3. Give an example of an entity, an attribute, and a key. Explain how data representing these would be stored in an information system.

4. Describe five examples of the categories of data that may be stored in a field.

5. Explain and give an example of how physical data organization may differ from logical data organization.

6. What are the three basic types of logical data structures?

7. List and explain four methods of record addressing.

8. List the steps necessary to access a record in an indexed-sequential file.

9. Explain two variations of direct addressing.

10. What are the relative advantages and disadvantages of the four basic methods of record addressing? Under what circumstances is each method most appropriate?

11. What are the two alternative types of data item which a pointer field may contain?

12. Explain the difference between using variable length pointer lists in linking a tree structure and using a child and twin pointers. What advantages does the latter approach have?

13. Describe some of the possible applications of chains in a data base system.

14. What are the advantages and disadvantages of using backward and/or parent pointers in addition to forward pointers in a chain?

15. What are the advantages and disadvantages of chaining records.

16. Explain the advantages and disadvantages of inverted files.

17. What are some of the limitations of traditional (non-data-base) data processing systems with regard to information retrieval? Explain several ways in which data base systems facilitate information retrieval.

18. List and explain several functions of a DBMS software package.

19. What were some of the items proposed in the April 1971 CODASYL Data Base Task Group report? What criticisms have been made of this report?

20. Name several of the commercially available DBMS software packages.

21. Summarize the advantages of data base systems in contrast with traditional data processing methods.

22. List some of the key steps which an organization must take in order to implement a data base system.

23. What are some of the uses of a data dictionary? Why should the accountant play a key role in the development of a data dictionary within an organization?

24. Briefly describe some significant aspects of the design of data base schemas.

25. Explain how a data base designer may be able to simplify the structure of a data base schema.

26. List some internal control concerns that must be emphasized in a data base environment.

Discussion Questions

27. What would be the advantages and disadvantages of integrating all of an organization's data into a single comprehensive data base? Would you favor such an approach? Explain.

28. What would be the advantages and disadvantages of having an industrywide standard with which all DBMS software packages conformed? Would you favor imposing such a standard? Discuss.

29. Does an auditor working for a public accounting firm need to have any knowledge of data base systems? Explain.

30. Discuss the potential impact of data base technology on the fundamental nature of accounting. Do you believe that this potential impact will ever be realized? Why or why not?

Problems and Cases

31. Using a data processing application to inventory record keeping as an illustration, identify one example of an entity, an attribute, a record, a data item, a repeating group, a primary key, and a secondary key.

32. Assume that 30 records with key values numbered sequentially from 721 to 750 are stored in blocks of six at five machine addresses numbered sequentially from 101 to 105.

Required

a) Prepare an index for this file segment.

b) Assuming an indexed-sequential file organization, explain how the system would access record number 740.

33. Assume that a customer account record labeled A1 owns three invoice records labeled from I1 to I3. Invoice I1 owns three line-item records labeled L1 to L3; invoice I2 owns two line-item records, L4 and L5; and invoice I3 owns four line-item records, L6 through L9.

Required

a) Draw a diagram showing how these records would be linked using variable length pointer lists. Show the presence of pointers within records in a manner similar to that shown in Fig. 8.9.

b) Draw a diagram showing how these records would be linked using child and twin pointers.

34. Assume that 4800 inventory records are to be stored in blocks of five at 1000 machine addresses numbered from 3000 to 3999. The division remainder method is to be used to assign the records to the storage addresses. You are to determine the storage address for each of the inventory records whose primary keys are listed below. **Hints:** (1) the prime number closest to 1000 is 997, (2) once you obtain a remainder, you must add a constant to it to obtain the address.

Key	*Address*
14958	_____
42871	_____
55833	_____
68797	_____
95714	_____

35. Refer to the set of hypothetical inventory records in Fig. 8.2. Assume that these are stored sequentially at machine addresses numbered from 1 to 9, and that we wish to use embedded pointers to chain together all items having the same color.

Required

a) Prepare a table with column headings "machine address," "stock number," "color," and "next C" (for the pointer to the next item of the same color). Fill in this table according to the specifications described above.

b) Invert this file on the secondary key "color" by means of an index.

36. Refer to the inverted lists in Fig. 8.13. Describe the process that the system would follow to answer the question "Which parts supplied by RST Mfg. are used in the Lodix product line?" Retrieve the appropriate part numbers from Fig. 8.11.

37. *Note:* To complete this problem, it is necessary that your school's library subscribe to *Datapro 70: The EDP Buyer's Bible,* or to a similar data processing library service.

Read the report entitled "A Buyer's Guide to Data Base Management Systems" in Volume 3 of *Datapro 70.* Using the comparison charts at the back of the report, identify five data base management systems available from five different vendors.

Required   Prepare a table listing the following information for each data base management system.

DBMS name	*DBMS #1*	*DBMS #2*	*etc.*

Vendor name
Current number of users
CPU's supported
Minimum memory requirements
Data base organization
Application languages
Inquiry/retrieval facility
Data dictionary support
Price

38. You are a systems analyst for the Consumer Electronics Co. The company has just acquired a data base management system, and one of the first applications of it will be to customer accounting. A credit memo form identical to that shown in Fig. 3.1 is used. You have been assigned to diagram the data structure of the credit memo as a first step in the application design. Use a format similar to that in Fig. 8.3. Note that the data base is to contain only the variable data on the form, not the constant data.

39. Consider the network data structure shown in Fig. 8.4. Draw a diagram showing how this network may be represented by a series of four CODASYL sets.

40. Consider the following data items composing an accounts receivable record which is to be incorporated into a data base system.

- Customer account number (primary key)
- Customer name
- Customer address
- Location code
- Credit rating code
- Credit limit
- Beginning account balance
- Current transactions (repeating group)
    Transaction type
    Document number
    Transaction date
    Amount
- Current balance

Required
Identify the data items within this record that are good potential candidates to be designated as secondary keys. Explain each of your choices.

41. You are to design a schema for a purchasing data base. This data base will encompass the data in five records that are presently maintained on magnetic tape files. These records, and their data content, are as follows.

(1) supplier record—supplier number, supplier name, supplier address, shipment terms, billing terms

(2) purchase order record—order number, supplier number, order date, buyer name

(3) purchase order line-item record—part number, part description, quantity ordered, quantity received, price, line total, requested delivery date

(4) parts inventory record—part number, part description, standard cost, quantity on hand, quantity on order

(5) part quotation record—part number, supplier number, quoted price

Required
a) Prepare a schema diagram. Use a format similar to that of Fig. 8.3. For each relationship between a pair of records, indicate by means of arrowheads whether it is a one-to-one, one-to-many, or many-to-many relationship.

b) Prepare a diagram (using the Fig. 8.3 format) showing the subschema that would be used by a program that adds new purchase order records to the data base.

c) Prepare a diagram (using the Fig. 8.3 format) showing the subschema that would be used by a program that enters records of receipts of parts on order into the data base.

d) Prepare a diagram (using the Fig. 8.3 format) showing the subschema that would be used by a program designed to generate a report that shows quotations and related supplier information for a specified part.

References
Ahituv, Niv, and Michael Hadass. "Identifying the Need for a DBMS." *Journal of Systems Management* (August 1980): 30–33.

Appleton, Daniel S. "What Data Base Isn't." *Datamation* (January 1977): 85–92.

Barnhardt, Robert S. "Implementing Relational Data Bases." *Datamation* (October 1980): 161–172.

Bonczek, Robert H.; Clyde W. Holsapple; and Andrew B. Whinston. "Aiding Decision Makers with a Generalized Data Base Management System: An Application to Inventory Management." *Decision Sciences* (April 1978): 228–245.

Canning, Richard G. "Planning for DBMS Conversions." *EDP Analyzer* (May 1978): 1–13.

_____. "Toward the Better Management of Data." *EDP Analyzer* (December 1976): 1–14.

Cardenas, Alfonso F. *Data Base Management Systems*. Boston: Allyn and Bacon, 1979.

Datapro Research Corporation. "A Buyer's Guide to Data Base Management Systems." In *Datapro 70: The EDP Buyer's Bible*. Delran, N.J.: Datapro Research Corporation, 1980.

Date, C. J. *An Introduction to Database Systems* (2nd ed.). Reading, Mass.: Addison-Wesley, 1977.

Kroenke, David. *Database: A Professional's Primer*. Science Research Associates, 1978.

McFadden, Fred R., and James D. Suver. "Costs and Benefits of a Data Base System." *Harvard Business Review* (January-February 1978): 131–139.

Martin, James. *Computer Data-Base Organization* (2nd ed.). Englewood Cliffs, N.J.: Prentice-Hall, 1977.

_____. *Principles of Data Base Management*. Englewood Cliffs, N.J.: Prentice-Hall, 1976.

Nolan, Richard L. "Computer Data Bases: The Future Is Now." *Harvard Business Review* (September-October 1973): 98–114.

Nusbaum, Edward E.; Andrew D. Bailey, Jr.; and Andrew B. Whinston. "Data-Base Management, Accounting, and Accountants." *Management Accounting* (May 1978): 35–38.

Parsons, Ronald G. "Whither DBMS Standards." *Infosystems* (September 1978): 64–68.

Rolfe, Michael, and Frank Kowalkowski. "How Successful Is Data Base Management?" *Infosystems* (March 1980): 56–64.

Romney, Marshall B. "Should Management Jump on the Data Base Wagon?" *Financial Executive* (May 1979): 24–30.

Ross, Ronald G. *Data Base Systems, Design, Implementation, and Management*. New York: AMACOM, 1978.

Schanstra, Carla. "Diminishing the DBMS Mystique." *Infosystems* (September 1978): 56–62.

Severance, Jay, and Ronald R. Bottin. "Work-in-Process Inventory Control through Data Base Concepts." *Management Accounting* (January 1979): 37–41.

Singel, John B., Jr. "Computer Data Base Systems: Who Needs Them?" *Price Waterhouse and Co. Review* (1975, No. 2): 18–27.

Walsh, Myles E. "Relational Data Bases." *Journal of Systems Management* (June 1980): 11–15.

Wiorkowski, Gabrielle K., and John J. Wiorkowski. "Does a Data Base Management System Pay Off?" *Datamation* (April 1978): 109–114.

Chapter 9

Real-Time Systems

Some data processing applications are characterized by a need for very fast processing and reporting of information. For example, a data processing system that supports bank teller operations must quickly provide current account balances and other customer information to enable the tellers to serve their customers without undue delay. Similarly, an airline reservations systems must provide current information concerning flight status and seat availability to enable airline personnel to adequately respond to customer requests for information and reservations. In both of these cases, quick access to current information has a significant impact upon the way that the organizations conduct their business affairs. In these cases the data processing is said to take place in *real-time* because it occurs simultaneously with the external operation (serving customers) in order that its output can guide or control the operation. A data processing system capable of performing in this fashion is called a *real-time system*.

An important concept in the definition of a real-time system is the concept of response time, or the time interval between data input and system response. Real-time systems are sometimes associated with immediate response. However, the length of response time which will qualify a given system as real-time is actually dependent upon the nature of the physical activity being controlled by the system. If the activity is the launching of a space satellite, a response time measured in fractions of a second is necessary in order for the system to control the activity effectively. If the activity occurs within a business environment, a response time of several seconds or even a few minutes may be adequate for control purposes. Thus the nature of the activity being controlled determines the response time necessary for a real-time system to effect control.

Although our definition of a real-time system is consistent with that provided by other authoritative sources,[1] it nonetheless leads us to a perplexing definitional dilemma. Specifically, in cases in which a system response after one hour or one day is useful in guiding or controlling a process, even a batch processing system or a manual system could qualify as a real-time system. Nonetheless, many authorities confine their discussion of real-time systems to online systems capable of fast response. Some authorities avoid this dilemma by using the term "on-line real-time" (OLRT) system, but this terminology is no longer commonly used.

Recognizing that the generally accepted definition of a real-time system may encompass batch or manual systems, the author has chosen in this chapter to limit the coverage to those real-time systems that are online and are capable of fast response. The discussion emphasizes the hardware and software components of such systems, and reviews some of their most common applications in business organizations.

Two other aspects of the definition of real-time system deserve comment at this point. First, note that the response of a real-time system is a form of feedback, and a real-time system is therefore one type of feedback control system. Second, it should also be noted that most real-time systems, particularly those in business, are subsystems of larger data processing systems. The real-time subsystem may only be applied to one particular activity, while processing related to all other activities in the organization is accomplished in batch mode. Both the real-time and batch processing applications would share the same central computer.

Two forms of online processing described in Chapter 6 were online updating and inquiry processing. Generally, online updating alone is not a form of real-time processing, because all that is accomplished in online updating is the updating of a record. The concept of online updating does not imply a system response. However, many real-time systems also perform online updating in conjunction with their real-time operation. On the other hand, inquiry processing is a form of real-time processing in cases where the response to the inquiry meets the condition of being timely enough to be useful for control purposes.

In addition to online updating and inquiry processing, a third function commonly performed by a real-time system is the initiation of a transaction as the by-product of another processing step. For example, after receiving data on a sale transaction, the system might print a shipping order authorizing delivery of the goods sold. As another example, the system might prepare a purchase requisition after receiving data on usage of raw materials. This function is called *dispatching*, and requires a very sophisticated real-time system.

A fourth function performed by some real-time systems is the actual management of the operations of a process, with a minimum of human intervention. Exam-

---

[1] *See for example Robert J. Thierauf,* Systems Analysis and Design of Real-Time Management Information Systems, *Englewood Cliffs, N.J.: Prentice-Hall, 1975, p. 6.*

ples of processes subject to real-time management are the optimal blending of raw materials and the scheduling of production operations. This type of application requires a very complex system. Because of their cost and complexity, systems of this type are common only in very large organizations.

Real-time systems are singled out for special study here because they offer accountants and others in business the chance to fulfill the potential of the computer as a tool of management. The reader will discover that real-time systems are also much more complex than conventional computer systems. The chapter will first discuss some of the complexities of the hardware and software in a real-time system, with special emphasis on the cost-performance trade-offs that affect system design. Then an analysis of some applications of real-time systems in business and accounting will follow.

Hardware for Real-Time Systems

The hardware required in a real-time computer system includes, in addition to the central processor, online file storage devices, data terminals located at major points of system usage, and a data communications network to connect the terminals with the central processor. Varying degrees of complexity are possible in the basic hardware configuration. The simplest configuration is illustrated in Fig. 9.1. In this configuration several[2] input-output terminals are linked directly to a central procesor. A system of this type is called a *simplex system* because there is only one central processor. A simplex system cannot be available for use at all times because of the necessity for regular preventive maintenance of the central processor, and because of the inevitability of occasional equipment malfunctions. Provisions for a manual backup system are thus necessary. To offset these disadvantages, however, the simplex system offers the advantage of real-time capability at the lowest possible cost and with a minimum of complexity in hardware and software system design.

A somewhat more complex real-time configuration is illustrated in Fig. 9.2. This is still a simplex system, but a *communications processor* (often called a *front-end processor*) has been added. The communications processor is a small computer that specializes in controlling the interaction between several terminals and the central processor. The communications processor serves as a buffer between the CPU and the terminals, storing input data until called for by the CPU and receiving output data from the CPU for transfer to the terminals. It also performs data conversion functions, translating from the data transmission code to the internal computer code and vice versa. Another of its functions is the detection and correction of parity errors in data transmitted by the terminals.

The communications processor shown in Fig. 9.2 is located at the site of the central processor. It is also possible to locate a communications processor at a site remote from the CPU and closer to the data terminals. In this case a data communi-

---

[2] *In Fig. 9.1 and the subsequent illustrations only three terminals are shown, though the actual number may vary from three to 100 or more in very large systems.*

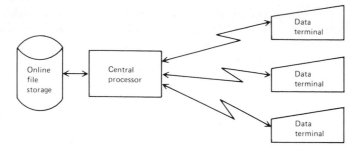

Fig. 9.1
Simplex system.

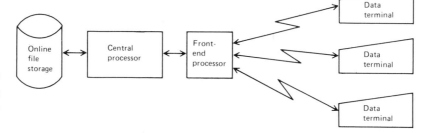

Fig. 9.2
Simplex system with
front-end communi-
cations processor.

cations link would be required between the communications processor and the CPU as well as between the terminals and the communications processor. If the system includes a large number of data terminals at many geographically scattered locations, then several communications processors might be used, each located relatively close to a different group of terminals.

The use of the communications processor provides several advantages. First, it relieves the central processor of communications work, which enables the CPU to perform its data processing chores more effectively. Second, the communications processor can perform some functions even while the CPU is not operative, including acceptance and storage of data (until the CPU is repaired) and routing of messages from one terminal to another. Third, if the location of the communications processor is remote from the CPU and relatively close to the terminals, then the reduction in the number of long-distance communications lines results in savings in communications costs. The main disadvantages of the communications processor are its extra cost and the increased system complexity that results from adding one more element capable of breaking down or causing errors in data transmission.

Several real-time configurations utilize more than one central processor to maximize the availability and reliability of the system. Two such systems that are best suited for business applications are described here. The first of these is the *duplex system* illustrated in Fig. 9.3. This configuration uses two central processors, the second of which can take over for the first during its scheduled maintenance or during an equipment failure. When the second computer is not substituting for the

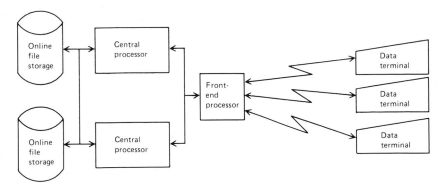

Fig. 9.3
Duplex system.

first, it generally performs batch processing or other jobs. The advantage of the duplex system is that it greatly increases the degree of availability of the system, which is a very important factor in some real-time systems. The major disadvantages are the increased system cost and the increased complexity of the software system required to accomplish the switchover of operations from one computer to the other.

A duplex system is design to meet the requirements of a single real-time function and a single class of users. In contrast, a *distributed processing* system uses multiple central processors to serve multiple real-time applications and/or multiple classes of users. Each CPU specializes in performing particular functions or serving a particular class of users. Data processing jobs, whether real-time or batch, are distributed among the processors according to which one can perform each job most efficiently. The central processors may all be located at the same site, but more typically are geographically scattered and connected by data communications lines, forming a *distributed network,* as illustrated in Fig. 9.4. This diagram shows five geographically scattered data processing systems linked by a network of data communications lines. Though not shown, front-end processors would probably also be used in such a system to interface between each CPU and its terminals. Also, some of the terminals might be located at a distance from the central processors and thus require additional data communications lines.

In a distributed network, there are several alternative patterns that may be followed with respect to the data communications links between the various computer systems. Fig. 9.4 illustrates a *ring network* configuration in which the data communication links form a loop or circular pattern. At the opposite extreme is the *star network* configuration, illustrated in Fig. 9.5, in which there is a central computer system to which all other computer systems in the network are linked. Between these two extremes there are various possible *hybrid network* configurations containing both ring and star patterns. For example, several large systems could be linked together in a ring configuration, while each also serves as the center of a star configuration consisting of smaller systems.

Distributed processing provides the advantages of increased system availability and faster system response time. System availability is increased because when one

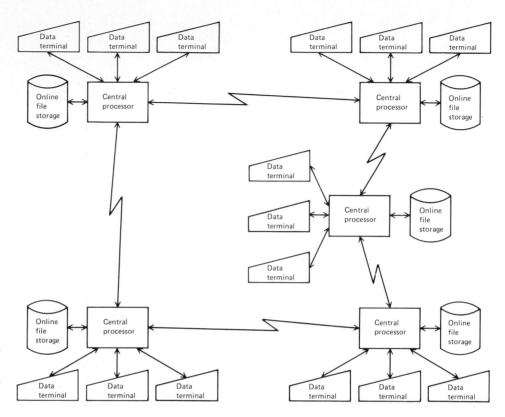

*Fig. 9.4
A distributed pro-
cessing network—the
ring configuration.*

CPU malfunctions or undergoes preventive maintenance, its work may be transferred to another CPU in the system. Response time is improved because the work
load can be distributed relatively evenly among the CPUs in order to minimize the
possibility of overloading the system.

Use of a distributed processing network provides even further advantages. Such
configurations enable a large organization with multiple divisions or branches to
realize the advantages of decentralized data processing without sacrificing the advantages of centralization. Divisional computer systems may be designed to meet the
particular needs of the divisional users, but the computational power of other computers in the network is also available when needed. Each division may maintain its
own data, readily accessible for its purposes, but these data are also available to
management at a headquarters location. These advantages are so substantial that
many authorities consider distributed processing networks to be the wave of the future in business data processing.

Up to this point we have discussed some of the ways in which the components
of a real-time system may be combined into a useful configuration. In the remainder
of this section we briefly examine some of the primary characteristics of each of the
four major hardware components of a real-time system.

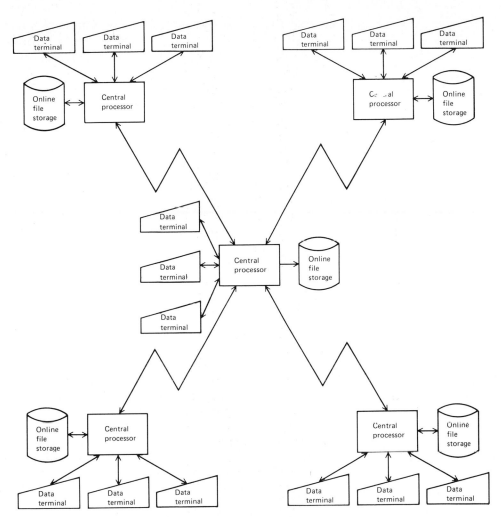

*Fig. 9.5
A distributed pro-
cessing network—the
star configuration.*

The central processor

Certain features of real-time operation demand that the central processor have capacity and capability beyond that required for simple batch processing operations. For one thing, the CPU must be capable of operating in a multiprogramming environment because a real-time system must handle many different activities at the same time. In addition, the control logic of the CPU must be capable of handling *program interrupts,* which are temporary stoppages in the execution of one program by the CPU in order that it can process a higher priority message or transaction which has demanded attention.

In a real-time system which utilizes more than one central processor, the system should also possess a multiprocessing capability. *Multiprocessing* refers to the simultaneous execution of two or more processing tasks (which may be part of the same job) by two or more processing units which are part of the same system. Each processor shares access to its main memory with the other processors. Note the distinction between multiprocessing, which involves multiple computers functioning simultaneously, and multiprogramming, which generally involves one computer which is rapidly switching back and forth among several jobs. Multiprocessing requires that each central processor possess additional control and interfacing capabilities.

Many of the features required of a computer performing real-time applications relate to the primary memory within the CPU. The most obvious requirement is for a larger memory capacity so that interrupted programs and data from uncompleted transactions can be stored while awaiting the attention of the computer. It is also desirable that the CPU have special features that facilitate the allocation of memory for various purposes and that keep track of committed and uncommitted memory blocks. Special features for memory protection are also essential to prevent the transfer of data into a memory area that is already in use. A well-planned system should also be capable of expanding by adding additional main memory units when needed.

A memory management technique designed to augment the capacity of a computer's primary memory is known as *virtual memory*. This involves using online secondary storage devices such as disks or drums as extensions of primary memory. Programs to be run on the system are divided into segments. Those segments of a program that are to be executed at a particular point in time are moved into primary memory, while the remainder of the program is stored on a secondary storage device. As the initial program segments are executed, program control will eventually pass to a segment on the secondary storage device, which is then read into primary memory. Program segments that are no longer needed in primary memory are written onto the secondary storage device. The virtual memory technique increases the number of programs that the system is able to process at one time, thereby increasing the efficiency of the system.

Online file storage

The file storage medium for a real-time application must have direct access capability. The two most common choices are magnetic disk and magnetic drum. A third possibility is the use of magnetic core as a secondary storage medium (rather than, or in addition to, its use in CPU primary storage). Further possibilities include magnetic bubble memories and charge-coupled device memories.

Choice among disk, drum, and core storage is primarily a trade-off between cost and access time. Disk storage provides the slowest access time, but it is also the least expensive. Core storage is the most expensive, but it provides the fastest access time. Drum storage is in the middle in both cases.

Three of the primary system characteristics affecting the choice among online storage media are the desired response time, the frequency of reference to the files, and the file size. If an extremely fast response is desired, drum or core storage may be desirable. In most business applications, a difference of a fraction of a second in response time will make little or no difference to the user. If there is a high frequency of references to a file, overall system efficiency may be improved by maintaining that file on a fast access drum or core memory. However, if the size of the file is large, disk storage may be favored because of its economy. In some large real-time systems these various considerations are compromised by use of disk storage for some files and either drum or core storage for others.

Another significant consideration relating to file storage in a real-time system is the provision for backup storage. In some systems in which constant availability of service is essential, duplicate files may be maintained. This is very expensive, not only because of the duplicate storage device but also because of the additional complexity of the software and the additional consumption of time to update both files. A less expensive alternative is to use disk file units with removable disk packs. Then if the file unit itself goes down, the disk pack can be removed and placed onto a backup file unit. If system availability at all times is not crucial, the system may be designed to reject file inquiries relating to a file which is down, though it may be possible to store file updates on another medium, such as tape, and process them once the file is restored to service.

Data terminals   The data terminal in a real-time system represents the point of interface between man and machine, and is therefore one of the more significant factors in the success of the system. There are two basic categories of terminals: (1) teleprinters; and (2) cathode ray tubes (CRTs), or display terminals. The latter may be either alphanumeric displays, which specialize in alphanumeric input and output (see Fig. 5.14), or graphic displays, which have the capability of displaying graphs and charts. Graphic display terminals are much more commonly used in engineering applications than in business, but their usage in business is growing. An example of a business-oriented graphics terminal is illustrated in Fig. 9.6.

Several factors influence the choice between teleprinters and alphanumeric displays in a real-time system. Cost considerations relating to the terminal alone favor the teleprinter, the cost of which may range from $600 to $3000, as compared to a range of $1000 to $10,000 for display terminals. Another factor favoring the teleprinter is that it automatically produces a paper copy of all input and output. Some display terminals have special units that will produce a copy of whatever is on the screen when desired, as exemplified by the unit shown in Fig. 9.6. Others are capable of storing internally more lines of data than can fit on the screen at any one time, in order that the operator can refer back to such data after it leaves the screen. However, both of these features significantly increase the cost of the display terminal. Primarily because of the cost factor, teleprinters were for many years more commonly used in business applications than display terminals.

Display terminals do possess several advantages over teleprinters, and their usage in business applications has grown in recent years to exceed that of teleprinters. Because they operate electronically rather than electromechanically, display terminals are generally more reliable than teleprinters. Also, display terminals are gener-

Fig. 9.6
*Business-oriented
graphics terminal
with attached
hard-copy unit.
(Courtesy of
Tektronics, Inc.)*

ally less noisy than teleprinters, which may be important if the terminal is to be operated in an environment such as a hospital. Another significant advantage of display terminals is their ability to display a data entry format to facilitate use of the terminal by inexperienced operators. For example, the terminal might display the format of a sales order to be filled in by a salesperson. Furthermore, the correction of errors in entered data is much easier using a display terminal than with a teleprinter. Still another advantage of display terminals is output speed, which becomes very significant if output quantities are large. The typical printing speed of a teleprinter is 15 characters per second, while CRT output speeds range from 60 to 240 characters per second.

Some advanced terminals are capable of being programmed and can interfere with such peripheral equipment as a disk or tape cassette drive and a printer. These are called *intelligent terminals.* They are actually small stand-alone computer systems which are also capable of functioning as terminals. The terminal portion of the system is generally a CRT that possesses all of the storage, formatting, and editing features mentioned above. The primary business and accounting applications of such devices involve online data entry. When several remotely located intelligent terminals are connected to a centrally located computer, the system is in effect a distributed processing network.

In some cases the cost savings and other advantages of online data entry may represent the primary justification for a real-time system. The main advantage of such a system is that files are up to date at all times, which facilitates management control in several ways. In addition, several other advantages are obtained. When an application is converted from batch processing to real-time, the equipment and personnel necessary for keypunching and verification are eliminated. The time-consuming operations of card reading and record sorting are no longer necessary. The time required for employees to fill out source documents is instead used for entering source data on the terminals, so that no increase in personnel is necessary. The possibility of errors in transcribing data from source documents onto cards, or loss of source documents in transit, is eliminated. The possibility of omission of relevant data from source documents is eliminated, because the computer can be programmed to accept only complete entries and ask for additional data if necessary. The possibility of erroneous source data entry is reduced because the computer can evaluate the reasonableness of critical data, the validity of record keys such as account numbers, and perform various other checks on the input.

Offsetting the advantages of online data entry listed above are the additional costs of the terminals and data communications facilities. It is likely that a real-time system will require more terminals than the number of keypunches it replaces because of the geographical dispersion of sources of data input and the slower speed of the operators. In most cases, however, more than one operator can share a single terminal. Another unfavorable factor is that the accuracy of data input in a real-time system is closely related to the degree of care that terminal operators are willing to take in entering and checking data. The decision of whether the cost savings and other advantages of online data entry outweigh the additional costs and other disadvantages must be based upon the unique circumstances of each individual case.

Data communications   The transmission of data from remote terminals to a central processor is generally accomplished through the facilities of the communications companies, the largest of which in the United States are the Bell System and Western Union. Numerous other telephone companies also offer data communication services, and there are a number of companies that provide specialized data transmission services of various kinds. The primary media used by these carriers to transmit data include satellite facilities, cables, and microwave radio facilities. Any organization operating a real-time system in which some of the components are geographically distant from others must utilize the services provided by the communications companies. However, if all components of the real-time system are located close together, then the use of "in-house" communication lines may eliminate the need to purchase outside data transmission services.

The carriers offer several choices of services to their data communications customers. With respect to speed of data transmission, communication lines fall into one of three categories: (1) *subvoice grade,* with speeds ranging up to 200 bits per second (bps), (2) *voice grade,* or normal telephone lines, with speeds ranging from

600 to 9600 bps, and (3) *wide-band,* with speeds ranging from 20,000 to 500,000 bps. The higher the speed of transmission of a line, the higher is its cost. The line speed required in a given case depends upon the expected utilization of the line. For example, if a line is to concurrently serve four terminals, each of which transmits and receives characters at 2400 bps, then the line speed should be at least 9600 bps.

With respect to usage of the facilities, the communications carriers offer three primary options. These are (1) leased lines (also called private lines), (2) switched lines (dial-up service using public lines), and (3) Wide Area Telephone Service (WATS). Leased lines are devoted exclusively to the use of a single customer. The cost of a leased line is fixed and is determined by the length of the line. Advantages of leased lines relative to the alternatives include lower error rates and the availability of faster rates of data transmission.

Both switched lines and WATS involve using the long-distance telephone service available to the general public. The difference between them lies in the rate structure. The cost of switched line service varies in proportion to the amount of time the lines are used. Under WATS the user pays a fixed charge for usage of a line up to a certain number of hours per month, and then pays an additional charge for extra usage which varies directly with the amount of extra usage. A single WATS line may be used for outward calls only, or for inward calls only, but not for both. The basic advantage of using the public telephone network, as opposed to a leased line, is flexibility—any telephone may be used for data transmission, and more than one computer system may be accessed from a single terminal.

A primary consideration in choosing among leased, switched, and WATS lines is cost, which in turn is dependent upon both volume of usage and distance between transmission points. At very low volumes of usage, switched line service is most economical because the user is charged only for the amount of time used. At very high volumes of usage, leased lines are more economical. A WATS line with a low monthly time allotment (such as ten hours per month) might be more economical at intermediate levels of usage, while a WATS line with a high monthly time allotment (such as 240 hours per month) is roughly comparable in cost to a leased line. As the distance between transmission points increases, switched lines and WATS lines tend to become relatively more attractive from an economic standpoint than leased lines.

An example should further clarify the economic factors affecting the choice among these three alternatives. Consider a company which wishes to connect a remote terminal to a processing center 835 miles away. Using Bell System rates in effect as of July, 1980, cost estimates for the three alternative forms of service are determined as follows.

(1) leased voice grade line—$96.28 for the first 25 miles, plus $1.18 for each of the next 75 miles, plus $0.70 for each mile over 100, plus $26.40 apiece for each of the two points serviced, for a total of $752.08 per month, regardless of the amount of usage.

(2) switched line—for points this distance apart, the weekday rate for each direct dialed call is $0.50 for the first minute, and $0.34 for each additional minute;

assuming an average of four minutes per call, this works out to an average of $0.38 per minute, or $22.80 per hour.

(3) WATS line—the rate is a function of the location of the two points and the distance between them; in this case, the rate is $238 for the first ten hours, and $17.85 per hour for each hour thereafter.

Once the distance between the two points has been used to make these determinations, the only other factor affecting cost is the volume of usage. Fig. 9.7 graphs the total monthly cost under each of these three alternatives as a function of the number of hours of use of the connection. The graph indicates that the use of switched lines is most economical up to a usage volume of approximately 12 hours per month; WATS lines are most economical for usage volumes ranging between 12 and 39 hours per month; and leased lines are most economical for usage volumes in excess of 39 hours per month. Note that the specific breakeven points will vary depending on the distance between the two points, but that the general shape of each of the three cost functions will always be as shown in Fig. 9.7.

The transmission of data over telephone lines is a form of analog transmission, in which signals are continuously variable, resembling waves. Computers generally only recognize digital transmission, in which signals are discretely variable. Examples of these two types of signals are shown in Fig. 9.8. In a data communications system, digital signals must be converted to analog form, which is called *modulation,* and then analog signals must be converted back to digital form, which is *de-*

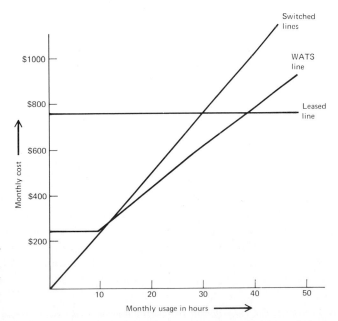

Fig. 9.7

Sample economic comparison of leased line, switched lines, and WATS line.

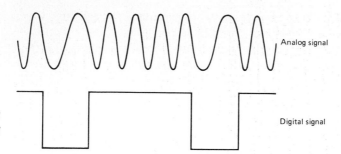

Fig. 9.8
Analog and digital
signals contrasted.

modulation. The device used to accomplish this task, both at site of the computer and at the site of the terminal, is called a *modem,* which is an acronym for MOdulator-DEModulator.[3] Some modems (also called *data sets*) are built into the telephone equipment for convenient use in a switched or WATS line hookup. A type of modem called an *acoustic coupler,* includes a cradle into which a conventional phone may be placed to establish a data hookup; these are often built into the terminal (see Fig. 9.9). Still other modems are separate devices with a direct electronic connection to terminals or other data processing equipment.

The network of communication lines which connects a centrally located computer with several geographically remote terminals may be configured in a number of ways. Three basic categories of configurations are point-to-point lines, multidrop lines, and the use of a line-sharing device that enables data from several lines to be combined on a single line. The simplest choice is the use of point-to-point lines, involving one line from each terminal to the central processor, as illustrated for an assumed system of terminals diagrammed in Fig. 9.10. The use of *multidrop lines,* illustrated in Fig. 9.11 for a set of terminals having the same relative relationship as those in Fig. 9.10, involves linking the terminals to each other, with only one or a few terminals linked directly to the CPU. All other terminals are indirectly linked to the CPU by means of lines that connect through other terminal locations. The use of a line-sharing device, in which incoming data from several terminals may be combined for transmission on a single line (or vice versa) is illustrated for the same terminal configuration in Fig. 9.12.

In a system using point-to-point lines, either leased lines, WATS lines, or switched lines may be used, whichever is most economical. In fact it is even possible to have a combination of different types of lines within the same network. The primary advantages of the point-to-point configuration over the others are (1) its simplicity in terms of hardware requirements; (2) its increased availability to users, who are rarely required to wait for service because other users have tied up the lines; and (3) its reliability in the sense that, if a line fails, only one user is affected. The primary disadvantage of this configuration is that it maximizes total line mileage in the network. Since most elements of data communications cost are directly related to

---

[3] *A few communications carriers offer digital data transmission services, which eliminate the need for a modem to perform the digital-analog conversions.*

*Fig. 9.9
Terminal with built-
in acoustic coupler
modem. (Courtesy of
Texas Instruments
Incorporated.)*

line mileage, this means that point-to-point lines are frequently more costly than alternative configurations.

A visual comparison of Fig. 9.10 with Fig. 9.11 should indicate the potential for reduction in line mileage (and data communications cost) from the use of multidrop lines. However, the multidrop configuration does have some disadvantages. First, the line cannot be shared by more than one message at a time, which means that when a message is being transmitted to or from one terminal, all other terminals must wait. This will cause system response times to be irregular and of greater average length, which could be undesirable from the standpoint of the system user. As the number of terminals on a particular multidrop line increases, this problem will intensify, which means that there is a limit on the number of terminals that feasibly may be connected to a given multidrop line. A second disadvantage is that the terminals required to use a multidrop line may be more expensive than necessary because they must contain sufficient intelligence to recognize which messages on the line are addressed to them and which are addressed to the other terminals. Still another disadvantage of a multidrop configuration involves its effect on system reliability. For example, if a line fails at a certain point in a multidrop configuration, then all terminals down the line from that point are cut off from the central computer. Finally, multidrop lines are the least flexible of the three basic configurations in the sense

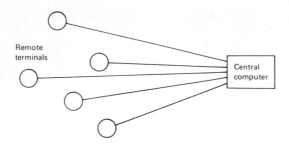

Fig. 9.10
Data communica-
tions network using
point-to-point lines.

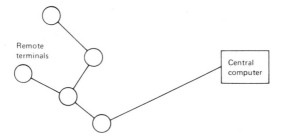

Fig. 9.11
Data communica-
tions network using
multidrop lines.

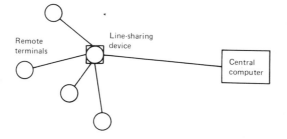

Fig. 9.12
Data communica-
tions network with
line-sharing device.

that all the lines must be leased, whereas switched or WATS lines may be used for some or all connections under the other two alternatives.

The two major types of line-sharing devices are the *multiplexor* and the *concentrator*. A multiplexor is a device that combines two or more incoming data signals from low-speed lines into one signal for transmission on a single high-speed line. As a result, several messages may be transmitted simultaneously between various terminals and the central computer, which eliminates or substantially reduces the wait time experienced by users of multidrop lines. A concentrator performs multiplexing functions plus other functions such as temporary data storage, data editing and control operations, and formatting. Some concentrators are minicomputers, while others are front-end communications processors geographically separated from the main computer.

The use of a line-sharing device in a data communications network also reduces total line mileage relative to a system using point-to-point lines. This is evident from a visual comparison of Fig. 9.10 with Fig. 9.12. However, the cost saving generated by this reduction in line mileage will be partially or wholly offset by the cost of the line-sharing equipment. Furthermore, a more expensive high-speed line is generally required to connect the line-sharing device to the central computer. Also, a large line-sharing network will generally be designed to provide a transmission capacity less than the maximum possible requirement, which means that during peak usage periods the system may be unavailable to some users if the entire capacity of the shared line is tied up by other users. In addition, system reliability is also a problem in the sense that a failure in the shared line will cause all users to be cut off from the system. Finally, an advantage of line sharing relative to the multidrop configuration is flexibility of choice among leased, switched, or WATS lines to connect each remote terminal to the line-sharing device; however, the shared line itself must be leased.

Although we have focused on the relative advantages and disadvantages of these three basic configurations, it should be pointed out that a large network may contain combinations of all three approaches. The network designer does not simply choose one of the three approaches for the entire network, but rather chooses the best approach for each individual terminal connection. Figure 9.13 illustrates a network in which all three approaches are represented. This figure also demonstrates the relationships that exist among the various hardware elements within a data communications network.

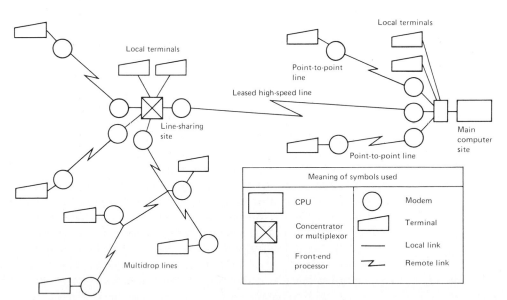

Fig. 9.13
A data communications network.

Software for Real-Time Systems

The software required in a real-time system is of a much higher level of complexity than that required in conventional systems. This is true simply because the number of functions which must be performed by the software is much greater in a real-time system. A partial list of some of these functions includes controlling input and output over a number of communication lines and to and from a number of terminals; controlling random access to data files; maintaining waiting lists, or queues, of input entries awaiting processing; administering a system of processing priorities and handling program interrupts; interfacing with other computers in a multicomputer system; responding to malfunctions in any of several components of the system; controlling the allocation of computer memory; and editing and validation of input data and control of errors.

The need for more complex software in a real-time system is attributable primarily to the presence of a data communications network that includes numerous terminals from which requests for service arrive in unpredictable patterns. To cope with this problem, special *communications control programs* have been developed to perform the operations necessary to manage the data communications activity and interact with the various terminals. These are a separate category of programs from the user's application programs and the operating system. They may be executed either by the main computer or by a programmable front-end processor if one is present in the system. A primary objective of communications control programs is to free the operating system from the task of managing data communication, which enables it to more efficiently perform its overall supervisory functions. In addition, they facilitate applications programming by providing macroinstructions that may be incorporated into application programs to handle data communications functions.

The accountant is interested in the software in a real-time system in several respects. First, he or she is concerned with the cost of software development, which could be a significant factor in the feasibility of a system. Second, he or she is concerned with the design of the application programs, most specifically those that will be applied to the accounting function. Finally, the accountant is concerned that all programs provide the degree of internal control necessary to the system. Three major internal control considerations in a real-time system are data reliability, security, and provision for an audit trail.

With respect to data reliability, one of the accountant's primary control tools, the principle of batching, is lost in a real-time system because transactions are processed individually rather than in batches. This tool must be replaced by a more elaborate system of validating input data at the point of entry into the system. Special programs or subroutines which test the reasonableness and validity of input data must be present in the system. These programs should be designed to request reentry of invalid data, and perhaps to request verification of the accuracy of all critical data. One aspect of a real-time system which is useful for control purposes is that data verification is done by the person in the system who is in the best position to verify source data accuracy—the operator who originates the source data.

One of the major problems of security in a real-time system is the prevention of unauthorized access to the system. In a conventional system, most or all of the data processing equipment is concentrated at a single physical location, so that control efforts can be focused there. In a real-time system, which has many terminals at several remote locations, the problem of unauthorized access is greatly magnified. The most common approach to this problem is to assign each person authorized to use the system a code number that is checked by the system software prior to allowing a user to have access to the system.

The problem of maintaining an audit trail is also greatly magnified in a real-time system. It is possible for a real-time system to be designed so that a transaction could be entered into the system without generating any documentary evidence of the transaction. Teletype terminals produce a paper copy of all activity, and some CRT terminals are also capable of producing a paper copy, which may be a useful form of documentary evidence. Of greater usefulness to the control and audit of real-time systems is the generation by the computer itself of a record, called a *transaction log,* of every transaction entered into the system. This log identifies the date and time of the entry, the terminal location and user code number, and all relevant data concerning the transaction itself. Generation of this log is one of the functions of the operational programs in a real-time system. Generally the log is initially stored on a random access file, to be written onto tape and/or printed out subsequently at periodic intervals.

The issues of data reliability, data security, and maintenance of audit trails in real-time systems are discussed in greater detail in Chapter 14.

Real-Time Business and Accounting Systems

Though real-time systems are generally more costly and complex than conventional data processing systems, their utilization has increased sharply in recent years, which reflects their high potential as a profitable tool of management. Realization of this potential has thus far been primarily limited to the area of control of operations, with benefits being generated from increased efficiency in the logistics function and from improvements in levels of customer service. There remains some controversy over the potential of real-time systems as tools of top management. This section will review the major issues in this controversy and then describe some existing applications of real-time systems in the control of business operations.

Total information systems for management

Much has been written about the utilization of real-time systems by top management. One important concept is that of the *total information system.* The primary characteristic of such a system is that all of the information necessary to manage an organization is collected, processed, and made available in an integrated data base at a centralized location. Integration of the data base implies that the information is organized in a manner which facilitates updating the information and preparing responses to inquiries. For the information system to qualify as "total," the data base must contain and integrate all of the information which is relevant to the management of the organization.

Utilization of such real-time systems by top management is possible in both the planning and control functions. In planning, the manager could use the system to test the outcomes of various decision alternatives by using a mathematical model to simulate the actual operation of the company. The quick response of the real-time system would enable the manager to "interact" with the model by performing several experiments in a short time period. In control, the real-time system would assist by keeping the manager informed of the existence of problem situations immediately as they occur, thus reducing the time lag between a deviation from plan and an adjustment.

John Dearden has analyzed carefully the functions of top-level managers and the promise of real-time systems, and concludes that the concept of a real-time information system for top management is a "myth."[4] Dearden delineates the primary functions of top management, including management control, strategic planning, personnel planning, and coordination. After examining each function in turn, he reasons that a real-time system would not improve management's performance in any of them. For example, with respect to management control, he points out that, "In most instances, when situations deteriorate to the point where immediate action is required, top management knows about it." With respect to the use of computer models in strategic planning, he states that the typical manager would be more inclined to assign such tasks to staff specialists, and that the computer can be used for this purpose without the need for a real-time system. In the functions of personnel planning and coordination, he sees no potential for application of real-time systems.

Dearden agrees with most other authorities that real-time systems can produce benefits when applied to operating management. However, he argues that it is a fallacy to equate the control problems of top management with the control problems of operating management. In a subsequent article, Dearden further attacks the concept of a total information system utilizing a fully integrated data base.[5] While stating that integration is a useful concept on a limited scale, he concludes that total integration is also a "myth" for most organizations.

In the several years since Dearden's papers were published, considerable progress has been made in the utilization of real-time systems to support management decision making. However, usually the decisions being aided by real-time systems are highly structured, limited in scope to a specific aspect of operations, and made at a management level below the top. At present, there is no evidence of any fundamental trends that would alter Dearden's basic conclusion that real-time systems to support top management functions are a remote prospect. While applications of real-time systems in operations management continue to grow, the idea of top level managers utilizing computer terminals in their offices to help them manage is still closer to a dream than to reality. This tends to support his contention that change, if

---

[4] *John Dearden, "Myth of Real-Time Management Information,"* Harvard Business Review, *vol. 44, no. 3 (May/June 1966), pp. 123–132.*

[5] *John Dearden, "MIS Is a Mirage,"* Harvard Business Review, *vol. 50, no. 1 (January/February 1972), pp. 90–99.*

it comes, will come gradually, leaving business executives plenty of time to adjust if necessary.

Real-time systems for operations management

While the potential of real-time systems for controlling the executive management process may still be uncertain, real-time systems are being applied to control a variety of operating processes in many business organizations. With the exception of process control applications that monitor physical processes such as petroleum refining or chemical production, virtually all of the major applications of real-time systems in business involve the collection and utilization of accounting data. The major characteristics of several such applications are described briefly in this section.

Sales order processing   This area is one in which many companies may find it possible to gain a significant competitive advantage from using a real-time system which shortens the time between receipt of customer orders and delivery. Such a system would maintain its finished goods inventory file online and would have data terminals distributed throughout its sales territory. Salespeople could call orders in to a regional data collection center at which the terminals are located, or alternatively each salesperson might be equipped with a small portable terminal with which he or she could enter orders directly from the customer's plant or office. If the terminal were a CRT, an invoice format could be displayed for the operator to fill in. The system would access the finished goods inventory file to confirm the availability and quantity of each item ordered, and this information would be relayed to the customer immediately. The finished goods inventory file would be updated as the orders were placed. All appropriate journal entries would be made immediately in the general ledger and the invoice could be immediately posted to the accounts receivable ledger if those files were online. If inventories were stored in a network of warehouses, a copy of the invoice could be transmitted to a data terminal at the warehouse closest to the point of delivery to initiate shipment.

In addition to speeding up the sales order-delivery cycle, the system described above could also have several other useful features. With the accounts receivable file online, a salesperson could answer customer inquiries about the status of the customer's account. The credit checking process could also be accomplished online as part of the order entry process. In addition, a sales analysis master file could be maintained online and updated as orders were placed. This file could be used by marketing executives to provide up-to-date information on sales trends, thus facilitating management control of the sales function. Furthermore, as the finished goods inventory balances of ordered items were updated, the updated balance of each item could be checked to determine if reordering or additional production were necessary to replenish the stock. A more extensive discussion of the use of such a system is provided in Chapter 16; in particular, see the systems flowchart in Fig. 16.11.

The hardware configuration required to implement a system of this sort could be any one of the configurations discussed earlier in the chapter. An indication of

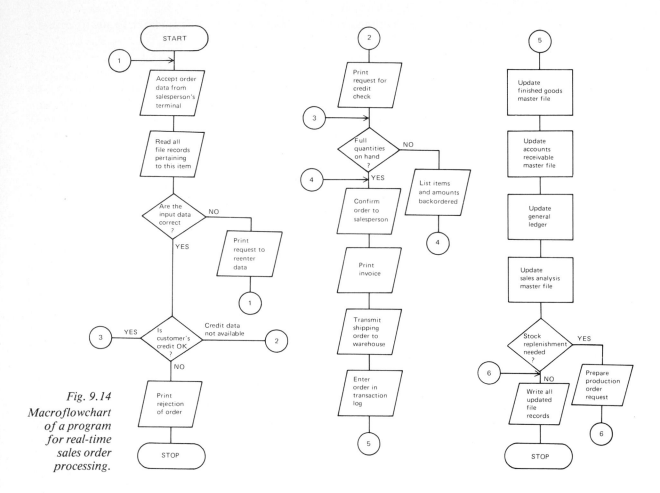

*Fig. 9.14
Macroflowchart
of a program
for real-time
sales order
processing.*

the nature of the application programs required for the system is provided by the macroflowchart in Fig. 9.14. It should be noted that most of the steps in the flowchart represent a series of more detailed program steps. In addition to the fact that sales orders are confirmed in real time, the system illustrated here is also significant from the standpoint of the complete integration which is achieved in the accounting function. One entry of data results in the updating of all accounting records affected by the data and initiates the preparation of all documents necessary for processing the transaction.

Transportation and travel reservations   Firms in these industries, notably the airline companies and major motel chains, were among the first to implement real-time systems. Applications involve processing and confirming customer reservations, and are actually quite similar to those involving the processing of sales orders. Data terminals are located at each reservations counter or motel lobby. Online file storage devices contain a record of the availability of services at future dates, such as available seats on airline flights or rooms at all motels in a chain. A customer may request a reservation in person or by phone. The reservation is entered on the data terminal, and if the requested seat, room, or other service is available, the file record is updated and the reservation is immediately confirmed to the customer.

In an airline reservations system, functions which may be performed in addition to maintaining records of seat availability and processing reservations include calculation of fares, updating sales and accounts receivable records, responding to customer requests for reconfirmation, and processing passenger check-ins. In a motel room reservations system, functions such as calculation of room charges, guest check-in and check-out, and revenue accounting are generally performed at each local unit rather than by the real-time system.

Banking systems   Savings banks were also among the first institutions to implement real-time systems, and such systems are now common in commercial banks as well. A real-time banking system is used to perform various functions for customers at bank teller windows. The primary function is checking the balance of a customer's account to determine whether it is large enough for a withdrawal being made by the waiting customer. In addition, deposits and withdrawals may be posted to customer accounts through the system. Hardware requirements for a real-time banking system include a data terminal for each teller window and online file storage to maintain a record of each customer's account.

The real-time banking system makes an up-to-date record of each customer's account available to every teller, even those at branches located at a distance from the main bank. Such systems enable banks to provide faster service to customers, which allows a reduction in the number of tellers required to wait on a given number of customers and reduces the amount of time each customer must wait for service.

Many banks which first obtained a real-time system to improve the efficiency of teller operations have since expanded its application into other areas, such as mortgages, commercial loans, consumer loans, and credit files. In recent years the concept of one gigantic real-time system to handle all banking transactions has emerged. Retail merchants would be tied into the banking network through point-of-sale terminals (see Chapter 5), and sales transactions would be immediately charged to the consumer's bank account and simultaneously credited to the merchant's account. Transactions among corporations and other institutions would be handled electronically rather than by check. Deposit of paychecks to the bank accounts of employees by their employers would also be done electronically. This concept has become known as *electronic funds transfer* (EFT).[6]

---

[6] *For more information about EFT, see John B. Benton, "Electronic Funds Transfer: Pitfalls and Payoffs," Harvard Business Review, vol. 55, no. 4 (July/August 1977), pp. 16–32, 164–173; Richard G. Canning, "The Impact of Corporate EFT," EDP Analyzer, vol. 15, no. 10 (October 1977), pp. 1–13; Rob Kling, "Value Conflicts and Social Choice in Electronic Funds Transfer System Developments," Communications of the ACM, vol. 21, no. 8 (August 1978), pp. 642–657; and Carol A. Schaller, "The Revolution of EFTS," The Journal of Accountancy, vol. 146, no. 4 (October 1978), pp. 74–80.*

Retail sales   Many retail organizations utilize real-time systems to perform credit checking and inventory control functions. Point-of-sale recorders have been specifically designed to serve as data terminals for this type of application. In such applications, a customer's credit standing may be checked at the time a credit transaction is initiated. The customer's account data is then accessed and updated, and a check against a credit limit may be made. If the credit sale is authorized, or if the sale is for cash, the inventory file is accessed and updated for the specific items of merchandise sold. Since this enables an up-to-date record of all inventory items to be maintained, the system can originate inventory reordering as needed.

Because of the expense of point-of-sale recorders or other data terminals, many retail organizations utilize real-time systems in which a centralized data terminal or group of terminals serves a number of retail counters or outlets. For example, in a large retail store with several branches, there might be one or more terminals centrally located at each branch store. Each sales clerk would dial a terminal operator within his or her own branch when a need to check credit arose. The terminal operator would then access the central computer system, obtain the necessary credit information, and respond to the sales clerk over the phone. A similar example is furnished by the large oil companies, in which each service station operator may dial a regional center from which terminal operators may make inquiries regarding the status of customer accounts. In most such systems, the retail clerk or attendant will not initiate the credit check unless the amount of the sale exceeds a specified sum, such as $50.00.

Manufacturing control systems   A real-time manufacturing control system is used to perform several functions relating to the scheduling and control of work in process. These functions include control of raw materials inventory, purchasing and receiving, scheduling of factory workers, scheduling of machine usage, quality control, control of finished goods inventories, and shipping. Unlike the airline, banking, and other real-time systems, the requirements of users of real-time manufacturing control systems are likely to vary greatly from firm to firm. Generally such systems require online file storage to maintain a current record of all work in process in the factory. Every change in status of a work in process item is recorded online as it occurs from data terminals located in the factory. For example, each time a worker completes a job, he or she enters all relevant data pertaining to the job into the system from the terminal.

The functions that may be performed in real time by a manufacturing control system include verifying the accuracy of data input; assigning workers and machines to jobs in accordance with an optimum schedule that takes into account job priorities, machine availability, and other conditions; responding to inquiries regarding the status of specific work in process items; and preparing purchase requisitions for raw materials whose balances fall below their reorder point. In addition, if it is economical, the cost control function can be performed in real time, with significant cost variances being reported to supervisors and to the plant superintendent as they occur.

The real-time manufacturing control system provides several advantages, foremost among which is the increased efficiency that can be achieved in manufacturing operations. Such a system helps to maximize machine utilization, minimize raw materials and work in process inventories, assure fast processing of rush orders, and also enables quick responses to changes in conditions, such as a machine breakdown. A more extensive discussion of these systems is provided in Chapter 18; in particular, see the systems flowchart in Fig. 18.16.

Review Questions

1. Define the following terms.

real-time	subvoice grade
real-time system	voice grade
dispatching	wide-band
simplex system	modulation
communications processor	demodulation
front-end processor	modem
duplex system	data set
distributed processing	acoustic coupler
distributed network	multidrop lines
ring network	multiplexor
star network	concentrator
hybrid network	communications control program
program interrupt	transaction log
multiprocessing	total information system
virtual memory	electronic funds transfer
intelligent terminal	

2. How short must the response time of a system be in order for the system to qualify as real-time?

3. True or false?
   a) A real-time system is a type of feedback control system.
   b) The central computer in a real-time system cannot be used for any functions other than the real-time application.

4. What are four general functions which may be performed by a real-time system? Which of these functions by itself is not a form of real-time processing?

5. What are the four general categories of computer hardware required in a real-time system?

6. What are the relative advantages and disadvantages of the following real-time system hardware configurations?
   a) simplex system
   b) simplex system with communications processor
   c) duplex system
   d) distributed processing network

7. Describe several features required of the central processor in a real-time system.

8. Identify several types of online file storage equipment that may be used in a real-time system.

9. Describe several factors that affect the choice among online storage media in a real-time system.

10. What are some choices available to the real-time system designer with respect to providing for backup file storage?

11. What are the primary factors affecting the choice between teleprinters and display terminals in a real-time system?

12. What are the primary advantages and disadvantages of utilizing online data entry in a computer system?

13. With respect to speed of data transmission, communication lines fall into one of three categories. What are these categories and what range of speed does each provide?

14. Describe three basic options offered by the communications companies to data transmission customers with respect to usage of facilities. Explain some of the advantages and disadvantages of each of these options.

15. Distinguish between analog and digital signals. What device is used to convert signals from one of these forms to the other?

16. Discuss the relative advantages and disadvantages of using either
    (a) point-to-point lines,
    (b) multidrop lines, or
    (c) concentration of lines in a central location as with a line-sharing device.

17. List several functions that must be performed by the software in a real-time system.

18. Describe three major internal control considerations in the design of real-time software systems.

19. Describe the ways in which a real-time system could be used by top management. What arguments have been made to support the contention that real-time systems are not useful to the top management function?

20. Describe briefly five examples of the use of real-time systems in the control of operating processes in business.

Discussion Questions

21. Discuss the definition of "real-time systems." Must a system have an online capability in order to qualify as a real-time system? Give an example of a real-time system that does not have an online capability.

22. At some future date, it is conceivable that all households and merchants would possess a computer terminal online to a communitywide real-time computer system. Discuss some of the ways in which the members of a household might use such a system.

23. Discuss the controversy over whether real-time systems are useful to top management executives in the performance of the management function. Do you feel that it would be worthwhile for each top executive in a large, multidivi-

sional company to have in his or her office a computer terminal linked to the company's central computer system? Describe circumstances in which it would definitely be worthwhile, or definitely not be worthwhile.

24. Discuss the relationship, if any, between the concepts of real-time system and source data automation.

25. Describe how a real-time system might be usefully applied within
    a) a university,
    b) a life insurance company,
    c) a hospital, and
    d) a construction company.

Problems and Cases

26. The Widget Manufacturing Company is planning to install a data terminal at its San Francisco regional sales office which would be online to its computer center in Los Angeles 400 miles away. One decision which must be made is whether to lease a line, obtain a WATS line, or use switched public lines. The monthly cost of a leased line would include a service charge of $140.50, plus mileage charges based upon the following rates.[7]

Mileage	0–100	101–250	over 250
Rate/mile	$1.64	$1.32	$0.85

The charge for a WATS line would be $330 for the first ten hours of usage per month and $25 for each additional hour. Public telephone rates are $0.48 for the first minute and $0.34 for each additional minute. It is estimated that the time required to enter a transaction over the terminal will average two minutes.

Required

a) Compute the monthly cost of the leased line.

b) At what average monthly volume of transactions would the total cost of the leased line be equal to the cost of using (1) the WATS line and (2) switched public lines? (Make each computation separately.)

c) Assume that an average volume of 810 transactions per month is expected. Which of the three alternatives would be least expensive? Show all supporting calculations.

d) Assume that a good portion of the transactions would be entered in groups of more than one, so that the extra rate for the first minute would be avoided for one half of all transactions if switched public lines were used. How would this affect your answer to part (c)?

---

[7] *In computing total monthly mileage charges using these rates, a separate calculation is needed for each individual mileage segment, with the results then added to obtain a total cost. For example, a line of 300 miles would cost $1.64 (100) + $1.32 (150) + $0.85 (50) = $404.50 per month.*

27. The Zion Company utilizes a real-time computer system for inventory control. Leased voice-grade data communication lines connect the main warehouse and computer center in Chicago directly with warehouses in Cleveland, Cincinatti, Detroit, and Pittsburgh. Monthly cost rates for these lines are:

Mileage	1	2–15	16–25	26–100	over 100
Rate/mile	$53.88	$1.90	$1.58	$1.18	$0.70

(**Note:** For an explanation of how these rates are used, see footnote 7.)

Distances from Chicago to the other four cities are:

From Chicago to	Cleveland	Cincinnati	Detroit	Pittsburgh
Distance in miles	350	302	298	472

The company is considering obtaining a multiplexor to be installed in its Cleveland warehouse. The voice-grade lines from Chicago to Cincinnati, Detroit, and Pittsburgh would then be replaced by leased voice-grade lines from Cleveland to Cincinnati, Detroit, and Pittsburgh. Distances from Cleveland to those cities are

From Cleveland to	Cincinnati	Detroit	Pittsburgh
Distance in miles	238	172	128

In addition, the line from Chicago to Cleveland would be conditioned to allow higher transmission speeds, and this would cost $50 per month. The multiplexor would cost $100 per month.

Required   Calculate the amount that the Zion Company would save per month by obtaining the multiplexor.

28. The First State Bank of Los Angeles is designing a real-time system for maintaining its customer accounts and processing inquiries from teller windows. Three files which will be maintained online are (1) individual checking accounts, (2) individual savings accounts, and (3) institutional checking accounts. The sizes of these three files are 20 million bytes, six million bytes, and eight million bytes, respectively. The frequency of file reference will be very high for the individual checking and savings accounts, but relatively low for the institutional accounts. A very fast response time is desired for all files.

Systems analysts for the bank are considering the use either of disk file storage for the three files, or drum storage for one of the files and disk for the other two. Rental charges and capacities for representative devices are provided below.

	Monthly rental per unit	Storage capacity per unit
Disk storage unit	$ 570	7.25 million bytes
Disk control unit*	525	
Drum storage unit	2500	3.9 million bytes
Drum control unit†	400	

*up to eight disk storage units may be attached to each control unit.

†one or two drum storage units may be attached to each control unit.

Required

a) Which one of the three files would be the best candidate for use of drum storage? Explain.

b) Determine the total file storage cost if all files are maintained on disk storage.

c) Determine the total file storage cost if the individual savings account file is maintained on drum and the other two are maintained on disk.

29. All other things being equal, explain the effect of each of the following factors on the choice between a teleprinter and a CRT display terminal for a given real-time application.

a) Volume of usage is very high.

b) Cost minimization is the prime objective.

c) It is essential to have a record of all terminal activity.

d) Graphic capability is desirable.

e) Each transaction requires entry of a dozen data elements, and the terminal operators are inexperienced.

f) System responses are voluminous and operator time is very valuable.

g) Minimization of machine noise is essential.

30. The Illinois Wholesale Liquor Corporation utilizes a real-time invoicing, inventory, and accounts receivable system. All sales orders are received in a central Sales Order Department, in which they are entered into the system by clerks utilizing CRT terminals. The system immediately transmits a shipping order to one of several warehouses, each of which has a teleprinter online to the system to receive these orders. The system also prepares six copies of a customer invoice for each order, and updates accounts receivable and finished goods master files. The firm's Financial Vice-President utilizes an office CRT terminal for occasional inquiry into the system. Periodic reports generated by the system include an inventory reorder report (daily) and an accounts receivable aging schedule (monthly).

Required   Prepare a systems flowchart of the system as described.

31. Prepare a macroflowchart of a program for processing airline reservations according to the procedures described below.

- The program begins processing when a reservations clerk types in a flight number, date, flight class, number of seats requested, etc. from a terminal.

- The program checks the validity of the flight number for the date specified. If the flight number is not valid, a reentry of data by the clerk is requested.

- The program checks whether the requested number of seats are available. If they are, it calculates the fare, reduces the seat inventory, prints a confirmation of the reservation over the terminal, and stops.

- If the seats requested are not available, the program checks whether seats of the alternative flight class are available on the same flight, and if they are it requests approval to reserve those seats from the clerk. If a favorable response is received, it calculates the fare, reduces the seat inventory, prints a confirmation of the reservation over the terminal, and stops.

- If alternative class seats are not available, or if the customer does not want the alternative class seats, the program prepares a list of alternative flights on the same date as the requested flight, and prints this list together with a request for the clerk to transmit either a termination signal or another reservation request.

- If a termination signal is received, the program stops.

- If a reservation request is received, the program begins the entire process over again by checking whether the requested flight number is valid for the date specified.

32. The Texas Machinery Distributing Company is a wholesaler of a variety of machinery products with headquarters and central warehouse in Houston, and sales offices in Dallas, Waco, Austin, San Antonio, Corpus Christi, Abilene, and Laredo, Texas. The Company has decided to install a real-time system for processing sales orders. The computer center is located in Houston, and one terminal will be located in each sales office.

A major concern of the company in the design of real-time system has been the cost of the data communications network. The company is considering four alternative configurations.

1) seven subvoice-grade leased lines, one each from Houston to each sales office,

2) a voice-grade line from Houston to Austin, and a communications processor in Austin to service six subvoice-grade leased lines from the other six sales offices,

3) dial-up service from each sales office to Houston,

4) a voice-grade line from Houston to Austin, and a communications processor in Austin to service dial-up from the other six sales offices.

Monthly cost figures obtained from the communications company for subvoice-grade and voice-grade leased lines are as follows.

Subvoice-grade	mileage	0–100	101–250	over 250
	rate/mile	$1.32	$1.06	$0.63

Voice-grade	mileage	1	2–15	16–25	26–100	over 100
	rate/mile	$53.88	$1.90	$1.58	$1.18	$0.70

(**Note:** For an explanation of how these rates are used, see footnote 7.)
The following table shows the distance in miles from Houston to the seven sales offices, and from Austin to the other six sales offices.

	Waco	Austin	Dallas	San Antonio	Laredo	Corpus Christi	Abilene
Houston	181	164	244	195	312	208	349
Austin	106	—	198	79	233	194	217

The table below shows the cost of a two-minute long-distance call from Houston to the seven sales office, and from Austin to the other six sales offices.

	Waco	Austin	Dallas	San Antonio	Laredo	Corpus Christi	Abilene
Houston	0.74	0.74	0.78	0.74	0.82	0.78	0.82
Austin	0.72	—	0.78	0.72	0.78	0.74	0.78

It is assumed that each call will consume approximately two minutes. The table below shows the expected average monthly volume of calls from each of the seven sales offices.

Office	Waco	Austin	Dallas	San Antonio	Laredo	Corpus Christi	Abilene
Monthly volume	200	450	650	500	150	350	200

If either alternative (2) or (4) is chosen, the communications processor will cost $500.00 per month.

Required   Determine the total monthly cost of the data communication network under each of the four alternatives.

33. Shown in Fig. 9.15 is a map illustrating the relative relationship of six major plants operated by the Gardiner Manufacturing Company.

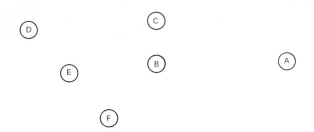

Figure 9.15

Gardiner's management wishes to provide a data communications link between its main computer center at point A and data terminals at the other five locations. The alternative network configurations have been narrowed down to three: (1) use multidrop lines, (2) locate a multiplexor at point B, lease a line to connect the multiplexor to the central computer, and lease four lines to connect the other four points to the multiplexor; (3) same as (2) except use switched lines to connect points C, D, E, and F to the multiplexor. Additional information follows.

■ The distances between each point and the other five points are indicated in Table 9.1.

Table 9.1

Distance from ⟍ to	A	B	C	D	E	F
A		200	220	370	300	280
B			50	180	100	100
C				160	130	150
D					80	140
E						60
F						

■ Leased lines that provide digital data transmission service will be used. Rates for these lines are as follows.

Mileage	1	2–15	16–25	26–100	over 100
Rate/mile	$56.36	$1.99	$1.66	$1.24	$0.73

(**Note:** For an explanation of how these rates are used, see footnote 7.)

■ Under alternative (1), there will be an additional service charge of $93.45 per month for each of the six points serviced.

■ Under alternative (2), the monthly service charge is $311 each for points A and B, and $93.45 each for points C, D, E, and F.

■ Under alternative (3), the monthly service charge is $311 each for points A and B only.

■ Separate mileage charges must be computed for each separate link in a multidrop line.

■ If multidrop lines are used, several "dumb" terminals would have to be replaced with "smart" terminals, which would raise equipment rental costs by $500 per month.

■ If the multiplexor is used, its monthly rental is $100.

■ If switched lines are used, the cost per minute for a long distance hookup between point B and the other four points is as follows:

Point B to	C	D	E	F
Rate/minute	$0.25	$0.30	$0.29	$0.29

■ The estimated volume of usage in terms of hookup hours per month for locations C, D, E, and F is as follows:

Location	C	D	E	F
Hours/month	20	10	15	12

■ The use of switched lines would require four modems at location B, and one at each of locations C, D, E, and F. Their monthly cost is $25 each.

Required   Compute the total monthly cost of data communications under each of the three specified alternatives.

34. The Establishment Manufacturing Corporation (EMC) has its headquarters and central data processing facility in Boston, and four regional data processing centers located in Hartford, New York City, Philadelphia, and Washington, D.C. EMC plans to establish a distributed data processing network by linking these centers together using data communications. Two plans are under consideration: (1) a star network in which separate lines would link Boston to each of the other four centers, and (2) a ring network which would include links from Boston to Hartford, Boston to New York City, Hartford to Philadelphia, New York City to Washington, and Philadelphia to Washington.

One of the factors affecting the choice among these alternatives is the cost of data communications. Leased wide-band lines would be used because of the high volume of data transmission expected. The rates that have been quoted are as follows.

Mileage	1–250	251–500	over 500
Rate/mile	$15.75	$11.05	$7.90

(**Note:** For an explanation of how these rates are used, see footnote 7.)

Table 9.2 shows the distance in miles between each of the pairs of cities.
In addition to the line charges, another element of cost is modems. Two high-

speed modems are required for each link between a pair of cities. The monthly lease cost of these modems is $215.

Table 9.2

Distance from \ to	Boston	Hartford	New York City	Philadelphia	Washington
Boston		93	204	302	440
Hartford			114	211	347
New York City				100	238
Philadelphia					142
Washington, D.C.					

Required Compute the total monthly data communications cost under each of the two alternatives under consideration.

References Benton, John B. "Electronic Funds Transfer: Pitfalls and Payoffs." *Harvard Business Review* (July/August 1977): 16–32, 164–172.

Canning, Richard G. "The Challenges of Distributed Systems." *EDP Analyzer* (August 1978): 1–14.

———. "An Update on Corporate EFT." *EDP Analyzer* (May 1980): 1–13.

Cushing, Barry E., and David H. Dial. "Cost-Performance Trade-offs in Real-Time Systems Design." *Management Advisor* (November/December 1973): 29–38.

Datapro Research Corporation. *Datapro 70, The EDP Buyer's Bible.* Delran, N.J.: Datapro Research Corporation, 1980. See especially the following reports.

"All about Alphanumeric Display Terminals," Volume 2 (June 1980).

"All about Communications Processors." Volume 3 (May 1980).

"All about Data Communications Facilities." Volume 3 (July 1980).

"All about Data Communications Multiplexors." Volume 3 (November 1979).

"All about Graphic Display Devices." Volume 2 (October 1979).

"All about Teleprinter Terminals." Volume 2 (September 1980).

"Buyer's Guide to Data Communications Monitors." Volume 3 (September 1980).

"How to Analyze Your Data Communications Needs." Volume 3 (January 1980).

Dearden, John. "Myth of Real-Time Management Information." *Harvard Business Review* (May/June 1966): 123–132.

———. "MIS Is a Mirage." *Harvard Business Review* (January/February 1972): 90–99.

Doll, Dixon R. *Data Communications: Facilities, Networks, and Systems Design.* New York: Wiley, 1978.

Evans, Roger L. "Basic Data Communication Techniques." *Mini–Micro Systems* (March 1980): 97–104.

_____. "Reducing Communication Line Costs with Multiplexors." *Mini–Micro Systems* (April 1980): 114–120.

Fitzgerald, Jerry, and Tom S. Eason. *Fundamentals of Data Communications.* New York: Wiley, 1978.

Frazer, W. D. "Potential Technology Implications for Computers and Telecommunications in the 1980s." *IBM Systems Journal* (Vol. 18 No. 2, 1979): 333–347.

Head, Robert V. "Real-Time Management Information? Let's Not Be Silly." *Datamation* (August 1966): 124–125.

Kallis, Stephen Λ., Jr. "Networks and Distributed Processing." *Mini–Micro Systems* (March 1977): 32–40.

Kiechel, Walter. "Everything You Always Wanted to Know May Soon Be On-Line." *Fortune* (May 5, 1980): 226–240.

Kling, Rob. "Value Conflicts and Social Choice in Electronic Funds Transfer System Developments." *Communications of the ACM* (August 1978): 642–657.

Martin, James. *Design of Man-Computer Dialogues.* Englewood Cliffs, N.J.: Prentice-Hall, 1973.

Moore, William G. "Going Distributed." *Mini–Micro Systems* (March 1977): 41–48.

Schaller, Carol A. "The Revolution of EFTS." *Journal of Accountancy* (October 1978): 74–80.

Statland, Norman, and Donald T. Winski. "Distributed Information Systems: Their Effect on Your Company." *Price Waterhouse and Company Review* (1978, No. 1): 54–63.

Stiefel, Malcolm L. "A Primer on Modems." *Mini–Micro Systems* (March 1980): 111–122.

_____. "What Is an 'Intelligent' Terminal?" *Mini-Micro Systems* (March 1977): 50–60.

Thierauf, Robert J. *Systems Analysis and Design of Real-Time Management Information Systems.* Englewood Cliffs, N.J.: Prentice-Hall, 1975.

Vanecek, Michael T.; Robert F. Zant; and Carl Stephen Guynes. "Distributed Data Processing: A New 'Tool' for Accountants." *Journal of Accountancy* (October 1980): 75–83.

Viggers, Thomas G. "Which Type of Terminal Is Right for You?" *Mini–Micro Systems* (July 1979): 97–103.

Part 3

Systems Management

Chapter 10

Basic Issues of Systems Management

The information systems function is a relatively new administrative unit in modern organizations. Management of this function has proven to be a difficult and complex task. This is because the information systems function is unique—it is based on a rapidly changing technology, the use of which cuts across traditional organizational lines in a very fundamental way. Further, the application of this technology continues to expand, and shows no signs of reaching a peak.

In this environment there have understandably been many failures in systems management. Some of these, such as massive cost overruns, computer frauds, and system malfunctions, have been well publicized. However, within the past few years there has gradually developed a body of knowledge relating to the successful management of the systems function. This body of knowledge represents a combination of the basic principles of management and an understanding of the unique issues raised by systems technology and its application. In Part 3 of this book (Chapters 10 through 15) this body of knowledge is reviewed and discussed.

In this chapter some of the most important issues associated with the management of the information systems function are identified and the related management policies and methods are discussed. The first such topic covered involves the allocation of organizational responsibilities necessary to provide effective direction and administration for the information systems activity. Next the important subject of long-range planning for information systems is explained. Other topics covered include internal pricing systems for computer services, obtaining the involvement of line managers in systems activities relating to their functions, and the institutional impact of automation.

In the remaining chapters of Part 3, various other topics relating to management of the information systems function are covered. Chapter 11 explains and illustrates some of the techniques of systems analysis and design, and discusses strategies relevant to the management of systems change. Chapter 12 discusses techniques and problems peculiar to the selection and acquisition of new systems of hardware or software. Chapter 13 covers the process of implementing a major systems change, and describes related techniques of project management and control. Chapter 14 examines the problems of data security, data integrity, and internal control in computer-based information systems and explains a variety of related policies, procedures, and techniques. Chapter 15 deals with the concepts and techniques of auditing of computer-based information systems.

Part 3 is written primarily from the broad perspective of management rather than from the more limited perspective of the accountant. This perspective encompasses the role of top management relative to information systems, as well as the functions of management within the information systems department. However, much of this material is relevant to the role played by accountants in modern organizations. For example, in many organizations the management of information systems is a direct responsibility of the accounting department. Even when this is not true, the accounting department is still likely to have some responsibility for such matters as long-range systems planning, internal pricing of computer services, cost analysis of systems, data security and integrity, and internal control of information systems. Furthermore, the accounting department is inevitably involved in systems activities because of its role as a primary user of information systems.

Organizing for the Systems Function

A critical factor in the success of information systems is the manner in which responsibilities for directing and administering the systems function are allocated within the organization. A major issue here is the appropriate organizational location of the systems function. Another important issue involves the composition and role of an information systems steering committee. In large multidivisional organizations, the question of whether the systems function should be centrally located and controlled or decentralized becomes important. These and related issues are discussed in this section.

Organizational location of the systems function

The introduction of information technology had a profound effect upon the structure of many organizations. The installation of a computer system in an organization creates a completely new department, with new responsibilities, a new set of employees, and new problems. Since computers began to be applied on a major scale in business in the 1950s, a wide variety of patterns of locating the computer activity in the organization has evolved. According to various surveys, the most common arrangement is for the top computer executive to report to the controller or financial vice-president. Another common approach consists of the top computer executive serving as a vice-president having equal status with the controller, treasurer, and other vice-presidents. A somewhat less common pattern, which exists when one of the major departments in a company has a special need for a computer unique to the company or industry, is for the computer activity to be located within a particular department, such as manufacturing or marketing. Still another possibility is for the information systems function to be combined with other administrative departments such as accounting and finance under the authority of a Vice-President for Administration, as illustrated in Fig. 10.1.

One factor that helps to explain the frequency with which the computer activity is located under the controller or financial executive is that early computer applications were primarily to accounting operations, such as payroll, billing, or inventory. These applications have been among the first to be automated because of their routine nature, which makes them relatively simple to program. Those who support the location of the computer function within the accounting department argue that it is only logical for the computer to be located within the department responsible for the majority of the data processing work load. They further argue that the major reorganization necessary to create a computer department separate from the accounting department is quite costly in terms of disruption of familiar organizational relationships. They cite the traditional role of the accounting department in supplying information to managers in all other functional areas, and argue that the separation of responsibility for information preparation between two major departments makes very little sense.

Those who oppose the location of the computer activity within the accounting department argue that the nature of computer applications has evolved to the extent that most or all departments in an organization are likely to be interested in applying the computer to their own individual needs or problems. They feel that accountants naturally possess certain biases that limit their capacity to manage the computer activity in a manner that encourages the profitable application of computers throughout the organization. For example, systems personnel responsible to a controller may have a tendency to favor the development of financially oriented applications. Similarly, computer operations personnel may feel obligated to give top priority in processing schedules to accounting work. They further argue that the narrow perspective of accountants leads to premature rejection of application whose benefits cannot be tangibly measured in dollars, and that systems designs prepared by accountants tend to emphasize processing efficiency rather than analysis of the information needs of users.

Those who favor the location of the computer activity in a separate department reporting to a top-level executive argue that this separation is necessary to free the computer facility from the biases of accounting management. They argue that specialists in accounting or any other functional area are generally not sufficiently well qualified to manage the computer activity. They feel that a top-level computer ex-

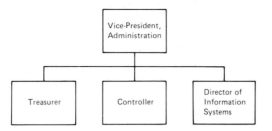

Fig. 10.1
Organization of the accounting, finance, and information systems functions under a Vice-President for Administration.

ecutive can make important contributions to top-management planning and control for the organization. They argue that this arrangement is the only one in which the top computer executive obtains the organizational status necessary to bring about integration of functions leading toward a total information system.

Creation of the position of Vice-President for Administration is advocated not only as a compromise in the computer location controversy but also as a more effective means of controlling administrative staff activities generally.[1] It reduces the potential for lack of objectivity on the part of the executive responsible for the computer system because the Vice-President for Administration is presumably a neutral officer. It also appeals to those who do not believe that a top computer executive is generally qualified to serve in a top-management position with vice-presidential status.

Several trends in recent years have reduced the significance of the computer location controversy. One is the development of new patterns of management of the systems function that increase the involvement of all users of computer services in determining the direction of information systems activities. These include systems steering committees, long-range planning procedures, and policies that enable users to "buy" computer services via a transfer pricing mechanism established by the organization. Such policies and procedures have tended to reduce the basis for conflict over decisions regarding the use of computer resources. Each of these is considered in greater depth later in this chapter.

A second trend is technological in origin—a movement toward small computers, computer terminals from which larger systems are accessible, simple programming languages, and "packaged" application programs. This makes computer resources more readily available to personnel throughout an organization, rather than completely concentrated under the control of a single department. This also tends to lead to a reduction of conflict over the use of systems development and data processing resources.

A third trend is philosophical, and consists of a growing disillusionment with the concept of a totally integrated management information system. Integration is being interpreted as a relative, rather than absolute, concept. Implementation of the concept is seen as practical only up to a point that falls short of a total system. For example, many manufacturing companies have found it worthwhile to integrate in-

[1] *See John Dearden, "MIS Is a Mirage,"* Harvard Business Review *(January/ February 1972), p. 98.*

formation systems for purchasing, inventory, production, and engineering functions. However, there is little or no common basis for integration of the information systems of, for example, the engineering, personnel, and sales functions. This trend in the thinking of systems theorists and practitioners[2] should tend to reduce pressures favoring top-executive status for the manager of the information systems department.

In summary, the issue of organizational location of the computer facility is an unresolved one, both generally and in many specific organizations. Recent trends seem likely to diminish the importance of the issue. One certainty is that each organization is unique, and each therefore must search for a means of organization best suited to its own individual circumstances.

The information systems steering committee

In recent years many organizations have found it useful to establish executive-level steering committees or advisory boards to oversee the information systems function.[3] Such committees should typically consist of the top computer executive and one or more other managers from the systems function, the controller, the financial vice-president, and all other functional vice-presidents or division heads whose areas of responsibility are significantly affected by the activities of the information systems function.

As an executive-level committee, the information systems steering committee should concern itself with broad policies and plans, and not get overly involved in technical details or administration of specific projects. It should meet only when necessary to carry out its functions. These functions should include review of proposals for major systems projects, review of long-range systems plans, monitoring of progress on major systems projects, approval of systems selection and acquisition decisions, review of the performance of the systems department, and consideration of organizational and key personnel changes relating to the systems department.

Effective use of an information systems steering committee provides several advantages. First, it provides a vehicle for productive top management involvement in the information systems function, a factor that has been found to correlate very highly with successful use of computers.[4] Second, it facilitates coordination and integration among departments and functions with respect to information systems activities. Third, it tends to reduce the conflict (mentioned earlier) over the best organizational placement of the systems function. Finally, it should lead to more effective management control over the allocation of resources in a manner that best reflects organizational goals.

[2] *For further elaboration of this point of view, see John Dearden, "MIS Is a Mirage,"* Harvard Business Review *(January/February 1972): 90–99, and Peter P. Schoderbek and Steven E. Schoderbek, "Integrated Information Systems—Shadow or Substance?"* Management Advisor *(November/December 1971): 27–32.*

[3] *Several examples are discussed by Richard G. Canning in "Do We Have the Right Resources?"* EDP Analyzer *(July 1975): 1–12.*

[4] Unlocking the Computer's Profit Potential *(New York: McKinsey, 1968); and Harold M. Sollenberger,* Management Control of Information Systems Development. *New York: National Association of Accountants, 1971.*

Centralization vs. decentralization of information systems

In a large multidivisional organization, one important issue that must be resolved involves the degree of centralization most appropriate for the information systems function. At one extreme is the highly centralized approach, under which there is a central data processing facility responsible for all aspects of the organization's data processing, including hardware selection and operation, software development and maintenance, data base design and administration, and planning and control of information systems resources. At the other extreme is the highly decentralized approach, under which each division operates its own independent data processing facility with little or no firmwide coordination or control. There is a wide variety of approaches that fall somewhere between these two extreme points. While most companies lean toward one or the other of these approaches, in practice there are few if any companies at either of the two extremes.

A highly centralized information systems function offers several advantages. One of these is the economies of scale provided by large computer systems; that is, the work load capacity per dollar spent on a computer increases substantially with the size of the computer.[5] Similar economies of scale apply to software, programming, and personnel costs. In addition, a larger computer facility may be more able to attract and retain more highly skilled technical, professional, and managerial personnel than would a smaller facility. Further, a common computer facility provides the opportunity for centralization of some administrative functions, such as billing, payroll, and purchasing, that can lead to substantial cost savings. Finally, a centralized systems function can develop and enforce standardized procedures and documentation, which facilitates communication, coordination, and control on an organizationwide basis.

A decentralized approach to the systems function also has advantages. Foremost among these is that there is closer proximity of the systems function to system users. As a result systems personnel generally have a better understanding of user needs and are more able and willing to respond to those needs. Also, divisional managers and personnel are more motivated to seek out profitable computer applications and participate in their development. In addition, decentralized computer facilities provide diffusion of the risk of system failure; that is, a system failure would affect only one division rather than the entire organization. Finally, expenditures for data transmission and other forms of communication are much smaller when separate divisional systems are used than when a central facility is set up to process data for the divisions.

Recent technological trends have caused many companies to be confronted abruptly by the centralization–decentralization issue. A common scenario involves a division or department that is dissatisfied with the service it receives from the central data processing facility, and decides to acquire its own mini- or microcomputer. Such temptations have been magnified in recent years by the declining size and cost of computer hardware and the increasing sophistication of computer users. How-

---

[5] *One rule of thumb which has been found to be accurate is that the rate of increase in computer power is proportional to the square of the rate of increase in computer cost. This is known as* Grosch's Law. *See Kenneth E. Knight, "Changes in Computer Performance,"* Datamation *(September 1966): 40–54.*

ever, it may not be in the long run best interests of a company to permit the proliferation of small computers to continue unchecked. Some form of coordination is
probably desirable, but it must be accomplished without stifling the initiative of
computer users.

Another technological development that has had a significant impact on this
issue is the increasing development and use of distributed processing networks. (See
Figs. 9.4 and 9.5.) Such networks make it possible to exercise centralized control
over the hardware configuration and technical support staff, while each location
performs its own systems analysis and design and data processing. Thus the organization can achieve some of the advantages of both centralization and decentralization.

More generally, it is coming to be recognized that the choice between centralization and decentralization of the information systems function is not one-dimen-
sional. That is, the systems function encompasses a wide variety of tasks, some of
which may be best performed on a centralized basis while others are best performed
at the divisional level. For example, Withington suggests that a central authority
should be responsible for hardware and software selection, design of data communications networks, and data base administration, while such functions as systems
analysis and programming are distributed among divisional or functional users of
systems resources.[6] Others such as Statland[7] and Buchanon and Linowes[8] argue that
each company must design its own hybrid organization for data processing, with
each function centralized or decentralized as appropriate. One thing is clear: the way
in which this problem is dealt with by today's organizations is going to have a significant impact upon the structure of information systems for many years to come.

Long-range Planning for Information Systems

Managerial planning for information systems involves decisions about the most
advantageous utilization of system resources in the future. These decisions, in turn,
affect the requirements of the system for additional hardware, personnel, and financial resources. The need for an effective system of long-range planning is especially
critical in large, computerized information systems.

The basic building block of information systems planning is the project development plan. Each such plan is a proposal to develop a particular application for the
computer system. One project plan might call for the development of a production
cost reporting system, while another proposes an online order entry system. Responsibility for the identification, selection, and implementation of new computer appli-

[6] *Frederic G. Withington, "Coping with Computer Proliferation,"* Harvard Business Review
(May/June 1980): 152-164

[7] *Norman Statland, "Organizing Your Company's EDP: Centralization vs. Decentralization,"* Price
Waterhouse Review, *vol. 20, no. 2 (1975): 12-17.*

[8] *Jack R. Buchanon and Richard G. Linowes, "Understanding Distributed Data Processing,"* Harvard
Business Review *(July/August 1980): 143-153, and "Making Distributed Data Processing Work,"* Harvard Business Review *(September/October 1980): 143-161.*

cations within an organization rests jointly with the systems development staff of analysts and programmers and the system user groups. At any given time, there may be several projects in the process of implementation or in the proposal stage.

The most important single decision made by an organization's management with respect to its information system is the assignment of priorities to the various systems projects under development. This decision defines the future direction of the information system and determines its ultimate success or failure as a profitable tool of management. The great significance of this decision dictates that it must be made at the top-management level and that it should not be left to computer specialists. The costs and benefits of each project proposal should be thoroughly analyzed to provide management with a basis for assigning priorities among competing projects. The priority assignment establishes which of these projects deserve a share of the organization's currently available systems development resources.

This section begins with a description of the appropriate content of each project development plan, then explains how the overall long-range systems plan is derived on the basis of the various individual project development plans. After a brief discussion of commonly observed patterns of evolution of the information systems function in modern business organizations, the section concludes with a discussion of the payoffs of systems planning.

Content of a project development plan

Each project development plan is basically an analysis of the requirements and expectations for a proposed computer application. Requirements are broken down into two categories, developmental and operational. Developmental requirements include all resources necessary to implement the new application. Operational requirements include all resources consumed by regular utilization of the new system subsequent to its implementation.

The resources required for development of a new computer application consist primarily of personnel work-hours. Each new application is really a software system which includes a set of programs and system documentation. The development of such a software system will consume the time of programmers, systems analysts, supervisors, and user group representatives. For each project, the number of work-hours required of personnel within each job classification should be estimated. A timetable should be established which indicates the number of weeks required to complete each step in the development process, and the number of work-hours required for each step. Network planning techniques such as PERT are often used for this purpose.

In addition to personnel work-hours, each development project will also consume some hardware resources. Computer time will be required to test and debug individual programs as they are written. As the project nears completion, the system as a whole must be tested and operators trained in its usage. If the system is to replace an existing system, parallel operation will be necessary. The computer time requirements for all of these activities should be specified with respect to the amount of time required and the timetable for utilizing that time.

An estimate of the financial resources needed for development of each application can be derived from the analysis of personnel, hardware, and other miscellaneous requirements such as supplies. These will consist primarily of personnel salaries and hardware utilization costs. All of the cost outflows should be classified into time periods to produce a project budget. The total of all of these costs, discounted if the time factor is significant, represents the total financial investment in the project.

The operational requirements of a computer application include the hardware time required for processing, the time of machine operators required to prepare input data and monitor the operation of the computer and other equipment, the time of programmers and analysts required to maintain the software system, and the supervisory time required for all of these activities. The project development plan should include a conversion of these requirements into financial terms. The operating cost estimate should be stated on a "per week" or "per month" basis.

Finally, each project development plan should include an analysis of the expected economic benefits of the new application. This analysis is essential to management's determination of priorities for proposed projects, as well as to the establishment of responsibility for the success of the project. Few general guidelines can be specified for this analysis, but one essential rule is that the users who will receive the benefits of a computer application must be involved in the estimation of its economic utility.

The overall systems plan

The individual project development plans form the basis for the overall long-range systems plan of an organization. For purposes of combining individual project plans in preparing an overall plan, the planned requirements for each individual project plan should be summarized in a form similar to that shown in Fig. 10.2. The requirements of all individual project plans (for those projects that have been accepted) may then be summed together to determine total resource requirements per month for all projects by category of resource. In addition, operational requirements for presently operating applications should be estimated from projections of growth in their current resource usage, and added to the total resource requirements. The result, as shown in Fig. 10.3, is a summary projection of total system resource requirements for the future. This diagram illustrates the three dimensions of long-range systems planning: requirements, time (months), and applications (development projects and current operations). Projections obtained from this process form the heart of the long-range systems plan.

From a planning perspective the resource requirement totals shown on the right in Fig. 10.3 are extremely valuable. In essence they show how much of each resource will be required during each future month in order to carry out the systems plan. Comparing these totals to currently available resources enables management to schedule the acquisition of any needed additional resources in an orderly manner. For example, once it is known when additional analysts, programmers, operators, and so forth will be needed, personnel can make arrangements for interviewing, hiring and training new employees, and promoting and reassigning existing employees,

REQUIREMENTS	DEVELOPMENT PHASE					OPERATION (per month)
	Month 1	2	3	4	etc.	
Personnel Man Hours						
Systems analysis						
Programming						
Operations						
Data preparation						
Other						
Hardware						
CPU time						
Disk storage						
Tape input/output						
Card input						
Print output						
Terminals						
Other						
Financial						
Salaries						
Hardware/Software						
Other						

*Fig. 10.2
Summary content of
a computer project
development plan.*

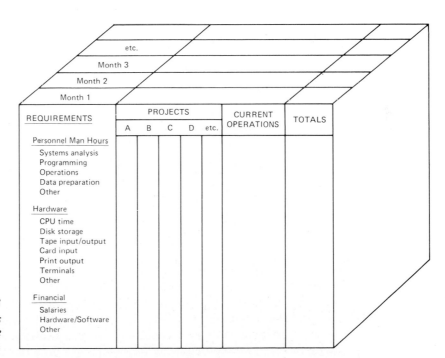

*Fig. 10.3
The three dimensions
of a long-range
systems plan.*

in order that positions are filled as they become available. This is a tremendous improvement on the haphazard approach to personnel management so often found in the data processing field.

The same point can be made with respect to computer hardware. There have been many cases in which an organization has waited until the capacity of its computer system is strained before realizing the need to obtain additional capacity. However, computer acquisition is a long and complex process, and one that should be undertaken in an orderly manner. The hardware requirement totals provided by the systems plan provide the information needed for this purpose. Once the appropriate time for adding new capacity or upgrading to a new system has been pinpointed, plans can be made to begin the process with sufficient lead time to enable an orderly transition.

In addition to project plans and resource requirement projections, a systems plan usually contains some narrative information as well. This might include a summary of the objectives of the information systems function, and an explanation of how they relate to organizational goals. Related to this would be a description of criteria for assigning project priorities. Another important element of such narrative information would be a survey of the most recent technological developments, as well as those expected in the near future and a discussion of both their implications for and possible application to systems operations within the organization.

A planning horizon of approximately five years is reasonable for the long-range systems plan. Projections should be reasonably firm for the first year of the plan, and moderately firm for the second year in the future. For the third and subsequent years, projections will be much rougher and plans will be stated in more general terms. The plan should be updated at least once each year.

The "stage hypothesis" of data processing growth

According to Richard L. Nolan, a prominent author and consultant in the information systems field, systems planning is greatly facilitated by the recognition that the data processing function in most business organizations evolves through six stages of growth.[9] These stages, together with a brief explanation of their characteristics, follow.

(1) *Initiation*—computer technology is introduced and applied to high-volume accounting applications for which cost savings are greatest.

(2) *Contagion*—computer applications proliferate in functional areas throughout the organization.

(3) *Control*—new computer applications are restricted, and the emphasis shifts to documenting and restructuring existing applications and the development of formalized systems for planning and controlling the computer resource.

(4) *Integration*—data base technology is introduced and existing applications are modified to utilize this new technology. There is a shift in emphasis from managing the computer to managing the company's data resources.

---

[9] See Nolan's "Managing the Crises in Data Processing," Harvard Business Review *(March/April 1979): 115–126. In an earlier article coauthored with Cyrus F. Gibson, Nolan had identified and described the first four stages.* See "Managing the Four Stages of EDP Growth," Harvard Business Review *(January/February 1974): 76–88.*

(5) *Data administration*—data base technology is used to integrate existing applications on an increasingly wider scale, and the data resource management concept is implemented throughout the organization.

(6) *Maturity*—the applications portfolio is complete, and its structure mirrors the organization and information flows in the company.

Nolan indicates that many large organizations have undergone the transition from stage 3 to stage 4 in recent years, and that this transition is characterized by explosive growth in data processing expenditures.

Nolan recommends that companies identify the stage that their data processing is in so that they may better understand their past problems and gain insight to their most promising future strategies. Benchmarks indicating which stage a company is in include the growth rate of the data processing budget, the extent of use of data base technology, the nature of data processing applications, the type of organization structure for data processing, the focus of data processing planning and control, and the depth of user involvement. Nolan stresses the importance of a formal data processing growth plan to smooth the evolutionary process. He also emphasizes the need to monitor new developments in information technology, and the importance of an effective senior-management data processing steering committee to establish priorities and formulate growth strategies. Finally, he suggests that companies must recognize and prepare for the fundamental organizational transition from computer management to data resource management because this will have a profound impact upon the way in which new applications are structured and the way in which systems for planning and controlling data processing are designed.

Advantages of systems planning

An effective program of long-range planning for its computer-based information systems pays dividends to an organization in several ways. The ability to approach hardware acquisition and personnel planning in a more systematic way has already been mentioned. Another important advantage is that the systems planning process provides a sound basis for selection of new computer applications. The alternative to long-range planning is to decide upon each proposal as it is made, independently of other proposals. Since all development projects consume the limited financial and personnel resources of the organization, it is essential that each of the potentially profitable computer applications be subjected to comparative scrutiny for identification and ranking according to their expected profitability, rather than be considered serparately. Only in this way can management maximize the return on its investment in computer systems.

Another advantage of systems planning is that it enables an organization's computer effort to be coordinated with its overall long-range planning program. This is important because the information system competes with many other functions, projects, and departments for a share of the available resources within the organization. The systems plan provides a better basis for deciding what portion of available organizational resources should be allocated to the information systems function. Projected financial requirements from the plan can be incorporated into the organization's budgeting system. Furthermore, if the organization revises its long-range goals and strategies, the systems plan provides a sound basis for appropriately revising project priorities and reassigning resources in an orderly fashion.

Long-range systems planning also enables better coordination among the various information subsystems within the total system. It also permits management to plan for the most effective utilization of new technological developments. Finally, the overall plan and the individual project plans provide standards for evaluating the performance of information systems managers and project development teams. In summary, the long-range systems plan is an essential cornerstone of good management of the information systems function.

Internal Pricing of Computer Services[10]

An important consideration relating to the management of the information systems function in all organizations is the extent to which users of computer services are charged for such services. A system of charging user departments for computer services is analogous to a system of transfer pricing of products exchanged between two divisions of the same company. Even though this system is simply an accounting procedure, it has a significant effect on the management and on the utilization of information system resources. In this section the objectives of a pricing system for computer services are explained, and several different approaches and techniques used in such systems are described and compared.

Objectives and criteria

Before settling on the details of a pricing system for computer services, it is necessary to consider what should be the most important objectives of the system, and what criteria will be used for selecting among alternative methods.

Among the objectives most often established are (1) equitable allocation of the computer resource to its most worthwhile uses while discouraging frivolous use, (2) motivation of computer management and personnel to provide efficient, high-quality service to users, (3) establishment of an objective basis upon which to evaluate the performance of computer management, and (4) encouragement of user interest and participation in the development and implementation of information systems. The relative importance attached to each of these objectives will vary depending on the specific needs and characteristics of the organization.

Numerous criteria have been proposed for systems of pricing computer services. For example, nearly all authorities agree on the importance of devising a charging system that is understandable to users. This encourages user decision making consistent with the most efficient allocation of the computer resource. Many experts also stress the importance of consistency or stability of charges, which means

[10] *Portions of this section are reprinted with permission from the author's paper "Pricing Internal Computer Services: The Basic Issues,"* Management Accounting *(April 1976): 47–50.*

that the same job processed at two different times under different work-load conditions should be charged the same price. Another important criterion is that charges be equitable in the sense that they are proportional to the amount of computer resources actually consumed by the user application. The charging system should be economical in the sense that the costs associated with the system itself should not be so great as to outweigh the benefits obtained from the system. These criteria may at times conflict so that value judgments may have to be made about which are more important in specific circumstances.

Selecting the allocation base

The allocation base refers to the measure of work performed by the computer system. A base is multiplied by a rate to arrive at a charge. Three different types of allocation bases may be used: a single factor base, a unit pricing base, and a multiple factor base.

Two commonly used single factor bases are wall clock time (WCT) and central processing unit (CPU) time. In both cases, a single measure of time usage is multiplied by a single rate to derive the charge. The simplicity of this approach makes it easily understood by users and easily implemented. Relatively minor changes in the operating system software enable the charge to be computed and reported as each job is being processed.

Disadvantages of single factor bases arise in a multiprogramming environment. WCT becomes very inconsistent, varying in accordance with the particular mix of jobs being processed. For example, a job that takes 15 minutes to complete when it is the only job being run may take 30 minutes when several other jobs are also being run.

Both WCT and CPU time also tend to be inequitable in the sense that charges are not related to the resources used. A job using five input/output devices could consume the same WCT or CPU time as a job using only two input/output devices, but to charge the same amount for the two jobs does not fairly reflect their differences in resource utilization. Once again, this disadvantage relates primarily to the multiprogramming environment in which system components not required in one job may be used by any other job being executed at the same time.

The unit pricing approach seeks to develop a single unit measure of work performed by the system that reflects all of the systems components available to the user during execution of the job. For example, the unit measure might be defined as the total amount of work the system can perform in one minute. For a given job this measure would be derived by counting the various operations performed by the system during execution, such as reading a card or printing a line, then applying a weighting factor to each count and summing the results. This unit measure would then be multiplied by a single rate to compute the charge.

The unit pricing approach has the advantage of producing a reasonably stable charge for a given equipment configuration, and it is reasonably equitable. Furthermore, each user's bill for services is uncomplicated, showing the total units consumed, the rate, and the total charge. A unit pricing system, however, is difficult to design and implement, and must be refined each time new equipment is added to the system. In addition, the concepts and techniques underlying the computation of the unit measure may not be easily understood by users.

A multiple factor base involves the use of a separate rate for each of the several system components used during the execution of a job. These components may include CPU time, core storage, cards read, cards punched, lines printed, tape accesses, disk accesses, and so forth. Each measure is multiplied by a separate rate and the resulting individual component charges are summed to arrive at a total job charge. This is probably the most equitable pricing approach for the user, and, in addition, the information generated by this approach may be used by the computer staff to evaluate and improve the efficiency of scheduling of computer operations.

A significant disadvantage of the multiple factor allocation base is that it is difficult and costly to develop and implement. Because of its complexities, it may also be confusing to users. Considerable testing of alternatives may be required before a particular scheme is chosen. Costs common to a number of system components—such as the wages of machine operators—must be allocated in some manner to the rates of the various components.

Setting rates   Rates charged for data processing services may be based upon three methods: full costing, market prices, or flexible pricing. Closely related to this issue is the question of whether the computer department is to be treated as a cost center or a profit center. Under the full costing method, rates charged for computer services are intended to generate revenues just sufficient to cover the costs of the computer center, which is consistent with the cost center concept. The use of market prices should provide an excess of revenues over costs, and is therefore consistent with the profit center concept. Flexible pricing is a technique which may be used in conjunction with either the cost center or profit center approach.

The full costing method (also called average cost pricing) requires that a rate, or rates, be computed on the basis of the actual total costs of the data processing operation. For example, where the single factor of CPU time is used as the allocation base, total cost is divided by total CPU time to derive a rate per hour. The rate is generally recomputed at short intervals, such as at the end of each month.

The full costing approach offers the advantage of simplicity. Charges are easily understood by users and are thus less subject to dispute. Furthermore, the rates may also be used for project costing and economic feasibility analysis of proposed new applications. Charges for computer services under this approach should be relatively low, thus encouraging fuller use of computer resources and stifling any desire by users to patronize outside service bureaus. Also, the use of a cost-based charge should tend to reduce the occurrence and intensity of disputes over the equity of charges. Such disputes are especially common when rates based upon market prices are used.

Full costing has its disadvantages. Since the rates are periodically revised, charges tend to be unstable over time because of changes in usage and total costs. When total use is relatively low, service rates tend to be high, which may discourage

desirable increases in demand. On the other hand, when use is high, rates are relatively low, which encourages increased use and aggravates the problem of under-capacity.

Full costing also fails to deal directly with the problem of an uneven work load characterized by periods of slack demand in the evenings and on weekends. Furthermore, it fails to recognize that some jobs deserve higher priority in terms of turn-around time than others. It also provides low motivation for data processing management to minimize costs, since users will be billed for actual costs whatever they may be.

Market prices generally provide a more stable charging rate for computer services. Furthermore, used in conjunction with the profit center concept, market prices provide a superior means of motivating the management of the computer facility. There is motivation not only to hold costs down but also to provide quality services that will maximize the satisfaction of user needs. The computer center manager becomes market oriented and seeks to develop and provide new services that take advantage of the best available technology for the benefit of users and the total organization.

The profit center approach also provides a better basis for economic evaluation of the computer facility by top management. Comparison of the return on investment of the computer facility with that of other divisions of the company gives some indication of whether the investment in computer resources is justified relative to alternative uses of corporate funds. If users are willing to pay the rates charged and to use most or all of the available capacity, a large profit should be generated to signal the need, as well as to provide justification, for additional investment in computer facilities.

There are also significant disadvantages to the use of market prices. Unless the computer center sells its services commercially, market prices may not be readily available. In such instances it is difficult to obtain a comparable market price. Therefore, costly, time-consuming negotiations between users and data processing management may be necessary. This also raises the issue of whether users should be permitted to use an outside service bureau when internal prices are too high. Finally, market prices do not solve the problems of handling peak demands and providing fast turnaround for high-priority work.

Flexible pricing involves adjusting prices for the purpose of stabilizing the demand for computer services. High rates are charged for services rendered during periods of peak demand, and for jobs requiring fast turnaround. In conjunction with a multiple factor allocation base, higher rates may be charged for heavily used system components in order to prevent those components from becoming bottle-necks. When system capacity is substantially increased (as it may be by the acquisition of a new computer), lower rates may be charged for a brief period in order to encourage users to consume the available capacity. Note that under flexible pricing, rates do not necessarily bear any relation to cost. Rates may be established to recover total costs, or to recover costs plus a profit.

If properly administered, a flexible pricing scheme may generate significant benefits. Those users whose needs are critical enough to justify fast turnaround and

service during peak periods will presumably be willing to pay higher rates, and those users whose needs are less critical will be encouraged to accept slower turnaround or processing during slack periods. Flexible pricing thus seeks to establish a stable and acceptable equilibrium between the supply and demand of computer services.

The use of flexible pricing adds to the complexity and expense of a charging system. In addition, prices may have to be changed frequently to accommodate changes in user behavior. Despite these disadvantages, the need to balance the work load of the computer facility over time is often important enough to justify the use of some form of flexible pricing. In a business data processing environment, flexible pricing for peak and slack period demand and for accommodation of differing turnaround requirements would seem to be the most appropriate forms.

In conclusion, the final choice of the allocation base and the technique of computing rates is a complex issue. A major factor in resolving this issue should be the degree of sophistication of computer management and users. If these groups possess a great deal of experience and expertise, the more complex techniques such as unit pricing, multiple factor bases, market prices, or flexible pricing may be appropriate. Otherwise the simple approach of full costing using a single factor base may be best.

Selecting new computer applications

When a pricing system for computer services is used, there is merit to the idea that computer users should be free to select among new computer applications. Under this approach computer applications would be selected for development only if a user department is willing to pay the systems development and operating costs out of its departmental budget. Proponents of user freedom to select new applications contend that such freedom makes users feel responsible for the success of the projects they select, thereby ensuring user involvement and motivation to achieve success. They argue further that user managers understand the needs of their own department better than anyone else, and are better able to evaluate the subjective benefits of proposed new applications. Thus if the data processing staff can provide a reasonably accurate forecast of cost, the user can evaluate whether the benefits outweigh the costs by a sufficient amount to justify the project.

There are disadvantages to this concept of user freedom to select new computer applications. Because of the relative newness and complexity of computer systems in many organizations, users may not be knowledgeable enough to make responsible choices. Also the development of integrated systems that cross departmental boundaries is often desirable and is made easier when the selection process is centralized. Furthermore, the centralized approach provides a better basis for long-range systems planning because such plans are not subject to constant change due to new user requests. Finally, there is merit to the idea of comparing all proposed applications at one time and assigning highest priority to those which are most consistent with overall organizational goals.

Resolution of this difficult question will obviously depend to a great extent on management's philosophy with respect to the general issue of centralization vs. decentralization. However, a compromise approach is used in many organizations.

Under this approach, users are free to accept computer projects costing less than a certain amount, but must seek approval at a higher level of authority for more expensive projects.

Advantages of pricing systems

Organizations that do not charge users for computer services frequently encounter serious problems. Users are motivated to request computer services without regard to cost. On the other hand, a user who is not charged for computer services is less likely to involve himself or herself in the development and implementation of computer applications, and such involvement is often critical to the success of the information system. Another problem is that it is difficult for management to evaluate the economic merits of requests by systems personnel for additional computer resources. If such requests are fulfilled, the computer budget may grow out of control, whereas denial of these requests may limit computer capacity to such an extent that user demand cannot be serviced adequately. Furthermore, the demand for computer services may exceed the supply during peak periods, but may be inadequate to provide full utilization of the system during slack periods.

A system of internal pricing for computer services should alleviate many of these problems. Users will request services only when they believe the benefits of such services outweigh the costs charged against their budgets. User managers are more likely to involve themselves in systems development and implementation in order to assure themselves that expected benefits will be realized, and that involvement enhances the likelihood of success. Because the computer function is paying its own way, increases in budget to enlarge system capacity are much easier to justify on an economic basis.

If a charging system includes a flexible pricing scheme to charge higher rates for peak period usage, then the problem of balancing the processing work load between peak and slack periods may be substantially reduced. Furthermore, if users are permitted the freedom to use the services of an outside service bureau in lieu of the internal computer function, a tremendous incentive is provided to the internal computer management to minimize its costs and maximize the quality of its services.

The difficulties in developing an internal pricing system are being reduced as computer manufacturers and software vendors develop packages and algorithms for job costing in multiprogrammed systems. As a result, systems of pricing for computer services are now recognized as an important cornerstone of sound computer management.

Management Involvement in the Systems Function

As mentioned earlier, the degree of management involvement with respect to the systems function has been found to correlate highly with success in the utilization of computer systems. When discussing management involvement in the systems function, it is helpful to distinguish two categories of management—executives at the top level of the organizational hierarchy, and managers of middle-level departments that make significant use of computer services.

The role of top management relative to the systems function encompasses the areas of planning, policy setting, performance review, and decision making. Top management should delineate the overall goals and objectives of the organization and identify what it feels are the key success factors in the organization's operations in order to provide guidance and direction to the systems activity. Top management should review long-range systems plans and strive to integrate such plans with the overall long-range planning effort of the organization. Top management should participate in major decisions relating to the systems function, including hiring of key personnel, acquisition of major equipment, and selection of major systems projects. Review of performance of the systems department, its key management personnel, and its major systems development projects is another important role of top management. The establishment of policies relating to project selection, pricing of computer services, organizational structure, and career paths for systems personnel is also important.

The role of user department managers primarily concerns the identification, selection, design, and development of new computer applications. User managers should participate in the determination of information requirements for their department's operations. They should cooperate with systems analysts in the estimation of costs and benefits for proposed systems applications. They should be willing to assign key members of their own staff to full-time participation in systems development projects, and should themselves be actively involved in directing and monitoring such projects. Furthermore they must make a financial commitment from their departmental budgets to support the development and operation of new systems.

Strategies for obtaining effective management involvement

It is relatively easy to identify what the roles of management should be with respect to the systems function. However, achieving effective management involvement to fulfill these roles has been one of the most difficult of all the problems of systems management. This section discusses some of the formal steps that can be taken to achieve effective management involvement in the systems function.

Perhaps the most critical barrier to effective management participation in systems activities is the communications gap that exists between operating managers having little or no technical expertise and systems personnel having great technical expertise but little understanding of line operations. This gap can probably never be eliminated, but it must be recognized and dealt with to the greatest extent possible.

The first step toward dealing with this problem is education and training. Large organizations may assign staff employees to the development of in-house training programs for management and systems personnel. Programs for management and systems users should focus upon the basic elements of systems technology, its terminology, its applications, its economics, and its evolution. Smaller organizations that cannot afford such in-house programs can make use of similar programs available from a variety of professional organizations such as the Association for Systems Management, the Data Processing Management Association, the American Institute of CPAs, and the National Association of Accountants. It should be noted that the success of such programs depends in large measure on the encouragement and support of top management, which should urge its subordinates to participate in such programs, and should back up its encouragement by taking account of such participation in the evaluation of employee performance.

A second approach to the management involvement issue relates to staffing policies. Too many organizations take the attitude that their systems department is a completely separate entity with respect to career paths of management and staff personnel. Such policies cannot help but widen the communications gap mentioned earlier. A more enlightened approach permits career paths to freely cross this boundary. Staff personnel in operating departments should be considered as candidates for assignment to positions in the systems department, and vice versa. It is particularly important that the systems department not be looked upon as a "dead end" in terms of career advancement but that systems personnel with good administrative skills be given the opportunity to move up the organizational hierarchy, possibly to executive status if merited by performance. This approach is obviously not a short-run solution to the issues of management involvement and the communication gap, but in the long run it may be the best possible solution.

Two policies whose effect is to enhance management involvement in the systems function have already been discussed in this chapter. One is the use of an information systems steering committee composed of top-level executives and systems personnel. Another is the use of a formal pricing mechanism for computer services. With respect to the latter, line managers are naturally more inclined to take interest in an activity which they are paying for through large allocations of their departmental budgets.

Another common approach is the use of project teams to carry out systems development work involving applications for the operating departments. Such teams include both systems analysts and programmers from the systems department and user department managers and staff from the appropriate operating departments. Some of these personnel may be assigned to the team on a full-time basis, others on a part-time basis. Such teams are formed when a systems development project is formally approved and they continue to function until the system is implemented. Once again it is necessary that the organizational reward structure clearly reflect management's desire for effective user department participation in such project teams.

In summary there are a variety of policies and procedures that can be used to foster management involvement in the systems function. However, nothing is quite so effective as a clear signal from the top level of the organization that such involvement is important and will be rewarded.

Impact of the Computer on Patterns of Organization

The advent of the computer and related information technology has had, and continues to have, a profound impact upon organizational patterns within the business world. One example concerning the issue of organizational location of the computer activity has already been discussed. At this point several other related issues of computer impact upon organizations are identified and briefly discussed.

**Centralization or
decentralization
of management**

Prior to the advent of computers a trend toward decentralization of management functions had existed in business. Large multidivision companies could not effectively make decisions for, and exercise control over, far-flung operating divisions. This was true because accounting, the primary information supplying function, did not have available the technology to provide company headquarters with adequate information on a timely basis that was necessary to make decisions at the operating level.

Some authorities predicted that the increased information processing capability provided by the computer could have the effect of eliminating this trend toward decentralization. The computer enables company headquarters to receive more timely and reliable information in greater quantities from the operating divisions. The use of real-time systems and distributed networks of computers linked by data communications is the ultimate expression of this trend. This would seem to provide top management with the capability to centralize decision making for operating divisions.

To date, no widespread trend toward recentralization of management control has been evident in multidivisional companies. Many companies have centralized certain administrative functions, such as customer accounting, purchasing, or cash management, but the primary motivation for this has been to improve efficiency rather than to centralize management control. At the same time, recent technological trends such as the advent of mini- and microcomputers and distributed processing networks have greatly enhanced the computer capability available to the divisions. Thus the divisions no longer simply provide input to a central computer facility but they also have their own processing facility as well. In short, modern computer technology can effectively support either a philosophy of centralization or a philosophy of decentralization, and it is up to each company to design a system that best fits its own philosophy and objectives.

**Effect on
management
tasks**

Another hotly debated issue has been the effect of information technology upon the functions performed by management, especially middle management. Some have suggested that computers would take over the routine decision-making functions of middle management, and result in a greater degree of centralization of creative activities within the higher management levels.[11] As middle management was eliminated, the shape of the organization structure would shift from the form of a triangle toward the form of an hourglass. Others suggest that computers will not eliminate middle management, but will remove the routine tasks from this group and give it more time to concentrate upon the creative aspects of its jobs. No clear pattern has yet emerged with respect to this question.[12]

---

[11] *The classic statement of this position is found in Harold J. Leavitt and Thomas L. Whisler, "Management in the 1980's,"* Harvard Business Review *(November/December 1958): 41–48.*

[12] *For further discussion of this subject, see Hak Chong Lee, "The Organizational Impact of Computers,"* Management Services *(May/June 1967): 39–43, and Charles W. Hofer, "Emerging EDP Pattern,"* Harvard Business Review *(March/April 1970): 16–31, 169–171.*

Examining this question very carefully, Whisler suggests that management functions can be delineated into four basic categories: (1) problem solving, (2) communication, (3) goal setting, and (4) pattern perception, or the recognition of problems and opportunities. He argues that computers possess advantages over human beings with respect to the functions of problem solving and communication of expected results. However, he does not foresee an ability for computers to replace managers with respect to goal setting, pattern perception, or the motivational aspects of communication.[13]

Effect on routine tasks   Still another major issue has been the effect of computer technology upon clerical workers, production line employees, and others whose jobs are routine and repetitive in nature. Prominent labor leaders and others have predicted that automation would cause mass unemployment by displacing thousands of clerical and production employees. This argument is countered by those who contend that computer technology enhances worker productivity, enables workers to escape from the drudgery of traditional industrial or clerical jobs, and opens up more creative jobs requiring knowledge, judgment, and higher levels of skill.

Has computer technology contributed to greater unemployment in our society? It is difficult to tell because computer technology has not been the only variable affecting employment. The unemployment rate in this country was about the same in 1968 that it was in 1948, but it has risen substantially since then. Employment in the data processing field has been growing rapidly for over 30 years. Other trends such as the increasing participation of women in the work force and changing government policies have also significantly affected the employment marketplace. Thus it is probably impossible to isolate the net effect of computer technology on unemployment rates.

One thing that now seems clear is that the computer's impact upon the nature of jobs is not something that is beyond our control. That is, it is possible to design man-machine systems in which the role of the employee involves little more than pushing buttons or reacting to the machine's needs, but it is also possible to design man-machine systems in which the judgment and creativity of the employee complements the speed, memory, and accuracy of the machine. In short, whether or not the new technology can eliminate the drudgery of menial jobs depends on the ingenuity of systems designers to devise systems that fulfill the promise of the computer era.

In summary, the long-range effects of computers upon traditional organizational structures and job responsibilities are not entirely clear. The major point of agreement is that the impact will be profound. Much speculation has been offered by experts on this subject, and the Lee and Hofer articles cited above provide a good synthesis of some of this literature. The process of change is made less orderly by the seemingly continuous advancements being made in information technology. The future promises to be hectic but interesting.

[13] *Thomas L. Whisler,* Information Technology and Organizational Change. *Belmont, Calif.: Wadsworth 1970: 24–26, 81–82.*

Review Questions

1. Explain why the management of the information systems function has proven to be such a difficult and complex task.

2. How is the study of information systems management relevant to the role played by accountants in modern organizations?

3. What are four existing patterns of location of the computer operation within business organizations?

4. What business data processing tasks were among the first to be automated and why?

5. Describe several arguments both favoring and opposing the location of the computer activity within the accounting department in organizations.

6. What arguments are advanced by those who favor the location of the computer activity in a separate department whose manager is a top-level executive in an organization?

7. What arguments are advanced by those who favor the creation of a position of Vice-President for Administration to whom the Controller, Treasurer, and Director of Information Systems would report?

8. Explain three trends of recent years in the systems field which have tended to reduce the significance of the computer location controversy in organizations.

9. Explain the role of an executive-level information systems steering committee. What should be the composition of such a committee? What advantages can be attained from effective use of such a committee?

10. List several arguments in favor of a centralized approach to the information systems function in a large organization.

11. List several arguments in favor of a decentralized approach to the information systems function in a large organization.

12. Describe some effects of recent technological trends on the issue of centralization vs. decentralization of the information systems function.

13. Explain why the assignment of priorities to proposed new computer applications is a very critical decision for an organization's management.

14. Describe in some detail the content of a systems project development plan.

15. Describe in some detail the content of an overall information systems plan for an organization.

16. What are the six stages of growth in the data processing function in most business organizations, according to Richard Nolan? What implications does this "stage hypothesis" have for systems planning?

17. Explain several advantages of long-range planning for information systems.

18. Explain briefly what a system of internal pricing of computer services is.

19. Explain some of the objectives that are often established for pricing of computer services.

20. Explain some of the criteria most often used in designing a system of pricing computer services.

21. Identify some alternative allocation bases for pricing of computer services, and describe their relative advantages and disadvantages.

22. Describe some alternative methods of setting rates for computer services, and explain their relative advantages and disadvantages.

23. What effect should the degree of sophistication of computer management and users have upon the selection of a system of pricing computer services?

24. When a system of pricing computer services is being used, what arguments favor permitting users to freely select new computer applications? What arguments oppose such an approach? Is there a possible compromise between these two points of view?

25. Explain several advantages of internal pricing of computer services.

26. Explain the role which top management should play relative to the systems function in an organization.

27. Explain the role which user department managers and personnel should play relative to the systems function in an organization.

28. What has been the most significant barrier to effective management participation in the activities of the systems function in most organizations?

29. Explain several strategies for obtaining effective management involvement in the systems function.

30. Identify and briefly discuss three issues of computer impact upon organizational patterns.

Discussion Questions

31. The approach to long-range information systems planning described in this chapter is obviously important for large organizations having extensive investments in computer facilities. Should small organizations, in which the computer department employs fewer than, say, ten persons, attempt to implement such planning programs? Discuss.

32. Do you believe that it is possible to generalize with respect to the proper organizational location of the computer activity in business? Why or why not? Discuss.

33. If a multidivisional company decides to adopt a decentralized approach to the information systems function, is there a role for long-range information systems planning in that company? Discuss.

34. Discuss the impact of computers and automation upon the nature of job responsibilities and upon unemployment in our society.

Problems and Cases

35. The Dobson Manufacturing Company has recently decided to replace its small business computer system with a large general-purpose computer system employing online terminals and real-time processing capability. The feasibility study that recommended this step was carried out by the Assistant Controller, who is also the manager of the current system, and by the Assistant Vice-President for Production, who is an expert in real-time production control systems. One of the first steps in planning for acquisition and implementation of the new

system is to decide how the change will affect the company's organization structure. The company is currently organized into five major functional areas: Production, Marketing, Personnel, Finance, and Accounting.

Some facts from the feasibility study which bear upon the decision are as follows:

■ The budget and staff of the new department will be three times as large as that of the old department.

■ The computer will perform all of the basic accounting functions previously performed by the small business computer system.

■ The primary justification for the new computer system is the contribution to profit which will be generated as a result of its immediate application to production planning and control.

■ Estimated usage of computer time by each of the five functional areas is expected to be as follows: Production—30 percent; Marketing—10 percent; Personnel—5 percent; Finance—5 percent; Accounting—50 percent.

■ High potential exists for profitable application of the new computer in Marketing, Personnel, and Finance, and total usage of computer time by these three areas should eventually reach 40 percent.

Required   Considering all aspects of the situation described, identify and discuss the relative merits of several alternative locations of the new computer facility within the organizational structure of the Dobson Manufacturing Company.

36. The Dooley Company operates its Data Processing Center as a cost center. Each year a budget for the center is developed by the company's Controller and the Manager of the Data Processing Center. The Manager's performance is evaluated on the basis of a comparison of actual costs incurred to budgeted costs.

The manager of the Data Processing Center is responsible for accepting or rejecting proposals from user departments for new applications. User departments are not charged for either programming work or data processing service. Some of the main problems relating to the operation of the Center have been as follows.

1) The Manager has complained that budget allowances are not sufficient to pay for necessary new equipment and personnel.

2) There is frequent uncertainty and disagreement regarding decisions on whether proposed new applications should be undertaken.

3) The Accounting, Production, and Marketing Departments have frequently disputed over whose applications should obtain priority in development and scheduling.

Required   a) Identify the policy or policies which are the probable cause of each of the problems cited above. Explain.

b) Describe an alternative system of management control which might be appropriate for the Data Processing Center. Explain how this approach would be implemented and how it might contribute to solution of the problems above.

37. The Perry Corporation has four new computer applications under development or scheduled to begin development shortly. The monthly requirements of these development projects for computer time and for system analyst-programmer time over the next two years are indicated below.

Months	Project A		Project B	
	System hours	Analyst-pro-grammer hours	System hours	Analyst-pro-grammer hours
1–6	20	240	30	352
7–12	75	380	30	400
13–18	80	100	100	550
19–24	88	110	150	120

Months	Project C		Project D	
	System hours	Analyst-pro-grammer hours	System hours	Analyst-pro-grammer hours
1–6	25	264	—	—
7–12	30	280	—	120
13–18	30	300	20	380
19–24	100	500	30	410

Operational requirements for the company's existing applications total 400 computer system hours and 200 analyst-programmer hours. These requirements increase by 10 percent at the end of each six-month period.

The firm presently employs six analyst-programmers who work eight hours per day for an average of 22 days each month. There are a total of 720 hours of available computer time per month (30 days × 24 hours per day). However, for each hour of computer time used, an average of only 80 percent is used for productive work, with the other 20 percent used for equipment maintenance, re-runs, etc.

Required

a) At what point in time will a significant increase in the capacity of Perry's computer system become necessary? Why?

b) Assume that a new computer system is to be acquired and that the conversion to this new system will be complete as of the first day of month 13. Further assume that one analyst-programmer will devote full-time effort to implementing this conversion during the six months preceding the first day of month 13. How many full-time analyst-programmers must Perry employ during each of the four six-month periods?

c) Assume that (1) the monthly salary of an analyst-programmer is $1000; (2) the monthly hardware rental and all other fixed costs for the present system total $8000, and will total $12,000 after the new system is implemented; (3) upon implementation the new system will exactly triple throughput (i.e., work formerly taking three hours on the computer will now take one hour); and (4) all variable costs relating to the operation of both the old and new systems, during both productive and nonproductive usage, total $10 per hour. Prepare a financial projection of the monthly total of these costs for each month over the two-year period.

38. The Maxwell Company uses unit pricing to compute charges to user departments for computer services. For each job run on the computer, the number of machine units (MU) is measured according to the following formula.

$$MU = .14 \times (.07C + .0002I) \times [13 + .3(.9D + .2D^2) + .1(T + .02T^2) + .4(.01R + .0002R^2)]$$

where C = CPU seconds, I = Input/output count, D = Disk drives used, T = Tape drives used, and R = Number of units of primary memory.

The charge for each machine unit is $10.

Required

a) What would be the total cost charged for a job that uses (1) 300 CPU seconds, (2) an input/output count of 10,000, (3) two disk drives, (4) four tape drives, and (5) 64 units of primary memory?

b) Suppose that you are interested in the incremental cost of various resources used on the job above. For example, the incremental cost of one disk drive would be the difference between the cost computed for part (a) and the cost that would have been computed if one less disk drive were used. Compute the incremental cost of

1)   one CPU second
2)   1000 input/output count units
3)   one disk drive
4)   one tape drive
5)   four units of primary memory

39. The Hunter Company uses a system of full costing in charging its computer using departments for computing services. Operating and cost data for a recent month are as follows.

Resource	Total cost	Units used
Central processor	$180,000	500 hours
Main memory	56,000	280,000 units
Disk/tape I/O	115,000	230,000 units
Card/print I/O	60,000	60,000 units
Total cost	$411,000	

Data on resources used by two jobs recently run on the computer system are as follows.

Resource	Accounting job	Engineering job
Central processor	1 hour	2 hours
Main memory	500 units	2000 units
Disk/tape I/O	500 units	100 units
Card/print I/O	500 units	40 units

Required

a) If the single factor base of CPU hours is used to price computer services, what will be the rate charged? How much would be charged to each of the two jobs described?

b) If a four-factor base is used, what will be the rates for each of the four factors? Under this scheme, how much would be charged to each of the two jobs?

c) Which of these two alternative pricing systems do you think is better? Discuss.

40. Stevens Chemical Company is a manufacturer of a wide variety of chemicals, including cleaning fluids, weed and bug sprays, lubricants, and several industrial chemicals used as raw materials by other firms. The company has total sales of about $100 million, and is made up of six operating divisions located in five southern states whose sales range from $6 million to $25 million. The company has always operated under a philosophy of decentralization, wherein each divisional management has authority to set prices, determine its product mix, and establish other policies. Company headquarters has exercised a loose form of budgetary control, generally approving budget requests submitted by divisions, and reviewing divisional performance to the extent necessary to reward division managements for successful performance and to make recommendations for improvement where appropriate. The company has operated profitably under this arrangement for several years, except that in the last two years one division has sustained a loss due to a combination of downward pressures on prices and large increases in selling and administrative costs.

The company's management has recently made a decision to acquire an advanced computer system that will be installed at company headquarters and will have data communications links to each of the divisions. Mr. Thomas Shockley, a former management consultant with the company's auditors and a specialist in data processing, has been hired as Assistant Controller to be in charge of the computer facility. Mr. Karl Pearson, formerly a controller at the largest of the company's operating divisions, has been the company's controller for the last ten years. The new computer is due to be installed within three months, and Mr. Shockley is in the process of supervising staff training, system design, and programming activities.

As a result of his work in preparing for installation of the new computer system, Mr. Shockley has proposed that the company adopt a philosophy of greater centralization of decision-making responsibility. He argues that the major reason for decentralization of such responsibility is that timely and relevant information is not available to top management to enable them to make major decisions for the divisions. He believes that the new computer system will make available to corporate headquarters enough relevant information on a timely basis to enable top management to effectively make major decisions for the divisions. Shockley has been authorized to develop a computer-based accounting system which will consolidate accounting functions for all of the divisions on the new computer; these functions include general ledger, billing, payroll, production and cost accounting, accounts receivable, accounts payable, inventory, budgeting, and performance reporting. Performance reports on each division, comparing actual with budgeted results, should be available to corporate headquarters each month, within a week from the end of the month, according to Mr. Shockley. A list of the functions which he feels should be centralized instead of performed at the divisional level includes (1) establishing pricing policies, (2) deciding on the product lines, (3) purchasing of raw materials, (4) scheduling of production, (5) extension of credit, (6) deciding on capital expenditures, and (7) deciding on salaries and promotions for divisional management personnel.

In discussions of Mr. Shockley's proposal by the company's top executives, Mr. Pearson has argued in opposition to the idea of centralization. He points to the company's long history of profitability under a philosophy of decentralization. He has expressed doubt that the new computer system will be able to provide company headquarters with information that is as reliable, timely, and complete as that available to the division managers. He feels that the freedom provided to division managers has been a significant factor in motivating them to perform successfully.

In response to Mr. Pearson's arguments, Mr. Shockley points out that the company's decision to acquire a computer system with real-time capability places it at a major crossroads. Top management must decide whether the computer will merely become an expensive form of mechanized bookkeeping, or an effective tool contributing to the profitable management of the company. He argues that centralized decision making is necessary because of the increasing lack of coordination of activities of operating divisions, as evidenced by some cases in which two different divisions have marketed competing products. He further argues that the new computer system will make it more efficient to centralize the administration functions than to continue the policy of decentralization. He cites the case of the division that has incurred operating losses as evidence of the need for more centralized financial control.

Required

a) Examine the list of functions which Mr. Shockley suggests should be centralized. Which of these functions do you feel could be more effectively performed if centralized? Which could be more effectively performed under decentralization? Explain.

b) Mr. Pearson has expressed doubt that the new computer system will be able to provide company headquarters with information that is as reliable, timely, and complete as that available to the divisional managers. Do you agree? Explain.

c) Mr. Shockley defines the issue at one point as "whether the computer will merely become an expensive form of mechanized bookkeeping, or an effective tool contributing to the profitable management of the company." Do you feel that this is the relevant issue in the case? Explain.

d) Are there any other alternatives to the strict centralization of decision making advocated by Mr. Shockley and the status quo defended by Mr. Pearson? Explain.

e) What action do you feel should be taken by the management of Stevens Chemical Company with respect to the proposal of Mr. Shockley? Which arguments do you feel are the most compelling and why?

References   Appleton, D. S. "DDP Management Strategies: Keys to Success or Failure." *Data Base* (Summer 1978): 3–8.

Borovits, I., and S. Neumann. "Internal Pricing for Computer Services." *The Computer Journal* (August 1978): 199–204.

Canning, Richard G. "Charging for Computer Services." *EDP Analyzer* (July 1974): 1–13.

_____. "Distributed Data Systems." *EDP Analyzer* (June 1976): 1–13.

_____. "Do We Have the Right Resources?" *EDP Analyzer* (July 1975): 1–12.

Cerullo, Michael J. "MIS: What Can Go Wrong?" *Management Accounting* (April 1979): 43–48.

Coughlin, Donald T. "Introduction to Cost Accounting for Data Processing Services." *The Internal Auditor* (June 1979): 80–89.

Cushing, Barry E. "Pricing Internal Computer Services: The Basic Issues." *Management Accounting* (April 1976): 47–50.

Dearden, John. "MIS Is a Mirage." *Harvard Business Review* (January/February 1972): 90–99.

Gibson, Cyrus F., and Richard L. Nolan. "Managing the Four Stages of EDP Growth." *Harvard Business Review* (January/February 1974): 76–88.

Gibson, Harry L. "Determining User Involvement." *Journal of Systems Management* (August 1977): 20–22.

Hofer, Charles M. "Emerging EDP Pattern." *Harvard Business Review* (March/April 1970): 16–31, 169–171.

Hunt, J. G., and P. F. Newell. "Management in the 1980s Revisited." *Personnel Journal* (January 1971): 35–43.

Joy, James J. "Pricing DP Services." *Journal of Systems Management* (November 1977): 36–41.

Knight, Kenneth E. "Changes in Computer Performance." *Datamation* (September 1966): 40–54.

Leavitt, Harold J., and Thomas L. Whisler. "Management in the 1980s." *Harvard Business Review* (November/December 1958): 41–48.

Lee, Hak Chong. "The Organizational Impact of Computers." *Management Services* (May/June 1967): 39–43.

Lucas, Henry C., Jr. "Measuring Employee Reactions to Computer Operations." *Sloan Management Review* (Spring 1974): 59–67.

McFarlan, F. Warren. "Problems in Planning the Information System." *Harvard Business Review* (March/April 1971): 75–89.

Nolan, Richard L., "Managing the Crises in Data Processing." *Harvard Business Review* (March/April 1979): 115–126.

_____. "Controlling the Costs of Data Services." *Harvard Business Review* (July/August 1977): 114–124.

_____. *Management Accounting and Control of Data Processing*. New York: National Association of Accountants, 1977.

_____. "Business Needs a New Breed of EDP Manager." *Harvard Business Review* (March/April 1976): 123–133.

Rush, Robert L. "MIS Planning in Distributed Data Processing Systems." *Journal of Systems Management* (August 1979): 17–25.

Schoderbek, Peter P., and Steven E. Schoderbek. "Integrated Information Systems—Shadow or Substance?" *Management Advisor* (November/December 1971): 27–32.

Sollenberger, Harold M. *Management Control of Information Systems Development*. New York: National Association of Accountants, 1971.

Statland, Norman. "Organizing Your Company's EDP: Centralization vs. Decentralization." *Price Waterhouse Review* (Vol. 20, No. 2 1975): 12–17.

Unlocking the Computer's Profit Potential. New York: McKinsey, 1968.

Whisler, Thomas L. *Information Technology and Organizational Change*. Belmont, Calif.: Wadsworth, 1970.

Withington, Frederic G. "Coping with Computer Proliferation." *Harvard Business Review* (May/June 1980): 152–164.

Chapter 11

Systems Analysis and Design

Two factors create the necessity for frequent change in the information systems of business organizations. One is the growth of business organizations themselves in a dynamic society, which produces both new demands for information and greater volumes of data processing. A second factor is the rapid improvement of information technology, which offers a potential competitive advantage to those firms which are among the first to innovate. Within the past two decades, both of these factors have operated to produce an atmosphere of hectic change for the information systems function in many organizations.

The concept of the system life cycle, introduced in Chapter 1, is a useful way of viewing the complex process of systems change. This process is diagrammed in Fig. 11.1. The cycle may be perceived as beginning at the point of recognition that a new system is needed. This recognition may be sparked by new information requirements, new technology, or simply by the inadequacies of an existing system to meet user needs. This is followed by the parallel processes of surveying the status of the existing information system and analyzing user requirements. These steps culminate in a synthesis phase in which a plan is developed for overcoming the deficiencies of the existing system. Next comes a more detailed design of the new system, followed by its implementation and operation. During the operating stage of its life cycle, an information system normally undergoes maintenance and minor modification. Ulti-

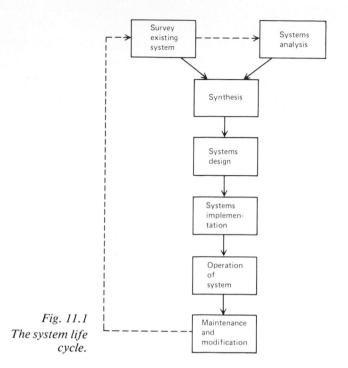

Fig. 11.1
The system life
cycle.

mately the system is found to be obsolete or inadequate, and the life cycle process begins anew.

The system life cycle concept is very general and may be applied to the entire information system or to any of its component parts, such as equipment, software, procedures, application subsystems, and so forth. In this chapter are examined the first four steps in the life cycle—survey, analysis, synthesis, and design. The implementation phase is covered in a subsequent chapter. Emphasis here is placed upon the objectives, policies, and techniques most commonly adopted at each step in the systems change process.

Systems analysts are people in an organization who are responsible for the development of information systems that employ available systems technology to satisfy user information requirements in an optimal manner. This generally involves the design of computer applications and the preparation of specifications for computer programming. The position requires both experience with systems technology and familiarity with the operations of the organization, for this person must serve to bridge the gap between the user and the technology. The systems analyst is the central figure in the system life cycle, playing a leading role in systems survey, analysis, synthesis, design, and implementation. Therefore, this chapter is written primarily from the perspective of the systems analyst.

Systems Analysis

As used in this section *systems analysis* refers to the process of examining user information requirements within an organization in order to establish objectives and specifications for the design of an information system. This section focuses upon broad policies, objectives, and frameworks which contribute to a successful strategy of systems change. Many of the specific techniques often associated with systems analysis are discussed later in this chapter in the sections on survey and design.

The systems approach

The systems approach to systems change emphasizes a number of specific approaches and policies relating to the planning of systems investigations. One is an emphasis on viewing problems and alternatives from the standpoint of the entire organization, rather than from the standpoint of any single department or interest group. Another is the requirement of a careful step-by-step approach to each task, which necessitates the thorough exploration of all implications and alternatives at each step in the project. A third useful approach is an emphasis on defining the objectives of the system as a framework for analysis of problems and opportunities.

Still another essential aspect of the systems approach to systems change is the use of the "team approach," in which systems specialists, operating managers, and other groups that are significantly affected by a systems change participate together in a coordinated effort throughout the various stages of the project. Use of the team approach to systems investigation reflects formal recognition of the fact that problems of major importance in an organization cannot be approached from a limited perspective. For example, accountants alone cannot design a reporting system that is to provide useful information to marketing executives. Similarly, computer specialists alone cannot be expected to design a computerized data processing system to replace an already operating manual system. Responsibility for such major projects should be assigned to a team whose members represent all of the diverse specializations relevant to the problem. Such an approach is not only likely to produce more effective results but also will facilitate the acceptance of the results by all parties concerned. Thus operating managers will feel more favorably disposed toward a system they helped to develop than toward one imposed upon them by what they consider "outside" forces.

In the context of computerized information systems, the most critical need for close cooperation arises between operating management and systems specialists. Operating managers often fail to recognize the potential benefits of computerization, whereas systems specialists often fail to understand the complexities of an operating system. If allowed to work in isolation from one another, these two groups may never feel compelled to respect each other's point of view. If obliged to work together on a project, the outcome of which will affect their own personal success, they are more likely to achieve a reconciliation of viewpoints sufficient to enable a working relationship to be established.

Perhaps the most important factor of all in successful planning for systems change is the involvement of top management. Such involvement begins with participation in the process of defining objectives for the information system. Top management must select the members of the project team, taking care to achieve a proper balance of operating managers and systems specialists. Top management must clearly define the responsibilities of the project team and demand from them a report containing a thorough analysis of the merits of all alternatives from the standpoint of the organization as a whole. Members of the project team must understand that they are responsible to top management for the eventual success or failure of the course of action they recommend.

Defining the objectives of the information system

The specific objectives of an information system are a function of the objectives of the organization that the system serves. Some authorities have suggested that every organization has a limited number of "key success factors" that must be identified to provide direction for systems planning.[1] By way of illustration, consider an automobile manufacturer, to whom the key success factors are product styling, manufacturing cost control, and an efficient dealer organization, according to Daniel. Identification of key success factors enables the systems planning and development group to focus upon the elements of the information system which are most vital to the success of the organization.

Certain general objectives, important in all information systems, may be identified. A partial list of these would include the following.

1. Usefulness—the system should produce information that is timely and relevant for decision making by management and operating personnel within the organization.
2. Economy—all component parts of the system, including reports, controls, machines, etc., should contribute a benefit value at least as great as their cost.
3. Reliability—system output should possess a high degree of accuracy, and the system itself should be capable of operating effectively even while a human component is absent or while a machine component is temporarily inoperative.
4. Customer service—the system should provide courteous and efficient customer service at points of interface with the organization's customers.
5. Capacity—the system should have sufficient capacity to handle periods of peak operation as well as periods of normal activity.
6. Simplicity—the system should be simple enough that its structure and operations can be easily understood and its procedures easily accomplished.
7. Flexibility—the system should be sufficiently flexible to accommodate changes of a reasonable magnitude in the conditions under which it operates or in the requirements imposed upon it by the organization.

[1] *See, for example, D. Ronald Daniel, "Management Information Crisis,"* Harvard Business Review *(September/October 1961): 111–121; William M. Zani, "Blueprint for MIS,"* Harvard Business Review *(November/December 1970): 95–100; and John F. Rockhart, "Chief Executives Define Their Own Data Needs,"* Harvard Business Review *(March/April 1979): 81–93.*

Thinking about systems problems in terms of objectives such as these helps to clarify the true nature of such problems. For example, the problem of maintaining adequate internal control must be examined as a trade-off between the objectives of economy and reliability. Similarly, the problem of cutting clerical costs must be analyzed in terms of a trade-off between the objective of economy on the one hand and capacity, flexibility, and customer service on the other. Once the objectives that are relevant to a particular problem are specified, a framework is provided for subsequent data collection and analysis. Of course it is impossible for any system to completely satisfy all of these objectives, but the objectives themselves do provide useful guidelines for systems planning.

Top-down vs. bottom-up approach

Two broad strategies of information systems analysis and design may be identified. The *bottom-up approach* seeks to develop an information system through an orderly process of transition, building upon transaction processing subsystems. As information needs are identified, these subsystems are modified and expanded to provide information for planning, control, and decision making as a by-product. The growth of the subsystems is planned and coordinated to achieve integration.

The *top-down approach* begins with a definition of both the organization's objectives and strategies, and proceeds to an examination of the decision-making process. Information requirements are determined according to what is needed for decision making. The information system is viewed as a total system, fully integrated, rather than as a collection of loosely coordinated subsystems. Top management participates more directly in the analysis and design process.

The top-down approach is obviously more consistent with the systems approach described earlier. Its potential flaw is that an organization may attempt to apply the approach on a scale which is too broad, in search of the elusive "total information system." This could lead to a dramatic failure. The best procedure is probably a combination of the top-down and bottom-up approaches that incorporates the systems approach but focuses upon one or a few subsystems at a time, taking into account the unique needs and capabilities of the particular organization.

Assessing the information needs of management

Because management decisions are based on information, it is axiomatic that the successful management of an organization is related to the effectiveness of its information system. In turn, the system's effectiveness depends upon the extent to which it satisfies the information needs of the managers and other users it serves. Therefore, the formal study of management's information requirements is an important part of systems analysis.

In practice, however, there seem to be many pressures that result in neglect of a systematic approach to assessing management's information needs. For example, managers may feel that they are too busy to participate seriously in such a project. Furthermore, there is a natural tendency in information processing to restrict input collection to only that data which is provided as a by-product of accounting transactions and clerical procedures. Typically, those responsible for data processing are more interested in and knowledgeable about procedures and equipment rather than management decision making. They may interpret volume of output as being synonymous with quality of output. In the face of such pressures, positive steps must be taken to assure that systems analysis and design give proper consideration to the information needs of management.

A proper analytical approach to assessing management's information needs should begin with an identification of the decisions for which management requires information. A useful framework for the study of management decisions is provided by Anthony,[2] who classifies management activities into the three broad categories of strategic planning, management control, and operational control. He defines *strategic planning* as the process of deciding on objectives of the organization, on changes in these objectives, on the resources used to attain these objectives, and on the policies that are to govern the acquisition, use, and disposition of these resources. *Management control* is the process by which managers assure that resources are obtained and used effectively and efficiently in the accomplishment of the organization's objectives. *Operational control* is the process of assuring that specific tasks are carried out effectively and efficiently. To clarify these definitions, Anthony presents a table, reproduced in Fig. 11.2, listing several types of decision-making activities which fall under each heading.[3]

Keen and Scott Morton[4] identify a second dimension by which management decisions may be characterized—that being the degree of structure they possess. At one extreme are *structured decisions,* which are repetitive and routine, and well enough understood to have been delegated to clerks or to have been automated on a computer. At the other extreme are *unstructured decisions,* which are nonrecurring and nonroutine to the extent that no framework or model exists for solving them, and the decision maker must rely primarily or exclusively on judgment and intuition. Between these extremes is a category of *semistructured decisions,* which are those which may be partially but not fully automated because they require subjective assessments and judgments in conjunction with formal data analysis and model building. Keen and Scott Morton propose that their three-way classification of decisions be merged with Anthony's framework to produce a two-dimensional taxonomy of decisions. They illustrate this taxonomy by means of a table, reproduced in Fig. 11.3, which contains an example of each of nine different categories of decisions.[5]

There is a rough correspondence between a manager's level in the organization and the nature of his or her decision responsibilities. That is, top management

[2] *Robert N. Anthony,* Planning and Control Systems, A Framework for Analysis *(Boston: Division of Research, Graduate School of Business Administration, Harvard University, 1965). Copyright © 1965 by the President and Fellows of Harvard College. The definitions in this paragraph are from pages 16–18.*

[3] *Ibid., p. 19.*

[4] *Peter G. W. Keen and Michael S. Scott Morton,* Decision Support Systems: An Organizational Perspective. *Reading, Massachusetts: Addison-Wesley Publishing Company, 1978, pp. 85–86.*

[5] *Ibid., p. 87.*

Strategic Planning	Management Control	Operational Control
Choosing company objectives	Formulating budgets	
Planning the organization	Planning staff levels	Controlling hiring
Setting personnel policies	Formulating personnel practices	Implementing policies
Setting financial policies	Working capital planning	Controlling credit extension
Setting marketing policies	Formulating advertising programs	Controlling placement of advertisements
Setting research policies	Deciding on research projects	
Choosing new product lines	Choosing product improvements	
Acquiring a new division	Deciding on plant rearrangement	Scheduling production
Deciding on non-routine capital expenditures	Deciding on routine capital expenditures	
	Formulating decision rules for operational control	Controlling inventory
	Measuring, appraising, and improving management performance	Measuring, appraising, and improving workers' efficiency

Fig. 11.2
Examples of activities in a business organization included in major framework headings.

Type of Decision	MANAGEMENT ACTIVITY			Support Needed
	Operational Control	Management Control	Strategic Planning	
Structured	1 Inventory reordering	4 Linear programming for manufacturing	7 Plant location	Clerical, EDP or management science models
Semistructured	2 Bond trading	5 Setting market budgets for consumer projects	8 Capital acquisition analysis	Decision support systems
Unstructured	3 Selecting a cover for *Time* magazine	6 Hiring managers	9 R&D portfolio management	Human intuition

Fig. 11.3
The Keen and Scott Morton decision taxonomy.

executives generally face unstructured or semistructured decision problems that involve strategic planning issues. Managers in the middle levels of the organizational hierarchy generally must deal with semistructured decision problems of a management control nature. Supervisors and employees at the lowest levels of the organization typically face semistructured or structured decision problems involving operational control. In any event, it is important to examine the types of decisions for which a manager is responsible as a first step in designing an information system to support that manager's activities, and the decision taxonomy presented above provides a useful framework for doing this.

To illustrate this point, consider a lower-level manager involved in operational control activities. The scope of authority of such a manager is typically limited to a particular department or a particular category of work. The decisions for which he or she is responsible are known, and these tend to be structured or semistructured decisions for which the required data and decision rules have been explicitly identified, perhaps in an operating manual. The information the manager needs must generally be detailed, accurate, short-term in perspective, provided frequently and regularly, and obtained from sources internal to the organization. If these needs for information are not being completely satisfied, the manager can probably identify what additional information should be available. As a result of these factors, the process of identifying the information requirements of lower-level managers does not usually present major problems.

At the other extreme is a top-level manager involved in strategic planning, whose scope of responsibilities encompasses the entire firm, and whose functions are defined according to such vague phrases as "setting objectives," "establishing policies," and "devising market strategies." To the extent that such a manager's decision problems can be explicitly identified, they tend to be unstructured or semistructured. The information required for this type of manager is primarily external information dealing with the product markets, the economy, the company's competitors, the availability of resources, and other environmental factors. Such information generally must also be highly summarized, encompass a broad time horizon, deal with a large number of variables, be future-oriented, and be available for demands that arise on an irregular and infrequent basis. Because of these factors, a top-level manager may find it difficult to specify information requirements. Thus a precise identification of the decision responsibilities and information requirements of top-level managers engaged in strategic planning is not a simple task.

Because most structured decision problems have already been successfully automated, and because most unstructured decision problems must be dealt with primarily by human intuition, Keen and Scott Morton suggest that the power of the computer can now be most effectively employed by developing systems to assist managers in semistructured decision situations. A system of this type is called a *decision support system,* which they define as "a conversational, interactive computer system with access through some form of terminal to the analytic power, models, and data base held in the machine."[6] Sprague and Watson state that "Evidence suggests many firms are moving to develop systems such as these that have as their main focus the support of managerial decision making."[7] Figure 11.4 illustrates the elements of a decision support system and their relationship to each other.[8]

[6] *Keen and Scott Morton,* Decision Support Systems, *p. 58.*

[7] *Ralph H. Sprague, Jr., and Hugh J. Watson, "Bit by Bit: Toward Decision Support Systems,"* California Management Review *(Fall 1979): 61.*

[8] *This figure is adopted with minor modification from Sprague and Watson's Fig. 1, p. 64.*

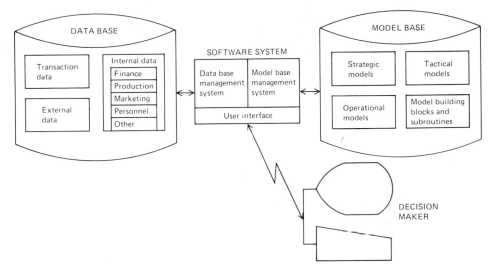

Fig. 11.4

Components of a decision support system. (Adapted from Fig. 1, p. 64, in Sprague and Watson's "Bit by Bit: Toward Decision Support Systems." © Copyright (1979) by the Regents of the University of California. Reprinted from California Management Review, *volume xxii, no. 1, by permission of the Regents.)*

The key element of any decision support system is the decision maker whom the system is designed to support. The system designer must fully understand the decision process from both a quantitative and a behavioral perspective, and must establish a combination of models, data bases, and software systems that can effectively supplement (rather than replace) the manager's judgment in making the decision. The key element of the software system is the user interface, which provides the user with a set of commands (verbs such as FIND, DISPLAY, GRAPH, etc.) that may be used to access and manipulate all of the other elements of the system. The user interface must be human-oriented rather than system-oriented in order to accommodate managers who lack the knowledge or inclination to deal with standard computer languages.

One early attempt to develop a computer-based system to support strategic planning decisions of a semistructured nature is represented by the management planning model developed by Gershefski for the Sun Oil Company.[9] This model utilized computer simulation to enable managers to explore the potential impacts of various decisions or policies in terms of profits, market share, and other objectives. This experiment was widely heralded as a breakthrough at first, but is now generally regarded to have been a failure. Keen and Scott Morton claim that a major reason for this failure was "the approach of defining the data base to be used and *then* finding the decisions it could support."[10] The point is that the systems analyst must first understand the decision process, and then build a system to support it.

Decision support systems should be viewed as a worthwhile extension of traditional data processing systems. Traditional systems capture transaction input, perform some structured tasks, and generate information useful to those who perform

[9] *See George W. Gershefski, "Building a Corporate Financial Model,"* Harvard Business Review *(July/August 1969): 61–72.*

[10] *Keen and Scott Morton,* Decision Support Systems, *p. 85.*

other structured tasks. Data base management systems enable a systematic integration of transaction data and other relevant internal and external data. Decision support systems appear to be the next logical extension of the use of computer technology in organizations. Viewed in this light, the concept of the decision support system provides a useful perspective the systems analyst can draw upon in preparing for and carrying out an assessment of management's information processing needs.

Systems Survey

Systems survey is the systematic gathering of facts relating to the existing state of an information system. It is generally done by a systems analyst. Its purpose is to obtain an accurate perspective on the existing system in order that areas of weakness causing problems can be identified, and that changes necessary to correct such weaknesses and resolve major problems can begin to be conceived. A systems survey may be carried out concurrently with systems analysis, or may be conducted separately as part of a more limited systems investigation.

The systems survey generally focuses on the visible components of an information system. These components include (1) resources, such as hardware, software, and personnel; (2) data, such as the system input, files, output, and documentation; and (3) activities, such as procedures, functions, and decisions. In this section several approaches and techniques for the systems survey are reviewed and discussed.

Human factors in systems survey

One of the primary sources of information to the systems analyst regarding the operation of an existing system is the people who are involved in operating it and utilizing its output. Thus the systems analyst needs to work closely with the people in a system during the survey phase of a systems investigation. Although this may occasionally involve merely recording observations, it will much more frequently require the systems analyst to conduct interviews with operating people and managers. To fulfill this aspect of the role effectively, the systems analyst needs to be sensitive to the feelings of people generally and aware of some of the more common human problems that arise in an organization during a systems investigation.

The presence in their midst of a systems specialist, who is a staff person or perhaps even an outsider, can be disconcerting to operating managers and personnel. The fact of the sudden interest in their work is an indication that a possible change may be under consideration. Requests for information and interviews are disruptive of the normal routine. In such a situation, the fear of uncertainty natural in people can generate mistrust and rumors, and perhaps be damaging to morale and efficiency.

Proper planning of systems investigations recognizes that people do not fear change by itself but do have a fear of the uncertainty that accompanies change. Such uncertainty should be minimized to the greatest possible extent. This can be accomplished by a policy of open communication with employees for the purpose of clarifying the intentions of the company regarding the investigation in progress. Generally the objective of such a policy should be to develop an attitude in employees that enables them to identify *with* the company and the system in its efforts toward improvement. The policy should prevent the formation of an employee attitude that perceives the company and the system as something having goals and plans separate from or even opposed to those of employees. Several more specific methods of accomplishing this objective are briefly discussed here.

As a first step in the survey phase of a systems investigation, the analyst should arrange to hold meetings with operating managers whose departments may be affected by the study. The scope of the study should be made clear as to whether a major change, such as automation, is being contemplated, or whether modifications of lesser magnitudes are the goal. The analyst should discuss the reasons for the study in positive terms, stressing the contribution that each department makes to the organization and the desire of company management to provide them with the best possible support. Stating objectives in negative terms, such as mentioning a need to correct existing problems, raise efficiency, or cut costs, should be avoided. The analyst should emphasize a personal need for the assistance of operating managers and their personnel in the project and encourage them to participate by offering their ideas and suggestions.

In cases in which the change being considered is very broad in scope, as in the case of a study to assess the feasibility of computerizing an existing manual or semi-automated system, the systems analyst must anticipate that many operating managers and their subordinates will fear the loss of their jobs, their seniority, or their status. Many personnel policies may be used to soften the impact of such major changes, and the analyst should make sure that management communicates its intentions in this regard to its employees. For example, existing employees may be given the first chance at new positions that become available and should be encouraged to test for such positions. Training programs may be offered by the company or by the firm from which equipment is being acquired. Communication with employees on this subject should stress the increased opportunities for advancement and more rewarding work that will result from the change.

In most medium-to-large-sized organizations, a policy of relocation of displaced employees in jobs of equal pay and status will be feasible. If hiring rates are temporarily reduced, the normal attrition of employees will enable such displaced personnel to be assimilated into the regular work force within a year or two. In the case of employees who are within a few years of retirement, it may be possible to arrange for an early retirement. In the case of persons whose employment is terminated, severance pay and assistance in obtaining new positions may be provided. Such policies may be expensive, but the decline in morale caused by the lack of such policies could be even more expensive. In any event, all such policies to be adopted should be communicated to employees, and the full backing and genuine interest of top management should be made clear.

The planning of a systems investigation should also take into account human factors and attitudes with respect to the top-management personnel who are closely involved with the study. One factor of primary importance is the willingness of top management to involve itself in monitoring and providing direction for the systems effort. Of equal importance is the concern of top management in maintaining an at-

mosphere of good human relations and high morale among employees. Also important is a willingness to adjust to changes in organizational relationships and to become familiar with a new pattern of systemization or a completely new technology.
To the extent that each of these factors is present in top management, the process of
systems change will be much easier to plan for and carry out.

**Review of system
documentation**

One important and useful source of facts about an information system is the documentation of the system. Ideally this should include complete procedures manuals,
organization charts, job descriptions, training materials, sample copies of documents and reports, file descriptions, flowcharts of systems, programs and document
flows, program listings, operating instructions for equipment, and so forth. One of
the systems analyst's first tasks in the systems survey should be to gather all of this
material that is available. If such material is not available or not complete, the
analyst will find it useful to develop it, at least in rough form.

It should be noted that such items of documentation as procedures manuals,
job descriptions, and flowcharts describe how the system is intended to work, but
this is not necessarily how it actually works. Throughout the systems survey, the
analyst should be alert for differences between the intended operation of a system
and its actual operation, for these often provide important insights to problems and
weaknesses.

The systems analyst should also carefully review the content and design of
documents and reports used in the information system. If a problem of lack of information exists at some point in the system, it could be that data from which to
generate that information are not being collected, or perhaps, once collected, are not
being processed properly or completely. If the problem is one of failure to collect the
necessary data, the need for redesign of input documents and procedures for recording input data is indicated. A review of documents and reports and the related data
collection and processing procedures may also provide useful insights on other types
of problems. For example, it may be that some data collection and processing steps
are being duplicated, in which case a consolidation of documents or reports, or an
integration of processing procedures might produce a cost savings. Similarly, a lack
of control might be corrected by instituting a change in the procedures for data
collection or processing, or perhaps by the prenumbering of a document.

**Document
flowcharting**

The preparation of document flowcharts is a useful technique of systems survey. A
document flowchart is a diagram illustrating the flow of documents relating to a
particular transaction through an organization. It provides the systems analyst with
a broad view of the formal communications network in an organization.

Information obtained from the review of systems documentation forms the primary basis for preparation of a document flowchart. After gathering this material,
the analyst must determine the departments, persons, and outside parties involved in
the operation or transaction being analyzed. All of the relevant documents and other
significant forms of communication that are part of the process must be established.

The place of origination of each document, its distribution, the purposes for which it is used, and its ultimate disposition should be determined.

As with other types of flowcharts, document flowcharts use a set of symbols with specialized meanings. However, there is very little standardization of document flowcharting symbols and their meanings. Figure 11.5 illustrates a set of symbols that have fairly widespread usage in document flowcharting. Note the equivalence of several of these symbols to those used in systems flowcharting (see Fig. 6.8). In fact some systems analysts incorporate some or all systems flowcharting symbols and conventions into their document flowcharts, in effect combining these two forms of flowcharting.[11] However, in this book document flowcharting is treated as a form of flowcharting separate and distinct from systems flowcharting. In addition to the sample document flowchart presented later in this section, several additional examples of document flowcharts may be found in Chapters 16 through 20.

The first step in drafting a document flowchart is to segment a blank page into columns by means of vertical lines. One column must be reserved for each entity involved in the process, including departments, persons, outside parties, and so forth. Each column is labeled at the top with the name of its respective entity. The origination of each document on a chart is done by the department or entity within which the document's flow begins. The name of each document is inscribed within the document symbol. The final disposition of a document, either by filing or by other means, is done in the department in which its flow terminates.

The document flowchart is generally assumed to represent a batch mode of processing. Thus each document shown on a chart represents a batch of like documents. Several copies of a given document might be prepared, in which case each copy is numbered on the flowchart to facilitate tracing the subsequent flow of each separate copy. To a limited extent, the use made of documents in various departments can be described in a few words on the flowchart. However, a more extensive description of the procedures and controls present in the system should be prepared separately as part of the documentation supporting the flowchart. A copy of each document shown on the flowchart should also be included in this supporting documentation.

As an illustration of how a document flowchart of an accounting procedure might be prepared, consider the following description of the processing of data relating to charges to patients by a hospital. When a patient enters the hospital, an admitting department prepares a record of admittance in four copies. It keeps one copy and sends one each to a medical records section, to the nurses' station on the floor on which the patient is located, and to the accounts receivable section. In accounts receivable, the admittance records are coded for keypunching by the data processing section and then filed by patient number. Requests for various services for patients originate at the nurses' station and are sent to various hospital departments, such as pharmacy, x-ray, or laboratories. All patient charges are originated in these departments, and a copy of each charge voucher is sent from the charging department to data processing, where they are keypunched. When the patient is re-

---

[11] *See problems 46 and 51 in this chapter for examples of this method.*

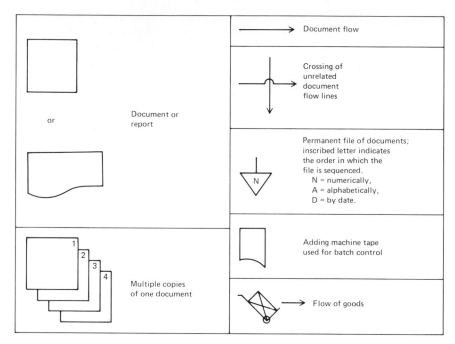

Fig. 11.5
Symbols for docu-
ment flowcharting.

leased, the nurses' station prepares two copies of a notice of release. One is sent to the medical records section where it is filed with the record of admittance. Another is sent to data processing where it is keypunched. Each day the data processing section processes admittance records, patient charges, and release notices against a patient accounts receivable file. One output of this process is a printout of charges to each released patient's account, which is provided to accounts receivable. The accounts receivable department then prepares three copies of a claim report, one of which it keeps, one of which is sent to the patient's insurance company, and one of which is sent to the medical records section to be filed with the record of admittance.

As indicated previously, the process of preparing a document flowchart is simplified if one begins by identifying all departments and other entities, and all documents involved in the process. From the description above, seven entities can be identified as participants in the document flow process. These are (1) the admitting department; (2) the medical records section; (3) the nurses' station; (4) the accounts receivable department; (5) the data processing section; (6) the service departments, which are lumped into one category because their roles in the document flow process are identical; and (7) the patient's insurance company. Seven documents can also be identified—(1) the record of admittance, (2) the coded admittance record, (3) the request for services for patients, (4) the patient charge voucher, (5) the notice of patient release, (6) the printout of charges to the released patient's account, and (7) the claim report. Once the process is analyzed in this manner, preparation of the document flowchart is relatively straightforward. A complete document flowchart of this process is shown in Fig. 11.6.

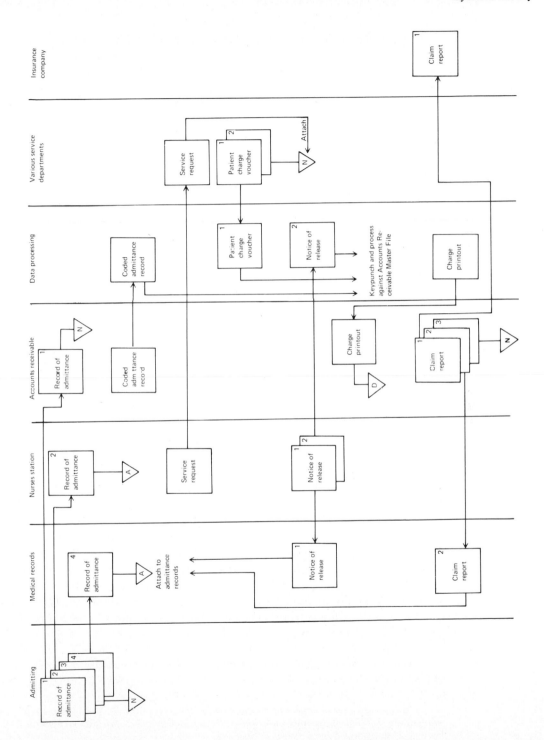

Fig. 11.6
Document flowchart of hospital accounting for patient records.

By integrating much of the material obtained in the review of system documentation, the document flowchart provides the analyst with a basic understanding of the process being charted. It may be used in several ways to pinpoint weaknesses in a system. It is particularly useful in analyzing the adequacy of control procedures in a system, such as internal checks and separation of functions. The document flowchart might also reveal inefficiencies present in a system, such as absence of adequate communication flows, an unnecessary complexity in document flows, or procedures responsible for causing wasteful delays. Document flowcharts may also be prepared as part of the systems design process, and should be included within the documentation of an information system.[12]

Volume analysis

Measures relating to the volume of processing are also important to the systems analyst at this stage. For each processing operation, an estimate of average volume should be obtained, as well as an assessment of the variability of volume, particularly with regard to the frequency and duration of periods of peak volume. Trends in the average and peak volume are also significant as indicators of future capacity requirements. Sometimes a relationship between processing volume and sales volume can be developed and used to generate predictions of future processing volume on the basis of available estimates of future sales volume. In addition to measures of volume, the analyst should obtain data on the percentage utilization of individual items of equipment and on the time required for, and time actually spent by, each employee in performing the tasks of which his job consists. All of these data are useful to the analyst in assessing the degree to which available processing capacity is being utilized by the current system, and the extent to which the capacity of the current system is sufficient to meet future processing requirements.

Work measurement

One well-developed set of techniques for obtaining and making use of data on the time required for employees to perform their jobs goes by the title of *work measurement*. This set of techniques is primarily applicable to jobs consisting of routine, repetitive clerical activities such as filing, typing, calculating, posting, sorting, and so forth, rather than to less structured functions such as management or creative work. To some extent, the applicability of work measurement techniques has declined in recent years, due both to a tendency toward relaxation of rigid work standards as part of an increased emphasis on employee morale and to the increasing degree of automation of routine clerical functions. However, the approach can potentially be very useful in some cases, and as such is worthy of at least a brief general description here.

A work measurement study begins by breaking down the routine functions in the department or process under investigation into the set of distinct tasks or activi-

---

[12] *For a more extensive treatment of the preparation of document flowcharts and their use in the evaluation of internal control, see Max Laudeman, "Document Flowcharts for Internal Control,"* Journal of Systems Management *(March 1980): 22–30.*

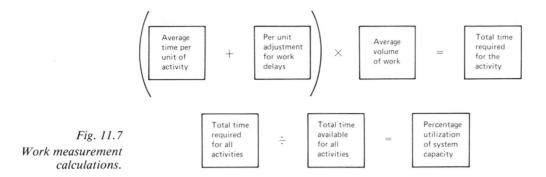

Fig. 11.7
Work measurement
calculations.

ties of which each consists. A time and motion study of each task is made to obtain a measure of the average time for performance of a single unit of each activity, such as the typing of a single purchase order or posting of transactions to a single account. Time and motion study involves observation of the performance of a task by a skilled employee and maintenance of a record of time spent. Observations should be taken at several different times to obtain a sample of observations representative of the various conditions under which the task is performed.

Once a measure of average time per unit of activity is obtained, it should be adjusted for work delays, such as interruptions, errors, machine breakdowns, and satisfaction of personal needs for rest or other relief. This adjustment is usually made in the form of a percentage of work time. For example, if ten percent of total work time is considered an adequate adjustment for work delays, then the average time per unit of activity is increased by ten percent to give an adjusted average time.

The next step is to multiply the adjusted average time per unit of activity by the average volume of units of activity in a processing cycle, which may be a day, week, or month depending on the operation. This gives the total time required for each separate activity during the processing cycle. Once this is done for all activities in the process or operation, the sum of the total times for all activities provides a measure of the total work time required in the operation during a processing cycle. At the same time, a measure of the total time spent on the job by all employees in the operation during a processing cycle can be determined. Dividing the total time required by the total available working time (see Fig. 11.7) provides a rough measure of the percentage utilization of available capacity in the operation.[13]

A work measurement study potentially can contribute a great deal toward accomplishing the objectives of a systems investigation. It may provide a basis for resolving the major problems that initiated the study by utilizing the available capacity of the current system rather than expanding that capacity, perhaps needlessly, through increased hiring or mechanization. It enables a judgment to be made of the

---

[13] *For a more detailed discussion of the application of work measurement methods, see Donald S. Anderson, "Supervisors as Work Measurement Analysts,"* Management Services *(January/February 1971): 20–26, and Robert I. Stevens and Walter J. Bieber, "Work Measurement Techniques,"* Journal of Systems Management *(February 1977): 15–27.*

extent to which the current system can accommodate expected increases in the volume of processing. As will be discussed in the next section, it provides a basis for a more equitable and efficient redistribution of work in an operation, which may be accompanied by the elimination of some jobs at a considerable cost saving. Finally, after a work measurement study has been completed, it is quite useful to adopt a permanent program of maintaining and updating work measurement data to provide standards for evaluating the performance of clerical employees.

Reliability analysis   A technique drawn from the engineering field has been proposed to measure in probabilistic terms the reliability of a data processing system in executing a particular task or set of tasks.[14] This technique is intended to assess the effectiveness of procedures which incorporate control checks, such as the use of a control total in posting a batch of transactions to an account. Such procedures might be broken down into the initial process itself, the control check, and the error correction step, as illustrated in Fig. 11.8.

The system reliability measure is computed from a series of reliability measures for the individual components of the process. The individual reliability measures required are the following probability estimates.

P = the probability that the original process (such as posting) is correctly executed.

D = the probability that the control check (such as comparison of control totals) will detect and signal an error given that one exists.

N = the probability that the control check will not signal an error if no error exists.

C = the probability that the error correction process will find and correct an error given that one exists and has been signaled.

F = the probability that, in the event that the control check signals an error when none exists, this will be discovered and the original process results allowed to stand.

Note that each of the parameters represents the probability of a correct system action, and that for each one there is a complementary probability of error. For example, $1 - P$ is the probability that the original process is incorrectly executed.

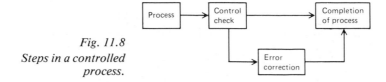

Fig. 11.8
Steps in a controlled
process.

[14] *Barry E. Cushing, "A Mathematical Approach to the Analysis and Design of Internal Control Systems,"* The Accounting Review *(January 1974): 24–41.*

Hypothetical Estimates	Calculations		
$P = 0.8$	(1) $P \times N$	$= (0.8)\,(0.9)$	$= 0.7200$
$D = 0.95$	(2) $P \times (1 - N) \times F$	$= (0.8)\,(0.1)\,(0.99)$	$= 0.0792$
$N = 0.9$	(3) $(1 - P) \times D \times C$	$= (0.2)\,(0.95)\,(0.98)$	$= \underline{0.1862}$
$C = 0.98$		R	$= 0.9854$
$F = 0.99$			

Fig. 11.9
Illustrative reliability calculations.

The *system reliability* is defined as the probability that the process will be completed with no errors. Completion of the process with no errors will occur when any two of the three steps preceding process completion (see Fig. 11.8) are correctly performed. Therefore, reliability (indicated by R) is equal to the sum of (1) $P \times N$, the probability that the process is executed correctly and the control step does not signal an error, (2) $P \times (1 - N) \times F$, the probability that the process is executed correctly, the control check erroneously signals an error, but the control error is discovered and the process results are not changed, and (3) $(1 - P) \times D \times C$, the probability that an error in the process is made, but that the control check signals an error and the proper correction is made. In terms of a formula, the system reliability is

$$R = [P \times N] + [P \times (1 - N) \times F] + [(1 - P) \times D \times C].$$

In Fig. 11.9 the calculation of system reliability is illustrated for a set of hypothetical component reliability estimates.

The reliability model can be extended to systems incorporating a series of control checks and to systems in which several types of errors having different probabilities may occur. It may also be extended to take into account the costs of control procedures and of undetected errors.

The reliability model provides a useful framework for collecting information about data processing activities and their associated controls and for evaluating the effectiveness of the controls. It also may be used in the systems design process to help decide whether new controls are needed. It may be applied to clerical procedures or to automated systems. Thus it is useful to the systems analyst in a variety of ways.

Interviews with personnel

An extremely useful source of facts and information during a systems survey is the interview. Interviews may be held with operating employees, supervisors, managers, or executives. The experience of such persons with the detailed workings of a system provides a valuable source of information for the analyst. Interviewees are likely to provide the analyst with some useful initial ideas about existing problems and possible solutions. Their familiarity with system operations enables them to provide valuable opinions regarding the feasibility of possible solutions suggested by the analyst.

A systems analyst should prepare for an interview by studying both the organization chart and the job description to learn the function of the interview subject, and making a list of points to be covered. During the interview, the analyst must take care to make the subject feel at ease, by being friendly and tactful. He or she should let the subject know the purpose of the interview and the time which will be required. Questions should deal with what the person's job consists of, how it relates to other parts of the system, how the person likes the job, and how the job itself might be improved. The analyst should take notes during the interview and should augment these notes with detailed impressions shortly after the completion of the interview.

Use of checklists

Another common technique of systems survey and analysis is the use of *checklists,* or standardized questionnaires dealing with some particular aspect of the information system. These generally consist of a comprehensive list of questions dealing with such things as the steps in an investigation process or the control procedures appropriate for a particular operation. Responses are generally limited to a yes or no, or perhaps to choice of a point on a scale. If the checklist is being used to evaluate some aspect of the system, a weighting factor may be assigned to each question reflecting its relative importance. Hence the checklist can be used to derive a "score" representing the effectiveness of the system. The checklist is useful to the analyst in studying and evaluating systems because it is standardized and comprehensive—considerable thought has been invested into its preparation and it is not likely that any important factors have been overlooked.[15]

Review of personnel

Another step in systems survey and analysis is a review of the capabilities of personnel in the performance of the functions for which they are responsible. A related step is the assessment of capabilities and aptitudes of personnel with respect to the adjustment necessary to implement and operate a more advanced system. As an aid in this step, the analyst should analyze the task content of each job in question, as well as the requirements for successful performance of the job. To provide a basis for evaluation, the analyst may observe employees at work, interview the employees and their supervisors, administer special tests, and review formal personnel evaluation records. Ultimately, the analyst must also apply his or her own judgment to arrive at evaluations which will be useful to the analysis and subsequent effort.

Problem analysis

Prior to completion of a systems survey it will be useful for the analyst to prepare a summary description of the problems that have been identified. Often the description of a systems problem will be suggestive both of the weaknesses that cause the problem and the corrective measures needed to resolve the problem. For example, a problem described as "lack of reliability of output" in a data processing system suggests a lack of certain internal check procedures, the initiation of which might well

---

[15] *An example of a checklist relating to forms design appears in Fig. 3.2. For an example of a checklist used to evaluate a computerized information system, see William G. Ramsgard, "Evaluate Your Computer Installation,"* Management Services *(January/February 1971): 37–41. For an example of an internal control questionnaire relating primarily to a manual system, see Howard F. Stettler,* Auditing Principles *(4th ed.), Englewood Cliffs, N.J.: Prentice-Hall, 1977, pp. 608–621.*

resolve the problem. Similarly, a problem of "lack of information by which to evaluate the performance of sales clerks" indicates that the identity of the salesperson is probably not being recorded on input documents at the point of sale. This suggests the solution of revising the design of sales documents and instituting a procedure whereby all sales clerks are required to enter their name or an identifying number on the sales document at the time of the sale. Some additional processing steps would also be required, including sorting all sales slips by sales clerk and accumulating a total number of sales and the total dollar amount of sales for each.

In other cases, however, the solution of a systems problem will be anything but obvious from its description. For example, a problem of "lack of current information on parts inventory balances" suggests the possible inadequacy of the entire materials inventory data processing system. Data collection procedures, documents, files, reports, processing methods, and use of equipment should all be reviewed to assess whether a correction of existing weaknesses will resolve the problem, or whether it will not be possible to remedy the situation without automating the system. Furthermore, the scope of the problem is such that the benefits of resolving it will have to be carefully weighed against the cost of doing so. It is probably safe to say that most systems problems possess at least this degree of difficulty, perhaps because the simple ones have already been solved.

Systems Synthesis

The synthesis phase of the system life cycle involves bringing together the results of the systems survey and of the analysis to devise recommendations for revision of the existing system and/or development of a new system. At the beginning of this stage the systems analyst should have an evaluation of the information needs of managers and other system users, an account of perceived problems in the existing system, and a complete description of the system and how it operates. Using these as the basis for the analysis, the analyst must determine what weaknesses are present in the existing system that cause each of the indicated problems. Then he or she must decide how each of the weaknesses can be corrected in such a way that the problems are resolved and the needs for information are satisfied. In some cases, the main question will be whether the existing system can simply be modified to correct its weaknesses, or whether it must be completely replaced by a newly developed system based upon a higher level of automation.

An important step in the synthesis phase is an evaluation of the relative merits of the alternative solutions under consideration. Each alternative should be assessed with respect to the initially stated objectives of the organization and the information system. The pivotal objective is that of economy, to which all other objectives are related. The cost factor may limit the extent to which other objectives can be achieved. Therefore, all cost factors relating to each alternative should be carefully measured, and the benefits of each alternative should be delineated. With respect to measurement of the benefits of the various alternatives, the participation of the users of the information systems is a necessary factor. The information developed from this analysis of alternatives forms the primary basis for management's final choice.

If one or more of the alternatives under consideration represents a major systems modification, or involves a large scale acquisition of computer hardware, software, or services, then a major feasibility study incorporating many factors must be undertaken. This topic is explored in the next chapter.

The climax of the period of systems synthesis is the presentation of recommendations to management. Depending on the preferences of management and the nature of the problem, such recommendations may be in the form of a delineation of alternatives, or the expression of a preference for a specific solution. In any event, management will be interested primarily in a summary of the major recommendations, the advantages and disadvantages of each, the estimated costs and cost savings generated by the changes, the data used as a basis for the recommendations, and the methods used in collecting the data. In addition to skills in analysis, design, and implementation of information systems, the systems analyst must possess a considerable measure of persuasive power and communicative skill to be successful in this stage of a systems investigation.

Systems Design

Systems design is the process of preparing detailed specifications for the development of a new system. The starting point of systems design is the development plan prepared during systems synthesis, as modified and/or approved by management. The design phase must fill in all of the details of this development plan in order that the new system may be successfully implemented.

Systems design begins with specification of the required system outputs, which includes the content, format, volume, and frequency of reports and documents. Next is the determination of the content and format of system inputs and files. Following these steps comes the all-important design of processing steps, procedures, and controls. At the completion of the systems design process, a plan for implementation of the new system should be prepared.

This section reviews some of the techniques used during the systems design process. Some other tools and techniques of systems design have already been covered in previous chapters. These include forms design (Chapter 3), coding (Chapter 3), systems flowcharting (Chapter 6), program flowcharting (Chapter 7), decision tables (Chapter 7), and document flowcharting (earlier in this chapter). To obtain a more complete feel for the nature of systems design, the reader may wish to review these other topics in conjunction with study of this section.

Output design

The basic objectives and general content of output reports and documents will have been determined as part of the systems analysis and synthesis. During the design phase the detailed content and format of system outputs must be established. At this point it is necessary to consult with the users of the system output to determine what specific pieces of data or information they require, how they use the data or information, and what format they would find best suited to their needs.

One useful tool for designing the format of computer output reports or forms is the *printer layout chart*. This chart, illustrated in Fig. 11.10, is a grid of empty

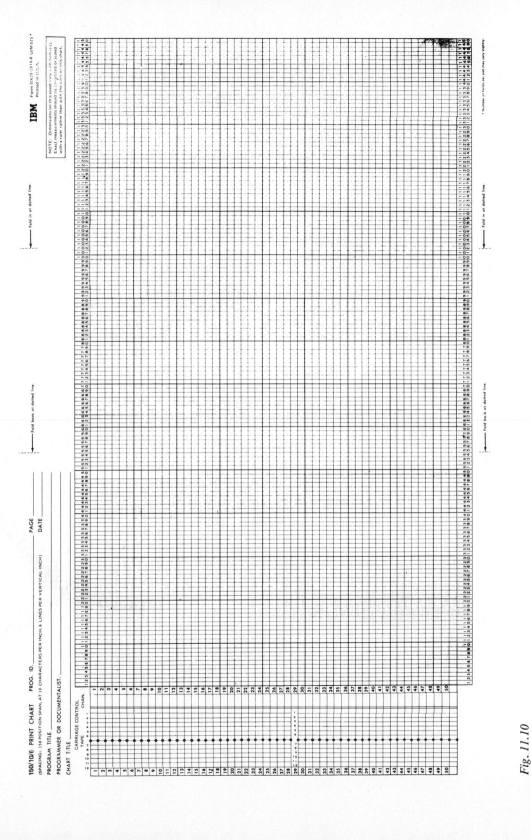

Fig. 11.10

Printer layout chart. (Courtesy of IBM Corporation.)

spaces containing 50 rows and 150 columns, which represent the printing spaces available on one page of computer printout. The systems designer can use several of these to experiment with various possible formats for computer-printed documents or reports. Sample outputs written on these charts can be shown to the eventual users of the output to obtain their preferences. When a format is settled upon, its print layout becomes a useful input to the program coding process.

In addition to the conventional tabular format of management reports, modern computer technology enables the preparation of reports in graphic form. Large volumes of data may often be condensed into a few pages of graphic reports. Such reports generally may be interpreted more quickly and more meaningfully than tabular reports, thereby enabling managers to make faster and better decisions. Some of the most commonly used forms of computer graphic output are bar charts, trendlines, and pie charts. These and several other forms of computer graphics are illustrated in Fig. 11.11.

In addition to the content and format of reports and other system outputs, another important aspect of report design is their timing. In this respect, four cate-

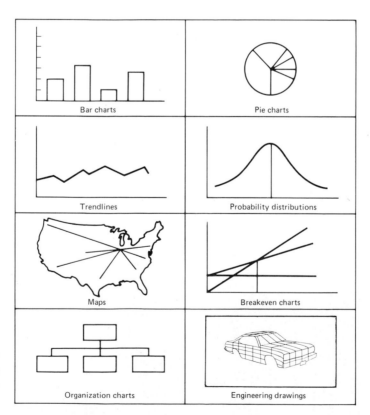

Fig. 11.11
Examples of
computer
graphic output.

gories of reports may be identified—(1) scheduled reports, (2) unscheduled special-purpose analyses, (3) triggered exception reports, and (4) demand reports. Scheduled reports have a prespecified content and format, and are prepared on a regular basis; examples include monthly departmental performance reports, weekly sales analyses, and annual corporate financial statements. Special-purpose analyses have no prespecified content or format, and are not prepared according to any regular schedule; rather, they are generally prepared in response to a management request to investigate a specific problem or opportunity.

Triggered exception reports have a prespecified content and format, but are prepared only in response to the presence of abnormal conditions which "trigger" the reporting process. Excessive absenteeism, cost overruns, inventory shortages, failures to meet sales quotas, and other situations that require immediate corrective action are the kinds of conditions that might trigger such reports. Demand reports also have a prespecified content and format, but are prepared only in response to a request from a manager or other employee. Both triggered exception reports and demand reports exemplify how the power of modern computer systems can be effectively used to facilitate the management process.

Input and file design

As with the system output, the general content of system inputs and files is established during systems analysis and synthesis. Thus the focus of systems design is primarily on the formats to be used. A useful tool of formatting of computer input and file records is the *record layout sheet,* which is a blank form upon which may be entered the content, position, format, and other characteristics of the record. An illustration of a partially completed record layout appears in Fig. 11.12. Once these are completed for all input and file records in a system, they are used in the process of coding the computer program.

Field Name	Account Number	Customer Name	Customer Address
Characteristics	Numeric; Key	Alphanumeric	Alphanumeric
Position	01-08	09-32	33-104

Region Code	Type Code	Salesman Name	Credit Rating
Numeric	Numeric	Alphanumeric	Alphanumeric
105-107	108-110	111-122	123-125

Credit Limit	Date of Last Sale	Account Balance
Money	Date	Money
126-134	135-140	141-149

Fig. 11.12
Record layout.

Work distribution analysis

Another systems design technique is an extension of work measurement referred to as *work distribution analysis*. This technique uses the total time requirements for each activity in a processing cycle, which are determined by work measurement, as a basis for equitable allocation of tasks to employees in an operation. The primary tool is the work distribution table, an example of which is shown in Fig. 11.13. All activities in an operation and the total time each requires are listed line by line on the left side of the table, and each employee's name is listed at the top of a separate column on the right side. Each activity is then allocated to one or more employees in such a way that the total working time for all employees equals the total number of hours for which each is employed per day. Slack time should be incorporated into the individual activity time estimates.

Certain aspects of the example in Fig. 11.13 have been oversimplified for illustrative purposes. First, each of the individual activities listed in the table normally would be broken down in much greater detail for purposes of work measurement. However, for purposes of work distribution analysis alone, this degree of consolidation is acceptable.

Second, the basis for assigning an activity to a particular employee is not indicated. The primary basis for such allocation should be the relative efficiency of each employee in the performance of each task; in this way the total utilization of employee time is minimized. Other considerations include the need to separate the performance of specific tasks for control purposes, or to provide variety in the job assignments to all employees.

WORK DISTRIBUTION TABLE					
Accounts Payable Department Activity	Hours per day	Employee			
		Smith	Jones	King	Evans
File purchase order copies	2				2
Match receiving reports with vendor invoices	1				1
Verify accuracy of vendor invoices	6	4	2		
Post receipts to filed purchase orders	5	4			1
Prepare vouchers and checks for payment	8		4	4	
File vouchers payable by due date	1		1		
Batch total day's vouchers to be paid	1		1		
File paid vouchers by vendor	4			4	
Total hours per day	28	8	8	8	4

Fig. 11.13
Sample work distribution table.

Work scheduling

Another factor essential to consider in the development of alternative job assignment plans is the set of scheduling constraints particular to the operation. These include the necessity for completing some tasks before others can begin, or to avoid the simultaneous scheduling of conflicting tasks. Work scheduling involves the assignment of a time dimension to task performance and machine utilization. While important in manual systems, scheduling is an even more critical factor in automated information systems.

Comprehensive approaches to systems design

In recent years, several comprehensive approaches to systems design have been developed and documented, and made available to organizations engaged in the development of information systems. The common feature of these approaches is the use of a set of standardized forms that are filled out by the systems designer to facilitate some aspect of the systems development process.

One such category of design aids focuses on the development of a comprehensive and standardized set of documentation of an existing system or of a system under development. Examples include ADS (Accurately Defined System) developed by NCR, SOP (Study Organization Plan) offered by IBM, and TAG (Time Automated Grid) also provided by IBM. These require the system designer to prepare precise output specifications, input requirements, descriptions of resources, activities, computations, logic requirements, and so forth. The resulting forms provide a basis for subsequent design and programming efforts.

A second category of design aids focuses more on the process of systems design. This category includes Honeywell's BISAD (Business Information Systems Analysis and Design) and Philips' ARDI (Analysis, Requirements Determination, Design and Development, Implementation and Evaluation). These provide a comprehensive description of the process of systems design and analysis, broken down into detailed steps with a variety of techniques provided to assist in performing each step. The systems designer would use an approach of this "checklist" type as a sort of guide through the development process in a systematic manner.

A third category of systems design aids includes those that attempt to use the computer to automate the systems design process. These methods are still being developed and are not yet in widespread use. They include ISDOS (Information System Design and Optimization System), developed at the University of Michigan, and the Hoskyns System, developed by a data processing consulting organization. To use these techniques the designer is required to complete a comprehensive description of system requirements and characteristics. These are coded on special input forms, which are processed through a system that generates a computer program, written in a language such as COBOL. Ideally, this program then becomes a part of the information system. In theory, this approach represents the highest possible level of systems development—automated systems design. In practice, there is still some question as to whether this technique will ever be feasible for large-scale systems design projects.

Review Questions

1. Define the following terms.

systems analyst	decision support systems
systems analysis	systems survey
bottom-up approach	document flowchart
top-down approach	work measurement
strategic planning	system reliability
management control	checklist
operational control	systems design
structured decisions	printer layout chart
unstructured decisions	record layout sheet
semistructured decisions	work distribution analysis

2. What are the primary factors that have made the present era a period of frequent change in the information systems of business organizations?

3. Identify and briefly describe the stages in the system life cycle.

4. Explain the role of the systems analyst, and describe the characteristics and abilities a person should possess to fill this role successfully.

5. List several aspects of what might be called the "systems approach" to systems investigations.

6. Describe the philsophy of the team approach to the analysis of information systems.

7. List several ways in which an organization's top management should be involved in the planning and administration of major systems change.

8. What is meant by "key success factors" within a business organization, and what is their importance to systems planning?

9. List several general objectives important in the analysis and design of information systems.

10. Explain the relative merits of the "top-down" and "bottom-up" approaches to systems analysis and design.

11. List several types of decision-making activities within the three major categories of Anthony's management framework.

12. Describe the decision taxonomy proposed by Keen and Scott Morton, and identify an example of one decision in each of their nine decision categories.

13. What significant differences exist among top-, middle-, and lower-level managers with respect to decision responsibilities and information requirements?

14. How are decision support systems related to traditional data processing systems?

15. A systems survey generally focuses on the visible components of an information system. What are these?

16. Detail the steps that a systems analyst should take to minimize the possibility of human problems in an information system during the period of systems survey.

17. What attitudes of top management should be taken into consideration by a systems analyst in planning a systems investigation?

18. List several items of system documentation that are an important source of information to the systems analyst during a systems survey. Why should caution be exercised in interpreting this material?

19. What weaknesses in an information system may be revealed by a review of the content and design of documents and reports?

20. Identify the symbols used in document flowcharting and indicate the meanings of each.

21. Describe the process of preparing a document flowchart.

22. What weaknesses in an information system may be revealed by an analysis of document flowcharts?

23. Describe the information the systems analyst should collect on volume of processing during a systems survey.

24. What is work measurement? For what types of jobs is this technique most appropriate? Give some examples.

25. Describe the steps necessary in a work measurement study to obtain (a) a measure of the total time required for each activity in a system during a processing cycle, and (b) a measure of the percentage utilization of system capacity.

26. List several ways in which a work measurement study can be useful to a systems investigation.

27. Explain the computation of the system reliability measure, and describe how it may be useful in systems investigations.

28. Describe briefly how the systems analyst should prepare for and conduct interviews with personnel during a systems investigation.

29. Explain how the use of checklists may be helpful to the systems analyst during a systems investigation.

30. Explain the purpose of the synthesis phase of the system life cycle. What activities are typically involved in this phase?

31. What steps are included in the systems design phase of the systems life cycle? Identify a number of techniques useful in systems design.

32. Explain how printer layout charts and record layout sheets are used in systems design.

33. Identify and describe four different categories of reports that may be prepared as output of an information system.

34. What is work distribution analysis? Draw an example of a work distribution table.

35. In work distribution analysis, what criteria may be used for assigning activities to employees?

36. Briefly describe some of the kinds of comprehensive, standardized approaches to systems design that have been developed in recent years. Identify the names of several of these.

Discussion Questions

37. The discussion of systems investigations in this chapter has been oriented toward a business organization. What significant differences in objectives and approaches would you expect in a system investigation of (a) a public school system, (b) a university, (c) a hospital, (d) an agency of government?

38. Your friend and fellow systems analyst, Joe Doakes, has made the following statement to you:

"The systems analyst does not have to be a psychologist, or be concerned with people problems in his work. His function is to determine the proper facilities, computer or otherwise, for performing the data processing functions of an organization. When this is finished he will then establish job specifications for employees in the system. He can perform these functions with a minimum of contact with people in the organization."

Do you agree with this statement? If not, what line of argument would you use in response to your friend?

39. It was suggested in this chapter that during a systems investigation an organization should make special efforts to ease fears among its employees about potential loss of jobs or seniority. However, it is also felt that one of the primary advantages of the mechanization of a system is the reduction in clerical costs. Are these two concepts inconsistent? What policies could be adopted in an organization during a systems investigation that would be consistent with both concepts?

40. Describe some examples of decisions in systems analysis that involve a trade-off between each of the following pairs of objectives.

a) economy and usefulness   b) economy and reliability
c) economy and customer service   d) simplicity and usefulness
e) simplicity and reliability   f) economy and capacity
g) economy and flexibility

41. In adopting a broad strategy for information systems analysis and design, would you favor a "top-down" approach, a "bottom-up" approach, or a compromise approach? Discuss.

Problems and Cases

42. From the description below of processing of casualty claims by an insurance company, prepare a document flowchart.

The process begins with the receipt by the claims department of a notice of loss from a claimant. The claims department sends the claimant four copies of a proof-of-loss form on which must be detailed the cause, amount, and other aspects of the loss. The claims department also initiates a record the claim at this time, which it transmits to the data processing section, where it is filed by claim number. The claimant must fill out the proof-of-loss forms in conjunction with an adjustor, who must concur in the estimated amount of loss. The claimant and adjustor both keep a copy of these forms, and send the other two copies to the claims department. The adjustor also submits a separate report at this point. On the basis of this information, the claims department authorizes a payment to the claimant, and forwards a copy of the proof-of-loss form to data processing. The data processing department prepares checks in payment of claims and mails them to the customer, removes paid claims from its file, and prepares a list of disbursements which it transmits to the accounting department.

43. Mr. Joe Grey, a senior consultant, and Mr. David Young, a junior consultant, were assigned by their firm to a systems analysis job for a client company. The objective of the study was to consider the feasibility of integrating and automating certain clerical functions. Mr. Grey had previously worked on jobs for this client, but Mr. Young had been hired only recently.

On the morning of their first day on the job, Mr. Grey directed Mr. Young to interview a departmental supervisor and learn as much as he could about the operations of the department. Mr. Young went to the supervisor's office, introduced himself, and made the following statement: "Your company has hired my firm to study the way your department works and to make recommendations as to how its efficiency could be improved and its cost lowered. I would like to interview you to determine what goes on in your department."

Mr. Young questioned the supervisor for about 30 minutes, but found him to be uncooperative. He then gave Mr. Grey an oral report on how the interview had gone and what he had learned about the department.

Required   Describe several flaws in the approach taken to obtain information about the operation of the department under study. How should this task have been performed?

44. As a systems consultant of wide repute, you have been invited to the executive offices of Consolidated Flypaper Corporation for an interview with the controller. The controller has indicated to you that he is concerned about the operation of the company's payroll processing system. Recent expansion of the company has placed a strain upon the system such that frequent overtime is necessary for regular processing to be completed.

The payroll and cost distribution sections of the company perform their functions almost entirely manually, with the only mechanical aids being typewriters and hand calculators. In addition to the problem of frequent overtime being necessary, the controller has indicated some additional problems with the system, including a lack of useful management reports that could be produced by the system and possible weaknesses in internal controls within the system. The controller has indicated that he is considering three possible alternatives, including hiring additional employees in the payroll and cost distribution sections, acquiring an electronic accounting machine for use in those sections, or installing a small business computer.

The controller has assured you that the president and other top executives of Consolidated Flypaper agree with the necessity of a systems study conducted by a qualified outsider. You have been introduced to the assistant controller, who performs internal auditing functions, and told that he is available to assist you full time if necessary.

You have agreed to accept this assignment, and have decided to send two of your assistants to complete the initial work while you finish another project.

You wish for your assistants to complete a preliminary evaluation of possible alternatives, which you will use in making a final decision and preparing recommendations.

Required

Prepare a schedule of activities to guide your assistants in performing their assignment. Be fairly explicit regarding the kind of information they might expect to find in a payroll processing system, how they should go about collecting it, and how to proceed in analyzing it. Please note that you are not being asked to give a solution to the problem, but only to describe, with reference to the particular situation, how a systems analyst would proceed with the initial phases of a systems investigation.

45. A reliability analysis of a data processing task and a related control procedure obtained the following parameter estimates.

$P = 0.84 \quad C = 0.98$
$D = 0.90 \quad F = 0.80$
$N = 0.95$

Required

Compute the system reliability measure for items processed through this system.

46. A partially completed charge sales systems flowchart appears in Fig. 11.14. The flowchart depicts the charge sales activities of the Bottom Manufacturing Corporation.

A customer's purchase order is received and a six-part sales order is prepared therefrom. The six copies are initially distributed as follows.

Copy No. 1—Billing copy, to billing department.
Copy No. 2—Shipping copy, to shipping department.
Copy No. 3—Credit copy, to credit department.
Copy No. 4—Stock request copy, to credit department.
Copy No. 5—Customer copy, to customer.
Copy No. 6—Sales order copy, file in sales order department.

When each copy of the sales order reaches the appropriate department or destination, it calls for specific internal control procedures and related documents. Some of the procedures and related documents are indicated on the flowchart. Other procedures and documents are labeled letters a to r.

Required

List the procedures or the internal documents that are labeled letters c to r in the flowchart of Bottom Manufacturing Corporation's charge sales system.

Organize your answer as follows. (Note that explanations of the letters a and b which appear in the flowchart are entered as examples.)[16]

[16] Question 2, Auditing Section, American Institute of Certified Public Accountants Examination, May 1979. Material from the Uniform CPA Examinations, copyright © 1979 by the American Institute of Certified Public Accountants, is reprinted with permission.

Flowchart symbol letter	Procedures or internal document
a	Prepare six-part sales order.
b	File by order number.

47. An inventory record contains the following data elements, each containing the number of characters indicated.

Part number	7
Description	20
Location code	4
Unit cost	8
Vendor code	5
Vendor name	20
Quantity on hand	5
Quantity on order	5
Reorder point	5
Order quantity	5

Required — Prepare a record layout sheet for this record.

48. Prepare a document flowchart of the process described in the paragraph below. Where necessary, add narrative explanation to your chart.

The billing department prepares five copies of each customer invoice, and a batch total of the sale amount on each invoice. Two copies of each invoice in the batch are sent, along with the adding machine tape containing the batch total, to the accounts receivable department. One of these copies is then immediately filed alphabetically by customer name. The other copy is used to post to accounts receivable ledger cards, which are pulled from a numerically sequenced file. As the posting is done, another adding machine tape is prepared in which the ledger balances before and after posting are entered as negative and positive amounts, respectively. At the completion of posting, the two batch total tapes are compared to check the accuracy of the process. Then the customer ledger cards are returned to their original file, and the second invoice copy is filed numerically by customer account number.

49. The Walla Walla Widget Company has completed a time and motion study of its Billing and Accounts Receivable Section. The results of that study in summary form follow.

Activity and Time Per Unit:

- Type an invoice in five copies from a copy of the sales order—196 seconds per invoice.
- Batch total the complete set of invoices for a day—three seconds per invoice.
- Separate copies of each invoice and send copies one and two to the mailroom—five seconds per invoice.

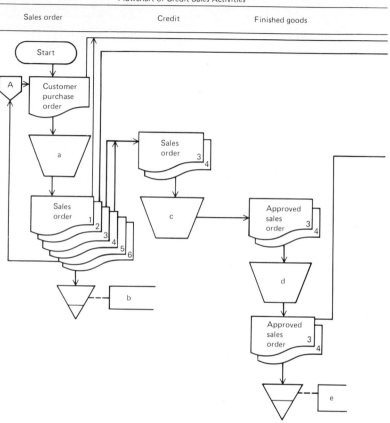

Figure 11.14

BOTTOM MANUFACTURING CORPORATION
Flowchart of Credit Sales Activities

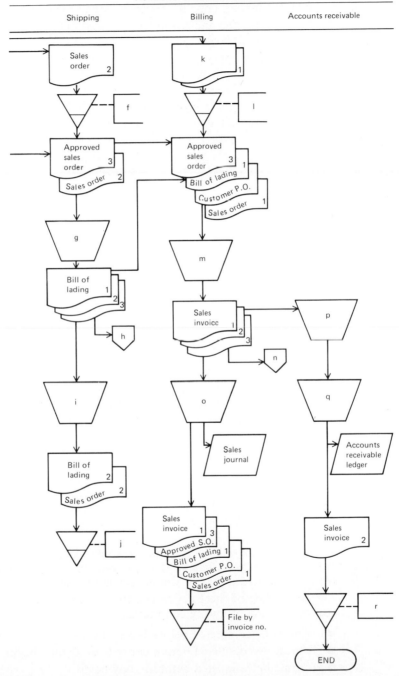

- File one invoice copy alphabetically—15 seconds per invoice.
- File one invoice copy numerically—one second per invoice.
- Post debits from another invoice copy to the accounts receivable ledger—30 seconds per invoice.
- Post cash receipts to the accounts receivable ledger from remittance advices—30 seconds per remittance advice.
- Total the balances of the accounts receivable ledger, and reconcile to sales, cash receipts, and yesterday's total—1000 seconds per day.
- Type customer statements from accounts receivable ledger—150 seconds per statement.

Information on daily volume is as follows

- Invoices—200 per day
- Remittances—100 per day
- Customer statements—there are 800 customer accounts. Statements are sent out in a monthly cycle such that about one-twentieth of all customer statements are sent out daily.

Other information

- A 20 percent allowance should be made for work delays and to provide sufficient slack time in the system to allow for periods of peak volume.

Required

a) What is the total work time required per day to perform all activities in this operation? Assuming three full-time workers (eight hours per day), what is the percentage utilization of capacity in this system?

b) Suppose the system employs two full-time workers (eight hours per day) and one part-time worker who works exactly the number of hours necessary to complete all work. Prepare a work distribution table showing how the various tasks might be allocated among these employees.

50. The Darwin Company has performed a work measurement study on one of its clerical departments. Activities performed within that department, and the number of hours per day consumed by each activity after adjustments for rest time and slack time, are as follows:

Activity	A	B	C	D	E	F	G
Hours/day	2	3	6	3	6	5	3

The department employs four persons: Adams, Baker, Clark, and Dill. Adams, Baker, and Clark work eight hours each day, from 8 A.M. to noon, and from 1 P.M. to 5 P.M. Dill works four hours each day, from 8 A.M. to noon. The scheduling of these activities and their assignment to the employees must conform to the following conditions.

- A must be completed before B may begin.
- B must be completed before either C or D may begin.
- E must be completed before F may begin.

- A, B, D, and G may be performed by only one person at a time. The other three activities may be separated among several employees working simultaneously.

- Because of internal control considerations, activity F must be performed by a person or persons different from those who perform activity G.

- G and D utilize the same machine, and thus cannot both be performed at the same time.

- No employee should spend over one half of his or her time on the job performing the same task.

Required

a) Prepare a work schedule containing four vertical columns, one for each employee, and eight horizontal rows, one for each hour between 8 A.M. and 5 P.M., excluding the noon hour. Assign each of the seven tasks to appropriate time periods within the work time of each employee. Be sure that your assignment is consistent with all of the conditions specified above.

b) Prepare in good form a work distribution table for this department's operations.

51. Charting, Inc., a new audit client of yours, processes its sales and cash receipts documents in the following manner.[17]

1. **Payment on account.**   The mail is opened each morning by a mail clerk in the sales department. The mail clerk prepares a remittance advice (showing customer and amount paid) if one is not received. The checks and remittance advices are then forwarded to the sales department supervisor who reviews each check and forwards the checks and remittance advices to the accounting department supervisor.

The accounting department supervisor, who also functions as credit manager in approving new credit and all credit limits, reviews all checks for payments on past due accounts and then forwards the checks and remittance advices to the accounts receivable clerk who arranges the advices in alphabetical order. The remittance advices are posted directly to the accounts receivable ledger cards. The checks are endorsed by stamp and totaled. The total is posted to the cash receipts journal. The remittance advices are filed chronologically. After receiving the cash from the previous day's cash sales, the accounts receivable clerk prepares the daily deposit slip in triplicate. The third copy of the deposit slip is filed by date and the second copy and the original accompany the bank deposit.

2. **Sales.**   Sales clerks prepare sales invoices in triplicate. The original and second copy are presented to the cashier. The third copy is retained by the sales clerk in the sales book. When the sale is for cash, the customer pays the sales clerk who presents the money to the cashier with the invoice copies.

A credit sale is approved by the cashier from an approved credit list after the sales clerk prepares the three-part invoice. After receiving the cash or ap-

[17] Adopted from Question 5, Auditing Section, American Institute of Certified Public Accountants Examination, November 1969: Copyright © 1969 by the American Institute of Certified Public Accounts, Inc., and reprinted with permission. The flowcharting symbols provided in the problem differ in some respects from those presented in this chapter. Nevertheless, the problem is illustrative of the usefulness of flowcharting to accounting systems work.

proving the invoice, the cashier validates the original copy of the sales invoice and gives it to the customer. At the end of each day the cashier recaps the sales and cash received and forwards the cash and the second copy of the sales invoices to the accounts receivable clerk.

The accounts receivable clerk balances the cash received with cash sales invoices and prepares a daily sales summary. The credit sales invoices are posted to the accounts receivable ledger and then all invoices are sent to the inventory control clerk in the sales department for posting to the inventory control cards. After posting, the inventory control clerk files all invoices numerically. The accounts receivable clerk posts the daily sales summary to the cash receipts journal and sales journal and files the sales summaries by date.

The cash from cash sales is combined with the cash received on account to comprise the daily bank deposit.

3. **Bank deposits.**   The bank validates the deposit slip and returns the second copy to the accounting department where it is filed by date by the accounts receivable clerk.

Monthly bank statements are reconciled promptly by the accounting department supervisor and filed by date.

Required   You recognize that there are weaknesses in the existing system and believe a chart of information and document flows would be beneficial in evaluating this client's internal control in preparing for your examination of the financial statements. Complete the flowchart, given in Fig. 11.15, for sales and cash receipts of Charting, Inc., by labeling the appropriate symbols and indicating information flows. The chart is complete as to symbols and document flows. The following symbols are used.

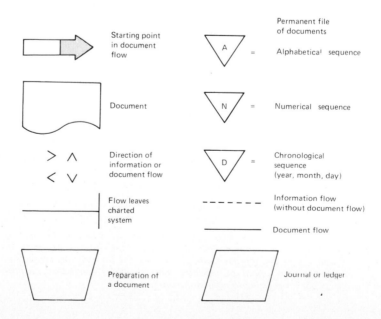

CHARTING, INC.
FLOWCHART FOR SALES AND CASH RECEIPTS

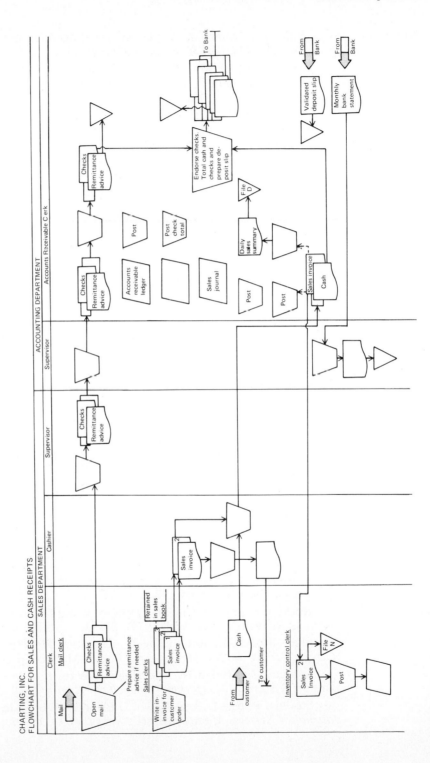

Figure 11.15

References   Anderson, Donald S. "Supervisors as Work Measurement Analysts." *Management Services* (January/February 1971): 20–26.

Anthony, Robert N. *Planning and Control Systems, A Framework for Analysis.* Boston: Division of Research, Graduate School of Business Administration, Harvard University, 1965.

Bonczek, Robert H.; Clyde W. Holsapple and Andrew B. Whinston. "Computer-Based Support of Organizational Decision Making." *Decision Sciences* (April 1979): 268–291.

Canning, Richard G. "Computer Support for Managers." *EDP Analyzer* (May 1979): 1–13.

————. "What Information Do Managers Need?" *EDP Analyzer* (June 1979): 1–12.

Cougar, J. Daniel, and Robert W. Knapp (eds.), *System Analysis Techniques.* New York: Wiley, 1974.

Cushing, Barry E. "A Mathematical Approach to the Analysis and Design of Internal Control Systems." *The Accounting Review* (January 1974): 24–41.

Daniel, D. Ronald. "Management Information Crisis." *Harvard Business Review* (September/October 1961): 111–121.

Davis, Gordon B. *Management Information Systems: Conceptual Foundations, Structure, and Development.* New York: McGraw-Hill, 1974.

Feeney, William, and Frea Sladek. "The Systems Analyst as a Change Agent." *Datamation* (November 1977): 85–88.

Gane, Chris, and Trish Sarson. *Structured Systems Analysis: Tools and Techniques.* Englewood Cliffs, N.J.: Prentice-Hall, 1979.

Gershefski, George W. "Building a Corporate Financial Model." *Harvard Business Review* (July/August 1969): 61–72.

Keen, Peter G. W., and Michael S. Scott Morton. *Decision Support Systems: An Organizational Perspective.* Reading, Mass.: Addison-Wesley, 1978.

Kotter, John P., and Leonard A. Schlesinger. "Choosing Strategies for Change." *Harvard Business Review* (March/April 1979): 106–114.

Laudeman, Max. "Document Flowcharts for Internal Control." *Journal of Systems Management* (March 1980): 22–30.

Paretta, Robert L. "Designing Management Information Systems: An Overview." *The Journal of Accountancy* (April 1975): 42–47.

Ramsgard, William C. "Evaluate Your Computer Installation." *Management Services* (January/February 1971): 37–41.

Rockhart, John F. "Chief Executives Define Their Own Data Needs." *Harvard Business Review* (March/April 1979): 81–93.

Shaw, Robert J., and Michael O. Regentz. "How to Prepare Users for a New System." *PMM & Co./Management Focus* (March/April 1980): 33–36.

Sprague, Jr., Ralph H., and Hugh J. Watson. "Bit by Bit: Toward Decision Support Systems." *California Management Review* (Fall 1979): 60–68.

Stevens, Robert I., and Walter J. Bieber. "Work Measurement Techniques." *Journal of Systems Management* (February 1977): 15–27.

Takeuchi, Hirotaka, and Allan H. Schmidt. "New Promise of Computer Graphics." *Harvard Business Review* (January/February, 1980): 122–131.

Teichroew, Daniel, and Hasan Sayani. "Automation of System Building." *Datamation* (August 1971): 25–30.

Welke, Richard J. "User-Oriented Approach to MIS." *CA Magazine* (August 1979): 62–68.

Wilkinson, Joseph W. "Effective Reporting Structures." *Journal of Systems Management* (November 1976): 38–42.

Zani, William M. "Blueprint for MIS." *Harvard Business Review* (November/December 1970): 95–100.

Chapter 12

Systems Evaluation and Selection

This chapter deals with the process of evaluating and selecting new systems and with the major factors which an organization should consider during this decision process. Note that the term "new systems" encompasses a variety of possible user situations. For example, it could refer to a potential computer user trying to decide whether to acquire its first computer system. Alternatively, it could refer to an established computer user who is considering replacement of a computer system. It could also apply to the acquisition of software packages, data communications services, time-sharing services, expanded equipment configurations, and so forth. Another possibility is that of an established computer user facing a choice among several new applications for the computer.

There are many similarities among the several user situations cited, but there are also important differences. This chapter approaches the topic of systems evaluation and selection from the perspective of the potential first-time computer user. Many of the concepts and approaches discussed are also applicable to the other user situations; however, when this is not true, the chapter elaborates on those considerations relevant to other specific circumstances.

In all cases, the first step in systems evaluation and selection should be a *feasibility study,* which is an investigation of whether the acquisition or development of a new system is practical. For first-time users, the next step is the *applications study,* which involves the preparation of a detailed description of the tasks which the new system is intended to perform. For any system being acquired from an outside party, the next step is to receive presentations from selected vendors, evaluate their relative merits, and make a final selection. This chapter covers each of these three major steps in the systems evaluation and selection process.

The Feasibility Study

Prior to a system feasibility study, an organization typically faces several alternatives. One obvious alternative is to continue using its existing information system, perhaps with some limited modifications. The potential first-time computer user may consider a service bureau, a time-sharing service, a used computer, a minicomputer, or a small business computer system in addition to a full-scale system purchased or rented from a computer manufacturer or leased from a third party. Established computer users seeking to upgrade their facilities obviously face a more limited array of choices. With respect to software, the established computer user must first decide what type of programs are needed, and then must decide whether to develop these internally or acquire them from software vendors—a classic "make-or-buy" decision.

One of the first steps in the feasibility study is to assign responsibility for carrying out the investigation. As with any systems study, one of the significant considerations here is that the group carrying out the study should include both persons with technical knowledge and persons with knowledge of and experience in the operation of the business. If the company has no previous experience with computers, persons with technical knowledge may not be available within the organization. In some such cases, it may be possible to utilize the services of a consulting firm, particularly one that has both technical competence and some familiarity with the company or the industry. In other cases, reliance may have to be placed upon representatives of a vendor. In companies in which a computer data processing function does exist, persons with technical competence can be obtained from within. To serve as a source of operating knowledge and experience, representatives should be obtained from top management, as well as from those operating areas that will be most involved in the utilization of a computer, such as accounting and production in a manufacturing company.

The inital phases of a feasibility study are very much similar to the initial phases of systems investigations generally. An emphasis should be placed upon defining objectives and delineating system requirements. The required system output includes management information, documents, files, and so forth. The existing system is subjected to a rigorous analysis to determine whether it can meet the current and future requirements in accordance with the objectives. If a long-range systems plan has been developed and put into effect, this process will be greatly facilitated.

Three dimensions of feasibility should be evaluated during a feasibility study. These are technical feasibility, economic feasibility, and operational feasibility.[1] *Technical feasibility* involves whether a proposed system is or is not attainable given the existing state of technology. *Economic feasibility* involves whether a proposed

---

[1] *George Glaser, "Plain Talk about Computers."* Business Horizons *(Fall 1967), pp. 33–38.*

system will or will not produce economic benefits that exceed its costs. *Operational feasibility* involves a determination of whether the system will be used and of how useful it will be within the operating environment of the organization.

The evaluation of technical feasibility can be left primarily to computer specialists and need not concern us here. Operational feasibility must be evaluated largely on a subjective basis, but its attainment obviously depends on the degree of involvement of top management and user groups in analysis and implementation, and on management's regard for the human factors in systems change. These topics are covered in Chapters 10 and 11.

The evaluation of economic feasibility, the primary concern of this section, involves a careful investigation of cost and benefit factors associated with each proposed alternative. Because an accountant is familiar with cost concepts, he or she can make a significant contribution to this evaluation. The basic framework for the evaluation is the capital budgeting model. This model requires that, for each alternative under consideration, dollar estimates be made of (1) the amount of the initial outlay, (2) the amount of operating costs and other cash outflows associated with the system during each period over the life of the system, and (3) the amount of cost savings and other benefits during each period over the life of the system. The choice among alternatives is then based upon the alternative that provides the highest net present value after discounting net cash flows at the organization's opportunity cost of capital.

If it is decided that the organization's existing information system is likely to be inadequate to meet its objectives and requirements, an investigation of the possible alternatives is initiated. An early attempt should be made by the study group to narrow the range of alternatives to a small set, in order to provide a focal point for subsequent efforts at data collection and review. The stated objectives and requirements provide guidelines for this process. Some alternatives may be eliminated at this point by the technical feasibility criterion. Operational feasibility, including such factors as the competence of personnel and their attitudes toward the various options, may rule out some other possibilities.

Once the feasibility study group has completed the initial culling of alternatives, the primary basis for subsequent analysis becomes the relative economic merits of the remaining alternatives. Whereas it is not too difficult to develop estimates of the initial outlay and operating costs required for a computer system, making reliable estimates of the amount of expected cost savings and other benefits can be quite a formidable task. Each of these categories of cost is now discussed in turn.

Costs of operating a computer system

The ongoing recurring costs of operating a computer system can be divided into three major categories—equipment costs, personnel costs, and overhead. Actually, the equipment costs may be either an operating cost if the system is rented or leased, or a part of the initial outlay if the system is purchased. Except in the case of very small systems, a majority of computer equipment is rented or leased, and therefore the presentation of this section assumes a rental arrangement. The relative merits of purchasing as opposed to renting or leasing a computer system are discussed in a later section of this chapter.

Equipment costs and capabilities vary over an extremely wide range. At the lower end of the scale are the microcomputer systems, which may be leased for as little as $100 per month. A typical business-oriented microcomputer system consists of a desktop unit containing a keyboard, CRT, and central processor with 16,000 bytes of primary memory, plus a separate cassette tape drive or flexible disk drive unit for mass storage, and a printer. Software typically includes BASIC language capability together with business and accounting application packages.

At the next level up the hardware scale are the business-oriented minicomputers, of which two catgories may be distinguished—(1) small accounting computers, also called electronic accounting machines, and (2) small business computers. A typical small accounting computer is a desk-sized unit consisting of a keyboard, serial printer, and central processing unit with 16,000 bytes of primary storage. Input/output and storage options include punched cards, paper tape, flexible disk drives, cassette tape drives, and/or magnetic ledger card devices. Software is often limited to standardized application packages designed for such accounting functions as billing and accounts receivable, payroll, and accounts payable. A configuration of this type may be leased for $200 to $400 per month.

A representative small business computer system contains a central processing unit with 16,000 to 64,000 bytes of primary storage, one or more disk drives, one or more CRT terminals, and a printer. Software includes a higher-level language such as BASIC or RPG, and various business-oriented application packages. Such a system may incorporate other forms of input/output and storage such as flexible disks, magnetic tape, or punched cards. A configuration of this type may be rented for $750 to $1000 per month.

At the next highest level are the medium-scale, general-purpose computer systems. An installation in this category might include a central processor with 500,000 to four million bytes of primary storage, several disk drives, one or more CRT terminals, one or more printers, and perhaps a card reader/punch or a group of magnetic tape drives. A configuration of this type may be rented for from $3000 to $15,000 per month.

At the upper end of the scale are the largest computer installations, which contain one or more central processors with a primary storage capacity of from two million to sixteen million bytes. Such a system would incorporate a large number and variety of input, output, and storage units, perhaps including specialized devices such as optical character readers, voice response units, or computer output microfilm devices. Average monthly rental of such large-scale systems ranges from $50,000 up.

Substantial as the costs of equipment rental may be, on the average they account for only 30 to 35 percent of the total costs of operating a computer installation. Personnel costs account for 45 to 60 percent of the total on the average and thus, with few exceptions, exceed the costs associated with the equipment.[2] A major portion of the personnel cost is for software development and maintenance, which takes the form of salaries of systems analysts, applications programmers, and systems programmers. Skilled people for these positions are in short supply, and so their salaries tend to be high. Also included in personnel costs are the salaries of computer operators, data preparation personnel, supervisory personnel, and data processing management.

The remainder of the costs of operation in a computer system include such categories as software, supplies, and overhead. Here software costs refer to the purchase or rental of program packages from manufacturers or independent software vendors. Supplies include paper, preprinted forms, punched cards, magnetic tapes, removable disk packs, and so forth. Overhead is composed of the cost of utilities, including power for the computer itself and for the air conditioning required by the computer, lighting, and telecommunications services. Equipment maintenance costs and insurance costs are other elements of overhead. Building occupancy costs should also be taken into consideration if there are cash flows or opportunity costs specifically identifiable with the occupancy of building space by the computer system. Taken together, these elements of cost may amount to from 10 to 20 percent of the total data processing budget.

For most organizations, the total data processing budget amounts to a relatively small percentage of gross revenues. According to one recent study, this percentage ranges from as low as two-tenths of one percent to as high as four percent.[3]

Initial outlay costs   For purposes of computing return on investment or net present value, the initial outlay costs of a system represent the investment component. These costs fall into several categories. First is the cost of organizational adjustment associated with the change. If the organization is acquiring a computer for the first time, many people will have to be hired for both managerial and operating positions, and some relocation of existing personnel may be necessary. For any type of systems change there will be costs associated with training of personnel. Steps should be taken to ensure that employee morale does not deteriorate as a result of a major systems change, and in some cases these steps could be expensive.

A second major portion of the initial outlay will be for preparation of the computer site. A microcomputer or minicomputer system requires little site preparation, but a larger general-purpose computer system often requires that considerable effort be devoted to the selection and development of a home for computer equipment and staff. Even if the site is to be part of an existing building, the cost of the remodeling necessary to accommodate a computer system is still likely to be substantial. The addition of electrical outlets, communications capacity, and raised floors will often

[2] *For an analysis of typical data processing budgets in a variety of industries, see Philip H. Dorn, "1979 DP Budget Survey," Datamation (January, 1979): 162–170.*
[3] *Ibid., pp. 164–165.*

be required. Space must also be provided to house systems analysts, programmers, data preparation personnel and equipment, supervisors, and so forth.

The initial systems analysis and programming is a third element that adds to the initial outlay cost. The operating system, utility routines, compilers, and so forth are obtained from the vendor. Some vendors charge for these separately, while others provide them as part of a package with the equipment. In addition to this software, however, much time and effort will be required to program the user's applications and to test and document them. Again, application programs may be obtained from the computer vendor or from other software suppliers, but such programs usually must be modified to fit the user's requirements, and this may consume a great deal of time. The development of a complete set of application systems documentation is also time-consuming. The cost of application systems development, documentation and testing primarily takes the form of salaries paid to systems analysts and programmers, but may also include rental of outside computer time for purposes of program testing.

A fourth portion of the initial outlay cost will be for the process of conversion itself. The cost of converting files to the storage media of the new system may be quite large if the old system is a manual one with files of printed documents. However, the main element of conversion cost arises from a period of parallel operation of the old and new systems prior to the final changeover. The major portion of conversion cost goes for wages and salaries of computer operators and other staff personnel. During the parallel operation period, these employees often must work long overtime hours, which adds even more to conversion costs.

Each of these activities requiring an initial outlay is part of the process of implementation, which is discussed in greater depth in the next chapter. The elements of cost attached to these activities are somewhat more difficult to estimate than operating costs. One rough rule of thumb is that such costs will be about equal to one year's operating costs. However, rules of thumb should not be substituted for careful analysis when so much is at stake in the decision.

Benefits of a computer system

The most difficult part of a feasibility study is to place a dollar value on the benefits that will come about as the result of computerization. Several different categories of cost savings and other benefits are usually cited as justification for computer acquisition, and some of the more significant of these are briefly discussed here.

Perhaps the most common expectation is that a new computer will result in cost savings due to reductions in clerical personnel. It is true that clerical cost savings are likely to represent one of the major benefits of computerization. However, from the standpoint of an analysis of cash flows it is necessary to consider the pattern of these savings over time. For example, if a policy of relocation of displaced personnel together with the reduction of hiring rates necessary for their assimilation is adopted, the clerical cost savings will be realized gradually rather than suddenly. Furthermore, it is reasonable to expect that the computer will continue to take over clerical functions after its implementation, and will thus effect a gradual increase in clerical cost savings over time. However, it is relevant to point out that most, if not all, savings from reductions in clerical personnel may be offset by the personnel costs relating to the staffing of the computer system.

Whereas clerical cost savings usually represent the primary initial justification for computer acquisition, the primary long-term justification for the computer must be its contribution to better management. The production management function is one area in which this contribution is often expected. More accurate and comprehensive information should be made available by the computer to enable production planning to be more sensitive to market conditions and to the availability of raw materials. Tighter control over waste and inefficiency in production can be accomplished with faster and more accurate production control information. Cost savings from greater production efficiency are difficult to estimate accurately, but they can be substantial. Care should be taken to separate those savings attributable solely to computerization from those that could be achieved by improvements other than computerization.

Another form of cost savings arises from having fewer funds tied up in working capital. The computer can help to reduce inventory balances by keeping a more accurate and up-to-date record and by automatically reordering items that need to be replenished. Accounts receivable balances can be reduced by means of faster billing and closer monitoring of past due accounts. Cash balances can be reduced because of more accurate forecasting of cash requirements. All of the funds thus freed can be invested in income-producing projects, thereby contributing to cash inflow.

Computerization can also help an organization provide better service to its customers. Increased control over inventories means fewer stockouts. Increased efficiency in the handling of customer orders means fewer errors and faster order handling and delivery. Increased automation enables faster responses to inquiries from customers or potential customers concerning the status of their account or the availability of a product. Advantages of this type are quite difficult to quantify. Nevertheless, they are real and should not be overlooked, particularly if the company operates in a highly competitive market.

Finally, the computer benefits which are perhaps the most difficult to quantify are those relating to improvements in management decision making. The computer provides management with more timely, more comprehensive, and more reliable information. It will provide a basis for better management control by spotlighting the extremes of good performance and bad performance in the organization. It offers the potential for development of planning models and quantitative techniques designed to support the decision-making process for critical management decisions. Such improvements will probably be realized gradually rather than quickly. Therefore, estimates of their contribution to cash flow should be conservative for the first few years after computerization.

On the basis of these tentative estimates of cash flows, the feasibility study group must formulate a recommendation either to discontinue further investigation of computer acquisition and maintain or modify the existing system or to go ahead with the plan for the new system. This decision should be made primarily on an economic basis. The best framework for making this decision is the capital budgeting model, in which all estimated future cash flows are discounted back to the present, using a discount rate that reflects the time value of money to the organization. From the resulting amount is deducted the initial outlay cost to obtain the *net present value*. A positive net present value is an indication that the alternative is economically feasible.[4]

Even if a decision is made at this point to halt the investigation and go no further in considering a new system, it is likely that the feasibility study will have produced some benefits through the correction of inefficiencies or the initiation of other improvements in the system. However, if the decision is made to go ahead with the system selection and acquisition effort, then the study group enters a new phase at this point, which is the detailed study of applications for the new system.

The Applications Study

The applications study phase of the systems evaluation and selection process involves a detailed description of the work load which the new system will be required to perform. While the information developed in the feasibility study will be a useful starting point, the objectives of the applications study require a much finer degree of detail than is required to evaluate economic feasibility. The primary goal of the the applications study is to produce a set of *specifications* that represent an itemized description of the data processing objectives and requirements of the organization. The specifications are provided to those equipment, service, or software vendors which the organization selects to submit proposals. The vendors who accept such invitations may then use the specifications as a basis for developing presentations geared to the specific requirements of the user organization.

Completion of the applications study and development of specifications are important steps for an organization that is preparing to procure systems or services from an external vendor. However, if the systems selection involves internal development and programming of information systems applications, with little or no impact on the organization's hardware or software configuration, then the applications study will be skipped and the study group will proceed directly to the design phase.

Content of specifications

A set of specifications typically includes certain general information, a detailed description of the user's applications, and an indication of the user's expectations of the vendors with respect to their presentations. Each of these categories of information is hereby examined in turn.

---

[4] *For an excellent treatise on capital budgeting, see Harold J. Bierman, Jr. and Seymour Smidt.* The Capital Budgeting Decision *(5th ed.), New York: Macmillan, 1980.*

General information A set of specifications should first include general background information on the company. A concise outline of the company's facilities, products, financial circumstances, and organization serves as an appropriate introduction. This should be followed by a more extensive description of the company's present data processing system, including major applications and existing equipment. A brief indication of the more serious inadequacies or problems with the present system could be useful here. Other general information should include the company's expectations with respect to the dates of submission of proposals and the date that the final decision on selection of a vendor will be made.

Description of applications The heart of the specifications will be a description of proposed applications. Each application should be treated separately. One of the most important elements in the presentation of an application will be the system flowchart, showing the input to and output from the computer runs. Input to the application should be further described by its sources, the operations performed on it prior to conversion to computer input, and its average and peak volume.

A specification of the contents of the master file is also a useful part of the description of each application. Record layouts describing the length, format, and other characteristics of each type of master file record should be included. The frequency and method of file updating, as well as the urgency and frequency of inquiries to the file, should be included in the description. The number of records contained in the file should be given and an estimate of the rate of growth expected in this number made.

The output required of each application should also be described. The points important to be clarified are (1) the information to be contained in each report and its format; (2) the average size (length) of each report; (3) the frequency with which each report is to be prepared and the necessity for timeliness in its preparation and distribution; and (4) the persons or locations to which each report is to be distributed.

Requirements for vendor presentation The third major category of information to be submitted in the specifications should be a list of major items the user company expects each vendor to cover in its proposal. Significant in this respect is first of all the hardware configuration proposed by the vendor, including a description of the central processor and its characteristics, the number and type of input and output units and a description of their speed and other vital characteristics, and the type of file media and related equipment. A topic important in the consideration of hardware will be its cost, which requires a description of alternative lease or purchase plans the vendor offers and other major terms of contract, such as length of lease and cancellation clauses. An indication of when installation could commence and an estimate of when it could be completed should also be included. Floor space required, electric power, and other aspects of the installation should be covered. Any user restrictions concerning cost, hardware characteristics, delivery date, or available floor space should be revealed.

The user will also expect the vendor to discuss system software in the proposal. Any user requirements regarding compiler languages are relevant. Any utility routines or application packages which the user feels are needed or desired should be discussed. The vendor should be expected to mention all compilers, assemblers, utility routines, and so forth that are proposed for the system and indicate what usage is recommended for each.

The vendor should also be required to submit a proposed processing schedule for the user. This will provide some assurance that the proposed system is actually capable of meeting the user's data processing requirements. The vendor should be requested to give attention to the effects of peak processing periods on the schedule.

The user will be interested in several other types of services provided by the vendor such as the facilities available for testing programs prior to installation, any training programs offered by the vendor for the user's employees, the amount of assistance available from the vendor during the preparation for installation and conversion, the arrangements for hardware maintenance, and the availability of backup facilities in the event of a system failure. Charges for any or all of these services should be included in the description.

Most of the major topics that would be covered in a set of specifications have been mentioned. In addition to these, the user may indicate some special requirements or restrictions that he or she wishes the vendor to recognize in his or her case. After the specifications have been provided to the vendors, the next step in the process is to await receipt of their various proposals. This is followed by the difficult process of evaluating the proposals and selecting a vendor.

Vendor Selection

The term "computer vendor" generally is interpreted as a reference to the relatively few large computer manufacturers. However, the computer industry contains a variety of firms. In addition to the major computer manufacturers, other major segments of the industry include minicomputer and microcomputer manufacturers, turnkey systems suppliers, mainframe replacement vendors, supplies vendors, service bureaus, time-sharing vendors, computer leasing companies, used-computer brokers, peripheral equipment manufacturers, facilities management vendors, EDP consultants, and software vendors. An organization considering computer acquisition may find it worthwhile to consider the services of firms in several of these industry segments in addition to, or as an alternative to, the major computer manufacturers. Certainly a restriction of consideration to the computer manufacturers alone is inappropriate. For one thing, many firms in other segments of the computer industry offer services or equipment equivalent to that of the manufacturers, but at a lower price. For another thing, if more alternatives are considered, the likelihood that the resulting system will more closely meet the needs and objectives of the user organization is increased.

Accordingly, one of the first steps in the vendor selection process is the determination of which type or types of vendor the organization wishes to consider. This must be followed by a determination of which specific vendors will be invited to submit proposals. To assist in this determination, the organization may classify the features it desires in its system as either "mandatory" or "desirable." Any vendors whose systems do not satisfy the mandatory requirements are automatically eliminated from further consideration. The remainder are invited to submit proposals by providing them with a "request for proposal," or "RFP," that consists primarily of the specifications developed in the applications study.

This section begins by briefly describing the products and services offered by firms in each of the computer industry segments mentioned above. Following this is a discussion of the vendor evaluation process. The section then concludes by examining the alternative methods of financing the acquisition of a computer system.

The computer industry

In the following paragraphs, fourteen categories of firms in the computer industry are described.

Computer manufacturers   Each of the major computer manufacturers is involved in most or all of the industry segments listed above. The distinguishing feature of the firms in this group is their production for commercial sale of a wide range of general-purpose computer systems. The primary computer manufacturer is IBM, whose share of the general-purpose computer market has ranged around 70 percent for the past several years. The policies and actions of IBM dominate the industry. Other computer manufacturers have had difficulty making a profit in this environment and several have dropped out of the market completely, including RCA in September 1971 and Xerox Data Systems in July 1975.

In addition to IBM, the other major computer manufacturers, in roughly the order of their market share, are Honeywell, the Univac Division of Sperry Rand, Burroughs, The National Cash Register Corporation (NCR), and Control Data Corporation. For most of these firms, the only effective way to compete with IBM has been to specialize in an area of the market in which IBM is relatively weak. For example, Control Data concentrates primarily on very large and fast computers for scientific applications, and thus sells many machines to research institutions and universities. Burroughs has a sizeable market share in the banking industry, and along with NCR has also concentrated heavily in the small business systems segment of the market.

Mainframe replacement vendors   The dominance of IBM in the general-purpose computer market segment has spawned a unique group of companies known as mainframe replacement vendors. These are companies that build and sell central processing units (or "mainframes") that may be substituted for those offered by IBM. Because they are based upon more advanced technology, the mainframe replacements are generally faster, smaller, and less expensive than their IBM counterparts. They are designed to operate using IBM operating systems and other software, and therefore little or no conversion costs are associated with the replacement of an IBM mainframe by one of these units. Offsetting the advantages of greater performance and lower cost is the risk of receiving a lesser quantity and quality of service from the mainframe replacement vendors than from IBM's renowned customer service staff. As a result it is generally only the more experienced computer users, with less dependence on the vendor's service staff, who should consider a mainframe replacement.

In recent years IBM has responded to the competitive pressures created by mainframe replacements by upgrading its technology and lowering its prices. In turn, other major computer manufacturers have been forced to do the same. From the standpoint of computer users, this has certainly been a positive development. However, it has also reduced the economic advantages of mainframe replacements.

Service bureaus   A data processing service bureau is an organization that provides data processing services, primarily batch processing, on its own equipment to users for a fee. For firms too small to afford the considerable investment of an "in-house" computer system, a service bureau may offer an attractice alternative. Because many users are sharing the computer facilities of the service bureau, the cost to each user is only a fraction of the total cost of a computer system.

Most data processing service bureaus charge a standard rate for time or perhaps for each item processed. They may add charges for materials, or perhaps a fixed fee to cover administrative costs. Service bureaus provide generalized programs for most standard applications, or will write a specialized program for a single user for an extra fee. Utilization of service bureaus requires the physical transporting of source document input to the bureau and of processed output to the user.

In addition to the cost advantages to small users, the use of data processing service bureaus affords several other advantages. A firm that has its own computer system may arrange for backup facilities to be made available through a service bureau. Such backup facilities would be helpful during a major equipment malfunction or during a period of peak processing volume. In addition, a service bureau may offer specialized equipment, programs, or expertise which would not otherwise be available to a computer user. Service bureaus also offer to users who are awaiting installation of a new computer system an opportunity to test programs on a computer model like the one being acquired.

Use of a service bureau also has disadvantages. The most significant of these relates to data security. Because the user of a service bureau must relinquish control of vital business data to the bureau, the user should assure himself or herself that proper control procedures are being followed and that proper security provisions are in effect. Another disadvantage is that the generalized programs offered by the service bureau may not exactly meet the data processing requirements of the user. In addition, the scheduling of a user's data processing work by a service bureau may cause the user to wait significantly longer for the work to be completed than if the user owned a facility or did the work manually.

Time-sharing vendors   The time-sharing vendor is an organization that provides for a fee the usage of a central computer and online file storage to users who obtain access through remote terminals and telecommunication lines. As with the service bureau, the primary advantage is the cost savings achieved through the sharing of a central computer system by many users. The time-sharing service differs from that of the service bureau in that the former is an online processing service, while the latter is a batch processing service. The most significant disadvantage of time-sharing is the high cost of data transmission over long distances.

The advent of commercial time-sharing services in the mid-1960s gave birth to the concept of the *computer utility*. According to this concept, computer service is like telephone or electric service, which is provided to subscribers by organizations having a monopoly on the service within a community. The computer utility would operate a large central computer system and provide service to its subscribers via telephone. Holders of this view felt that computer utilities were inevitable due to the tremendous economies of scale in computer systems. However, the uniqueness of each user's needs, the problems of data security, and the cost of data transmission have thus far prevented the large-scale computer utility from becoming a reality.

Three basic categories of time-sharing services are available. One is a problem-solving or scientifically oriented service. This type of time-sharing service is the most common and has several advantages. First, it provides computer availability to organizations that do not have access to private facilities at a relatively low cost that varies with usage. Second, it provides an interactive capability. This means that the user can obtain a problem solution quickly and then structure another problem based upon that solution, and so on. A third important advantage is that time-sharing vendors generally offer several specialized library programs, many of which a user might find to be helpful.

The second basic category of time-sharing service is business-oriented batch processing, in which the input consists of transaction data and the output consists of documents and reports. In addition to a terminal, the user of this service may also have a special printer or other specialized input-output equipment. Because business applications generally involve high volumes of data input and output and because the cost of data transmission is high, this type of service is often not economical relative to the service bureau. In addition, the problems of data security and control are perhaps even more serious than those in service bureaus because of shared file storage. The main advantage of this service is that it provides a real-time capability, which in some cases may improve the efficiency of the user's operations or provide the user with a significant competitive advantage.

The third type of service offered by time-sharing vendors is an information utility service. This service provides the user with access to a large centralized data base containing information relevant to specific needs of each user. One example related to accounting is a credit reference service. The centralized data base of such an organization contains credit information on all potential credit customers within a community. Subscribers may obtain access to this information via telephone whenever a customer applies for credit.

The cost of a time-sharing service generally includes a fixed monthly charge for the terminal and other equipment and variable charges for terminal hookup, central processor time, and file storage used. The cost of a terminal varies widely, but generally ranges between $100 and $500 per month. The charge for terminal hookup time is usually between $5 and $30 per hour. The charges for central processor time and file storage are generally small relative to terminal and hookup costs. However, pricing patterns among time-sharing vendors are quite diverse, and so the potential user is well advised to shop around for a vendor whose pricing policies are most favorable relative to the expected usage pattern.

Minicomputer manufacturers   Several manufacturers are in the minicomputer segment of the computer industry. These companies offer a high-performance product that is fast, reliable, inexpensive, and possessed of all of the logical capabilities of large computers. However, these companies have traditionally not placed a great deal of emphasis on peripheral equipment, high-level languages, or systems support. As a result, the major market for minicomputers has been among users who possess sufficient technical skills to utilize them successfully despite these handicaps. These include scientists, engineers, and researchers. In recent years the emphasis of most minicomputer manufacturers has shifted toward the business-oriented user, but the addition of new capabilities to these systems obviously tends to erode their cost advantages. Nevertheless, the minicomputer represents a strong and growing element of the computer industry.

Several companies within this industry segment offer a type of computer known as the electronic accounting machine, so called because it was originally designed as an upgraded version of the electromechanical bookkeeping machines that were very popular prior to the 1970s. These systems provide a low-cost automated accounting capability for small business applications. The vendors typically attempt to provide a level of software and supporting services appropriate for the relatively unsophisticated computer user. Due to the relatively low cost and the large potential market, this segment of the computer industry is expected to grow substantially over the next few years.

Turnkey systems suppliers   Because minicomputer manufacturers have generally not been strong in providing software and services to first-time small business computer users, another group of companies has emerged to fill this void. These companies are called turnkey systems suppliers because their systems are (theoretically) delivered to customers ready to use by simply turning them on. A turnkey systems supplier does not manufacture computer equipment, but instead buys equipment from a minicomputer manufacturer and then writes application software that is tailored both to that equipment and to the user needs of its customers. The most successful turnkey systems suppliers target their offerings to specific classes of customers, such as automobile distributors, medical clinics, or food wholesalers, in order to develop the specialized expertise necessary to provide high-quality service. As a result, turnkey systems suppliers are an option that should be given serious consideration by a first-time computer user.

Microcomputer manufacturers   In the late 1970s another wave of small computers entered the market place, creating still another industry segment. Because the computers are even smaller, faster, and less expensive than minicomputers, they have been tabbed microcomputers, but they are also called desktop computers or personal computers. These machines are perhaps best suited for the businessperson who is a sole proprietor of a very small business. They may be used for file processing applications which have a limited volume of input, output and storage; for computational applications such as discounted cash flow analysis, forecasting, and engineering problem solving; and for household applications such as budgeting and checking account record keeping. They are ideal for professionals, such as engineers, architects, or accountants, who are willing and able to program in simple languages such as BASIC and who wish to have an inexpensive computer for both business and personal use. However, they generally do not have the capacity to meet the data processing requirements of larger companies.

Computer-leasing companies   These companies usually offer a computer user an opportunity to lease a computer system at rates below the rental rates charged by the manufacturers. Offsetting this basic advantage is the basic disadvantage that these leasing contracts are for a long-term period with no options to cancel. Thus the flexibility and avoidance of risk present in rental contracts with the manufacturer is not present in contracts with leasing companies. These companies basically provide a financing alternative to purchasing or renting, and this option has proven attractive to many organizations. According to one estimate, over 35 percent of the general-purpose computer systems in use are financed in this manner.[5]

Used-computer brokers   These organizations operate primarily as agents for sellers of used computers, assisting them in finding a buyer. Their fee is determined as a percentage, commonly 10 percent, of the selling price. Used equipment prices range from as low as 10 percent for older equipment to as high as 90 percent for newer equipment. In addition to the cost advantage, the used-computer broker can often provide immediate delivery of equipment, whereas delivery of new equipment usually requires a delay of from three to twelve months. While first-time computer users may wish to consider the used computer alternative, most buyers of used computers are well-established users who wish to upgrade their facilities and know exactly what equipment they want. As the total number of computer systems in use continues to increase, the market for used computers has grown rapidly, passing the $1 billion mark in 1976 according to one estimate.

Peripheral equipment manufacturers   These firms manufacture a variety of input, output, and memory devices. Though the computer manufacturers are a major segment of this group, there are a large number of independents. Relative to central processor units, peripheral equipment represents 60 percent of the dollar value of all computer hardware sales. From the user's point of view, the most significant thing about this industry segment is that the independents may offer price and performance advantages over the computer manufacturers. Some may offer devices that

[5] "User Ratings of Computer Systems," Datapro 70: The EDP Buyer's Bible. *Delran, N.J.: Datapro Research Corporation, June 1980, p. 50b.*

are equivalent to those of IBM, for example, but at a lower cost. Others may offer devices technologically superior to those available from the computer manufacturers at equivalent prices.

Facilities-management vendors   A facilities-management vendor is an organization that contracts to manage the data processing facilities of a user for a fee. In most cases the hardware is owned or leased by the user and is located at the user's site. The facilities-management firm operates under guidelines and schedules established by the user. Banks, insurance companies, and hospitals are among the most significant users of facilities-management services.

Facilities management offers several advantages, the most significant of which is the reduction of staffing problems relating to the computer facility. Qualified EDP personnel are in short supply, and users of smaller systems have difficulty attracting qualified people and evaluating their work. Another advantage is the control of costs and efficiency that is provided by a contract that establishes a schedule and specifies a fee. Other advantages include availability of specialized knowledge and expertise, the ability to balance staff levels over periods of high and low volume, and the possibility of more effective security and control being implemented.

For the company contemplating acquisition of its first computer system, a facilities-management firm can provide useful assistance in vendor selection as well as manage the system through implementation and the early period of operation. Facilities-management personnel should be familiar with a wide range of equipment and software available on the market.

Facilities management does have significant disadvantages. A primary one is that a major segment of the user's operation is turned over to the control of outsiders. The personnel provided by a facilities-management vendor may not be as sensitive to the needs and objectives of the user organization as would be the user's own personnel. Facilities management is probably not an appropriate alternative to consider for an organization that has an effectively operating computer system staffed with experienced and qualified personnel.

EDP consultants   The two foremost types of firms that offer independent EDP consulting services are the major private consulting firms and the large public accounting firms. Both employ people who specialize in EDP consulting. A service of this type is often invaluable to the user considering computer acquisition for the first time. With little knowledge and no experience, first-time buyers are often taken advantage of by equipment salespeople whose primary objective is to make a sale. The experience and objective viewpoint of the EDP consultant helps to ensure that decisions are based upon facts and needs rather than emotions.

Software vendors   Firms in this industry segment specialize in the development and marketing of program packages. These include standardized applications packages, utility programs, data base management systems, report generators, data communications software, and operating systems. Prior to IBM's unbundling of hardware and software prices in 1969, most software development work by these vendors was done under contracts with users. The unbundling stimulated the development of a market for software products. As with peripheral equipment, the software products available from the independent software vendors may offer price or performance advantages over those available from the computer manufacturers.

Supplies vendors   This market segment consists of a large number of firms that sell magnetic tape, disk packs, punched cards, preprinted computer forms, and related computer media and accessories. Among these are the large computer vendors, but neither they nor any other firms have a dominating influence on this market. According to one estimate, sales revenues from these products amount to over 4 percent of all data processing expenditures. Significant price and product quality differences do exist in this market, and so computer users are well advised to shop carefully for their computer supplies.

Summary   The division of the computer industry into the fourteen segments described here does not represent a standardized or generally accepted method of classification. There are certainly some other less significant segments not described here, and there are other ways of subdividing these segments. Once again the major purpose of this discussion was to point out the wide variety of options open to the computer user.

For the potential first-time computer user, minicomputer or microcomputer manufacturers, turnkey systems suppliers, service bureaus, time-sharing vendors, and used-computer brokers, in addition to the major computer manufacturers, may be considered as alternatives during the feasibility study. The advice of EDP consultants may be useful in carrying out the feasibility study. If the decision is made to acquire a computer system, either a facilities-management vendor or an EDP consultant may provide useful assistance in preparing specifications and evaluating vendor proposals.

Once the applications study has been completed, the specifications are provided to a number of computer manufacturers (generally three to five) who are invited to submit proposals. The time lapse between providing a vendor with the specifications and receiving the proposals averages about two months. During that period each of the different vendors may desire clarification of various aspects of the specifications, and the company should be prepared to provide such guidance. In the next section, the criteria for evaluating vendor proposals are discussed.

After a vendor for the main system has been selected, the user may wish to consider alternative sources of peripheral equipment, software, or supplies. Vendor selection must be followed by a decision of how to finance the computer acquisition. At this point, computer-leasing companies may be considered. A subsequent section of this chapter discusses purchasing and leasing as alternative means of financing.

Evaluation of vendor proposals   After the proposals of all vendors have been received, the difficult choice among equipment configurations and vendors must be made. The most important factors in the selection of an equipment configuration are hardware and software performance and cost. One popular means of comparing the hardware and software performance of computer systems is the *benchmark problem*. This is a data processing task typical of the jobs a new computer system will be required to perform, and that therefore provides a useful means for making a comparison among proposed systems. A second approach is to develop a performance-cost ratio for each proposed system. The problem with this approach is that it is difficult to reduce all of the various aspects of system performance to a formula that is to be solved to provide a number representing a comparable measure of performance. A third approach is the use of mathematical models to simulate the performance of each proposed system relative to the complete processing requirements of the user.

A thorough analysis of the proposed processing schedule of each vendor also provides an indication of the capability of the proposed hardware and software to accomplish the required data processing functions of the user company. Necessary for making a determination of whether the schedule allows enough time to complete each application is knowledge about rated speeds of each hardware item, including the average speed of the central processor in executing a typical mix of instructions. Because many business data processing applications are input/output bound, the speeds of input/output hardware may often determine the rate at which each application can be processed. The time required for each unit of activity multiplied by the volume of activity for each application provides a fair measure of the total time required for each in the schedule. The schedule should also make allowances for periods of peak volume.

Another significant factor in equipment selection is the compatibility of the proposed system with the user company's present data processing system. This is particularly important if the user company is already automated and is seeking to obtain more capacity. A closely related factor is the *modularity* of a proposed system, which is its capacity to be expanded with a minimum of difficulty to meet growth in the user company's needs. Modularity relates both to hardware and software. For example, the capacity of a sytem may be expanded by adding more primary storage, faster input/output equipment, or a faster central processor. Hardware changes, particularly a change in CPU, will require changes in software. The ease with which such changes can be made is what is referred to as modularity.

In some cases there may be specific criteria of critical importance to the selection decision. For example, in the selection of an online system to support customer service activities or key operating functions, response time and equipment reliability are critical factors. For another example, if the system is to be used for storage and retrieval of sensitive data, the security features of the hardware and software become a critical factor.

Still another important element of the equipment selection decision is the choice among vendors. The reputation of each vendor and the support that each is able and willing to provide to the user are very significant. Support consists of such things as training for user personnel; use of equipment for testing purposes; contracts for maintenance; assistance in systems analysis and design, in implementation, and in eliminating bugs during the early stages of operation; and provision for system backup in the event of failure. The relationship between a computer vendor and a user company is complex and has many facets. During the period of implementation especially, this relationship will be a very close one. Throughout the period of their association, the user company will be placing reliance upon the vendor. The choice of vendor is thus a decision that must be carefully weighed.

Outside sources of information should not be overlooked during the vendor selection process. For example, other users of a vendor's systems may provide useful insights regarding system performance and vendor support. A somewhat more objective source of information is the user ratings of computer hardware and software systems regularly compiled and published by organizations such as the Datapro Research Corportion.[6] These ratings are based upon comprehensive surveys of large numbers of computer users, and are widely regarded as a valuable source of information on user opinions.

Many authorities recommend the use of an objective procedure for evaluating the overall merits of vendor proposals, taking into account all of the relevant criteria. One such approach is known as *point scoring*. Under this procedure the various criteria are listed and a weighting factor is applied to each criterion according to its relative importance to the user. Then each vendor is assigned a score on each criterion according to how well its proposal measures up to the ideal for that criterion. Summation of the scores for the individual criteria then gives an overall score that may be used to compare the various vendors. A simple illustration of how this form of point scoring might work is provided in Fig. 12.1.

Point scoring provides a useful way of obtaining an overall view of the vendor proposals and how they compare. The process of selecting criteria and assigning weights and points tends to focus attention on the factors relevant to the decision process. However, care must be taken to avoid placing too much emphasis on the outcome of the point-scoring technique. It should be kept in mind that both the weights and the points are assigned subjectively, and therefore a sizeable margin for potential error should be provided in interpreting the results. For example, the results shown in Fig. 12.1 are too inconclusive to support a final decision that vendor #3's proposal is best. It would be appropriate in this case to experiment with other possible values of weights and point assignments and study the impact of the alternative values on the result.

Another objective technique for evaluating the relative merits of proposed systems is known as *requirements costing*. Under this approach a list is made of all of the required features for the new system. Then, if any feature is not present in a particular system, an estimate is made of the cost to purchase or develop that feature for that system. Therefore, the total cost for each system is computed by adding its acquisition cost to the cost of purchasing or developing any additional required features not possessed by the system. The resulting sums represent the total costs for systems having all of the required features, and thus provide an equitable basis for comparing the alternative systems.

Neither requirements costing nor point scoring is totally objective. The disadvantage of point scoring is that it does not incorporate dollar estimates of costs and

---

[6] *Ibid., pp. 50a–50yy.*

Criterion	Weight	Vendor # 1	Vendor # 2	Vendor # 3
Hardware performance	60	40	60	50
Software capability	70	55	40	60
System reliability	40	25	30	35
Rental cost	60	60	35	50
Ease of use	40	30	25	35
Ease of conversion	20	15	20	15
Modularity	40	30	40	30
Vendor support	40	40	30	30
Documentation	30	25	20	20
TOTALS	400	320	300	325

Fig. 12.1
The point scoring method of evaluating vendor proposals.

benefits. Requirements costing partially overcomes this problem, but generally overlooks intangible factors such as system reliability and vendor support. The ideal selection technique would be one that reduces all factors to dollar estimates of costs and benefits. While it is generally not possible to reduce factors such as those listed in Fig. 12.1 to precise dollar terms, an attempt to do so may be no more subjective than the point-scoring approach. In any event, the final choice among vendor proposals is not likely to be a clear-cut decision. In the final analysis this decision cannot be based solely upon objective criteria, but must rely to some extent on subjective factors.

Financing system acquisition

Closely related to the choice among vendor proposals is the selection of a method of financing the acquisition of major items of equipment or software. The three primary alternatives are purchasing the system, renting it from the vendor, or leasing it from either the vendor or a computer-leasing company.

The major difference between renting and leasing is in the length of the agreement. A rental contract may generally be terminated by giving 90 days prior notice, whereas a lease contract may be written to cover a fixed period of from two to ten years. Rental payments are higher than lease payments for the equivalent hardware. Rental contracts often include an extra charge for usage of the computer for more than 176 or 200 hours during a month. Lease contracts typically do not contain extra use charges, and usually provide the user (lessee) with an option to purchase the system at a specified price at the conclusion of the lease term. Under both rental and lease plans, the manufacturer provides maintenance of the equipment and the charge for this service is included in the monthly payment.

The terms of equipment purchase from a computer manufacturer are relatively straightforward. Computer equipment prices generally average between 25 and 50 times the monthly rental charges for the same hardware. Equipment maintenance must be handled by separate contract payable on a monthly basis. For the protection of the user, a purchase contract may include provision for a penalty payment in the event of late delivery and a commitment to provide maintenance service during the first 90 days after installation.

The relative economic merits of purchasing a computer system as opposed to either renting or leasing it are highlighted in Fig. 12.2. This illustration shows the annual cash flows over an eight-year life for a computer system that could be purchased for $1,080,000, or rented for $25,000 per month ($300,000 per year). Under

Year =	0	1	2	3	4	5	6	7	8
PURCHASE:									
a. Purchase payment	$1,080,000	—	—	—	—	—	—	—	—
b. Depreciation (8/36, 7/36, etc.)	—	$240,000	$210,000	$180,000	$150,000	$120,000	$90,000	$60,000	$30,000
c. Maintenance	—	30,000	30,000	30,000	30,000	30,000	30,000	30,000	30,000
Tax saving from:									
d. Investment tax credit [10% of a]	(108,000)	—	—	—	—	—	—	—	—
e. Deductible expenses [50% of (b + c)]	—	(135,000)	(120,000)	(105,000)	(90,000)	(75,000)	(60,000)	(45,000)	(30,000)
f. After-tax cash outflow (inflow) [a + c − d − e]	972,000	(105,000)	(90,000)	(75,000)	(60,000)	(45,000)	(30,000)	(15,000)	—
g. Cumulative cash outflow [f + previous g]	972,000	867,000	777,000	702,000	642,000	597,000	567,000	552,000	552,000
RENTAL:									
h. Rental payment	—	$300,000	$300,000	$300,000	$300,000	$300,000	$300,000	$300,000	$300,000
i. Tax saving [50% of h]	—	(150,000)	(150,000)	(150,000)	(150,000)	(150,000)	(150,000)	(150,000)	(150,000)
j. After-tax cash outflow	—	150,000	150,000	150,000	150,000	150,000	150,000	150,000	150,000
k. Cumulative cash outflow [j + previous k]	—	150,000	300,000	450,000	600,000	750,000	900,000	1,050,000	1,200,000

Fig. 12.2

Comparative cash flows: purchase vs. rental of a computer system.

the purchase plan, an investment tax credit of 10 percent may be taken at the time of purchase. Depreciation is computed on a sum-of-years'-digits basis, at the rate of 8/36 of purchase price in the first year, 7/36 in the second year, and so forth. Maintenance charges are a constant $30,000 per year. The tax savings are computed based on the tax-deductible expenses (depreciation and maintenance) assuming a 50 percent marginal tax rate (i.e., 50 percent of $240,000 + $30,000 in year 1). The after-tax cash flow is actually an inflow because the tax savings more than offset the maintenance payment in every year except the last. The cumulative cash flow represents the net total of all current and prior years' cash flows as of the end of each period.

The patterns of cash flow under both rental and lease plans are similar, although the amounts would differ. The rental or lease payment is tax deductible, and so the after-tax cash flow is equal to the total payment to the vendor minus the tax saving. By comparing the cumulative cash flows for rental with those for purchase, it is evident that rental is significantly more expensive over the long run, although this effect takes about four to five years to be realized.

Two other cost factors not reflected in Fig. 12.2 also favor purchasing. One is that equipment owned by the user has a residual value on the used-computer market. A second is that a purchaser does not pay extra use charges. However, the overall cost advantage of purchasing would be somewhat offset if the analysis was adjusted to take into account the time value of money, because the purchase requires an immediate outlay while both rental and lease contracts call for deferred payments. Even taking this into account, however, purchasing still has a lower total cost, and this represents its primary advantage.

Despite its higher cost, renting a computer system does have significant advantages. One is the avoidance of the large initial outlay of cash. A second is the flexibility provided by the ability to cancel the rental arrangement after giving a 90-day notice. The most important aspect of this flexibility is the avoidance of risks from being "locked-in" to a particular system. Examples of such risks are the risk that the equipment configuration may become obsolete as more efficient and less costly equipment becomes available in the market; the risk that the equipment rented may not perform as expected; the risk that the user may outgrow the equipment configuration sooner than expected; and the risk that the level of support provided by the vendor may not be adequate.

In terms of cost and risk, lease contracts fall in between purchase and rental contracts. Lease payments are smaller than rental payments, but leasing is still not as economical as purchasing in the long run. The lessee does not own the equipment and so, to some extent, avoids the risks of ownership by the ability to terminate the lease arrangement once the contract runs out. The length of a lease can be negotiated, and longer-term contracts require smaller monthly payments. Other advantages of leasing are the avoidance of extra use charges and the availability of the option to purchase.

Basically, then, the choice of a method of financing system acquisition involves a trade-off between the risks of a long-term commitment and cost factors as measured by cash flow analysis using present value methods. Each organization must decide for itself which of the options best fits its requirements. According to one survey of a sizeable number of users of general-purpose computer systems, 52 percent have purchased their systems, 38 percent have leased from third parties, and the remainder have rented or leased them from the manufacturer.[7]

Review Questions

1. Define the following terms.

   feasibility study   specifications
   applications study   computer utility
   technical feasibility   benchmark problem
   economic feasibility   modularity
   operational feasibility   point scoring
   net present value   requirements costing

2. What are the three major steps in the systems evaluation and selection process?

3. What should be the qualifications of the persons who carry out a feasibility study?

4. Outline and briefly describe the steps in a feasibility study.

5. Identify three dimensions of system feasibility and explain how each should be evaluated.

6. What three categories of cash flow estimates should be made during a computer feasibility study? List several individual elements within each category. Once these estimates have been made, what basic framework should be used in evaluating the feasibility of alternatives?

7. Briefly describe a typical equipment configuration within each of the following categories of computer system: (a) microcomputer, (b) small accounting computer, (c) small business computer, (d) medium-scale, general-purpose computer, and (e) large-scale computer. What would be an average monthly rental for each?

8. List several categories of personnel that are necessary in a computer system. How does the total operating cost expended for personnel generally compare with the total operating cost expended for equipment in a computer system?

9. Other than hardware and personnel costs, what are some of the categories of costs incurred by a data processing facility?

10. What percentage of a total organizational budget is generally consumed by expenditures on data processing?

11. What is the difference between a feasibility study and an applications study?

12. What is the goal of an applications study?

---

[7] *Ibid.*, p. 50b.

13. Outline and briefly describe the content of a set of specifications.

14. Describe in detail the information that should be contained in a description of input, files, and output for an application in a set of specifications.

15. Describe in detail the information that a company should request a vendor to include in its presentation of a proposed computer system for the company.

16. Briefly describe the steps in the vendor selection process.

17. List and briefly describe fourteen major segments of the computer industry. At what point in the computer acquisition process would the products or services of each segment be considered?

18. List several criteria that should be used by a company to select a computer vendor from among several that have presented proposals. What techniques might be used as a basis for the final selection?

19. Explain how the capability of a proposed computer system to meet a processing schedule might be evaluated.

20. Explain the characteristics of purchase, rental, and lease contracts as methods of financing computer system acquisition. What are the advantages of each to the user?

Discussion Questions

21. Discuss the role of the accountant in the computer acquisition process. Should the accountant play an active role or should all of the work done be left to computer experts? In what aspects of computer acquisition might the expertise of the accountant produce a useful contribution?

22. Computer manufacturers generally employ very competent personnel who will assist a customer in designing a system for no charge or for a relatively small fee. Being good businesspeople interested in repeat sales, representatives of a computer manufacturer will certainly consider very seriously the needs and objectives of the customer. Why, then, should a firm contemplating the acquisition of a computer system for the first time consider employing the relatively expensive services of an EDP consultant?

23. While reviewing a list of benefits from a computer vendor's proposal, you note an item which reads "improvements in management decision making—$50,000 per year." How would you interpret this item? What influence should it have on the computer acquisition decision?

24. You are participating in a feasibility study for a company that is considering the acquisition of its first computer system. The company's management has decided that a warehouse adjoining the main plant should be used to house the computer system if it is acquired. This warehouse was built only five years ago, but the company has not used it since discontinuing a major product line three years ago. The warehouse was rented briefly to another firm, but is not presently in use for any purpose.

    You feel that the warehouse would make an excellent location for a new computer facility. How should a cost of space utilization for the computer facility be determined for inclusion in the feasibility study? Discuss.

25. The Schulte Corporation has recently decided to replace its computer system with a larger, more advanced model. Proposals have been received from three vendors. As Chairman of the Evaluation Committee, you have prepared a list of nine criteria for comparing these proposals, and have ranked each vendor on a scale of 1 to 10 on each criterion. The criteria and assigned ranks are as follows.

   1. Hardware performance: vendor A–9, vendor B–8, vendor C–6.
   2. Software capability: A–8, B–6, C–7.
   3. System reliability: A–7, B–9, C–6.
   4. Rental cost: A–7, B–6, C–9.
   5. Ease of use: A–7, B–8, C–7.
   6. Ease of conversion: A–8, B–9, C–6.
   7. Modularity: A–8, B–9, C–5.
   8. Vendor support: A–6, B–9, C–7.
   9. Documentation: A–8, B–7, C–6.

   You have prepared a tentative set of weightings for the nine criteria as follows: Hardware performance—50, software capability—50, system reliability—30, rental cost—30, ease of use—50, ease of conversion—20, modularity—20, vendor support—50, documentation—20. Upon reviewing these with the Manager of Information Systems, you recieve the following reaction: "These weights are generally fine, except that vendor support isn't that critical to us any more. We have an experienced and capable staff. I'd give that a weight of only about 20. On the other hand, software capability is extremely critical. How good is the operating system? What kind of utilities, data management packages, and compilers are they offering? I think that ought to rate a 70."

   Required
   a) Prepare a point-scoring analysis of the three vendor proposals using your tentative set of weights.
   b) Prepare a point-scoring analysis using the weights as adjusted by the Manager of Information Systems.
   c) What conclusions can you reach as a result of this analysis? Discuss.

26. The Valentine Company is acquiring a new computer system, and must decide how the acquisition is to be financed. If the system is purchased, it will cost $550,000, and the separate maintenance contract will cost $2000 per month. An investment tax credit of 7 percent could be taken. The machine would be depreciated using the sum-of-years'-digits method with an estimated useful life of ten years. Assume a marginal income tax rate of 50%. Trade-in value of the machine would be about $360,000 at the time of purchase, and would decline at approximately $3000 per month for each month thereafter. Assume that there is no salvage value.

   If the system is leased, the monthly payment will be $12,000 per month, which includes maintenance. There will be no extra use charges. The lease contract could be canceled at the end of any one-year period at no penalty. An option to purchase is included in the lease contract that specifies that the customer may purchase the system at the end of any year at the following prices.

End of year	1	2	3	4	5	6–10
Purchase price	$500,000	$430,000	$360,000	$290,000	$220,000	$150,000

Required

a) Prepare for both the purchase and the lease situation a schedule of annual and cumulative cash flows at the beginning of the first year and during each year for ten years afterward.

b) Management is interested in the impact of the trade-in value on the comparison of purchasing to leasing. Prepare a schedule showing the "net purchase cost," which is the cumulative cash outflow under purchasing minus the trade-in value, over the ten-year period.

c) Considering only the cash flow considerations and ignoring the effects of discounting of cash flows, which of the two choices is more attractive?

d) If the cash flows were discounted, how would this affect the relative attractiveness of leasing and purchasing?

e) Cite some factors in addition to those mentioned above which would have some bearing on the decision.

27. You are an accountant employed by the Argus Corporation. You are serving as an accounting consultant to a software evaluation and selection project. The choice has been narrowed down to three software packages (call them package #1, package #2, and package #3), and you have decided to use requirements costing to make the final choice.

You have gathered the following information.

■ Argus has identified five features that it would like the system to have. Label them A, B, C, D, and E.

■ Package #1 costs $100,000, and possesses all of the desirable features except E. However, an optional routine that incorporates E can be purchased for an additional $20,000.

■ Package #2 costs $80,000 and possesses all features except B and E. However, feature B could be developed at a cost of $25,000, and feature E can be developed for $10,000.

■ Package #3 costs $80,000, and possesses all features except B and D. For this package, feature B could be constructed for $25,000, and feature D for $15,000.

Required

a) Determine the total cost required to buy each package and, where necessary, modify it to contain all desirable features. Which package looks best?

b) Suppose that you could develop feature E for package #1 for a cost of $10,000, which would mean that you wouldn't have to buy the optional subroutine associated with this feature. How would this change (if at all) your answer to part (a)?

c) Suppose that the project team decides that feature D is an unnecessary luxury that need not be developed. How would this change (if at all) your answer to part (a)? (Note: Ignore the changes in assumptions mentioned in part (b).)

d) List some factors other than package features and costs that might affect your choice among these three packages.

28. You are a systems consultant for Cooper, Price, and Arthur, CPAs. During your country club's annual match play tournament, your second-round opponent is Mr. Frank Fender, owner of a large automobile dealership. During the course of the round, Fender describes to you a proposal he has recently received from Turnkey Systems Corporation to install a computer in his dealership. The computer would take over data processing for inventories, receivables, payroll, accounts payable, and general ledger accounting. Turnkey personnel would install the system and train Fender's employees. The proposed system is to cost $70,000.

Suppose that Fender asks your opinion of this proposal. Without going into too much detail, identify the major themes you would try to touch upon in responding to his inquiry.

29. **Note:**   To complete this problem, it is necessary that your school's library subscribe to *Datapro 70: The EDP Buyer's Bible,* or to a similar data processing library service.

Read the report entitled "All about Small Business Computers" in Volume 1 of *Datapro 70.* Using the comparison charts at the back of the report, identify five small business computer systems manufactured by five different companies.

Required   Prepare a table listing the following information for each computer.

Name of computer	Computer #1	Computer #2	Etc.
Internal storage			
Capacity of basic system, bytes			
Maximum capacity, bytes			
Access time, microseconds			
Mass storage capabilities			
Floppy disk drive (yes or no)			
Pack disk drive (yes or no)			
Input/output devices			
Punched card reader-speed			
Punched card punch-speed			
Line printer-speed			
Reel-to-reel tape drive-speed			
CRT (yes or no)			
Software support			
COBOL (yes or no)			
BASIC (yes or no)			
Multiprogramming (yes or no)			
General accounting packages (yes or no)			
Data base management system (yes or no)			

Name of computer	Computer #1	Computer #2	Etc.
Pricing			

Purchase price of basic system, $
Monthly rental of basic system, $

30. You are an administrative services specialist for the CPA firm of Xeron, York, and Zapata. The Avalon Electronics Company, one of your firm's clients, has asked you to study for them the feasibility of computer acquisition. The company has a sales volume of $10,000,000 and has been having some problems with profit margins, making only a 2 percent return on sales as opposed to the industry average of 10 percent.

The applications which Avalon would like to automate initially are payroll, accounts receivable and billing, parts inventory, finished goods inventory, and general ledger. A need for frequent inquiry into the parts inventory and finished goods inventory files exists. The firm also expects to grow by a factor of 50 percent in the next five years. You have determined that the required equipment configuration includes a central processor with 64,000 character storage capacity, a disk drive unit with 27 million character storage capacity, a flexible disk input/output unit, three CRT display/keyboard units, and a line printer that operates at 160 lines per minute. Monthly rental for a configuration of this sort would be $1200.

You estimate costs of systems personnel as follows: one systems analyst-programmer at $1200 per month, one operator at $800 per month, and one full-time and one half-time CRT operator at $600 and $300 per month, respectively. Monthly rental of software would total $500 per month, and other miscellaneous overhead would total about $700 monthly.

Initial outlay costs for this system would include expenditures for site preparation, file conversion, hiring and training of personnel, and modification and testing of programs. You estimate that these costs will total $18,000.

You have estimated that the new computer system would generate cost savings in two primary areas, which are clerical costs and inventory carrying costs. Implementation of the new system would initially reduce the number of people in accounts receivable and billing from four to one, and in payroll, from two to one. Each of these employees makes $700 per month. Also the number of people in the parts inventory section could be reduced from four to two. These people each make $600 per month.

If Avalon does not computerize, in five years six people will be needed in accounts receivable and billing instead of four, three will be needed in payroll instead of two, and six will be needed in parts inventory instead of four. If the firm does computerize, no new people would be required in these areas in five years, and in addition the accounts payable and job order cost functions could be computerized by that time, saving a net of three additional employees. You estimate that the net impact of these factors will be that clerical cost savings will increase by 30 percent per year each year through the first five years following installation of the computer, if the computer is acquired.

You feel confident that the increased efficiency in reordering and control of parts inventory resulting from computerization would reduce the company's inventory balance of $750,000 by 20 percent. The funds thus freed would generate savings at an annual rate of 10 percent (the firm's cost of capital). You estimate that the amount of cost savings from inventory reduction will increase by 10 percent per year over the next five years if the computer is acquired.

Although you did not attempt to estimate the dollar amount, you feel that significant intangible benefits would accrue to the firm if it acquired a computer. These include improved production efficiency, better customer service, and better management reports and decision making.

You have estimated that after five years Avalon will require a CPU with 128,000 characters of main memory, an additional disk drive, an additional CRT terminal, and several additional programs. You project that this represents an increase in hardware and software rental charges of approximately 20 percent per year. In addition, another full-time CRT operator will have to be hired, and the salaries of all computer personnel will have to be increased regularly; this translates into an average annual increase in computer personnel costs of 15 percent. Finally, overhead costs will increase at an annual rate of 10 percent.

Required

a) Calculate the total monthly operating costs required for the proposed system during the month immediately following its implementation. Determine the total monthly cost savings from personnel reductions and inventory reductions during that month.

b) To simplify your analysis, assume that monthly costs and cost savings remain constant from month to month within each year, and that the percentage increases described in the problem all take place at once as Avalon Electronics moves from one year into the next. Prepare a schedule showing total monthly operating costs (in each of the four major categories described in the problem) for years one through five; and showing total monthly cost savings (in each of the two major categories given) for years one through five.

c) Convert the monthly cost and cost savings totals computed in part (b) to annual figures. Then prepare a table with six columns and four rows as follows: columns for the initial outlay and each of the first five years; and rows for cost, cost savings, net inflow or outflow (cost savings minus cost), and cumulative inflow or outflow. Complete the table. What is the payback period for the computer acquisition?

d) (Optional for those students who have studied discounted cash flow analysis.) What is the net present value of the computer acquisition investment?

e) Identify some factors not reflected in the calculations outlined above that should also be considered in the feasibility decision. Considering all factors, would you recommend that Avalon Electronics acquire a computer at this time? Why or why not?

References   Bierman, Harold, Jr., and Seymour Smidt. *The Capital Budgeting Decision* (5th ed.). New York: Macmillan, 1980.

Caswell, Stephen A. "Computer Peripherals: A Revolution Is Coming." *Datamation* (May 25, 1979): 83–87.

Cortada, James W. *EDP Costs and Charges: Finance, Budgets, and Cost Control in Data Processing.* Englewood Cliffs, N.J.: Prentice-Hall, 1980.

Cunningham, Peter A., and Walter P. Smith. "Computer Services: A Menu of Options." *Datamation* (May 25, 1979): 89–91.

Datapro Research Corporation. *Datapro 70: The EDP Buyer's Bible.* Delran, N.J.: Datapro Research Corporation, 1980.

Dorn, Philip H. "1979 DP Budget Survey." *Datamation* (January 1979): 162–170.

Geran, Michael J. "Mainframes: How Long the Mainstay for Their Vendors?" *Datamation* (May 25, 1979): 98–102.

Kelley, Neil D. "The Impact of Buying or Leasing." *Infosystems* (May 1980): 78–81.

King, John Leslie, and Edward L. Schrems. "Cost-Benefit Analysis in Information Systems Development and Operation." *Computing Surveys* (March 1978): 19–34.

King, Karl G., and Mark L. Hildebrand. "How to Help a Client Select a Data Processing System." *The Practical Accountant* (September 1979): 43–53.

Lipsher, Laurence E. "Selecting a Minicomputer." *Journal of Accountancy* (June 1979): 61–64.

Miller, Frederick W. "Used Computers: A Lower Cost Alternative." *Infosystems* (March 1980): 66–70.

Milne, Bruce. "Staying Alive in the Turnkey Systems Business." *Mini-Micro Systems* (May 1979): 127–130.

Page, John R., and H. Paul Hooper. "How to Buy a Computer." *The CPA Journal* (September 1979): 39–45.

Radell, Nicholas J. "Optimizing the Management Consultant." *Data Management* (August 1977): 32–36.

Schmedel, Scott. "Taking on the Industry Giant: An Interview with Gene M. Amdahl." *Harvard Business Review* (March/April 1980): 82–93.

Szatrowski, Ted. "Rent, Lease, or Buy?" *Datamation* (February 1976): 59–68.

Weinberg, Steven J. "Why Choose an Accounting Software Package?" *Management Accounting* (February 1980): 44–47.

Wooldridge, Susan. *Software Selection.* New York: Petrocelli, 1973.

Chapter 13

Systems Implementation

After the systems analysis and design have been completed and management has approved the recommendations of the systems study group for system modification or choice of a vendor from whom to acquire equipment, the focus of the systems investigation is transformed dramatically from the realms of analysis, deliberation, and creative thinking to the realm of action. The plans and theories of the systems study group must be put into practice in the arena of the real world. This period of time, between the acceptance of recommendations by management and the acceptance of the new system as an operational success, is referred to as the period of systems implementation.

Depending on the size of an organization and the level of sophistication of its information system, a systems implementation project could involve either a major revision to a manual system, conversion from a manual to an automated system, or conversion from an automated system to a larger and/or more advanced automated system. Within a computer system, implementation often refers to the development of and conversion to a major software system. However, systems implementation generally involves the performance of a fairly well-defined set of activities. The first section of this chapter will discuss the steps in the implementation process, using implementation of a computer system as the primary point of reference. The second and final section of the chapter provides an extensive discussion of *PERT* (Program Evaluation and Review Technique), which is a commonly used technique for the planning and scheduling of complex projects such as systems implementation.

The Implementation Process

Any major implementation project will involve the following activities: planning and scheduling of the implementation process, organizational planning and personnel administration, final systems design and testing, establishment of standards of performance and control procedures, site preparation, conversion from old to new system, and follow-up review and evaluation of results. This section discusses each of these activities in detail. Whereas most of the discussion relates directly to computer implementation, many of the concepts also apply to major revision of manual systems or major software development projects.

Planning and scheduling

During the implementation period, many varying activities will be proceeding simultaneously. A great deal of planning and coordination is necessary to ensure that these activities are accomplished smoothly and with dispatch. Responsibility for the performance of each function must be fixed, and a timetable for the completion of each task must be established. Estimates of the cost of each activity must be developed for purposes of preparing a financial budget. Provisions should be made for monitoring the performance of all activities and making adjustments where necessary to ensure continued progress. These activities are generally the responsibility of an implementation team composed of users, executives, and systems personnel.

Two techniques that provide an explicit framework for scheduling, coordinating, expediting, and monitoring the progress of the implementation effort are PERT (to be discussed later in the chapter) and the *Gantt chart*. The Gantt chart is a form of bar chart adapted to project planning and control. Project activities are listed on the left-hand side of the chart, and units of time in days or weeks are shown across the top. Corresponding to each activity, a bar is drawn showing the time period over which that activity is expected to be performed. A sample Gantt chart illustrating these concepts appears in Fig. 13.1.

As a project proceeds, a procedure should be adopted for recording the completion of each activity on the Gantt chart. In Fig. 13.1 the procedure used for this purpose is to fill in the open space within each bar in proportion to the percentage of completion of each activity. Then at any time it is possible to determine quickly which activities are on schedule and which are behind schedule. This capacity to show in graphic form the entire schedule for a large, complex project, including progress to date and current status, is the primary advantage of the Gantt chart.

Rather than focus on implementation techniques, some authorities stress the importance of implementation strategies in planning for systems implementation. For example, Alter describes a strategy he calls "implementation risk analysis."[1] This involves identifying in advance those conditions that decrease the likelihood of successful implementation. These conditions, called "risk factors," include such things as nonexistent or unwilling users, large numbers of users, inability to specify usage patterns in advance, inability to predict and cushion impact on all parties, lack

---

[1] *Steven L. Alter,* Decision Support Systems: Current Practices and Continuing Challenges. *Reading, Mass.: Addison-Wesley, 1980, Chapter 7.*

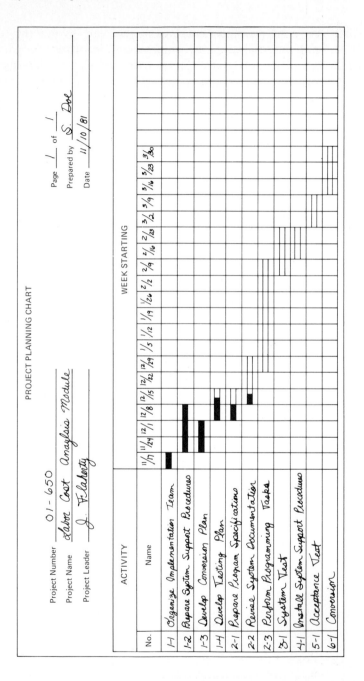

Fig. 13.1
Sample Gantt chart.

or loss of management support, and lack of experience with similar systems. Once the potential risk factors are identified for a particular system, implementation strategies are devised to cope with each risk factor. Among the possible implementation strategies are the testing of prototype systems, the use of an evolutionary approach, simplifying the system, obtaining user participation or commitment, obtaining management support, providing training, providing for ongoing user assistance, and tailoring the system to the user's capabilities. Alter goes so far as to suggest that if adequate implementation strategies cannot be devised to deal with the identified risk factors, then the project should be either abandoned or deferred.

Organizational planning and personnel administration

Any change in established routines of work in an organization requires attention to the human factors involved in the change. As in systems analysis and design, the participation of employees in the process of implementation will tend to prevent serious problems of resistance to change. A policy of communicating openly and honestly with employees during this period is advisable. Management and the systems group should be alert to sense any deterioration in employee morale or other serious problems, and should be prepared to take appropriate steps to deal with such problems.

In a company acquiring a computer for the first time, the areas of personnel and organization planning will require much greater attention than will those areas in a company that is merely converting from one computer system to another. The latter company will experience many of the same problems, but on a much smaller scale. Examples of problems commonly confronted are communication with employees, adjustment of organization structure, selection of personnel, relocation of displaced personnel, and personnel training.

Communication with employees   The period prior to computer installation can be a very difficult one from the standpoint of an organization's relationship with its employees. Once the fact is known that a computer will soon be installed, the natural reaction of employees to the uncertainty of the situation is one of apprehension. If it remains unchecked, such apprehension could well degenerate into an attitude of resistance and distrust.

If proper employee relations policies are adhered to during the initial period of systems survey and analysis, communication with employees prior to computer installation will follow naturally. Employees should be made aware of the possibility that the organization will undergo a major systems change, and they should be informed of management's plans for personnel in the event of such a change. Management must now provide evidence that it fully intends to honor the reassurances made during the survey. Specific plans relating to relocation of displaced personnel, staffing of new positions from the existing employee group, training programs offered to employees, and so forth should be announced. Even though such announcements may not placate everyone in the short run, their long-run effect will almost certainly be better than policies of silence or glib reassurance. Either of these latter policies is likely to generate resentment, resistance, and a loss of morale among employees, and perhaps cause the company to lose employees with a high potential for success in the new system.

Announcements to employees regarding computerization should always emphasize the positive aspects of the change—opportunities to devote more attention to the creative aspects of one's job while the computer performs the routine functions, opportunities for more rapid advancement and higher salaries, and so forth. The need for cooperation of employees at all levels of the organization to facilitate successful implementation should be stressed. Throughout the entire employee relations effort, the interest and concern of top management should be made clear.

Adjustment of organization structure   A company's first venture into computerization of data processing will require significant adjustments to its organization structure. A new set of departments will have to be staffed. Major categories of jobs to be established and defined include analyst, programmer, computer operator, and various managers. The problem of the appropriate level in the organization structure for the head of data processing will have to be resolved. The structure of the data processing department itself will have to be established. Even a company converting from an existing computer system to a larger or more advanced system may be faced with problems of expansion of the data processing organization, or a major change in its status in the company organization.

Selection of personnel   Once the personnel needs have been specified, the task of filling these needs must begin. Considerations relating to employee morale indicate that employees whose jobs may be replaced or significantly altered by computer acquisition should be given the first chance at testing for positions in the new system. It may even be easier to train these people in computer operations than to orient computer specialists to the company's operations and procedures. It is likely, however, that some positions will have to be filled by outsiders.

Once again the problems faced by a company computerizing for the first time are much greater in the area of personnel selection than they are for other firms. Such a company should probably seek professional assistance for this purpose. Usually such assistance can be obtained from the vendor. Computer work demands a unique set of aptitudes and abilities, including logical thinking, attention to detail, problem-solving ability, and the capacity to tolerate frustration and hard work. Selection of supervisory personnel in this field requires even greater care. These problems are compounded by the existence of a shortage of qualified computer specialists in the labor market.

Relocation of displaced personnel   Computerization will result in the elimination of a number of clerical and some supervisory positions. The manner in which this problem is approached will have a significant effect upon employee morale and loyalty. As stated above, some of these employees may be capable of obtaining positions in the new system. Others may be transferred to other departments within the organization. Since the period of preparation for installation will extend up to a year or more, the suspension of hiring when combined with the normal rate of attrition, which is generally high among clerical employees, may effect a partial solution to the problem of personnel displacement. For those employees who are nearing retirement age, the opportunity for early retirement can be provided. In those cases in which there appears to be no alternative to termination of an employee's services, the company should give a generous separation bonus and assistance in finding a comparable position in another organization.

A company's treatment of personnel displaced as a result of computer acquisition will affect the loyalty and morale not only of employees directly affected but of all employees throughout the organization. A company's actions in this regard will be interpreted as a reflection of its attitude toward its employees in general. The problem is even more serious as it relates to displaced supervisors, who may have given many years of loyal service to the company and will probably be most difficult to relocate in comparable positions. Careful planning and an attitude of social responsibility are requisites for the organization to successfully resolve these problems.

Personnel training   The task of training employees for their positions in the new system is one for which assistance from the vendor is usually available. Special classes in programming and computer operation are conducted by most computer manufacturers. Training of analysts and supervisory personnel must be much broader in perspective, with emphasis on orientation to the company's operations and policies as well as on technical factors. Personnel in areas of the organization outside of the computer activity should not be neglected in this process. Such personnel should be given orientation sessions designed to develop their understanding of the new system and what it can accomplish for them. Top- and middle-level managers should be encouraged to make requests for information and reports that would be useful to them and that could be made available under the new system.

Final systems design   The core of the implementation process is the detailed design of the new system. The preliminary systems design developed during the survey and analysis stage, as modified to obtain management approval, provides the starting point for the final systems design. For each application of the computer, the content and format of input, output, and file records must be established, and the relationships of individual record types within the overall data base must be specified. The flow of documents and reports within the organization must be modified to incorporate the role of the computer. Detailed document flowcharts and systems flowcharts are the primary design tool for this purpose.

The programming process is a major part of the final systems design. As outlined in Chapter 7, the steps in the programming process include preparation of program flowcharts and decision tables, coding the program modules, deskchecking the code listings, compiling the program modules, and correcting the programs for diagnostic messages indicating errors in program code. If the programs are being developed for a new computer system that has not yet been installed, the compilation and correction process will require the use of outside equipment, generally provided by the vendor. Another important part of the programming process is the compilation of final systems documentation in the form of a system reference manual for users, analysts, and programmers. Closely related to this is the preparation of operating documentation in the form of run manuals to assist computer operators in running the programs on the computer.

Also during the final systems design process, plans must be developed for the conversion to the new system. Training programs must be prepared. Plans for testing the new systems and programs must be established. A detailed conversion plan and schedule should be prepared. A processing schedule for the new system should be established. The necessary forms and supplies for the new system should be procured. These steps help to ensure a smooth conversion from the old system to the new one.

Testing   Before a newly designed system is implemented, it must be subjected to extensive testing to establish its logical correctness and consistency with design specifications. Documents and reports, processing procedures, computer programs, and other elements of the system should all be given a trial run in circumstances as realistic as possible. Three commonly used forms of testing are walkthroughs, processing of test transactions, and acceptance testing.

A *walkthrough* is a meeting at which a detailed review of system procedures or program logic is carried out in a step-by-step manner. Such a meeting may take place at any point in the systems design process. Walkthroughs during the early stages of systems design are generally attended by systems analysts, managers, and other system users, and deal with the contents of inputs, files, and outputs, and with data and information flows through the organization. Walkthroughs during the later stages of systems design are generally attended by programmers, and deal with the logic and structure of program code. To be most effective, walkthroughs should be scheduled to occur on a regular basis throughout the final systems design process.

The processing of test transactions is designed to check a program's response to all possible combinations of input and file data which it may encounter. Appropriate controls and routines for dealing with input errors and other unusual conditions should be incorporated into each program, and hypothetical test transactions and file records must be devised specifically to test their adequacy and completeness. For a large program consisting of several modules, each module is first tested independently, and then the program as a whole is tested. For each test transaction, the correct system response must be specified in advance in order to provide a basis for evaluation of the test results. Whenever the test results indicate that a significant change must be made in a program, the proposed change should be reviewed and approved by system users. As with program compilation, if the programs are being developed for a new computer system that has not yet been installed, then the program tests must be performed on outside equipment.

An *acceptance test* is a systems test in which test transactions and test acceptance criteria are developed by the system users, who also review the test results and decide whether the system is acceptable to them. Acceptance testing generally follows the processing of test transactions by the systems development team, and immediately proceeds the conversion process. Rather than using hypothetical transaction and file records, an acceptance test generally uses copies of real transaction and file records. Users may actually participate in such steps as preparing records for computer input, reviewing computer outputs, and processing computer generated documents. Any final decisions to accept the system or to require specific modifications are the responsibility of the users.

Establishment of standards and controls

An essential aspect of the final systems design phase of implementation is the establishment of job performance standards and control techniques and procedures for the new system. Often these factors are not considered until after the new system becomes operational, and this can lead to many unanticipated problems. Planning for assignment of job responsibilities must take internal control considerations into account. Job descriptions and work schedules should make provision for the execution of control procedures. Personnel selection should be affected by the performance standards attaching to each position to be filled. Documentation standards and data security provisions should be formulated. Error checks should be built into all computer software systems, and procedures must be developed to guide system operators or users in responding to various error conditions that may be identified by the system. A policy of continuous planning for and evaluation of the new system should be devised. The significance of these various factors is such that the next chapter is devoted entirely to an extensive treatment of them.

Site preparation

Once a specific equipment configuration has been selected, requirements for a site can be determined and work can begin on the selection and preparation of the site. A computer site should be located as centrally as possible to facilitate the frequent communication required between the computer activity and all other operations in the organization. Space will have to be provided not only for equipment and operators but also for storage of cards, tapes, and other supplies, and for the offices of analysts, programmers, and supervisors. The site should be laid out to facilitate efficient operation. The possibilty of future expansion of the system should also be considered in site selection and preparation.

Depending on the size of the equipment configuration being acquired, computer installation may require extensive physical changes in the location selected. A micro- or minicomputer may require very little in the way of physical site preparation, but a larger system may require additional electrical outlets, data communications facilities, lighting, and air conditioning. Security measures such as fire protection and emergency power supply may also be necessary. Some companies have constructed a separate building or an expansion of their existing building specifically to house their computer center. Thus site preparation can be quite costly, but it usually does not create major problems, such as those that may be encountered in connection with personnel adjustments and systems design. The vendor is usually able and willing to provide competent assistance in this task.

Conversion   One of the first major activities in the conversion phase of systems implementation is the conversion of master files from old to new system media. If the old system is a manual one, this process will be difficult and time-consuming. It will involve transcribing the data from each record on file to the new storage medium, which could be ledger cards, punched cards, magnetic tape, or magnetic disk. Care must be taken to ensure the reliability of the data converted. If the system conversion is from one computer system to another, the conversion of files from one computer data media to another generally will not be a significant problem.

If the program of preparation for installation has been adequately planned, the installation of the equipment should occur almost simultaneously with the completion of program testing, conversion of files, employee training, and site preparation. The next major activity during the period of conversion is *parallel operation* of new system and old system to provide a final test of the new system. Both systems will be operated on a full-time basis, and their output compared. Differences must be analyzed to determine their cause, and the new system should be modified appropriately.

The period of parallel operations is one of the most costly and demanding in the entire computer acquisition process. Most employees connected with the project will be required to work long hours of overtime to operate both systems, compare results, and make necessary adjustments. These factors argue for minimizing the length of this period. However, successful implementation will require extensive testing of the reliability of the new system, and this fact argues for a longer period of parallel operations. Generally, three or four parallel runs of each application are sufficient to eliminate most of the major problems in a newly designed system. Since some applications will be run daily, others weekly, others monthly, and so forth, the period of parallel operations will be very hectic for a month or two and then gradually wind down to final conversation after three or four months.

Many small organizations do not have the staff, or cannot afford the expense, for a full parallel operation. An alternative approach to final systems testing is called a *pilot operation*. This form of testing involves a sample of transactions. The sample may include historical records that have already been processed, or artificial transactions devised to test the system under various unusual conditions. The results of such tests would be compared with those previously generated by the manual system, or with those predetermined for artificial transactions. Because the volume of sample transactions is much smaller than regular processing volume, a pilot operation is less expensive and less time-consuming than parallel operation.

Follow up

After a new system has been in operation for a brief period, perhaps two to four months, the systems group should perform a follow-up analysis and appraisal of its performance. The analysis should be designed to reveal and correct any weaknesses in the new system that have become evident. The extent to which the new system is meeting its planned objectives should be evaluated. The adequacy of standards and controls to keep the system operating as expected should be assessed. Major differences between actual and expected performance should be brought to the attention of management, and necessary adjustments should be initiated. The system should be analyzed through observation and interviews with employees to discover weaknesses, which should then be corrected. Even after the system review study is complete, continuous attention should be given to the possibility of correcting weaknesses and improving the system.

PERT: A Project Scheduling Technique

The Program Evaluation and Review Technique is a useful management tool for planning, coordinating, and controlling large, complex projects such as computer implementation. The development and initial application of PERT was done in connection with the development of the Polaris submarine by the United States Navy in the late 1950s. PERT has since been used for many applications in business. An extensive discussion of PERT is presented here to develop an understanding of and appreciation for the usefulness of this analytical technique in systems implementation. According to one recent survey of systems management techniques, PERT was used in project planning in 39 percent of the systems projects included in the survey.[2]

PERT concepts and definitions

The PERT technique involves the diagrammatical representation of the sequence of activities comprising a project by means of a network consisting of arrows and nodes (see Fig. 13.2). Arrows in a PERT network represent "tasks" or "activities," which are distinct segments of the project requiring an expenditure of time and resources. Nodes in a network symbolize "events," or milestone points in the project representing the completion of one or more activities and/or the initiation of one or more subsequent activities.[3] An event is thus a point in time and does not consume any time in itself as does an activity.

The first step in applying PERT to project planning is to determine all of the individual tasks in the project that are separate and distinct from all other tasks. Then all of the immediate predecessor tasks must be established for each task. That is, if task A is the immediate predecessor of task B, then task A must be completed before task B is begun, and task B may be begun immediately upon completion of task A. Some tasks may have several immediate predecessors, and such a task may

---

[2] John H. Lehman, "How Software Projects Are Really Managed," Datamation *(January 1979): 124.*

[3] *In a variation of these conventions used by some PERT analysts, nodes represent activities and arrows represent the time sequence of activities.*

Activity	Time (days)	Predecessor activities
A	3	None
B	8	None
C	6	A
D	0	A
E	7	B,D
F	4	C

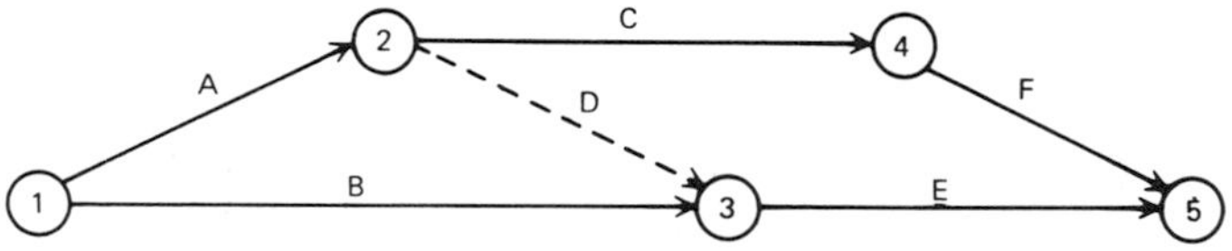

Fig. 13.2
A simple PERT network.

not be begun until all of its immediate predecessors have been completed. Once all of the activities in a project have been determined and their precedence relationships established, the PERT network can be drawn.

One of the primary aspects of the PERT technique is the analysis of the network in terms of the time required to complete each activity and the project as a whole. For each separate activity an estimate of completion time in hours, days, weeks, or months must be made. Once this is completed, the next step is to determine the network's *critical path,* the path of activities from beginning event to ending event that requires the greatest total expenditure of time. The sum of the estimated activity times for all activities on the critical path is the total time required to complete the project. These activities are "critical" because any delay in their completion will cause a delay in the project. Activities not on the critical path are not critical, since they will be worked on simultaneously with critical path activities and their completion could be delayed up to a point without delaying the project as a whole.

Consider the simple PERT network illustrated in Fig. 13.2. Note how the network itself is constructed from the precedence relationships shown in the figure. The example illustrates a common PERT convention—the labeling of activities with capital letters and of events with numbers. Also illustrated is a new concept, the "dummy activity," D, represented by the dashed arrow in the network. This activity is not really an activity at all in that it does not require any expenditure of time or resources. However, it is required in the network to show that activity A is an immediate predecessor of activity E. This relationship could not be represented by routing the arrow symbolizing activity A into the node preceding activity E because that would imply that activity B is an immediate predecessor of activity C, which is not true.

There is a total of only three paths through the network of Fig. 13.2. A comparison of the total time required for each of these paths reveals that the path consisting of activities B and E requires the greatest total expenditure of time, fifteen days, and is therefore the critical path. The paths consisting of activities A, D, E, and of A, C, F require a total of ten and thirteen days, respectively. Activities not on the critical path can be delayed without delaying the project, and are thus said to have a quantity of *slack time*. Because any delay in a critical path activity will delay the project as a whole (in this case beyond fifteen days), critical path activities have zero slack time. A procedure for calculating the quantity of slack time for all activities not on the critical path will be presented shortly.

Most projects to which PERT is applied are sufficiently complex that the total number of paths through the network will be quite large. Thus a more efficient procedure for finding the critical path must be used than complete enumeration of all paths. The first step in such a procedure is to find the earliest completion time for each activity and event in the network, proceeding in sequence from early events to later events, or from left to right in the network itself. The earliest completion time for an event is the greatest of the earliest completion times of all activities immediately preceding the event. The earliest completion time for an activity is the sum of the estimated time for the activity and the earliest completion time of its predecessor event. The earliest completion time for the final network event is the total required project completion time.

In terms of the illustration of Fig. 13.2, the earliest completion time for activity A and event 2 is three days, and for activity B is eight days. For event 3 the earliest completion time is the greater of the earliest completion times of the two activities preceding it, namely B and D. The earliest completion time for activity D is the zero days for the activity itself plus the three days earliest completion time for its predecessor event 2, or three days. This is less than the eight days earliest completion time for activity B, which indicates that the earliest completion time for event 3 is eight days.[4] Extending this analysis, we find that the earliest completion time for activity C and event 4 is six plus three, or nine days. The earliest completion time for activity F is thirteen days, and for activity E is fifteen days. Therefore the earliest completion time for event 5 and for the project as a whole is fifteen days.

The next step in the procedure for finding the critical path is to find the latest time that each activity could be completed without delaying the project beyond the total required time already determined. For activities terminating at the ending project event, the latest time is equal to the total required project time. Determination of the latest time for other activities in a network can be done most easily by starting with activities near the end of the network and proceeding from right to left to activities at the beginning of the network. The latest time for an event and for all activities leading into that event is equal to the smallest of the remainders obtained by subtracting the activity time for each activity starting at the event from the latest time for the activity. Figure 13.2 shows that the latest time for activities E and F is fifteen days. The latest time for event 4, and therefore for activity C, is fifteen minus four, or eleven days. The latest time for event 3, and therefore for activities B and D, is fifteen minus seven, or eight days. To determine the latest time for activity A, the

---

[4] *This point is often confusing to students, who point out that the quickest path to event 3 is the path consisting of activities A and D that takes only three days. To eliminate this misconception note that* all *of the activities in the network, including A, B, and D, must be performed, and event 3 represents the completion of* both *activities B and D.*

comparison mentioned above must be made. The latest time for activity C minus the activity time of C is eleven minus six, or five days. The latest time for activity D minus the activity time of D is eight minus zero, or eight days. The smaller of these two figures, five days, is the latest completion time for event 2 and activity A.

Continuing the procedure, the next step is to calculate the slack time for each activity. An activity's slack time will be equal to its latest completion time minus its earliest completion time. The earliest, latest, and slack times for all activities in the sample problem are summarized in Fig. 13.3. Critical path activities are identified by the slack time calculation. All activities revealed by this calculation to have zero slack time are critical path activities. Note that it is possible for a network to have more than one critical path. For example, if the time required for activity A in this illustration had been five days instead of three, the path containing activities A, C, and F would also have been a critical path.

Knowledge of which activities in a project are critical is extremely useful to management for planning and control purposes. There is usually ample reason for management to desire to complete a project as quickly as possible. A major reason is that while resources such as staff and equipment are at work at one job, they cannot be put to work on other jobs. Waste and inefficiency in resource utilization can be very expensive in terms of revenue lost (sometimes called opportunity cost). The faster one project can be completed, the faster the resources used on it can be transferred to other revenue-producing activities.

For planning and control purposes, a critical path activity is obviously one requiring a maximum of management attention if the total project completion time is to be minimized. Such activities should be monitored very closely to ensure that delays in their completion will be rendered unlikely. On the other hand, activities not on the critical path require less management attention and monitoring. The larger the slack time for an activity, the less closely it needs to be monitored.

The PERT technique is useful not only at the beginning of a project but also throughout the entire period during which the project is being worked on. As individual activities are completed, their estimated completion times can be replaced in the network by their actual completion times. This adjustment may cause the critical path itself to change, and so the slack time for all activities needs to be continually recalculated to provide a basis for dynamic project control. As work on the project proceeds, a measure should be maintained of how much ahead or behind schedule the project is. If the project is behind schedule, the network can be used to determine which activities are the best candidates for an effort at acceleration of completion times. Thus PERT can be a useful management tool during the entire period of project execution.

Activity	Earliest time	Latest time	Slack time
A	3	5	2
B	8	8	0
C	9	11	2
D	3	8	5
E	15	15	0
F	13	15	2

Fig. 13.3
Solution data for
sample problem.

Activity	Time (weeks)	Predecessor activities	Activity description
A	36	None	Physical preparation (including vendor lead time)
B	4	None	Organizational planning
C	2	B	Personnel selection
D	2	A	Equipment installation
E	10	C	Personnel training
F	15	C	Detailed systems design
G	9	F	File conversion
H	4	F	Establish standards and controls
I	9	H	Program preparation
J	9	I	Program testing
K	20	D,E,G,J	Parallel operations
L	8	I	Finalize system documentation
M	20	K,L	Follow-up

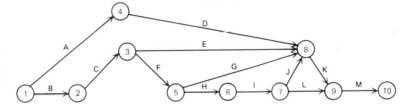

Fig. 13.4
PERT network of the computer implementation process.

PERT applied to computer implementation

Figure 13.4 provides an illustration of a PERT network representing the activities involved in implementing a computer system. The activity times shown in the illustration correspond to those required for a medium- to large-scale installation. A smaller-size installation might require less time, whereas a very large installation might require more time, but the activities and precedence relationships represented by the network itself are applicable to any computer implementation project.

For review purposes, the reader should verify that the critical path for this network consists of activities B, C, F, H, I, J, K, and M, that the total required project time is 83 weeks, and that the slack time for activities A, D, E, G, and L are 5, 5, 27, 13, and 21 weeks, respectively.

Other applications of PERT

PERT generally is useful to the administration of complex projects of a nonroutine or nonrecurring nature. For an operation which is routine or repetitive, such as mass production, a great deal of past experience is generally available for planning and control purposes. PERT is of little use in such a situation. Some of the most common and successful applications of PERT have been to research and development activities, construction projects, and the marketing of new products.

PERT with uncertain time estimates

In a real-world application of PERT to a complex project, the estimates of completion times for activities will seldom be certain. To cope with the uncertainty in activity time estimates, the application of PERT in practice usually proceeds by estimating three possible duration times for each activity. These are a most optimistic estimate of required time (labeled a), a most likely estimate (m), and a most pessimistic estimate (b). A weighted average of these three time estimates is then calculated to establish the "expected completion time" for the activity. The weighted average formula applies a weight of one to both the most optimistic and the most pessimistic estimates and a weight of four to the most likely estimate. The formula is thus as follows.

$$\text{Expected time} = \frac{a + 4m + b}{6}.$$

The expected completion time may be looked upon as an average or mean figure. This formula has nothing in the nature of a theoretical proof to support it, but in actual applications it has been proven to provide time estimates accurate enough to be more useful than the single-valued estimate, which often turns out to be too low.

A measure of the relative dispersion of completion time around the expected completion time for an activity is the standard deviation. A formula for computing the standard deviation of completion time for an activity from the estimates of most optimistic and most pessimistic time as follows.

$$\text{Standard deviation (activity)} = \frac{b - a}{6}.$$

Again this formula has no theoretical justification, but has been proven in practice to provide a reasonably accurate measure of dispersion.

When expected activity times and their standard deviations are computed in this manner, the PERT network is solved using the expected activity times. The total required project time obtained is thus an expected or mean time. Therefore the probability that the project will be completed within this expected total time is exactly 0.5 or one half. The standard deviation of total project time around this mean expected time is computed using the following formula:

$$\text{Standard deviation (project)} = \sqrt{\begin{array}{l}\text{the sum of the squares of}\\ \text{the standard deviations of}\\ \text{all critical path activities.}\end{array}}$$

Using this standard deviation and a table of areas under the normal curve, the probability of completing the project within any given time period can be determined.

PERT under uncertainty: an example

Consider the PERT network shown in Fig. 13.5. Estimates of most optimistic, most likely, and most pessimistic completion times in days for each activity are given. In addition, both the expected completion time and standard deviation for each activity have been computed according to the above formulas and are also included in the illustration. The reader should verify the accuracy of these calculations, and should verify also that the critical path consists of activities A, D, and G with a total expected project completion time of 23 days.

Calculation of the standard deviation of completion time for the project as a whole according to the formula is as follows.

$$\begin{aligned}\text{Standard deviation (project)} &= \sqrt{2^2 + 2^2 + 1^2}\\ &= \sqrt{9}\\ &= 3.\end{aligned}$$

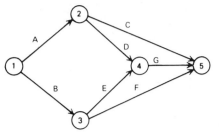

Activity	A	B	C	D	E	F	G
Most optimistic time	6	5	4	4	4	4	2
Most likely time	9	8	7	7	7	10	5
Most pessimistic time	18	17	22	16	10	22	8
Expected time	10	9	9	8	7	11	5
Standard deviation	2	2	3	2	1	3	1

Fig. 13.5

Sample PERT network with related time data.

The usefulness of this approach stems from the determination of the probability of getting the project finished within some specified time period. For example, suppose we want to know the probability of completing the project in 27 days or less. The first step is to compute z, which is the number of standard deviations from the mean represented by our given time of 27 days. If we label the given time G.T., the mean expected time E.T., and the project standard deviation S.D., the formula for z is as follows.

$$z = \frac{G.T. - E.T.}{S.D.}.$$

For 27 days, z is computed as follows in this example.

$$z = \frac{27 - 23}{3} = 1.3.$$

The next step in this analysis is to find the probability associated with the calculated value of z by referring to a table of areas under the normal curve such as that shown in Fig. 13.6. In the example, a z of 1.3 corresponds to a probability of .90320. This is interpreted to mean that the probability of completing the project within 27 days or less is .90320. For review purposes the reader may wish to verify that the probabilities of getting the project done within 17, 20, and 29 days are .02275, .15866, and .97725, respectively.

Knowledge of the probabilities associated with various possible values of project completion time may be very valuable to management for planning purposes. It allows management to judge the probable length of time for which the resources required for the project will be tied up at work on the project and therefore unavailable for other useful work. If management can also estimate the cost per day of utilization of the resources, the probability of various total costs for the project can be determined. For example, if the cost per day of the resources required for the sample problem of Fig. 13.5 is $1000, then the probability that the total resource cost for the project will be $23,000 or less is 0.5; that it will be $27,000 or less is .90320; and so on. If the project represents something for which a contract price is being negotiated, information of this sort would obviously be very valuable to management.

z = Number of standard deviations from the mean

P = Probability that the actual value of the variable will be z or less.

z	P	z	P	z	P
−3.0	.00135			1.0	.84134
−2.9	.00187	−0.9	.18406	1.1	.86433
−2.8	.00256	−0.8	.21186	1.2	.88493
−2.7	.00347	−0.7	.24196	1.3	.90320
−2.6	.00466	−0.6	.27425	1.4	.91924
−2.5	.00621	−0.5	.30854	1.5	.93319
−2.4	.00820	−0.4	.34458	1.6	.94520
−2.3	.01072	−0.3	.38209	1.7	.95543
−2.2	.01390	−0.2	.42074	1.8	.96407
−2.1	.01786	−0.1	.46017	1.9	.97128
−2.0	.02275	0.0	.50000	2.0	.97725
−1.9	.02872	0.1	.53983	2.1	.98214
−1.8	.03593	0.2	.57926	2.2	.98610
−1.7	.04457	0.3	.61791	2.3	.98928
−1.6	.05480	0.4	.65542	2.4	.99180
−1.5	.06681	0.5	.69146	2.5	.99379
−1.4	.08076	0.6	.72575	2.6	.99534
−1.3	.09680	0.7	.75804	2.7	.99653
−1.2	.11507	0.8	.78814	2.8	.99744
−1.1	.13567	0.9	.81594	2.9	.99813
−1.0	.15866			3.0	.99865

Fig. 13.6
Probabilities associated with values of z or less under the normal curve.

The Critical Path Method

It is also possible to introduce cost considerations into a PERT analysis in another way. For example, it may be possible to reduce the completion time of one or more activities by accelerating the work effort on the activity. However, it is likely that such accelerated effort will require an extra expenditure of cost, such as that required for overtime pay for employees. Thus the benefit from reducing the total completion time of a project by accelerated efforts on certain activities must be balanced against the extra cost of doing so. A related problem is to determine which activities must be accelerated to reduce the total project completion time. This form of analysis is referred to as the Critical Path Method (CPM). Though worthy of mention, CPM will not be illustrated here.[5]

Review Questions

1. Define the following terms.

PERT   parallel operation
Gantt chart   pilot operation
walkthrough   critical path
acceptance test   slack time

2. What basic change of emphasis takes place in a systems investigation when work on implementation begins?

[5] *For a presentation of CPM, see Jerome D. Wiest and Ferdinand K. Levy,* A Management Guide to PERT/CPM *(2nd ed.). Englewood Cliffs, N.J.: Prentice-Hall, 1977, Chapter 5.*

3. List several categories of activities commonly performed as part of a systems implementation project.

4. Describe some of the planning and scheduling considerations important to systems implementation.

5. Explain the concept of implementation risk analysis.

6. Describe in detail the activities in the area of personnel and organizational adjustment that should be performed by a company preparing for computer installation.

7. What steps should a company take to cope with problems of employee morale that may arise when plans to acquire a computer become known to employees?

8. Describe in some detail the major activities in the final systems design phase of preparation for computer installation.

9. Identify and describe three commonly used forms of systems testing.

10. Describe several factors that should be taken into account during systems implementation with respect to the establishment of standards and controls for the new system.

11. Describe in some detail the process of preparing a site for the physical location of a computer system in a business organization.

12. Outline and describe the major activities in a company during the conversion phase of computer implementation.

13. Explain what is meant by parallel operation and pilot operation. Compare and contrast these two concepts.

14. What are the major considerations in the decision of how long the period of parallel operations should be? What is the usual length of this period?

15. Describe the process of the follow-up review to a systems investigation.

16. What do the arrows and nodes in a PERT network signify?

17. What is a "dummy activity" in a PERT network, and why is it sometimes necessary for networks to contain such activities?

18. Explain how PERT is useful to management planning and control of large complex projects.

19. List four common applications of PERT in business.

20. Explain how cost considerations might be introduced into an analysis using PERT.

Discussion Questions

21. Modeling techniques such as PERT are often based upon assumptions or estimates which are frequently inaccurate. Discuss the implications of this observation for the usefulness of such techniques.

22. Assume that you are a systems consultant advising a firm's management on implementation of a new computer system. Management has decided not to retain several employees after the system is implemented. Some of these employees have many years of service to the firm. How would you advise management to communicate this decision to its employees?

Activity	A	B	C	D	E	F	G	H
Activity time	6	3	5	4	3	7	4	6
Predecessors	none	none	B	A,C	A,C	B	D	E,F

Figure 13.7

Problems and Cases

Required

23. Given in Fig. 13.7 are a set of activities, single activity time estimates, and precedence relationships for a project.

    a) Construct a PERT network for this project.

    b) Determine the critical path and the total completion time for the project.

    c) For each activity, determine the earliest completion time, the latest completion time, and the slack time.

24. Shown in Fig. 13.8 is a list of project activities accompanied by the scheduled starting time and completion time of each activity.

Required

    a) Using a format similar to that illustrated in Fig. 13.1, prepare a Gantt chart for this project.

    b) Assume that it is February 16, and activities A and B have been completed, activity C is half completed, activity F is 25 percent completed, and the other activities have not yet commenced. Record this information on your Gantt chart. Is the project behind schedule, on schedule, or ahead of schedule? Explain.

    c) Note that the project parameters given for this problem are identical to those given in problem 23. Discuss the relative merits of the Gantt chart and the PERT technique as tools for project planning and control.

25. A construction company has contracted to complete a new building and has asked for assistance in analyzing the project. Using the Program Evaluation and Review Technique (PERT), the network in Fig. 13.9 has been developed.[6]

    All paths from the start point to the finish point, event 6, represent activities or processes that must be completed before the entire project, the building, will be completed. The numbers above the paths or line segments represent expected completion times for the activities or processes. The expected time is based upon the commonly used, 1-4-1, three-estimate method. For example, the three-estimate method gives an estimated time of 4.2 to complete event 1.

Required

    a) The critical path (the path requiring the greatest amount of time) is

       (1) 1-2-5-6

       (2) 1-2-3-4-6

       (3) 1-3-4-6

       (4) 1-7-8-6

       (5) 1-9-6

[6] *Question 5, Item A, Accounting Practice Section, Part I, American Institute of Certified Public Accountants Examination, May 1971. Material from the Uniform CPA Examinations, copyright © 1971 by the American Institute of Certified Public Accountants, is reprinted with permission.*

Activity	Starting date, Monday, week of:	Ending date, Friday, week of:
A	Jan. 5	Feb. 9
B	Jan. 5	Jan. 19
C	Jan. 26	Feb. 23
D	Mar. 2	Mar. 23
E	Mar. 2	Mar. 16
F	Feb. 2	Mar. 16
G	Mar. 30	Apr. 20
H	Mar. 23	Apr. 27

Figure 13.8

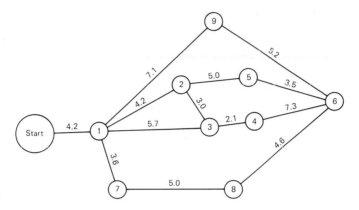

Figure 13.9

b) Slack time on path 1–9–6 equals
   (1) 4.3
   (2) 2.8
   (3) .9
   (4) .4
   (5) 0

c) The latest time for reaching event 6 via path 1–2–5–6 is
   (1) 20.8
   (2) 19.3
   (3) 17.4
   (4) 16.5
   (5) 12.7

d) The earliest time for reaching event 6 via path 1–2–5–6 is
   (1) 20.8
   (2) 16.9
   (3) 16.5
   (4) 12.7
   (5)   3.5

e) If all other paths are operating on schedule but path segment 7–8 has unfavorable time variance of 1.9,
  (1) the critical path will be shortened.
  (2) the critical path will be eliminated.
  (3) the critical path will be unaffected.
  (4) another path will become the critical path.
  (5) the critical path will have an increased time of 1.9.

26. Shown in Fig. 13.10 is a PERT network and a related set of activity time estimates, in weeks.

Required

a) Determine the expected completion time of each activity.
b) Determine the earliest expected completion time, latest expected completion time, and slack time of each activity.
c) What is the total project completion time, and what activities are on the critical path?
d) Determine the standard deviation of expected completion time for only those activities on the critical path.
e) Determine the standard deviation of expected completion time for the project.
f) Determine the probability that the project will be completed within (1) 41 weeks, (2) 47 weeks, (3) 50 weeks, (4) 59 weeks.

27. Refer to the PERT network of the computer implementation process in Fig. 13.4. Using *months* as the basic unit of time, prepare a Gantt chart for the project represented in the figure. Assume that each activity is scheduled to begin immediately following the scheduled completion of any predecessor activities. Also, to simplify your analysis you may assume that four weeks = one month.

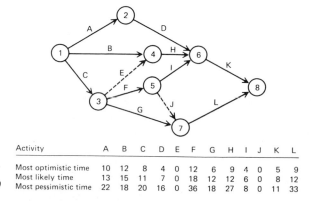

Activity	A	B	C	D	E	F	G	H	I	J	K	L
Most optimistic time	10	12	8	4	0	12	6	9	4	0	5	9
Most likely time	13	15	11	7	0	18	12	12	6	0	8	12
Most pessimistic time	22	18	20	16	0	36	18	27	8	0	11	33

Figure 13.10

28. Benjamin and Watson Enterprises has decided to acquire a new computer system, and is presently entering a twelve-month implementation period. A schedule of activities for this period follows.

Beginning of:	Activity:
Month 1	A Data Processing Manager-Programmer is hired. That person is responsible for final systems design and program flowcharting.
Month 5	A Programmer is hired. The coding process is begun.
Month 6	A Keypunch Operations Supervisor is hired and immediately assumes responsibility for keypunching the programs.
Month 7	Program testing is begun, which requires rental of outside facilities. The rental contract with the company renting the building selected as the computer site is terminated. The remodeling of this site in preparation for installation is begun.
Month 10	Two keypunch operators are hired. The file conversion process begins.
Month 11	Site remodeling, program testing, and file conversion are completed. The computer is installed and two computer operators are hired. Parallel operation begins.
Month 13	Parallel operation is completed and final changeover to the new system is achieved.

The monthly costs attached to these various implementation activities include the following.

Salaries	
Data Processing Manager-Programmer	$1800
Programmer	1200
Keypunch Operations Supervisor	800
Keypunch Operator	600
Computer Operator	800
Overtime during parallel operation	1500
Rental of time for program testing	300
Remodeling of site	800
Computer rental	4000
Miscellaneous overhead after system is installed	500

In addition, the future site of the computer is presently being rented out at $600 per month.

Required Prepare an implementation cost schedule for the twelve-month implementation period. Show each cost as a one-line item, and show the total cost incurred during each of the twelve months. Also show the total cumulative cost as of the end of each month.

29. Shaky Construction Company has an opportunity to submit a bid for the construction of a new apartment building. From specifications provided by the developer, a PERT network for the project has been developed, and is shown

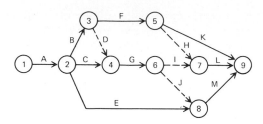

Activity	a	m	b	Activity description
A	5	8	17	Excavate basement
B	5	8	11	Build concrete elevator tower
C	3	5	7	Pour concrete foundation
D	0	0	0	Dummy activity
E	6	9	18	Excavate parking ramp area
F	5	8	17	Install temporary manual elevator
G	5	7	12	Erect main building
H	0	0	0	Dummy activity
I	0	0	0	Dummy activity
J	0	0	0	Dummy activity
K	4	7	10	Install automatic elevator
L	7	10	31	Complete interior work
M	4	6	11	Erect parking ramp

Figure 13.11

in Fig. 13.11. Also shown for each activity are estimates of most optimistic, most likely, and most pessimistic completion times in weeks (*a, m,* and *b,* respectively).

Required

a) Compute the expected completion time for all activities in the project.

b) Determine the network critical path and the total expected completion time for the project.

c) Determine the standard deviation of completion time for the project.

d) Shaky's management policy with respect to submitting bids is to bid the minimum amount which will provide a 92 percent probability of at least breaking even. Materials for this project will cost $900,000 and all other costs will vary at a rate of $10,000 per week for every week spent working on the project. What amount should be bid under this policy?

e) Assume that Shaky's bid was accepted and that the project has been in progress for 20 weeks. Activities A, B, and C have been completed. Activities E, F, and G are in progress, with the estimates in Fig. 13.12 made of time required to complete them.

No change has been made in the time estimates for activities K, L, and M. Draw a revised PERT network representing the remainder of the project (excluding completed activities). Determine the critical path for the remainder of the project and the remaining project completion time.

Activity	a	m	b
E	1	2	3
F	3	5	10
G	3	6	9

Figure 13.12

References   Alter, Steven L. *Decision Support Systems: Current Practice and Continuing Challenges.* Reading, Mass.: Addison-Wesley, 1980.

Donaldson, Hamish. *A Guide to the Successful Management of Computer Projects.* New York: Halsted, 1978.

Kotter, John P., and Leonard A. Schlesinger. "Choosing Strategies for Change," *Harvard Business Review* (March/April 1979): 106–114.

Lehman, John H. "How Software Projects Are Really Managed," *Datamation* (January 1979): 119–129.

Lucas, Henry C. "Unsuccessful Implementation: The Case of a Computer-Based Order Entry System," *Decision Sciences* (January 1978): 68–79.

Metzger, Philip W. *Managing a Programming Project.* Englewood Cliffs, N.J.: Prentice-Hall, 1973.

Powers, Richard F., and Gary W. Dickson. "MIS Project Management: Myths, Opinions, and Reality," *California Management Review* (Spring 1973): 147–156.

Shaw, John C., and William Atkins. *Managing Computer System Projects.* New York: McGraw-Hill, 1970.

Szweda, Ralph A. *Information Processing Management.* Princeton: Auerbach, 1972.

Wiest, Jerome D., and Ferdinand K. Levy. *A Management Guide to PERT/CPM* (2nd ed.) Englewood Cliffs, N.J.: Prentice-Hall, 1977.

Chapter 14

Internal Control in Computer-Based Information Systems

In Chapter 4 we discussed general concepts of internal control, and illustrated their application to manual data processing operations. Now that we have developed a more complete understanding of computer data processing, and of the planning and development of computer-based information systems, it is appropriate to consider the application of internal control concepts in organizations using a computer-based information system. The importance of an understanding of internal control in computer-based information systems is underscored by the following conclusion from a recent survey of internal control in American corporations.

> *The aspect of internal control that troubles executives most, and which we consider to be most serious, is the increasing dependence of companies on computers for operational effectiveness and for financial reporting. Technological progress in data processing has greatly increased a number of internal control risks, and these are compounded by a substantial shortage in adequately trained data processing and internal audit personnel.* [1]

In short, the widespread use of computers to support operating functions and to process accounting data in modern corporations has led many authorities to question the adequacy of internal control systems in these corporations.

---

[1] *Robert K. Mautz, Walter G. Kell, Michael W. Maher, Alan G. Merten, Raymond R. Reilly, Dennis G. Severance, and Bernard J. White,* Internal Control in U. S. Corporations: The State of the Art. *New York: Financial Executives Research Foundation, 1980, p. 8.*

According to the Auditing Standards Executive Committee of the American Institute of CPAs,

The objectives and the essential characteristics of accounting control do not change with the method of data processing. However, organization and control procedures used in electronic data processing may differ from those used in manual or mechanical data processing. [2]

This chapter covers a variety of internal control policies, procedures, and techniques relating to computer-based information systems. However, the reader should note that these specific controls are invariably based upon general control concepts such as responsibility accounting, organizational independence, internal check, and numerous others.

The chapter is divided into four major sections. In the first are discussed both the internal organization of a typical computer data processing facility and the control considerations relevant to the design of this organization structure. In the second are discussed management control policies and procedures relating to computer personnel, computer operations activities, and the systems development process. The third section describes a variety of control standards and policies applicable to the operation of a computer facility. Control procedures and techniques involved in the actual processing of data on a computer system are explained in the fourth and last section.

Organization of the Information Systems Function

There are two basic subdivisions of the information systems function. One is the operations activity, which is concerned with the day-to-day processing of data on the computer system. The other is the systems activity, which involves the development and maintenance of the computer software, particularly application programs, but also including utility routines, data management systems, and the operating system as well. Within these broad areas are found a number of more specific functions, typically allocated among several departments.

This section is divided into two parts. In the first are described the roles and responsibilities of the various departments or individuals within the information systems organization structure. The second focuses on the internal control considerations relevant to the allocation of those responsibilities.

Information systems responsibilities

Figure 14.1 provides an illustration of a typical organization structure for the information systems function in a larger company. Of course the exact allocation of responsibilities within the systems function will vary from one organization to another, depending on specific needs and circumstances. Therefore, this chart is not intended to represent a prescription for systems organization in all companies but

[2] *Auditing Standards Executive Committee, American Institute of Certified Public Accountants.* The Effects of EDP on the Auditor's Study and Evaluation of Internal Control, *Statement on Auditing Standards 3. New York: American Institute of Certified Public Accountants, Inc., 1974, p. 4.*

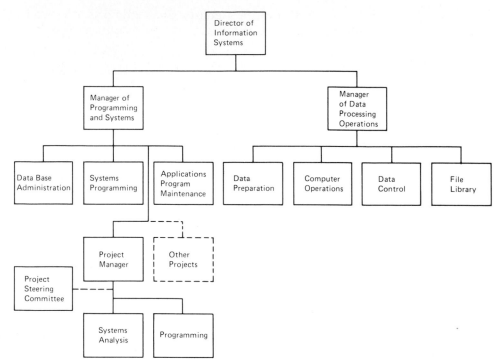

Fig. 14.1
Organization of the
information systems
function.

instead is merely an example consistent with organizational patterns found in many companies that can serve as a vehicle for discussion.

As discussed in Chapter 10, the top executive of the information systems function may or may not be a vice-president having equal status with other top-level executives in the organization. The position as a member of top management affords participation in setting objectives for the organization, in long-range planning to meet objectives, in establishing broad policies for the organization, and in top-management decision making. One of the primary contributions to these activities is his or her ability to articulate the extent to which the information system can contribute to the achievement of plans and objectives and the execution of policies and decisions. The position also allows the encouragement of the profitable use of the information system in all other functional areas of the organization.

Regardless of whether the top computer executive has the status of vice-president, he or she must perform the role of manager of the systems activity, whose responsibilities include the development of profitable new applications and the efficient processing of existing applications. He or she is accountable for the costs associated with the equipment and personnel required for the system, and is responsible for maintaining a modern, up-to-date facility that takes maximum advantage of new technological developments. Such responsibilities require a good combination of administrative skills and technical competence.

The Manager of Programming and Systems is responsible for managing the development of new information systems applications and for the maintenance and improvement of existing programs and data bases. He or she must establish and enforce standards for systems design, programming, and system documentation. The manager is responsible for planning and controlling the implementation of new systems applications, and is accountable for the costs and progress of systems development efforts. Responsible to him or her are specialists in data base administration, systems programming and applications program maintenance as well as managers of various systems development projects.

The data base administration function is responsible for the design and control of the organization's data bases. The data base administrator must establish the appropriate content and format of data records, the structure of data relationships, the appropriate data names and key fields. He or she controls and monitors data base usage through the assignment of user passwords and the collection of statistics on utilization of data and programs, and also is concerned with efficient use of physical data storage equipment. The data base administrator must maintain a close liaison with system users, providing documentation and other aids to the effective use of data base systems.

The systems programming group is responsible for the effective functioning of the operating system, utility routines, compilers, data base management systems, and other software. They also provide technical support to the data base administrator and to applications programmers on matters relating to the systems software. Another systems programming responsibility is the implementation of enhancements to the systems software to improve the efficiency of operation of the computer system.

Applications program maintenance personnel are responsible for the design, development, programming, and testing of modifications and extensions to existing application programs. The program maintenance function is described briefly in Chapter 7. In some organizations this activity actually consumes more effort than the development of new application programs.

Project managers direct a group of analysts and programmers in the process of designing and implementing new systems applications. They are responsible for planning, administering, and controlling all phases of the development effort for a specific project. As discussed in Chapter 10, a project steering committee consisting of users, management representatives, and senior systems personnel should be appointed to provide guidance to the project manager during this process. As indicated on the chart, there will often be more than one project under development in an organization at any given time.

The systems analysis function involves the design of computer applications to satisfy user needs in an organization. The position of systems analyst requires both experience in systems design and familiarity with the operations of the organization, for this person must serve to bridge the gap between the user and the technology of the computer system. The programming function involves converting the designs of the analyst into a set of computer instructions. Programming is generally regarded as a lower-level position than systems analysis because the position does not require the same degree of familiarity with the organization's operations. The specific steps involved in the programming process are described in Chapter 7.

The Manager of Data Processing Operations is responsible to the top computer executive for the day-to-day performance of data processing operations. Once new systems designs have been fully implemented, their successful execution becomes the responsibility of this department. As shown, a common pattern of division of responsibilities within this department involves separation among the functions of (1) data preparation, (2) computer operations, (3) file custodianship, and (4) data control.

The data preparation function involves the preparation and verification of source data for computer processing. Depending on the type of data input used, this may involve keypunching, key-to-tape encoding, key-to-disk equipment, or online data terminals. This function may also include the operation of peripheral equipment such as sorters, remote job entry devices, or data communications equipment.

The computer operations function actually runs the computer and its related input, output, and storage devices. Included are such activities as loading card decks, mounting tapes and disk packs, and monitoring and responding to console messages. In a multiprogramming environment in which several programs may be running simultaneously, the computer operator's job is dynamic and exacting.

The data control function maintains a record of all work in process, monitors the flow of work within and through the processing department, and distributes systems output upon completion of processing. The data control group is also responsible for checking the accuracy of input and output against preestablished control totals, for ensuring that established control procedures are adhered to during processing operations, and for following up on errors identified by computer editing and validation programs.

The file librarian function is responsible for maintaining a separate storage area, the file library, for control of files and programs stored on cards, magnetic tape, or disk packs. The file librarian should maintain an inventory of all files and programs in the library, and should keep a record of files and program copies checked out for use by other systems personnel.

In many computer installations there are additional functional specializations not mentioned here, such as data communications specialists, operations research personnel, scheduling personnel, a planning director, and training specialists. On the other hand, in a small installation many of the functions shown in Fig. 14.1 might be combined. Some perspective on the relative proportions of employees in these various functional specialties is provided by a recent survey of 131 large computer sites. According to this survey, the typical large company employs about 250 people in its computer facility, including 17.1 percent in data entry, 23.1 percent in computer operations, 12 percent in systems analysis, 22.3 percent in programming, 6.7 percent in systems programming, 4.8 percent in management, and the remaining

14 percent in other support functions.[3] Furthermore, the basic separation of systems development and maintenance from data processing operations was found in virtually all of the computer sites surveyed.

Organizational independence within the systems function

The effective achievement of organizational independence in a computer-based information system requires a clear division of authority and responsibility among the following functions: (1) systems analysis and programming, (2) computer operations, (3) file library, and (4) data control. The most critical separation is that between systems analysis and programming on the one hand and operations personnel on the other. As pointed out by the Auditing Standards Executive Committee,

> *Frequently, functions that would be considered incompatible if performed by a single individual in a manual activity are performed through the use of an EDP program or series of programs. A person having the opportunity to make unapproved changes to any such programs performs incompatible functions in relation to the EDP activity.[4]*

According to this description, a programmer or systems analyst who was permitted to operate the computer, or a computer operator who had unrestricted access to program copies and detailed documentation, performs incompatible functions. Organizational independence thus requires that programmers and analysts not have access to the computer room, and that operators have access to programs and documentation only when authorized and supervised.

Separation of the analysis and programming function from other functions should be accompanied by a policy of formal authorization for necessary program changes. A written description of such changes and the reasons for them should be submitted to the data processing manager, chief analyst, or some other person in a position of authority, whose authorization should be required prior to testing such changes, and whose approval of test results should be required prior to final implementation of program changes. Complete documentation of all program changes should be retained.

The computer operations function is particularly sensitive from a control standpoint and thus requires additional controls. Close and effective supervision of the operations activity is one such control. Another is a policy of rotation of operations personnel among jobs and shifts in order to avoid having any single operator who always processes the same job. Still another useful control procedure is a requirement that a minimum of two qualified personnel be on duty in the computer room during all processing. In addition, a copy of the printout from the computer console should be maintained as a record of processing. This console log should be reviewed

---

[3] *From a study conducted by International Data Corp., as reported in Bruce P. Hoard, "Division of 250 Employees Found Typical MIS Profile,"* Computerworld *(August 25, 1980): 4.*

[4] *Auditing Standards Executive Committee, op. cit., p. 5.*

periodically for any evidence of irregularity in connection with manual intervention by the operator during regular processing.

The Auditing Standards Executive Committee also stresses the importance of effective library control over data files: "A person in a position to make unapproved changes in EDP data files performs incompatible functions."[5] Separation of the file librarian function accomplishes this control by limiting all access to data files except by authorized personnel under authorized conditions. The file librarian also keeps a record of all such usage, and this record should be periodically reviewed for evidence of unusual circumstances.

For organizations large enough to afford a greater degree of specialization, the separate data control function provides an additional measure of organizational independence. The presence of data control personnel further inhibits the possibility of unauthorized access to the computer facility, provides an additional element of supervision of computer operations personnel, and contributes to more efficient data processing operations.

For micro- or minicomputer installations too small for separation of functions to be practical, other elements of internal control should be stressed in order to compensate for the potential control deficiencies. These compensating controls include restrictions on physical access to the equipment; the use of locks and keys on the machine itself; greater emphasis on user participation in such internal control procedures as transaction authorization, batch total checks, and output reviews; automatic preparation of a transaction log for review by management; sound personnel practices, including bonding of key data processing personnel; and software controls relating to online access and data entry.[6]

Management Control of the Information Systems Function

The folklore of the computer industry includes numerous stories of poorly run computer facilities, systems projects whose completion time and cost requirements far exceed expectations, and even some projects which were never successfully implemented after consuming millions of dollars worth of developmental effort. To a great extent situations of this type represent failures of management control. The basic principles of responsibility accounting are directly relevant to the information systems function. The effective application of these principles, by means of documenting personnel activities and reporting on the performance of systems staff personnel and managers, greatly reduces the possibility of major cost overruns or spectacular project failures, and substantially improves the efficiency and effectiveness of the information systems function.

---

[5] *Auditing Standards Executive Committee, p. 5.*

[6] *For a look at this issue in greater depth, see Harry Zimmerman, "Minicomputers: The Challenge for Controls,"* The Journal of Accountancy *(June 1980), pp. 28–35; or William G. Birtle, Barry D. Hawkins, and Walter D. Pugh, "How to Evaluate Accounting Controls in a Minicomputer Installation,"* The Practical Accountant *(August 1980), pp. 47–53.*

Some key elements of management control of the systems function have been discussed in prior chapters. One is the long-range systems plan that, like all plans, provides a framework for management control and a standard against which performance may be measured. A second such element is a system of charging user departments for computer services, which provides important feedback to both the users themselves and to top-level systems managers and their superiors on the overall performance of the systems function. A third is a project development plan for each major systems project, often accompanied by a Gantt chart or a PERT schedule, which provides a basis for control of the systems development effort.

This section describes three additional elements of management control over the systems function. First is the measurement and evaluation of the performance of programmers and systems analysts. Second is the control of systems projects under development by means of periodic progress reviews and post-implementation follow-up. Third is the measurement and evaluation of performance of the computer operations activity and its personnel.

Programmer/ analyst performance evaluation

A key element of performance evaluation of systems personnel is the collection of information on the specific activities in which those personnel have been involved. This requires the use of a time-reporting system under which each analyst and programmer is required to account daily for how his or her time was spent, with activities classified according to the projects and programs worked on as well as the type of work performed. An example of a daily time sheet for this purpose is shown in Fig. 14.2. Note that the information collected on this form provides input not only for employee performance evaluation but also for project cost accumulation and reporting.

Because the analysis and programming effort involved in large systems development projects may span a long period of time, it is a mistake to wait until the project is completed to evaluate the performance of the analysts and programmers involved. Instead each project should be broken down into a series of small parts, or modules, each of which may be assigned to a single individual. For each module certain objectives are established, such as test specifications for a section of program code, or documentation specifications for a portion of the systems design. Estimates incorporated in the project plan provide standards of quality, time, and cost against which the performance of the person assigned to the job may be evaluated. The evaluation itself is performed immediately upon completion of each module.

With respect to programming, it is possible to develop rough measures of accomplishment for comparative purposes. The number of instructions which a completed program module contains may be divided by the number of hours spent by the programmer in preparing the module to provide a measure of "instructions per hour." This measure may then be used to compare the relative efficiency of all programmers within the organization. Further provisions have to be made to take into account factors such as the differences in size and complexity of programs and the variations in experience levels of programmers. Nonetheless, this approach in its

NAME __A.E. Neumann__   EMPLOYEE NO. __39070__   DATE __5/22/81__

TIME CHARGED TO		TYPE OF WORK										
PROJECT	PROGRAM	SYSTEM ANALYSIS	SYSTEM DESIGN	DETAIL DIAGRAMMING	PROGRAMMING	TESTING AND DEBUGGING	CONVERSION AND PARALLEL	DOCUMENTATION	TRAVEL	TRAINING	MEETING	OTHER*
1260	007				2							
8971	012			1								
6407	023			1								
6407	024				2							
0705	101					1		1				
TOTALS				2	4	1		1				

*For "Other" categories, use the project code indicated below.

9000-1 Vacation
9000-2 Holiday
9000-3 Personal Time
9000-4 Illness
9000-5 Professional or Technical Societies

Fig. 14.2
Daily time sheet for programmers and analysts. (This figure and also Figs. 14.3, 14.4, and 14.5 are reprinted with permission from Rudolph E. Hirsh, "Data Processing Can Be Cost-Controlled," Price Waterhouse Review (Summer 1970)).

simplest form does at least furnish some objective information with which to control programming activities, and it also provies a basis for estimating the time and cost requirements of future developmental projects.[7]

If a reasonably standard measure of "instructions per hour" can be developed, it becomes possible to budget programmer hours, and then to prepare programmer performance reports that compare these estimates to actual performance and determine variances. An example of such a performance report is shown in Fig. 14.3.

With respect to systems analysis, measures of employee performance cannot be quite as precise. Time and cost standards are more difficult to develop in the absence of a unit of work such as number of instructions. However, the quality of documentation prepared may be evaluated, and over a period of time a reasonably accurate subjective impression may be formed of how efficiently an analyst performs his or her assigned tasks. Since much of the analyst's job requires interaction with system users on the one hand and with programmers on the other, skill in interpersonal relations is an important factor in the success of employees assigned this role.

Systems project controls

The systems development process should be subject to strict management control. One key element of this control is the assignment of responsibility for the success of each project to a project manager and a project team. Another is the project development plan that divides the project into phases, with time and cost estimates for each phase. The plan should specify *project milestones,* or significant points in the developmental effort at which a formal review of progress is made. An important element of such progress reviews is a comparison of actual completion times for each project phase with estimated completion times. Data on the actual completion times can be accumulated from the daily time sheets filled out by programmers and analysts. Figure 14.4 provides an illustration of a possible format for such a progress report.

In addition to the time and cost analysis, a project progress review should consider a number of other factors; for example, the adherence of the project team to quality standards for documentation, program testing, and system auditability. In addition, estimates of remaining project completion times, costs, and benefits should be reevaluated based upon the additional experience gained since the previous progress review. If this reassessment reveals a significant change in expectations, the entire project timetable should be revised, and it may even be necessary to consider whether the project should be completely halted.

Another important aspect of project control is the follow-up review subsequent to implementation of a new computer application. This should be done periodically for all applications for the purpose of evaluating whether each is generating economic benefits in excess of costs in an amount consistent with the original project proposal and development plan. Any significant unfavorable variance should require an explanation from the persons responsible for the original estimates and

---

[7] *Further discussion of programmer performance evaluation is provided by Trevor D. Crossman, "Taking the Measure of Programmer Productivity,"* Datamation *(May 1979): 144–147.*

NAME   NORMAN, A.E.   REPORTING PERIOD   7/16-31/81

PROJECT AND PROGRAM	*IF COM-PLETE	DESCRIPTION	LANGUAGE	NO. OF INSTRUC-TIONS	PROGRAMMING HOURS				COMPUTER TEST HOURS			
					PERIOD	TO DATE ACTUAL	TO DATE ESTIMATED	VARIANCE	PERIOD	TO DATE ACTUAL	TO DATE ESTIMATE	VARIANCE
0041/012	*	TRAVEL EXPENSE DISTB.	COBOL	425	—	13	15	−2	—	2	2	0
0702/009	*	UPDATE CUSTOMER FILE	COBOL	650	—	64	50	+14	—	19	7	+12
0705/101	*	PRINT MAIL LABELS	COBOL	40	2	6	5	+1	1	2	1	+1
1260/007		TIME CARD EDIT	COBOL	512	2	24	20	+4	—	4	5	−1
6407/023		STORES ISSUE REGISTER	COBOL	375	1	9	7	+2	—	—	—	—
6407/024		STORES ISSUE TOTALS	COBOL	185	2	5	5	0	—	—	—	—
8971/012		OPTIMIZE MAINTENC.	COBOL	94	1	12	10	+2	—	2	2	0
TOTALS				2,281	8	133	112	+21	1	29	17	+12

Fig. 14.3
Programmer performance analysis.

PROJECT IDENTIFICATION 0702. CUSTOMER FILE PROCESSING

STATUS AS OF 7/31/81

PROGRAM	DESCRIPTION	TARGET DATE	SYSTEM ANALYSIS	SYSTEM DESIGN	DETAIL DIAGRAMMING	PROGRAMMING	TESTING AND DEBUGGING	CONVERSION AND PARALLEL	DOCUMENTATION	TRAVEL	TRAINING	MEETINGS	COMPUTER TIME	KEYPUNCH AND DATA PREP.	COST
0000	GEN. PROJECT	6/2/0							5	8	1	4	2		$ 177
0001	INPUT EDIT	7/9/0							8			2	4	1	330
0003	CREATE FILE	8/4/0	1			30	4	7	9				3	1	541
0004	SELECT 01	8/6/0		2	2	15	13	6	6				1	2	962
0007	SELECT 02	9/1/0				10	11	4	7				2	2	510
0009	UPDATE	9/1/0	1			12	13	1	2				1	3	638
0015	RESTARTS			2	7		4	9				1			453
	TOTAL THIS PERIOD		2	4	9	37	45	27	37	8	1	7	13	9	$3,611
	TOTAL TO DATE		46	35	42	128	105	44	69	16	16	21	39	15	$9,771
	ESTIMATE		50	30	40	135	120	40	70	18	10	5	25	20	$8,607
	VARIANCE		-4	+5	+2	-7	-15	+4	-1	-2	+6	+16	+14	-5	+$1,164

Fig. 14.4
Systems project progress report.

should initiate efforts to correct the situation if possible. These follow-up reviews not only help to control project development activities but also to encourage more accurate and objective initial estimates of project costs and benefits.

Control of computer operations

A basic element of computer operations control is the data processing schedule. The schedule is prepared at the beginning of each shift by a supervisor or scheduling clerk. It should assign each incoming job to an appropriate time period in a way that maximizes the productive utilization of all available equipment to the greatest possible extent. The schedule should also provide time for necessary preventive maintenance and should allow some slack time for the inevitable equipment malfunctions requiring corrective maintenance and for occasional reruns of incorrectly processed work.

Evaluation of the performance of all machine operators should be based upon a comparison of actual processing time with scheduled processing time for all jobs run by each operator. Of course, actual processing time must be adjusted for losses of productive time due to malfunctions or other factors not under the control of the operator. Furthermore, the scheduled processing time must be adjusted for variations in actual volume of processing from average volume to provide an equitable standard.

The performance of input preparation personnel may be evaluated in two ways. One is by measuring their output in terms of keystrokes per hour or some similar measure and then comparing each individual operator's rate to an average or standard. A second is to measure the error rate of all input preparation work in terms of the percentage of errors discovered by key verification or by editing routines built into the computer programs. Obviously, these two approaches complement each other, because one is basically a measure of efficiency and the other is a measure of quality.

Also useful for computer operations control is data on machine utilization for the computer hardware. The simplest way to collect such data is to require each shift operator to fill out a daily computer log indicating the jobs processed or other events occurring during the time available. An example of a form for this purpose is illustrated in Fig. 14.5. In addition, whenever productive computer time is lost due to equipment malfunction, operator error, or other problems, a separate form should be filled out specifying the amount of time lost and identifying the cause of the problem.

Data collected in this fashion provides useful input to a number of management reports and analyses. For example, computer time recorded for testing of systems under development can be charged to the specific project. Also, the lost time data can be aggregated weekly or monthly to provide an analysis of the causes of lost time. Finally, the daily computer logs themselves can be aggregated to provide a breakdown of total available computer time for each week or month into categories such as (1) productive time, (2) idle time, (3) reruns, and (4) machine maintenance

SYSTEM TYPE AND NUMBER __570/50-1__   DATE __5/22/81__

PROJECT PROGRAM IDENTIFICATION	PROGRAMMER ACCT CODE MODE	OPERATOR ACCT CODE MODE	ELAPSED TIME START	STOP	TOTAL	COMPUTER TIME START	STOP	TOTAL	LOST TIME CODE	Trouble Report Number	OPERATOR	COMMENTS
0001/000		30	0801	0857	56	4625	4718	93			J.C.	
1214/004		10	0858	1004	66	4718	4828	110			J.C.	
0705/101	13	11	1005	1100	55	4828	4920	92			J.C.	
0041/012		10	1102	1240	98	4920	5083	163			J.C.	
1600/008		10	1241	1243	2	5083	5086	3	42	2-14	L.B.B.	
0705/101	13	12	1245	1314	29	5086	5134	48			L.B.B.	

OPERATION CODES:

10 – PRODUCTION   20 – IDLE   30 – PREVENTIVE MAINTENANCE
11 – DEBUGGING   21 – SPECIAL   31 – UNSCHEDULED MAINTENANCE
12 – ASSEMBLY   22 – POWER OFF

LOST TIME CODES:

40 – LOST TIME-COMPUTER   43 – LOST TIME-PROGRAM
41 – LOST TIME-OPERATOR   49 – LOST TIME-OTHER
42 – LOST TIME-INPUT DATA

Fig. 14.5
Daily computer log.

and downtime.[8] Reports of this type are extremely useful to systems management in evaluating the efficiency of the computer operations activity, scheduling future processing operations, estimating operating costs for new projects, and establishing management policies for the operations function.

There are a number of ways of using the computer itself to collect and report information on the effectiveness of computer usage. *Hardware monitors* are devices that may be connected to a computer to collect information on the percent utilization of various system resources (CPU, channels, etc.) and on the number of occurrences of particular events (disk accesses, print lines, etc.). *Software monitors* are programs which may be linked to the operating system for the same purpose. *Job accounting routines* are programs, also linked to the operating system, to measure and record resource utilization for each job processed in order to facilitate cost accounting and charging computer users for services. These tools also provide a source of useful information for systems management.

Procedural and Security Controls for the Computer Facility

The Auditing Standards Executive Committee suggests a two-way classification of data processing controls: "Some EDP accounting control procedures relate to all EDP activities (general controls) and some relate to a specific accounting task, such as preparation of account listings or payrolls (application controls)."[9] Among the most critical general controls are those relating to the plan of organization of data processing activities and the separation of incompatible functions, discussed earlier in this chapter. This section covers the remaining general controls, including documentation standards, data security procedures, physical protection of computer facilities, insurance, provisions for backup, hardware controls, and computer security planning. The next section covers application controls.

Documentation standards

Good documentation is an important asset to the efficient operation and control of a computer-based information system. Data processing management must establish and enforce standards that specify what documentation is required for projects under development and for fully implemented systems. An important part of the progress reviews of systems projects involves a management review of the adequacy of documentation. There is a natural tendency for many systems analysts and programmers to view documentation as a necessary evil at best, and so management must continually stress its importance as part of a professional approach to systems work.

---

[8] *According to a 1971 survey conducted by the consulting firm of A. T. Kearney & Co., the breakdown of available time among 22 more efficient computer-using companies into these categories was (1) 81 percent, (2) 10 percent, (3) 6 percent, and (4) 3 percent. See Walter Schroeder, "The EDP Manager—and the Computer Profit Drain,"* Computers and Automation *(January 1971): 14–18.*

[9] *Auditing Standards Executive Committee, SAS 3, p. 3.*

Documentation may be classified into three basic categories—(1) administrative documentation, (2) systems documentation, and (3) operating documentation. Administrative documentation represents a description of overall standards and procedures for the data processing facility, including policies relating to justification and authorization of new systems or systems changes, standards for systems analysis, design and programming, procedures for file handling and file library activities, and so forth. Systems documentation includes a complete description of all aspects of each systems application, including narrative material, charts, and program listings as described in Chapter 7. Operating documentation includes all information required by a computer operator to run the program, including the equipment configuration used, variable data to be entered on the computer console, descriptions of conditions leading to program halts and related corrective actions, and so forth.

The purposes served by well-planned and enforced documentation standards within an organization are many. Among the benefits resulting from good documentation are facilitation of communication among system users, analysts, and programmers during systems development; facilitation of regular progress reviews of systems development work; provision of a reference and training tool for systems users, machine operators, and newly hired employees within the systems function; and simplification of the program maintenance function.

Good documentation is particularly important in view of the high rate of turnover among systems analysts and programmers. If a programmer leaves an organization in the middle of a major project, much time may be wasted by colleagues attempting to continue the work if the programmer has not maintained up-to-date documentation. If a programmer responsible for developing some of the existing applications in a system leaves without having provided adequate documentation, the making of necessary changes in those applications may be extremely difficult, perhaps almost as difficult as developing completely new programs. These potential problems underscore the necessity of requiring analysts and programmers to adhere to documentation standards in their work.

Protection of facilities

An organization's investment in computer facilities often amounts to hundreds of thousands or millions of dollars. It follows that this equipment should receive adequate physical protection. Access to the computer system itself and to all online data terminals should be restricted at all times to authorized personnel only. The temptation to locate the computer facilities in a glass-encased "showcase" should be avoided, for this presents an inviting target for ill-intentioned persons. Contingency plans for protection of equipment during natural disasters or riots should be established.

Data security

Good internal control in a computer installation requires that provisions be made for protection of files and programs from unauthorized disclosure or accidental destruction. The requirements of authorization and supervision for the removal of tapes or disk packs from a tape library represent an essential element of such control. Both the computer room and the file storage locations should be protected against fire, dust, excesses of heat or humidity, or other adverse conditions.

Tape rings and file labels are useful devices in protecting against accidental writing over or erasure of files. A *tape file protection ring* is a device that, when inserted on a reel of magnetic tape, permits writing on the tape. In the absence of the ring, the tape may not be written on, and the data on the reel is protected. Thus the tape ring is removed when any application is processed for which the tape file need only be read. File labels are both internal and external. An external label is merely a gummed paper label attached to a tape reel or disk pack, upon which may be written the file identification, data processed, and other information. Internal file labels are the first and last records in a tape or random access file. The first record, or *header label,* is read by the computer prior to processing and is checked against the program to ensure that the file is the correct one for the program. The last record, or *trailer label,* indicates the end of the file and may contain control totals for checking against those accumulated during processing.

In addition to protection against loss or destruction, an information systems control plan should also make provisions for reconstruction of records, should such loss actually occur. Duplicate tapes of programs and important files should be stored in a location away from the computer facility as a protection against a major disaster such as fire or flood. One data retention procedure used most commonly with magnetic tape files is known as the *grandfather–father–son concept.* Under this plan the three most recent master files are all retained, with the son file being the most recent. If the processing to produce the son file from the father file is accomplished with no errors or destruction of records, the grandfather file is then no longer needed and can be reused as the new son file at the next file update. If an error or loss of records does occur in the father and/or the son file during processing, the grandfather file can be used as a basis for reconstruction.

With respect to disk files, a file security program requires that the contents of the file be duplicated, generally by writing the file onto magnetic tape. If transactions are processed in batches, the duplicate serves as the father file in the event of errors or destruction of data in the updating process. If transactions are processed online, a log of all transactions may also be recorded on disk or tape which, together with the most recent duplicate copy of the file, could be used to reconstruct the current disk file.

With respect to highly confidential data, protection against unauthorized disclosure is provided by a paper shredder and by cryptographic protection. A shredder may be used to chop and mutilate confidential papers and printouts, such as customer listings, research data, and payroll registers, once they are no longer needed. Cryptographic protection involves the translation of data into a secret code for storage purposes or prior to data transmission. The data may then be translated back to meaningful form for authorized usage. Cryptographic protection is particularly important when confidential data are being transmitted from remote terminals because data transmission lines can be electronically monitored without the user's knowledge.

Insurance

In addition to physical protection of facilities and data security procedures, an insurance program is an essential control device. Major risks to be insured against include fire, flooding, severe weather, riots, and sabotage. The fidelity bond (see Chapter 4) provides insurance against the risk of loss from embezzlement. Fidelity bonds are particularly essential in small installations in which extensive separation of functions is not possible. In some installations that handle work for outsiders in addition to their own work, liability insurance for losses incurred due to errors in performing the work may be necessary.

Backup systems and procedures

Another form of protection against risk consists of backup systems and procedures. With respect to disasters that could completely disable a computer facility, an organization should have a disaster recovery plan that will prepare it to recover its data processing capacity as smoothly and quickly as possible. This plan should establish priorities for the recovery process, such as by identifying those applications most critical in keeping the organization running. A key element of the plan is an arrangement with the vendor or a service bureau that permits usage of their facilities in the event of an emergency. Also essential for disaster recovery is the storage of duplicate copies of critical files and programs in a location away from the organization's main computer center.[10]

Backup procedures must also be established to deal with temporary hardware failures that inevitably occur. In some cases, hardware failures in system components can be isolated, enabling the remainder of the hardware system to continue operation, though in a less efficient mode, until the malfunctioning component is fixed. This is referred to as *graceful degradation*. In a real-time system for which maintaining a constant level of service is essential, some hardware components may be duplicated in order that the system can switch to the backup component if necessary. The duplex system (see Chapter 9) is an example in which the CPU itself is duplicated, but it is also possible to duplicate other components, such as terminals or multiplexors.

Hardware controls

Several control features are built into the hardware in a computer system. One example is *duplicate circuitry* in the arithmetic unit of the central processor that results in duplicate performance of computations and subsequent comparison of the two results. *Dual reading* is another hardware control in which records on cards, tape, or random access media are read twice by separate reading components, and the results of both read operations compared. Still another hardware control is the *echo check,* in which the accuracy of data transmission to an output device is checked by comparing a signal sent back to the computer from the output device with the data originally sent.

---

[10] *For further discussion of disaster recovery plans and backup facilities, see Larry Lettieri, "Disaster Recovery: Picking Up the Pieces,"* Computer Decisions *(March 1979): 16–22, 27; and Wayne L. Rhodes Jr., "Second Site Protection,"* Infosystems *(September 1980): 46–52.*

Hardware controls may also be used to help control access to a computer system. Many computer systems may be switched off and on using a lock and key similar to an automobile ignition. Also, some computer terminals may be given an electronic identification number that enables the central processor to recognize whether or not it is being accessed from an authorized terminal.

The use of the parity bit to check the accuracy of data transfer within a computer system is one type of hardware control already discussed. (See Chapter 6.) Two-dimensional parity checking is an extension of parity checking commonly used for data transmission over telecommunication facilities. This involves use of a redundant column of check bits for each record in addition to a redundant row of check bits. The parity checking is thus done both vertically and horizontally. This form of control is important in telecommunications because noise bursts frequently cause two or more adjacent bits to be lost or picked up. A vertical parity check alone would not catch all such errors.

Two additional hardware controls that help to prevent processing errors are *preventive maintenance* and *uninterruptible power systems.* Preventive maintenance involves regular testing of all system components and replacement of those found to be in a weak condition. This greatly reduces the likelihood of a system failure during regular operations. An uninterruptible power system consists of an auxiliary power supply which operates as a buffer between the power input from the electric company and the power usage by the computer. Such systems smooth out the flow of power to the computer, eliminating loss of data that might be caused by momentary surges or dips in power flow. In the event of complete power failure, uninterruptible power systems provide a backup power supply to keep the computer operating without interruption until regular power is restored.[11]

Computer security planning

Many authorities in the systems field are now advocating a systematic approach to the management of data processing security that may be referred to as "computer security planning." Under this approach an organization attempts to identify all possible threats or hazards associated with its data processing equipment and operations. Then it attempts to assess vulnerabilities, i.e., threats for which there is a lack of protection, and risks, i.e., the likelihoods that each threat will actually come to pass. Finally, it attempts to estimate the exposure for each threat, which is the harm or loss that will be suffered if the threat actually does come to pass.

Based upon the vulnerability and risk analysis outlined above, the organization then prepares a computer security plan that attempts to (1) minimize the likelihood of each threat, (2) minimize the exposure if the threat is not avoided, and (3) provide for recovery from the damage associated with any threats that are not avoided. The elements of such a computer security plan are the internal control policies and proce-

---

[11] *The cost and benefits of uninterruptible power are discussed in greater depth in Neil D. Kelley, "The Economics of Uninterruptible Power,"* Infosystems *(September 1980): 55–64.*

dures described throughout this chapter; however, data security procedures, system access controls, and backup systems are generally emphasized. The advantage of the computer security planning approach is that it helps the organization to select that set of control policies and procedures that optimizes the level of computer security relative to cost.[12]

Application Controls

Application controls are those that relate to specific processing jobs as they are performed at the computer facility. They involve the data inputs, files, programs, and outputs of a specific computer application, rather than the computer system in general. Their primary objective is to maintain the accuracy of the system's outputs, data files, and transaction records. They include batch totals, source data controls of various kinds, programmed input validation routines, control over the errors and exceptions revealed by other controls, checkpoint/restart recovery procedures, and online data entry controls.

Batch totals

Batch totals are as essential to computerized batch processing as they are to manual data processing. In a computerized batch processing application, batch totals are accumulated manually from source documents prior to input preparation. The original totals are then compared with machine-generated totals at each subsequent processing step. Any discrepancy may indicate a loss of records or errors in data transcription or processing.

Three forms of batch totals commonly used in computer systems are *financial totals, hash totals,* and *record counts.* A financial total is simply the total of a dollar field in a set of records, such as total sales or total cash receipts. A hash total is a total generated from a field that would usually not otherwise be added, such as a total of all customer account numbers or employee identification numbers. A record count is a total of the number of input documents to a process or of records processed in a run.

One special form of batch total is the *cross-footing balance test.* This can be performed only on a set of data that is additive horizontally (across several columns) as well as vertically (down each column). When the column that contains the horizontal sums of all the other columns is added downward, the resulting total should also equal the horizontal sum of all the other column totals. For example, the sum of the gross pay column in a payroll application should equal the sum of the net pay column plus all deductions columns.

For large volumes of data, the effective use of batch totals requires that they be accumulated for smaller subsets of the total set of records, such as for every 50

---

[12] *For further discussion of computer security planning, see K. S. Shankar, "The Total Computer Security Problem: An Overview,"* Computer *(June 1977): 50–62; and Richard G. Canning, "The Security of Managers' Information,"* EDP Analyzer *(July 1979): 1–13.*

items. In this way any errors that are encountered will be isolated among a smaller group of records, making it easier to find the specific record or records which are in error.

Source data controls

These include a number of checks on the accuracy and completeness of computer input prior to processing. One form of checking the accuracy of input data is keyverification, which may be done using a key-to-tape encoder or other key-operated data entry device. (See Chapter 5.) Where keyverification is not considered to be essential or is too expensive, a substitute source data control is the visual inspection of printed input listings prior to processing.

Another source data control is *check digit verification,* which may be performed by any data entry device having a processing capability, including a key-to-disk-to-tape system or an intelligent terminal. In check digit verification, all authorized identification numbers contain a redundant digit, called the check digit. This digit is a numerical function of the other digits in the number. For example, in the number 90614, the last digit, 4, could be generated by subtracting the sum of the first four digits from the next highest number ending in zero $(20 - 16 = 4)$. The number 41365 would fail this test. To use check digit verification, the microprocessor within the data entry device must be programmed to perform the check digit test each time an identification number (such as a customer account number or employee number) is entered. If an error in the keying of an identification number occurs, check digit verification will probably (but not certainly) detect the error and signal the operator. As a result, most such errors may be corrected prior to submission of the input for computer processing.

As is the case in manual systems, sequentially prenumbered forms provide a useful form of control over source documents to computer systems. In a computer system, control of sequentially prenumbered forms is facilitated by using the computer to determine and report the numbers of forms that have not been processed. The forms containing these numbers can then be traced in order to ensure that all data that should be processed is eventually received by the system.

The turnaround document is defined in Chapter 5 and described as a means of reducing the data preparation work load. Since turnaround documents are automatically prepared as computer output, the data they contain is generally much more accurate than if they had been manually keyed. As a result, when they return to the system as computer input, their greater reliability provides better internal control.

Various activities of the data control function (described earlier in this chapter) contribute significantly to source data control. When source data are received for processing, data control personnel check for necessary user authorizations, and record the name and source of the transactions, the record count, control totals, and other relevant information concerning the input in a control log. Data control personnel then monitor the progress of the source data through the data preparation process, expediting the process when necessary to meet the processing schedule, re-checking record counts and control totals after the data preparation process is completed, and initiating any necessary corrections to the data prior to submitting them for computer processing.

Input validation routines

Input validation routines are programs or routines therein that utilize the computer to check the validity and accuracy of input data. These are also called *edit programs,* and the specific types of accuracy checks they perform are called *edit checks.* In many cases input validation is performed by a separate program prior to regular processing, in which case any errors discovered may be corrected before the input is processed (see Fig. 14.6). In other cases input validation is performed as part of regular processing, in which case input records rejected as invalid must be resubmitted in the next regular processing run.

There are several different types of edit checks used in input validation routines. A *sequence check* is a check on whether a batch of input data is in the proper numerical or alphabetical sequence. A *field check* is a check on the characters in a field to ensure that they are of the class the field is supposed to contain. For example, a field check on a numeric field would indicate an error if it revealed that the field contained blanks or alphabetic characters. A *sign check* is a check to assure that the data in a field are of the appropriate arithmetic sign. For example, data in a field such as inventory balance should never have a negative sign.

Other edit checks include the *validity check,* which tests identification numbers or transaction codes for validity by comparison with ones already known to be authorized. For example, in a sequential file updating process, any transaction for which the control field value does not match that of an existing file record, and that is not coded as a new record to be added to the file, should be flagged as invalid. Check digit verification may be performed in an input validation routine in the same way that it is performed when input is prepared. Still another common form of edit check is a *limit check,* which is a test to ensure that a numerical amount in a record does not exceed some acceptable limit that has been predetermined. For example, the hours-worked field in a payroll processing run may be checked to assure that no input record contains hours worked in excess of 60 in a single week. A *reasonableness test* is a check of the logical correctness of relationships among the values of data items on an input record and its corresponding file record. For example, a journal entry that debits inventory and credits wages payable is not reasonable. Similarly, the quantity received of inventory items might be tested for reasonableness by checking whether it exceeds twice the value of the order quantity of the item.

One other form of edit check is the *redundant data check.* This check requires that two identifiers be included for each input transaction record that is to be updated in order to confirm that the correct match will be obtained by cross-checking. For example, if both the customer account number and the first five letters of the customer's name are included on the input record, the system can check, after ob-

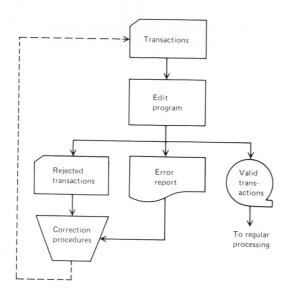

Fig. 14.6
Edit program.

taining a match on account number, whether the first five letters also match those on the file. This check has the purpose of preventing the posting of transactions to the wrong master file records.

Control of errors and exceptions

An essential aspect of internal control in a computer-based information system is the procedures for investigation and correction of errors identified by edit programs, batch total checks, and other source data controls. If a data control department exists, this function is often one of its responsibilities. Procedures for correction and reentry of erroneous input should be prescribed, and data control personnel are responsible for making sure that such procedures are carried out accurately. Corrected input should again be submitted to validation routines, for the error rate on error corrections is perhaps higher than on any other type of transaction. Exceptions encountered during processing, such as transaction amounts or file balances that exceed prescribed limits, should be investigated to reveal their cause. User department personnel should be notified of those errors caused by incorrect input submitted by them.

A useful technique for controlling data processing errors and exceptions is maintenance of an error log. For every error, the information initially recorded in the log would include the type of record, the transaction identification number, the processing date, the specific field in error, and the error type. As errors are corrected and the corresponding data successfully resubmitted to the system, the status of the error record in the log would be changed from "open" to "closed," and a notation of the resubmission date and the cause of the error would be entered. The error log may be maintained manually by data control personnel, or it may be maintained by the computer. Periodically, the error log may be used to prepare management reports summarizing the number of errors by record type, by error type, and by cause. Also, reports listing all outstanding errors should be regularly provided to operations supervisors to enable them to follow up on uncorrected errors and make sure that all errors are corrected as quickly as possible.

Online access controls

Virtually all modern data processing systems may be accessed from terminals located at a distance from the central computer site. This means that system access controls must include not only restrictions on physical access to the central computer but also controls over access to the system from online terminals. Restrictions on physical access to terminals arc helpful, but not always effective. Therefore, online access controls are primarily focused on the systems software that controls the interaction between terminal users and the system.

One type of online access control mentioned previously is to provide each terminal with an electronic identification number. The system is then programmed to accept commands and transactions only from terminals having authorized identification numbers. Also, those online systems that need to be operational only during business hours (such as a banking system) may be programmed to enable a supervisor to deactivate the system by signing off from a terminal at the end of each day. Then the system would accept no morc transactions until the supervisor activated it by signing on at the beginning of the next day.

The most essential and universally used form of online access control is a system of user codes and passwords. Under this system each authorized user is assigned a unique user code number and password that must be keyed into the system prior to using it. If the user cannot supply an authorized code number and password, the system shuts off service to the terminal. Once an authorized code number and password have been accepted by the system and the user is allowed to proceed, the system may apply a *compatibility test* to transactions or inquiries entered by the user. This checks whether the user having the code number given is authorized to initiate the type of transaction or inquiry being entered. For example, factory employees would not be authorized to make entries involving accounts payable. This helps to prevent both unintentional errors and deliberate attempts to manipulate the system.

In order to perform compatibility tests, the system must maintain an internal *access control matrix* consisting of (1) a list of all authorized user code numbers and passwords, (2) a list of all files and programs maintained on the system, and (3) a record of the type of access each user is entitled to have to each type of file and program. "Type of access" refers to the things that the user is authorized to do to the file or program; examples of possible types of access include (1) no access permitted, (2) access only to summary information, (3) read and display individual records, and (4) various combinations of types of changes, including modifying field values within a record, adding a new record, deleting an existing record, or redefining the record structure. An example of an access control matrix appears in Fig. 14.7. According to the access codes assigned to the various users in this example, user 12345-ABC

USER IDENTIFICATION		FILES			PROGRAMS			
Code number	Password	A	B	C	1	2	3	4
12345	ABC	0	0	1	0	0	0	0
12346	DEF	0	2	0	0	0	0	0
12354	KLM	1	1	1	0	0	0	0
12359	NOP	3	0	0	0	0	0	0
12389	RST	0	1	0	0	3	0	0
12567	XYZ	1	1	1	1	1	1	1

Codes for type of access:
0 = No access permitted.
1 = Read and display only.
2 = Read, display, and update.
3 = Read, display, update, create, and delete.

Fig. 14.7
Access control matrix.

is permitted only to read and display file C, and is permitted no access of any kind to any other file or program. User 12359–NOP may perform any and all operations on file A, but may access no other file or program. User 12389–RST is apparently a programmer who is authorized to make any type of change in program 2 and also to read and display records in file B. User 12567-XYZ, probably a supervisor, is authorized to read and display the contents of any and all files and programs.

A system of online access controls based upon user code numbers and passwords is effective only as long as each user's code number and password remain a secret to everyone except the user. For this reason, the system should be programmed never to display or print a user code number or password, and users should be cautioned not to disclose theirs to other persons. In addition, all passwords should be modified frequently to reduce the likelihood that a current password will become known to someone other than its authorized user. One other procedure useful to the maintenance of system security is for the system to record all attempts to access it from an unauthorized terminal or using an unauthorized user code number or password. Periodic review of this record by a security officer should disclose attempts by unauthorized persons to access the system.

Online data entry controls

This category includes all controls over the accuracy and integrity of input data entered into the system from online data terminals. Most controls in this category are specialized forms of input validation routines which are unique to online systems. In addition, many of the edit checks described in the previous section are useful in online systems as well as in batch systems. These include field checks, validity checks, limit checks, reasonableness tests, and the redundant data check.

If the personnel assigned to enter data input are generally inexperienced in the use of systems or terminals, then the system may be programmed to control the data entry process using a technique known as *prompting*. Under this approach the system displays a request to the user for each required item of input data, and then waits for an acceptable response before requesting the next required item. An alternative procedure for this purpose is called *preformatting,* which involves the display of a document format containing blanks for the data items which the user must fill in. If preformatting or other free form methods of data entry are used, the system should also perform a *completeness test* on each input record to check whether all of the data items required for a particular transaction have in fact been entered by the terminal operator.

Any errors or possible errors in online data entry detected by input validation routines should cause an error message to be displayed to the terminal operator. Because terminal operators are often inexperienced system users, the error message should be as clear as possible with respect to which item is in error, what the error is, and what the operator should do. The system should then recheck the operator's response to the error message prior to accepting any further transaction input.

After all data for a transaction have been entered by a terminal operator, another technique for checking their accuracy is to have the system send certain data back to the terminal for comparison with the data originally sent. This is called *closed loop verification.* For example, the terminal could count the number of bits sent for each message, and the system could count the number of bits received and transmit this bit count back to the terminal for comparison to the terminal's count. If the two counts are not equal, a data transmission error has occurred, and the terminal can retransmit the transaction. Closed loop verification may also involve participation on the part of the terminal operator. For example, if one of the data items being entered is an item number or account number, the system may retrieve the item description or account name, display it on the operator's terminal, and wait for confirmation from the operator that the description or name corresponds to the number the operator entered. This form of closed loop verification is an alternative to the redundant data check as a protection against entering a valid but incorrect identification number.

In remote batch processing systems, in which several transactions are being entered in a batch, it is useful for the terminal operator to number each transaction sequentially. In this way if a system malfunction occurs that temporarily shuts down the system, the number of the last transaction processed can be provided to the operator by the system once service is restored. This helps to ensure that no transactions are lost, or that none are inadvertently entered twice, as a result of a system malfunction.

Other programmed controls   In addition to batch totals, label checking, and input validation, there are other control procedures that may be incorporated into the application programs. *Overflow procedures* are one example. These are programmed routines for dealing with an arithmetic result that exceeds the capacity of the computer's numeric storage register. Since this could only happen with an abnormally large number, this condition invariably indicates an error of some kind. Thus a routine designed to react to this problem should print out and flag all the details of the transaction for manual review.

For large batch processing jobs requiring a runtime of an hour or more, there is a danger that a hardware failure midway through the job could necessitate running the entire job a second time. Such hardware failures cannot be prevented, but their consequences to large jobs can be mitigated through the use of *recovery procedures*. One such procedure is the taking of *checkpoints* at periodic intervals during the processing of the program. A checkpoint is an exact copy of all of the data values and status indicators relating to the program at some point in time. The checkpoint is generally written from primary memory onto a disk or tape file. If a hardware failure occurs between checkpoints, then the job can be restarted after the hardware is repaired by reading in the last checkpoint, rather than going back to the beginning of the job.

A complementary recovery procedure for data files is called *rollback*. Under this procedure a log of the pre-update values is prepared for every record that is updated within a particular interval. Then if a hardware failure occurs that could have caused erroneous data to be written on the file, the log is processed to "rollback" the file, restoring all records updated since the beginning of the current interval to their correct values at that point. The file updating process then resumes from that point.

Application controls: an example

To illustrate the use of many of the application controls described in this section, consider the example of a credit sales transaction. At a minimum the required input data will include (1) the customer's account number, (2) the inventory item number, (3) the quantity sold, (4) the sale price, and (5) the delivery date. If the customer purchased more than one type of inventory item, then the inventory item number, quantity sold, and price fields will occur more than once in the sales transaction record. To process this transaction, the system must access each inventory master record to subtract the quantity sold from the quantity on hand, and access the master customer account record to add the total sale amount to the customer's account balance.

If these sales transactions are being processed in batches, then the following batch totals may be prepared manually (with the help of an adding machine) by the persons who assemble the batches of sales documents for submission to data processing, (1) a record count of the number of customer transactions, (2) a record count of the number of inventory transactions, (3) hash totals of the quantity sold and price fields, and (4) a financial total of the total dollar sales (price × quantity). If the data are then keyed onto a machine-readable medium using a "smart" data entry device, such as a shared processor key-to-disk-to-tape system, then these batch totals can be accumulated by that system during the keying process, and checked against the original batch totals immediately upon completion of the keying process. In addition, such a system could perform check digit verification on the account numbers and item numbers, perform a limit check on the delivery dates, and perform a field check for numeric characters in the quantity, date, and price fields. As a result, a number of possible errors in the input data would be discovered (and corrected) prior to submitting the data for processing on the main computer.

Alternatively, if the data are keyed onto a machine-readable medium using a "dumb" data entry device, such as a conventional keypunch, then keyverification may be used to compensate for the device's inability to perform the functions of the "smart" machine. Furthermore, the records might subsequently be processed on the computer by an edit program (see Fig. 14.6), which would transcribe them to a faster input medium (i.e., cards to tape), and perform the various processing functions of the "smart" data entry device, including accumulating the batch totals and performing check digit verification, limit checks and field checks. Transaction batches that pass the edit program's tests would be ready for submission to file update processing, while those batches in which the edit program identifies errors would be investigated, corrected, and resubmitted to the edit program.

Once the input records are ready for processing against the master files, care must be taken to ensure that the right copies of the master files are loaded on the system. The disk packs or tape reels containing the customer and inventory master files should have external labels containing their name and processing date, and the operator should check these labels carefully prior to loading the files. Both files should also have an internal header label containing this information, and the file update program should be designed to check these header labels prior to accepting any transactions for processing. Each master file may also include a trailer label containing a record count and one or more other file totals, and these would be checked and updated during the file update processing run.

Because the file update program accesses the customer and inventory master file records, it can perform additional tests on the accuracy of the input data. These include (1) validity checks on the customer account numbers and inventory item numbers, (2) sign checks on inventory balances on hand after subtracting sales quantities, (3) limit checks on the total amount sold to each customer relative to that customer's credit limit, (4) limit checks on the sale price of each item sold relative to the permissible range of prices for that item, and (5) reasonableness tests of the quantity sold of each item relative to normal sales quantities for that item. In addition, to prevent the possibility that valid but incorrect account numbers or item numbers might be entered, redundant data such as the customer name and item description could be included in each input record and cross-checked against the corresponding values in the respective master files. This would prevent the posting of the credit sale to the wrong customer account, or the posting of the inventory reduction to the wrong inventory master record.

Outputs of the file update processing run will include billing and/or shipping documents, and a control report. Data control personnel should be responsible for distributing all copies of the billing and shipping documents to the appropriate departments or persons within the organization. The control report will contain batch totals accumulated during the file update run, and a listing of any transactions rejected by the input validation routines within the file update program. The batch totals should be reconciled to those prepared prior to the file update run, and any rejected transactions or discrepancies in batch totals should be investigated and corrected by data control personnel.

If the sales transactions are being entered using an online system rather than using batch processing, then all of the data entry controls must be concentrated on the interaction between the terminal user and the system. The first step is for the system to check the validity of the terminal itself and of the user code number and password entered by the user when the system is first accessed. Personnel authorized to enter sales transactions should be provided with user code numbers and passwords that do not permit them to enter any other types of transactions or commands.

To assist authorized personnel in entering sales transactions, the system may be programmed to list a series of requests for the customer account number, item number, and other required data. After each request, the system would wait for a valid response from the terminal operator prior to making the next request. Alternatively, the system could display a blank sales transaction format and wait for the operator to complete it. As the data are entered, the system would perform validity checks, field checks, limit checks, sign checks and reasonableness tests in the same manner as the batch processing system. However, a significant advantage of the online system for data entry is that if the system detects errors it can notify the terminal operator immediately and thus initiate a real-time correction and reentry of the data in question.

To prevent entry of valid but incorrect account numbers or item numbers, redundant data could be entered and cross-checked, as in the batch processing system. Alternatively, a form of closed loop verification could be used in which the system receives only the account number and item number from the terminal, retrieves the customer name and item description corresponding to these numbers from the master files, and displays these on the terminal. The terminal operator would then visually examine the name and description, and either signal the system to proceed if these were correct, or enter a corrected account number or item number if the system displays the wrong name or description.

It should be clear from this example that the design of a system of application controls requires ingenuity and care. Each significant item of input data should be checked by at least one method. However, cost–benefit relationships must also be considered in designing application control systems. Generally, tests performed by the computer, such as edit checks, are less costly and more effective than tests, such as keyverification and visual inspection, performed by people. Also, it is preferable to catch data entry errors as soon as possible after they are made, because this enables such errors to be corrected more easily.

Review Questions

1. Define the following terms.

project milestones	edit program
hardware monitors	edit check
software monitors	sequence check

job accounting routines

tape file protection ring

header label

trailer label

grandfather-father-son concept

graceful degradation

duplicate circuitry

dual reading

echo check

preventive maintenance

uninterruptible power systems

financial total

hash total

record count

cross-footing balance test

check digit verification

input validation routine

field check

sign check

validity check

limit check

reasonableness test

redundant data check

compatibility test

access control matrix

prompting

preformatting

completeness test

closed loop verification

overflow procedures

recovery procedures

checkpoint

rollback

2. Generally speaking, how do internal controls change in electronic data processing systems as compared to manual systems?

3. What are the two basic subdivisions of a typical information systems department?

4. Describe the nature of the roles played by a top computer executive who is also a member of the top management group in a business organization.

5. Describe the functions performed by a manager of programming and systems, a data base administrator, a systems programmer, an applications maintenance programmer, a project manager, and a systems analyst in a typical data processing department.

6. Describe the functions performed by a manager of data processing operations, an input preparation department, a computer operations department, a file librarian, and a data control group in a typical data processing department.

7. Which functions within an information systems department should be organizationally independent, and why?

8. What procedures should be utilized in a computer system to control program changes?

9. What elements of internal control should be stressed in a micro- or minicomputer installation that is too small for separation of functions to be practical?

10. Identify several key elements of management control of the systems function.

11. Explain how the performances of systems analysts and computer programmers should be evaluated.

12. Describe how management control of project development activities should be maintained.

13. Describe several elements of a program of management control of computer operations.

14. Explain the distinction between general controls and application controls in an EDP system.

15. Identify and describe three categories of systems documentation.

16. What reasons exist for maintaining up-to-date documentation in a computer system?

17. What provisions should be made in a computer system to protect files, programs, and equipment from loss or destruction? What provisions for reconstruction of records in the event of loss should be made?

18. What forms of insurance should be maintained as part of the control plan for a computer installation?

19. Describe several approaches to the use of backup facilities or procedures for prevention of losses due to systems malfunctions or natural disasters.

20. Describe several types of computer hardware controls.

21. Explain the concept of computer security planning. What is its primary advantage?

22. What types of errors are batch totals intended to reveal? Describe four types of batch totals and give an example of each.

23. Describe several types of source data controls that might be used in a computer installation.

24. Identify and describe several edit checks that might be included in an input validation routine, and given an example of each.

25. What procedures should be established for control over errors and exceptions in a computer-based system?

26. Explain the nature and purpose of online access controls. Describe several examples and explain how each might be utilized.

27. What are online data entry controls? Describe several examples and explain how each might be utilized.

28. List several edit checks that are equally useful in both batch and online processing systems.

29. Describe three categories of programmed controls over computer data processing and give an example of each.

30. Describe an example of how various application controls might be applied to the processing of sales transactions.

Discussion Questions

31. Many persons believe that programming is basically a creative activity, and should therefore not be subject to cost controls and other managerial regulation. Discuss this point of view.

32. A computer implementation project is often performed in a state of crisis, with the implementation group working feverishly to keep pace with the implementation schedule. In this atmosphere, corners are often cut with respect to documentation and programmed controls. What arguments do you feel would be effective to prevent such cutting of corners, even though doing so could delay implementation?

33. Theoretically a control procedure should be adopted if its benefit value exceeds its cost. Explain how the benefit value and cost of the following controls can be estimated:
    a) separation of functions,
    b) data security provisions,
    c) turnaround documents,
    d) input validation routines.

34. Discuss how reliability analysis (see Chapter 11) could be applied to the design and evaluation of internal controls in a computer-based information system. For which types of internal controls would it probably be most useful, and why?

Problems and Cases

35. Prepare a segment of a program flowchart showing how a check of a header label by a program would work.

36. Prepare a systems flowchart illustrating the grandfather-father-son concept.

37. What control or controls would you recommend in a computer system to prevent the following situations from occurring?
    a) The "time worked" field for salaried employees is supposed to contain a "01" for one week. For one employee, this field contained the number 40 and a check for $6,872.51 was accidentally prepared and mailed to this employee.
    b) A programmer obtained the master payroll file tape, mounted it on a tape drive, and changed his own monthly salary from $1400 to $2000 through the computer console.
    c) A bank programmer wrote a special routine, punched a set of cards for the routine, obtained the program that calculates interest on customer accounts, and processed the cards against the program to add the routine to the program tape. The routine adds the fraction of a cent of each customer's interest, which would otherwise be rounded off, to her own account.
    d) The master accounts receivable file on disk was inadvertently destroyed and could not be reconstructed after being substituted for the accounts payable file in a processing run.
    e) Loss of almost all of its vital business data from a fire which destroyed the room in which a company stored its magnetic tape files.
    f) A programmer quit the firm in the middle of a programming assignment. Because no other programmers could make sense of the work already completed, the project was begun over from scratch.
    g) A salesperson keying in a customer order from a remote terminal entered an incorrect stock number. As a result, an order for 50 typewriters was placed for a customer who had intended to order 50 typewriter ribbons.
    h) A janitor cleaning out the drive-in booths in a bank entered a $1000 credit to his own account over an online terminal.

i) A salesperson provided with a terminal with which to enter customer orders used it to initiate a $500 increase in his own monthly salary.

j) A salesperson keying in a customer order from a remote terminal inadvertently omitted the delivery address from one order.

k) A company's research and development center utilized remote terminals tied into its computer center 100 miles away. By utilizing a wiretap, the company's largest competitor was able to steal secret plans for a major product innovation.

l) Because of failure in a $400 multiplexor serving terminals at eight drive-in windows, a bank was forced to shut down the windows for two hours during a busy Friday afternoon.

m) A twenty-minute power failure that shut down a firm's computer system resulted in loss of data for several transactions that were being entered into the system from remote terminals.

n) During payroll processing, an error correction entry performed by the console operator resulted in the unintentional recording of data on the payroll master tape file, which destroyed several records on that file.

o) During keypunching of customer payment records, the digit "0" in a payment of $123.40 was mistakenly punched as the letter "O." As a result, the transaction was not correctly processed and the customer received an incorrect statement of account.

p) After updating the inventory master file maintained on magnetic tape, the old master tape was removed for use in other applications. The updated master was then accidentally mislabeled and its contents subsequently erased. Considerable difficulty was encountered in reconstructing the master inventory file.

38. Consider the following set of numeric computer input data.

Employee number Col. 1–3	Pay rate Col. 4–6	Hours worked Col. 7–8	Gross pay Col. 9–13	Deductions Col. 14–18	Net pay Col. 19–23
121	250	38	$9500	01050	08450
123	275	40	11000	01250	09750
125	200	90	16000	02000	12000
122	280	40	11200	11000	00200

Required

a) From the data above calculate one example hash total, record count, and financial total.

b) For each of the controls listed below, give a specific example from the four records above of an error or probable error that would be caught by the control.

field check   reasonableness test
sequence check   cross-footing balance test
limit check

39. Check digit verification schemes apply a series of mathematical operations to the first $n - 1$ digits of an n digit number to determine the correct value of the nth digit. Assume that check digit verification is to be applied to a five-digit number. One check digit scheme, called the "simple sum" method, would determine the sum of the first four digits and subtract that sum from the next highest multiple of ten to obtain the check digit. Another scheme, called the "2–1–2" method, would compute a weighted sum of the first four digits, with the first and third digits from the right (excluding the check digit) weighted by a factor of two, and the second and fourth digits from the right weighted by a factor of one. This sum is then subtracted from the next highest multiple of ten to obtain the check digit.

Listed below are two columns of five-digit numbers. All six of the numbers in the left-hand column are valid according to both check digit methods described above. (You might want to verify this.) The numbers in the right-hand column are erroneous versions of their column counterparts. The first two contain single transcription errors, in which one digit has been copied incorrectly. The second two contain transposition errors, in which two digits have been transposed. The third two are completely garbled.

14267	14567
23573	28573
32582	35282
43274	43724
50609	36609
92487	65937

Required

a) Determine which of the numbers in the right-hand column would fail check digit verification under (1) the simple sum method, and (2) the "2–1–2" method.

b) Extrapolating from the results of part (a), can you form any general conclusions about the relative effectiveness of the two check digit methods with respect to the different types of errors?

40. Your company has procured a number of minicomputers for use in various locations and applications. One of these has been installed in the stores department which has the responsibility for disbursing stock items and for maintaining stores records. In your audit you find, among other things, that a competent employee, trained in computer applications, receives the requisitions for stores, reviews them for completeness and for the propriety of approvals, disburses the stock, maintains the records, operates the computer, and authorizes adjustments to the total amounts of stock accumulated by the computer.

When you discuss the applicable controls with the department manager, you are told that the minicomputer is assigned exclusively to that department and that it therefore does not require the same types of controls applicable to the large computer systems.

Required   Comment on the manager's contentions, discussing briefly five types of control that would apply to this minicomputer application.[13]

41. Shown in Fig. 14.8 are data relating to the evaluation of programming job performance by four programmers employed in the Welfare Department.

Performance factor	Programmer			
	Adams	Baker	Cline	Davis
Instructions per hour	12	15	12	15
Program complexity	Low	Medium	Medium	Low
Years of experience	6	1	2	4

Figure 14.8

Required   a) Which programmer's performance is best? Explain.

b) Which programmer's performance is worst? Explain.

c) Can you rank the other two programmers in terms of performance? Why or why not?

42. You are the data security administrator for a small computer installation. This system uses two programs—a payroll processing system and an inventory processing system—and maintains three files—a payroll master file, an inventory master file, and a master transaction log. You are to establish an access control matrix that permits varying levels of access authority with respect to these systems and files to the following system users.

a) salesperson—read and display records in the inventory master file.

b) inventory control analyst—read, display, update, create, and delete records in the inventory master file.

c) payroll analyst—read, display, and update records in the payroll master file.

d) personnel manager—read, display, update, create, and delete records in the payroll master file.

e) payroll programmer—perform any and all operations on the payroll system, plus read and display payroll master file records and transaction log records.

f) inventory programmer—perform any and all operations on the inventory system, plus read and display inventory master file records and transaction log records.

g) data processing manager—read and display any and all programs and files.

h) yourself—perform any and all operations on any and all programs and files.

---

[13] *Question 18, Part II (Internal Audit Techniques). From* The Certified Internal Auditor Examination, *1976. Copyright © 1976 by the Institute of Internal Auditors, Inc. Reprinted by permission of the Institute of Internal Auditors, Inc., 249 Maitland Ave., Altamonte Springs, Fla. 32701.*

You will assign each user a six-character user code, and select access authority codes for each user based upon the following access authority coding system.

0 = no access permitted.

1 = read and display only.

2 = read, display, and update.

3 = read, display, update, create, and delete.

Required   Prepare the access control matrix.

43. The Foster Corporation recently fired its Director of Information Systems after experiencing several years of budget overruns in systems development and computer operations. As an internal auditor with computer management experience, you have been appointed as Interim Director and charged to investigate the problems which the department has experienced.

A significant obstacle to your investigation has been a lack of written information about the activities of the department or the policies under which it was managed. The previous director apparently managed in an informal manner, communicating assignments, standards, and performance evaluations to his employees verbally. This style of management was apparently popular with many employees, but unpopular with many others, some of whom have left the company.

The major systems project under development is a Management Information System. Objectives for this project are loosely defined, although a good deal of analysis, design, and programming has been completed. The project director estimates that this project is roughly half finished.

The computer operations department runs jobs on an "as received" basis. The operations supervisor suggests that a newer, faster, and more reliable system is needed to satisfy demand during peak periods and to cope with expected growth in processing requirements.

Required   Identify and briefly describe several elements of control that appear to be lacking in this situation and that you feel should be implemented in the Information Systems Department.

44. You have been engaged by Central Savings and Loan Association to examine its financial statements for the year ended December 31, 1967. The CPA who examined the financial statements at December 31, 1966 rendered an unqualified opinion.

In January 1967 the Association installed an online-real-time computer system. Each teller in the Association's main office and seven branch offices has an online input-output terminal. Customers' mortgage payments and savings account deposits and withdrawals are recorded in the accounts by the computer from data input by the teller at the time of the transaction. The teller keys the proper account by account number and enters the information in the terminal keyboard to record the transaction. The accounting department at the main office has both punched card and typewriter input-output devices. The computer is housed at the main office.

Required

You would expect the Association to have certain internal controls because an online-real-time computer system is employed. List the internal controls that should be in effect solely because this type of system is employed, classifying them as

a) those controls pertaining to input of information, and

b) all other types of computer controls.[14]

45. You are performing an audit of the EDP function of a chemical company with about $150 million in annual sales. Your initial survey discloses the following points.

1. The EDP manager reports to the director of accounting who, in turn, reports to the controller. The controller reports to the treasurer who is one of several vice-presidents in the company. The EDP manager has made several unsuccessful requests to the director of accounting for another printer.

2. There is no written charter for the EDP function, but the EDP manager tells you that the primary objective is to get the accounting reports out on time.

3. Transaction tapes are used daily to update the master file and are then retired to the scratch tape area.

4. A third-generation computer with large disk capacity was installed three years ago. The EDP activity previously used a second-generation computer, and many of the programs written for that computer are used on the present equipment by means of an emulator.

5. You observe that the output from the computer runs is written on tape for printing at a later time. Some output tapes from several days' runs are waiting to be printed.

6. The EDP manager states that the CPU could handle at least twice the work currently being processed.

Required

a) Identify the defect inherent in each of the six conditions shown above.

b) Briefly describe the probable effect if the condition is permitted to continue.[15]

46. Prepare a flowchart of a program incorporating several control features as described below.

A file is read that contains an employee identification number, a department number, employee name, pay rate, hours worked, gross pay, net pay, and total deductions. The program performs various control checks and edits as follows.

a) Sequence check—the cards are checked to assure that they are in numerical sequence by employee identification number.

b) Field check—the department number is checked to assure that it contains numeric data.

[14] Adapted from Question 2, Auditing Section, American Institute of Certified Public Accountants Examination, May 1968. Copyright © 1968 by the American Institute of Certified Public Accountants, Inc., and reprinted with permission.

[15] Question 19, Part II (Internal Audit Techniques). From The Certified Internal Auditor Examination, 1977. Copyright 1977 by the Institute of Internal Auditors, Inc. Reprinted by permission of the Institute of Internal Auditors, Inc., 249 Maitland Ave., Altamonte Springs, Fla. 32701.

c) Validity check—the employee identification number is checked to ensure that it is either less than 2500 or greater than 4300.

d) Limit checks—pay rate and hours worked are checked to ensure that they do not exceed $18.00 and 70, respectively.

e) Sign check—net pay is checked to ensure that it is positive.

f) Edit check—gross pay for each record is tested to ensure that it is equal to the product of pay rate and hours worked.

g) Cross-footing balance test—at the completion of processing, the total of gross pay is compared with the sum of the total of net pay and of deductions.

h) Control totals—a hash total of employee identification number, a record count, and financial totals of gross pay and total deductions are accumulated during processing and checked for accuracy against predetermined control totals read from the trailer label.

If an error is encountered by checks (a) through (f), the record data are printed out together with an error message. Each record should be checked for the existence of all of these conditions, so some records may be printed out more than once with more than one error message. When processing is completed, messages should be printed out indicating whether or not conditions (g) and (h) are satisfied.

References

Allen, Brandt. "Embezzler's Guide to the Computer." *Harvard Business Review* (July/August 1975): 79–89.

_____. "The Biggest Computer Frauds: Lessons for CPAs." *The Journal of Accountancy* (May 1977): 55–62.

American Institute of Certified Public Accountants. *Controls over Using and Changing Computer Programs.* New York: American Institute of Certified Public Accountants, Inc., 1979.

Auditing Standards Executive Committee, American Institute of Certified Public Accountants. *The Effects of EDP on the Auditor's Study and Evaluation of Internal Control.* Statement on Auditing Standards 3. New York: American Institute of Certified Public Accountants, Inc., 1974.

Birtle, William G.; Barry D. Hawkins, and Walter D. Pugh. "How to Evaluate Accounting Controls in a Minicomputer Installation." *The Practical Accountant* (August 1980): 47–53.

Canning, Richard G. "Are We Doing Things Right?" *EDP Analyzer* (June 1975): 1–12.

_____. "The Security of Managers' Information." *EDP Analyzer* (July 1979): 1–13.

Crossman, Trevor D. "Taking the Measure of Programmer Productivity." *Datamation* (May 1979): 144–147.

Davis, James R. "EDP Control Means Total Control." *Management Accounting* (January 1977): 41–44.

Hansen, William A. "The Operator's Changing Status." *Datamation* (January 1979): 189–193.

Hirsch, Rudolph E. "Data Processing *Can* Be Cost-Controlled." *Price Water-house Review* (Summer 1970): 65–72.

Kelley, Neil D. "The Economics of Uninterruptible Power." *Infosystems* (September 1980): 55–64.

Lettieri, Larry. "Disaster Recovery: Picking Up the Pieces." *Computer Decisions* (March 1979): 16–22, 27.

Lyons, Norman R. "Segregation of Functions in EFTS." *The Journal of Accountancy* (October 1978): 89–92.

Martin, James. *Security, Accuracy, and Privacy in Computer Systems.* Englewood Cliffs, N.J.: Prentice-Hall, 1973.

Mason, John O., Jr., and Jonathan J. Davies. "Legal Implications of EDP Deficiencies." *The CPA Journal* (May 1977): 21–24.

Matthews, Joseph R. "A Survey of EDP Performance Measures." *Government Data Systems* (July/August 1978): 29–32.

Mautz, Robert K.; Walter G. Kell; Michael W. Maher; Alan G. Merten; Raymond R. Reilly; Dennis G. Severance; and Bernard J. White. *Internal Control in U.S. Corporations: The State of the Art.* New York: Financial Executives Research Foundation, 1980.

Meyer, Carl H., and Walter L. Tuchman. "Putting Data Encryption to Work." *Mini-Micro Systems* (October 1978): 46–52.

Parker, Donn B. *Crime by Computer.* New York: Scribner's, 1976.

Price Waterhouse & Co. *Guide to Accounting Controls: EDP.* New York: Price Waterhouse & Co., 1979.

Rhodes, Wayne L. "Second Site Protection." *Infosystems* (September 1980): 46–52.

Romney, Marshall. "Fraud and EDP." *The CPA Journal* (November 1976): 23–28.

Schroeder, Walter, J. "The EDP Manager—and the Computer Profit Drain." *Computers and Automation* (January 1971): 14–18.

Shankar, K. S. "The Total Computer Security Problem: An Overview." *Computer* (June 1977): 50–62.

Stanford Research Institute. *Systems Auditability & Control Study, Data Processing Control Practices Report.* Altamonte Springs, Fla.: The Institute of Internal Auditors, Inc., 1977.

Stimler, Saul. *Data Processing Systems: Their Performance, Evaluation, Measurement, and Improvement.* Trenton, N.J.: Motivational Learning Programs, Inc., 1974.

Sykes, David J. "Protecting Data by Encryption." *Datamation* (August 1976): 81–85.

Thorne, Jack F. "Control of Computer Abuses." *The Journal of Accountancy* (October 1974): 40–48.

Wood, C.; E. B. Fernandez; and R. C. Summers. "Data Base Security: Requirements, Policies, and Models." *IBM Systems Journal,* Vol. 19, No. 2 (1980): 229–252.

Zimmerman, Harry. "Minicomputers: The Challenge for Controls." *The Journal of Accountancy* (June 1980): 28–35.

Chapter 15

Auditing of Computer-Based Information Systems

To complete this unit on the management of information sytems, this chapter describes the concepts and techniques used in auditing computer-based systems. As discussed in Part I, the internal audit function in an organization is a key element of management control, providing an independent appraisal of management performance as well as a review of the effectiveness of the internal control system. The rapid growth of the internal auditing profession in recent years reflects a growing recognition of the importance of the internal auditor on the management team.

Of course there are a number of other categories of auditors in addition to internal auditors. For example, the General Accounting Office of the United States Congress and various legislative audit agencies of state governments employ auditors to evaluate management performance and compliance with legislative intent in government departments and bureaus. The Defense Contract Audit Agency of the Department of Defense employs auditors to review the financial records of companies having defense contracts with the government. Public accountants, or "external auditors," provide an independent review of the financial statements of publicly held corporations. While this chapter is written primarily from the perspective of the internal auditor, many of the concepts and techniques discussed here are equally applicable to these other types of auditing.

The American Accounting Association has prepared the following general definition of *auditing*.

Auditing is a systematic process of objectively obtaining and evaluating evidence regarding assertions about economic actions and events to ascertain the degree of correspondence between those assertions and established criteria and communicating the results to interested users. [1]

Certain aspects of this definition are of particular interest. For example, note that the auditor *objectively* obtains and evaluates evidence. Objectivity is critical to the credibility and usefulness of the auditor's findings, which is why the audit function should be organizationally independent of those functions it is assigned to review. Also, auditing is described as a *systematic process,* which suggests a step-by-step approach characterized by careful planning and judicious selection and execution of appropriate techniques. A later section of this chapter reviews the steps in the auditing process. Furthermore, note that much of auditing involves the collection, review, and documentation of *audit evidence.* Finally, in developing recommendations the auditor uses *established criteria* as a basis for evaluation. With respect to audits of computer-based information systems, these established criteria are the principles of management and control of information systems described in the previous five chapters in Part III.

The advent of electronic data processing has had a major effect upon auditing, due primarily to the absence of a visible audit trail in computerized systems. More specifically, computerized data processing systems maintain files on media that are machine readable, such as magnetic tape or disk. File content may be printed out infrequently or at irregular intervals. A history of the activity relating to each individual file may not be maintained. In online processing, even a printed record of input may not be produced.

The importance of internal control and the natural tendency toward elimination of visible audit trails in computerized information systems underscore the need to involve the auditor in the systems design process. In this role, the auditor may suggest the incorporation of necessary internal controls and audit trails into new systems while they are being developed, and while there is still time to implement such suggestions economically. This will not only minimize the need for expensive modifications of systems after implementation, but should also reduce the extent of testing required during the regular audit process.

The first reaction of auditors to the use of computers in data processing was to attempt to perform their audits with the printed records and output provided by the system, ignoring the computer and its programs. This approach was referred to as auditing "around" the computer. The assumption underlying this approach was that if a sample of system output was correctly obtained from system input, then the processing itself must be reliable. This was a reasonable approach fifteen or twenty years ago when knowledge of electronic data processing among auditors was limited. However, both the increasing difficulty of applying this approach to a dis-

---

[1] *Committee on Basic Auditing Concepts,* A Statement of Basic Auditing Concepts. *Sarasota, Fla.: American Accounting Association, 1973, p. 2.*

appearing audit trail and the development of better methods of auditing computer systems have combined to discredit the old approach of auditing "around" the computer.

The alternative to auditing "around" is referred to as auditing "through" the computer. This approach uses the computer itself to check the adequacy of system controls and the accuracy of system output. Most of the auditing techniques discussed in this chapter involve auditing "through" the computer.

However, if auditors must work directly with the computer, then they must possess some degree of computer expertise. According to a recent study, modern organizations have tried several approaches to the development of such expertise on their internal audit staffs, including (1) training data processing specialists in audit concepts and methods, (2) training internal auditors in data processing techniques and practices, and (3) supplementing the internal audit staff with a few data processing specialists.[2] That study concluded that a combination of the second and third approaches appears to be most effective at the present time. However, in the long run the acquisition of computer science expertise by accounting and auditing students during their professional education may offer the greatest promise of resolving this problem.

The chapter is divided into five major sections. In the first section the scope and objectives of internal audit work are briefly described. The second section provides a brief overview of the steps in the auditing process. The third section deals with the process of evaluating internal controls in a computer-based information system, and explains several techniques used for this purpose. In the fourth section, techniques for evaluating the reliability and integrity of financial and operating information maintained on the computer are described. The fifth section discusses the review of performance of systems management and operations in a computer-based information system.

Scope and Objectives of Audit Work

According to the *Standards for the Professional Practice of Internal Auditing* promulgated by the Institute of Internal Auditors in 1978

The scope of the internal audit encompasses the examination and evaluation of the adequacy and effectiveness of the organization's system of internal control and the quality of performance in carrying out assigned responsibilities.[3]

The Institute further delineates five specific standards dealing with the following aspects of the scope of audit work.

[2] *Stanford Research Institute,* Systems Auditability & Control Study, Data Processing Audit Practices Report. *Altamonte Springs, Fla.: The Institute of Internal Auditors, Inc., 1977, Chapter 5.*

[3] *Institute of Internal Auditors,* Standards for the Professional Practice of Internal Auditing. *Altamonte Springs, Fla.: The Institute of Internal Auditors, Inc., 1978, p. 3.*

1. Reliability and integrity of information.
2. Compliance with policies, plans, procedures, laws, and regulations.
3. Safeguarding of assets.
4. Economical and efficient use of resources.
5. Accomplishment of established objectives and goals for operations or programs.

This section describes each of these five standards and discusses their implications with respect to computer-based information systems.

The first internal audit scope standard states that

> *Internal auditors should review the reliability and integrity of financial and operating information and the means used to identify, measure, classify, and report such information.*[4]

In modern organizations, much of the information referred to in this standard is maintained on a computer system. Therefore, the auditor must have a clear understanding of how this information is processed on the computer in order to meet this standard. Furthermore, the auditor will have to rely on the computer in order to access the information to be reviewed. To best fulfill the requirements of this standard, the auditor should actually use the computer itself as a primary tool for carrying out many of the necessary auditing procedures.

The second standard states that

> *Internal auditors should review the systems established to ensure compliance with those policies, plans, procedures, laws, and regulations which could have a significant impact on operations and reports and should determine whether the organization is in compliance.*[5]

Numerous examples exist of policies, plans, procedures, laws, and regulations relating to computer-based information processing, including policies for hiring, assignment, evaluation and promotion of EDP personnel, operating procedures for data processing equipment, three- or five-year plans for the information processing facility, and laws and regulations dealing with corporate financial reporting, information privacy, and internal controls. Therefore, reviewing compliance with matters such as these requires a considerable amount of review of the information processing facility itself.

According to the third scope standard,

> *Internal auditors should review the means of safeguarding assets and, as appropriate, verify the existence of such assets.*[6]

---

[4] *Ibid., p. 3.*

[5] *Ibid., p. 4.*

[6] *Ibid., p. 4.*

Modern organizations generally use computers to account for and control such assets as inventories, plant and equipment, and receivables. Furthermore, many organizations use their computer to prepare checks. In such cases, a review of the means of safeguarding assets is to a great extent a review of computer processing of asset information. Furthermore, in order to verify the existence of recorded assets, the auditor must use the computer to obtain a listing of the assets to be verified.

The fourth standard is that

> *Internal auditors should appraise the economy and efficiency with which resources are employed.*[7]

The standard is applicable to all operations, departments, and managers within the organization, including the systems department. Information processing resources include both data processing equipment and personnel such as systems analysts, programmers and equipment operators. In Part III of this book a number of principles underlying the effective and efficient use of these resources have been discussed. It is the proper application of these principles that the auditor must review in order to comply with this standard.

According to the fifth scope standard,

> *Internal auditors should review operations or programs to ascertain whether results are consistent with established objectives and whether the operations or programs are being carried out as planned.*[8]

Again, this is a standard that is applicable to all parts of an organization. In the systems management area it applies to such things as feasibility studies for new systems, long-range information systems plans, and system project development activities.

In conclusion, the scope of internal auditing work can be divided into three major categories. The first of these is the *internal control audit,* the scope of which roughly corresponds to the second and third standards discussed above. The second major category is the *financial audit,* which correlates with the first of the five scope standards.[9] The third major category, corresponding to the fourth and fifth scope standards, is the *management audit,* often referred to as the *operational audit.* These three major categories are each described in turn in the three final sections of this chapter. A fourth category of lesser general importance, which is not discussed further in this chapter, is referred to as the *compliance audit.* This type of audit is a subset of the work referred to in the second scope standard, and specifically deals with an organization's compliance with laws, contract provisions, government regulations, and other obligations to external parties.

---

[7] *Ibid., p. 4.*

[8] *Ibid., p. 4.*

[9] *Note that since the first standard refers to both "financial and operating information," it would perhaps make better sense to use the term* information audit. *However, because of the traditional emphasis of internal auditors on financial information, the term* financial audit *has become generally accepted, even though the scope of such audits is expanding to encompass nonfinancial information.*

An Overview of the Auditing Process

Whether performed by internal, external, or governmental auditors, and whether their scope involves internal controls, financial information, or management performance, all audits consist of a very similar sequence of activities. Generally, the auditing process may be divided into the following four steps.

1. Planning.
2. Evidence gathering.
3. Evidence evaluation.
4. Communication of results.

This section of the chapter discusses some of the major factors involved in each of these four steps.

Audit planning

The first step in audit planning is to establish the scope and objectives of the audit. These depend on who the audit is for and what type of audit is desired. For example, the independent audit of financial statements of publicly held corporations is directed at corporate stockholders, and has the purpose of evaluating the fairness of presentation of corporate financial statements. The scope and objectives of internal audits vary widely, but are generally established either implicitly or explicitly by management.

Once the audit scope and objectives are defined, the auditor must develop (or reestablish) a general familiarity with the operations of the entity to be audited. Discussions with management personnel and a review of summary documentation and operating information are useful for this purpose. This should enable the auditor to identify any potential audit risks or problems to which he or she may be exposed.

To conclude the planning stage, the auditor prepares a preliminary audit program that delineates the nature, extent, and timing of specific audit tests and procedures that will achieve the desired audit objectives and minimize the audit risks. In conjunction with this step, a preliminary time budget for the audit is prepared, and audit staff members are assigned to perform specific portions of the audit work. This audit program is "preliminary" in the sense that it may be revised during the audit if necessary in view of the audit findings.

Collection of audit evidence

Audit evidence is gathered by means of a number of different kinds of tests and procedures. These include (1) *observation* of the operating activities of the audited organization and its employees, (2) *physical examination* of the quantity and/or condition of tangible assets such as equipment, inventory, or cash, (3) *confirmation* of information accuracy by means of written communication with independent third parties, (4) *inquiry* directed at employees of the audited organization, often facilitated by questionnaires or interview checklists, (5) *recalculation* of quantitative information on records and reports, (6) *vouching,* or examining the accuracy of documents and records, especially by means of tracing the information through the processing system to its source, and (7) *analytical review* of relationships and trends among financial and operating information in order to detect items that should be further investigated. A given audit will generally consist of several tests and procedures from most or all of these categories. It is also appropriate to point out that many audit tests and procedures cannot feasibly be performed on the entire population of activities, records, assets, or documents under review, and so must be performed on a sample basis.

Evaluation of audit evidence

Three broad options available to the auditor at the evaluation stage are (1) to decide that the evidence supports a favorable conclusion with respect to the operations, controls, or information being audited, (2) to decide that the evidence supports an unfavorable or negative conclusion, or (3) to decide that the available evidence is inconclusive and that more evidence should be collected.

In making the evaluation decision, the auditor utilizes the concepts of *materiality* and *reasonable assurance.* That is, the auditor desires reasonable assurance that there is not a material error or deficiency in the information or process being audited. The concept of reasonable assurance implies that the auditor does not seek complete assurance because to do so would be prohibitively expensive; however, this also implies that the auditor is willing to accept some degree of risk that the audit conclusion will be incorrect. The concept of materiality recognizes that some errors or deficiencies are bound to exist in any system, and therefore the auditor should focus on detecting and reporting only those errors and deficiencies that could possibly have a significant impact on decisions. Determining what is and what is not material in a given set of circumstances is primarily a matter of judgment. It should be noted that consideration of materiality and reasonable assurance is important at the audit planning stage, when the auditor is deciding how much audit work is necessary, as well as at the evidence evaluation stage.

As the audit proceeds, it is important that the auditor carefully document his findings and conclusions in a set of audit working papers. Documentation should occur at all stages of the audit, but it becomes especially critical at the evaluation stage when final conclusions must be reached and supported.

Communication of audit results

Once the audit work is completed and final conclusions have been reached, the auditor prepares a report of his findings and recommendations. This report is provided to management, shareholders, the board of directors, or other appropriate parties. At some point following the communication of audit results, it may be desirable for the auditor to perform a follow-up study to ascertain whether his recommendations have been implemented.

Internal Control Audits of Computer-Based Information Systems

In performing a study and evaluation of internal control in a computer-based information system, the auditor should attempt to accomplish the following six objectives.

Objective 1:   To ascertain that the design and implementation of application programs is performed in accordance with management's general and specific authorization.

Objective 2:   To ascertain that any and all changes in application programs have the authorization and approval of management.

Objective 3:   To ascertain that provisions exist to ensure the accuracy and integrity of computer processing of files, reports, and other computer-generated records.

Objective 4:   To ascertain that application program source data that is inaccurate or not properly authorized is identified and dealt with in accordance with prescribed managerial policies.

Objective 5:   To ascertain that computer operators and other persons with online access to the system cannot accomplish unauthorized modification of input, output, programs, or data files.

Objective 6:   To ascertain that provisions exist to protect data files from unauthorized access, modification, or destruction.

This section discusses each of these objectives in turn, focusing on the auditing techniques and procedures available to accomplish them.

As a framework for the discussion of each objective, the "conceptually logical approach" to internal control evaluation advocated by the American Institute of Certified Public Accountants (AICPA) is used. This approach involves the following four steps.[10]

1. Consider the types of errors and irregularities that could occur.
2. Determine the accounting control procedures that should prevent or detect such errors and irregularities.
3. Determine whether the necessary procedures are prescribed and are being followed satisfactorily.
4. Evaluate any weaknesses, i.e., types of potential errors and irregularities not covered by existing control procedures, to determine their effect on (a) the nature, timing, or extent of auditing procedures to be applied and (b) suggestions to be made to the client.

The determination of "whether the necessary procedures are prescribed," mentioned in 3, is called the *system review,* whereas the determination of whether these procedures "are being followed satisfactorily" is done via *tests of compliance.*

---

[10] *American Institute of Certified Public Accountants,* Codification of Statements on Auditing Standards, Numbers 1 to 15. *New York: AICPA, 1977, Section 320.65.*

Generally, the system review will consist of such audit procedures as review of system documentation and inquiry of personnel. Audit procedures most commonly associated with tests of compliance include observation of system operations, test checking of system inputs and outputs, tracing of transactions through the system, and confirmation of system data with third parties.

Generally, if the EDP control system does not appear to satisfy one or more of the six objectives, the auditor should consider whether or not compensating controls exist with respect to the particular errors or irregularities in question. It is not surprising that the control objectives are to some extent overlapping with respect to certain types of errors and irregularities because the concept of redundancy is central to many kinds of control systems. Therefore, control weaknesses in one area may be acceptable if they are compensated for by control strengths in other areas.

Once the auditor has completed the system review and tests of compliance with respect to each objective, and has considered the adequacy of compensating controls, he or she should have a clear understanding of the kinds of errors and irregularities that could occur. This provides a sound basis for developing recommendations to management, and for determining the appropriate extent of reliance on the EDP control system for financial auditing purposes.

Objective 1: program development

The focus of the first objective is on the program development process, particularly as it relates to accounting application programs. Essentially, two things could go wrong in this process. First, inadvertent errors could be introduced into the programs through misunderstanding of system specifications or simply careless programming. Second, unauthorized instructions could be deliberately included in the programs by persons whose motives are contrary to those of management.

The control procedures that should prevent these problems involve the quality and integrity of the process of systems analysis, design, and implementation. Generally, the specifications for application programs should have the authorization and approval of management, and in particular the approval of those functional departments and other system users whose operations are affected by the new system. A thorough process of testing and approval of test results for new systems should be in use. Finally, the system itself and all related authorizations and approvals should be well documented.

The auditor who actually participates in the systems design process as a member of the project development team is in a position to influence the project manager to follow these preferred practices. However, there is a danger in this situation that the auditor will lose the objectivity necessary to perform an independent evaluation function. Therefore, the auditor's role should be limited to an independent review of, rather than participation in, systems development activities. Furthermore, there is no requirement that such a review take place after the systems development process is completed. Independent reviews by auditors during the systems development process will be much more effective in achieving audit objectives.

During the system review stage of the examination, the auditor should obtain copies of written policies and procedures pertaining to systems development, and review those standards relating to authorization and approval of new systems; involvement of user departments and other appropriate personnel in the systems design process; review and evaluation of programmer output; documentation of new systems; testing of new systems; and review and approval of tests results. The auditor should also discuss these prescribed policies and procedures with management, system users, and EDP personnel to obtain their understanding of how such policies and procedures are intended to be applied. Finally, the auditor should review in some detail the application systems documentation.

Tests of compliance with respect to systems development policies should include interviews with managers and system users, which attempt to ascertain the extent of their actual involvement in the design and implementation of specific application systems. In addition, evidence of such involvement, in the form of participation in systems development groups and signed approvals at various stages of the development process, should be sought. In the former case this involves review of minutes of meetings of systems teams. In the latter case this requires review of system specifications, preliminary system design documentation, test data specifications, test results, and records of final conversion for signatures evidencing the necessary authorizations and approvals.

Among the most important controls over new system development is the processing of test data. The auditor should review thoroughly all available client documentation relating to the testing process, and should ascertain that all program routines affecting accounting data were tested. This involves an examination of the test specifications, a review of the test data, and an evaluation of test results. When unexpected test results were obtained, the auditor should ascertain how the problem was resolved.

The review and evaluation of internal controls relating to EDP systems development should be performed for each significant application program. However, once the review has been completed for a particular application, it need not be done again in future years. Therefore, the auditor should regularly perform such a review only for newly developed application programs. For ongoing applications after the initial review, the auditor's concern shifts to controls over program changes, which are the focus of the second of our six objectives.

If the auditor concludes that system development controls for a particular application program are inadequate, the inadequacy may be compensated for by the presence of strong processing controls (see Objective 3). However, such reliance upon compensatory processing controls would require that the auditor obtain persuasive evidence of compliance with these controls through such techniques as independent processing of test data. If it is not possible to obtain such evidence of effective compensating controls, then the auditor may have to conclude that a material weakness in internal control exists such that the risk of significant errors or irregularities in application programs is unacceptably high.

Objective 2: program changes

The things that could go wrong with respect to program changes are essentially the same as with new program development. First, inadvertent errors could be introduced into programs undergoing an authorized change either because of a misunderstanding of change specifications or careless programming. Second, unauthorized instructions could be deliberately inserted into existing programs. These problems could potentially affect not only application programs but also systems programs, such as utilities and operating systems. Accordingly, the suggested internal controls and audit procedures discussed in this section apply to all types of programs used by the computer department.

Internal controls should exist that ensure the authorization, documentation, review, testing, and approval of all program changes. In addition, however, controls must exist to prevent deliberate and unauthorized program modification. These include separation of the programming, operations, and file librarian functions, and procedures to control access to computer equipment and program files.

With respect to authorized program changes, part of the auditor's system review should include the examination of written policies and standards, as well as discussions with EDP management concerning how these policies and standards are intended to be implemented. The auditor should also review organization charts and job descriptions and make related inquiries to ascertain the existence of separation of the functions of programming, computer operations, and file librarian. Written policies pertaining to control over access to computer equipment, program files, and program documentation should be examined. Discussions with EDP management, programmers, operations personnel, and the file librarian will help the auditor understand how the written policies and procedures are intended to be implemented.

An important part of the auditor's tests of compliance with respect to these controls is the observation of EDP operations. The auditor should attempt to ascertain that systems analysts, programmers, and other nonoperations personnel do not have unrestricted access to computer equipment or program files. The effectiveness of the supervision of computer operations should be evaluated. The auditor should observe whether application program usage records are consistently maintained by a file librarian and, if they are, should review those records for evidence of any unusual access to program files.

In many modern organizations, greater emphasis is being placed upon remote terminals and minicomputers located in centers of activity at a distance from the central computer site. In this situation the concept of "restricted access" takes on new dimensions because it is far more difficult to restrict access to a multitude of separate locations than to a single centralized location. In this type of environment, the auditor should attempt to ascertain that only a limited number of persons is authorized to operate each terminal or minicomputer, and that access is restricted by means of supervisory controls, password access controls built into the systems software, controls over equipment keys and, wherever possible, by locating the equipment in a limited access area.

Tests of compliance relating to authorized program changes should begin with a review of the documentation of such changes and the related authorizations and approvals. Particular attention should be given to the authorization for the changes, evidence of review and approval of changes in program code, and the quality of testing of the modified program. Note that it is important to test the entire program rather than just the portion that was modified, in order to prevent a programmer from inserting an unauthorized routine into a separate part of the program during the process of making an authorized program change.

A powerful tool for testing for the presence of unauthorized program changes is a source code comparison program.[11] This program will perform a detailed match of the current version of the application program with a previous version. The auditor should have thoroughly tested the previous version or have other good reasons to have confidence in its integrity. The output of this process is a report identifying the differences between the two programs. The auditor must then review each difference to ascertain that it represents an authorized change.

Two additional techniques that involve using the computer to detect unauthorized program changes are *reprocessing* and *parallel simulation*. To use the reprocessing technique, the auditor must verify the integrity of a copy of the application program, and then save that copy for future use. At subsequent intervals on a surprise basis, the auditor uses the previously verified version of the program to reprocess data that have been processed by the current version, and the output of the two runs is compared. Any discrepancies in the two sets of output are then investigated to ascertain their cause. Parallel simulation works in a similar fashion, except that instead of using a previously verified copy of the application program, the auditor writes his or her own version of the program, or of those parts of the program that are of audit interest. The auditor's version of the program is then used to reprocess the data, and the output is compared with the output from the current version of the program.

The auditor's review of program change controls should encompass each significant application program, and should be repeated periodically. In fact, whenever the organization is implementing a major change in an application program, the auditor should be called in to observe the testing and implementation, review related authorizations and documentation and, if necessary, perform independent tests. If this is not done, and the auditor's subsequent examination reveals inadequacies in the program change controls, it may not be possible to rely on the system with respect to the accuracy of program outputs subsequent to the change. In addition, the auditor should always perform some program tests on a surprise basis, as a precaution against unauthorized program changes that may be inserted after the auditor's examination is completed, and then removed prior to the next scheduled audit.

If the auditor concludes that internal controls over program changes are deficient, and especially if this deficiency is caused by a lack of separation of functions

---

[11] *A specific program for this purpose is described by Donald L. Adams in "Alternatives to Computer Audit Software,"* The Journal of Accountancy, *November 1975, page 56.*

or inadequate restrictions on access to equipment or program files, the possibility that the auditor can place any reliance on EDP controls is remote. If such controls are present but are only partially effective, then the presence of excellent processing controls together with the auditor's independent tests of such controls may compensate for such deficiencies.

Objective 3: processing

At the stage of processing input data on the computer to update files or to generate documents and reports, several things could go wrong. Incorrect or unauthorized source data could fail to be detected. Attempts to correct inaccurate data could fail, or could introduce additional errors. Correct input or file data could be inadvertently rendered incorrect through improper operating procedures,[12] system malfunctions, or program errors of either a deliberate or unintentional nature. Computer output could fail to be properly distributed or become available to unauthorized persons. Our third objective is to ascertain that processing controls[13] exist to prevent, or to detect and correct, these kinds of problems.

The processing controls that should be present in a well-managed data processing facility include file labeling techniques, reconciliation of output control totals, maintenance of a console log, incorporation of data edit routines and other programmed controls into application programs, effective supervision of computer operations, good operating documentation and run manuals, preparation of file change listings and summaries for user department review, the use of vendor-supplied hardware and system software controls, and the maintenance of proper levels of temperature, humidity, and other environmental conditions in the computer facility.

The auditor's system review with respect to processing controls should include an examination of written installation standards relating to file labeling, console logs, control totals, environmental controls, and output distribution. Copies of operator's run manuals should be reviewed. The nature of processing controls used in specific accounting applications should be ascertained by a review of application documentation. Vendor literature describing available hardware and system software controls should be examined. Finally, the auditor should interview computer operators, operations supervisors, EDP management, and other appropriate personnel to develop an understanding of how these various types of controls are intended to be applied in practice.

If the auditor suspects or uncovers evidence indicating that a particular application program may contain significant flaws, then a detailed review of some or all of the program logic may be necessary. This is a time-consuming procedure that requires the auditor to be proficient in the programming language. Therefore, it would

---

[12] *Computer operators could also deliberately introduce unauthorized or erroneous data; this is covered by Objective 5.*

[13] *The term* processing controls *as used here encompasses both* processing controls *and* output controls *as these terms are defined by the AICPA in* Codification of Statements on Auditing Standards, *Section 321.08.*

be used only when no alternative method is available to accomplish the auditor's objective. To perform such a review, the auditor would normally refer to systems flowcharts, program flowcharts, and other program documentation in addition to a listing of the program source code. There are several software packages the auditor may use to assist in this review, including (1) *automated flowcharting programs,* which interpret the program source code and generate a program flowchart corresponding to it; (2) *automated decision table programs,* which generate a decision table representing the program logic; (3) *scanning routines,* which search a program for occurrences of a specified variable name or other combinations of characters; and (4) *mapping programs,* which can be activated during regular processing of application programs to identify those portions of the application program that are not executed.

As a part of the tests of compliance with respect to processing controls, the auditor should evaluate the adequacy of controls prescribed by run manuals and other operating documentation, and then observe computer operations for evidence that these prescribed controls are actually being followed. Specific things that the auditor should observe are the reconciliation of output control totals, handling of application program error listings, logging of console intervention by the computer operator, label checking and other file handling operations, and adherence to prescribed environmental controls. The auditor should also evaluate the organization's practices relating to the use of available hardware and system software controls, and then observe the actual application of these practices.

The auditor's tests of compliance should also include a review of the console log for evidence that all operator intervention is in accordance with prescribed policies and procedures. The auditor should make an independent test of the reconciliation of a sample of output control totals with corresponding input totals, and follow up on any discrepancies. The auditor should also observe the distribution of outputs of accounting application programs and determine that all recipients of such outputs are properly authorized. Ideally, the output distribution function should be the responsibility of data control personnel rather than computer operators.

Certain types of accounting transactions are sensitive from the standpoint of internal control. Among these are changes in customer credit ratings, product prices, and employee pay rates. Also in this category are transactions generated automatically by the computer system as a by-product of routine processing. The auditor should obtain evidence that output listings of these kinds of transactions are regularly reviewed by appropriate user departments. The auditor may also wish to verify a sample of these transactions by comparing them with user department records or by confirmation.

The auditor should evaluate the adequacy of data edit routines incorporated into client application programs, and then review the output of such programs for evidence that such edit tests have been applied. Client procedures for follow up and correction of edit errors should be observed and evaluated. Additional assurance as to the adequacy of client data editing may be obtained by using computer audit software[14] to independently edit selected accounting files. As mentioned earlier, the use of test decks is an additional method of testing the data edit provisions that have been incorporated into application programs. Furthermore, live processing of test transactions without the knowledge of computer operators enables the auditor to test the client's operating procedures for dealing with unusual or erroneous transactions.

Generally, it will be necessary for the auditor to reevaluate the client's processing controls periodically in order to justify continuing confidence in them. If the auditor concludes that the organization's processing controls are not satisfactory with respect to some or all application programs, he or she may nonetheless decide that internal controls in the related user departments (user controls), and source data controls are strong enough to compensate for such deficiencies. However, if these alternative controls are not sufficient to compensate for the deficiencies in processing controls, then the auditor must conclude that a material weakness exists in the organization's internal control system.

Several specialized techniques exist that enable the auditor to use the computer to perform compliance tests of data edit routines and other programmed controls in application programs. These include (1) processing of test data, (2) program tracing, and (3) embedded audit modules. In the following paragraphs, the nature and application of each of these techniques are explained.

Processing of test data   Processing of test data involves the introduction of hypothetical transactions into a computer system to check the completeness and accuracy of the system's processing and control procedures. Previous chapters have referred to this technique as an important means of testing new computer programs before they become operational. It is sometimes referred to as the "test deck" approach because punched cards were once the primary medium for introducing the test transactions. This technique is designed to test system compliance with respect to processing controls associated with an application program.

Figure 15.1 contains a systems flowchart representing an overview of the test data process. As a first step in this process the auditor reviews the system's documentation to develop a clear understanding of the nature and function of the program being tested. He or she should identify the edit routines, programmed controls, and alternative logic paths present, and then prepare a set of hypothetical transactions containing both valid and invalid data designed to test all portions of the program having audit significance. Examples of the kinds of invalid data that might be included are records with missing data, fields containing unreasonably large amounts, unusual relationships among data in two or more fields, invalid account numbers or processing codes, nonnumeric data in numeric fields, records out of sequence, illogical accounting journal entries, and so forth. Some transac-

---

[14] *The nature and application of computer audit software is explained in the following section of this chapter dealing with the financial audit of computer-based information systems.*

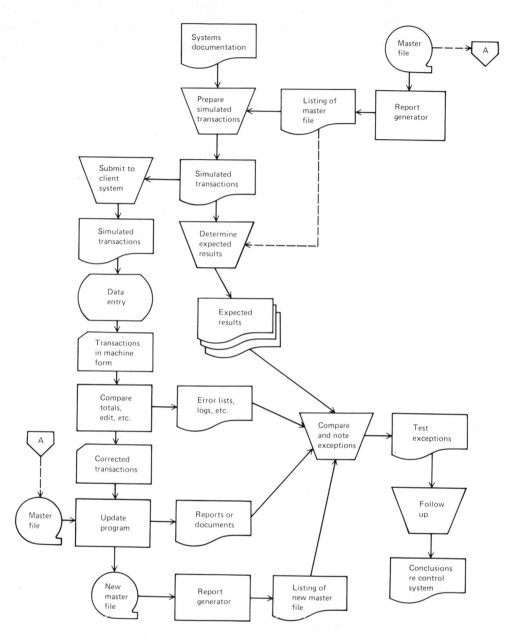

Fig. 15.1
Overview of test data
process.

tions should contain multiple errors. In addition, all of the alternative logic paths should be checked for proper functioning by one or more of the test transactions.

To facilitate the preparation of test transactions, the auditor may obtain a listing of actual transactions, as well as of test transactions used by the programmer. However, the availability of the programmer's test data may be useful for reference purposes, but does not relieve the auditor of the responsibility to perform an independent test using independently prepared test data. If available, the auditor may use a *test data generator* program to automatically prepare a set of test data based upon specifications describing the logical characteristics of the program to be tested.

Once the hypothetical transactions have been prepared, the auditor should review a listing of the current version of the master file or files maintained by the application program, and manually determine what the expected results of processing the test transactions should be. The test data are then introduced into the system, either as source documents (as shown in Fig. 15.1), or in machine-readable form at a subsequent processing step. Alternatively, the auditor may process the test data independently of the organization's data processing personnel.

After the test data are processed, the actual system output, including error reports or logs, documents, reports, and file update listings, is compared to the predetermined correct output. Any discrepancies indicate a potential lack of compliance with appropriate processing controls, and should be thoroughly investigated to determine their cause.

Although the processing of test transactions is a very effective means of testing system compliance with processing controls, it does have some disadvantages. The auditor typically must spend considerable time developing an understanding of the system and preparing an adequate set of test transactions. Furthermore, care must be taken to ensure that the test transactions do not affect the company's actual master file records. This might involve procedures to reverse the effects of the test transactions, or perhaps a separate run in which the test transactions are processed against a copy of the master file rather than against the real file. However, the use of a separate run removes some of the reality that is obtained from processing the test transactions along with the regular transactions. A further problem is that these special procedures may reveal the existence and nature of the auditor's test to the employees of the computer facility. Thus these procedures may be less effective than a concealed test would be.

Program tracing   *Program tracing* is a technique that enables the auditor to obtain a detailed knowledge of the logic of an application program, as well as test the program's compliance with its control specifications. To use this technique, the auditor processes the application program either with regular or test transactions, but activates a trace routine built into the system software. This routine will cause the computer to print out in sequential order a list of all of the application program steps (line numbers or paragraph names) executed during the program run. This list is intermingled with the regular program output so that the auditor can observe the precise sequence of events that took place during program execution. The auditor then reviews a copy of the source program in conjunction with the trace output to confirm his or her expectations of the way the program works.

This technique may enable the auditor to detect the presence of unauthorized program instructions, incorrect logic paths, or unused program sections within application programs. Such conditions should then be investigated further to ascertain their cause and effect. Program tracing can be a very effective computer auditing technique. However, it is also time-consuming and requires that the auditor be proficient in the programming language used by the application program.

Embedded audit modules *Embedded audit modules* are special portions of an application program designed to perform functions of particular use to auditors. For example, such modules might be designed to monitor all transaction activity and notify the auditor of any transactions having special audit significance, such as unauthorized attempts to access the system or dollar amounts in excess of prescribed limits. In one variation of this approach known as *real-time notification,* the auditor is informed of such transactions immediately as they occur by means of a message printed on the auditor's terminal. A more common approach is for the system to write all relevant information concerning such transactions on a tape or disk file called the *audit log.*[15] The auditor then periodically requests a printout of the audit log and investigates the transactions on it.

Another variation of this technique is known as *tagging.* Under this approach, selected records are marked with a special code. As the application programs process these records, the audit modules will capture all data relating to the marked records on a file that can subsequently be reviewed by the auditor. This enables the auditor to observe in detail all aspects of the processing of particular transactions through the information system.

Objective 4: source data

The focal point of Objective 4 is the accuracy and integrity of the data input to application programs. The errors or irregularities that could occur are that inaccurate or unauthorized source data could be introduced into the system and posted to system files by the computer. Internal controls should exist which will prevent, detect, and correct inaccurate or unauthorized source data. Among the most important of such controls is the existence of an independent data control function assigned responsibility for source data accuracy and integrity. Specific control techniques include user authorization of source data, desk-checking of input data listings, check digit verification during data encoding, keyverification of important data items, reconciliation of data input, the use of turnaround documents where feasible, the use of edit programs to check source data accuracy prior to processing, and special handling of any input errors discovered by these other controls.

As part of the system review, the auditor should examine organization charts and job descriptions to ascertain the existence of a data control function that is organizationally independent of user departments or the computer operations function. Written descriptions of the general procedures used for control of source data should be reviewed. The documentation of significant accounting applications should be examined to develop an understanding of the flow of accounting data to

---

[15] *A colorful acronym sometimes used to describe the audit log is* SCARF, *which stands for "System Control Audit Review File."*

and from the EDP function, and of the specific source data control procedures applied to such data. One tool the auditor may use to document the results of a review of source data controls for a particular application is the *input controls matrix,* (see Fig. 15.2) which shows the control procedures applied to each field of an input record. The auditor should also obtain a copy of the signatures or other forms of authorization required for each significant type of input transaction. Finally, the auditor should interview system users, EDP management, and data control personnel to develop an understanding of how the prescribed source data control procedures are intended to be applied.

In a small business data processing operation, or in a minicomputer installation located in a department or small division of a larger company, it is unlikely that an independent data control function will exist because it is simply not economically feasible. To compensate for this lack, other control procedures must be that much stronger. These include user department controls over data preparation, batch control totals, edit programs, system access restrictions, and error handling procedures. These controls should be the focus of the auditor's system review and compliance tests whenever there is no independent data control function in the installation being reviewed.

Tests of compliance with respect to source data controls should include observation of the operations of the data control function to ascertain its independence from other functions within the EDP department, as well as from user departments. The degree of control exercised over the data control log should also be observed. To verify the fact that batch control totals are being properly applied, the auditor should trace a sample of control totals through the input process. Control totals provided by user departments should be compared to those recorded in the data control log and to those generated by the computer during the preparation of input listings or the running of data edit programs. Any exceptions to proper reconciliation of control totals should be investigated. Finally, the auditor should compare a sample of transactions from computer listings of edited transactions to the data on the original source documents, and investigate any significant discrepancies.

Using the list of required source data authorizations obtained during system review, the auditor should examine samples of accounting source data for evidence that proper authorizations were present and were checked by data control personnel prior to acceptance of the data for computer processing. Any significant exceptions to proper source data authorization should be investigated by the auditor. Furthermore, the auditor should observe the performance of specific input verification procedures, such as checking for authorizations, review of input listings, logging, check digit verification, keyverification, reconciliation of input control totals, and processing of edit programs. Of particular importance here is observation of procedures used to control exceptions, such as transactions that fail check digit tests or edit program error listings.

A technique enabling comprehensive testing of both source data controls *and* processing controls is called the *mini-company test* or *integrated test facility* (ITF). This is an extension of the concept of test data processing that involves introducing a

INPUT CONTROLS	Employee number	Last name	Department number	Transaction code	Week ending (date)	Regular hours	Overtime hours			Comments
Batch totals					√	√				
Hash totals	√									
Record counts										Yes
Cross-footing balance										No
Key verification	√				√	√				
Visual inspection										All fields
Check digit verification	√									
Prenumbered forms										No
Turnaround document										No
Edit program										Yes
Sequence check	√									
Field check	√		√		√	√				
Sign check										
Validity check	√		√	√						
Limit check					√	√				
Reasonableness test					√	√				
Redundant data check	√	√	√							
Completeness test				√	√	√	√			
Overflow procedure										
Other:										

RECORD NAME: Employer Weekly Time Report

Fig. 15.2 Input controls matrix.

small set of records representing a fictitious entity into the master files of the system under review. The fictitious entity might be a dummy division, department, branch office, customer, etc. Test transactions may then be processed against these fictitious master records without affecting the real master records. Further, the test transactions may be processed along with the real transactions, and the employees of the computer facility need not be aware that the testing is being done. The integrated test facility therefore eliminates two of the primary disadvantages of processing test data, in that there is no need to reverse the effects of test transactions on the actual master file records, and the existence of the test can be concealed from the employees whose work is being checked. However, care must be taken in designing the integrated test facility to ensure that it does not cause real transactions to be initiated unnecessarily, and that its fictitious records are not aggregated with regular records during the preparation of summary reports for management.

Even though the prescribed source data controls may not change from year to year, the strictness with which they are applied may change. Therefore, the auditor who intends to rely upon EDP source data controls should perform compliance tests of them on a regular basis. If the auditor concludes that source data controls are not adequate with respect to a particular application system, other controls that may compensate are user department controls, and computer processing controls. If these other controls do not compensate for the inadequacies in source data controls, then the auditor may have to conclude that the EDP internal control system as a whole is unsatisfactory.

Objective 5: operations

The focus of Objective 5 is upon persons who operate computer equipment. Specifically it concerns the possibility that such persons may use the computer to deliberately introduce unauthorized transactions or program changes into the system. In this regard the term "computer operator" encompasses not only persons who run computer equipment at central data processing sites but also those who have online access to the system from remote terminals.

Effective internal control over computer operations requires that this function be organizationally independent of the programming, data control, and file librarian functions. Responsibility for supervision of computer operations should be assigned to a qualified employee. The access of computer operators to systems documentation and to program and data files should be controlled. There should be a data processing schedule indicating when each significant application is to be processed, and records of actual system utilization should be collected and compared with the schedule. The duties of computer operators should be periodically rotated, and vacations for them should be mandatory. In addition, such processing controls as data editing, control totals, and maintenance of a console log are also effective with respect to computer operations. Particularly important is that all of these provisions should be applied not only to day shift operations but also to evening and overnight shifts.

Access to the central computing facility and to remote terminals should be controlled both by sound personnel practices and by physical security measures such as door locks and alarms. Online access to the central computer and its files should be controlled by employing user passwords and related system software access controls. Transactions entered on an online basis should be recorded by the system in a transaction log for subsequent review and analysis.

To develop an understanding of management-prescribed internal controls relating to computer operations, the auditor should review organization charts, job descriptions, policy and procedure manuals, operator run manuals, system documentation, and related materials. This understanding should be supplemented by discussions with EDP management, operations supervisors, systems programmers, and other appropriate employees.

In a small-business environment, separation of functions and restricted access to equipment may not be economically feasible. To compensate for lack of these controls in such situations, the auditor must ascertain that other operations controls are strong enough to compensate. In particular, a strong system of password access controls is especially critical. Authorization and supervision of equipment use and externally maintained control totals are also helpful.

The auditor's tests of compliance of operating controls should begin with observation of the computer operations function. Evidence should be obtained that access to computer equipment is controlled according to prescribed policies, that console logs, equipment utilization records, and error transaction logs are conscientiously maintained, that operators do not have unrestricted access to system documentation, program tapes, and data files, and that operations supervision is consistent and effective. As implied earlier, such observation should encompass evening and overnight shifts if significant application programs are processed at those times. The audit log concept described earlier in this chapter is a useful extension of the auditor's capacity to observe computer operations.

The auditor's tests of compliance should also include a review of operator work records for evidence of compliance with rotation and vacation policies. The auditor will wish to compare equipment utilization records with processing schedules for evidence of any unusual discrepancies between actual and scheduled processing times.[16] The auditor should also review the console log for evidence that it is complete, that it is periodically reviewed by appropriate persons outside the operations function, and that it contains no indications of unusual or unauthorized operator intervention. The auditor should probe any questionable console log entries to determine whether they were investigated by appropriate personnel and how they were resolved.

If erroneous transactions detected by source data or processing controls are recorded in an error log by operators or data control personnel, the auditor should examine the error log to determine that the disposition of errors is properly noted and that errors are not allowed to remain unresolved for an excessive period of time. The auditor may wish to test check the recording, investigation, and correction of a sample of errors. Any errors recorded in the log that have not been resolved within a reasonable time period should be investigated by the auditor.

With respect to remote online access to the system, the auditor's tests of compliance should include observation and inquiry concerning access to and operation of computer terminals. The auditor should evaluate the adequacy of system software access control methods, and of password assignment procedures. Processing of a sample of password assignment requests should be investigated for evidence of compliance with prescribed procedures. The auditor should examine a sample of assigned passwords and their associated access authority for evidence that password holders may have access authority incompatible with their other responsibilities. Online transaction logs should be examined for evidence that they are regularly reviewed by appropriate personnel, and that any unauthorized online access or attempts to initiate improper transactions are identified, investigated, and adequately resolved.

If the auditor concludes that computer operation's personnel have the opportunity and ability to initiate unauthorized computer transactions, then the only other controls that could possibly compensate for this deficiency are excellent user department controls. Essentially user personnel would have to be able to recognize any-

---

[16] *It should be noted that in advanced systems employing multiprocessing, it is more difficult to predict how long a particular job should take because that depends on the mix of other jobs that happen to be using the system's resources at the time.*

thing unusual in the output they receive from the computer. Otherwise the auditor should conclude that the EDP internal control system is seriously deficient.

Objective 6: data files

Objective 6 is concerned with the accuracy, integrity, and security of data stored in machine-readable files. In the absence of good controls, stored data could be modified in an unauthorized manner, inadvertently or intentionally destroyed, or be made available to persons outside the organization against the wishes of management.

As part of the system review, the auditor should examine job descriptions, policy and procedure manuals, and related documentation to ascertain the existence of such controls as a separate file librarian function, restrictions on access to disk and tape files as well as to systems documentation, maintenance of a usage log for these materials, use of both internal and external file labels, maintenance of file control totals by persons independent of data processing, provisions for reconstruction of lost data or files, use of offsite locations for storage of duplicate copies of critical data, and special controls over master file conversions during system changeovers. The auditor should also discuss with EDP management and file librarians the way in which these controls are intended to be applied.

The auditor's tests of compliance with data controls should include observation of the file librarian's activities to ascertain that other systems personnel are not permitted unrestricted access to data files, that a usage record for such data files is maintained, and that the file librarian is not permitted to operate computer equipment. The auditor should determine that someone with appropriate authority is responsible for regular review of the librarian's usage records, and follow up in cases of unauthorized or unscheduled usage. The auditor may also wish to investigate a selected number of cases of unusual access to data files.

When data control personnel regularly check data file control totals with corresponding user totals maintained outside of the EDP function, the auditor should test check a number of these comparisons for accuracy. Simultaneously the auditor may wish to foot the data file using a computer audit software package to check the accuracy of the file totals maintained by the EDP function.

As part of the observation of computer operations, the auditor should ascertain that operating personnel are adhering to prescribed file security provisions, such as the checking of file labels, preparation of duplicate files, and prompt removal of duplicate file copies to offsite storage locations.

Whenever the implementation of a new EDP system requires that data files be changed from one storage medium to another (especially from a written medium to a machine-readable medium), the auditor should be concerned that this file conversion process is properly controlled. The auditor should evaluate the prescribed file conversion controls, and test the conversion of files by comparing selected records from the new file to their counterparts on the old. The auditor may wish to independently perform a series of edit checks on the new file using a computer audit software package. Ideally, EDP personnel will inform the auditor when important conversions of files are scheduled, in order that the auditor may be present to observe the process and accompanying control procedures.

The most significant deficiency in file security would be lack of proper separation of functions accompanied by failure to restrict access to sensitive data files. If such deficiencies are present, then the auditor must conclude that there are material weaknesses in the EDP internal control system. Alternatively, if such controls are only partially deficient, or if other file security controls are not satisfactory, strong controls over processing, operations, and user functions may compensate, and reliance on the EDP internal control system may be possible.

Conclusion

Application of the concept of auditing by objectives as explained above provides focus to the auditor's study and evaluation of EDP internal controls. The auditing by objectives approach may be implemented by means of an audit procedures checklist organized around the six objectives. Such a checklist should direct the auditor to reach a separate conclusion regarding the extent of achievement of each objective, and suggest appropriate compensating controls when a particular objective is not fully achieved. When distinct application programs are being reviewed, separate versions of the checklist should be completed for each significant application. This approach represents a comprehensive, systematic, and effective means of evaluating internal controls in a computer-based information system.

One other conclusion may be formed based upon the nature of several of the auditing techniques reviewed in this section. Techniques such as real-time notification, the audit log, tagging of transactions, and the integrated test facility all should be incorporated into a system during the design process, rather than as an afterthought once the system has been implemented. Also, many of the application control techniques the auditor expects to find in a system are easier to design into the system in the first place than to attach later on. These points give added emphasis to the importance of involving the auditor in the systems design process while there is still time to adopt his or her suggestions for incorporating control techniques and audit features into new application systems.

Financial Audits and Computer Audit Software

As explained earlier in this chapter, the first of the five standards dealing with the scope of internal audit work is that

Internal auditors should review the reliability and integrity of financial and operating information and the means used to identify, measure, classify, and report such information.[17]

And of course the primary objective of the external auditor is to evaluate the information reported by management in annual financial statements. The *general* methodology for this type of audit work is discussed extensively in numerous stan-

[17] *Institute of Internal Auditors, p. 3.*

dard textbooks on auditing,[18] and so is not belabored here. Accordingly, this section deals with *specific* auditing procedures and techniques directed at auditing financial and operating information maintained on a computer system.

In those situations in which the computer plays a significant role in processing, storing, and reporting the information subject to audit, the auditor should generally audit *through* the computer if practical. This means that the auditor should use the computer to the maximum extent feasible in (1) gathering evidence about the reliability of internal controls in the systems that produced the information (using the methodology explained in the previous section), which evidence will influence the auditor's preliminary judgments concerning the accuracy of the system outputs, and (2) performing a variety of auditing operations on the computer files used to store the information. These latter operations are performed using computer programs written especially for auditors called *Generalized Audit Software Packages* (GASP), or simply *computer audit software*. Several packages of this type are available from software vendors as well as from the larger public accounting firms. This section describes the nature of computer audit software and explains how it may be applied in the auditing process.

In Fig. 15.3 is a systems flowchart that provides an overview of the processing steps required to utilize a GASP. Once the auditor has established the audit objectives of the application, obtained knowledge of the format and content of the files to be audited, designed the format of the desired audit reports, and determined the operations necessary to accomplish the objectives and produce the reports, all of these details concerning the application are encoded by the auditor on a set of preformatted specification sheets. The data on the specification sheets are keypunched onto a deck of cards, which is then processed as input to the GASP. This step generally results in a computer program, or set of programs, either in machine language or in a higher-level language such as COBOL. In the latter case the higher-level language program must then be compiled before being processed. In essence, the GASP is a computer program that generates other computer programs based upon the auditor's specifications, and it is these other computer programs which perform the audit functions.

In the next step the source files containing the information subject to audit are processed as input to the audit program generated by the GASP. Usually there is a series of such computer runs, each designed to perform selected auditing operations as necessary to produce one of the specified audit reports. A general list of the functions performed by computer audit software appears in Fig. 15.4. Frequently, the major objective of the first of these computer runs is to extract specific information of interest to the auditor from the source file or files, and reformat it into an audit work file. The desired audit reports are then generated by a subsequent series of computer runs which use the audit work file as input.

[18] *For example, see Alvin A. Arens and James K. Loebbecke,* Auditing: An Integrated Approach *(2nd ed.), Englewood Cliffs, N.J.: Prentice-Hall, 1980, or Jack C. Robertson,* Auditing *(Rev. ed.), Dallas: Business Publications, Inc., 1979.*

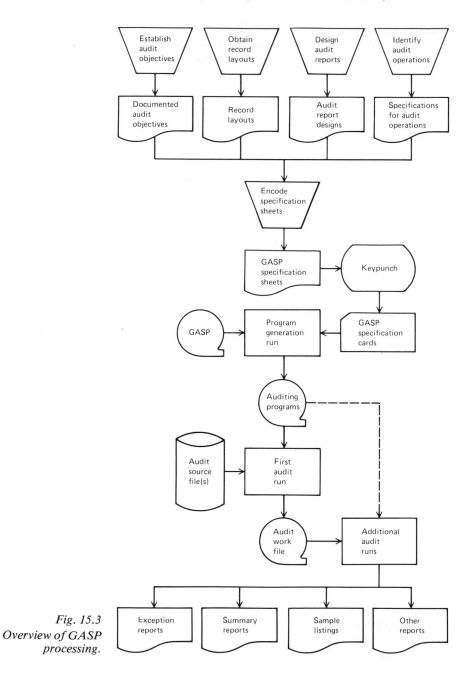

*Fig. 15.3
Overview of GASP
processing.*

The primary purpose of the GASP is to assist the auditor in reviewing and retrieving information stored on computer files. Note, however, that the use of a GASP is normally one of the first steps in the financial audit. Once the auditor

FUNCTION	EXPLANATION
REFORMATTING	Audit software extracts relevant information from source files, rearranges it as required by the auditor, and creates audit work files from it.
CALCULATION	Audit software can perform the four basic arithmetic operations: add, subtract, multiply, and divide.
LOGICAL OPERATIONS	Audit software can perform logical operations such as comparing data values, selecting records based on specified criteria, and editing data for consistency and completeness.
DATA EDITING	Audit software can perform numerous edit checks on the data content of machine readable records.
FILE MANIPULATION	Audit software can perform basic file handling operations such as sorting and merging.
REPORT GENERATION	Audit software can generate standard audit documents and reports such as confirmations and aging schedules, and other reports in formats specifically designed by the auditor.
STATISTICS	Audit software can select random samples, compute means and variances, and perform other basic statistical functions.

*Fig. 15.4
General functions of
computer audit
software.*

ADVANTAGE	EXPLANATION
ACCESS	Audit software provides improved access to data stored in machine readable form.
SCOPE	Audit software enables the auditor to examine more records than would otherwise be possible.
COST	Audit software reduces the cost of auditing in large organizations which are extensively computerized.
INDEPENDENCE	Audit software is used under the auditor's control, thereby lessening the auditor's dependence on EDP personnel.
SIMPLICITY	Audit software is easy to learn about and to use, and requires only minimal knowledge of computer technology.
GENERALITY	Audit software performs a variety of auditing tasks, and can function in a variety of auditing environments.
UNDERSTANDING	A by-product of using audit software is that the auditor gains a better understanding of the information system.

*Fig. 15.5
Summary of audit
software advantages.*

receives the reports prepared by the GASP application, most of the audit work still remains to be done. Items listed on exception reports must be investigated, file totals and subtotals must be verified against other sources of information such as the general ledger, and items selected for audit samples must be examined and evaluated. In summary, while the advantages to the auditor of using a GASP (summarized in Fig. 15.5) are numerous and compelling, a computer program cannot replace the auditor's judgment or free the auditor from significant participation in all phases of the audit.

An example of a GASP application

In this section the functions that can be performed using computer audit software are explained in greater detail using as an example the audit of accounts receivable information produced by a computerized order entry, billing, and customer accounting system.[19] Assume that this system maintains an accounts receivable master file and transaction detail files for sales on account, cash collections, and credit memos. The auditor has obtained copies of record layouts for these files, which are reproduced in Fig. 15.6. The following specific objectives for the GASP application have been delineated by the auditor: (1) recalculate the current balance of every master record from the previous balance and the intervening transactions, and identify all accounts having an incorrect current balance, (2) sum the current balance, credit sales, cash collections, and credit memo amounts for verification of their totals against other independently maintained information, (3) perform edit checks on selected fields in each file to confirm the reliability of data editing performed within the EDP function, (4) check the transaction files for any records that do not match with a master record, (5) prepare an aging schedule of the receivables and an analysis of accounts having current balances in excess of their credit limit, in order to evaluate the sufficiency of the allowance for uncollectible accounts and to assess the performance of the credit department, (6) select a sample of accounts for confirmation in order to verify the existence and accuracy of the receivables recorded on the master file, and (7) analyze cash collections and credit memos subsequent to the test date for those customers who do not respond to confirmation requests. In the

RECORD NAME: *Accounts Receivable Master*

FIELD NAME	Account Number	Name	Address				Credit Code	Credit Limit	Previous Balance	Current Balance
			Street	City	State	Zip				
POSITION	1-6	7-31	32-56	57-74	75-76	77-81	82-83	84-91	92-99	100-107

RECORD NAME: *Sales Detail*

FIELD NAME	Account Number	Transaction Code	Transaction Date	Invoice Number	Amount	
POSITION	1-6	7	8-13	14-18	19-26	

RECORD NAME: *Cash Collections Detail*

FIELD NAME	Account Number	Transaction Code	Transaction Date	Reference Number	Amount	
POSITION	1-6	7	8-13	14-18	19-26	

RECORD NAME: *Credit Memo Detail*

FIELD NAME	Account Number	Transaction Code	Transaction Date	Credit Memo Number	Amount	
POSITION	1-6	7	8-13	14-18	19-26	

Fig. 15.6
Record layouts for accounts receivable system.

[19] *Systems of this kind are described more fully in the next chapter.*

following paragraphs, the steps necessary to accomplish these objectives using computer audit software are described. The reader should note that each of the general audit software functions delineated in Fig. 15.4 is utilized one or more times in the course of this application.

A systems flowchart showing the sequence of computer operations necessary to accomplish the first six objectives appears in Fig. 15.7. Input to the first computer run consists of all four of the source files, each sequenced by account number. If any of these files had originally been in some other sequence (for example, the transaction files might have been maintained in sequence by transaction date), then a previous run using the GASP to sort these records by account number would have been necessary.

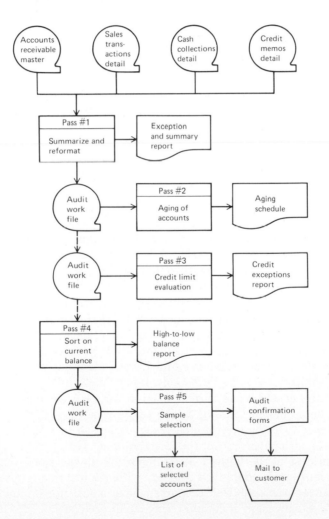

Fig. 15.7
Application of computer audit software to accounts receivable.

One objective of this first pass is to merge the data from all four files into a single information set for each customer, and then extract from this customer information set only that information necessary to perform the subsequent auditing operations. The information so extracted is recorded on an audit work file. In this case assume that the auditor elects to include the following items in his or her work file: (1) account number, (2) name, (3) address, (4) credit limit, (5) current balance, (6) last invoice (sale) date, (7) last invoice amount, (8) last credit (payment or credit memo) date, and (9) last credit amount. For each account record, an audit record containing these data is created, and these audit records are written in sequential order onto a separate file.

This first run also performs a variety of tests on the information recorded on each of the four input files, and prints an exception report containing the results of these tests. For each customer information set, all sales on account are added to the previous balance, and all cash collections and credit memo amounts are subtracted; if the result is not equal to the current balance amount, data pertaining to the account are printed on the exception report. A series of edit checks could also be performed on selected data from each of the four types of records, with all erroneous records listed on the exception report. Among the edit checks that could be performed in this case are validity checks on the transaction codes and dates, a completeness test of each type of record, a sign test of the current balance, field checks of all numeric fields, and a sequence check of each file based on account number. Furthermore, any transaction detail records that lack an accounts receivable master record having the same account number would be listed on the exception report. All significant exceptions identified by these checks should be investigated by the auditor to ascertain their cause and evaluate their implications with respect to the overall reliability of the accounts receivable information.

Additional operations performed during this first pass are footing the amount fields for cash collections, sales on account, credit memos, and account balances, and printing a summary report containing these file totals. These may then be compared with corresponding totals from the sales and cash receipts journals and the general ledger accounts for credit sales, sales returns and allowances, and accounts receivable. If these totals cannot be reconciled, then there may be a serious deficiency in the quality of the information maintained by the system.

On the second pass, the audit work file is processed to generate an aging schedule for the receivables. Most audit software contains built-in logic specifically designed to perform aging operations. Immediately following this step a third pass is made during which the current balance for each customer is compared with the credit limit, and all accounts having balances in excess of the credit limit are printed on a report. During this third pass, the total of all such balances, as well as the total excess of such balances over the corresponding credit limit, can be accumulated, and then printed at the bottom of the report. Both the aging schedule and the credit exceptions report could then be used by the auditor to appraise the adequacy of the allowance for uncollectible accounts, and as a basis for evaluating the credit department's effectiveness in administering credit policies.

On the fourth pass, the records on the audit work file are re-sorted into sequence from high to low current balance. Each account is classified into a dollar range based upon its current balance; for example, over $20,000, $19,501 to $20,000, $19,001 to $19,500 and so on down to $0 to $500. A summary report is printed that lists the number of accounts and the cumulative dollar amount within each range. This report is useful to the auditor in designing a sampling plan for selecting accounts to be confirmed. For example, the auditor may decide to select all accounts over $15,000, 10 percent of the remaining accounts over $5,000, 2 percent of the remaining accounts over $1,000, and 1 percent of the accounts of $1,000 or less. This type of sampling plan, called *stratified sampling,* enables the auditor to include in the sample a relatively high percentage of the total number of *dollars* in the population, even though the sample may include a very low percentage of the total number of *accounts.* The high-to-low balance summary report helps the auditor decide how many strata to use and what strata boundaries to establish.

Once the sampling plan has been established, the resorted audit work file is input to a fifth pass that selects the specific accounts to be included in the sample. A list of these accounts is printed for the auditor. In addition, virtually all audit software packages have a built-in formatting capability for audit confirmations, and this pass results in the printing of these confirmations for the accounts in the sample. The auditor will then supervise the mailing of these confirmation forms to the customers.

Generally there will be some customers who do not respond to confirmation requests. However, the auditor can obtain evidence concerning the validity of those accounts by examining subsequent collections from those customers. In this case, for example, the auditor might wait a month or so after sending out the confirmations, and then write a program using the audit software package to scan the cash collections and credit memo files and identify and print records of all cash collections and credit memos for those customers in the sample who did not respond to the confirmation request.

Once the auditor has obtained and examined confirmation responses and other relevant evidence, the results of the sample must be evaluated. Some audit software packages have the capability of statistically evaluating sample results by computing means, variances, confidence intervals, sampling risks, and so forth. A common approach when the GASP does not possess this capability is to use a separate time-sharing program for the statistical evaluation.

In summary, the use of a GASP in this illustration provided the auditor with the ability to quickly and inexpensively review the accounts receivable information, identify questionable records that should be investigated further, prepare several summary reports, select a sample of accounts for confirmation, and automatically print the confirmation forms. Furthermore, it is quite significant that the auditor is able to do these things independently of EDP personnel. However, the results obtained from using the GASP generally represent only the first step in the audit. Once these results are made available to him or her, the auditor must still investigate exceptions, audit sample items, independently verify file totals, evaluate the significance of summary reports, and perform numerous other auditing procedures.

Management Audits of Computer-Based Information Systems

The steps involved in a management audit of a computer-based information system, and many of the techniques and procedures used, are very similar to those used in internal control audits or financial audits. The basic differences involve the scope and objectives of the management audit. Whereas the scope of the internal control audit is confined to internal controls, and the scope of the financial audit is confined to the output of information systems, the scope of the management audit is much broader, encompassing all aspects of the management of the information systems activity. Furthermore, the objectives of management audits involve evaluating such factors as effectiveness, efficiency, and the accomplishment of organizational objectives. This section briefly outlines some of the most significant aspects of the management of computer-based information systems, in order to provide a framework for understanding the scope of management audits of such systems. The section concludes with a brief discussion of the application of standard auditing procedures and techniques to the performance of management audits.

The principles of good systems management provide a standard against which the attributes of an actual system can be measured. Many of these principles have been described at length in the previous five chapters of Part III. Accordingly, what is presented here is simply an outline of major topics intended to refresh the reader's memory.

Our outline divides systems management principles into six basic categories: (1) organizational arrangements, (2) systems planning, (3) personnel policies, (4) management of systems development projects, (5) financial controls, and (6) computer operations. Organizational arrangements include such matters as the role and responsibilities of the MIS director, the existence and effective functioning of an MIS steering committee, and the proper distribution of functions within the systems department. Systems planning encompasses the prioritization of potential systems development projects, the preparation of systems development plans, the projection of future hardware and personnel requirements, and the preparation of an overall long-range financial plan for the systems development activity that is integrated with the organization's long-range planning process. Personnel policies include standards for hiring, training, and assigning EDP personnel; establishing job descriptions and performance standards; evaluating employee performance; and effectively involving appropriate management personnel in such activities as systems planning, project selection, and development of new systems.

Good principles of management relating to systems development projects include the use of feasibility studies and other systematic project or vendor selection methods, the preparation of systems development schedules and budgets, the establishment of project milestones, the regular use of project progress reviews, and adherence to good documentation standards. Financial controls encompass the application of responsibility accounting and reporting standards to systems departments and projects, including the use of financial budgets and performance reports, and the use of a system of charging computer users for the cost or value of the computer services they consume. Computer operations management involves the use of a data processing schedule, the maintenance of activity logs, the existence and use of good operating documentation such as run manuals, the use of computer hardware and software performance monitors, adherence to a regular equipment maintenance schedule, and proper controls over equipment access.

The process of performing a management audit parallels the process of performing an internal control audit or a financial audit. The first step is planning, during which the audit scope and objectives are established, a preliminary review of the system performed, and a tentative audit program prepared. Evidence gathering includes such activities as review of operating policies and documentation, inquiry of management and operating personnel, perhaps aided by the use of questionnaires or checklists, observation of operating functions and activities, examination of financial and operating plans and reports, tests of accuracy of operating information, and tests of compliance with prescribed policies and procedures.

At the evidence evaluation stage, the auditor is basically measuring the actual system against an ideal system that would follow all of the best principles of systems management. One important consideration here is that the *results* of management policies and practices are more significant than the policies and practices themselves. That is, if excellent results are being achieved through policies and practices that are theoretically deficient, then the auditor must carefully consider whether recommended improvements would substantially improve results. In any event, the auditor should thoroughly document the findings and conclusions, and communicate the audit results to management in an effective manner.

To be a good management auditor probably requires some degree of management experience. Persons with excellent backgrounds in auditing but without management experience often lack the perspective necessary to understand the management process. Thus the ideal management auditor is probably a person with training and experience as an auditor, but also with a few years' experience in a managerial position.

Review Questions

1. Define the following terms.

auditing	automated decision table programs
internal control audit	scanning routines
financial audit	mapping programs
management audit	test data generator
operational audit	program tracing
compliance audit	embedded audit modules
confirmation	real-time notification
vouching	audit log
analytical review	tagging
materiality	input controls matrix
reasonable assurance	mini-company test

tests of compliance	integrated test facility
reprocessing	generalized audit software packages
parallel simulation	computer audit software
automated flowcharting programs	stratified sampling

2. Why is it said that the audit trail has disappeared in computerized data processing systems?

3. Distinguish between auditing "around" and auditing "through" the computer.

4. Describe the five standards of internal auditing that deal with the scope of internal audit work. Briefly explain how each standard applies to the audit of computer-based information systems.

5. Describe the four major stages of the auditing process.

6. Identify several auditing tests and procedures used for purposes of collecting audit evidence.

7. In evaluating audit evidence, what are the auditor's options with respect to possible conclusions? What role do materiality and reasonable assurance play in forming these conclusions?

8. Identify six objectives of internal control audits of computer-based information systems.

9. List the four steps in the AICPA's "conceptually logical approach" to internal control evaluation. Where do "system review" and "tests of compliance" fit into this approach?

10. Explain the concept of compensating controls. How do they affect the auditor's study and evaluation of internal control?

11. With respect to the program development process, (a) what are the potential control problems, (b) what internal controls should be present, (c) what should the auditor examine during the system review, (d) what tests of compliance can the auditor perform, and (e) what compensating controls may exist in the event that program development controls are inadequate?

12. With respect to program changes, (a) what are the potential control problems, (b) what internal controls should be present, (c) what should the auditor examine during the system review, (d) what tests of compliance can the auditor perform, and (e) what compensating controls may exist in the event of inadequate program change controls?

13. Explain how a source code comparison program works. Why is this particularly valuable to the auditor?

14. With respect to computer processing of data, (a) what are the potential control problems, (b) what internal controls should be present, (c) what should the auditor examine during the system review, (d) what tests of compliance can the auditor perform, and (e) what compensating controls may exist in the event that processing controls are inadequate?

15. Explain why the auditor might decide to perform a review of program logic. What are some of the tools available to assist the auditor in this process?

16. Explain in detail the steps that an auditor would follow in processing test data to test the adequacy of computer processing controls.

17. What are some of the disadvantages to the auditor of processing test data?

18. Explain how the auditor would use the technique of program tracing.

19. With respect to computer source data controls, (a) what are the potential control problems, (b) what internal controls should be present, (c) what should the auditor examine during the system review, (d) what tests of compliance can the auditor perform, and (e) what compensating controls may exist in the event that source data controls are inadequate?

20. In what ways does the *mini-company test* eliminate two of the disadvantages of processing test data?

21. With respect to the operation of computer equipment, (a) what are the potential control problems, (b) what internal controls should be present, (c) what should the auditor examine during system review, (d) what tests of compliance can the auditor perform, and (e) what compensating controls may exist in the event that operating controls are inadequate?

22. With respect to controls over computer data files, (a) what are the potential control problems, (b) what internal controls should be present, (c) what should the auditor examine during system review, (d) what tests of compliance can the auditor perform, and (e) what compensating controls may exist in the event that control over data files is inadequate?

23. Describe in general the steps that an auditor follows in using a generalized audit software package.

24. Describe in general the functions that can be performed by computer audit software.

25. Explain several of the advantages to the auditor of using computer audit software.

26. Explain why the use of computer audit software does not replace the need for the auditor's judgment.

27. Describe the steps followed in applying computer audit software to the audit of accounts receivable.

28. What are the similarities and differences between management audits and financial or internal control audits?

29. Briefly outline some of the primary aspects of management of computer-based information systems that are the potential objects of a management audit.

30. Outline the steps in the process of performing a management audit.

Discussion Questions

31. Discuss the extent to which the auditor should be a "computer expert" in order to effectively perform audits in an organization with a computer-based information system.

32. Should the internal auditor be extensively involved as a member of systems development teams that design and implement computer-based information systems? Why or why not? Discuss.

33. If an organization's internal audit department needs to develop an EDP auditing capability, do you feel that the best approach would be (a) to train computer specialists in auditing, (b) to train auditors in data processing, (c) to employ computer specialists on the audit staff who will work with regular auditors on EDP audit teams, or (d) some other approach? Discuss.

Problems and Cases

34. You are an internal auditor for the Quick Manufacturing Company. You are participating in the audit of the company's computer-based information system. The company uses the computer in most of its significant accounting applications. You have been reviewing the internal controls associated with these computer systems. You have studied the company's extensive documentation of its systems, and you have interviewed the EDP Manager, Operations Supervisor, and other employees in order to complete your standardized computer internal control questionnaire.

You report to your supervisor that the company has designed an excellent and comprehensive set of internal controls into its computer systems. The supervisor thanks you for your efforts, and asks you to prepare a summary report of your findings for inclusion in a final overall report on accounting internal controls.

Required   Aren't you forgetting an important audit step? Explain. Then list five examples of specific audit procedures that you might recommend be performed before you reach a final conclusion.

35. As an internal auditor, you have been assigned to evaluate the controls and operation of a computer payroll system. The audit technique which you will be using is online testing of the computer systems and/or programs by submitting independently created test transactions with regular data in a normal production run.

Required   a) List four advantages of this technique.

b) List two disadvantages of this technique. [20]

36. You are the director of internal auditing at a university. Recently, you met with the manager of administrative data processing and expressed the desire to establish a more effective interface between the two departments.

Subsequently, the manager of data processing requested your views and help on a new computerized accounts payable system being developed. The manager recommended that Internal Auditing assume line responsibility for auditing suppliers' invoices prior to payment. The manager also requested that Internal Auditing make suggestions during development of the system, assist in its installation, and approve the completed system after making a final review.

Required   State how you would respond to the administrative data processing manager, giving the reason why you would accept or reject each of the following.

a. The recommendation that your department be responsible for the preaudit of suppliers' invoices.

b. The request that you make suggestions during development of the system.

c. The request that you assist in the installation of the system and approve the system after making a final review. [21]

---

[20] *Question 6, Part II (Internal Audit Techniques). From* The Certified Internal Auditor Examination, *August, 1974. Copyright 1974 by the Institute of Internal Auditors, Inc. Reprinted by permission of the Institute of Internal Auditors, Inc., 249 Maitland Ave., Altamonte Springs, Fla. 32701.*

[21] *Question 13, Part I (Principles of Internal Auditing). From* The Certified Internal Auditor Examination, *1977. Copyright 1977 by the Institute of Internal Auditors, Inc. Reprinted by permission of the Institute of Internal Auditors, Inc., 249 Maitland Ave., Altamonte Springs, Fla. 32701.*

37. You are involved in the internal audit of accounts receivable, which represent a significant portion of the assets of a large retail corporation. Your audit plan requires the use of the computer, but you encounter the reactions described below.

   a. The computer operations manager says that all time on the computer is scheduled for the foreseeable future and that it is not feasible to perform the work for the auditor.

   b. The computer scheduling manager suggests that your computer program be cataloged into the computer program library (on disk storage) to be run when computer time becomes available.

   c. You are refused admission to the computer room.

   d. The systems manager tells you that it will take too much time to adapt the computer audit program to the EDP operating system and that the computer installation programmers would write the programs needed for the audit.

Required   For each of the four situations described, state the action the auditor should take to proceed with the accounts receivable audit.[22]

38. You are auditing the financial statements of Aardvark Wholesalers, Inc. (AW), that is a wholesaler having operations in twelve western states, and total revenues of around $15 million. AW uses a computer system in several of its major accounting applications. Accordingly, you are undertaking to study AW's internal control relating to its computer system.

   You have obtained a manual containing job descriptions for key personnel in AW's Information Systems Division. Excerpts from these include:

   Director of Information Systems. Reports to Administrative Vice President. Responsible for defining the mission of the Information Systems Division in the organization, and for planning, staffing, and managing a department that optimally executes this mission.

   Manager of Systems and Programming. Reports to Director of Information Systems. Responsible for managing a staff of systems analysts and programmers whose mission is to design, program, test, implement, and maintain cost-effective data processing systems. Also responsible for establishing and monitoring documentation standards.

   Manager of Operations. Reports to Director of Information Systems. Responsible for cost-effective management of computer center operations, enforcement of processing standards, and for systems programming, including implementation of vendor upgrades of operating systems.

   Keypunch Shift Supervisor. Reports to Manager of Operations. Responsible for supervision of keypunch operators and monitoring of data preparation standards.

   Operations Shift Supervisor. Reports to Manager of Operations. Responsible for supervision of computer operations staff and monitoring of processing standards.

---

[22] *Question 15, Part II (Internal Audit Techniques). From* The Certified Internal Auditor Examination, *1977. Copyright 1977 by the Institute of Internal Auditors, Inc. Reprinted by permission of the Institue of Internal Auditors, Inc., 249 Maitland Ave., Altamonte Springs, Fla. 32701.*

Data Control Clerk. Reports to Manager of Operations. Responsible for logging and distribution of computer input and output, monitoring of source data control procedures, and custody of program and data files.

Required

(a) Prepare an organization chart for AW's Information Systems Division.

(b) Comment on the adequacy (from an internal control standpoint) of this organization structure; specifically,

  (i) what, if anything, is good about it?

  (ii) what, if anything, is bad about it?

  (iii) what, if any, additional information would you require before you could make a final judgment on the adequacy of AW's separation of functions in the Information Systems Division?

39. You are a manager for the regional CPA firm of Dewey, Cheatem, and Howe. Upon reviewing working papers prepared by staff accountants working under you on the Welfare Department audit, you find that the test data concept was used to test the Department's Welfare Accounting program. Specifically, a duplicate copy of the program and of the welfare accounting data file were obtained, and the test transaction deck used by the department's programmers in preparing the program was borrowed. These were processed on DC&H's home office computer, and a copy of the edit summary report listing no errors was included in the working papers, along with a notation by the Audit Senior that the test indicates good application controls.

You note that the quality of the audit conclusions obtained from this test are flawed in several respects, and decide to require your subordinates to perform the test over again.

Required

Identify three problems (or potential problems) with the way that this test was performed. For each of the problems that you identify, suggest one or more procedures that may be performed during the revised test in order to avoid flaws in the audit conclusions obtained from it.

40. The Robinson's Plastic Pipe Corporation uses a computerized inventory data processing system. The basic input record to this system has the format shown in Fig. 15.8.

You are performing an audit of source data controls for this system. You have decided to use an input control matrix for this purpose.

Figure 15.8

PARTS INVENTORY TRANSACTION FILE		
Field name	Field type	Positions
Item number	Numeric	1–6
Description	Alphanumeric	7–31
Transaction date	Date	32–37
Transaction type	Alphanumeric	38
Document number	Alphanumeric	39–46
Quantity	Numeric	47–51
Unit cost	Monetary	52–58

Required   Prepare an input controls matrix using the same format, and listing the same input controls, as the one in Fig. 15.2, except replace the field names shown in the figure with those of the inventory transaction file shown above. Place checks in the cells of the matrix that represent input controls you might expect to find with respect to each field.

41. You are an internal auditor for the Military Industrial Company. You are presently involved in preparing test transactions for the company's weekly payroll processing program. Each input record to this program contains the following data items.

Spaces	Data item
1–9	Social security number
10	Pay code (1 = hourly; 2 = salaried)
11–16	Wage rate or salary
17–19	Hours worked, in tenths
20–21	Number of exemptions claimed
22–29	Year-to-date gross pay
30–80	Employee name and address

The program performs the following edit checks on each input record.

■ field checks to identify any records not having numeric characters in the fields for wage rate/salary, hours, exemptions, and year-to-date gross pay.

■ validity check of the pay code.

■ limit check to identify any hourly employee records having a wage rate higher than $20.00.

■ limit check to identify any hourly employee records having hours worked greater than 70.0.

■ limit check to identify any salaried employee records having a salary greater than $2000.00 or a salary less than $100.00.

Those records that do not pass all of these edit checks are listed on an error report. For those records that do pass all of these edit checks, the program performs a series of calculations. First, the employee's gross pay is determined. Gross pay for a salaried employee is equal to the salary amount contained within spaces 11–16 of the input record. Gross pay for an hourly employee is equal to the wage rate times the number of hours up to 40, plus one and one-half times the wage rate times the number of hours in excess of 40.

The program computes federal withholding tax by multiplying gross pay times a tax rate determined for each employee based upon the table in Fig. 15.9. The program next computes state withholding tax by multiplying gross pay times a tax rate determined for each employee based upon the table in Fig. 15.10. The program then computes FICA tax withholdings by multiplying gross pay by 6 percent, except that no FICA taxes are withheld once year-to-date gross pay exceeds $25,000.

Number of Exemptions	GROSS PAY RANGE			
	$0-99.99	$100-249.99	$250-499.99	Over $500
0-1	.06	.12	.18	.24
2-3	.04	.10	.16	.22
4-5	.02	.08	.14	.20
Over 5	.00	.06	.12	.18

Figure 15.9

Number of Exemptions	GROSS PAY RANGE	
	$0-249.99	Over $250
0-3	.03	.05
Over 3	.01	.03

Figure 15.10

The program next computes the employee's pension contribution, which is 3 percent of gross pay for hourly employees, and 4 percent of gross pay for salaried employees. Finally, the program computes the employee's net pay, which is gross pay minus tax withholdings and pension contribution. Once all of these calculations have been completed for one employee record, the program prints that employee's paycheck and summary earnings statements, and then proceeds to the next employee input record to perform edit checks and payroll calculations, continuing this cycle until all input records have been processed.

For the moment, you are concerned only with preparing a set of test transactions containing one of each possible type of error, and another set of test transactions that will test each of the computational alternatives one at a time. Transactions to test for multiple errors in one record, or to test for multiple combinations of logic paths, are to be developed later.

Each test transaction you prepare need not include a social security number or an employee name and address (your assistant will add those after reviewing a file printout). Accordingly, each of your test transactions will consist of a series of 20 characters representing data in spaces 10–29 of an input record. For example, a test transaction for an hourly employee having a wage rate of $9.50, who worked 40 and five-tenths hours, who claims two exemptions, and who has year-to-date gross pay of exactly $12,000, would be 10009504050201200000.

Required

a) Prepare a set of test transactions, each of which contains one of the possible kinds of errors tested for by the edit checks. Determine the expected results of processing for each of these test transactions.

b) Prepare a set of test transactions, each of which tests one of the ways in which gross pay may be determined. Determine the expected gross pay for each of these transactions.

c) Prepare a set of test transactions, each of which tests one of the ways in which federal withholding tax may be computed. Determine the expected value of federal withholding tax for each of these test transactions.

d) Prepare a set of test transactions, each of which tests one of the ways in which state withholding tax may be computed. Determine the expected value of state withholding tax for each of these test transactions.

e) Prepare a set of test transactions, each of which tests one of the ways in which FICA withholding tax may be computed. Determine the expected value of FICA withholding tax for each of these test transactions.

f) Prepare a set of test transactions, each of which tests one of the ways in which the pension contribution may be computed. Determine the expected value of the pension contribution for each of these test transactions.

42. An auditor is conducting an examination of the financial statements of a wholesale cosmetics distributor with an inventory consisting of thousands of individual items. The distributor keeps its inventory in its own distribution center and in two public warehouses. An inventory computer file is maintained on a computer disk and at the end of each business day the file is updated. Each record of the inventory file contains the following data.

- Item number
- Location of item
- Description of item
- Quantity on hand
- Cost per item
- Date of last purchase
- Date of last sale
- Quantity sold during year

The auditor is planning to observe the distributor's physical count of inventories as of a given date. The auditor will have available a computer tape of the data on the inventory file on the date of the physical count and a general purpose computer software package.

Required
The auditor is planning to perform basic inventory auditing procedures. Identify the basic inventory auditing procedures and describe how the use of the general purpose software package and the tape of the inventory file data might be helpful to the auditor in performing such auditing procedures.

Organize your answer as follows.[23]

Basic inventory auditing procedure	How general purpose computer software package and tape of the inventory file data might be helpful

[23] *Adapted from Question 5, Auditing Section,* American Institute of Certified Public Accountants Examination, *November 1978. Copyright © 1978 by the American Institute of Certified Public Accountants, Inc., and reprinted with permission.*

494   Auditing of computer-based information systems

43. The Thermo-Bond Manufacturing Company maintains its fixed asset records on its computer. Data content of the fixed asset master file includes the following items.

Item number	location	description
1	1–6	Asset number
2	7–30	Description
3	31	Type code
4	32–34	Location code
5	35–40	Date of acquisition
6	41–50	Original cost
7	51–56	Date of retirement*
8	57	Depreciation method code
9	58–61	Depreciation rate
10	62–63	Useful life (years)
11	64–73	Accumulated depreciation at beginning of year
12	74–83	Year-to-date depreciation

*For assets still in service, retirement date is assigned the value 99/99/99.

Required

Explain several ways in which a generalized computer audit software package could be used by an auditor to assist in achieving audit objectives relating to the audit of Thermo-Bond's fixed asset account.

44. You are auditing the financial statements of the Preston Manufacturing Company. At the beginning of the current fiscal year, the company converted its general ledger accounting from a manual to a computer-based system. The new system involves the use of two computer files, the contents of which are indicated in Fig. 15.11.

Each day, as detailed transactions are processed by Preston's other computerized accounting systems, summary journal entries are accumulated; and at the end of the day are added to the general journal file. At the end of each week, and also at the end of each month, the general journal file is processed against the general ledger control file to compute a new current balance for each account, and to print a trial balance.

Your review and evaluation of internal controls with respect to this particular system has led to the conclusion that *no reliance* can be placed on those controls in performing the financial audit.

You have decided to use your firm's generalized computer audit software package to perform certain procedures and tests on these files. You have available to you

(a) a complete copy of the general journal file for the entire year

(b) a copy of the general ledger file as of the fiscal year end (i.e., current balance = year-end balance), and

(c) a printout of Preston's year-end trial balance listing the account number, account name, and balance of each account on the general ledger control file.

GENERAL JOURNAL		
Field name	Field type	Size
Account number	Numeric	6
Amount	Monetary	9.2
Debit/credit code	Alphameric	1
Date (MM/DD/YY)	Date	6
Reference document type	Alphameric	4
Reference document number	Numeric	6

GENERAL LEDGER CONTROL		
Field name	Field type	Size
Account number	Numeric	6
Account name	Alphameric	20
Beginning balance/year	Monetary	9.2
Beg-bal-debit/credit code	Alphameric	1
Current balance	Monetary	9.2
Cur-bal-debit/credit code	Alphameric	1

Figure 15.11

Required

Assume that you are using a Generalized Audit Software Package with a comprehensive set of capabilities. Prepare an application design for this problem, including

(a) a description of the data content of each output report, preferably in the form of a tabular layout chart of the report format.

(b) accompanying each report from part (a) a description of the auditing objectives of each report, and how the report would be used in subsequent auditing procedures to achieve those objectives.

(c) a detailed system flowchart of the application.

References

Adams Donald L. "Alternatives to Computer Audit Software." *The Journal of Accountancy* (November 1975): 54–57.

_____, and John F. Mullarkey. "A Survey of Audit Software." *The Journal of Accountancy* (September 1972): 39–66.

American Institute of Certified Public Accountants, *Codification of Statements on Auditing Standards, Numbers 1 to 26* (New York: AICPA, 1980).

Arens, Alvin A., and James K. Loebbecke. *Auditing: An Integrated Approach.* Englewood Cliffs, N.J.: Prentice-Hall, 1980.

Auditing Advanced EDP Systems Task Force, AICPA. *Management, Control and Audit of Advanced EDP Systems* (New York: AICPA, 1977).

Auditing Electronic Funds Transfer Systems Task Force, AICPA. *Audit Considerations in Electronic Funds Transfer Systems* (New York: AICPA, 1978).

The Canadian Institute of Chartered Accountants, Study Group on Computer Control and Audit Guidelines. *Computer Audit Guidelines.* Toronto, Canada: Canadian Institute of Chartered Accountants, 1975.

Canning, Richard G. "The Importance of EDP Audit and Control." *EDP Analyzer* (June 1977): 1–14.

Cash, James I. Jr.; Andrew D. Bailey, Jr.; and Andrew B. Whinston. "A Survey of Techniques for Auditing EDP-Based Accounting Information Systems." *Accounting Review* (October 1977): 813–832.

Committee on Basic Auditing Concepts, *A Statement of Basic Auditing Concepts*. Sarasota, Fla.: American Accounting Association, 1973.

Computerized Inventory Systems Task Force, AICPA. *Audit Approaches for a Computerized Inventory System*. New York: AICPA, 1980.

Computer Services Executive Committee, AICPA. *The Auditor's Study and Evaluation of Internal Control in EDP Systems*. New York: AICPA, 1977.

Computer Services Executive Committee, AICPA. *Computer-Assisted Audit Techniques*. New York: AICPA, 1979.

Crouse, David W. "Risk Analysis in an EDP Audit Environment." *The Internal Auditor* (December 1979): 69–77.

Institute of Internal Auditors, *Standards for the Professional Practice of Internal Auditing* Altamonte Springs, Fla.: The Institute of Internal Auditors, Inc., 1978.

Jancura, Elise G. "Technical Proficiency for Auditing Computer-Processed Accounting Records," *The Journal of Accountancy* (October 1975): 46–59.

————. "The Auditor's Responsibilities in Examining Computer Processed Records." *International Journal of Government Auditing* (July 1975): 13–17.

Lowe, Ronald L. "Auditing the Corporate Information System." *CPA Journal* (November 1977): 35–40.

MacNab, Seaforth B. "Debugging the EDP Auditor." *The Internal Auditor* (February 1979): 72–82.

Mair, William C.; Donald R. Wood; and Keagle W. Davis. *Computer Control & Audit*. Altamonte Springs, Fla.: Institute of Internal Auditors, Inc., 1978.

Mastromano, Frank M. "The Changing Nature of the EDP Audit." *Management Accounting* (July 1980): 27–30, 34.

Nottingham, C. "Conceptual Framework for Improved Computer Audits." *Accounting and Business Research* (Spring 1976): 140–148.

Perry, William E., and Henry C. Warner. "Systems Auditability: Friend or Foe?" *Journal of Accountancy* (February 1978): 52–60.

Pound, G. D. "A Review of EDP Auditing." *Accounting and Business Research* (Spring 1978): 108–128.

Reneau, J. Hal. "Auditing in a Data Base Environment." *Journal of Accountancy* (December 1977): 59–65.

Richardson, Dana R. "Auditing EFTS." *Journal of Accountancy* (October 1978): 81–87.

Robertson, Jack C. *Auditing*. Dallas: Business Publications, Inc., 1979.

Stanford Research Institute. *Systems Auditability & Control Study, Data Processing Audit Practices Report*. Altamonte Springs, Fla.: The Institute of Internal Auditors, Inc., 1977.

Venecek, Michael T., and George Scott. "Data Bases—The Auditor's Dilemma." *The CPA Journal* (January 1980): 26–35.

Weber, Ron. "An Audit Perspective of Operating System Security." *The Journal of Accountancy* (September 1975): 97–100.

Wilkins, Barry J. *The Internal Auditor's Information Security Handbook.* Altamonte Springs, Fla.: The Institute of Internal Auditors, Inc., 1979.

Part 4

Accounting Information Systems Applications

Chapter 16

Accounting Information Systems for Marketing Management

All business organizations must produce a product or provide a service for which a market demand exists. From this market demand must be generated a stream of revenue sufficient to cover the firm's costs and expenses, replace its assets, and provide its capital suppliers with a return on their investment. The accounting information system plays an important role in this revenue generation process because it is a primary source of information to the executives who manage the marketing function. The accounting system is also responsible for processing all customer transactions.

It is therefore evident that a close relationship must exist between the accounting and marketing functions in a business organization. This chapter explores the general nature of that relationship. The decision responsibilities and information requirements of the marketing function are described, and the role of the accounting information system in meeting these information requirements and in processing sales transactions is explained and illustrated. The discussion is intended to be general in nature rather than descriptive of the real system of a specific company.

The remaining chapters in Part IV examine the relationship of the accounting information system to other functional areas of management within a typical business organization. Chapters 17 and 18 cover the logistics function, while Chapters 19 and 20 cover the personnel and finance functions, respectively. The purpose of these chapters is to integrate and illustrate the application of the concepts, tools, and technology covered in the first three sections. In particular, the concepts of control and

Fig. 16.1
Marketing organiza-
tion structure.

organization, the tool of flowcharting, and the technology of computer-based information systems are stressed.

In Part IV, the various subsystems of the accounting information system are discussed separately rather than as one total system. This is done primarily as a matter of convenience of presentation, however, and should not obscure the fact that the various functional areas are very much interdependent in terms of both operations and information. As the reader proceeds through Part IV, the interrelationships among the various information subsystems should be noted.

The Marketing Management Function

In Chapter 2 it is emphasized that knowledge of the organization structure of a company provides the systems analyst with important insights into the decision responsibilities and information requirements of the various managers and personnel within the organization. This and subsequent chapters apply this concept by illustrating typical forms of organization within each of the several functional areas of business firms. The illustrations provide a framework for discussion of decision responsibilities and information requirements within each functional area. Figure 16.1 provides an example of a typical marketing organization structure. Each of the executive positions shown in the chart is examined in this section.

The top marketing executive

The Vice-President of Marketing is responsible to the company President for the effective planning, coordination, and control of the marketing effort. The position requires participation in companywide planning, specifically as it relates to marketing activities, as well as participation with other top level executives in the establishment of pricing policies that encompasses not only setting base prices but also instituting discount policies, credit terms, and warranty policies. The Marketing Vice-President also may participate in forming the most significant policy decisions relating to the specific areas for which marketing staff executives are responsible, such as new product introduction or the planning of a major advertising campaign. The role requires review and evaluation of the performance of subordinate executives.

The Marketing Vice-President in a business organization may be looked upon as a strategist seeking an optimal allocation of "scarce resources" to achieve the maximum advantage for the firm in the environment of the marketplace. Scarce resources include personnel—staff specialists and sales force—and funds. The Marketing Vice-President must allocate these resources among such activities as selling effort, advertising and promotional campaigns, marketing research studies, and so forth. Environmental forces include customers, competitors, the economy, and government.

To fulfill responsibilities of the position, the Vice-President of Marketing relies on extensive information obtained from various sources. The planning function requires environmental information on such matters as economic trends, competitors' plans, and customers' attitudes, as well as internally generated information such as sales forecasts and market research studies. The pricing decision requires all of the kinds of information above plus internal information on the cost of products and the cost of credit and warranty policies. The control function requires information as a basis for evaluating the performance of all subordinate executives.

Director of sales   The Director of Sales is responsible for the effectiveness of the selling effort within the firm, and also participates in the planning of sales with the Marketing Vice-President to establish standards and quotas for the sales force. If the firm's products are consumer goods sold through wholesale and retail outlets, the Director of Sales will be involved in the selection of the most effective of such distribution channels. The Regional Sales Managers who report to the Director of Sales have similar responsibilities on a smaller scale. The Director of Sales must review, evaluate, and control the performance of the Regional Sales Managers who, in turn, must review, evaluate, and control the performance of their respective sales forces.

Sales forecasts provide the Director of Sales and the Regional Sales Managers with an information base for planning the sales effort. Similarly, reports of actual sales, or *sales analyses,* provide an information base for control. Sales analysis reports may classify sales in several ways. To the Regional Sales Manager, classification by salesperson is most meaningful as a tool for evaluating salespeople. To the Director of Sales, a sales analysis by regions and perhaps by territories within regions is useful. To individual salespeople, sales analysis by customer is very useful.

Whereas a sales analysis reports only sales volume, a *profitability analysis* breaks down the marginal contribution to profit made by each territory, customer, distribution channel, or other unit. Profitability is a function of both the volume and profit margin of a product. Reports of this nature are even more useful to sales managers and the sales force for planning and control than sales analyses because they indicate directly the marginal contribution to profit of each individual selling activity. However, such reports are more difficult for an information system to generate because they require variable product cost data in addition to sales volume data.

Also useful in controlling the selling effort are analyses of the activities of individual salespeople, including customers called upon, time spent with each, literature distributed, demonstrations presented, and so forth. Individual salespersons require certain operational information for use in executing sales transactions such as information on the availability and location of inventories, the time required for delivery to a customer, the credit standing of a customer, etc. In addition, information on the incremental cost of various selling activities is useful to salespeople and sales managers for purposes of cost control. Important in this respect are analyses of the incremental costs of calling on a particular class of customer, of utilizing a particular type of distribution channel, or of serving a particular territory.

Director of advertising and promotion

The Director of Advertising and Promotion is responsible for planning and control of promotional activities. Together with a staff, the Director plans advertising campaigns and other promotional strategies, such as dealer incentives, contests, and trade show displays, and then must coordinate the execution of these strategies and evaluate their effectiveness as a basis for subsequent planning. The Director must allocate a limited promotional budget among various product lines, territories, etc., to obtain maximum results.

Sales and profitability analysis information that provides breakdowns by territory, by product line, and perhaps by customer is relevant to the planning and control of advertising and promotion. Information on customer attitudes and plans is also useful for planning. Information on the cost of individual advertising and promotional campaigns is necessary for control purposes. Information that specifically relates sales and profit performance with advertising and promotional efforts is especially useful for planning and control.

Director of product planning

The Director of Product Planning is responsible for planning the characteristics of the product line. This involves decisions relating to such factors as styling and packaging, as well as to the planning and introduction of new products. Also involved is the function of reviewing the performance of existing products—their sales, profitability, and potential—and deciding or recommending whether any such products should be removed from the product line.

Sales analyses and profitability analyses by product line are vital to the product planning function. Information on present and future product costs is also useful to decisions on styling, packaging, and the deletion of products from the line. Information on customer attitudes is important to decisions on styling and new product introduction. Projected cost and revenue information is essential for making recommendations on new product introduction.

Director of customer service

The Director of Customer Service is responsible for policies and decisions relating to the servicing of customer needs after the sale of the product. The Director may administer a staff that responds to customer complaints or which reviews the adequacy of retail facilities, and may administer a maintenance organization if the product is a technical one. The basic objective is to ensure that a customer achieves the level of satisfaction of needs or desires expected from the product.

The information used in the Customer Service function is for the most part obtained directly from customers and includes requests for information or technical assistance, complaints, requests for maintenance, and so forth. Information on the incremental cost of customer service activities and the performance of customer service personnel is useful for purposes of control.

Director of marketing research

The Director of Marketing Research is responsible for planning and administering the data gathering and analysis activities of the Marketing Research Staff. This staff carries out special studies of consumer behavior and other subjects of interest to marketing executives. The Director must allocate scarce resources among alternative projects and interpret the results of such projects for other marketing executives and top management. Marketing Research studies are often a primary basis for planning in such areas as new product introduction, advertising, and pricing. For the most part the Marketing Research Staff is not a user, but a producer, of information, which it generates from data collected by means of scanning the environment.

Sources of Marketing Information

In terms of volume of information, the accounting information system is the primary source of marketing information in most business organizations. However, a well-managed marketing activity cannot rely solely on financial information, and must therefore exploit other sources of information, including its own salespeople and staff personnel, other departments within the firm, and the environment. This section discusses the nature of the data collected and the information generated from each of these sources.

The accounting information system

The accounting information system is a source of two basic types of information to marketing management: information generated from the processing of sales orders, and cost reports and analyses.

Sales order processing   The sales order processing cycle begins with the initiation of an order by a customer and ends with the delivery of goods to the customer. The basic data source is the sales invoice, an example of which is illustrated in Fig. 16.2. The invoice serves as a record of the sales transaction, and copies sent to the customer provide notice that shipment has been made and payment is due. In addition, items that were ordered but not shipped due to insufficient supply are listed as *back-*

NEEDMORE MANUFACTURING COMPANY						

987 Glendale Needmore, Tx 78799   Tel. 512/836-0107   Invoice No. 10001

INVOICE

Customer Order No. 45236	Order date 7/10/81	Salesperson Code 24 − 76	Customer Account No. 24 − 93106			

Sold to: Ship to:

Hardware Wholesalers   Same
1006 East 61st
Austin, Texas 78744

Shipper	Date shipped	Invoice date	Terms of sale
Austin Trkg. 24061	7/12/81	7/12/81	2/10, net 30

Item code	Description	Quantity ordered	Back ordered	Quantity shipped	Unit price	Item total
10562	Hammer	100		100	$ 1.00	$100.00
20651	Sickle	50	20	30	1.75	52.50
38214	Hoe	50		50	2.50	125.00
	Rake	80	30	50	3.25	162.50
	Freight					5.61
	Total					$445.61

Fig. 16.2
Sales invoice.

ordered, which means that they will be shipped as soon as the stock is replenished. Note how much of the data collected on the sales invoice is coded to facilitate subsequent processing. For example, the salesperson's number, customer account number, and item code provide a basis for generating sales and profitability analyses by salesperson, by customer, and by product. In addition, the invoice itself is numbered to provide a basis for future reference and audit.

Data from the sales invoice represent one of the primary inputs to the marketing data base, which in turn is the major repository of information useful to marketing management. The marketing data base contains information relating to finished goods inventories, customers, and sales. The finished goods inventory information is used to check on inventory availability at the time of the sale. Customer records include accounts receivable and credit history information that may be used as a basis for evaluating the credit worthiness of a customer who has placed an order. The sales information is used to generate the various sales analysis reports that provide vital management information to marketing executives.

Sales analysis reports generally present dollar and/or unit sales for the most recent period (week or month) and for the year to date. In addition, for comparison purposes it is useful if sales quotas and/or prior year sales are reported along with actual sales for the current period. An example of a report analyzing sales by territory, and by salesperson within territory, is provided in Fig. 16.3. A report of this type would be useful to the sales manager of a territory for purposes of evaluating the territory's sales force. Similarly, a report analyzing sales by territory within a

Period ending: March 31, 1981			Territory:	East Texas		
Salesperson	Period	Actual sales	Prior year	% Change	Quota	% Variance from quota
Benjamin, H.L.	This month	$ 5,000	$ 4,000	+ 25%	$ 4,800	+ 4%
	Year to date	12,000	11,500	+ 4%	12,500	− 4%
Carlton, J.C.	This month	$ 4,000	$ 3,800	+ 5%	$ 4,500	− 11%
	Year to date	10,500	11,000	− 5%	13,000	− 19%
Territory totals	This month	$30,000	$28,550	+ 5%	$35,000	− 14%
	Year to date	85,000	84,000	+ 1%	95,000	− 11%

Fig. 16.3
Sales analysis by salesperson and territory.

region would be useful to a regional sales manager in evaluating territorial sales managers, whereas a report of aggregate sales by region would be useful to the Director of Sales in evaluating regional sales managers.

Within a typical business organization, sales may be analyzed according to several detailed and aggregate classifications to provide useful information to various marketing executives at all levels of the organization. In addition to breakdowns by salesperson, territory, and region, sales may be analyzed by individual product, product class, major customers, type of customer, distribution channel, and so forth. Furthermore, reports may be prepared in which sales are detailed according to two or more classification categories. Examples would include a breakdown of sales by product for key customers, or by type of customer for each territory. Sales analyses are useful not only because they provide a historical summary for control purposes but also because they provide information relevant to planning advertising and promotional campaigns, selling activities, price changes, composition of product lines, and other marketing activities.

Profitability analysis reports are generated from sales records together with product cost data. Such reports generally may be prepared using the same categories of classification as sales analyses. An example of a profitability analysis by product class and model for a customer is illustrated in Fig. 16.4. This sample report reveals that the contribution margin (excess of revenues over variable costs) for this customer exceeds the amount budgeted, primarily because unfavorable volume variances for low margin products in each class are more than offset by favorable volume variances among high margin products. This type of information is useful both to salespeople and sales managers for purposes of allocating sales effort among products and customers. Similar product profitability breakdowns may be generated by distribution channel, by territory, or by salesperson. Aggregate product profitability information may also be generated for use by top level marketing executives in product planning.

ATLANTA WHOLESALE APPLIANCE COMPANY

Account number: 16520

Date: October 31, 1981

*- - - - - - - - - - - Year-to-date Totals - - - - - - - - - -

Product		Per unit gross margin	1980 actual	Unit sales 1981 actual	1981 budget	Actual contribution margin	Budgeted contribution margin	Variance
Class	Model							
Refrigerator	RF-10	$ 40	1,800	2,000	2,100	$ 80,000	$ 84,000	$ (4,000)
Freezer	RF-14	60	3,500	4,000	4,100	240,000	246,000	(6,000)
	RF-16	80	3,000	3,600	3,500	288,000	280,000	8,000
	RF-20	100	1,200	1,500	1,400	150,000	140,000	10,000
Freezer	F-16	75	1,100	1,280	1,300	96,000	97,500	(1,500)
	F-20	90	1,500	1,750	1,800	157,500	162,000	(4,500)
	F-24	130	600	750	700	97,500	91,000	6,500
Totals, all products						$1,109,000	$1,100,500	$ 8,500

*Fig. 16.4
Profitability analysis
by product for key
customer.*

A third major category of information generated from the processing of sales orders includes various analyses of sales trends. For example, projections developed from sales trends are useful for purposes of forecasting sales; sales forecasts, in turn, can be utilized in the planning and control of marketing activities. Further, analyses of historical sales trends contribute to evaluating the success of various marketing actions, such as advertising campaigns, special promotions, or price changes.

The procedures involved in processing sales order transactions, maintaining the marketing data base and generating the various reports are described in detail in a later section of this chapter.

Cost reports and analyses   All cash disbursements made by an organization must be recorded by its accounting system. A good system will record enough information about the nature and purpose of each disbursement to enable useful reports to be generated. One significant example is information about product costs. This information is used in establishing pricing policies, in product planning, and in various profitability analyses. Manufacturing companies generally maintain fairly elaborate cost accounting systems to generate accurate and useful product cost data.

To be most useful, product cost information should be segregated according to the fixed and variable components of manufacturing costs and selling expenses. For purposes of marketing cost control, each detailed element of selling expense should also be segregated into its fixed and variable elements. Ordering information in this way enables marketing management to evaluate the incremental cost of various alternative marketing actions under consideration.

Though incremental product cost information is very useful to marketing management, it is also very difficult for an accounting system to provide. The primary problem is that not all cost elements are either rigidly fixed or directly variable with unit sales volume. In addition, the accounting systems of many firms are designed to fulfill external reporting requirements, which dictate that the cost per unit of a manufactured product must include all manufacturing costs, including both fixed and variable costs. Selling expenses are generally reported as one lump sum or according to functional classifications, with no recognition given to their fixed and variable components. Most data classification systems, such as charts of accounts, were originally designed primarily to facilitate external reporting. In order for accounting information systems to provide incremental cost information, each type of cost must first be separated into fixed and variable components, and then systems of data collection and classification must be redesigned to facilitate the necessary processing steps.

In addition to product cost information, a firm's accounting information system should provide cost reports by responsibility centers within the marketing department. These reports compare costs incurred to budgeted costs for each responsibility center. Such reports are useful to marketing executives for controlling the allocation of budgeted funds to their most profitable uses. In addition, project cost reports comparing and analyzing estimated and actual costs for significant marketing projects should be prepared. Examples of such projects would include market research studies, advertising campaigns, and other promotions and surveys.

The accounting information system must also participate in the preparation of revenue cost projections upon which decisions regarding new product introduction are based. While records of sales of similar products provide one basis for revenue projections, per unit cost projections are developed using the estimates of labor and material requirements obtained from the engineering department. An estimate of the amount of the initial cash outlay for promotion and new equipment is also required. Once all cash flow projections have been made, the decision should be based upon a capital budgeting analysis that predicts the expected present value and risk factors involved in the decision. Accounting executives are generally familiar with capital budgeting techniques and should participate in the development of these analyses.

Several subsystems of the accounting information system contribute to the generation of cost information and reports of the type discussed in this section. The next four chapters discuss further the structure and operations of these subsystems.

The marketing department

A significant share of the information that the marketing department uses for marketing management is typically generated from within the department. One significant data source in this category is the salesperson's call report, an example of which is illustrated in Fig. 16.5. This report is intended to be filled out by each salesperson for each call he or she makes on a customer, whether or not the customer makes a purchase. All firms would not necessarily find it appropriate to collect and utilize

SALESPERSON ACTIVITY REPORT

Salesperson number

Name

Date of call

Time spent

Account data

Name _____   Acct. number _____

Address _____   Buyer's name _____

_____

Type of store	Account status	Order status
Furniture sales	Prospect	Order received
Local dept. store	Old account	Will send later
Dept. store chain	New account	Won't buy now
Other	No interest	No interest

Comments

Fig. 16.5
Sales person's call report.

data of this sort, but when the technique is employed, it yields a very useful source of information for evaluation of the sales force and of feedback from customers regarding their needs of, and opinions on, the firm's products.

The marketing research studies prepared by the Marketing Research Department constitute a second significant source of marketing information within the marketing department. These studies may range from pilot studies of consumer reaction to the introduction of a new product or to a new advertising campaign in a limited market area, to general surveys of customer attitudes throughout the country. Such studies may be performed as needed by other marketing departments or on a regular basis. The primary source of data input for these studies is the external environment. The Marketing Research Staff applies its expertise in statistical sampling and statistical inference techniques to "process" these data into information. Marketing research information is potentially useful to almost all marketing decisions involving the planning function.

A third important source of marketing information within the marketing department consists of sales forecasts. Estimates provided by the sales force play a major role in developing such forecasts, although historical records of past sales are also important. Sales forecasts are used as a basis for planning the activities of the entire firm, and are also very useful as standards for management control of the sales force. Statistical techniques such as exponential smoothing or regression and correlation analysis may be used to generate these forecasts.

Other internal sources

In addition to the accounting and marketing departments, other departments within a firm may contribute significantly to the flow of information to marketing personnel. For example, the production and/or engineering department may provide information relating to product quality or design useful to product planning or to salespeople. The economics department, if one exists, may provide useful analyses of the economy or of the particular industrial field within which the firm operates. The personnel department may provide information relating to potential marketing department employees. In many firms, a smooth interface between the marketing department and a research and development department is essential to product planning. While information from all of these sources may be important, it is generally neither as regular nor as voluminous as the information provided by the accounting department or that generated within the marketing department itself.

External information sources

Much useful marketing information may be obtained directly from scanning the external environment without the need for an intermediate data processing step. One type of information that fits within this category relates to the activities and plans of competitive firms. Information about the nature of the products, prices, and advertising of competitors is very useful to marketing planning. Information about the plans of competitors, while not easily obtained, is also extremely useful. Trade publications, the promotional literature of competitors, and communication with customers are potential sources of this information.

General information on economic and industry trends may also be obtained directly from the environment. Information on demographic characteristics of the market—rural vs. urban; population, education, and income levels; population in various age groups; etc.—falls in this category. The United States Bureau of the Census and other federal and state government agencies comprise one important source of such information. Trade associations that gather, analyze, and distribute information relating to a particular industry are another.

There are definite problems with respect to deciding what environmental information is needed and establishing a regular mechanism for its acquisition and analysis. Unlike accounting information, environmental information is not made available automatically as the by-product of some other essential business process. Marketing executives must accept the responsibility for becoming familiar with external information sources and obtaining the environmental information of most relevance to their particular functions.

The Sales Order Processing System

The general nature of the input to and output from the sales order processing system has already been discussed. This section will outline the accounting transactions involved in the process, examine the content and structure of the marketing data base, and then describe in detail an example of (1) a manual system, (2) a computer-based batch processing system, and (3) a real-time system for processing sales orders and generating marketing information.

The accounting transactions

The primary accounting journal entry reflecting sales order processing appears as follows.

Accounts Receivable	XXX
Sales	XXX

Almost all sales of a manufacturing company, as well as a significant portion of the sales of retail companies, are recorded in this manner. For firms that maintain inventory on a perpetual basis, these sales entries are accompanied by the following entry.

Cost of Goods Sold	XXX
Finished Goods Inventory	XXX

Certain variations from these basic entries may also occur. For example, when a customer returns merchandise, or asks for an adjustment in price because of damaged merchandise, the following entry is made.

Sales Returns and Allowances	XXX
Accounts Receivable	XXX

These journal entries represent the most important transactions that are initiated as a result of sales order processing. Transactions involving the collection of accounts receivable are treated in Chapter 20.

In manual systems, journal entries are usually recorded either in a general journal or on a journal voucher. The manual systems described in Chapters 16 through 20 assume that journal vouchers (see Fig. 16.6) are used. In this way, illustrative document flowcharts of these systems (such as Fig. 16.8) show the exact point in the system at which journal vouchers are prepared for each of the important journal entries initiated by the process.

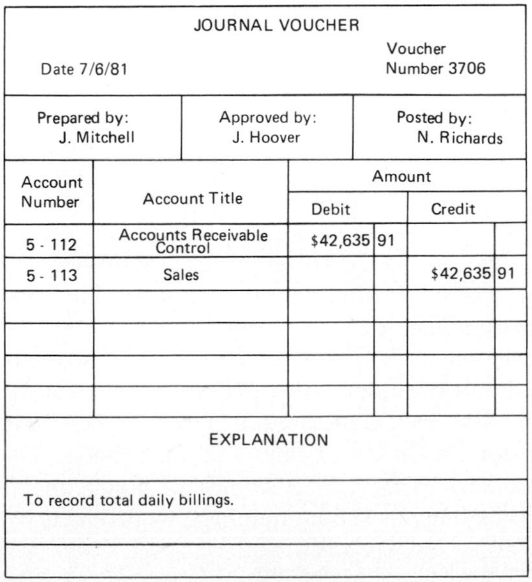

JOURNAL VOUCHER

Date 7/6/81   Voucher Number 3706

Prepared by: J. Mitchell   Approved by: J. Hoover   Posted by: N. Richards

Account Number	Account Title	Debit	Credit
5 - 112	Accounts Receivable Control	$42,635 91	
5 - 113	Sales		$42,635 91

EXPLANATION

To record total daily billings.

*Fig. 16.6
Journal voucher.*

The marketing data base

An example of the data content and organization of a marketing data base appears in Fig. 16.7. This data base is essentially a network consisting of two interrelated families of records. One of these families includes finished goods inventory data, while the other includes customer data. In addition, transaction records such as the production order, sales invoice, credit memo for sales returns and allowances, cash receipt, and salesperson's call report are associated with one or both of these families.

Each customer record in the system contains a single value for all of the data fields listed under "Customer File." In addition, each customer record owns one or more "Customer Transaction" records; that is, Customer Transaction is a repeating group with respect to the Customer File. In turn, each Customer Transaction record is a summary of the data contained in a Sales Invoice, Credit Memo, Cash Receipt, or Salesperson's Call Report. The "Transaction Type Code" and "Document Number" in the Customer Transaction record enable the system to access a more detailed transaction record (for example, a complete sales invoice) when necessary. At any given time only transactions from the current month or year will be stored in the marketing data base, although records of older transactions may be stored offline.

Basic inputs to the customer file portion of the marketing data base include routine sales and cash receipts transactions, credits for sales returns and allowances, salesperson's call reports, and nonroutine adjustments such as changes of address, addition of new credit customers, bad debt writeoffs, and corrections of errors. Basic outputs include statements of account that are mailed to customers each month, responses to requests for credit approval for individual customers, and various reports such as the accounts receivable aging schedule.

Each finished goods inventory record in the marketing data base contains a single value for each of the data fields listed under "Finished Goods Inventory" in Fig. 16.7. Furthermore, each finished goods inventory record owns one or more "Finished Goods Transaction" records, each of which is a summary of a production order, sale, or sales return transaction. When it is necessary to access the detailed transaction record (such as a complete production order) from the transaction summary record, the "Transaction Type Code" and "Document Number" fields provide the required reference data.

Basic inputs to the finished goods inventory portion of the marketing data base include records of sales transactions, production orders initiated, and production orders completed, as well as miscellaneous additions, corrections, and adjustments. The data stored here provide important reference information for production planning, warehouse and stockroom operations, and selling operations. Basic outputs that may be generated include a *stock status report,* which is a listing of data values for each inventory record; a report of items out of stock or below the prescribed minimum stock level; or an analysis of product turnover.

A marketing data base structured as outlined above contains most of the data necessary to generate a variety of sales analysis reports. These would include sales analysis by customer, by type of customer (if a subcode for type of customer is included in each customer's account number), by product, by product class (if a sub-

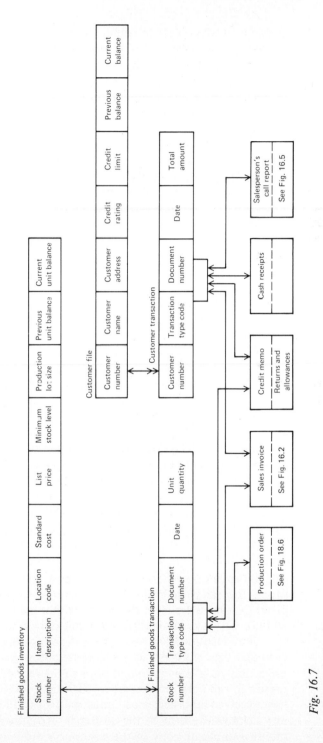

Fig. 16.7
Marketing data base.

code for product class is included in each inventory stock number), by salesperson (coded on the invoice), by territory (if a subcode for territory is included in each salesperson number), or by any number of cross-classifications of the categories above. Note, however, that the most useful form of sales analysis is one in which current sales data are compared with sales quotas and/or prior year's sales figures for comparable periods, and performance variances or percentage changes are highlighted. To enable this system to generate this type of report, it could be assumed that monthly quotas and prior year's monthly sales totals are simply an additional type of finished goods and customer transaction record that may be stored in the data base for this purpose.

In a manual data processing system or a conventional computer-based batch processing system, the marketing data base exists in the form of a series of separately maintained files. For example, there might be separate files for customer data, finished goods data, sales data, salesperson's call reports, and so on. Updating each of these files for input transactions requires a separate set of procedures. In addition, each file is separately processed to generate output reports, and such reports can reflect only that information that is contained on the specific file from which it was generated. Furthermore, output reports are generally prepared only at predetermined intervals (such as monthly), and must usually conform to a predesigned fixed format.

In contrast, if the marketing data base is maintained using a data base management system of the kind described in Chapter 8, then it is possible to combine many of the separate updating procedures referred to above into an integrated data base maintenance process. For example, merely adding a new sales invoice to the data base automatically initiates the necessary update of inventory records for shipments *and* the update of the customer's record for the credit sale. The same would be true for any other type of transaction affecting the marketing data base. Also, the data base management system would enable users to generate at any time they desire a report in any format they wish to specify, and the content of such a report is not limited to that of a particular record but rather may include any of the data items contained in the marketing data base. Thus the marketing function provides ample demonstration of the advantages of data base concepts and techniques.

A manual system   The document flowchart in Fig. 16.8 illustrates one example of a manual system for processing sales orders in a manufacturing company. Most such companies will differ in some ways from this example, but the general pattern of information flow will not vary a great deal from the illustration in most cases.

The illustration shows the sales order process beginning with the receipt of the customer's purchase order, which is used to prepare a sales order. Actually the sales order may have been prepared prior to the receipt of the purchase order by a salesperson in the field or by a sales order clerk receiving telephone orders. Once they have received an order, most industrial firms will transmit some form of documentary acknowledgment to the customer. As shown in the illustration, this is commonly a duplicate copy of the customer's purchase order.

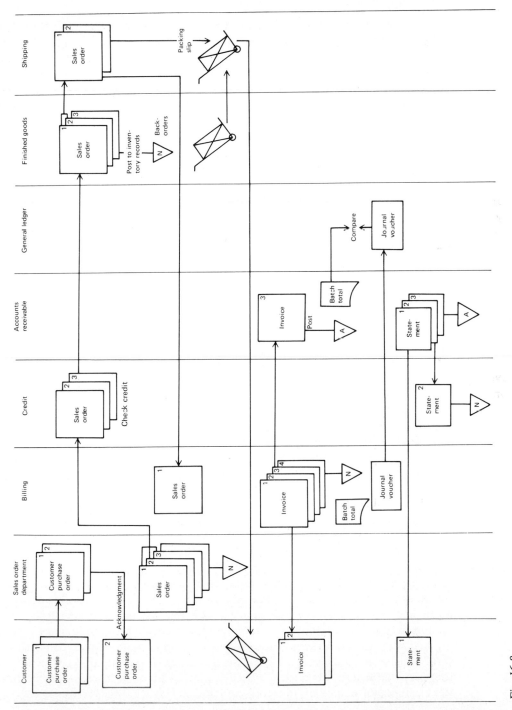

Fig. 16.8

Document flow in a manual system for sales order processing.

The sales order contains basically the same data as the invoice except for such things as item *extensions* (price times quantity calculations), shipping charges, taxes, invoice total, and credit terms. In cases in which the quantity delivered is less than the quantity ordered, the extra units are backordered. A notation is made in the finished goods file so that when the stock is replenished the goods will be shipped automatically to the customer. Many firms, particularly those in which backordering is not common, do not use a separate sales order document. Instead, they begin to prepare the sales invoice immediately upon receipt of orders, and use extra copies of the invoice in place of the several copies of the sales order.

One copy of the sales order is filed numerically in the sales order department. Three other copies are sent to the finished goods storeroom or warehouse. If the customer's credit is not established, the sales order may be routed through the credit department, where a credit check is performed before shipment is authorized. In the finished goods storeroom the products ordered are retrieved from available stock. The sales order serves as an authorization to release the goods to the shipping department, and is used as a source document to post shipments to the finished goods inventory file. If any goods ordered are backordered, a notation to that effect is made on the sales order, and one copy is filed by storeroom personnel for future reference.

Those goods in stock are assembled and transferred to the shipping department, along with two copies of the sales order. To acknowledge the transfer of responsibility for these goods from the storeroom to shipping, an employee of shipping will sign a copy of the sales order indicating the exact quantities to be shipped. This copy will then be sent to billing. The remaining copy of the sales order may be enclosed as a *packing slip* with the goods as they are shipped to the customer.

In the billing department the sales order evidencing the transfer of goods to shipping provides the basis for preparation of the invoice. After the invoice is prepared, the first (and often a second) copy is sent to the customer. Another copy is sent to the accounts receivable department where it is used to post the billing to the customer's account and is then filed alphabetically by customer name. One other copy of the invoice is filed by invoice number in the billing department.

An example of the use of batch totals for contol purposes is found in this process. The billing department compiles a batch total of the amount billed on all invoices in a batch. Once preparation of the batch is complete, the billing department uses the batch total to prepare a journal voucher. The journal voucher contains the summary entry debiting accounts receivable and crediting sales for the total amount billed, and is sent to the general ledger clerk. In the accounts receivable department, as invoices are posted to the subsidiary ledger, another batch total is prepared. This second batch total is compiled by summing the individual ledger balances after posting and subtracting the sum of the individual ledger balances prior to posting. This total is also sent to the general ledger section where it is compared to the amount of the entry on the journal voucher. Any discrepancy between these two totals indicates the existence of one or more errors, which can then be discovered and corrected.

Periodically, usually at the end of each month, the accounts receivable department may prepare a statement of each customer's account, detailing transactions in the most recent period and indicating the total amount due on account from the customer. One copy of this statement is sent to the customer, another is kept by accounts receivable, and another may be sent to the credit department for their records. Statements of this sort are commonly prepared and utilized by retail businesses, but are generally not used in regular dealings between industrial firms.

Organizational independence with respect to the sales order process is achieved by separation of the custodial functions performed by finished goods and shipping from the recording functions performed by billing and accounts receivable, and from the authorization functions performed by the sales order and credit departments. This separation of duties helps to ensure that only goods intended for shipment to customers are removed from the finished goods storeroom, and that all such goods are shipped only to authorized customers and are properly billed.

Special procedures must be established for handling sales returns and allowances. Each adjustment should be approved by a person in a position of responsiblity, such as the Credit Manager. The basis for approval should be a letter from the customer. Issuance of a credit memo formally recognizing the adjustment should, in the case of sales returns, also require a receiving report as verification of the return of goods. A copy of the credit memo is sent to the customer, another is filed, and another is used as a source document for posting to the accounts receivable ledger. At the end of a day or week, the person authorizing these credits should prepare and send to the general ledger clerk a journal voucher containing a summary entry for all sales returns and allowances during the period.

In a manual system, the regular preparation of reports such as sales and profitability analyses may not be feasible. In very small companies, no such reports need be generated because the manager or owner probably knows enough about the customers and sales. Somewhat larger companies may obtain a limited analysis of sales by recording all sales in specially formulated journals in which, for example, separate rows are used for each product, separate columns for each time period, and separate pages for each salesperson. The data on such journals may then be aggregated across one or more of these dimensions to provide summary analyses of sales by product or by salesperson for particular periods of time.

A computer-based batch processing system   A document flowchart of the sales order and accounts receivable process for a typical manufacturing company that uses a computer-based system appears in Fig. 16.9. It is assumed that the system uses magnetic tape input and maintains master files on magnetic disk. Once again, it must be emphasized that the illustration is not intended to demonstrate how the process should be accomplished but merely to show one example of how it might be done.

A comparison of Fig. 16.9 with its manual counterpart, Fig. 16.8, reveals that procedures relating to sales order preparation, credit checking, order assembly in

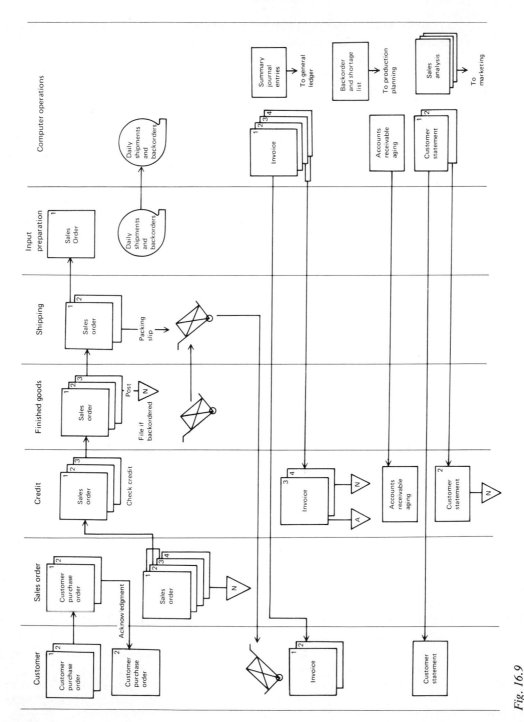

Fig. 16.9   Document flow in computerized batch processing of sales orders.

finished goods, and shipping are the same. However, the functions of billing and accounts receivable have been replaced by data processing. When the shipping department is finished with a sales order, it sends a copy indicating which items were shipped and which were backordered to the input preparation department. This department keys and verifies a tape record for each individual item shipped or backordered. These records become input to a series of computer runs that produce invoices, update the accounts receivable master file, update the finished goods inventory master file, produce a list of inventory items that are out of stock or in short supply, update the master sales file, produce a sales analysis report at the end of each week or month, produce customer statements of account at the end of each month, and produce an aged accounts receivable schedule at the end of each month. A systems flowchart of the computer operations necessary to accomplish these various processes appears in Fig. 16.10.

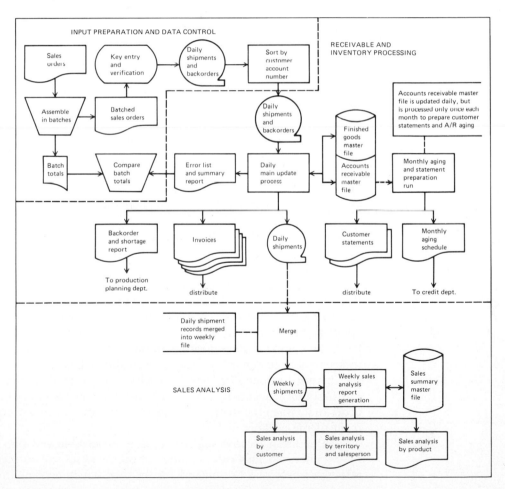

Fig. 16.10 System flow in computerized batch processing of sales orders.

To simplify its interpretation, the systems flowchart is separated by dashed lines into three separate categories of operations. These are (1) input preparation and data control, (2) accounts receivable and inventory processing, and (3) sales analysis. Each of these three sets of operations is discussed in turn in this section. Also discussed are a number of control policies and procedures relating to these processes.

Input preparation and data control   Each day this operation begins with the assembly of sales orders in batches and the preparation of batch totals. For each batch of sales orders, control totals that could be accumulated include record counts of the total number of sales orders, shipments, and backorders as well as hash totals of customer account numbers, inventory stock numbers, or the number of units ordered. The batch totals are retained and compared to summary totals generated by subsequent computer processing to help ensure that no records are lost during processing or improperly processed. The next step in input preparation is the keying and verification of a shipment or backorder record for each item ordered. It is assumed that these records are keyed onto magnetic tape using a key-to-tape encoder or key-to-disk-to-tape system. The computer is then used to sort these magnetic tape records into sequential order according to the customer account number.

There are several alternative means by which these input preparation operations could have been accomplished. For example, the shipment and backorder records could have been keyed into punched cards and sorted on a card sorter. Alternatively, these records could be keyed onto a diskette and then transferred to magnetic tape or disk for sorting and processing. Another alternative used by many mailorder companies is to send the customer a preprinted order form on which items to be ordered may be marked; when returned, such forms can be read by optical character recognition equipment and recorded on magnetic tape.

Accounts receivable and inventory processing   The main step in this operation is the daily processing of shipment and backorder records to update the accounts receivable and inventory master files. In the manual system, these steps are performed by employees in the accounts receivable and finished goods inventory departments. Because the input records are sequenced by customer account number, the accounts receivable master file is accessed sequentially during this run. Therefore, finished goods inventory records must be accessed randomly using the stock number as the key. The updating process results in the addition of the amount billed to each customer to that customer's accounts receivable balance, as well as the subtraction of the quantity shipped of each inventory item from that item's balance on hand. Furthermore, backorder records are posted to the appropriate inventory master in order that, when the stock is replenished, the system can automatically initiate shipment of the backordered goods.

In addition to updating the accounts receivable and finished goods inventory master files, the daily main update run produces several outputs. One is a tape containing records of all shipments for the day, which becomes input to sales analysis processing. Another output is a report of backordered items and other inventory items for which the balance on hand is below the minimum stock level; this report is provided to the production planning department to aid in decisions regarding which items should be produced. Also generated are four copies of a customer invoice for each order, which are distributed as shown in Fig. 16.9. In the manual system, the invoice preparation function is performed by employees in the billing department.

A fourth output of this run is a listing of error transactions and summary information. Error transactions include any input records that failed an input validation test or other processing check in the program. This list should be provided to the data control clerk for follow up and error correction. The summary report includes batch totals accumulated during the run that are compared with those calculated manually prior to keying. Also included on the summary report are (1) the summary journal entry debiting accounts receivable and crediting sales, and (2) if a perpetual inventory system is used, the summary journal entry debiting cost of goods sold and crediting finished goods inventory. These summary journal entries may be posted to the general ledger either manually, by a separate computer run, or (if the general ledger is maintained online) by directly accessing the affected general ledger records at the conclusion of the main update run.

The other process illustrated in this section of the flowchart is a monthly run utilizing the accounts receivable master file as input. This run results in the preparation of statements of account, which are mailed to customers, and an aging schedule of accounts receivable, in which each customer's account is categorized according to whether and by how much it is past due. The aging schedule is submitted to the credit department for use in customer credit checks, and to initiate special collection procedures when necessary.

Sales analysis   The illustration assumes that sales analysis operations are performed weekly, although a monthly cycle is also quite common. It is also assumed that a magnetic disk master file summarizing previous sales activity is maintained as a source of data for preparing sales analysis reports. Before these reports can be prepared, this sales summary master file must be updated for sales transactions of the most recent week. In turn, this requires that the daily shipments tape must be merged into a single weekly shipments tape, which is then processed against the sales summary master at the end of each week. This process is performed sequentially by customer account number, and therefore sales analysis reports by customer or by customer class may be prepared as a by-product of the update run.

Next, the sales summary master file may be sorted into sequence by salesperson number, and then subsequently by product stock number, in order to generate sales analysis reports by territory and salesperson,[1] and by product item and product class. Alternatively, the use of a direct access storage medium such as magnetic disk permits separate indices to be maintained for the sales summary master file—one

[1] *This assumes that each salesperson serves within a single territory only, so that sales for a territory is simply the sum of the total sales for all salespersons assigned to that territory.*

for salesperson numbers and one for product stock numbers. Because these indices would be in sequential order (though the records are not), these various sales analysis reports could be produced without the need for intermediate sorting steps. Once the preparation of the various sales analysis reports is completed, they are distributed to the appropriate executives in the market department.

Control policies and procedures   A number of control policies and procedures should be integrated into the computerized processing of sales orders. Two examples already mentioned are the key verification of shipment and backorder records, and the preparation and checking of batch totals. Several other examples may be cited. In the area of data security, each of the tape and disk files used in this system should have both internal and external labels to ensure that no file will be inadvertently processed by the wrong program. Backup copies of the three master files stored on magnetic disk should be periodically written onto magnetic tape, and subsequent transaction tapes saved to permit reconstruction of any master file whose contents are destroyed. Tape file protection rings should be removed from the transaction and backup tapes saved for this purpose in order to prevent such tapes from being written on. Current copies of these tape and disk files, when not in use, should be stored in a tape library and removed only for authorized purposes. Backup copies of master files and transaction records should be stored in a secure off-site location.

In the area of processing controls, input validation routines should be included in each file maintenance program in the system. Examples of the edit checks that might be included in these routines are field checks on all numeric fields in the input data; sequence checks of the input records; validity checks on customer account number, inventory stock number, and salesperson number; and reasonableness tests of price and quantity data from the orders. The list of error transactions produced by each file maintenance run should be reviewed by data control or supervisory personnel, and each error transaction should be corrected and resubmitted into the system.

Variations from the basic transactions, such as new customer accounts, sales returns and allowances, or corrections and adjustments of file records, would normally be included in the regular file processing runs. Keypunching personnel should check for the appropriate approval on source documents for transactions of this type. Input records for these items would include a transaction code identifyng the nature of each record for the program. Each updating program would then check for and report any records having invalid transaction codes.

A real-time system   A systems flowchart of a real-time sales order processing system is illustrated in Fig. 16.11. The general characteristics of this system were described in Chapter 9 and will be reviewed only briefly here. This section will emphasize the differences between the real-time and batch processing systems and will also describe control procedures and techniques appropriate for the real-time system.

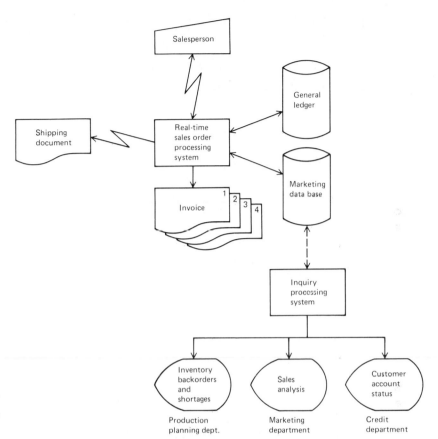

Fig. 16.11
Real-time sales order
processing system.

As shown in the flowchart, a salesperson using the real-time system may obtain access to the system from the field, either through a portable terminal or through regional centers. The salesperson may check the availability of inventory items for the customer, check the customer's credit and the status of the account, initiate a transaction, and confirm the transaction immediately to the customer. A shipping order is quickly transmitted to a terminal in the stockroom or a warehouse if prompt shipment is desired. The transaction is immediately posted to the appropriate records within the marketing data base, and to the general ledger.

Multiple copies of the invoice for each transaction may be printed out immediately as the order is processed. Alternatively, in order to avoid tying up a printer permanently for this purpose, the invoice data could be spooled onto a tape or disk file. Then all invoices could be printed out in a batch once a day or at some other regular interval.

In a batch processing system such as the one described in the previous section, management reports are printed at regular intervals. In a real-time system that incorporates an inquiry processing capability, the need for regular preparation of printed management reports is reduced or eliminated. Instead, each manager uses a terminal to access the marketing data base and retrieve relevant management information. For example, as illustrated in Fig. 16.11, production planners can obtain on demand a list of inventory items backordered or in short supply to assist them in scheduling production. Similarly, sales analysis reports in any desired format can be obtained by marketing executives using a terminal. Credit managers can obtain a receivables aging schedule at any time, or inquire into the current status of a specific customer's account.

In addition to these differences in management reporting, this example illustrates several other major differences between batch processing and real-time systems. For example, in the batch processing system, entering data into the system requires several steps. First, the source document (the sales order) has to be prepared, approved by the credit department, used by the finished goods storeroom personnel in retrieving the goods for shipment, and finally used as a source document for keying and verifying shipment and backorder records. Once the data are recorded on machine readable media (cards or tape), they must be sorted and read in separately for each separate file update. The existence of these several steps in the batch processing system means that (1) there are several possibilities for errors to occur, and (2) the entire process consumes a sizable quantity of time.

In contrast, the real-time system replaces document preparation, keying, sorting, and reading with a single step—the keying of the relevant data into the system using a terminal. Credit checking is done automatically and all of the files are updated in one process, without reloading and re-sorting of tapes or disks. The general ledger is also updated in this process, with no separate procedures being required. Basically, the real-time system accomplishes, in a single automatic process, the same result that requires several different steps, all requiring manual intervention, in the batch processing system.

The real-time system does have a major disadvantage with respect to control of data accuracy: there is only one point in the system at which the accuracy of data can be controlled—the point of entry of data into the system. If the system accepts inaccurate data, the chance to discover and correct the error before it contaminates all files, documents, and reports is lost. However, in another sense this fact is an advantage. It means that control of data accuracy can be focused at a single point, the point of data entry, with the assurance that if all errors are prevented there, no subsequent errors are likely.

The first essential control feature of a real-time sales order processing system is the assignment of a unique user code to each salesperson. The user code number of each salesperson should be known only to that person. Each time the salesperson desires access to the system, the user code number is the first item of data to be entered. The system should check the validity of the user code number before accepting any further instructions or data from the salesperson. Furthermore, each salesperson's user code number should contain an internal code that defines the transactions he or she is authorized to initiate and the files to which he or she is authorized to have access. A salesperson should be restricted to initiating only sales orders and inquiring only into the marketing data base.

Another control feature over data entry into a real-time system is simplicity of operator data entry procedures. This might be effected by displaying an invoice format for the salesperson to fill in, or by writing questions on the terminal that ask the salesperson for each required item of data. The system thereby guides the salesperson through the data entry process, and will not accept the order until all of the required data have been entered.

One major form of data control lost in a real-time system is the batch total. Since transactions are entered one at a time as they occur, there is no such thing as a batch of input records in a real-time system. Responsibility for controlling the accuracy of data input in a real-time system therefore shifts more heavily to data editing routines programmed into the system. With respect to sales order data, the first of these should be a validity check on the customer account number and on the inventory stock number of each item ordered. The system should accept orders from new customers to whom no account number has been assigned, but should not initiate shipping papers until a credit check is performed.

To ensure that the salesperson does not enter a valid but incorrect account number or stock number, a redundant data check may be used. This would require that the salesperson also enter the first few letters of the customer name and the item description. The system could then check whether the number and letters provided by the salesperson match those in the customer account record and the inventory stock record. Alternatively, closed loop verification could be used for this purpose. Given only the account number and item numbers, the system could retrieve the customer name and item descriptions from the files and display these data back to the salesperson's terminal for verification.

Another type of edit routine in this system would be a field check to ensure that the quantity and price fields contain numeric data only. In addition, if the salesperson enters item prices, the accuracy of the prices entered may be tested by comparing them to the list prices on file in the marketing data base.

The various types of reasonableness tests constitute still another class of input validation checks that may be included in this system. First, the reasonableness of the product relative to the customer might be tested. For example, it would not be reasonable for a men's clothing store to order women's underwear. For another example, the reasonableness of the quantity ordered relative to the product might be tested. An order for a large quantity of a large product, such as 500 magnetic disk drive units, would not be reasonable. Conversely, an order for a very small quantity of a small product, such as ten punched cards, would not be reasonable.

If any of these editing routines detect a possible error, the salesperson is requested to reenter the item in question. After all data have been entered and have passed the various edit routines, the system may print or display critical data back to the salesperson, requesting verification of its accuracy. This step would detect data transmission errors in which the data were entered correctly, but were incorrectly transmitted to the system.

The design of a system of editing routines requires ingenuity and care. All of the techniques described above would not necessarily be appropriate for a given user. The system designed must balance cost and risk factors in a manner appropriate for the organization using the system.

Still another aspect of the overall control of the real-time sales order processing system involves the maintenance of a transaction log. Such a log is useful both for audit purposes and because it enables reconstruction of the marketing data base in the event of its accidental destruction. The transaction log could be maintained on a separate disk unit or on magnetic tape, and would be printed out periodically. The marketing data base would also be periodically written onto magnetic tape. Therefore if any portion of the data base were destroyed, it could be reconstructed using the most recent tape listing and the transaction log.

Review Questions

1. Define the following terms.

   sales analysis stock status report
   profitability analysis extensions
   backorder packing slip

2. Describe or illustrate an example of a typical marketing organization structure. Why is an understanding of the marketing organization structure necessary to the analysis of marketing information systems?

3. Describe the decision responsibilities and information requirements of
   a) the top Marketing executive,
   b) the Director of Sales,
   c) the Director of Advertising and Promotion,
   d) the Director of Product Planning,
   e) the Director of Customer Service, and
   f) the Director of Marketing Research.

4. Describe the nature of the marketing information provided, and the related data sources used, by
   a) the Accounting Information System,
   b) the Marketing Department,
   c) other sources of information within the business organization, and
   d) external information sources.

5. Describe in detail the data recorded on a sales invoice.

6. Describe in detail the data recorded on a salesperson's call report.

7. What are the accounting journal entries that summarize the activities involved in the processing of sales transactions?

8. Describe the data content and organization of the marketing data base.

9. Describe the nature and purpose of a journal voucher.

10. What departments in a manufacturing company might be involved in the manual processing of sales and maintenance of accounts receivable? What documents might be involved and what information would each contain? Where would each originate and to whom would it be distributed?

11. What control procedures are involved in manual processing of sales orders and accounts receivable in a typical manufacturing company?

12. What procedures might be established for handling backordered goods in a manual data processing system? in a computerized data processing system?

13. How is organizational independence achieved with respect to sales order and accounts receivable processing?

14. Describe an appropriate set of procedures for processing sales returns and allowances.

15. Describe the similarities and differences in processing of sales order transactions in a typical manufacturing company using a computer rather than a manual data processing system. Emphasize documents, departments, and reports involved in the process.

16. What control procedures might be involved in batch processing of sales transactions by a typical manufacturing company that uses a computer data processing system?

17. Explain how the use of magnetic disk storage permits both the accounts receivable and finished goods inventory master files to be updated for sales activity in a single computer run. Would this be feasible if both of these master files were stored on magnetic tape?

18. Explain how a summary master file of sales data stored on a magnetic disk may be processed to generate sales analyses by customer, by salesperson, and by product without the need for intermediate sorting operations.

19. Prepare a systems flowchart of a real-time system for processing sales orders.

20. Describe some of the major differences between a computerized batch processing system and a real-time system for processing sales orders.

21. Describe several control procedures and techniques appropriate for a real-time sales order processing system. What is the major difference in emphasis between these techniques and those in a batch processing system?

Discussion Questions

22. This chapter primarily emphasized the marketing information requirements of a manufacturing firm with a large sales force. Compare the organizational structure, information requirements, and data sources of this type of organization with those of

a) a large retail organization,

b) a firm which does all selling by direct mail,

c) a large motel chain, and

d) a hospital.

23. Some companies have created the post of Product Line Manager within the Marketing Department. There may be several Product Line Managers, each responsible for a related group of products. Discuss the effects on decision responsibilities and information requirements within the Marketing Department of this type of organization.

24. Create a definition for the term "marketing information system." Discuss the conceptual and operational relationships between marketing information systems and accounting information systems.

Problems and Cases

25. As a systems analyst for the Dolphin Motor Company, you have been asked to design a computer report that will analyze product sales by dealers. The company sells three major lines of cars—the Dolphin, the Eagle, and the Flyer—and all dealers carry all three lines. Assume that space constraints limit the report such that a maximum of eight columns of data may be placed across the width of a page. Of course, there are no constraints regarding how many lines of data may be used for each dealer.

    In designing the report, you may make any reasonable assumptions about the availability of data. Make sure that you take into account the need for effective presentation of information, the need for standards of comparison, and the principle of management by exception.

26. Shown in Fig. 16.12 is a document flowchart of sales order, billing, and accounts receivable procedures (including everything except cash receipts) for Tabco Manufacturing, Inc. What changes would you recommend to improve control and efficiency?

27. What controls in a sales order processing system are designed to provide the best protection against the following errors or manipulations?

    a) Theft of goods by shipping department personnel, who claim that subsequent shortages are due to errors made by personnel in the finished goods storeroom.

    b) An error in posting from a copy of an invoice to the accounts receivable ledger.

    c) Sale to a customer who is four months behind in making payments on his account.

    d) Failure to send a bill for goods ordered and shipped to a customer.

    e) Sale and shipment of goods to a fictitious customer.

    f) Authorization of a credit memo for a sales return when the goods were never actually returned.

    g) Billing a customer without recording the account receivable, in order to conceal theft of subsequent collections.

    h) Billing a customer for the quantity of raw materials ordered, when the quantity shipped was actually less than the quantity ordered due to an out-of-stock condition.

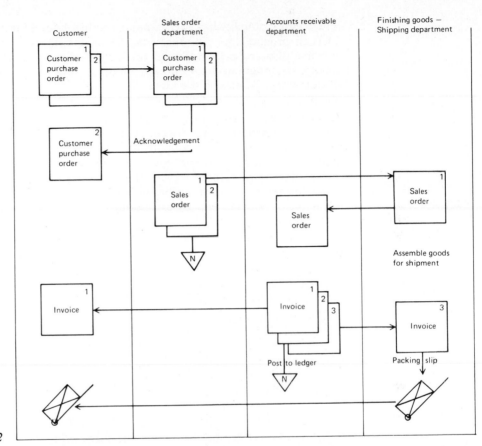

Figure 16.12

28. Your company has just acquired a data base management system, and one of the first applications of it will be to marketing data. A sales invoice form identical to that in Fig. 16.2 is used. You are to diagram the data structure of the invoice as a first step in the application design. Use a format similar to that in Fig. 16.7. Note that the data base will contain only the variable data on the invoice, not the constant data.

29. Cragg and Company utilizes a real-time sales order processing system. Sales orders are entered into the system by salespeople utilizing portable data terminals from customer offices. For each sale, the salesperson enters his or her personal user code number, the customer's account number, and the item number, quantity ordered, and price of each item sold.

Required   Describe several means by which the system should be programmed to check the accuracy and validity of the input data entered by salespeople. Relate your answer specifically to the data items mentioned.

30. The Rigby Company has twelve major product lines with twenty to thirty items in each product line. Product Line Managers have been selected to assume product planning responsibilities for each product line. As a systems analyst in charge of designing marketing information systems, you wish to show these Product Line Managers the kind of information that can be made available to them.

Required

Design a computerized sales analysis report that analyzes sales by product item within each product line. Assume that space constraints limit the report such that a maximum of eight columns of data may be placed across the width of a page. In designing the report, you may make any reasonable assumptions about the availability of data. Make sure that you take into account the need for effective presentation of information, the need for standards of comparison, and the principle of management by exception.

31. Elite Publishing Company has established a subsidiary, Business Book Club, Inc. (BBC), that will operate as described below.

BBC's editors will select from among recently published books in the business area those it feels will be of most interest to businesspeople. These books can be purchased in large lots at approximately 40 percent of list price. BBC plans to sell these books to its club members at approximately 75 percent of list price.

Solicitation of new customers will be done through advertising by direct mail and in selected publications. Such advertisements will offer four free books if one is purchased and if the purchaser agrees to become a member of the club. Each club member will be sent a list of new selections each month. Members are not required to buy any books. After purchase of four books a member is sent a list of selections from which he or she may choose a free book.

You have been called upon to design a computerized billing and book inventory system for BBC. Assume that you have asked various managers about their information needs and find that the advertising manager wants to know which advertising media are more effective, the credit manager wants to know which accounts are more than 90 days past due, and the editors want to know which books are best-sellers.

Required

a) Identify the master files you feel should be maintained in this system and list the data content of each.

b) Identify the input transactions that will be necessary for this system to process, and the output documents and reports that the system must be designed to produce.

c) Assume that transaction inputs will be recorded on magnetic tape, and that the master files will be stored on magnetic disk units. Prepare systems flowcharts of all computer runs necessary to process the inputs, maintain the master files, and generate the outputs for your system.

32. George Beemster, CPA, is examining the financial statements of the Louisville Sales Corporation, which recently installed an offline electronic computer. The following comments have been extracted from Mr. Beemster's notes on computer operations and the processing and control of shipping notices and customer invoices:

- To minimize inconvenience, Lousiville converted without change its existing data processing system, which utilized tabulating equipment. The computer company supervised the conversion and has provided training to all computer department employees (except keypunch operators) in systems design, operations, and programming.

- Each computer run is assigned to a specific employee, who is responsible for making program changes, running the program, and answering questions. This procedure has the advantage of eliminating the need for records of computer operations because each employee has responsibility for his or her own computer runs.

- At least one computer department employee remains in the computer room during office hours, and only computer department employees have keys to the computer room.

- System documentation consists of those materials furnished by the computer company—a set of record formats and program listings. These and the tape library are kept in a corner of the computer department.

- The Company considered the desirability of programmed controls but decided to retain the manual controls from its existing system.

- Company products are shipped directly from public warehouses which forward shipping notices to general accounting. There a billing clerk enters the price of the item and accounts for the numerical sequence of shipping notices from each warehouse. The billing clerk also prepares daily adding machine tapes ("control tapes") of the units shipped and the unit prices.

- Shipping notices and control tapes are forwarded to the computer department for keypunching and processing. Extensions are made on the computer. Output consists of invoices (in six copies) and a daily sales register. The daily sales register shows the aggregate totals of units shipped and unit prices which the computer operator compares to the control tapes.

- All copies of the invoice are returned to the billing clerk. The clerk mails three copies to the customer, forwards one copy to the warehouse, maintains one copy in a numerical file, and retains one copy in an open invoice file that serves as a detailed accounts receivable record.

Required   Describe weaknesses in internal control over information and data flows and the procedures for processing shipping notices and customer invoices and recommend improvements in these controls and processing procedures. Organize your answer sheets as follows.[2]

Weakness	Recommended improvement

---

[2] *Question 6, Auditing Section,* American Institute of Certified Public Accountants Examination, *May 1972. Material from the Uniform CPA Examinations, copyright © 1972 by the American Institute of Certified Public Accountants, is reprinted (or adapted) with permission.*

33. When a shipment is made, the Shipping Department prepares a shipping order form. This form is in three copies. The first copy is sent out with the goods to the customer as a packing slip. The second copy is forwarded to the Billing Department. The third copy is sent to the Accountant. When the Billing Department receives the second copy of the shipping order, it uses the information thereon to prepare a two-part sales invoice. The second copy of the shipping order is then filed in the Billing Department. The first copy of the sales invoice is sent to the customer. The second copy of the sales invoice is forwarded to the Accountant. Periodically, the Accountant matches the copy of the shipping order with the copy of the sales invoice and files them alphabetically by customer name. Before doing so, however, the Accountant uses the copy of the sales invoice to post the sales entry in the subsidiary accounts receivable ledger.

Required

a) For use in appraising internal control, prepare a flowchart covering the flow of documents reflected in the above situation.

b) List those deficiencies and/or omissions revealed by the flowchart which would lead you to question the internal control.[3]

References

Arthur Anderson & Co. *A Guide for Studying and Evaluating Internal Accounting Controls.* Chicago: Arthur Andersen & Co., 1978.

Bentz, William F., and Robert F. Lusch. "Now You Can Control Your Product's Market Performance." *Management Accounting* (January 1980): 17–25.

Doppelt, Neil. "Down-to-Earth Marketing Information Systems." *Management Advisor* (September-October 1971): 19–26.

Goodman, Sam R. "Sales Reports That Lead to Action." *Financial Executive* (June 1973): 20–29.

Jackson, Barbara B., and Benson P. Shapiro. "New Way to Make Product Line Decisions." *Harvard Business Review* (May-June 1979): 139–149.

Price Waterhouse & Co. *Guide to Accounting Controls: Revenues and Receivables.* New York: Price Waterhouse & Co., 1979.

Savesky, Robert S. "How Good Is Your Company's Sales Forecast?" *Price Waterhouse Review.* Vol. 22, No. 2 (1977).

Sterling, T. D. "Consumer Difficulties with Computerized Transactions: An Empirical Investigation." *Communications of the ACM* (May 1979): 283–289.

[3] *Adapted from Question 11, Internal Audit Techniques Section. From the* Certified Internal Auditor Examination, *August 1974. Copyright 1974 by the Institute of Internal Auditors, Inc. Reprinted by permission of the Institute of Internal Auditors, Inc., 249 Maitland Ave., Altamonte Springs, Fla. 32701.*

Chapter 17

Accounting Information Systems for Logistics Management I

Logistics management involves planning and controlling the physical flow of materials through an organization. In most cases these materials are inventories—either product inventories in a retail organization, or inventories in various stages of production in a manufacturing organization. In some firms (transportation companies are a good example) the materials with which logistics management is concerned are fixed assets, such as jet planes, railroad cars, or taxicabs. In still other cases involving service organizations such as professional accounting firms, the primary logistics problems relate to the assignment of personnel. Construction companies may have the most complex logistics problems of all, for they must plan and control the flow of inventories, assets, *and* personnel between various construction sites.

The information requirements of the logistics management function are the subject of this and the following chapter. From the discussion above, the difficulty of generalization with respect to logistics management should be evident. However, for the sake of simplicity, these chapters will focus upon the most common and familiar example of logistics management—the production operations of a typical manufacturing company. As a starting point for this approach, Fig. 17.1 illustrates the organization structure of the production department of a typical manufacturing company.

The logistics function is very closely interrelated with the marketing, personnel, and finance functions in most organizations. These interrelationships are manifested

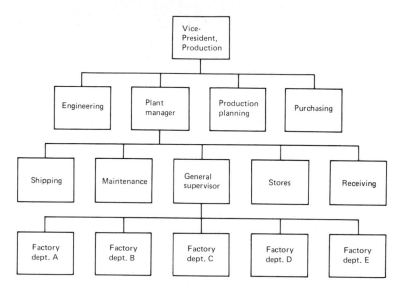

Fig. 17.1
Production depart-
ment organization.

by numerous shared data bases and interdepartmental communication flows. Simplicity of presentation demands that the logistics function be examined separately from the other functions, which unfortunately tends to de-emphasize the significance of such interrelationships. The reader should be alert to the evidence of these interrelationships as he or she proceeds through this and the other chapters in Part IV.

The logistics management function may be divided into two subfunctions: (1) purchasing and inventory management, and (2) production management. Purchasing and inventory management, the subject of this chapter, is relevant to retail organizations as well as to manufacturing firms. Production management and its related information flows is the subject of Chapter 18.

The Purchasing and Inventory Management Function

The purchasing function is the primary management function in the purchasing and inventory management system. The basic decisions for which the purchasing department is responsible include (1) the quantity to be purchased, (2) the timing of purchases, and (3) the vendor from whom to purchase.

Deciding upon the quantity and timing of each item purchased is called the inventory control function, and was discussed briefly in Chapter 4 as an example of a feedforward control system. The inventory control function has been the frequent subject of applications of mathematical modeling techniques. The basic objective is to determine for each inventory item the order quantity and reorder point that minimize the sum of the costs of ordering the item, carrying the item in inventory, and being out of stock. Application of the mathematical models requires that these three cost factors be quantified, that the future requirements for the item be known or estimated, and that an estimate of vendor lead time be prepared.[1]

The information required for estimating future requirements for an item and vendor lead time can be generated by formal information systems within an organization. In a retail organization, future demand can be estimated by applying forecasting techniques to historical records of past sales. In a manufacturing organization, future requirements can be accurately estimated if production planning is effectively integrated with sales forecasting. Vendor lead time can be estimated if formal records of past dealings with vendors are maintained.

Inventory costs are generally the most difficult elements of the model to estimate. Carrying costs include all costs that vary with the quantity of goods in inventory. The most significant element of carrying cost is the opportunity cost of the funds tied up in inventory. Stated another way, this cost represents the revenue lost from investing funds in inventory rather than in revenue generating activities. Other elements of inventory carrying cost include the incremental costs of spoilage, breakage, pilferage, obsolescence, insurance, taxes, and space utilization. Ordering cost refers only to those costs that vary with the number of orders placed, and generally involves the costs of processing the order and the fixed costs of shipping. Stockout cost, which involves lost goodwill or inefficiencies in operations, is practically impossible to measure, and is therefore usually the subject of arbitrary estimates.

In general, mathematical modeling techniques are applied only to the high-cost, high-usage items of inventory. For low-cost, low-usage items, carrying and ordering costs are so insignificant that reorder point and order quantity can be set with the sole objective of eliminating stockouts. Once the order quantity and reorder point of an item are determined, they are stored along with other data pertaining to the item in the master inventory file. Clerks or machines then are responsible for applying these policies to determine the timing and size of individual orders.

An alternative to the mathematical modeling approach to inventory control in a manufacturing company is called *materials requirements planning* (MRP). Under this approach, the production planning department prepares a schedule of the quantities of each product to be manufactured during, for example, the next three months. Based upon this schedule, it may then be determined exactly what quantities of raw materials, parts, and supplies will be required, and at what points in time. This enables the purchasing department to purchase exactly those items that are needed for delivery when they are needed, thereby minimizing the need for safety stock as a hedge against the uncertainty of production requirements. Thus MRP enables the reduction of materials inventory levels, but places much greater demands

---

[1] *For an extensive coverage of mathematical modeling techniques of inventory control, see Harvey M. Wagner,* Principles of Operations Research *(2nd ed.). Englewood Cliffs, N.J.: Prentice-Hall, 1975, Chapter 19.*

upon the information system to maintain accurate inventory records.[2]

The other significant management decision made by the purchasing function is selection of vendors for inventory items. In a retail organization, there are buyers who specialize in related lines of merchandise. When the decision is made to carry a particular type of merchandise in the store, it becomes the buyer's responsibility to select a supplier. Examples of factors relevant to the decision are price, reliability, product styling, brand image, and quality. Information on prices and styles is provided by representatives of the various suppliers. Information on brand image and quality should be known to the buyer from his or her knowledge about the lines of merchandise in which he or she specializes. Information on reliability—the supplier's history of meeting quantity specifications and delivering goods promptly —should be maintained as part of a vendor history file within the purchasing department.

In a manufacturing organization, the selection of vendors for raw materials is made when the engineering department provides the specifications for a new part to the purchasing department. Purchasing then prepares requests for price quotations that are sent to potential suppliers. Once these price quotations are received, the purchasing department selects a vendor for the item. The decision is based not only on price but also on reliability, quality, and perhaps whether a given supplier is also a significant customer. Records of dealings with vendors should be maintained to provide information about reliability, and product quality. The quality of a vendor's products can be measured in terms of how frequently products received from the vendor fail to pass inspection or testing performed by the receiving department.

Once a vendor has been selected for a product, the identity of the vendor becomes a part of the master inventory record of that product. Vendor selection thus does not have to be performed each time the product is ordered. However, the identity of possible alternative vendors may also be included in the file, in case the primary vendor is temporarily out of stock. Periodically decisions may be made to change primary vendors for some products if a primary vendor does not provide satisfactory service or goes out of business.

The Purchasing and Inventory Data Processing System

The accounting transactions

The basic accounting journal entries that summarize the purchasing process vary depending on whether the firm uses a perpetual or periodic inventory accounting system. In a perpetual system one basic entry is used to record purchases.

```
Raw Materials Inventory   XXX
    Accounts Payable             XXX
```

Purchase returns and allowances are reflected as a reversal of that entry. If inven-

[2] For further discussion of MRP, see Jeffrey G. Miller and Linda G. Sprague, "Behind the Growth in Materials Requirements Planning," Harvard Business Review, Vol. 53, No. 5 (September-October 1975): 83–91; and Daniel P. Keegan, "Some Second Reflections on MRP," Price Waterhouse & Company Review (1977, No. 3): 38–43.

tory counts reveal that actual quantity on hand is less than the quantity recorded, the Raw Materials Inventory account is written down and the debit entered to Cost of Goods Sold or to a special loss account.

If a periodic inventory system is used, purchases are recorded by the following journal entry.

Purchases	XXX	
Accounts Payable		XXX

Purchase returns and allowances are recorded in a special contra-account as follows.

Accounts Payable	XXX	
Purchases Returns and Allowances		XXX

Periodically a complete physical inventory is taken, and the following journal entry is made.

Inventory (Ending)	XXX	
Cost of Goods Sold	XXX	
Purchases		XXX
Inventory (Beginning)		XXX

This entry adjusts the inventory balance to its correct level and records Cost of Goods Sold for the period as the total of Purchases for the period plus the net reduction (or minus the net increase) in the Inventory account.

The purchasing data base

An example of the data content and organization of a purchasing and raw materials inventory data base appears in Fig. 17.2. This data base is structured as a network consisting of two interrelated families of records. One of these families contains raw materials inventory data, while the other contains data on raw materials vendors. Transaction records associated with one or both of these families include materials inventory requisitions, purchase requisitions, price quotations, purchase orders, inventory receipts, purchase returns and allowances, vouchers payable, and cash disbursements.

Each raw materials inventory record in the data base contains a single value for all of the data fields listed under "Raw Materials Inventory," with the "Item Number" serving as the primary key. In addition, each raw materials inventory record owns one or more "Raw Material Transaction" records. In turn, each Raw Material Transaction record is a summary of the data contained in a Materials Requisition, Purchase Requisition, Price Quotation, Purchase Order, Receiving Report, or Purchase Return. The "Transaction Type Code" and "Document Number" in the Raw Material Transaction record permit the system to access a more detailed transaction record (for example, a complete purchase order) whenever necessary.

In a manual data processing system, a materials ledger card (see Fig. 17.3) for each inventory item is commonly maintained by the accounting department or a pro-

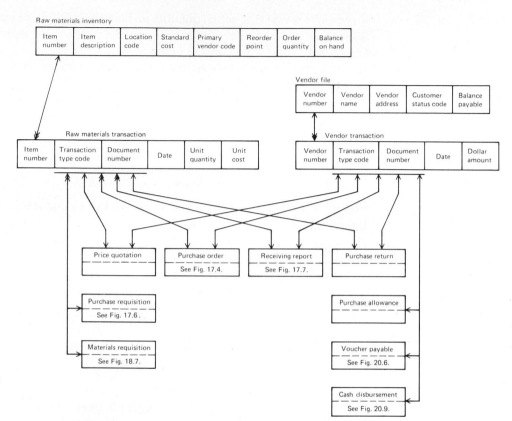

*Fig. 17.2
Purchasing and in-
ventory data base.*

duction department. The data shown in the top portion of the materials ledger card are essentially equivalent to the data in the "Raw Materials Inventory" record of the data base, while the data shown under "Transactions" in the lower left portion of the card are similar to those contained in the "Raw Material Transaction" record in the data base. One significant difference is that the materials ledger card does not contain unit cost information for every transaction—a common limitation of manual systems for inventory record keeping. In an automated system, all inventory receipts would be recorded at their purchase cost, while all issues would be recorded on a FIFO, average, LIFO, or other cost basis. Also note that the materials ledger card maintains a record of the quantity available, which is the sum of the quantity on hand and the quantity on order. The quantity available is not stored separately in the data base, but may be computed at any time for any inventory item using data available elsewhere in the data base.

Updating the raw materials inventory portion of the data base consists primarily of appending new transaction records to the data base, creating a new "Raw Material Transaction" summary record for each new transaction, and adjusting the appropriate fields within the "Raw Materials Inventory" master record. This should

MATERIALS LEDGER CARD

Item number: 5216408		Description: bearing		Reorder point: 150		

Location		Standard unit cost	Vendor		Order quantity	
Row 26	Bin 12	$1.40	Code 3621	Name Needmore Mfg.	500	

Transactions					Balances		
Date	Reference	Issued	Rec'd	Ordered	On hand	On order	Available
1/2/81	P.O. 1008			500	0	500	500
1/7/81	Rec. 1095		300		300	200	500
1/9/81	Req. 1056	200			100	200	300
1/14/81	Rec. 1208		200		300	0	300
2/4/81	Req. 1128	200			100	0	100
2/9/81	P.O. 1101			500	100	500	600
2/16/81	Rec. 1375		500		600	0	600

Fig. 17.3
Sample materials ledger card.

be done daily, because the inventory data serve as an important reference for personnel in production planning, purchasing, and production operations. In a manual system, this update is accomplished by posting the transaction data to the materials ledger card, and recalculating the "On Hand," "On Order," and "Available" balances. Other inputs include nonroutine transactions such as error corrections or changes in location, standard cost, or primary vendor. Outputs from processing the inventory data base include stock status reports, exception reports on high- and low-activity items, and purchase requisitions or purchase orders to replenish the stock of low balance items.

Each vendor record in the purchasing and raw materials inventory data base contains a single value for each of the data fields listed under "Vendor File" in Fig. 17.2, with the "Vendor Number" serving as the primary key. In addition, each vendor record owns one or more "Vendor Transaction" records; in turn, each Vendor Transaction record is a summary of data contained in a Price Quotation record, Purchase Order, Receiving Report, Purchase Return or Allowance record, Voucher

Payable, or Cash Disbursement record. The "Transaction Type Code" and "Document Number" in the Vendor Transaction record enable the system to access one of these more detailed records whenever necessary.

In a manual data processing system, it is not uncommon that no master file dealing exclusively with vendors is maintained. Instead, records of dealings with particular vendors are scattered throughout files of disbursement vouchers, purchase orders, and receiving reports. In some manual systems, a file of ledger cards summarizing financial transactions with each vendor may be maintained.

The vendor file portion of the purchasing and inventory data base may be updated daily or weekly. Basic inputs include orders, receipts, disbursement authorizations, and other transactions of the kind listed above and shown on Fig. 17.2. As these are added to the data base, new Vendor Transaction records are created, and when necessary the "Balance Payable" field in the Vendor File is updated. Other inputs include nonroutine transactions such as a change in a vendor's address or customer status, or an error correction.

The primary output documents generated from the data base are checks in payment of accounts payable. Useful output reports that may be produced include cash flow commitment schedules and vendor performance reports. A cash flow commitments schedule represents a summarization by expected payment date of cash payment commitments as reflected in disbursement vouchers and purchase orders, and would be prepared weekly to assist financial executives in short-run budgeting of cash flows. A vendor performance report is a summary of past dealings with a particular vendor, including price quotations, orders placed, late shipments, early shipments, shipments rejected for poor quality, and shipments of the incorrect quantity. Virtually all records within the vendor file portion of the data base provide source data for this report. The vendor performance report enables purchasing management to continuously monitor vendor conduct, and is an important input to the vendor selection decision. It may be generated weekly, monthly, or on demand, depending on how critical vendor performance is to the organization.

In a manual data processing system, a file of open purchase orders (that is, orders that have not yet been completely filled) plays a central role in purchasing operations. This file would consist simply of purchase order documents, such as the one shown in Fig. 17.4. Such a file is often maintained manually for reference purposes even when the purchasing function is automated. Basic inputs to the open purchase order file are new orders placed and receipts of goods on order. If partial shipment is received, a notation of the receipt may be posted to the appropriate purchase order record. Once a purchase order is completely filled, it should be removed from the open purchase order file. The file itself provides an important source of information for purchasing, accounting, and production personnel.

Purchase order records that are also maintained on a computer file would contain essentially the same data as shown in Fig. 17.4, with the purchase order number serving as the control field. However, automating the maintenance of purchase order records enables the preparation of such useful reports as a cash flow commitments schedule and a list of orders for which delivery is past due.

NEEDMORE MANUFACTURING COMPANY

| PURCHASE ORDER | 987 Glendale Needmore, Texas 78799 | No. 12153 |

TO   Avalon Electronics
     401 Cherry Street
     Waco, Texas 78123

Show the above order number on all invoices and shipping papers

| Vendor number 8015 | Order date 3-14-81 | Req. number 27654 | Buyer Dave Watson | Terms 2/10 |

| F.O.B. Shipping point | Ship via express | Deliver on At once | Remarks |

Item number	Part number	Quantity	Description	Price
1	86402	20	Transistor	$1.44
2	78712	20	Diode	1.65
3	81296	10	Capacitor	2.40

Buyer _____

Fig. 17.4
Sample purchase
order.

A manual system

The document flowchart of Fig. 17.5 illustrates one example of a manual system for processing purchase transactions in a manufacturing company. Most companies will differ in some respects from this example, but the general pattern of information flow, even in nonmanufacturing organizations, will not vary a great deal from the illustration in most cases.

As the illustration shows, the purchasing process begins with the initiation of a purchase requisition by the inventory clerk. The purchase requisition, illustrated in Fig. 17.6, indicates that the supply of an item of inventory is low and a reorder is necessary. The quantity required and the number of the primary vendor are also indicated. One copy of each requisition prepared is sent to the purchasing department and a second is filed by requisition number by the inventory clerk.

Using the purchase requisitions, the purchasing department prepares purchase orders. In some cases, the purchasing department may utilize a vendor other than the primary vendor, or may change the order quantity to comply with the vendor's shipping quantity per package. Several copies of each purchase order are prepared. Two are generally sent to the vendor, with the request that one be returned as an acknowledgment. At least one copy is filed in the purchasing department, and other copies may be sent to the inventory clerk, accounts payable, and receiving.

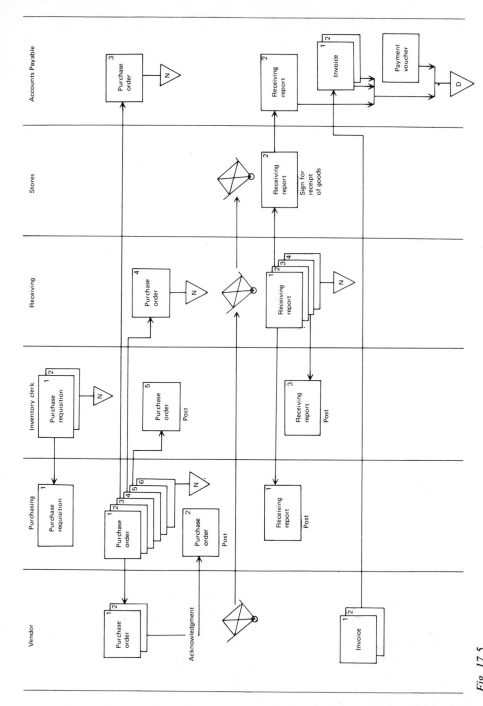

Fig. 17.5
Document flow in a manual system for processing purchase transactions.

NEEDMORE MANUFACTURING COMPANY		Req. No. 1245			
PURCHASE REQUISITION		Date 2/10/81			
Date needed 2/15/81		Vendor code 3725	Prepared by J. Trimble	Department stores	
Part number	Quantity	Description	Quantity on hand	Reorder point	Reorder quantity
72142	450	Shaft	40	100	400

Fig. 17.6 Sample purchase requisition.

The purchasing department records the receipt of acknowledgments from vendors, and also the receipts of items ordered, in the open purchase order file. Purchasing department personnel are responsible for following up on orders for which no acknowledgment has been received or for which delivery is overdue. In the event that goods received are damaged or do not not pass quality inspection, the receiving report will so indicate, and the purchasing department must correspond with the vendor to arrange an appropriate adjustment.

Another copy of the purchase order is provided to the inventory clerk for posting to the "on order" field of the raw materials inventory records. Still another copy should be provided to the receiving department. This copy is filed by purchase order number and checked by receiving personnel when the goods are received to verify that the goods were actually ordered. For control purposes, the quantity ordered should not be included on this copy. This will encourage the receiving department personnel to carefully count the quantity of each item received.

When the goods are received by the receiving department, a document recording the receipt is prepared. An example of this document, called a receiving report, is illustrated in Fig. 17.7. Inspectors in the receiving department examine the goods for damage or poor quality, and an indication of acceptance or rejection of the goods is made on the receiving report. The receiving department files one copy of each receiving report by its document number. Another copy is routed to the purchasing department for posting to the open purchase order file. Still another copy is sent to the inventory clerk, where it is posted to the master inventory file. The receipt will increase the quantity on hand in the file and decrease the quantity on order. A final copy accompanies the goods to the storeroom and then is sent to the accounts payable department.

The transfer of custody of goods from the receiving department to the parts storeroom is a significant event for control purposes. The transfer of accounting control for the goods should be evidenced by the signature of stores personnel on the

```
┌─────────────────────────────────────────────────────────┐
│              RECEIVING REPORT                            │
│                                    No. 6405              │
├──────────────┬────────┬─────────────┬───────────────────┤
│ Prepared by  │  Date  │ "P.O." number│    Vendor         │
│              │        │             │                   │
├─────────┬────┴──┬─────┴─────────────┴───────────────────┤
│ Quantity│ Units │ Description                           │
├─────────┼───────┼───────────────────────────────────────┤
│         │       │                                       │
├─────────┼───────┼───────────────────────────────────────┤
│         │       │                                       │
├─────────┼───────┼───────────────────────────────────────┤
│         │       │                                       │
├─────────┴───────┴───────────────────────────────────────┤
│  Delivered by      Inspected by _____      │
│                    Remarks:                              │
│  Shipping weight                                         │
└─────────────────────────────────────────────────────────┘
```

Fig. 17.7
Sample receiving report.

copy of the receiving report. Stores personnel must verify that the correct items have been received in the appropriate quantities prior to signing the receiving report because they are responsible for subsequent shortages. The signed copy of the receiving report is immediately routed to the accounts payable department. The signature ensures the accounts payable personnel that the goods for which they approve payment are safely in the custody of storeroom personnel.

The accounts payable department receives vendor invoices requesting payment for goods delivered. Before approving these invoices for payment, accounts payable clerks check each one against its corresponding receiving report and purchase order. The department maintains its own file of open purchase orders for this purpose. The purchase order is checked to ensure that the goods were ordered and that the quantities received and prices charged are consistent with the order. If the shipment is a partial shipment, the quantity received is posted to the purchase order. The receiving report is checked to ensure that the quantities received are equal to the quantities invoiced. The accuracy of the extensions on the vendor's invoice must be verified. Once all of these steps have been completed, a voucher is prepared that authorizes the cash disbursement in payment of the invoice. These documents are then filed according to the due date of the invoice. Cash disbursement procedures are discussed in Chapter 20.

Organizational independence with respect to the purchasing function is achieved by separation of the operating function performed by the purchasing department from the custodial functions performed by the receiving and stores department. Furthermore, both of these functions are separated from the recording functions performed by the accounts payable department and the inventory clerk. This separation helps to ensure that only authorized orders are placed, and that all goods that are ordered are actually received and are properly and accurately recorded.

Another significant control procedure with respect to raw material inventories is the reconciliation of actual inventory quantities with the inventory records. This may be done on a periodic basis, with high-cost and high-usage items being reconciled more frequently than low-cost, low-usage items. In addition this reconciliation should also be performed whenever it becomes obvious that there is a discrepancy; for example, when the inventory record shows a negative balance or when no parts are available even though the record shows a positive balance. These reconciliations should be performed by accounting department personnel who are independent of both inventory record keeping and stores.

The control policies exercised with respect to the purchasing operation and personnel are also important. Budgetary control over the cost of purchased raw materials might be achieved by a standard cost system in which the purchase price variance is the responsibility of the purchasing department head. Budgetary control over the purchase of supplies, or of merchandise in a retail organization, is often exercised over the department requesting the supplies or merchandise rather than over purchasing. To control the possibility that purchasing personnel might favor certain vendors who offer them gifts or kickbacks, a policy that no such gifts may be accepted by purchasing personnel should be enforced. Use of the purchase requisition as the basis for purchase order preparation also provides control in this sense in that the requisition evidences a definite need for the goods by the company. Finally, it may also be a good control policy to require that all purchasing employees involved in vendor selection make known any significant financial interest they may have in supplier companies.

A computer-based batch processing system

A document flowchart of the purchasing process for a typical manufacturing company that uses a computer-based system appears in Fig. 17.8. It is assumed that the system uses magnetic tape input and maintains master files on magnetic disk. The illustration is merely an example rather than a description of the actual system of a real company. Much of the description is also applicable to nonmanufacturing organizations.

A comparison of Fig. 17.8 with its manual counterpart in Fig. 17.5 reveals that the computer has completely replaced the manual system's inventory clerk. However, the functions performed by purchasing, receiving, stores, and accounts payable are very similar in both systems. One minor difference is that the accounts payable department now prepares two copies of the voucher. One is filed in voucher number sequence, with the supporting invoice and receiving report documentation attached. The second copy is provided to the input preparation department as a source document for a computerized cash disbursements system (described in Chapter 20). Another difference is that the computer prepares purchase orders instead of the purchasing department. In addition, the computer generates two reports for the purchasing department and one for the controller, which may not have been available in the manual system.

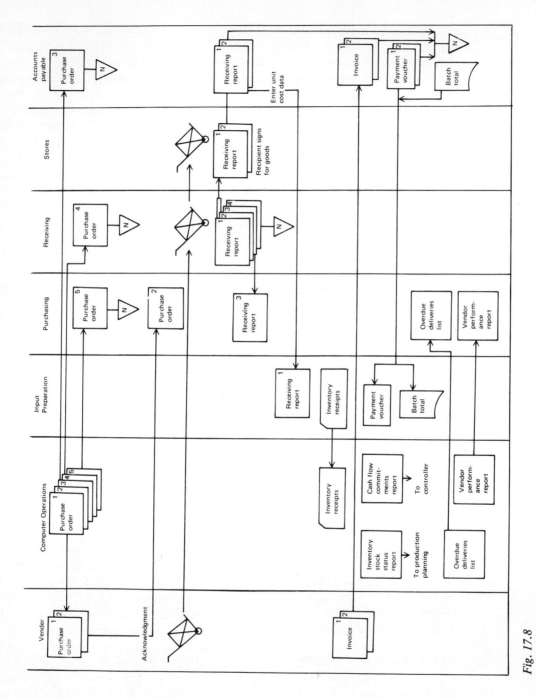

Fig. 17.8
Document flow in computerized batch processing of purchase transactions.

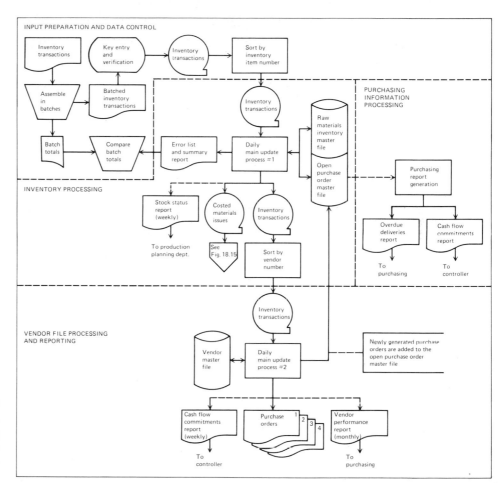

*Fig. 17.9
System flow in computer-based batch processing of purchasing and inventory transactions.*

A systems flowchart of the operations involved in the computerized purchasing system appears in Fig. 17.9. For purposes of simplification, the flowchart is separated by dashed lines into four major categories of operations: input preparation and data control, inventory processing, purchasing information processing, and vendor file processing and reporting. After coverage of each of these four areas of operation, this section concludes with a discussion of control policies and procedures in the system.

Input preparation and data control   Each day this operation begins with the assembly of inventory transaction source documents in batches and the preparation of batch totals. Note that inventory issues and other inventory transactions are processed along with receipts in one integrated process. The origination of issue documents is covered in Chapter 18.

Control totals that might be obtained for each batch of inventory transactions include record counts of the total number of transactions, the total number of issues, and the total number of receipts, as well as hash totals of all inventory stock numbers, the number of units issued, and the number of units received. These batch totals are retained for comparison with those generated after the inventory update run. If any discrepancies are found in the comparison of batch totals, they may indicate that some records were lost or improperly processed. Subsequent checking in detail of those specific batches for which a discrepancy exists should enable discovery and correction of any errors.

The next step in input preparation is keying and verification of inventory transaction records from the batched source documents. It is assumed that these records are keyed onto magnetic tape using a key-to-tape encoder or key-to-disk-to-tape system. Alternative methods of input preparation include the use of punched cards or diskettes as an input medium.

Following the preparation of input records, the next step is to sort them into sequence by inventory item number. If the records are on magnetic tape as shown in Fig. 17.9, this step is performed on the computer using a tape sort program. The records are then ready for processing to update the raw materials inventory master file.

Inventory processing   This step is performed daily and involves one main updating program. The inventory transaction records on magnetic tape are input to this program. The program sequentially accesses the raw materials inventory master file and updates the appropriate master file record for each transaction. This is the task performed by the inventory clerk in the manual system. Furthermore, for inventory receipt transactions this program randomly accesses the appropriate purchase order master record, appends the quantity received to the appropriate line-item subrecord of the purchase order, subtracts the quantity received to determine a revised quantity on order, and then deletes from the file any purchase orders that have been completely filled. In the manual system, these steps are performed in the purchasing department.

This update run also generates a magnetic tape file containing costed materials issue records. Each record on this tape indicates the cost of an inventory item issued into production, determined on a FIFO, LIFO, or other basis from the cost data recorded on the inventory file. This tape is used in a computerized system of accounting for materials costs in production, as explained in Chapter 18.

Two output reports are also generated by the raw materials inventory updating program. One is a list of error transactions flagged by one or more input validation routines of the update program. This report also contains the batch totals mentioned above and summary journal entries for the inventory transactions, including the debit to raw materials inventory and the credit to accounts payable for inventory receipts. The second output report is a stock status report on the inventory file. The dashed line to this report indicates that this report is printed only once each week, rather than every day. Copies of the stock status report might be provided to stores' personnel for reference in storeskeeping operations, and to production planning personnel for use in planning future production.

Another function of the materials inventory update program is to identify all inventory items for which the quantity available has fallen below the reorder point, so that an order for these items may be initiated. For such items a reorder record is created and added to the inventory transaction tape. When this program is finished, the inventory transaction tape is resorted by vendor number for subsequent processing to update the vendor master file.

Purchasing information processing Two reports may be generated using the data available in the open purchase order master file. One is an overdue deliveries report, which lists those orders for which the promised or expected delivery date has passed without the order having been received. This report is provided to the purchasing department for their use in following up on these orders, and would probably be prepared weekly. The other report is a schedule of cash flow commitments as reflected in outstanding purchase orders. This report would be provided to the controller or treasurer for use in planning short-run cash flows, and would also probably be generated on a weekly basis.

Vendor file processing and reporting The vendor file processing program has two primary functions. One is to update the vendor master file for orders, receipts, returns, allowances, and any other transactions with each vendor. The other is to generate purchase order documents. Input to this program consists of the inventory transactions tape, which has been sorted into sequence by vendor number. The vendor master file may then be accessed sequentially to update the master record corresponding to each transaction.

If there are one or more purchase requisition or inventory reorder records for a particular vendor, then a purchase order to that vendor is initiated. For each purchase order, the vendor's name and address, shipping arrangements, and credit terms are pulled from the vendor master file. The quantity to be ordered and other relevant inventory data are obtained from the input record. A purchase order number is assigned sequentially to each order according to the next highest number available on the open purchase order master file. An original and three copies of each new purchase order are then printed out, and the new purchase order record is also added to the open purchase order master file.

Two reports may be prepared as a by-product of the vendor file processing run. One is a short-run cash flow commitments schedule, based upon disbursement authorization records contained in the vendor master file. Like its counterpart generated from the open purchase order master, this report would probably be prepared once weekly, and would be provided to the controller or treasurer for use in short-term cash management. The second report deals with vendor performance, and represents a summary of past transactions with particular vendors, highlighting such matters as compliance with requested delivery dates, discrepancies between quantities ordered and quantities received, discrepancies between prices quoted and prices billed, and number of defective items received. This report would probably be generated monthly for each vendor, or on a demand basis when requested for a specific vendor. The vendor performance report goes to the purchasing department for use in vendor selection.

Control policies and procedures   Among the control policies and procedures that might be used in this system for computerized batch processing of purchasing and inventory information are two that have already been mentioned—keyverification of inventory transaction records and batch totals. This section will discuss other examples in the areas of data security and input validation.

Data security in this operation primarily involves the master disk files of open purchase orders, raw materials inventory, and vendor records, as well as the tapes of inventory transactions and costed materials issues. Each of these files should have appropriate internal and external labels to prevent their being processed by the wrong program or on the wrong date. Tape file protection rings should be removed from the transaction tapes after they are written to prevent the data on them from being written over or erased during subsequent processing. Duplicate versions of the three disk master files should be periodically written onto magnetic tape, and subsequent transaction tapes saved to permit reconstruction of any master file whose contents are destroyed. Current copies of these tape and disk files should be stored in a file library when not in use, and removed only when properly authorized. The backup copies of these files should be stored in a secure offsite location.

The inventory update program should contain an input validation routine that performs various edit checks on the inventory transactions. These would include a validity check on transaction codes, on the inventory item number, and on the vendor number. Check digit verification might be performed on stock numbers for all transactions adding new master records to the file. A field check should be performed on numeric fields in each record such as quantity and unit cost. The input records should be checked for correctness in sequence, and any records out of sequence should be rejected. A reasonableness test might also be performed on the quantity and unit cost on each input record relative to the corresponding values of those items on the inventory master file. Any issue transactions that reduce the balance on hand as recorded in the inventory master to a negative amount should be flagged for review. The list of error transactions containing items that fail to pass one or more of these tests should be reviewed by data control personnel, and each error should be corrected prior to resubmitting the transaction in the next day's run. Similar edit checks might also be included in the vendor file processing run.

Possible real-time applications   Except for certain unique situations, real-time systems have not generally been applied to the purchasing function. The unique situations are those in which buyers must make quick decisions based upon circumstances that may change rapidly. The stockbroker is one example of a buyer in this situation. Most brokerage houses do utilize a real-time system with display terminals that provide them with current stock quotations.

One possible application of a real-time system to the purchasing operation of the "typical" company as described in this chapter involves the receiving function. Terminals could be made available in the receiving department for use in entering all inventory receipts data into the system. The most useful real-time feature of such a system might be its ability to identify critical items of inventory at the time of their arrival at the plant. A list of critical or out-of-stock inventory items would have to be maintained on disk and checked by the system each time the receipt of an item was entered. If an item were identified as critical, a message would be printed or displayed on the receiving department terminal requesting that the operator inform the appropriate department manager concerning the item's arrival.

Review Questions

1. What is logistics management? Give some examples of the various kinds of materials flows involved in logistics management within different kinds of organizations.

2. Describe or illustrate an example of a typical production organization structure. Why is an understanding of the production organization structure necessary to the analysis of logistics information systems?

3. What are three basic decisions for which the purchasing department is responsible? Describe the decision criteria and related information requirements for making these decisions.

4. Describe two alternative approaches to the inventory control function.

5. What accounting journal entries summarize the activities involved in the processing of purchase transactions?

6. Describe the data content and organization of the purchasing and raw materials inventory data base. Identify input transactions to this data base, and output reports generated from it.

7. What departments in a business organization might be involved in the manual processing of purchase transactions? What documents might be used and what data would each contain? In what department would each document originate, and where and for what purposes would each be distributed?

8. Describe the nature and purpose of (a) the purchase requisition, and (b) the receiving report.

9. What control policies and procedures are involved in manual processing of purchase transactions in a typical business organization?

10. How is organizational independence achieved with respect to the processing of purchase transactions?

11. Describe possible similarities and differences in processing of purchase transactions using a computer, rather than a manual system. Emphasize documents, departments, and reports involved in the process.

12. Explain how and by what department in an organization each of the following reports might be used:
    a) stock status report,   b) cash flow commitments summary,
    c) overdue deliveries listing, and   d) vendor performance report.
13. Describe several control policies and procedures that might be used in batch processing of purchase transactions by a business organization using a computer.
14. What circumstances make it worthwhile to apply a real-time system to the purchasing function? Give an example.
15. Describe the nature and function of a real-time system applied to the receiving function of a typical business organization.

Discussion Questions

16. The purchasing process described in this chapter related to a single plant or store. What differences would exist in the information system of a multiplant or multistore company in which the purchasing operation is centralized?
17. The computerized system described in this chapter prepared purchase orders as one of its outputs. A simplifying assumption was made that each item of inventory was purchased from only one vendor. Under what circumstances might it be more appropriate to select a vendor at the time of placing the purchase order? How would the design of the computerized system have to be revised to do this?

Problems and Cases

18. What internal controls relating to a purchasing procedure would provide the best protection against the following situations?
    a) A purchasing agent ordering unnecessary goods from a company of which he is one of the officers.
    b) A vendor overcharging for goods purchased.
    c) An error in the vendor's favor in calculating the total on an invoice.
    d) Theft of inventory by stores personnel, who claim to have never received the goods from the receiving department.
    e) A vendor invoicing the company for a greater quantity of goods than were received.
    f) A vendor delivering unordered goods and sending an invoice requesting payment for them.
    g) A vendor sent two copies of an invoice. The copies became separated and eventually two checks in payment of the two copies of the same invoice were prepared and mailed.
19. Long, CPA, has been engaged to examine and report on the financial statements of Maylou Corporation. During the review phase of the study of Maylou's system of internal accounting control over purchases, Long was given the document flowchart for purchases shown in Fig. 17.10.

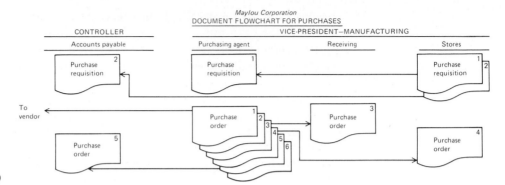

Figure 17.10

Required   a) Identify the procedures, relating to purchase requisitions and purchase orders, that Long would expect to find if Maylou's system of internal accounting control over purchases is effective. For example, purchase orders are prepared only after giving proper consideration to the time to order, and quantity to order. Do not comment on the effectiveness of the flow of documents as presented in the flowchart or on separation of duties.

b) What are the factors to consider in determining

  i) the time to order?

  ii) the quantity to order?[3]

20. You are to design an integrated system for processing purchase transactions using magnetic disk file storage. The system maintains an inventory master file, an open purchase order master file, and a vendor history file, all on the disk. System inputs are receipts and issues of inventory keyed in as they occur from receiving or stores. System outputs are batches of purchase orders, each in four copies, and periodically generated reports of cash flow commitments, overdue deliveries, and vendor performance.

The system outputs are generated by programs that are separate from the main update program. The main program begins by updating the inventory master file. If the balance of the item falls below its reorder point, the item is written onto a reorder file on a separate disk. This file is processed at the end of each day to prepare the purchase orders.

The main program then updates the open purchase order file for inventory receipts. If a receipt completes the purchase order, the purchase order is deleted from the file, and vendor performance data obtained from the completed purchase order is then processed to update the appropriate vendor history record.

The purchase order preparation program operates on the reorder list after that list has been sequenced by vendor code number. This program accesses the vendor history file to obtain the name and address associated with each vendor

[3] *Question 4, Auditing Section,* American Institute of Certified Public Accountants Examination, *November, 1978. Material from the Uniform CPA Examinations, copyright © 1978 by the American Institute of Certified Public Accountants, is reprinted with permission.*

number from the reorder file. It then generates the completed production order, adds it to the open purchase order file, and writes the purchase order.

Required

    a) Prepare a systems flowchart of this system.

    b) Prepare a macroflowchart of the main update program.

    c) Prepare a macroflowchart of the purchase order preparation program.

21. Figure 17.11 shows a document flowchart of purchasing and cash disbursement procedures for EBM, Inc. As a systems analyst, point out the weaknesses in the procedures, and describe inefficiencies or manipulations that could occur as a result of these weaknesses.

22. What internal controls in a computerized inventory update program should provide the best control over the following situations?

    a) Posting of an inventory receipt to the wrong file record due to an incorrect item number.

    b) Failure to process several inventory transactions because the cards were lost while being brought to the computer center from the keypunch room.

    c) Processing of an issue transaction in which the quantity issued was erroneous, with the result that the on-hand balance in the inventory record fell below zero.

    d) Erasure of the only copy of the inventory master tape due to inadvertent use of the tape as an output file in another program.

    e) Posting of an inventory receipt on which the item cost was erroneously keypunched as $20.00; the correct unit cost was $2.00.

    f) Due to several miscellaneous errors occurring over a period of several years, a large discrepancy arose between the quantity on hand of an important subassembly and the balance on hand according to the inventory master.

23. Culp Electronics Company processes inventory receipts as they arrive at the receiving dock by means of online data terminals located in the Receiving Department. All of the six Receiving Department employees have been taught to operate the terminals. Each inventory receipt entered into the system is processed to update the appropriate records in both (1) an inventory master file and (2) a file of open purchase orders.

Required

    a) What items of data should be entered into the system each time an operator uses the terminal to report the receipt of a shipment?

    b) Describe several means by which the system could be programmed to check the accuracy and validity of the input data entered from the Receiving Department. Relate your answer specifically to the data items mentioned in part (a).

24. The Doyle Company processes its inventory transactions by computer. Data on inventory receipts, issues, and other file changes are keyed directly from source documents onto magnetic tape using key-to-tape encoders. The transaction tape is then sorted and processed to update an inventory file maintained on a magnetic disk unit. Outputs of this process include a list of items to be reordered on magnetic tape, a printed stock status report, and a summary printout listing error transactions and run totals.

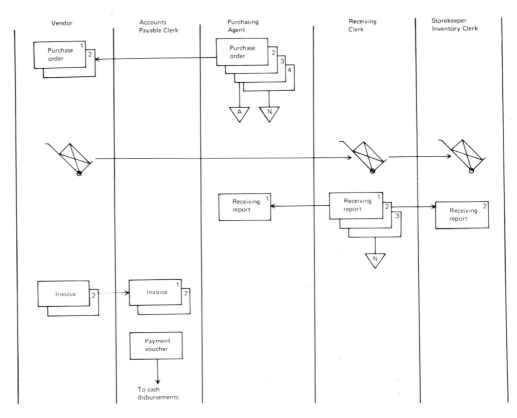

Figure 17.11

Required
a) Prepare a systems flowchart of all operations described above.

b) Describe a comprehensive set of control policies and procedures for this computerized inventory processing system. Describe the nature and purpose of each policy or procedure. Be sure to relate each policy or procedure specifically to the data and operations of the system as described above.

25. Your company has just acquired a data base management system, and one of the first applications of it will be to purchasing data. A purchase order identical to that in Fig. 17.4 is used. You are to diagram the data structure of the purchase order as a first step in the application design. Use a format similar to that in Fig. 17.2. Note that the data base will contain only the variable data on the purchase order, not the constant data.

26. The accounting and internal control procedures relating to purchases of materials by the Branden Company, a medium-sized concern manufacturing special machinery to order, have been described by your junior accountant in the following terms:

After approval by manufacturing department supervisors, materials purchase requisitions are forwarded to the purchasing department supervisor who distributes such requisitions to the several employees under his control. The latter employees prepare prenumbered purchase orders in triplicate, account for all numbers, and send the original purchase order to the vendor. One copy of the purchase order is sent to the receiving department in which it is used as a receiving report. The other copy is filed in the purchasing department.

When the materials are received, they are moved directly to the storeroom and issued to the supervisors on informal requests. The receiving department sends a receiving report (with its copy of the purchase order attached) to the purchasing department and forwards copies of the receiving report to the storeroom and to the accounting department.

Vendors' invoices for material purchases, received in duplicate in the mailroom, are sent to the purchasing department and directed to the employee who placed the related order. The employee then compares the invoice with the copy of the purchase order on file in the purchasing department for price and terms and compares the invoice quantity received as reported by the shipping and receiving department on its copy of the purchase order. The purchasing department employees also check discounts, footings, and extensions after which they initial the invoice to indicate approval for payment. The invoice is then submitted to the voucher section of the accounting department where it is coded for account distribution, assigned a voucher number, entered in the voucher register, and filed according to payment due date.

Required   Discuss the weaknesses, if any, in the internal control of Branden's purchasing and subsequent procedures. Suggest supplementary or revised procedures for remedying each weakness with regard to (a) requisition of materials and (b) receipt and storage of materials.[4]

27. You have been engaged by the management of Alden, Inc., to review its internal control over the purchase, receipt, storage, and issue of raw materials. You have prepared the following comments which describe Alden's procedures.

■ Raw materials, which consist mainly of high-cost electronic components, are kept in a locked storeroom. Storeroom personnel include a supervisor and four clerks. All are well trained, competent, and adequately bonded. Raw materials are removed from the storeroom only upon written or oral authorization of one of the production foremen.

■ There are no perpetual-inventory records; hence, the storeroom clerks do not keep records of goods received or issued. To compensate for the lack of perpetual records, a physical-inventory count is taken monthly by the storeroom clerks who are well supervised. Appropriate procedures are followed in making the inventory count.

■ After the physical count, the storeroom supervisor matches quantities counted against a predetermined reorder level. If the count for a given part is below the reorder level, the supervisor enters the part number on a materials-requisition list and sends this list to the accounts-payable clerk. The accounts-payable clerk prepares a purchase order for a predetermined re-

---

[4] Adapted from Question 4, Auditing Section, American Institute of Certified Public Accountants Examination, May 1963. Copyright © 1963 by American Institute of Certified Public Accountants, Inc., and reprinted with permission.

order quantity for each part and mails the purchase order to the vendor from whom the part was last purchased.

■ When ordered materials arrive at Alden, they are received by the storeroom clerks. The clerks count the merchandise and check to see that the counts agree with the shipper's bill of lading. All vendors' bills of lading are initialed, dated, and filed in the storeroom to serve as receiving reports.

Required   Describe the weaknesses in internal control and recommend improvements of Alden's procedures for the purchase, receipt, storage, and issue of raw materials. Organize your answer sheet as follows.[5]

Weaknesses	Recommended improvements

28. Anthony, CPA, prepared the flowchart (Fig. 17.12) which portrays the raw materials purchasing function of one of Anthony's clients, a medium-sized manufacturing company, from the preparation of initial documents through the vouching of invoices for payment in accounts payable. The flowchart was a portion of the work performed on the audit engagement to evaluate internal control.

Required   Identify and explain the systems and control weaknesses evident from the flowchart. Include the internal control weaknesses resulting from activities performed or not performed. All documents are prenumbered.[6]

References   Arthur Andersen & Co. *A Guide for Studying and Evaluating Internal Accounting Controls.* Chicago: Arthur Andersen & Co., 1978.

Bonczek, Robert H., Clyde W. Holsapple, and Andrew B. Whinston. "Aiding Decision Makers with a Generalized Data Base Management System: An Application to Inventory Management." *Decision Sciences* (April 1978): 228–245.

Burton, Terence T. "Get Back to Basics with MRP." *The Internal Auditor* (October 1979): 66–76.

Donelson, William S., II. "MRP—Who Needs It?" *Datamation* (May 1979): 185–194.

Hall, Robert W., and Thomas E. Vollmann. "Planning Your Material Requirements." *Harvard Business Review* (September–October 1978): 105–112.

---

[5] *Question 6, Auditing Section,* American Institute of Certified Public Accountants Examination, *November 1973. Material from the Uniform CPA Examinations, copyright © 1973 by the American Institute of Certified Public Accountants, is reprinted (or adapted) with permission.*

[6] *Question 6, Auditing Section,* American Institute of Certified Public Accountants Examination, *November 1975. Material from the Uniform CPA Examinations, copyright © 1975 by American Institute of Certified Public Accountants, is reprinted (or adapted) with permission.*

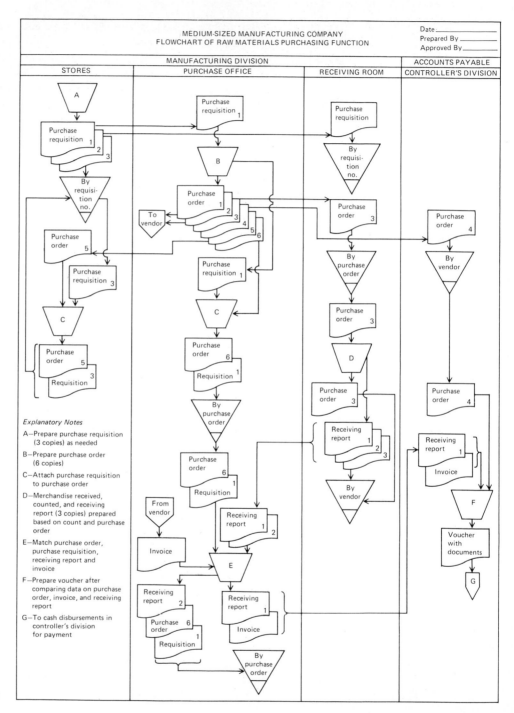

Figure 17.12

Keegan, Daniel P. "Some Second Reflections on MRP." *Price Waterhouse & Company Review* (1977, No. 3): 38–43.

Miller, Jeffrey G., and Peter Gilmour. "Materials Managers: Who Needs Them?" *Harvard Business Review* (July–August 1979): 143–153.

Miller, Jeffrey G., and Linda G. Sprague. "Behind the Growth in Materials Requirements Planning." *Harvard Business Review* (September–October 1975): 83–91.

Price Waterhouse & Co. *Guide to Accounting Controls: Purchases & Payables*. New York: Price Waterhouse & Co., 1979.

Chapter 18

Accounting Information Systems for Logistics Management II

Chapter 17 discusses information systems serving the purchasing function. In a retail or wholesale organization, purchasing represents the primary factor in logistics management. However, in a manufacturing organization, the purchasing function is only the beginning of the materials flow process. The second major step in this process is the production operation. The nature of the production management function, and of the information systems that serve it, comprises the subject of this chapter.

The Production Management Function

Referring to the organization chart in Fig. 17.1, we observe that the production management function is primarily the responsibility of the production planning department, the plant manager, the general supervisor, and the various production department supervisors. Generally the production planning department is responsible for planning and scheduling of production, while the plant manager, general supervisor, and departmental supervisors are responsible for the coordination and control of production operations. Important service functions to these activities are performed by the engineering, maintenance, and stores departments.

**Production
planning**

The production planning function involves determining what should be produced and when it should be produced. Closely related to production planning is the engineering function of determining how a given product should be produced.

Deciding what should be produced consists basically of establishing the appropriate quantities of each product to be manufactured during a given time period. The decision process encompasses the specification of a suitable mix of styles, sizes, colors, and other features. For those firms that manufacture goods to customer orders, this aspect of production planning may be quite simple, especially if there is a large *backlog* of orders that have been received but not filled. However, those firms that manufacture goods for inventory must utilize information on both current inventory levels and forecasted sales by product for making these decisions.

The engineering function involves establishing, for each product or subassembly the firm manufactures, the standard quantity of each raw material or part required for the product, the precise labor operations required for each product, the standard amount of time each operation should consume, and the work station or machine at which each operation should be performed. These specifications are developed for a product at the time when it is first introduced into the firm's product line, and may be revised periodically thereafter. Materials specifications for a product are embodied in a document called a *bill of materials,* illustrated in Fig. 18.1. Labor operations, with their corresponding machine requirements and standard time requirements, are indicated on a document called an *operations list* or *routing sheet,* illustrated in Fig. 18.2. Copies of both of these documents are prepared and kept current by the engineering department for every item produced, and are used extensively in production planning and control. In a firm that uses a standard cost system, the standard materials cost per unit and standard labor rate per operation might also be included on the bill of materials and operations list, respectively.

Planning the specific time at which product items will be manufactured is referred to as production scheduling. The scheduler must know what quantities of each product are to be produced, what resource requirements exist for each product, and what resources are available. Determination of the quantities to be produced is the stage in production planning that precedes scheduling. Resource requirements are then established by multiplying the quantity of each product to be produced by the standard per unit requirements specified in the bill of materials and operations list for the product. Three types of resources—materials, labor, and equipment—must be brought together at the same point in time for production to occur. The availability of these resources is made known to the scheduler by materials stock status reports, personnel reports, and machine availability and capacity reports. The scheduler must coordinate the work of all production employees and the use of all available machines and materials throughout the plant to achieve maximum production at a minimum expenditure of time and resources. His or her output is a production schedule for each factory production department—a schedule that indicates

BILL OF MATERIALS

Assembly No. 2742816	Assembly Name Miniature Calculator	Page 1 of 2	Approved by FDK	Date 1-9-81

Part Number	Description	Quantity per Assembly
7054396	Calculator Unit	1
4069136	Lower Casing	1
1954207	Screw	8
3099218	Battery	1
4069245	Upper Casing	1
1954209	Screw	6

Fig. 18.1
Bill of materials.

OPERATIONS LIST

Stock number	Description		Date prepared	By	
Dept. no.	Oper. no.	Operation description	Machine requirements	Stand. hours	Set-up hours

Fig. 18.2
Operations list.

what jobs must be performed within that department during the period covered by the schedule.

Finally, the production scheduler must know the relative priorities of the various items in the process of production. Some items will have high priority because they are out of stock, backordered, rush ordered, or behind schedule for a promised delivery date. Such high-priority items must be given preference over lower priority items in production scheduling and operations.

Operations control   The operations control function includes all activities related to expediting, coordinating, and controlling the operations of the various production departments. At least three basic standards—time standards, cost standards, and quality standards—must be met in this function. Time standards are embodied in the operations lists, which, in turn, are embodied in the production schedule. The control function with respect to time standards is carried out by production department supervisors, who must coordinate the operations of the workers and equipment under their direction to complete the scheduled production. The performance of the supervisors is evaluated by the general supervisor and plant manager on the basis of comparison of scheduled unit production with actual unit production. The supervisors must also observe the priorities attached to various production jobs; their success in this regard is also an important element of performance.

The control function with respect to cost standards is also carried out by production department supervisors; the results can be evaluated by the plant manager and general supervisor on the basis of reports generated by the cost accounting department. The decisions of the departmental supervisors regarding the assignment of workers to jobs are made in accordance with the experience, efficiency, and quality of each employee's work. The quality of those decisions, and the quality of each supervisor's supervision, are reflected in materials usage costs and labor costs. Other decisions of the departmental supervisors are reflected in overhead costs such as repairs and maintenance, supplies, small tools, power, and so forth. A good cost accounting system uses the standard material and labor requirements developed by the engineering department to provide a standard cost per unit for all production work performed. Cost accounting reports such as the one illustrated in Fig. 18.3 compare actual costs within each department to standard costs, and thus provide important feedback to departmental supervisors on their performance. Similar reports are provided to the plant manager and the general supervisor for use in evaluating their own performance and that of the supervisor under their supervision.

The quality control function may be performed by the engineering department and/or by a separate inspection or quality control department. The function involves testing or inspecting completed items of production for defects in materials or workmanship. It is often performed on a sample basis, in which case the entire lot of completed items is not inspected unless a certain portion of the sample is found to be defective. All defective units are returned to the appropriate factory department for reworking. Costs of reworking should generally be charged to the supervisor in whose department the defective work occurred. Information needed to perform this function is provided by the engineering department. However, quality results as determined by this function are reflected in production costs related to reworking, and are thus relevant to performance evaluations of department supervisors and the general supervisor.

One other important production control function is the *expediting* or *dispatching* function. This function involves monitoring the progress of production, particularly of high priority items. The expediter must have knowledge of the current status of all work in process. He or she is frequently called upon to report such information in response to a customer request. The expediter is responsible for maintaining a smooth flow of production through the factory, and may authorize deviations from the production schedule if neccessary to accomplish this goal. The expediter must also report significant deviations from scheduled production to the plant manager, the general supervisor, and the production planning department.

DAILY LABOR COST EFFICIENCY REPORT										
Dept. no. 473 Machining			Supervisor: Oscar Nagursky				Date: Feb. 28, 1981			
Employee		Order No.	Operation		Stand. Rate	Hours		% Efficiency	Total Cost	
No.	Name		No	Description		Actual	Stand.		Actual	Stand.
4099	Jones, Harold	1406	352	Drill	3 00	3 6	3 5	97	10 80	10 50
4099	Jones, Harold	1406	382	Burr	3 00	4 4	4 0	91	13 20	12 00
4166	Bond, Jim	1381	425	Grind	2 90	3 0	3 6	120	8 70	10 44
4166	Bond, Jim	1406	392	Bore	2 90	5 0	5 5	110	14 50	15 95
	Dept. Totals					128 0	125 4	98	362 20	356 20

Fig. 18.3
Labor cost efficiency report for a production department.

The Production Information System

Most manufacturing organizations have two primary information subsystems for production management. One concerns the physical operations and elements of production, while the second concerns the cost elements of production. In automated systems, these two subsystems tend to become integrated, and so this chapter covers both subsystems. This section reviews the accounting transactions arising from production operations, describes and illustrates the production data base, and then discusses examples of manual, computerized batch processing, and real-time information systems for production management.

The accounting transactions

All of the accounting transactions pertaining to production operations within a company are internal transactions, which means that there is no outside party to these transactions. Two basic accounting journal entries summarize the activities of the production process. The first of these follows.

```
Work-in-Process Inventory   XXX
     Raw Materials Inventory        XXX
     Payroll                        XXX
     Manufacturing Overhead         XXX
```

This is a composite entry representing the charging of the three major categories of manufacturing cost to production in process. The raw materials inventory portion of the entry is generally made at the beginning of production of a batch of units, when materials are issued for production from the storeroom. The payroll portion of the entry is made every week or every other week, depending on how frequently production employees are paid. The overhead portion of the entry represents overhead applied to work in process rather than actual overhead incurred. It is necessary to make this distinction because manufacturing overhead costs, unlike materials and labor, cannot be traced directly to units of work in process. Therefore, overhead is generally applied at a standard rate, using direct labor hours or direct labor costs as a base.

The actual overhead costs are recorded by the accounting department as they are incurred. Numerous factory overhead accounts, including supplies, indirect labor, small tools, overtime premium, power and other utilities, insurance, taxes, maintenance, and depreciation, are debited for these costs. These detailed overhead accounts are coded both by type of cost and by the department for which the cost is incurred. Credits are made to accounts payable, payroll (for indirect labor, overtime premium, etc.), and other accounts (accumulated depreciation, accrued taxes, etc.). At the end of each reporting period (generally monthly), all balances in these detailed overhead accounts are closed to the manufacturing overhead control account. The net balance remaining in the manufacturing overhead control account after the closing represents overapplied or underapplied overhead. In a standard cost system, this difference is broken down into standard overhead cost variances. The net difference is eventually written off to cost of goods sold.[1]

There are two alternative techniques of cost accounting for work-in-process inventories. These are called *job order costing* and *process costing*. In job order costing, manufacturing costs are accumulated by production jobs in process, and there is a single work-in-process control account representing the total amount charged to all jobs in process. In process costing, manufacturing costs are accumulated by departments, and there are separate work-in-process accounts for each department. Therefore, in process costing the transfer of work in process from one department to another is accompanied by a journal entry transferring the accumulated manufacturing costs from one department's work-in-process account to the other's. Firms that produce goods to specific customer orders generally utilize job order costing, whereas firms that produce goods for inventory may use either job order or process costing. The systems described and illustrated in this chapter are based on the model of a firm that produces goods for inventory and uses a job order costing system.[2]

The second basic accounting journal entry relating to the production process follows.

Finished Goods Inventory	XXX	
Work-in-Process Inventory		XXX

This entry reflects the completion of production goods and their transfer from the final assembly department into the finished goods storeroom, or to the shipping department for shipment to warehouses or customers.

The production data base

Taking a broad view, the production data base in a manufacturing company may be looked upon as a set of closely related data bases, including the marketing data base (discussed in Chapter 16), the purchasing and materials inventory data base (discussed in Chapter 17), the product structure data base, and the production work-in-

[1] For a more extensive discussion of accounting for overhead costs, see Charles T. Horngren, Cost Accounting: A Managerial Emphasis *(4th ed.). Englewood Cliffs, N.J.: Prentice-Hall, Inc., 1977); Chapters 4 and 9.*

[2] For a more extensive coverage and comparison of job order and process costing, see Charles T. Horngren, op. cit., Chapters 4 and 17.

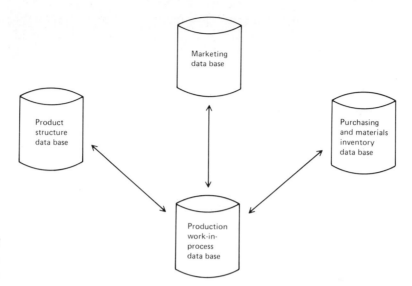

Fig. 18.4
Overview of produc-
tion data base.

process data base, which is the heart of the system. This is illustrated in Fig. 18.4. The marketing data base indicates the demand rate and finished goods inventory level of all manufactured products, thereby enabling the preparation of a master production plan for the organization. The master production plan shows the quantity of each product to be manufactured each week for several weeks into the future.

The product structure data base details the engineering specifications for each product, including the quantities of various raw material items required and the exact sequence of operations performed in the manufacturing process. Thus the product structure data base essentially consists of the bill of materials and operations list for each product.

The purchasing and materials inventory data base shows the quantities of each item of raw materials inventory that are on hand or on order. This information is essential to the determination of a detailed production schedule. In turn, the master production plan, in conjunction with the bills of materials, indicates the quantities of various items of raw materials that need to be ordered. As materials are issued into production, the on-hand balances of the appropriate inventory accounts are reduced accordingly.

As shown in Fig. 18.4, the production work-in-process data base is the core of the production data base. Figure 18.5 provides an example of the data content and organization of a production work-in-process data base. This data base contains a series of records for each production order currently being processed in the factory. This includes a master work-in-process record, a set of materials requisition records for each type of material used in the product, and a set of operations records for each scheduled production operation required in manufacturing the product. These records are structured as a tree, with the master work-in-process record representing the parent and the materials requisition and production operations records repre-

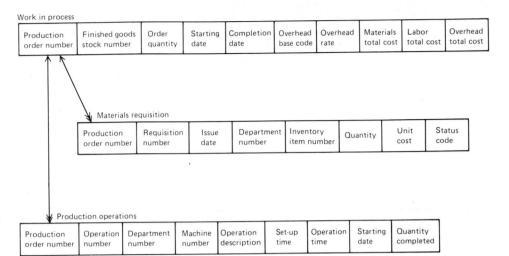

*Fig. 18.5
Production work-in-
process data base.*

senting the children. Production order number serves as the primary key for work-in-process records, each of which contains accumulated manufacturing cost data and an entry for the order quantity and scheduled completion date.

The primary inputs to the production work-in-process data base are newly initiated production orders and records of activities completed within the factory. The initiation of production orders is based upon the master production plan. Access to the product structure data base permits a complete set of material requisition records and production operations records to be generated. These are linked to a work-in-process master record to form a tree, which is then added to the data base. Next, as materials are issued into production in the factory, records of the actual quantity and cost are entered, and the requisition "status code" is changed from "scheduled" to "issued." Records of quantity, time, and cost of completed labor operations are also entered into the data base, updating the appropriate production operations records and adding to the accumulated materials and overhead costs in the work-in-process master. Eventually the last product is transferred to the finished goods storeroom; this causes the removal of the complete tree of the production order record from the data base, and initiates an increase in the on-hand quantity in the finished goods inventory section of the marketing data base.

Several output documents and reports may be generated from the production work-in-process data base. One is a production order, illustrated in Fig. 18.6, that provides the factory and the production planning department with a written reference document for each production order in process. Another is a materials requisition, illustrated in Fig. 18.7, that authorizes the transfer of raw materials from the storeroom to the appropriate factory department. Each day the production operations records are processed sequentially by department number and machine number to prepare complete production schedules for each department. Daily reports on labor cost efficiency (see. Fig. 18.3) and materials usage efficiency may be generated

MILL WORK TICKET

M.O. ITEM	CUSTOMER	SHIP-TO NO.	CUSTOMER NO.	CUSTOMER ORDER NO.	DATE PROM.	QUAL.	SPEC NO.	PROC NO.
123456 00	FISH STEEL	1240	1011	12C418-11	4-217	CQ	1420	711

PRODUCT GROUP	ORDERED WEIGHT	INGOT SPEC CODE	HEAT NO.	PRODUCT SIZE-IN. T-W-L
HR F PKL SULF HVY OIL ME COIL	24.000	107 3412	27463	.125 X 56.5 X COIL

OPER NO	FAC NO	OPERATION DESCRIPTION	SIZE T W L	PROC CODE	DATE SCHD	LIFTS SCHD	WEIGHT SCHED	SPECIAL INSTRUCTIONS	X O	SP NO
05	00	PROVIDE STEEL	4.0 X 54.0 X112.0		203	4	27200			
10	12	HR 1FIN COIL	.125 X 56.5 XCOIL	212	205	4	24800	CONTACT MET B14 ROLLING		
15	22	PKL OIL ME		111	210	4	24300	CUT OUT WELDS		
20	81	PACKAGING		714	214	4	24300	USE CUST SKIDS		
25	91	SHIPPING	.125 X 56.5 XCOIL		217	4	24300	NO DELIV FRI PM		

Fig. 18.6 *Production order. (Reprinted by permission from* Primary Metals—Basic Production Planning and Control System, *Vol. 1. Copyright © 1971 by International Business Machines Corporation.)*

MATERIALS REQUISITION No. 14160

Date	Department Issued to	Production order no.

Item No.	Item description	Quantity	Cost/unit	Total cost

Received by ____________ Date ________

Fig. 18.7 *Materials requisition.*

by comparing actual and planned quantities. As production orders are completed, summary cost reports may be prepared for the accounting department.

In a manual data processing system, two sets of records are generally maintained for each production order in process. First, the production planning department maintains records of open production orders, entering written notes of completed operations. Second, the cost accounting department maintains work-in-process cost records detailing the accumulated manufacturing costs for each production order in process. The open production order file serves as an important reference regarding the status of orders in process, and also serves as a production schedule by identifying those operations currently due to be performed.

PRODUCTION ORDER COST SUMMARY				
Order no.	Item no.	Item description		
Quantity started		Date started	Quantity completed	Date completed

Direct materials costs

Date	Dept. no.	Req. no.	Description	Total cost	

Direct labor costs

Date	Dept. no.	Oper. no.	Description	Total hrs.	Total cost	

Applied manufacturing overhead costs

Date	Dept. no.	Basis of application	Total cost	

*Fig. 18.8
Work-in-process cost
summary sheet.*

The work-in-process cost records may consist simply of a cost summary sheet, as illustrated in Fig. 18.8. The cost accounting department records the data on these records from source documents evidencing material and labor usage in production. As explained earlier, overhead costs charged to work-in-process represent applied rather than actual costs. Once a production order is completed, the cost data on this record are summarized to determine total and per unit cost for the items produced.

When a manufacturing company converts from a manual to an automated data processing system for production data, the open production order file and the work-in-process cost file are prime candidates for integration. This is because both files are organized according to production orders in process. The combined master file would contain complete data on operations, quantities, and costs for each order. Ultimately, an integrated file of this type will evolve into a production work-in-process data base of the kind illustrated in Fig. 18.5. The data base approach is proving to be extremely effective in maintaining production records and scheduling and controlling production activities in many manufacturing companies.

A manual system   A document flowchart of a manual system for processing data relating to production operations appears in Fig. 18.9. Once again it must be emphasized that this and all subsequent illustrations are examples, rather than descriptions, of a real system. The production area is one in which the differences between firms are often quite significant. However, for most manufacturing firms the general pattern of information flows is likely to be somewhat similar to that shown.

The illustration shows that production data processing begins in the production planning department. This department reviews current sales forecasts from the marketing department, finished goods stock status reports from the finished goods department, and raw materials stock status reports from the inventory clerk. On the basis of these inputs, the department decides the types and quantities of products which will be produced during the next period. The operations list is then used as a basis for generating production orders, and the materials specifications list is used to prepare materials requisitions for each production order.

One copy of each production order is sent to the cost accounting department, where it is used to establish a work-in-process record for the job. A second copy is sent to the production department in which the work is to begin. This copy will accompany the work in process on its way through the factory. A third copy is retained by production planning and filed in the open production order file.

The production planning department also prepares several copies of a materials requisition (see Fig. 18.7) authorizing the transfer of raw materials from the stores department to the appropriate factory department. The items and quantities listed on the materials requisition are determined according to the specifications provided on the bill of materials. For each production order, one or more materials requisitions may be issued by production planning—one for each department to which materials are issued according to the bill of materials. In some cases all materials may be issued to one department, whereas in other cases various portions of the materials may be issued to several different production departments as the work proceeds through the factory.

One copy of each materials requisition is filed by requisition number in the production planning department. Three other copies of each are sent to the raw materials storeroom, where they provide authorization to the stores supervisor to release the goods to the factory. When this transfer occurs, the person receiving the materials signs the form and has the cost per unit data entered by the inventory clerk, who retains one copy and transmits another copy to cost accounting for entry to the work-in-process master. The recipient of the goods retains the third copy to be attached to the factory copy of the production order. The inventory clerk posts each requisition to the issues and on-hand fields of the raw materials inventory master and, after each batch is posted, prepares a journal voucher of the debit to work in process and credit to raw materials inventory that is sent to the general ledger clerk.

The production planning department also prepares daily production schedules for all factory production departments. The basis for preparing these schedules is the open production order file, which is kept current to reflect all operations remain-

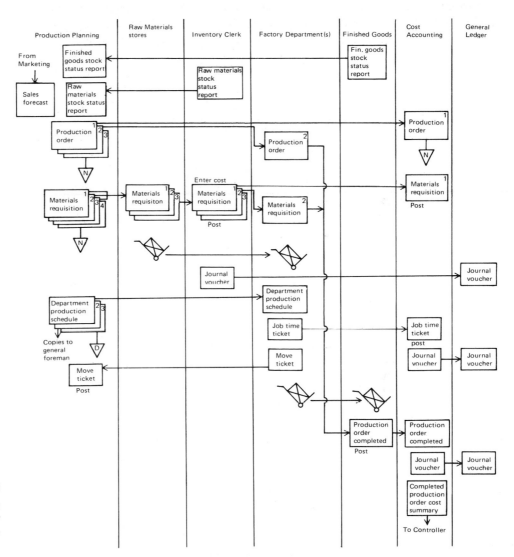

Fig. 18.9
Document flow in a manual system for processing of production data.

ing to be performed on all outstanding production orders. The production schedule for each department lists all operations to be performed in the department each day, including the production order number, the machine number, quantity, total time required, start and stop time, priority of the order, the location from which the work in process is to arrive, and the location to which it must be sent when completed. Each departmental production schedule must, of course, properly reflect the availability of machine time and labor in the department. A copy of each department's production schedule is sent at the beginning of each day to the department supervisor. Another copy of each is sent to the general supervisor, while a third copy is filed by date in the production planning department.

In the individual factory departments the production schedule provides a guide to the supervisor in assigning workers to jobs. Departures from the schedule may be necessary in the event of machine breakdowns, employee absenteeism, unavailability of materials, the need to rework some materials, and so forth. Supervisors must observe the priority status of each job to the maximum extent possible if it becomes necessary to depart from the schedule. As each factory employee completes the operation to which he or she is assigned, a job time ticket (see Fig. 18.10) is prepared detailing the work performed. All job time tickets are approved and signed by the department supervisor and sent to the cost accounting department for posting to the work-in-process cost summary sheets.

The transfer of work-in-process from one work station or department to another as operations are completed is recorded on a document called a move ticket. Move tickets are provided to production planning as a source for updating the production order file. The final move ticket, signed by an employee in finished goods, records the transfer of the product to the finished goods storeroom. When this copy of the move ticket is received by production planning, the corresponding production order may be removed from the open production order file.

The cost accounting department is responsible for maintaining the file of work-in-process cost records. New records are added to this file upon receipt of new production orders initiated by production planning. Materials costs are posted to this file from copies of materials requisitions. Direct labor costs are posted from job time tickets. Overhead costs are often applied on the basis of direct labor hours or direct labor costs, and therefore are posted at the same time as labor costs. The cost accounting department initiates a journal voucher reflecting each batch of job time tickets posted that contains a debit to work-in-process and credits to payroll and manufacturing overhead. This journal voucher is transmitted to the general ledger clerk, and posted to the general ledger.

When the finished products are transmitted to the finished goods storeroom from the factory, the production order and attached materials requisitions accompany them. This completed production order is used by finished goods personnel to post to the finished goods inventory file. The copy is then transmitted to cost accounting, where it provides the basis for closing the work-in-process record of the job. After each batch of these is processed, a journal voucher is prepared by the cost accounting department indicating the debit to finished goods inventory and credit to work-in-process. The voucher is transmitted to the general ledger clerk for posting to the general ledger. The cost accounting department also prepares for the controller a completed production order cost summary, which contains an outline of all materials, labor, and overhead costs accumulated for the job.

The cost accounting department is responsible for the periodic preparation of departmental cost performance reports for the various production departments. Actual materials usage and labor costs for this purpose are accumulated from mate-

JOB TIME TICKET			
Date	Dept. no.	Department name	
Prod. ord.	Oper. no.	Operation description.	
Employee no.		Name	Hourly rate
Start time	Stop time	Total hours	Quantity completed
Approved by _____ Department foreman			

Fig. 18.10
Job time ticket.

rials requisitions and job time tickets. Actual overhead costs are obtained from a summary analysis of the factory overhead ledger provided by the accounting clerk responsible for maintaining that ledger. This analysis indicates the total of each type of overhead cost incurred by each factory department. The cost accounting department maintains current standard costs for materials usage, labor, and overhead, and these standard costs are also used in preparing performance reports. As indicated in the report illustrated previously in Fig. 18.3, each departmental cost performance report is a summary and comparison of actual and standard costs for the most recent period, with cumulative totals encompassing several recent periods perhaps also provided. Copies of each of these reports are sent to the appropriate departmental supervisors, and duplicate copies of all reports may be provided to the general supervisor, the plant manager, the controller, and other executives.

Organizational independence with respect to production processing operations is achieved by separation of the authorization function performed by the production planning department from the recording functions performed by the inventory clerk, the cost accounting department, and the general ledger clerk, and from the operating and custodial functions of the various factory departments and the raw materials and finished goods storerooms. This separation of duties provides assurance that all movements of materials in the firm are properly authorized and accurately recorded.

The most significant control problems in the production area are prevention of loss of inventories and the maintenance of efficient production operations. Controls over loss of inventories, in addition to separation of duties, include effective supervision by factory supervisors and stores supervisors, limitations on access to the storerooms containing raw materials and finished goods, and physical security measures such as the placing of plant protection personnel at factory gates. Also important are the documentary controls on all transfers of materials within the factory. In the case of all such transfers, the recipient of the materials must sign a document acknowledging the receipt and verifying the accuracy of the amount recorded on the document. The document, which may be a materials requisition or a move ticket, is then immediately routed to a recording center, such as cost accounting or production planning. If materials shortages do occur, this system enables tracing the responsibility for the shortages to a specific department.

Control of production efficiency is provided by comparisons of actual production with scheduled production and by departmental cost performance reports. Comparisons of actual and scheduled production by the departmental supervisors, general supervisor, and production planning department establish a basis for daily control of operations. The expediting function, which closely monitors the progress of high priority items through production, and brings any delays to the attention of the appropriate managers, also contributes to the day-by-day control of production efficiency. Departmental cost performance reports measure production efficiency in financial terms, on a daily, weekly, or monthly basis. In the long run, departmental cost performance reports contribute to control of production efficiency by encouraging supervisors and managers to improve their decisions, policies, and procedures.

One other aspect of production control not reflected in the flowchart is quality control. The quality inspector's station is often the last factory department through which a product passes before it reaches the finished goods storeroom. If the product passes inspection, the inspector's report is attached to the move ticket that acknowledges receipt of the goods in the finished goods storeroom. These documents are routed to production planning. Any items that do not pass inspection are sent back to the appropriate factory department, and an inspector's report indicating the rejection is routed to production planning. The latter department must then include the necessary rework operations in preparation of subsequent production schedules. Periodically prepared summaries of work failing to pass inspection may be used by production management to pinpoint quality control problems within the factory.

The flowchart also does not indicate the special procedures that are necessary in the event that actual materials usage is greater than or less than the amount requisitioned. If the supervisor decides a larger quantity of materials is needed, he or she must inform the production planning department of the items and quantities required. The production planning department issues another materials requisition, which undergoes processing identical to the original version. To provide control over materials issued in this manner, the authority to initiate requests for additional materials must be restricted to supervisors only, since supervisors will eventually be held accountable for the excess materials costs.

If a quantity of raw materials is left over after production within a department is completed, the departmental supervisor must prepare two copies of a returned materials report. These copies are taken, together with the materials themselves, to the raw materials storeroom. There the custodian signs one copy acknowledging receipt of the exact items and quantities indicated on the report, and this copy is sent to cost accounting for posting to the work-in-process master file. The other copy is provided to the inventory clerk for posting to the raw materials inventory file.

A computer-based batch processing system

A document flowchart of the production information system of a typical manufacturing company using computerized batch processing appears in Fig. 18.11. As in previous descriptions of batch processing systems, it is assumed that master files are maintained on magnetic disk storage, and that magnetic tape is used for data input.

A comparison of Fig. 18.11 with its manual counterpart, Fig. 18.9, reveals that the computer has replaced the inventory clerk and has assumed many of the clerical functions performed within the production planning and cost accounting departments. The production planning department decides what is to be produced on the basis of the same information—sales forecasts and inventory status reports—but this information is prepared by computer instead of by various other departments. Production planning prepares a set of manufacturing authorizations indicating the quantity of each product to be produced and the relative priorities of each product. This is provided to the input preparation department and becomes input to a computerized process that prepares production orders, materials requisitions, and production schedules. The open production order file, maintained by the production planning department in the manual system, and the work-in-process master file, maintained by the cost accounting department in the manual system, are instead maintained together as a single integrated file by computer.

The functions performed by raw materials stores, the various factory departments, the finished goods department, and the general ledger clerk are quite similar in the two systems. The factory departments must route the job time tickets and move tickets to input preparation instead of to cost accounting and production planning. Factory supervisors must still manually prepare requisitions for excess materials needed or reports for unnecessary materials returned in the event that actual usage varies from the amount originally requisitioned. The finished goods department is no longer responsible for maintaining the finished goods master file, which is instead maintained by computer. The general ledger clerk receives journal vouchers as computer printouts rather than as manually prepared documents. Actually, the general ledger function itself could easily be computerized, and a system incorporating this feature is described in Chapter 20.

Figures 18.12, 18.13, and 18.15 illustrate by means of systems flowcharts the computer operations involved in (1) production order and materials requisition preparation, (2) production scheduling, and (3) cost accounting. This section discusses each of these three areas of computer operations in turn, and describes control policies and procedures directly applicable to these operations.

An important feature of the computerized production information systems described and illustrated here is the integration of open production order and work-in-process data. The combined file resulting from the integration of these two files is referred to as the "production order cost and operations data file." The control field for this file is production order number, and the file contains both physical and cost data for all operations and materials connected wtih the order. In addition, it is assumed that standard cost data are recorded on this file. In each of the three areas of computer operations covered in this section, the production order cost and operations data file is the key master file in updating and reporting processes.

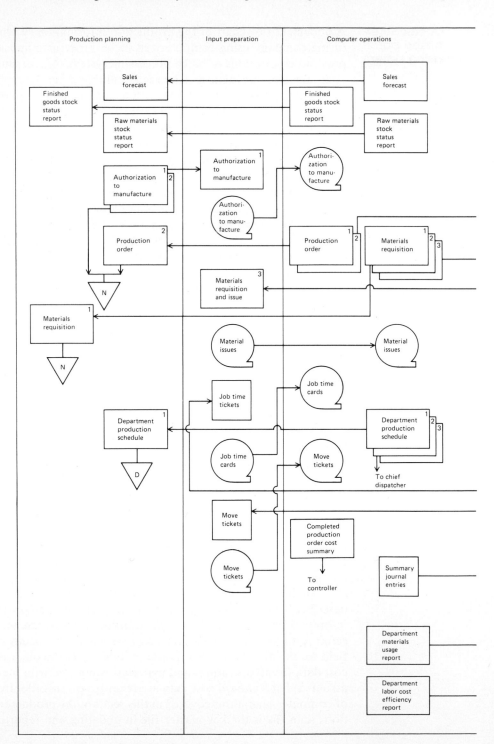

Fig. 18.11
Document flow in computerized batch processing of production data.

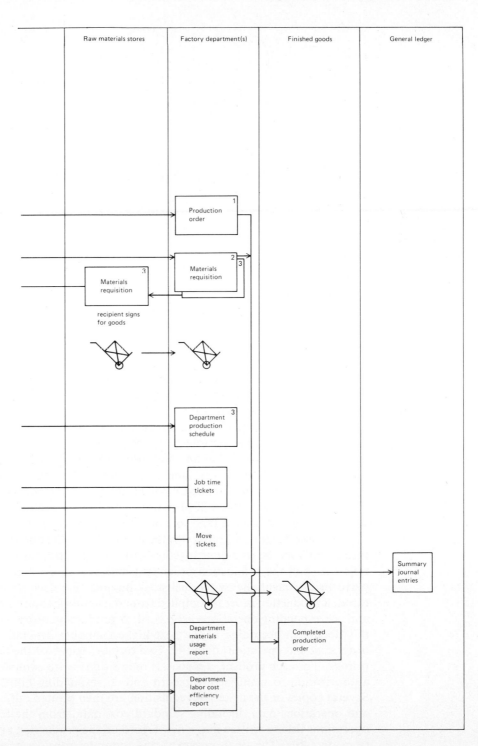

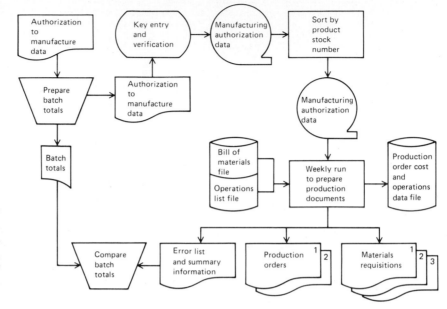

Fig. 18.12
Computerized batch
processing system for
preparation of pro-
duction orders and
materials requisi-
tions.

Preparation of production planning documents   The input preparation and computer processing operations necessary to prepare production orders and materials requisitions are illustrated in Fig. 18.12. These operations are initiated once each week by receipt of "authorization-to-manufacture" documents or lists from the production planning department. Batch totals prepared from these documents might include a record count and hash totals of product stock number and quantity to be produced. After keying and verification, the authorization-to-manufacture records are sorted into sequence by product stock number, which is the same sequence followed for the bill of materials file and operations list file. The sorting step is performed using a tape sort program on the computer.

The next step in this process is the processing of the authorization-to-manufacture records on the computer together with the operations list file, the bill of materials file, and the production order cost and operations data file. This process is performed sequentially by product stock number. For each product to be manufactured, a production order is compiled from the authorization-to-manufacture record and corresponding operations list record. A production order number is assigned to this document according to the next highest number available on the production order cost and operations data file. Two or more copies of the production order are printed. For each product, a materials requisition is also compiled from data on the authorization to manufacture record and corresponding bill of materials record. Several copies of the materials requisition are then printed out. All of the materials and operations data, including standard cost data, from the bill of materials and operations list are written into a new record on the production order cost and operations data file. The final output of this computer run is a printed listing of error

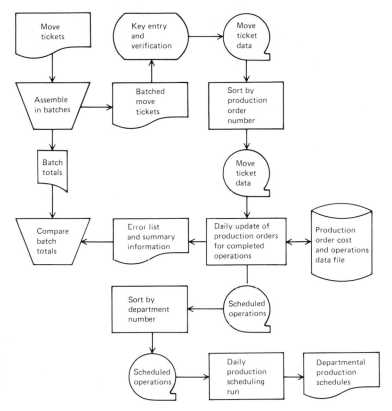

Fig. 18.13
Computerized batch
processing system for
production
scheduling.

transactions, batch totals, and other summary information that is compared with the manually generated batch totals as a means of data control.

Production scheduling   This activity is assumed to be performed daily in the computerized system as in the manual system. A systems flowchart of the process appears in Fig. 18.13. The process begins with the updating of the production order cost and operations data file for move tickets evidencing the completion of an operation at one work station and the transfer of the work to the next scheduled work station. Move tickets are received during the shift from the factory and assembled into batches at the completion of the shift. Batch totals will include a record count as well as hash totals of production order number and quantity of units completed. The batched move tickets are then keyed onto tape and verified, after which they are sorted by production order number for processing against the production order cost and operations data file.

The collection and preparation for computer processing of source data on production operations is a common application of source data automation. This observation applies to source data such as that recorded on move tickets and job time tickets. Numerous portable data recorders exist that are designed primarily for collecting production data in machine readable form. Also used are data collection terminals with which factory employees may enter production data by means of setting various switches indicating the operation number, start and stop time, quantity completed, and so forth. Such terminals may be directly online to the computer or connected to an offline tape drive or card punch that records data from all terminals for subsequent batch processing. Also common is the use of turnaround documents upon which production order number, operation number, department number, and related data may be prepunched at the time of preparation of the production orders. As the operations are completed, the employee number, time worked, and quantity completed may be entered on the card in predefined fields for mark sensing. An example of a prepunched card for job time recording upon which production data is recorded for mark sensing upon completion of operations is illustrated in Fig. 18.14.

The processing of move tickets against the production order cost and operations data file updates the record of operations performed on that file, and therefore keeps current the records of operations still remaining to be performed for each production order. Two outputs are generated from this process. One is the familiar printed listing of error transactions and summary information. Batch totals on this printout are compared with those prepared manually prior to processing to check on the reliability of the processed input records. The other output is a tape listing of operations scheduled for performance during the forthcoming shift. Each record on this list includes the production order number, operation number, department number, work station number, quantity to be completed, and standard time requirement for each operation, as well as an indication of the priority of each operation and the appropriate sequence of performance of operations. This tape is then sorted by department number and processed by a special program that prepares departmental production schedules for all production departments. This program contains data on machine and labor capacity of each department. Often programs of this sort may be very sophisticated, having a capability to generate schedules that represent the optimum assignment of resources for maximum production.

Fig. 18.14
Turnaround document for collection of production data using mark sensing. (Reprinted by permission from Basic Applications-System/360 Model 20, *Copyright © 1971 by International Business Machines Corporation.)*

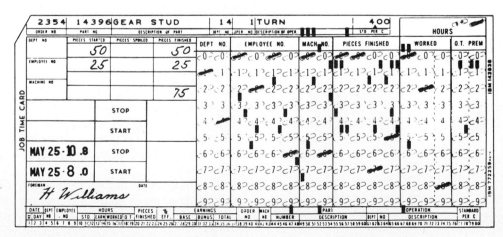

Cost accounting   A systems flowchart of daily computerized operations for cost accounting appears in Fig. 18.15. All of the operations shown are assumed to be performed once daily. To simplify the illustration and accompanying discussion, the chart is divided by means of dashed lines into three separate application areas —materials costing, labor costing, and finished goods file updating.

Materials costing operations utilize the costed material issues tape generated as an output of updating the raw materials inventory file as illustrated in Fig. 17.9. Each record on this tape contains the requisition number, production order number, code number of the department to which the materials were issued, quantity issued, and unit cost from materials requisitions evidencing issues from stores into production. This tape must be sorted into sequence by production order number prior to processing against the production order cost and operations data file. The computer run updates the material usage and cost records in this file. As outputs of the run emerge (1) a printed list of error transactions and summary information, which includes the summary journal entry debiting work-in-process and crediting raw materials inventory, and (2) a tape of material usage data, containing actual vs. standard usage and resulting cost variances for all completed operations. The latter tape is sorted by department number and processed to generate daily material usage reports for each production department.

Labor costing operations begin each day with the assembly of job time tickets into batches and computation of batch totals. Among the batch totals prepared might be a record count of the number of job time tickets and hash totals of employee number, pay rate, and hours worked. Job time records are then keyed onto magnetic tape, verified, and sorted into sequence by production order number for processing against the poduction order cost and operations data file.

In many firms the generally high volume of job time records, together with the relatively large data content of each record, will justify a more automated form of data preparation than the one illustrated. As described in conjunction with processing of move tickets, several possible techniques of source data automation may be used for this purpose, including portable data recorders, factory data collection terminals, or turnaround documents.

The next step in this operation is the processing of job time records to post the time of completion of operations and labor rate data to the production order cost and operations data file. If manufacturing overhead is applied on the basis of direct labor hours or direct labor cost, this process also calculates applied overhead costs and records these costs in the file. One output of this process is a printed listing of error transactions and summary information that includes the summary journal entry debiting work in process and crediting the payroll and manufacturing overhead control accounts. The report also contains the batch totals accumulated during the run, which are then compared with those compiled prior to input preparation as a data control check.

A second output of this processing run is a tape of labor cost efficiency data. This tape contains the actual and standard time and standard labor rate of all operations performed by all production employees during the day. The tape is sorted by

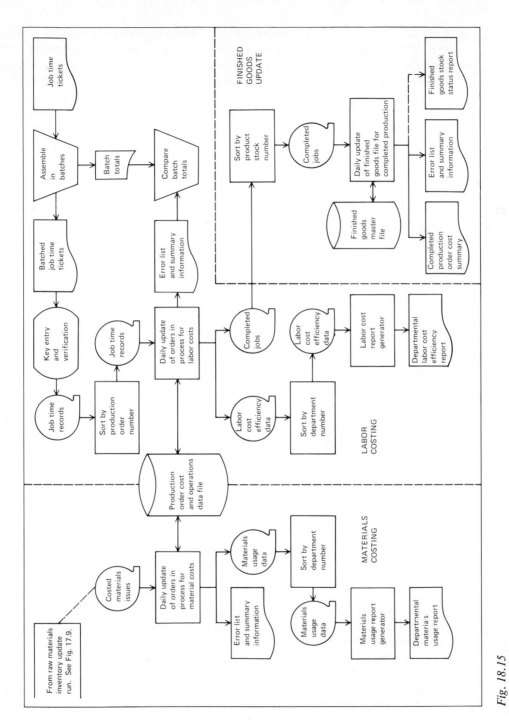

Fig. 18.15
Computerized batch processing system for cost accounting.

department number and employee code, and is then processed to generate for each production department a daily labor cost efficiency report similar to the one illustrated in Fig. 18.3.

The other output of this process is a tape listing of all cost data for production orders that are completely finished as a result of the operations represented by the job time cards. All records of such orders can be eliminated from the production order cost and operations data file because they no longer represent work-in-process inventory, nor do they require any further production scheduling. The completed jobs tape is sorted by finished goods inventory stock number and is processed to update the finished goods inventory master for the completed stock. The printed listing of error transactions and summary information generated from this run contains, among other things, the summary journal entry debiting finished goods and crediting work in process for the cost of manufacturing the items. The second printed report generated by this run is a series of completed production cost summaries for each product completed. Each of the summary reports on this printout details all production costs for the particular production order, and might follow a format similar to the cost summary sheet illustrated in Fig. 18.8.

The third and final report printed out by this run is a finished goods stock status report. As indicated by the dashed line in the illustration, this report is assumed to be prepared once each week rather than once a day, though the latter frequency could certainly be adhered to if considered beneficial. Because the report represents the third printed output of this run, some special provision may have to be made if the organization does not have three printers. One possibility is to write the finished goods stock status report on tape for subsequent printing. Another possibility is to store all data for the relatively small error list and summary report inside the computer until the completion of processing, at which time they would be printed out at the end of one of the other reports.

Control policies and procedures   Batch totals, turnaround documents, and key-verification are methods of control over the computerized production information system that are discussed above. The topics of data security and input validation as they relate specifically to this system are now addressed.

The focal point of data security in this system must be the production order cost and operations data file. If this file is destroyed, the basis for production scheduling and costing of work in process is lost. A duplicate copy of this file should be prepared at the completion of each day's processing. This copy and all subsequent transaction tapes, including the manufacturing authorization data tape, the move ticket data tape, the costed materials issues tape, and the job time records tape, should be saved to permit reconstruction of the current version of the file if necessary. Internal and external labels identifying the files and their dates of expiration should be used to help prevent the accidental destruction of one of these files. The tape file protection ring should be removed from all current versions of the tape files to protect against their being written on. The disk pack containing the current copy of the production order cost and operations data file should be stored in a file library when not in use, and removed only for authorized purposes. The backup copy of the master file and the related transaction tapes should be stored in a secure offsite location.

Three other master files maintained on disk in this system are the bill of materials file, the operations list file, and the finished goods master file. Disk packs containing these files should also be stored in the file library when not in use, and should be protected by the use of internal and external labels. Other tape files, including the scheduled operations tape, the materials usage data tape, the labor cost efficiency data tape, and the completed jobs tape, should be secured while in use by the removal of tape file protection rings and the use of internal and external labels.

Each of the five major file updating programs in the production information system should contain an input validation routine that performs several edit checks on each input transaction. Because each of these processes is performed in sequential order, a sequence check on the input records should always be performed. A validity check of the value in the control field of each input record must always be performed in a sequential file updating program. In addition, when updating the production order cost and operations data file for move tickets and job time tickets, the validity of the operation number, department number, and work station or machine number should be checked. When this file is updated for material issues, the validity of inventory stock number and department number should be checked. These validity checks are accomplished by comparing the values of these items on the input records with the values of the same items in the master record.

Field checks and reasonableness tests should be performed on the values of all numeric items that are not validity checked. The fields involved are quantity to be produced on the authorization-to-manufacture records, quantity completed on move tickets, quantity and unit cost on material issues, hours worked, pay rate and quantity completed on job time tickets, and quantity completed and unit cost on finished job records. The reasonableness of values for each of these items is tested by comparison with average or expected values recorded on the master files.

A final set of edit checks is necessary in all programs that update the production order cost and operations data file. In explanation, note that this file includes records of scheduled operations and requisitioned materials that are updated as operations are completed and materials are issued. Because of this, the programs that update the file can be written to detect any unreported operations performed and materials issued. For example, if the completion of operation A has not been recorded, but the completion of operation B that follows A has been recorded, an error exists—either A has been completed but not recorded, or B has been improperly recorded as complete. Similarly, if an issue of materials has not been recorded, but the completion of an operation requiring those materials has been recorded, an error exists. All discrepancies of this type should be reported on the list of error transactions.

Further control over production information processing is accomplished by review and follow-up on the various error transaction reports. This function should be the responsibility of personnel other than operators or programmers, preferably data control personnel or a supervisor. The source of each error transaction should be traced as a means of ensuring the accuracy of error corrections and identifying potential weak areas of control. Error corrections should be prepared and submitted to the system as quickly as possible.

A real-time system

In a manual or computerized batch processing system for production information processing, the cycle of planning and control information flows is repeated primarily daily or weekly. Production scheduling is done daily. Most production orders are initiated at the beginning of each week. Production cost data may be reported daily, weekly, or even monthly. In small firms, an information flow cycle of this length may be acceptable. As firms grow larger, the production management function will employ expediters to monitor production work requiring closer attention than that provided by daily or weekly feedback. At some point in the growth of a manufacturing firm, the use of an online computer system to provide real-time scheduling and control of production operations becomes economically feasible.

A system flowchart of a real-time production information processing system appears in Fig. 18.16. Online input devices are available within each department in the factory. These input devices could be keyboard data terminals, or they could be other types of data collection devices, such as optical readers that can interpret mark-sensed cards. Input data entered by factory workers using these devices would include the production order number, operation number, employee number, machine number, and materials quantity of all work performed, both at the time of starting and completing the work. Input data recording the movements of work-in-process from one work station to another would also be entered by factory personnel.

Because factory workers are prone to make errors in entering input data, the real-time production information system must utilize input validation routines and other techniques for maximizing the accuracy of data collection. Some data collection devices utilize card input, so that cards with some prerecorded data can accompany work-in-process and be used by each worker to enter input. Other devices can read an employee's number from a specially prepared identification badge. Input validation routines can compare entered data with data from schedules and, if significant differences are discovered, can request the worker to check the data for errors and reenter the data if necessary.

Input data on all factory activities are entered into the system as they occur. Therefore, the production data base contains current information on the status of all production orders, employees, machines, materials, costs, schedules, and so on. All of these status records are updated in a single integrated process as inputs recording the completion of an operation or the movement of materials are received from the factory. Furthermore, as illustrated in Fig. 18.4, the production data base links this current status information on production work-in-process to the engineering specifications within the product structure data base, and to raw materials and finished goods inventory information within the purchasing and marketing data bases.

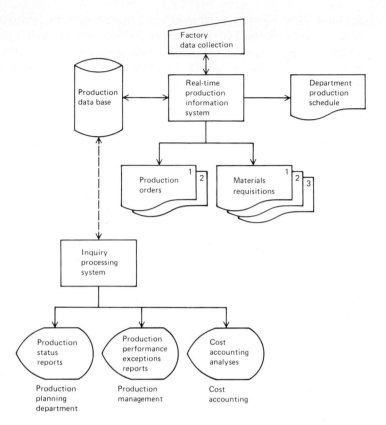

Fig. 18.16
Real-time production
information system.

In this system new production orders may either be triggered automatically or may be initiated by the production planning department. If the data base incorporates a master production plan indicating the quantity of each product scheduled for completion each week, then the system may be programmed to automatically initiate materials purchase orders, production orders, and materials requisitions at the necessary points in time. In addition, if special orders or rush orders are received, the production planning department may use its online terminal to enter the relevant data and initiate preparation of the necessary documents. The system prints multiple copies of production order and materials requisition documents as required.

The system also prepares departmental production schedules at the beginning of each factory shift, but has the capability to adjust scheduled operations on a real-time basis in response to changing conditions in the dynamic factory environment. Examples of such changing conditions include machine breakdowns, employee absenteeism or illness, operations which are not completed within the scheduled time, faulty materials, introduction of rush orders, and so forth. As such conditions are reported to it, the system reacts quickly to adjust its status records and reschedule operations in an optimal fashion.

An online inquiry processing system provides immediate access to the production data base for the cost accounting department, the production planning department, and other production executives using online display terminals. This system may be used to make inquiries into the current status of work in process, or to request reports analyzing production cost and efficiency. The content and format of such reports may either be predesigned, or may be determined by the user at the time of the inquiry.

The primary advantages provided by a real-time production information system involve improvements in the efficiency of operations through better scheduling and faster control reporting. With respect to scheduling, the objectives are to achieve maximum factory throughput and machine utilization while minimizing both the value of work-in-process inventories and the completion time of all orders in accordance with their relative priorities. With respect to production control, a real-time system can provide online monitoring of critical situations. For example, the system can check the status of rush orders at periodic intervals and prepare a report on any rush orders falling behind schedule. Scheduled operations on which no operator has reported starting or completing can be reported to the appropriate supervisor. Data input of questionable accuracy can be reported for follow-up and possible subsequent correction. Significant cost overruns can be reported as they occur if desired. Raw materials inventory can be reordered immediately as materials usage lowers available quantities below the reorder point. Current information is always available on the status of work in process in response to inquiries from management or production personnel.

Review Questions

1. Define the following terms.

backlog	expediting
bill of materials	dispatching
operations list	job order costing
routing sheet	process costing

2. Describe in general the decision responsibilities and information requirements of the production planning function.
3. What are three basic types of standards that must be met in the production operations control function? What information, from what sources, is required in controlling operations to achieve each standard?
4. Identify the two primary information subsystems in production planning and control.
5. What are the accounting journal entries that summarize the activities involved in the production process?
6. Explain the distinction between applied and actual overhead costs. Why is it necessary to use applied overhead costs in production costing?
7. Identify the relationships that exist between the production work-in-process data base and other data bases in a manufacturing company.

8. Describe the data content and organization of the production work-in-process data base. Identify the primary inputs to and outputs from this data base.

9. What departments in a business organization might be involved in the manual processing of production information? What documents and reports might be used, and what information would each contain? In what department would each document or report originate, and where and for what purpose would each be distributed?

10. What functions must be separated to achieve organizational independence with respect to production information systems?

11. What control policies and procedures are important in a production information processing system?

12. What special control procedures are necessary in a production information system in the event that actual materials usage is greater than or less than the amount originally requisitioned?

13. Describe possible similarities and differences in processing of production information using a computer system rather than a manual one. Emphasize documents, departments, and reports involved in the process.

14. Describe or illustrate how production orders and materials requisitions might be prepared by computer.

15. Explain several ways in which source data automation might be applied to the collection of data on production operations.

16. Explain or illustrate how the computer might be used to prepare production schedules for factory departments.

17. Describe several control policies and procedures that might be used in batch processing of production information by a typical manufacturing company utilizing a computer system.

18. Prepare a system flowchart of a real-time system for processing information for production planning and control.

19. What techniques could be used in a real-time production information system to minimize the possibility of acceptance of inaccurate input data?

20. Explain several advantages provided by a real-time production information system.

Discussion Questions

21. This and the preceding chapter primarily emphasized the logistics information requirements of a manufacturing firm. Discuss the basic similarities and differences in organization structure, information requirements, and data sources between the logistics system of a manufacturing firm and that of

   a) a transportation company, such as a railroad or airline,

   b) a construction company, or

   c) a professional service firm such as a public accounting partnership.

22. Would it be worthwhile for a manufacturing firm to have a real-time system that reports production cost variances on an hour-by-hour basis? Discuss.

Problems and Cases

23. What control policies and procedures in a production information system would provide the best control over the following situations?

   a) A production order was initiated for a product for which demand no longer exists.

   b) Items of in-process inventory were stolen by a production employee.

   c) The "rush order" tag on a partially completed production job became detached from the materials and lost, causing a costly delay in completing the job.

   d) A production employee prepared a materials requisition, used the document to obtain $300 worth of parts from the parts storeroom, and stole the parts.

   e) A supervisor's insistence that every worker in his department must learn to use every machine in his department resulted in an increase in the proportion of work done by the department that failed to pass quality control tests.

   f) A production worker entering job time data over a terminal mistakenly entered 3000 instead of 300 in the quantity completed field.

   g) A dishonest parts storeroom employee issued quantities of parts 10 percent lower than indicated on several materials requisitions, and stole the excess quantities.

   h) Incorrect keypunching of the production order number from a materials requisition caused a materials issue to be posted to the wrong production order.

24. Your company has just acquired a data base management system that will first be applied to production data. You are to design the product structure segment of the data base, which will include a bill of materials and operations list for each product. Currently these specifications are maintained on documents identical in format to those in Figs. 18.1 and 18.2. Prepare a data base design diagram for the product structure, using a format similar to that of Fig. 18.5.

25. Assume that you are a management consultant for a large public accounting firm. One of your firm's clients is the Willard Corporation, a medium-sized manufacturing firm. Willard's Controller has recently come to you for advice regarding the following problems.

   ■ The proportion of customer orders filled by the promised delivery date has declined from 90 percent to 50 percent within the past year.

   ■ Production costs have risen dramatically because of increased charges for overtime, rework, and idle time waiting for materials or machines.

   ■ The company has doubled the number of expediters employed from three to six with no noticeable lessening of the problems.

   What are some important questions you would ask the Controller in attempting to gain insight into these problems? Relate your questions specifically to the company's production information system and its approach to production management.

26. Your company has just acquired a data base management system that will first be applied to cost accounting data. These data are presently accumulated manually on production order cost summary forms identical to that shown in Fig.

18.8. You are to diagram the data structure of the production order cost summary segment of the data base as a first step in the application design. Use a format similar to that of Fig. 18.5.

27. In Fig. 18.17 is a document flowchart of data flows relating to production operations for the April Manufacturing Company.

Required

a) Describe several deficiencies in internal control in the system shown in Fig. 18.17. For each deficiency, indicate an error, manipulation, or inefficiency that could result.

b) Indicate the best means of remedying each deficiency described in part (a).

28. The Caesar Manufacturing Company uses sheet metal and other uncut and unshaped raw materials in its production process. Accordingly, control of materials usage and spoilage is a significant management problem. The company

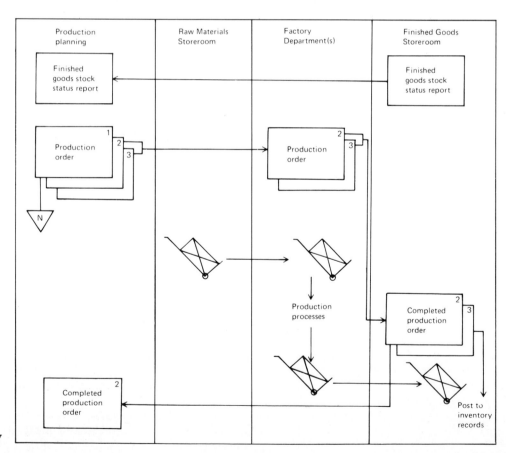

Figure 18.17

utilizes a standard cost system that specifies standard materials usage for each operation performed in production. Each departmental supervisor is responsible for materials usage variances arising from operations performed by the employees under his or her supervision on the machines in the department. The primary means of control available to supervisors are the assignment of employees to machines and supervision of employee work.

Required   Design a format for a daily materials usage report for a factory department. Make any reasonable assumptions about the availability of data for inclusion in the report. Make sure that you take into account the need to relate the report to the supervisor's objectives and decision alternatives. The report should present the vital information effectively and use the principle of management by exception.

29. The Miller Manufacturing Company maintains an online production work-in-process data base and updates it using a real-time factory data collection system. Upon completing a job, a factory employee enters (1) his or her employee number, (2) the machine number, (3) the production order number, (4) the operation number, and (5) the quantity completed. The system notes the time of each transaction, performs a variety of edit checks on the data input and, if the data are accepted, updates the appropriate records on the data base.

Required   Prepare a program flowchart of an input validation routine that checks the accuracy of each item of input data listed above. Note that it will be helpful for the system to access some data within the data base as a means of checking some or all of the input items. However, your flowchart should stop short of illustrating update procedures.

30. The Gibson Manufacturing Company utilizes an online production information system that has access to the following files stored on an online disk unit.

a) A production order file, which keeps track of the operations performed and still to be performed, the quantities in process, and the accumulated materials, labor, and overhead cost for all outstanding production orders.

b) A finished goods inventory file, which includes data on the quantity and production cost of all finished products in stock.

c) An employee data file, which is keyed by employee number and includes the employee's pay rate and all other essential payroll data.

One of the programs in this system processes data on completed operations entered by factory employees using terminals. For each operation completed, the following data are entered: production order number, operation number, employee number, quantity completed, start time, and stop time. The program performs various edit checks and validity checks on data entered. If the input is valid, the program updates the production order record for completion of the operation and corresponding labor cost data. If the operation represents the completion of the entire production order, the program updates the finished goods inventory file for the completed stock, writes a completed production order cost summary report on a separate disk file for subsequent processing by another program, and removes the completed production order record from the production order file.

Required

Prepare a macroflowchart of the program described above. Assume that the checking of whether the input data is valid represents one macrostep. Show all necessary input and output steps and each major decision and processing step, as required to complete the necessary processing.

31. Processing of production orders in the Monahan Manufacturing Company is performed as follows. At the end of each week the production planning department prepares a list of products and quantities to be produced during the next week. Using this list as a source, data entry personnel key "authorization to manufacture" records onto magnetic tape. This tape is sorted by the computer into product stock number sequence, and then processed together with an operations list file on magnetic tape to generate production orders. For each new production order, the program (1) prepares three copies of a production order document, (2) writes the production order onto a disk file of open production orders, and (3) punches an operations card for each operation to be performed on the production order.

The operations cards are used as turnaround documents. They are distributed to the factory departments where each operation is to be performed. After completing an operation, factory employees mark the elapsed time, quantity completed, etc., on the card and submit it to the data processing center. There a reproducer is used to mark sense and punch the data entered by the factory employees into the card. The cards are converted to magnetic tape using an off-line converter. The magnetic tape records are then sorted by production order number and processed to update the open production order master. After the master has been updated for all completed operations, the program generates departmental production schedules for the next day.

Required

a) Prepare a systems flowchart of all operations described.

b) Describe several control policies and procedures that should be incorporated into this computerized system. Indicate the purpose of each policy or procedure. Relate your answer specifically to the computer-related activities described in the case.

c) Explain how departmental production schedules may be generated from the updated production order master file without sorting that file by department number.

References   Appleton, Dan. "A Manufacturing Systems Cookbook, Part I." *Datamation* (May 1979): 179–184.

Arthur Andersen & Co. *A Guide for Studying and Evaluating Internal Accounting Controls.* Chicago: Arthur Andersen & Co., 1978.

Carbone, Frank J. "Automated Job Costing Helps Mulach Steel Stay Competitive." *Management Accounting* (June 1980): 29–31.

Caspole, John M. "Costing from a Data Bank." *Management Accounting* (July 1972): 47–50.

Hayes, Robert H., and Roger W. Schmenner. "How Should You Organize Manufacturing?" *Harvard Business Review* (January–February 1978): 105–118.

Karchner, Quentin L., Jr. "How One Plant Automated Its Collection of Data." *Management Accounting* (September 1980): 45–48.

Mammone, James L. "A Practical Approach to Productivity Measurement." *Management Accounting* (July 1980): 40–44.

Price Waterhouse & Co. *Guide to Accounting Controls: Purchases & Payables* New York: Price Waterhouse & Co., 1979.

Severance, Jay, and Ronald R. Bottin. "Work-in-Process Inventory Control through Data Base Concepts." *Management Accounting* (January 1979): 37–41.

Wright, Oliver W. *Production and Inventory Management in the Computer Age.* Cahners Publishing Co. Inc., 1974.

Chapter 19

Accounting Information Systems for Personnel Management

Personnel management involves planning, coordinating, and controlling the use of human resources within an organization. Information systems for personnel management are concerned with the processing of information about people within an organization—their recruitment, training, safety, and compensation. The accounting information system generates much useful information to personnel management through systems for processing employee payrolls. This chapter briefly reviews the personnel management function, discusses the nature and sources of personnel information, and finally explores in more detail the payroll processing system.

The Personnel Management Function

A typical organization structure for the personnel management function is illustrated in Fig. 19.1. However, the personnel management function in an organization does not take place entirely within the personnel organization. Every supervisor within an organization plays a major role in the management of the personnel under his or her supervision. In this sense, the personnel management function is the most decentralized of all of the management functions. The personnel organization is responsible for those personnel management activities that are most conveniently performed on a centralized basis. This section will review the personnel management responsibilities and related information requirements of the typical departmental supervisor, as well as of the top personnel executive and the various personnel staff functions.

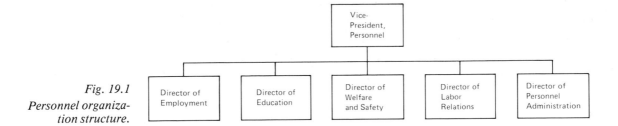

Fig. 19.1
*Personnel organiza-
tion structure.*

**The top personnel
executive**

The place of the top personnel executive in the organizational structure varies from company to company. In some companies, he or she is a vice-president with status equal to that of the vice-presidents for production, marketing, and finance. In other companies the position is subordinate to the vice-president for production. In the latter case responsibilities of the top personnel executive would primarily involve production employees, and executives in other functional areas would hold primary responsibility for personnel management within their respective areas.

Because of the increasing recognition of the importance of human resources to the business organization, the top personnel executive is increasingly being accepted as a participant in top-management planning for corporate resource allocation. In this role he or she contributes a perspective on the personnel management implications of corporate plans for expansion or contraction of operations. The formal output of this process should be a staffing plan, which forecasts the organization's needs for personnel of various skills and levels of education and experience. In addition, the top personnel executive is responsible for developing recommendations to top management concerning companywide personnel policies. Examples of such policies include hiring practices, job performance standards, health and safety standards, and wage and salary plans.

The top personnel executive is also responsible for the administration of the various personnel staff functions. The staffing plan provides a basis for planning and controlling the activities of employment and education and training. Major decisions in the areas of welfare and safety, labor relations, and personnel administration require the approval of the top personnel executive. The development of a personnel management organization, the delegation of authority to carry out personnel management activities, and the monitoring of performance of those activities are further administrative functions of the top personnel executive.

The information needs of the top personnel executive are broad. On the one hand, he or she requires quantitative information concerning the number of existing employees in various skill and experience categories, trends in hours worked, efficiency, accident rates, turnover and absenteeism, future staffing requirements, cost of alternative wage and salary proposals, existing labor market conditions, and so forth. Formal information systems are typically designed to fulfill many of these information requirements. On the other hand, the top personnel executive requires qualitative information involving such factors as employee motivation, morale, abilities, interpersonal relationships, etc. Factors of this sort are not as easily evaluated by formal information systems. However, information of this type is one of the primary products of informal information channels within an organization.

The personnel staff functions

The personnel staff functions of employment, education and training, welfare and safety, labor relations, and personnel administration are representative of the way in which personnel management responsibilities are functionally allocated in many large organizations. The primary responsibilities of each of these staff functions are reviewed briefly here.

The Director of Employment is responsible for such activities as the development of job specifications, recruiting, interviewing and testing of potential employees, and maintaining files of job applicants. The Director is also in charge of hiring, placement, and counseling, and may play a role in decision making with respect to promotions, and terminations. Programs for recruitment, hiring, training, and advancement of members of minority and disadvantaged groups are an important aspect of this function. The information requirements of the Director of Employment are both internal and external. The primary internal information need concerns staffing requirements within the firm—both job specifications and quantity requirements. The primary external information need concerns sources of staffing, such as employment agencies, training schools, and college placement offices.

The Director of Education and Training is responsible for developing the skills of personnel at all levels of the organization. At the lowest level this involves the training of machine operators and clerks. At a higher level it encompasses the training of supervisors and staff personnel. At its highest level it concerns the development of executive skills and experience. Essential to the administration of training programs are such factors as organization and planning of the training program; development of training materials; selection of trainees, instructors, and training site; and evaluation of results. Administration of executive programs includes determination of desired executive capabilities, selection of candidates, choice of a program of development, and evaluation of results.

The Director of Welfare and Safety is responsible for establishing and enforcing health and safety standards within the organization. With respect to health, this function involves maintaining employee medical records, administering physical examinations at the time of employment and periodically thereafter, and providing first-aid and other medical services. With respect to safety, such matters as the establishing of safety rules, planning for the use of protective clothing and mechanical safeguards, administering a program of safety education, and investigating the causes of accidents are involved.

In an organization that has a significant percentage of employees belonging to a union, the Director of Labor Relations plays an important role. This individual has the primary responsibility to prepare for and conduct collective bargaining negotiations with union representatives. Other responsibilities include handling of grievances and arbitration with respect to the union contract, and maintaining compliance with federal and state labor legislation.

The personnel administration function encompasses a variety of personnel services. These include wage and salary programs, profit sharing and incentive plans, pension plans, executive compensation packages, group insurance plans, employee credit unions, plant cafeterias, in-house publications, recreation programs, and employee suggestion plans. The function also includes the maintenance of up-to-date personnel records on all employees within the organization.

The departmental supervisor

Each departmental supervisor within an organization is directly responsible for the day-to-day planning, coordination, and control of that department's employees, and must organize the tasks to be performed, assign employees to jobs, coordinate their activities, motivate them, monitor their performance, evaluate their abilities, provide on-the-job training, and enforce company policies.

Much of the information required by the departmental supervisor to perform the personnel management function may be obtained simply from observation and experience. However, the formal information system provides useful supplementary information. This would include statistics concerning the productivity (output per work hour) of each employee at each job within the department. Among other useful information regarding individual employees are rate of absenteeism and tardiness, quality of work performed, and level of skills. Qualitative assessments provided by other employees or supervisors concerning personality and character may also be useful.

Sources of Personnel Information

The primary sources of personnel information are the accounting information system and the personnel department. Personnel information is also obtained from other sources inside the business organization as well as from external sources. This section reviews the nature of the information available from each of these sources.

The accounting information system

The payroll processing system is the traditional channel within which personnel information is generated from accounting data. The human resource accounting system is a new channel for such information and is, in fact, used in only a very small number of companies, primarily on an experimental basis. Both of these systems are discussed here; the payroll processing system is discussed in greater detail in a subsequent section. Cost estimation for wage negotiations is a third source of accounting information for personnel management discussed in this section.

The payroll processing system   With respect to the processing of factory payrolls, the two basic input documents are the job time card and the employee clock card. The nature and use of the job time card as a source of data for labor cost distribution is described in Chapter 18, and two examples of job time cards are illustrated in Figs. 18.10 and 18.14. The employee clock card, illustrated in Fig. 19.2, indicates the total number of hours the employee spends at work each day. This document serves as the basic input to the payroll calculation and paycheck preparation function.

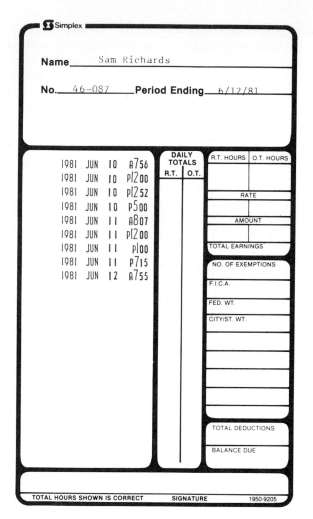

Fig. 19.2
Employee clock card.
(Courtesy of Simplex
Time Recorder Co.,
Gardner,
Massachusetts.)

With respect to the processing of payrolls for clerical, sales, and salaried employees, the nature of data input is somewhat different. Because administrative and selling expenses are not charged to production in process, the job time card is not used. However, a form similar to a job time card may be used if administrative expenses are charged to specific projects, such as a software development project, a sales promotion, or a research and development project. The employee clock card may be used for those clerical employees who are paid on an hourly basis, but is not needed for those paid a salary. The monthly gross pay of a salaried employee is a known constant, except in those cases in which some salaried employees are paid for overtime work. For salespeople paid on a commission basis, sales data are required for payroll processing.

Another basic class of inputs to the payroll processing system includes additions, deletions, and adjustments of various kinds to employee payroll records. The category of adjustments includes salary or wage rate changes, address changes, departmental transfers, changes in tax exemptions, changes in deduction authorizations, and so forth. The volume and variety of these transactions is often quite large.

Among basic outputs of payroll processing are employee paychecks and earnings statements and various reports required by governmental authorities. However, a variety of useful personnel information may be generated as a by-product of payroll processing. Reports that measure employee efficiency or productivity are one example. From the job time cards, the average time spent by each production employee in performing each job operation can be determined. For each operation the average time spent by all employees in performing that operation can be derived. If a standard cost system or work measurement system is used, a comparison of average actual time to standard time provides a measure of the efficiency with which each operation is being performed. The relative efficiency of each employee can be generated by taking a weighted average of his or her efficiency in all of the various operations performed by that person. Finally, the aggregation of these statistics by department provides a measure of departmental efficiency useful in evaluating the performance of departmental supervisors. If a standard cost system is employed, efficiency measures in the form of labor cost variances can also be provided. An example of a report containing information of this type is illustrated in Fig. 18.3.

Several other types of reports and analyses may be generated from payroll processing. These include reports of absenteeism and tardiness by employee; analyses of indirect labor by type of cost—supervision, materials handling, inspection, etc.—and by department; reports on actual and standard labor costs for completed production orders; analyses of overtime pay by department; analyses of fringe benefit costs; and reports on sales commission expenses. Also valuable in staff planning are certain aggregate statistics accumulated during payroll processing, such as total number of employees, total hours worked, total labor cost, average wage rate, rate of absenteeism, rate of turnover, and average and total fringe benefit costs. These statistics are most meaningful when trends in their values are analyzed and correlated with each other and with other factors. For example, useful management information may be obtained from correlating the rate of turnover with average hours worked per employee, or the rate of absenteeism with the number of units that fail to pass quality control inspection.

Human resource accounting   The basic philosophy of human resource accounting is that human resources are assets, and that the investment in acquiring and developing these resources should be accounted for as an asset. Expenditures for hiring and training, which would be expensed in conventional accounting systems, are capitalized and allocated to individual employees. As with the cost of other assets, this cost is amortized over the expected useful life of the asset. The net investment in an employee who is terminated is written off as a loss.

Useful information for staff planning is provided by the human resource accounting system. The year-to-year change in the total balance of the human resources account (annual investment minus amortization and turnover losses) provides an indication of management's performance in maintaining and developing human assets. Adding the human resources account into the total asset base may provide more significant measures of return on investment. Information concerning the probable loss of human resources is useful to decisions regarding employee lay-offs. Finally, capital investment information may be more meaningful if each investment proposed includes an analysis of the human resources that must be invested in the project and those that will be consumed by the project.

Human resource accounting is a new and unconventional technique. It is not recognized for tax purposes or for financial reporting under generally accepted accounting principles. Its uses imposes additional requirements for data collection and processing, record keeping, and reporting upon accounting information systems. Despite these disadvantages, human resource accounting seems likely to become an important element of accounting information systems in an age during which human knowledge and ability is recognized as being of critical importance to the modern business organization.[1]

Cost estimation for wage negotiations   Contract negotiations with labor unions require management to make trade-offs between such factors as the wage rate, paid vacations, paid holidays, contributions to employee insurance and pension plans, overtime premiums, and so forth. Each of these factors has a cost, and management should be provided with estimates of the cost implications of various alternative contract proposals to use as a basis for bargaining. Cost accountants and payroll accountants are in the best position to develop such estimates, and should therefore participate in this aspect of collective bargaining. Accounting systems should be designed to facilitate the preparation of whatever kinds of information management deems useful for this purpose.[2]

The personnel department   Much valuable information for personnel management is generated by and maintained within the personnel department. One of the best sources of information is the personnel data file, in which is maintained a complete record of each employee in the organization. This record includes such data as the physical characteristics of

---

[1] For further discussion of human resource accounting, see R. Lee Brummet, Eric G. Flamholtz, and William C. Pyle, "Human Resource Accounting—A Challenge for Accountants," The Accounting Review (April 1968): 217–224; and Mohammad A. Sangeladji, "Human Resource Accounting: A Refined Measurement Model," Management Accounting (December 1977): 48–52.

[2] For an extensive treatment of this topic, see Harry C. Fisher, The Uses of Accounting in Collective Bargaining, Institute of Industrial Relations, University of California, Los Angeles, 1969. Also see Walter A. Hazelton, "How to Cost Labor Settlements," Management Accounting (May 1979): 19–23.

the employee, background of education and experience, basic payroll information, quantitative and qualitative evaluations of past performance, state of health and medical history, results of tests of ability and aptitude, and so forth. This data file provides a basic source of information for decisions regarding assignment of employees to positions, approval of raises and promotions, and selection of supervisory and management trainees. If properly organized to facilitate information retrieval and aggregation, the employee data base can also be a useful tool for companywide staff planning.

Other information developed and maintained by the personnel department includes job specifications, which detail the training and experience required to qualify for each job in the organization; aggregate safety and accident statistics; forecasts of staffing requirements by job category within the organization; and records and statistics concerning training programs, health services, employee credit unions, and other employee services.

Other internal sources

One of the primary sources of personnel information is the departmental supervisor, who is responsible for providing merit evaluations of the employees under his or her supervision. These are basically qualitative evaluations of such factors as personality, initiative, attitude, judgment, and character. Departmental supervisors also supply the personnel department with information concerning the staffing requirements of their department in terms of the number of employees required and the desired qualifications.

Other functional departments within the firm may also contribute worthwhile information for personnel management. For example, the engineering department may develop job time standards for use in evaluating employee performance. The legal department may provide advice concerning legal aspects of employee relations. The economics department may provide special studies of labor market conditions and their implications for hiring policies or wage negotiations.

External information sources

External sources of information for personnel management include employment agencies, labor unions, vocational and training schools, university placement offices, and various governmental agencies. Information regarding potential employees may be obtained from employment agencies, schools, personal references, and in some cases labor unions. Labor unions also serve as a spokesperson for employees with respect to their satisfaction with the existing labor contract, and the topis that will most concern them during negotiation of the next contract. Various agencies of state and federal government often make available research studies or statistical compilations concerning such factors as labor market conditions, prevailing wage rates, levels of unemployment, industry accident rates, and so forth. College placement offices provide statistics on expected number of graduates by area of specialization. Personnel managers must be familiar with all of these various external sources of personnel information.

The Payroll Processing System

The general nature of the input to and output from payroll processing has already been reviewed. This section will outline the accounting transactions involved in the process, describe in detail the data maintained in the payroll master file, and then explore in some depth examples of a manual payroll system and a computer-based payroll system.

The accounting transactions

There are two basic accounting journal entries that reflect payroll processing. The first of these shows payroll cost distribution to various expense and inventory accounts.

Work-in-process inventory	XXX	
Manufacturing overhead	XXX	
General and administrative expense	XXX	
Selling Expense	XXX	
Payroll		XXX

The debit portions of this entry are classified according to the type of cost and the department number of the employee, and are accumulated for purposes of preparing departmental cost performance reports. The work-in-process portion of the entry is further classified and accumulated by production order as explained in Chapter 18.

The second of the two basic accounting journal entries in payroll processing reflects the payroll calculation and paycheck preparation process.

Payroll	XXX	
Federal Income Tax Withholdings Payable		XXX
FICA Tax Withholdings Payable		XXX
State Income Tax Withholdings Payable		XXX
Group Insurance Premiums Payable		XXX
Pension Fund Withholdings Payable		XXX
Savings Bond Deductions Payable		XXX
Union Dues Deductions Payable		XXX
Cash		XXX

The deduction accounts shown in the entry represent the most common payroll deductions. After the payroll preparation is completed, the total balance in each of these liability accounts is paid with a single check. The credit to cash represents the total of all employee paychecks issued. The debit to the payroll control account in this entry should be exactly equal to the total credit to this account in the previous entry.

The payroll data base

In manual data processing systems, a payroll master file is generally maintained by the accounting department, and a personnel master file is maintained by the personnel department. Since the entity—the employee—around which these files are organized is the same for both files, they are a prime candidate for integration when the organization converts to an automated system. Thus the payroll data base may be looked upon as a subset of the personnel data base.

An example of the data content and organization of a payroll data base is illustrated in Fig. 19.3. The figure indicates that there is a one-to-one relationship between an employee's personnel records and his or her payroll record. The payroll segment of the data base is in the form of a two-level tree, in which a series of deduction records form a repeating group within the employee payroll record.

Several fields shown within the payroll data base require further explanation. The "pay basis" code indicates whether the employee is paid on a hourly, salaried, or other basis. The "debit code" indicates the account to which the employee's gross pay is charged—direct labor, indirect labor, sales commission, etc. The "number of exemptions" and "marital code" are required for computing federal income tax withholdings. For each employee there will be a separate deduction record for each type of deduction from that employee's gross pay, including federal and state taxes, social security taxes, life and health insurance premiums, pension fund contributions, savings bond purchases, union dues, and so forth. Each deduction record contains codes identifying the type of deduction and the basis or rate of calculation. Quarterly and year-to-date totals of gross pay, net pay, and each type of deduction must be maintained for periodic reporting to the federal government.

The payroll data base is updated once at the end of each payroll period for all adjustments to employee records, new hires, terminations, and time worked data for hourly employees. The output of this process includes employee paychecks and earnings statements and a *payroll register,* which is a listing of payroll data for each employee for the current payroll period. A separate *deduction register* may also be prepared detailing the miscellaneous deductions of each employee. These two reports are illustrated in Fig. 19.4. At intervals other than during payroll preparation, the payroll data base is used to prepare various reports for managers and the government.

The processing of payroll transactions affects not only the payroll data base but also numerous other data bases within a business organization. For example, new hires, terminations, job transfers, pay increases, and similar transactions must also be posted to the personnel data base. If payroll and personnel records are properly integrated, then only one updating process will be required to post these transactions to all affected records. For another example, the debit distribution of the gross payroll must be posted to several data bases, including the production work-in-process data base (see Chapter 18), and numerous overhead and expense ledgers within the accounting data base (see Chapter 20). In a highly automated system, these operations could be integrated with payroll processing, but most business organizations have not yet achieved such a high level of integration.

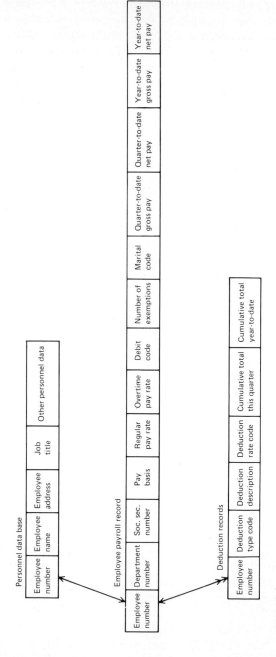

Fig. 19.3
Payroll data base.

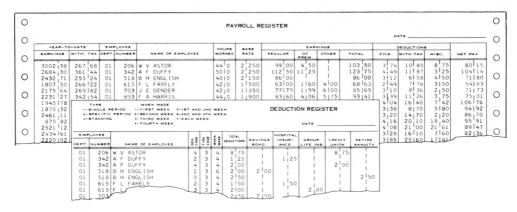

Fig. 19.4
Payroll and deduction registers. (Reprinted by permission from Basic Applications—System/360 Model 20. *Copyright © 1971 by International Business Machines Corporation.)*

A manual system   Figure 19.5 illustrates one example of a manual system for processing a factory payroll. Unless otherwise indicated in the discussion, the flowchart is also applicable to the processing of an office employee payroll. A payroll master file is maintained by the payroll department. Terminations, hirings of new employees, changes in employee wage rates, tax status, or deduction authorizations, and any other changes in this file that affect payroll preparation must be approved by the personnel department, which also maintains a record of this data for each employee in a personnel data file. Good internal control requires that the internal audit department periodically compare the payroll data in the payroll master file with that in the personnel file to prevent unauthorized changes in the payroll master.

Regular payroll processing begins with the collection of employee time worked data. The flowchart illustrates this process with respect to factory employees. The job time ticket is filled out by each employee for each job upon which he or she works during the day. For control purposes, each job time ticket should be verified and signed by the departmental supervisor.

Each day the job time tickets are transmitted to the timekeeping department where they are reconciled to the employee clock cards. The clock cards are generally prepared by using a time clock upon which employees punch in and out of work. The reconciliation step is a check that the total time spent at work by each employee is equal to the sum of the time spent on all production orders upon which the employee worked during the day. This internal check helps to ensure the accuracy of input data regarding time worked by factory employees prior to its use in various subsequent processing steps.

Time worked data for salaried employees does not need to be provided to the payroll department. Time worked data for factory service department or office employees who are paid on an hourly basis is generally provided by use of a time clock or by departmental supervisors. If salespeople are paid by commission, the payroll department must receive the required input from one of the marketing or sales departments.

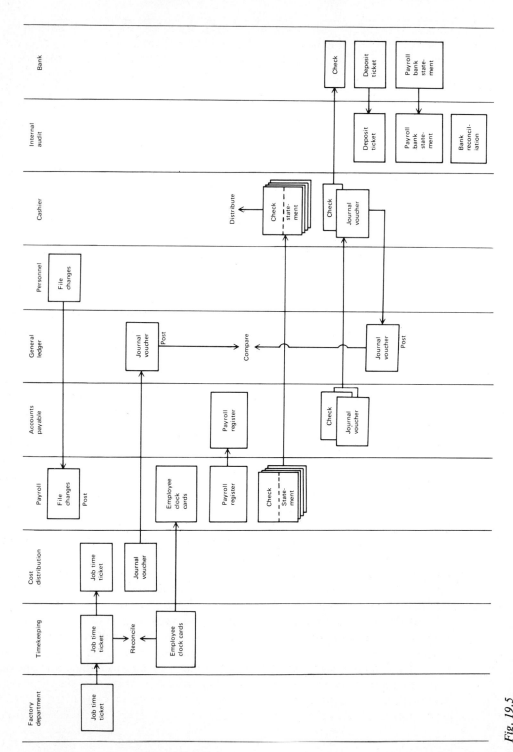

Fig. 19.5

Document flow in a manual system for payroll processing.

After reconciliation to employee clock cards, the job time tickets are provided to the cost accounting department for purposes of payroll cost distribution. At this point, direct labor costs are allocated to the various work-in-process accounts, and a journal voucher recording a debit to work-in-process inventory and credit to payroll is initiated and transmitted to the general ledger clerk. As explained in Chapter 18, applied factory overhead may also be calculated at this point, and would therefore be included on this journal voucher. The distribution of payroll costs to the various subsidiary ledger accounts of the manufacturing overhead ledger, the selling expense ledger, and the general and administrative expense ledger is not shown on the chart. This function is typically performed by the payroll department in a manual system, which department would then also be responsible for preparing the journal voucher summarizing the distribution.

Employee clock cards are provided to the payroll department where, together with the payroll master file, they provide the basis for preparation of employee paychecks and the payroll register. Once gross pay and all deductions have been computed and entered into the payroll register, net pay can be determined. When preparation of the payroll register is completed, the accuracy of net pay calculations is checked by cross-footing, or determining the sum of the gross pay, net pay, and deductions columns for all employees, and then comparing total gross pay with the sum of total net pay and deductions. Following this internal check, the individual paychecks and earnings statements are prepared and transmitted to the cashier for distribution to employees.

Next the payroll register is provided to the accounts payable department. On the basis of the column totals of the payroll register, a journal voucher recording the debit to the payroll control account and credit to cash and the various deduction accounts is prepared. At the same time, a check is prepared which authorizes the transfer of the net pay total from the firm's regular bank account to its payroll bank account. This check and journal voucher are provided to the cashier, who signs and deposits the check and forwards the journal voucher to the general ledger clerk. The payroll register is retained to provide an audit trail of the payroll process.

At this point, the general ledger clerk has received two journal vouchers. One records a debit to the payroll control account for the gross pay of factory employees, and the other a credit for the same item. The amount of these two entries to the payroll control account should be exactly equal. If the amounts are not equal, an error has occurred either in direct labor cost distribution or paycheck preparation, and the error must be discovered and corrected. This form of internal check is called a *zero balance check* because the balance of the payroll control account should be zero after these entries are made. Similar checks could be made on the payroll distribution to manufacturing overhead, selling expense, and general and administrative expense.

The use of a separate payroll bank account improves internal control because it facilitates the preparation of bank reconciliations. It is much easier to prepare two separate reconciliations, and to trace the source of any discrepancies, than to prepare one large reconciliation of a single account. Periodically the internal audit department must prepare the reconciliation of the payroll bank account. The payroll bank statement, deposit tickets, and cancelled paychecks provide a basis for this function.

Organizational independence with respect to payroll processing is achieved by the multitude of functional separations that exist in the system. Perhaps the most significant of these is the separation of timekeeping from payroll preparation, which tends to prevent errors or manipulations involving submission of time data for terminated or nonexistent employees. This type of error or manipulation is also inhibited by separation of payroll preparation from paycheck distribution, together with special procedures for handling unclaimed paychecks. Separation of the personnel function from the payroll preparation function along with periodic comparison of the payroll records of both functions tend to prevent errors or manipulations with respect to the payroll master file. Separation of the timekeeping function from the factory departments tends to prevent errors or manipulations involving input data for factory employees. Separation of the cost distribution and payroll preparation functions tends to prevent errors or manipulation in the distribution of payroll costs or the calculation of gross pay. Finally, the separate internal audit function provides an independent check on the operation of the entire payroll system.

Special control procedures are necessary in a payroll processing system for handling unclaimed paychecks. If paychecks are distributed by hand to employees, unclaimed paychecks for terminated or absent employees will be fairly common. Even if paychecks are distributed by mail, some may occasionally be returned for lack of a forwarding address. In any event the unclaimed paycheck indicates the possibility of manipulation. The internal audit department should trace the preparation of such paychecks to the original timekeeping records, and should check the payroll master file against the personnel master in all such cases. The internal audit department should make further attempts to distribute such checks to the proper persons and, if unsuccessful, should lock them up for safekeeping and eventually destroy them.

The internal audit department is also responsible for certain other internal control activities with respect to payroll processing. A sample of payroll calculations may be reviewed in detail for each payroll period. Payroll calculations of paychecks for employees of the payroll department should be reviewed frequently in detail. Periodically internal audit personnel should take charge of the distribution of paychecks to employees to ensure that all paychecks prepared are being received by bona fide employees.

The payroll processing function is one of the most time-consuming clerical functions in many organizations. In a manual payroll processing system it may be difficult to both complete payroll preparation and cost distribution and generate useful reports concerning labor costs, production efficiency, and so forth. Several devices have therefore been developed to facilitate payroll processing. One device is the payroll board, which is a type of pegboard designed so that several records may be written simultaneously using carbon paper. An example is illustrated in Fig. 19.6. In the board shown in the illustration, data written onto the employee earnings state-

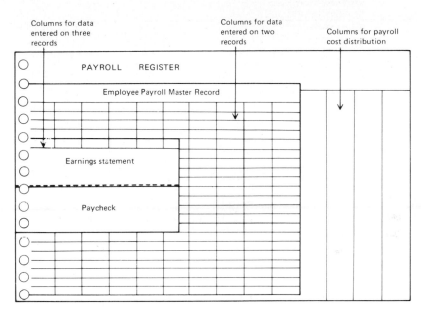

Columns for data
entered on three
records

Columns for data
entered on two
records

Columns for payroll
cost distribution

PAYROLL   REGISTER

Employee Payroll Master Record

Earnings statement

Paycheck

Fig. 19.6
Payroll board for
simultaneous writing
of payroll records.

ment are simultaneously written onto the employee payroll master record and the
payroll register. This data would include the employee's name and number, the date,
hours worked, gross pay, itemized withholdings, other deductions, and net pay.
Certain other data, such as check number and year-to-date earnings totals, are simultaneously written onto the employee payroll master record and the payroll register. The payroll cost distribution is entered only in the payroll register.

**A computer-
based batch
processing system**

Because of the volume and complexity of payroll processing, and the routine nature
of payroll calculations and records, this operation has generally been one of the first
to be computerized in most organizations. A document flowchart of a computer-
based system for processing a factory payroll in a typical manufacturing company
appears in Fig. 19.7. It is assumed that the payroll processing is performed in batch
mode using magnetic tape input and magnetic disk file storage. A comparison of this
system with its manual counterpart of Fig. 19.5 reveals that the computer has replaced the functions of cost distribution and payroll preparation, but that many of
the other functions remain unchanged.

The payroll master file is maintained by the computer operations department
on magnetic disk. File changes must be authorized by the personnel department, and
are then transmitted to the input preparation department for keying onto magnetic
tape. Job time tickets and employee clock cards are prepared in the same manner as
described for the manual system, but both of these input documents are also routed
to input preparation for keying onto tape.

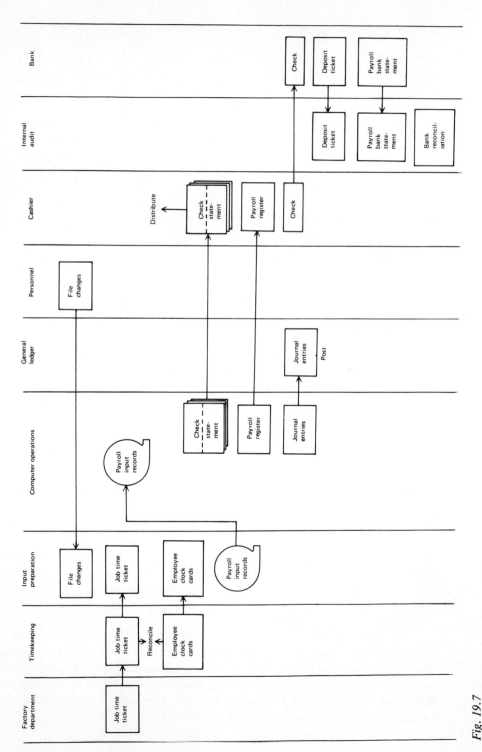

Fig. 19.7
Document flow in a computerized batch processing system for payroll processing.

As in the manual system, employee checks and earnings statements are sent to the cashier for distribution to employees. At the same time, the payroll register is sent to the cashier, who prepares the check to authorize transfer of funds to the payroll bank account. The journal entry printouts are provided to the general ledger clerk for posting. As in the manual system, the internal audit section is responsible for preparing a reconciliation of the payroll bank account.

After the various input records have been keyed and verified, the input tape is taken to computer operations for processing. The computerized processing of job time data to update records of cost and operations performed for production in process is discussed in Chapter 18 and illustrated in Fig. 18.15. The systems flowchart of Fig. 19.8 illustrates the computer processing of file changes and employee time card data to update the payroll master file and to prepare employee checks and earnings statements, the payroll register, and the summary payroll journal entry. The data preparation process generates batch totals and magnetic tape records sorted into sequence by employee number. The payroll register generated by the file update program is on magnetic tape, and must be processed again to prepare a printed payroll register.

Some of the internal controls described for the manual payroll processing system are replaced in the computerized system by new sets of controls. For example, such batch totals as record counts of the number of employee time records and the number of file changes of each type, as well as hash totals of employee numbers and hours worked, should be prepared from source documents and compared to those accumulated during processing. Batch totals from the payroll master file itself, including the number of employees and a hash total of employee wage rates, should also be accumulated during processing and printed out for comparison to personnel department records. The keying step should be controlled by keyverification and the use of check digit verification on employee numbers. Furthermore, a printout of file change records might be prepared and sent to the personnel department for verification of the integrity of all file changes processed.

Other important areas of control with respect to computerized payroll processing include data security and input validation. For example, the payroll master file and the payroll transactions and payroll register tapes should make use of both internal and external labels to prevent accidental processing of these files by the wrong program. A backup copy of the payroll master file should be written onto magnetic tape at the completion of the file update process, and stored in a secure offsite location. Tape file protection rings should be removed from the payroll transaction tape, the payroll register tape, and the backup master file tape to prevent them from being accidentally written on during processing. The disk pack containing the current copy of the payroll master file should be stored in the file library when not in use, and removed only for authorized purposes. Edit checks within the main payroll program should include a sequence check, validity check on employee number, field check and limit check on hours worked, and reasonableness tests on rate increases and other file changes affecting the payroll computations. The validity of the computations might also be tested by means of a limit check on gross pay and net pay. Any

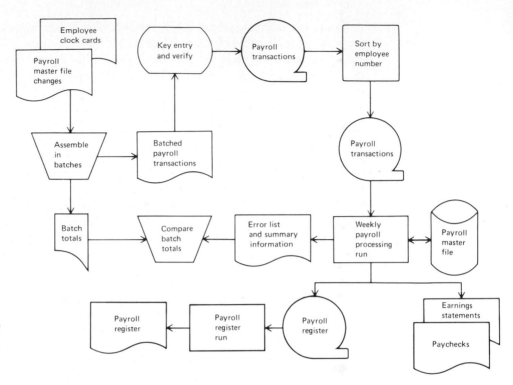

Fig. 19.8
Systems flow in computerized batch processing of payrolls.

records that violate one or more of these edit checks should be printed on the error list for subsequent follow-up and resubmission by someone independent of programming and operations.

Real-Time Systems for Personnel Management

The use of real-time systems for payroll processing is very uncommon because there is almost no need for immediate access to payroll data. The processing of payroll transactions occurs on a regular cycle, once each week or month, and all such transactions are processed together. This makes the payroll application ideally suited for batch processing. However, as described in Chapter 18, the processing of job time and job cost data on a real-time basis as part of a real-time production order processing system is fairly common.

With respect to personnel management in general, the use of real-time systems offers significant advantages in some cases. Such cases involve organizations in which employee skills are an extremely important resource, and decisions involving the selection and assignment of the human resource are frequently made. One example would be large organizations of professional people, such as management consultants, engineers, or lawyers, that sell the services of their employees for a fee, and that often must search for an employee whose specialized qualifications best meet the requirements of a client. Other examples include large placement services or employment agencies and military organizations. Large multidivisional corporations may also be interested in applying this approach to their top-managerial and staff personnel.

A real-time personnel management system of this type would center around a personnel data base maintained on direct access storage. The data base would be indexed according to classifications of skills, experience, and other qualifications possessed by employees. A software system would be designed to facilitate searching the data base for the names of employees possessing certain desired combinations of characteristics. For example, an employee may be sought who possesses an educational background in engineering and management, experience in industrial engineering, and the ability to speak a foreign language. If such an employee existed, that person's name could be retrieved by the system in a matter of seconds or minutes, and that person's qualifications listed or displayed for review by management. By means of the index of skills, the personnel data base becomes a *skills inventory file*.

Review Questions

1. Define the following terms.

   payroll register   zero balance check
   deduction register   skills inventory file

2. In very general terms, what is personnel management and what type of information is processed by an information system for personnel management?

3. Describe or illustrate an example of a typical personnel organization structure. Describe the responsibilities of each separate personnel function within the organization.

4. Describe the information requirements of the top personnel executive in an organization.

5. Describe the personnel management responsibilities and related information requirements of the typical departmental supervisor within an organization.

6. Describe the nature of the personnel information generated by
   a) the accounting information system,
   b) the personnel department,
   c) other sources of information within the business organization, and
   d) sources external to the business organization.

7. What input data is required for processing the payrolls of
   a) factory employees,
   b) salaried employees, and
   c) salespeople paid on a commission basis?

8. Identify several examples of nonroutine file maintenance transactions involving the payroll master file.

9. What is human resource accounting and how is it different from conventional accounting? Illustrate by means of sample journal entries.

10. What accounting journal entries summarize the activities involved in payroll processing?

11. Describe in detail the data content of a payroll data base.

12. What departments in a manufacturing company might be involved in the manual processing of payrolls? What documents might be processed and what data would each contain? Where would each originate, and where and for what purposes would it be distributed?

13. Describe several control procedures that might be used in a manual system for payroll processing.

14. How is organizational independence achieved with respect to payroll processing?

15. Explain some of the control procedures in payroll processing commonly performed by internal auditing personnel.

16. What is a payroll board and how might it be used?

17. Describe the similarities and differences in processing of payrolls in a typical business organization using a computer rather than a manual data processing system. Emphasize documents, departments, and reports involved in the process.

18. What internal controls might be used in computerized payroll processing?

19. Why is it uncommon for real-time systems to be applied to payroll processing?

20. What type of organization would utilize a real-time system for personnel management? Explain how such a system would be useful.

Discussion Questions

21. Do some research to discover how financial accounting theorists define the term ''asset.'' Are human resources considered as assets under this definition? Is it possible to record human resources as assets under generally accepted accounting principles? Should it be possible to do so? Discuss.

22. Do you expect that in the near future most large firms will utilize a real-time personnel management system? Discuss.

23. Does a good departmental supervisor really need quantitative information, such as measures of employee productivity, to adequately perform the personnel management function? Discuss.

Problems and Cases

24. The Future Corporation is a small manufacturing concern in Aggie, Texas. It maintains one plant and employs 50 workers in its operations. The employees are paid weekly. The department supervisors supply the payroll clerk with signed time sheets. The clerk compares the time sheets with the time cards and prepares the checks. The checks are then given in sealed envelopes to the supervisors, who in turn give them to the respective employees. Comment on the internal control in the company's payroll system.

25. You are engaged in auditing the financial statements of Henry Brown, a large independent contractor. All employees are paid in cash because Mr. Brown believes this arrangement reduces clerical expenses and is preferred by his employees.

During the audit you find in the petty cash fund approximately $200, of which $185 is stated to be unclaimed wages. Further investigation reveals that Mr. Brown has installed the procedure of putting any unclaimed wages in the petty cash fund so that the cash can be used for disbursements. When the claimant to the wages appears, he or she is paid from the petty cash fund. Mr. Brown contends that this procedure reduces the number of checks drawn to replenish the petty cash fund and centers the responsibility for all cash on hand in one person inasmuch as the petty cash custodian distributes the pay envelopes.

a) Does Mr. Brown's system provide proper internal control of unclaimed wages? Explain fully.

b) Because Mr. Brown insists on paying salaries in cash, what procedures would you recommend to provide better internal control over unclaimed wages?[3]

26. What controls in a manual system for processing factory payrolls are designed to provide the best protection against the following errors or manipulations?

a) The carrying of names of former employees on the payroll after their termination in order to receive and cash their paychecks.

b) Incorrect recording of hours worked on a job.

c) A dishonest payroll employee overstating the pay rate or hours worked of friends in order that their paychecks are higher than they should be.

d) A factory employee punches a friend's clock card in at 1:00 and out at 5:00 while the friend spends the afternoon playing golf.

e) An arithmetic error in calculation of gross pay for a factory employee.

f) Incorrect calculation of federal income tax deduction such that gross pay does not equal the sum of all deductions plus net pay.

g) The cashier pocketing and cashing unclaimed paychecks of terminated employees.

h) An arithmetic error in the calculation of labor costs allocated to jobs in process.

27. Prepare a record layout for the following payroll transactions that are to be processed as input to a computerized payroll data base identical to that in Fig. 19.3.

a) Add an employee payroll record for a newly hired employee.

b) Change an existing employee's number of exemptions.

c) Add a deduction record for an employee who authorizes a monthly savings bond deduction.

d) Change an employee's regular pay rate.

---

[3] *Question 3, Auditing Section,* American Institute of Certified Public Accountants Examination. *November 1961. Copyright © 1961 by the American Institute of Certified Public Accountants, Inc., and reprinted with permission.*

28. The Kowal Manufacturing Company employs about 50 production workers and has the following payroll procedures.

    The factory supervisor interviews applicants and on the basis of the interview either hires or rejects the applicants. The applicant who is hired prepares a W-4 form (Employee's Withholding Exemption Certificate) and gives it to the supervisor. The supervisor writes the hourly rate of pay for the new employee in the corner of the W-4 form and then gives the form to a payroll clerk as notice that the worker has been employed. The supervisor verbally advises the payroll department of rate adjustments.

    A supply of blank time cards is kept in a box near the entrance to the factory. All workers take a time card on Monday morning, fill in their names, and note in pencil on the time card their daily arrival and departure times. At the end of the week the workers drop the time cards in a box near the door to the factory. The completed time cards are taken from the box on Monday morning by a payroll clerk. Two payroll clerks divide the cards alphabetically between them, one taking the A to L section of the payroll and the other taking the M to Z section. Each clerk is fully responsible for a section of the payroll. The clerk computes the gross pay, deductions, and net pay, posts the details to the employee's earnings records, and prepares and numbers the payroll checks. Employees are automatically removed from the payroll when they fail to turn in a time card.

    The payroll checks are manually signed by the chief accountant and given to the supervisor. The supervisor distributes the checks to the workers in the factory and arranges for the delivery of the checks to the workers who are absent. The payroll bank account is reconciled by the chief accountant who also prepares the various quarterly and annual payroll tax reports.

    List your suggestions for improving the Kowal Manufacturing Company's system of internal control for the factory hiring practices and payroll procedures.[4]

29. The Karras Corporation is a large multidivisional enterprise. One of its divisions is located in Farmbelt, Iowa. In the spring of 1978 the personnel manager of the Farmbelt Division and an assistant went on a recruiting trip to several midwest business schools. Four graduating business school students were hired as management trainees. The total cost of the recruiting trip was $2000.

    In the summer of 1978 the four management trainees were sent to Chicago for a corporate training program. Travel and lodging for the trip cost $1200. Corporate headquarters charged the division $400 per trainee as the cost of the training session. Upon completion of the training program, each of the four new employees was assigned to an assistant manager position at the Farmbelt Division.

    In late 1978 Karras Corporation's top management decided to institute an extreme cost-cutting campaign for the year 1979. The Manager of the Farmbelt Division wondered whether to retain the services of the four new assistant managers. The Manager had planned to assign them to permanent management positions in July 1979. If they were released, their salaries of $8400 each for the

---

[4] *Question 2, Auditing Section,* American Institute of Certified Public Accountants Examination, *May 1964. Copyright © 1964 by the American Institute of Certified Public Accountants, Inc., and reprinted with permission.*

first six months of 1979 could be saved. However, four new employees would eventually have to be recruited, trained, and allowed to gain some experience for the four management positions that would be open July 1979.

a) Show by means of journal entries how the recruiting, training, and travel expenditures would be treated using conventional accounting principles.

b) Show by means of journal entries how the recruiting, training, and travel expenditures would be treated using human resource accounting.

c) If the four new assistant managers are released, what journal entry would be made in (1) a conventional accounting system; (2) a human resource accounting system?

d) Would the conventional or human resource accounting system provide more meaningful information in this case for purposes of deciding whether to release or retain the four assistant managers? Explain.

30. Describe internal controls in a computerized system for payroll processing that are designed to provide the best protection against the following errors or manipulations.

a) Overstatement of an employee's wage rate on the payroll master file.

b) Placing the name of a fictitious employee on the payroll master file.

c) Entry of 80 as the value of hours worked on a particular date for an employee who only worked eight hours on that date.

d) A computer operator entering a payroll transaction card to increase the operator's own salary by 50 percent.

e) A programmer obtaining the payroll master file and entering an increase in his own salary.

f) Accidental erasure of a portion of the payroll master file tape by a computer operator making an error correction entry over the console.

g) Destruction of a large portion of the payroll master file when the disk pack containing the file was used as a scratch file for another application.

31. The Sharpesville Insurance Company utilizes a computer-based system with disk file storage. Among the files it maintains on disk are a salesperson's payroll master sequenced by salesperson number, and a policyholder's master sequenced by policy number.

Each salesperson's monthly gross pay is equal to $500 plus commission. Each salesperson's commission is calculated as 5 percent of all premiums collected during the first year of the policy from policyholders who purchased from the salesperson, and 1 percent of all premiums collected during the next four years from those policyholders.

Each day the policyholder's master file is updated for new policies sold and premium payments received on outstanding policies. All premium payments are collected on a monthly basis. At the end of each month, the policyholder's master and salesperson's payroll master are processed to generate salesman's paychecks. Each salesperson's paycheck and payroll statement data are punched onto cards, which are subsequently processed on an interpreter and distributed to salespersons. Other outputs from this run include three printed reports—a payroll register, a listing of all policyholders who did not pay their premium for the month, and a summary report.

a) What data must be contained in each policyholder master record in order for that file to be used as described above in generating salespersons' payroll data? (Do not mention policyholder master data that are not used in generating salespersons' payroll data.)

b) Prepare a systems flowchart of the monthly payroll processing run described above.

c) Assume that the processing illustrated in part (b) is done sequentially. What operation must then be performed on the policyholder's master file prior to the run?

d) What accounting journal entry would be accumulated in the run and printed out as part of the summary information? (Show accounts debited and accounts credited.)

e) Prepare a macroflowchart of the monthly payroll processing program. The flowchart should include (1) separate input and output symbols for each file processed in the run; (2) decision symbols necessary to accomplish sequential processing, to determine whether or not to include each policyholder on the listing of policyholders behind on premium payments, and to determine the appropriate rate to be used in calculating the salesperson's commission; and (3) a single processing step representing calculation of net pay, and all processing steps necessary to accumulate gross pay.

32. The Mayberry Corporation has acquired a tape-oriented computer system that will perform several clerical functions previously done manually. You have been called upon to design a computerized system for one of these functions—the processing of factory payrolls.

The computerized system will include a medium-sized central processor, several tape drive units, one card reader, one printer, and several keypunch and verifier units. No other hardware is available for use in payroll processing.

You have investigated the existing manual system and have discovered that it operates in the following manner. Employee clock cards are maintained in the timekeeping department, each of which contains an employee number and name and the time clocked in and out of work for each day of the week by the employee. All of these cards are sent to the payroll department at the end of each week. The payroll department also receives data on new employees, employee terminations, changes in address or deductions, and other nonroutine payroll transactions from the personnel department. The payroll clerks perform all steps necessary to prepare employee paychecks and earnings statements, to prepare a payroll register (weekly listing of payroll data for each employee), and to maintain payroll records as required for producing quarterly and annual summary reports on employee earnings and withholdings as required by the government.

Your discussions with various system users have produced one major finding. Factory supervisors are unanimous in requesting a weekly report on employee tardiness and absenteeism, which would include such data as the average number of hours lost through lateness and absenteeism per week during the current year for each employee in the supervisor's department.

Required   a) Describe the data content of any master file or files necessary to perform the payroll processing by computer.

b) Prepare a systems flowchart representing a preliminary design of the computerized payroll processing system. Show all operations required, commencing with receipt of source documents and terminating with production of all necessary system outputs. For simplicity, do not include in this preliminary design any internal control operations.

33. The Darwin Department Store pays all of its employees on a salaried basis. Payroll processing is done once monthly by computer. The payroll master file is maintained on a disk file. The only transaction inputs to the run are file changes on magnetic tape. Outputs include (1) a report listing error transactions and summary information, (2) employee checks and earnings statements on punched cards, and (3) a payroll register on magnetic tape. The processing is done sequentially. The check and earnings statement cards are subsequently processed on an offline device to print the appropriate data on the face of the cards. The payroll register tape is also processed by a utility routine to prepare a printed payroll register printout.

Required   a) Explain what is meant by "file changes" in the description above. Give four examples you would expect to find in this process.

b) Prepare a systems flowchart of the computer processes described above.

c) List the components of the hardware configuration necessary to accomplish all phases of the processing described in the case subsequent to keypunching. Be sure to allow for necessary offline operations.

d) Describe a comprehensive set of control policies and procedures for this payroll processing application. For each policy or procedure, indicate its objective and exactly how it would operate. Be sure to relate each policy or procedure specifically to the payroll processing system described above.

34. You are reviewing audit work papers containing a narrative description of the Tenney Corporation's factory payroll system. A portion of that narrative is as follows.

Factory employees punch time clock cards each day when entering or leaving the shop. At the end of each week the timekeeping department collects the time cards and prepares duplicate batch-control slips by department showing total hours and number of employees. The time cards and original batch-control slips are sent to the payroll accounting section. The second copies of the batch-control slips are filed by date.

In the payroll accounting section payroll transaction cards are keypunched from the information on the time cards, and a batch total card for each batch is keypunched from the batch-control slip. The time cards and batch-control slips are then filed by batch for possible reference. The payroll transaction cards and batch total card are sent to data processing where they are sorted by employee number within batch. Each batch is edited by a computer program which checks the validity of employee number against a master employee tape file and the total hours and number of employees against the batch total card. A detail printout by batch and employee number is produced which indicates batches

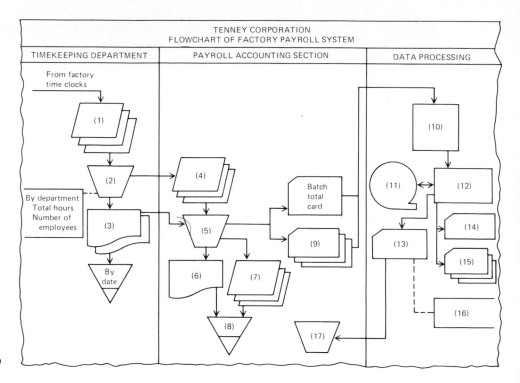

Figure 19.9

that do not balance and invalid employee numbers. This printout is returned to payroll accounting to resolve all differences.

In searching for documentation you found a flowchart (Fig. 19.9) of the payroll system which included all appropriate symbols (American National Standards Institute, Inc.) but was only partially labeled. The portion of this flowchart described by the above narrative appears in Fig. 19.9.

Required

a) Number your answer 1 through 17. Next to the corresponding number of your answer, supply the appropriate labeling (document name, process description, or file order) applicable to each numbered symbol on the flowchart.

b) Flowcharts are one of the aids an auditor may use to determine and evaluate a client's internal control system. List advantages of using flowcharts in this context.[5]

35. In connection with an examination of the financial statements of the Olympia Manufacturing Company, a CPA is reviewing procedures for accumulating direct labor hours. The CPA learns that all production is by job order and that all employees are paid hourly wages, with time-and-one-half for overtime

[5] *Question 7, Auditing Section,* American Institute of Certified Public Accountants Examination, *November 1974. Material from the Uniform CPA Examinations, copyright © 1974 by the American Institute of Certified Public Accountants, is reprinted (or adapted) with permission.*

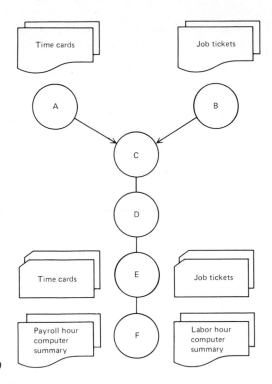

Figure 19.10

hours. Olympia's direct labor hour input process for payroll and job-cost determination is summarized in the flowchart shown in Fig. 19.10.

Steps A and C are performed in timekeeping, step B in the factory operating departments, step D in payroll audit and control, step E in data preparation (keypunch), and step F in computer operations.

Required

For each input processing step A through F
a) list the possible errors or discrepancies that may occur, and
b) cite the corresponding control procedure that should be in effect for each error or discrepancy.

Note: Your discussion of Olympia's procedures should be limited to the input process for direct labor hours, as shown in steps A through F in the flowchart. Do not discuss personnel procedures for hiring, promotion, termination, and pay rate authorization. In step F do not discuss equipment, computer program, and general computer operational controls.

Organize your answer for each input-processing step as follows.[6]

Step	Possible Errors or Discrepancies	Control Procedures

References

Brummet, R. Lee; Eric G. Flamholtz; and William C. Pyle. "Human Resource Accounting—A Challenge for Accountants." *The Accounting Review* (April 1968): 217–224.

Campion, William M., and Richard M. Peters. "How to Analyze Manpower Requirements Forecasts." *Management Accounting* (September 1979): 45–50.

Fahnline, R. H. "The Skills Inventory Put On." *Journal of Systems Management* (May 1974): 14–21.

Famularo, Joseph J. (ed.). *Handbook of Modern Personnel Administration.* New York: McGraw-Hill, 1972.

Fisher, Harry C. *The Uses of Accounting in Collective Bargaining.* Institute of Industrial Relations, University of California, Los Angeles, 1969.

Foulkes, Fred K. "The Expanding Role of the Personnel Function." *Harvard Business Review* (March-April 1975): 71–84.

_____, and Henry M. Morgan. "Organizing and Staffing the Personnel Function." *Harvard Business Review* (May–June 1977): 142–154.

Hazelton, Walter A. "How to Cost Labor Settlements." *Management Accounting* (May 1979): 19–23.

Kaumeyer, Richard A. *Planning and Using Skills Inventory Systems.* New York: Van Nostrand Reinhold, 1979.

Price Waterhouse & Co. *Guide to Accounting Controls: Employee Compensation & Benefits.* New York: Price Waterhouse & Co., 1979.

Sangeladji, Mohammad A. "Human Resource Accounting: A Refined Measurement Model." *Management Accounting* (December 1977): 48–52.

Chapter 20

Accounting Information Systems for Financial Management

Financial management involves decisions relating to sources of financing for, and uses of financial resources within, an organization. Financial information is any information concerning the flow of dollars through the organization. Virtually all activities and decisions within an organization are reflected in financial information. The financial management function and systems for providing financial information are thus vital to all business organizations, as well as to most other types of organizations. This chapter discusses the nature of the financial management function, and of systems for generating financial information, within the typical business organization.

The Financial Management Function

The financial management function encompasses both the role of treasurership, or administration of the finance function, and controllership, or administration of the accounting function. In many business organizations, the treasurership and controllership functions are combined organizationally under the authority of an Executive Vice-President for Finance. An example of an organization structure of this type is illustrated in Fig. 20.1. The controllership function encompasses the collection and processing of transaction data and the reporting and interpretation of financial information. To the modern business organization, attempting to generate an economic profit from scarce resources in a competitive environment, the avail-

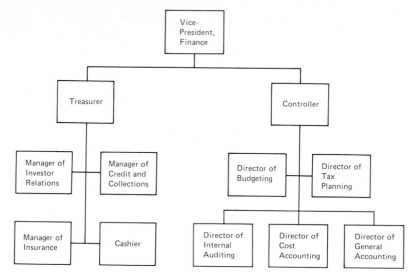

Fig. 20.1
Organization struc-
ture for financial
management.

ability of relevant, timely, and reliable financial information is essential. Because of the importance of the financial reporting and interpretation activity, the controller has become an important participant in managerial decision making at the top level.

The controllership function and its subsidiary functions—budgeting, tax planning, internal auditing, cost accounting, and general accounting—are discussed in Chapter 2 and elsewhere throughout this book. Therefore, the remainder of this section concentrates upon the functions of the top financial executive, the treasurer, and the various staff functions reporting to the treasurer. Each of these is discussed here in turn.

The top financial executive

The top financial executive, often having the title of financial vice-president, is responsible both for administration of the functions under his or her authority and for making decisions and recommendations involving the most important aspects of the finance function. Into the latter category fall decisions concerning long-term financing, dividend policy, capital budgeting, short-term management of cash flows, and allocation of resources within the enterprise.

Decisions concerning long-term financing are generally made very infrequently in most business organizations, perhaps only once every few years. However, each major decision in this area will have a significant impact upon the firm's success and growth over an extended period of time. The two most crucial aspects of the long-term financing decision are timing and sources. The timing aspect involves determining the point in time at which entry into the capital markets can be achieved on terms most favorable to the firm. Selecting the sources of long-term financing involves choices among such alternatives as issuing bonds, common stock, or preferred stock. Dividend policy is also closely related to long-term financing because another source of long-term funds consists of retained earnings that are not paid out as dividends.

Much of the information required for decisions on long-term financing is external information concerning, for example, the state of the economy and its impact on stock and bond prices, interest rates, and the capital markets generally. Internally generated information useful to decision making in this area includes long-term past and future information regarding the firm's financial position and earnings performance. The basic financial statements generated by the accounting function—balance sheet, income statement, etc.—provide a perspective on past trends and present conditions in this regard. Major plans developed by top executives, and financial projections generated on the basis of such plans, are also an important source of information input.

Planning and control of capital expenditures are other areas of decision making in which the top financial executive is deeply involved. The planning of capital expenditures involves determining the total size of the capital expenditures budget for the firm each year or quarter, and choosing among alternative fixed asset purchases. The control of capital expenditures deals with establishing policies for granting approval of expenditure requests and following up on the execution of the expenditure and the installation of the asset.

The information required for capital expenditure planning consists primarily of estimates of cash inflows and outflows and of risk factors associated with alternative fixed asset purchases. The discounting technique should be applied to cash flow estimates to derive a net present value for each alternative investment.[1] The availability of funds for capital expenditures may be estimated on the basis of sales forecasts and earnings projections. Information for control of capital expenditures begins with the formal request for authorization of the expenditure, which indicates the costs associated with the purchase, the expected benefits, and the projected revenues or cost savings. When the asset is purchased and received, a record of all vital data relating to the asset should be prepared and maintained for as long as the asset is owned and used. Other control information may be generated from follow-up studies that evaluate the accuracy of the original cost and revenue estimates.

Planning and control of operating expenditures are other areas of major concern to the top financial executive. These involve the preparation of annual operating budgets for departments and divisions within the organization, and the establishment of systems of control reporting that generate comparisons of actual performance of each department or division with the operating budget. Finally, planning and control of operating expenditures involve the interpretation of reported operating performance to provide a basis for managerial decisions and actions.

---

[1] *For an extensive treatment of capital budgeting and cash flow discounting, see Harold Bierman and Seymour Smidt,* The Capital Budgeting Decision *(5th ed.). New York: Macmillan, 1980.*

The treasurer   The treasurership function is primarily concerned with the management of short-term cash flows and with policymaking and administration with respect to various staff functions under the treasurer's authority. Cash management involves decisions relating to the investment of cash balances in excess of short-term cash requirements and decisions on timing and sources of short-term cash borrowing. Alternatives for short-term cash investment include United States Treasury bills, bank certificates of deposit, and commercial paper. Alternative sources of short-term borrowing include trade credit, commercial bank unsecured credit, and secured loans using inventories or accounts receivable as collateral.

The information requirements of short-term-cash management involve both external and internal information. Decisions on investment of idle cash require information on the nature, yield, and maturity dates of various alternative investments. Decisions on short-term borrowing utilize information relating to sources of supply. The timing decision primarily depends on internal information concerning when excess cash balances will be available, or when short-term borrowing will be required. Short-term cash budgets that project weekly or monthly cash flows for the immediate future are one source of such information. These budgets may be supplemented by revenue projections generated from accounts receivable data, and by cash outflow projections generated from accounts payable and purchase commitments data.

Manager of investor relations   The manager of investor relations has the responsibility of developing and maintaining a satisfactory market for the firm's securities. This entails communications with stockholders; with security analysts, who advise investors; with stock exchanges, through which securities are traded; with investment bankers, through whom new securities are issued; and with the Securities and Exchange Commission, which regulates the securities markets. The information requirements of this position are primarily external. The stockholder recordkeeping system provides some information of use to the investor relations manager, such as reports on the holdings and dealings of the company's largest shareholders. In addition, much company information is funneled through the investor relations manager and reported to stockholders, security analysts, and others interested in the company's activities.

Manager of credit and collections   The manager of credit and collections has the responsibility of developing and administering policies relating to the granting of credit and collection of accounts. Credit granting policies, credit limits, and collection procedures must be tight enough to avoid tying up funds in accounts receivable that could be profitably invested elsewhere. On the other hand, such policies and procedures must be loose enough to avoid the loss of sales and customers. The manager of credit and collections must find the optimum point of trade-off between these two objectives.

Some of the information requirements of the credit and collections function are external. For example, information on the credit worthiness of new customers is required to decide whether and to what limit to extend credit to them. Primary external sources of credit information include Dun & Bradstreet, which provides credit reports and ratings on business firms, and local credit bureaus, which provide credit reports on individuals. Much internal information should also be available to assist in credit decisions. Records of the payment history of a customer are useful to making decisions on whether to extend further credit. Records of current past due balances are also relevant to the credit granting decision, and necessary to the decision of whether to initiate special collection procedures. Reports analyzing customer accounts written off as uncollectible are constructive in the establishment of credit granting policies.

Manager of insurance

The manager of insurance is responsible for identifying and evaluating potential losses to the firm that are insurable, selecting the appropriate mix of insurance coverage and other methods for dealing with the potential losses, obtaining insurance coverage on terms favorable to the firm, and administering the firm's various insurance contracts. This responsibility requires the use of both external and internal information in decision making. External information requirements include knowledge of the characteristics and costs of various types of available insurance coverage. Examples of internal information requirements are measures of potential loss from physical damage to assets, disability or death of key employees, criminal action, and fraud or negligence on the part of employees. In the case of physical damage to assets, accounting records provide some useful information. However, in the case of the other types of losses mentioned, accurate measures of size and likelihood of potential loss may be hard to develop from available information. For administration of insurance programs, the insurance manager must receive information concerning payment of premiums, execution of new insurance contracts in accordance with established policies, maintenance and funding of reserves for self-insurance, and reporting and collection of claims.

Cashier

The function of cashier is primarily administrative rather than being a policymaking or decision-making function. The cashier is responsible for endorsing, depositing, and maintaining a record of cash receipts, and for reviewing disbursement authorizations, signing and distributing checks, and maintaining a record of cash disbursements. This function also encompasses the maintenance of banking arrangements for the organization.

The Financial Information System

This section reviews the basic accounting transactions reflecting the processing of information for financial management, describes the data content and organization of the financial accounting data base, and discusses and illustrates examples of manual and computer-based information systems for financial management. The systems illustrated are not those of any real organization, but are intended to be representative of financial information systems in general.

The accounting transactions

Numerous accounting transactions summarize the processing of data from which accounting information for financial management is generated. The most significant of these are reviewed here.

Cash receipts and disbursements   With respect to cash receipts, the primary accounting journal entry follows.

Cash	XXX	
Accounts Receivable		XXX

This summary entry is typically made daily for the complete batch of cash receipts processed during the day. Other miscellaneous accounts that reflect less regular sources of cash receipts include notes receivable, sales of fixed assets, and miscellaneous income from dividends, interest, or rentals.

The primary cash disbursement transactions are reflected by the following journal entry.

Accounts Payable	XXX	
Cash		XXX

This entry is also generally made each day to summarize the preparation and distribution of a batch of checks. Credits to accounts payable originate from purchases of inventory and fixed assets, and from the incurrence of costs and expenses.

Another cash disbursement transaction reflecting a high volume of individual transactions appears thus.

Wages and Salaries Payable	XXX	
Cash		XXX

The liability account is originated weekly or monthly as payrolls are processed, and represents the difference between gross pay and all deductions. The entry itself reflects the distribution of paychecks to employees.

A third cash disbursement entry that represents the most regularly recurring transaction with stockholders follows.

Dividends Payable	XXX	
Cash		XXX

The liability account itself is originated by debiting the Retained Earnings account. This transaction is generally executed quarterly and the entry summarizes the distribution of a batch of dividend checks to all stockholders. Most corporations utilize the services of a bank as transfer agent, which involves administering records of share transfers among stockholders. Many firms also have their transfer agent process dividend payments as well. Systems for administering capital stock records are not discussed further in this chapter.

Cost and expense distribution   Various accounting processes culminate in the recording of costs and expenses. A composite entry reflecting several of the most significant of these processes follows.

Manufacturing Overhead	XXX	
Selling Expense	XXX	
General and Administrative Expense	XXX	
Accounts Payable		XXX
Payroll		XXX
Accumulated Depreciation		XXX
Supplies		XXX
Accrued Expenses Payable		XXX
Allowance for Bad Debts		XXX

The accounts debited in the above composite entry are control accounts, each of which encompasses a large number of subsidiary cost and expense accounts. Examples of the subsidiary accounts include wages and salaries expense, depreciation, insurance, taxes, utilities, advertising, supplies, travel, and bad debts. These debits arise from several processes. Perhaps the primary source is the debit distribution generated from the daily preparation of disbursement vouchers, which establish and authorize payment of accounts payable. The debit distribution summarizes the accounts to which the total amount payable is apportioned. The payroll entry is made as payrolls are processed weekly or monthly. The debit to supplies expense and credit to supplies inventory is made as supplies requisitions are processed, but is subject to adjustment as periodic inventories of supplies are taken. The depreciation and accrual portions of the entry, including the estimate of bad debts expense, are generally made at the end of each month.

Fixed assets   The recording of fixed asset acquisitions is reflected by the following journal entry.

Fixed Assets	XXX	
Accounts Payable		XXX

If the asset is a very large purchase, the credit portion of the entry may be partly recorded to a long-term liability account. Very small asset purchases may simply be expensed for the sake of convenience. This entry generally arises as part of the debit distribution of accounts payable, as described above. The volume of such transactions is usually minimal in relation to other debits arising from accounts payable processing.

Financial statement preparation   Standard practice calls for most firms to prepare balance sheets and income statements monthly. Prior to this, a variety of *adjusting entries* must be made. These include accrual of expenses incurred but not yet paid, such as interest, wages and salaries, and utilities; expiration of prepaid expenses, such as depreciation, insurance, and supplies; accrual of revenue earned but not yet collected; recognition of the earned portion of revenues collected in advance; and other special entries such as adjustment of the inventory accounts to record the results of a physical inventory, or the elimination of profits and account balances arising from intercompany transactions. Following the preparation of financial statements, a series of *closing entries* are made. These reflect the zeroing out of all revenue and expense account balances and the transfer of the net credit or debit (net income or loss) to the retained earnings account.

The financial accounting data base

The overall structure of the financial accounting data base is illustrated in Fig. 20.2. The key master files in this data base are traditionally referred to as *ledgers;* this term is a carryover from manual systems in which these files are often maintained in bound ledger books. The *general ledger* is a master file in which a record is maintained for each and every account in the organization's accounting system. The key field for the general ledger consists of the account codes that comprise the chart of accounts, illustrated in Figs. 3.4, 3.5, and 3.6. A *subsidiary ledger* is a master file of accounting records for a specific category of accounts. The most significant subsidiary ledgers are accounts receivable; inventory including raw materials, work-in-process, and finished goods; fixed assets; accounts payable; manufacturing overhead; selling expense; and general and administrative expense.

The basic format of all ledger accounts is identical, whether they are maintained manually or by computer. Each contains a key field (account number), an account name, an account balance as of the beginning of the current period, and a current account balance. In addition, each contains an itemization of all transactions affecting the account during the current period. Each transaction contains a notation referencing a source document or journal. The classic example of this format is the "T-account" that should be very familiar to all accounting students. In this format, the transaction record is a repeating group within the ledger record, as reflected by the double arrows pointing to the transaction record from the ledger records in Fig. 20.2. Also indicated by Fig. 20.2 is the fact that each source document record may support one or more transaction records.

The relationship between general ledger records and subsidiary ledger records requires that for each subsidiary ledger there will be a single general ledger control account. The balance of the control account represents the sum total of the balances of all of the accounts in the subsidiary ledger. When a batch of transactions is recorded in a subsidiary ledger, the total amount of all those transactions is simultaneously recorded as a single transaction in the general ledger control account. For some general ledger accounts, such as cash, prepaid expenses, bonds payable, and retained earnings, there is no subsidiary ledger. Therefore, as implied by Fig. 20.2, transaction records affect these accounts directly rather than indirectly through a subsidiary ledger.

Several examples of subsidiary ledgers have been discussed and illustrated in previous chapters. For example, the finished goods inventory file and customer file discussed in Chapter 16 and illustrated in Fig. 16.7 are equivalent to a finished goods inventory ledger and accounts receivable ledger, respectively. Also, the raw materials inventory file and vendor file discussed in Chapter 17 and illustrated in Fig. 17.2 are equivalent to a raw materials inventory ledger and accounts payable ledger, respectively. Note that the data base structure corresponding to all four of those

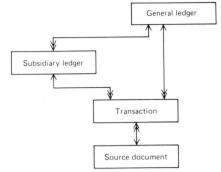

Fig. 20.2
*Structure of the fi-
nancial account-
ing data base.*

subsidiary ledgers is identical to the general structure shown in Fig. 20.2—that is, each subsidiary ledger record owns a series of transaction records, and each transaction record is related to a source document record. Also note, however, that each subsidiary ledger record format may go beyond the basic format described earlier to contain data fields unique to the particular entity, such as the customer credit rating or the inventory location code.

In manual accounting systems, all transactions are initially recorded in a *journal,* which lists the amounts debited or credited to each ledger account affected by each transaction. There are special journals for high volume transactions such as cash receipts, cash disbursements, purchases, and sales, as well as a general journal for all other transactions. One of the most time-consuming of accounting operations is the posting of transactions from journals to ledgers. However, note that in a data base system the input of a source document record into the system automatically results in the creation of a transaction record, and that each transaction record is automatically linked (or "posted") to the appropriate ledger record by virtue of the fact that it contains the appropriate account number. Thus in a data base system the need for a separate posting operation is eliminated, and the system no longer maintains journals. However, if desired for auditing purposes, a journal can be prepared from the transaction records stored in this system. For example, a cash receipts journal for October 13, 1983 might be generated using a command such as "PRINT ALL TRANSACTION RECORDS HAVING TRANSACTION CODE = CR AND DATE = 101383."

In manual accounting systems, ledger records are often maintained on specially formatted cards such as the materials ledger card illustrated in Fig. 17.3. Another example is provided by the fixed asset ledger card shown in Fig. 20.3. Processing of fixed asset transactions in both manual and computer-based systems is discussed later in this chapter. The basic input transactions include the purchase of new fixed assets, additions to or major repairs on existing assets, and disposal through sale or scrapping of existing assets. Records of accumulated depreciation for each asset are also commonly maintained on the ledger card. The fixed asset ledger is used as a basic reference for general accounting, capital budgeting, insurance administration,

PLANT AND EQUIPMENT HISTORY LEDGER		
Kelly Manufacturing Corp.	1234 Fifth St.	Albany, NY 12205

Item No. 6648	Serial No. 613440736	Dept. No. 407

DESCRIPTION	MANUFACTURER
IBM 4331 Processor, Model K2 Mainframe Memory–2 megabytes	IBM Corporation Data Processing Division 1133 Westchester Ave. White Plains, NY 10604

COST INFORMATION				RECORD OF IMPROVEMENTS		
Item	Date	Ref.	Amount	Date	Ref.	Amount
Acquisition	6/30/80	V-1089	$150,000 —			
Transportation In			—			
Installation Cost	6/30/80	V-1274	2,000 —			
Subtotal			$152,000 —			
Estimated Salvage Value			8,000 —			
Depreciable Cost			$144,000 —			

DEPRECIATION RECORD										
Year	1980	1981	1982	1983	1984	1985	1986	1987	1988	19__
Rate	25%×½	25%								
Beginning Balance	$144,000	$126,000								
Annual Depreciation	18,000	31,500								
Adjustments to Depr.	—	—								
Reserve Balance	18,000	49,500								
Net Book Value	134,000	102,500								

Fig. 20.3 Fixed asset ledger record.

and tax planning. Outputs that may be generated from the file of fixed asset ledger records include summary analyses of depreciation or asset cost by type of asset, by department, or by division.

The data content and organization of the manufacturing overhead ledger, the selling expense ledger, and the general and administrative expense ledger correspond almost directly to the basic format of all ledger accounts as described above. The beginning balance of all accounts in these ledgers is always zero because they are closed to the profit and loss summary at the end of each period. Little descriptive information other than an account title is included in these account records. Each transaction subrecord within each subsidiary account contains the transaction date, amount, and disbursement voucher or other source document reference number. The only difference between these ledgers lies in the type of accounts included in each. Constituting the manufacturing overhead ledger are such accounts as inspection, supervision, maintenance and other indirect labor, small tools, factory utilities, depreciation on plant and factory equipment, and so forth. The selling expense ledger is comprised of accounts for salaries and commissions of salespeople, salaries of sales supervisors and clerical staff, shipping expenses, depreciation of selling facilities and equipment, supplies, postage, advertising, travel, etc. The general and administrative expense ledger includes accounts for executive and clerical salaries, depreciation and rental of office facilities and equipment, supplies, postage, travel, contributions, and income taxes.

The cost and expense ledgers are updated for accounting transactions arising from accounts payable debit distribution, payroll processing, and depreciation, accruals, and other end-of-period adjustments. The most important reports generated from this file are departmental performance reports comparing the actual expenses incurred in each department, obtained from the ledger, with budgeted expenses, and perhaps also with expenses incurred for the same period in the previous year.

The data content and organization of the general ledger also corresponds to the universal ledger format described above. The inputs and outputs associated with the general ledger should be familiar to all accounting students. The inputs consist of debit and credit transactions recorded in journals or on journal vouchers (see Fig. 16.6). The primary outputs are the financial statements, including the balance sheet, income statement, and funds flow statement. For internal reporting purposes, financial statements for subsidiaries and divisions are also prepared, and these often include comparisons of current statement information with budgeted amounts.

Most modern organizations use budgeting in financial planning and control. This means that there must be a master file of budget information for each general ledger account, as well as for each cost and expense subsidiary account. There are several possible approaches. For example, budget data could be included within the general ledger records themselves, or could be contained on a separate master budget file. Each budget record could contain an estimate of the monthly increases and decreases in the account over the budget horizon, or could contain a formula by which such budget estimates could be computed. A commonly used formula for cost and expense accounts consists of an estimate of the fixed portion of the cost or expense for the period, plus the variable rate of the cost or expense, together with the base to which the rate is applied. For example, indirect labor for the assembly department might be budgeted at $1000 per month (the fixed portion) plus ten cents (the variable rate) per direct labor hour (the rate base). Therefore, the budget record for the indirect labor account would contain separate fields for the monthly fixed cost, the variable cost rate, and a code indicating the base to which the variable cost rate is applied.

The master budget is updated periodically to reflect current information with respect to budget estimates. Many reports for control purposes are generated as output of the master budget. Reports comparing actual and budgeted expenses by department and division are essential for performance evaluation and feedback to managers. Such reports are prepared monthly, quarterly, and annually. The master budget may also be used to generate cash flow budgets on a monthly basis.

Manual systems   Manual data processing systems for processing cash receipts and cash disbursements are described in this section and illustrated by means of document flowcharts. Brief descriptions of systems for maintaining the fixed asset ledger and the general ledger are also included. Emphasis is placed upon data flows and internal control provisions of these systems.

Cash receipts   Figure 20.4 illustrates the process of receiving payments on account for a typical manufacturing company. It is assumed that the company receives most such payments by check through the mail. These are opened in the mail room, where a list of all receipts in a batch is prepared, perhaps in the form of an adding machine tape. All checks are sent to the cashier's department for endorsement and deposit in the bank. The batch total accumulated in the mail room is used by the cashier's department as a check on the accuracy of the deposit. On the basis of the deposit, the cashier's department prepares a journal voucher debiting cash and crediting accounts receivable. This is sent to the general ledger section.

Enclosed with each customer's payment should be a *remittance advice,* which indicates the invoices, statement, or other items for which the payment is made. If most of its customers are small companies or individuals, a company should request that the customer return one copy of the invoice or statement with the payment, and this then serves as a remittance advice. Remittance advices are separated from checks in the mail room and sent in a batch to accounts receivable, where they are posted to individual accounts. At the completion of the posting process, a new balance of accounts receivable is calculated, and the total change in accounts receivable is determined. This total change is then compared by the general ledger section to the amount of the journal voucher from the cashier's department. If the two amounts do not agree, an error has occurred that must be discovered and corrected.

The accounts receivable clerk should periodically check the status of all open customer accounts. Any accounts for which payment is significantly past due should be brought to the attention of the manager of credit and collections. This information might be reported in the form of an aging schedule of all past due accounts. On the basis of this feedback, the manager of credit and collections may decline to provide further credit to these customers, and may also initiate special collection procedures. In the event that account write-offs become necessary, their initiation should occur in the credit department after all attempts to collect the account have proven unsuccessful. The credit department would prepare a journal voucher recording the debit to allowance for bad debts and the credit to accounts receivable for posting by the general ledger clerk. A copy of the write-off authorization would also be sent to the accounts receivable clerk for posting to the subsidiary ledger account.

The internal audit department plays an important role in the control of the cash receipts process. It receives a copy of the batch total of cash receipts from the mail room each day and a copy of each deposit slip. At the end of each month it receives a bank statement, on the basis of which it prepares a bank reconciliation. Part of the work involved in preparing the bank reconciliation will be to compare each batch

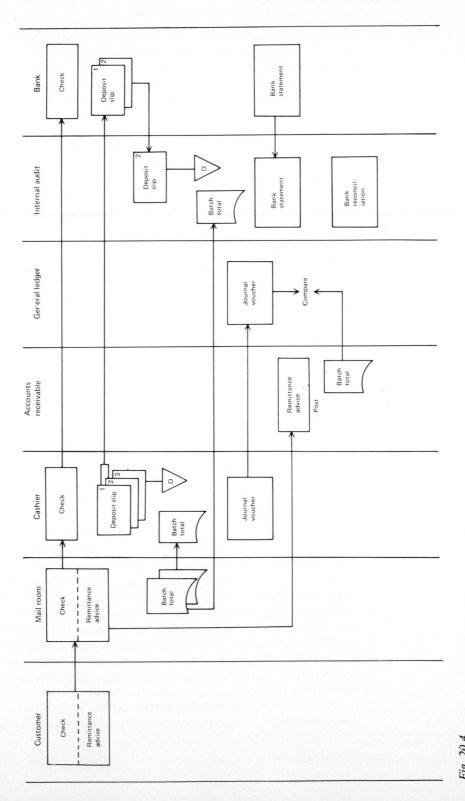

Fig. 20.4
Document flow in a manual system for processing cash receipts.

total with its corresponding deposit slip and bank statement entry. This check should reveal any errors or irregularities that occur after a proper batch total is accumulated in the mail room.

Organizational independence with respect to the cash receipts process is achieved by separation of the recording functions from the custodial function. Recording functions are performed by mail room personnel and by accounts receivable. The custodial function consists of the authority to endorse and deposit checks, which is the responsibility of the cashier. With respect to account writeoffs, separation of their authorization from the maintenance of the account records and the handling of cash receipts is essential. The independently performed functions of the internal auditor also impose a control check on the process. The batch total procedure and preparation of the bank reconciliation provide further control.

The establishment of procedures to control sales of merchandise for cash is a major concern of retail enterprises. The most critical point in the process from a control standpoint is the point of the transaction itself. Once the transaction is properly recorded, a firm basis for control has been established. Two factors are most useful in securing control at the point of the transaction itself. One is the use of cash registers, whose control features include a display window in which the amount rung up for a sale is shown, provision for issuing a receipt for each sale to the appropriate customer, and a locked-in paper tape record of each transaction. The second critical control factor is close supervision of personnel.

Many organizations use a form of internal check to control the cash sales process subsequent to the recording of the sale. Sales slips are prepared at the point of sale, and at the end of each day are processed in a batch to update sales records. A batch total of cash sales is obtained from this process. Also at the end of each day, cash from each register is collected and cash register tapes are used as a basis for preparing a deposit slip and a journal voucher to record the debit to cash and the credit to sales. The totals obtained from these two processes are then reconciled, with adjustments made for credit sales, payments by check, sales returns, and like factors. If a discrepancy exists, steps can be taken to discover and correct the error.

Cash disbursements   A document flowchart of a manual system for processing cash disbursements is illustrated in Fig. 20.5. The accounts payable department maintains a file of invoices approved for payment by due date of the invoice. Approval of invoices for payment is made by the accounts payable department for inventory purchases on the basis of purchase orders and receiving reports. For costs and expenses and fixed asset purchases, payment authorization may be provided by the signature on the invoice of the department head to whose department the cost, expense, or asset is charged. For each invoice, or each set of invoices from one vendor, which has been approved for payment, a *disbursement voucher* is prepared. The disbursement voucher, illustrated in Fig. 20.6, is simply an authorization to pay a vendor for the invoices and amounts shown on the voucher.

Three copies of each disbursement voucher are prepared for each approved invoice and filed by due date together with all supporting documents. At the same

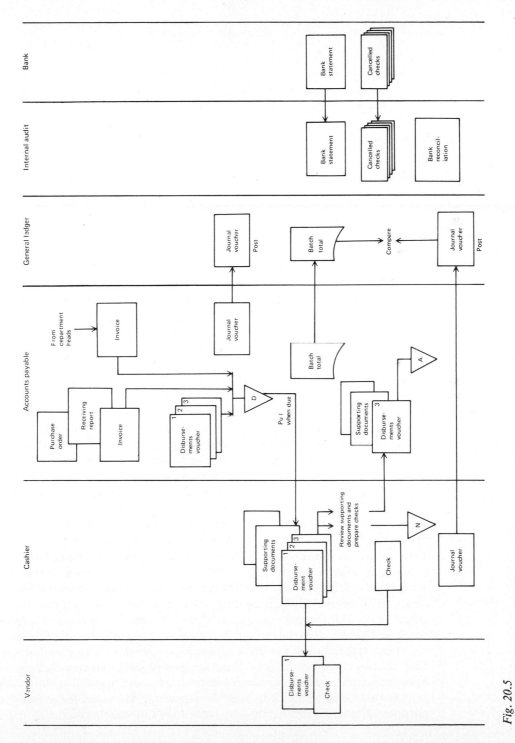

Fig. 20.5 Document flow in a manual system for processing cash disbursements.

Voucher No. 1623   THE NEEDMORE MANUFACTURING COMPANY
                          Needmore, Texas

Remit to: Avalon Electronics   Date entered:
              401 Cherry Street   5/14/73
              Waco, Texas 78123

Your invoice		Memo	Invoice Amount	Returns & allowances	Discount	Net remittance
Date	Number					

*Fig. 20.6
Disbursement
voucher.*

time, the accounts payable department prepares the debit distribution; this details the accounts to which all debits arising from recognition of accounts payable are charged. After the processing of each day's batch of vouchers is completed, the accounts payable department prepares a journal voucher summarizing the debit distribution and indicating the total credit to accounts payable. The journal voucher is provided to the general ledger clerk for posting to the general ledger and the cost and expense subsidiary ledgers.

Each day the file of vouchers payable on that day is pulled. A batch total of the net amount to be remitted is prepared, and the disbursement vouchers and all supporting documents are provided to the cashier. The supporting documentation for each voucher is reviewed by the cashier, who then prepares and signs a check in payment of the voucher. For control purposes, a second person, perhaps the treasurer, may also review supporting documents and countersign each check. All supporting documents should be stamped paid or otherwise clearly marked to preclude their reuse to authorize disbursements. The checks are then mailed out together with a copy of the voucher, which serves as a remittance advice. A second copy of the disbursement voucher is filed by the voucher number. The supporting documents, including the vendor invoice and, where applicable, the receiving report and purchase order, are attached to the other copy of the disbursement voucher and returned to the accounts payable department for filing in the alphabetical vendor file. The cashier also prepares for each daily batch of checks a journal voucher that reflects the debit to accounts payable and the credit to cash, and that is transmitted to the general ledger clerk. This journal voucher is checked against the batch total prepared by the accounts payable department and is then posted to the general ledger.

The preparation of the bank reconciliation by the internal auditors provides a final control check on the cash disbursements process. All cancelled checks should be examined to ascertain the date of endorsement and name of endorser. All checks paid should be accounted for as either cancelled, outstanding, or voided. For this purpose, of course, checks must be sequentially prenumbered.

Organizational independence with respect to the cash disbursements process is obtained by separation of the recording and authorization functions performed by the accounts payable department and the general ledger clerk from the custodial function of the cashier, under whose authority checks are prepared, signed, and distributed. Other control procedures that reinforce the effectiveness of this separation include periodic reconciliation of the accounts payable control account balance with the total of the vouchers awaiting payment; the batch total of vouchers due for payment each day, prepared before the vouchers are transmitted to the cashier and checked after all checks have been prepared and mailed against the resulting journal entry; dual signing of the checks; and the preparation of the bank reconciliation.

In many firms it is convenient to be able to make some small cash disbursements in cash rather than by check. In such cases, a petty cash fund may be established from which such disbursements can be made. Use of the "imprest" system for maintaining such funds provides control over the cash disbursed in this manner. Under this system, the amount of the fund is set at some specified amount, such as $100. A petty cash fund custodian is made solely responsible for the fund, and this person should not have any other cash handling or recording functions. The appointed individual must prepare a petty cash voucher for all disbursements made from the fund, and obtain the signature of the payee on each voucher. The fund custodian retains these vouchers so that at any given time the total amount of the vouchers plus the cash remaining in the fund should equal the total amount of the fund. The internal auditor may periodically make surprise counts of the fund to verify this condition.

When the amount of the petty cash fund is low, the fund custodian provides all petty cash vouchers to the accounts payable department. On the basis of these supporting documents, a disbursement voucher is prepared authorizing replenishment of the fund in the exact amount of the total of all the petty cash vouchers. The cashier then prepares and signs a check from this disbursement voucher to accomplish the replenishment. Petty cash vouchers must be marked paid at this time to prevent their reuse. Furthermore, the cashier should verify the unexpended balance of the fund at this time. The replenishment check should bring the fund balance up to its specified maximum level.

Fixed assets The primary procedures and controls in connection with accounting for fixed assets relate to the maintenance of the fixed asset ledger and the acquisition of new assets. In most firms this is a very small job requiring only a few minutes or hours each month. The paid disbursement vouchers and their supporting documentation provide source documents for the origination of asset records in the fixed asset ledger. This ledger is used for preparation and recording of depreciation. It may also be used to record appraisals for insurance purposes.

Control over the fixed assets themselves requires that the serial number and location of each asset be recorded in the fixed asset ledger. All transfers of an asset from one location to another should be authorized and documented, with the resulting documentation serving as a basis for recording such transfers in the fixed asset ledger. Periodically an inventory of fixed assets should be taken and the asset ledger adjusted if necessary. Reconciliation of the asset ledger to the fixed asset control account from time to time is also a necessary control procedure.

For control of fixed assets it is also essential that retirements of fixed assets be approved by a specified individual, and that a system exists to ensure prompt and accurate recording of such retirements. The journal voucher recording a sale or scrapping of an asset must be prepared with reference to the asset ledger to ensure proper recording of the gain or loss as well as removal of the cost and accumulated depreciation from the books.

Control procedures for fixed asset acquisition are also essential. Authorization for each asset purchase should be made by a designated manager on the basis of a request form that delineates the cost factors associated with the asset and the reasons for its purchase. Many firms utilize a system whereby asset purchases involving small amounts may be approved by lower-level managers, such as the general supervisor or director of sales, from their departmental capital expenditure budgets. Larger purchases require approval at higher levels, and very large purchases require the approval of the president and board of directors. Formal capital budgeting analysis, including cash flow projections and discounted present value calculations, should accompany these large proposals. Follow-up reports should be prepared on large projects to evaluate whether the expected results were actually achieved.

General ledger   This function primarily involves posting from journal vouchers, or from the general journal, to the general ledger accounts. Because the volume of work is typically quite small, this function is often combined with maintenance of the factory overhead ledger, the selling expense ledger, the general and administrative expense ledger, and the fixed asset ledger. Journal entries are generated from many different sources within the accounting department as by-products of almost all processing of accounting data. The general ledger clerk should check the equality of debits and credits for all journal entries prior to posting. At the end of each month, the general ledger clerk prepares and posts accrual and adjusting entries and prepares a post-closing trial balance to check the equality of debits and credits in the general ledger. All control accounts should be reconciled to the subsidiary ledgers at this time. Once any necessary corrections have been made, the closing entries are performed and the monthly financial statements are prepared.

Computer-based batch processing systems   This section describes and illustrates computer-based systems for batch processing of (1) cash receipts, (2) cash disbursements and accounts payable debit distribution, (3) fixed asset records, and (4) the general ledger. The systems described use magnetic tape input and maintain all master files on magnetic disk. System flows and controls are emphasized. The reader should find it interesting to examine the similarities and differences between these systems and their manual counterparts.

Cash receipts   Procedures for receipt of payments on account in a computer-based system would vary from those in a manual system only in that the data processing department would perform the function of posting payments to the accounts instead of the accounts receivable department. A systems flowchart of this process as performed by a data processing department appears in Fig. 20.7. Each day the process begins with assembly of remittances in batches and preparation of batch totals for control purposes by personnel in the mail room. The documents are then transmitted to the input preparation department, where they are keyed onto magnetic tape. The key-to-tape encoder may also be used to keyverify the records at this time. As described in examples in earlier chapters, alternative forms of input that are often used include punched cards, diskettes, and online data entry.

In many organizations, the remittance advice is a turnaround document—a punched card or OCR document sent to the customer as a bill or statement with the request that it be returned with the customer's payment (and not folded, spindled, or mutilated!). When the turnaround document and payment are received from the customer, the payment must be checked for agreement to the amount billed. If the payment and the amount billed agree, the turnaround document may be used as an input record with no additional keying of data. The use of turnaround documents not only speeds up the data entry process but also increases its accuracy because the data on the turnaround document are recorded automatically by the system as a byproduct of computerized billing or statement preparation. In order to speed up the file updating process, turnaround document records are often transferred from OCR documents or punched cards (slow input media) to magnetic tape (much faster) prior to being processed against the master file.

The next step in the process is to sort the magnetic tape records into sequence by customer account number, the key field for the accounts receivable master file. Since the accounts receivable master is on magnetic disk, this step could conceivably be skipped and the input records processed randomly, making use of the direct access feature of the disk. However, the activity ratio for cash receipts transactions is generally high enough so that it is more efficient to sort the records first and then process them sequentially.

After sorting, the remittance records are processed to update the accounts receivable master file. Each remittance is posted to its corresponding master record, and the current account balance in the record is reduced by the amount of the remittance. In addition to the updated version of the accounts receivable master, this run produces a printout of error transactions and summary information, including batch totals and the summary journal entry debiting cash and crediting accounts receivable; and a printed report projecting short-term cash inflows resulting from customer payments on account balances due. The latter report, useful to short-term cash management by the treasurer, would probably be generated only once a week, as shown, rather than once a day.

Internal control procedures instituted in this system should include (1) keyverification of critical data on remittance records, or alternatively the use of turnaround

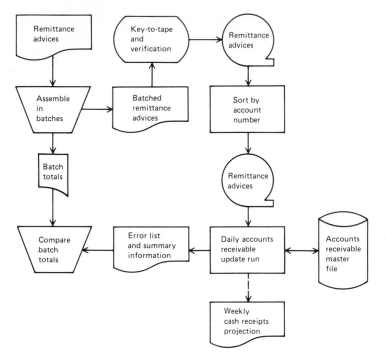

*Fig. 20.7
System flow in computerized batch processing of cash receipts.*

documents; (2) batch totals including a record count of remittances, a hash total of customer account numbers, and a financial total of remittance amounts; (3) data security provisions with respect to the transaction tape and master file disk pack, including the use of internal and external labels, offsite storage of a backup copy of the master file, and the use of a file library with controlled checkout procedures; and (4) an input validation routine in the main update program that performs such edit checks as a sequence check, field checks on all numeric data, validity check on account numbers, and a comparison of the amount remitted with the amount due. Furthermore, the batch totals on the error and summary printout must be compared with those generated prior to processing, and the error transactions themselves must be reviewed, corrected, and resubmitted as quickly as possible.

In retail firms, several techniques of source data automation may be applied to the recording of cash received over the counter. Some companies of this type attach to each inventory item a machine-readable tag containing stock number, cost, price, and other information. When a sale is made, the tag is removed and provided to data processing. Another possibility is the utilization of cash registers that produce a machine-readable record of each sale, usually in the form of punched paper tape or a magenetic tape cassette. Still another possibility is the use of an online point-of-sale recorder equipped with a wand that can interpret universal product code imprinted on price tags.

Cash disbursements   The basic difference between a manual and computerized cash disbursements system is generally the automation of accounts payable record keeping and of check preparation. A systems flowchart of this process as performed by computer appears in Fig. 20.8. Each day this process begins with the assembly of those vouchers that have been approved for payment in batches for keying onto tape. Batch totals that might be prepared at this time include a record count of the number of vouchers, a hash total of vendor numbers, and a financial total of the amount to be added to the accounts payable master.

Each disbursement voucher in this system would contain, in addition to the data shown on the sample voucher illustrated in Fig. 20.6, an indication of the account or accounts to which the amount of each voucher is to be charged. For all purchases of inventory, the appropriate account number is the same—the raw materials inventory account. For purchase of fixed assets or incurrence of costs and expenses, the appropriate account number or numbers are entered on the vendor invoice in the department in which payment of the invoice was authorized. These account numbers are then transcribed from invoice to voucher as the voucher is prepared. Keyed onto tape from each disbursement voucher are (1) a record of the payment authorization, which will be added to the total amount payable to the vendor in the accounts payable master file, and (2) one or more debit distribution records that indicate the ledger account or accounts to which each amount payable is to be charged. Thus the debit distribution records form a repeating group within each disbursement authorization record.

Once the disbursement transactions have been keyed onto magnetic tape, they must be sorted into sequential order by vendor account number prior to the main file update run. This step is performed by the computer under the control of a tape sort program. Next, the sorted transaction tape is processed as input to the accounts payable update run. This run adds each disbursement record to the corresponding accounts payable master record, and increases the total balance due in each master record by the amount of the authorized disbursement.

The accounts payable update run produces four outputs. First, the update program examines the due date of all items in the file, and prepares a check and remittance advice in payment of all due invoices, while simultaneously deleting these paid invoices from the master file record. The program also prepares a cash disbursement register, or check register (see Fig. 20.9), that is simply a listing of the check number, amount, vendor, and other relevant data from each check written. The check register is a key element of the audit trail for cash disbursements. In this system the check register is shown to be recorded on magnetic tape for subsequent conversion to a printed report. The third output is a magnetic tape file containing all of the debit distribution records; these will be processed as input to the general ledger in an operation described subsequently in this chapter. The other output of this run is a report listing error transactions and summary information. In addition to identifying disbursement transactions that do not pass field checks, validity checks, and other input validation tests, this report also lists any transactions for which the total of all debits in the debit distribution records is not equal to the total authorized disburse-

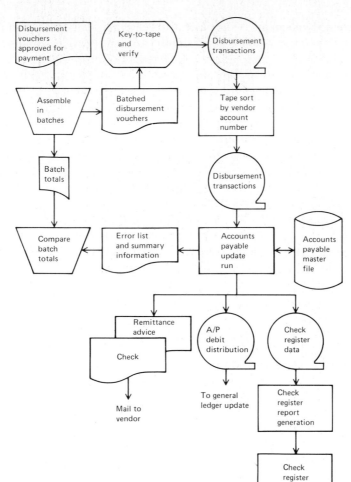

Fig. 20.8
System flow in computerized batch processing of accounts payable.

CASH DISBURSEMENTS REGISTER									
Date: Jan. 11, 1981									
Chk. No.	Vendor No.	Vendor Name	Account Payable dr.		Discount cr.		Cash cr.	
1045	63218	National Supply	$ 512	67	$ 10	25	$ 502	42
1046	17641	Ross Mfg.	$ 95	07	$	95	$ 94	12
1047	41524	Northern Metal Prod.	$ 742	72	$ 14	85	$ 727	87
1048	36602	Webster Bros.	$4,208	18	$ 84	16	$4,124	02

Fig. 20.9
Cash disbursements register.

ment according to the corresponding payment authorization record. The summary information includes an analysis of the accounts payable control account, including its beginning balance, total increases from newly authorized disbursements, total decreases from checks written, and ending balance.

In a fully integrated information system, the accounts payable master file would become part of a vendor master file, an example of which is shown in Fig. 17.2. As explained in Chapter 17 and illustrated in Fig. 17.9, two additional reports could be generated from such a file. These are a summary of cash flow commitments by due date, which would be generated weekly to assist financial executives in short-term cash management; and a vendor performance report prepared monthly or on demand to assist purchasing agents in vendor selection.

Several control procedures relating to this system have already been mentioned, including keyverification of critical input data from the disbursement vouchers, the use of batch totals, and the incorporation of input validation routines into the accounts payable update program. Also important are data security provisions with respect to the accounts payable master file and the various transaction files. The specifics of application of all of these control procedures should by now be familiar to the reader and are not elaborated on here.

Fixed assets   A systems flowchart of monthly batch processing of fixed asset records by computer appears in Fig. 20.10. Fixed asset transactions are of several different types, and may be recorded on various types of source documents. These transactions include new asset purchases, sales or scrappings of existing assets, location transfers, revisions to estimated useful life, major additions or writedowns, and several other kinds of adjustments. Even then, the monthly volume of these transactions is usually not great, and so it is assumed in the illustration that only one set of batch totals is prepared. Among the batch totals prepared would be a record count of the total number of transactions, record counts of the number of transactions of each type, a hash total of asset numbers, and a financial total of new asset purchases and other transactions affecting the dollar balance of the ledger records.

After batch totals are prepared, the fixed asset transactions are keyed onto tape and verified, and then are sorted by asset number for processing to update the fixed asset ledger. This main updating program must be written to identify the transaction code of each record and carry out the appropriate steps for each type of transaction. One output of this monthly run is simply a report listing the contents of the file for reference purposes. Another output is a tape listing of all depreciation charges and the overhead or expense account to which each is charged. This tape is sorted by account number and processed to update the general ledger in an operation described in the next section. The other output is a report listing error transactions and summary information, including batch totals and summary journal entry. If new asset purchases are recorded in the accounts payable debit distribution, this summary entry will record only the effects of such asset transactions as sales, writeoffs, or writedowns.

The batch totals on the summary printout must be compared to those accumulated prior to processing, and any errors revealed by this comparison or the error

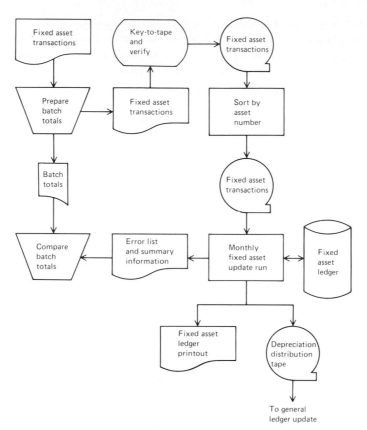

*Fig. 20.10
Computerized batch
processing of fixed
asset records.*

listing should be traced to their cause, corrected, and resubmitted to the system. Other internal control procedures in this system include keyverification of critical data on each transaction, data security provisions with respect to the fixed asset ledger file, and an input validation routine in the fixed asset update program. The input validation routine could be quite cumbersome in this program because a different set of edit checks must be used on each type of transaction, and there is a large variety of transaction types.

General ledger   In the manual system described earlier in this chapter, it is assumed that subsidiary ledgers for manufacturing overhead, selling expenses, and general and administrative expenses are maintained separately from the general ledger. This is done primarily for convenience and to permit clerical specialization. However, in a computerized system, integration of these subsidiary ledgers with the general ledger provides greater advantages than does maintaining them separately. The system described in this section therefore assumes that the general ledger contains all of the detailed cost and expense accounts.

The computerized general ledger may be updated several times during a month. The systems flow of this updating process, illustrated in Fig. 20.11, is actually a composite of updating processes that take place at different times and frequencies during a month. The accounts payable debit distribution tape, prepared as a by-product of daily input preparation for accounts payable processing (see Fig. 20.8), would be processed against the general ledger daily or weekly. The payroll distribution tape, a product of the processing of indirect factory labor and office payrolls, would be processed subsequent to each payroll operation, that might be weekly, bi-

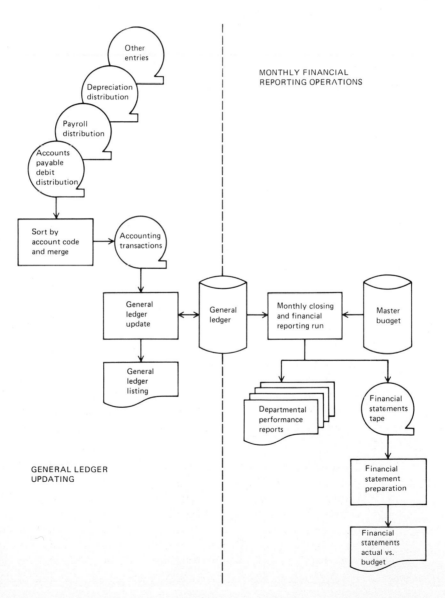

Fig. 20.11
Computerized batch
processing of general
ledger updates and
finanical reports.

weekly, or monthly. The depreciation distribution tape, an output of fixed asset processing (see Fig. 20.10), would be processed once a month following the fixed asset update run. Other entries include summary entries from various daily or weekly batch processes, which should be posted as they occur, and end-of-month accrual, adjusting, and miscellaneous entries. Once each week a printout of the general ledger is obtained for reference purposes.

At the end of each month, the master budget is processed with the final monthly version of the general ledger to prepare various financial reports. It is assumed that both of these files are sequenced by department number, which is the major key within the account number. This run generates departmental performance reports comparing actual and budgeted cost for all production departments, factory service departments, and selling and administrative units within the organization. An example of such a report is illustrated in Fig. 20.12. Reports aggregating these financial data for summarization of the performance of higher-level managers (see Fig. 2.5) cannot be printed in the same pass, but may be recorded on tape for subsequent printing. As an example, the financial statements, which aggregate data from all departments according to account codes, are shown to be recorded on tape as an output of this run, after which this tape is processed to print a report comparing projected and actual financial results. In addition to generating these various reports, the run closes all revenue and expense account balances to the retained earnings account and prepares a beginning general ledger for the next period.

In a fully integrated accounting information system in which the general ledger is maintained online at all times, it is possible to post almost all accounting transactions automatically to the appropriate general ledger accounts as a byproduct of other accounting operations. For example, as disbursement authorization transac-

Fig. 20.12
Cost performance report for a production department.

OPERATING PERFORMANCE SUMMARY					
Department: # 473 Machining				Supervisor Oscar Nagursky	
Cost element	Month ending 2/28/81			Year to date		
	Budget	Actual	Over (under) budget	Budget	Actual	Over (under) budget
Controllable overhead						
Indirect labor	$4,750	$4,608	$(142)	$9,300	$9,248	$(52)
Idle time	250	304	54	480	502	22
Tools and supplies	880	856	(24)	1,720	1,702	(18)
Maintenance	750	802	52	1,450	1,638	188
Rework	120	70	(50)	230	180	(50)
Miscellaneous	200	230	30	380	370	(10)
Total controllable overhead	$6,950	$6,870	$(80)	$13,560	$13,640	$80
Direct labor	$13,200	$13,256	$56	$26,000	$26,384	$384

tions are being processed to update the vendor (accounts payable) master file, the system could access the appropriate general ledger accounts randomly to post the debit distribution for each transaction. The total credit to accounts payable would be posted to the general ledger control account at the completion of processing. Similar general ledger posting subroutines could be incorporated into payroll processing, inventory processing, fixed asset processing, accounts receivable processing, and all other computerized accounting systems. Under this approach there would probably be a few transactions, such as capital transactions and month-end accruals, which would not originate from any other process and therefore would have to be prepared specifically for processing against the general ledger. Except for these few transactions, the need for frequent batch processing operations to update the general ledger would be eliminated by this technique. Furthermore, the general ledger account balances would be more current, which would make it more worthwhile for users to initiate online inquiries to the general ledger, or request reports from it on a demand basis.

Possible real-time applications

The processing of financial information is not a common area for application of real-time systems. This is true generally because decisions involving financial information do not require great speed. Perhaps the reason for this is that financial events are more predictable than are events involving production or marketing. Therefore, careful planning can be accomplished so that decisions can be effectively made in advance of events rather than immediately as events occur.

One possibly useful application of real-time systems to financial information involves inquiry processing. An online financial information system would enable immediate response to inquiries concerning comparisons of current expenditures with budgeted expenditures, up-to-date calculations of profit center contribution, or information required for audit investigations. Whether such responses would be needed immediately for effective decision making is another question.

If cash receipts processing is converted to an online basis, the keying of receipts data onto tape is replaced by the keying of receipts data into a terminal. Such a system would make the accounts receivable records only slightly more current than a batch processing system operating on a daily cycle. Similarly, conversion of cash disbursements processing to an online basis involves replacement of the keying of disbursement voucher records and debit distribution records by the keying of this data into a terminal. This system also fails to add much to the currency of payables and ledger account data. However, in both of these cases, savings would result from online verification of input data and from elimination of keyverification, sorting, and batch input operations.

One application of real-time systems to financial management that has great potential is the area of mathematical models for financial planning. Such models enable managers to experiment with alternative decisions or policies that are under consideration, with the model predicting the financial outcome of each alternative. The primary advantage of immediate response in a system of this sort is the capability of interaction with the model that is available to the system user. That is, upon receipts of a system response to a user experiment, the user may formulate a second experiment based upon the results of the first. This process may be continued through a series of many experiments. The real-time capability of the system therefore generates considerable savings in timeliness of information over the use of batch processing, in which each experiment in a series would require a separate computer run. As managers formulate and test possible decision alternatives, they receive continuous feedback from the model that guides their subsequent formulations. This process of interaction of the manager with the system enhances considerably the usefulness of both the system and the model.[2]

Review Questions

1. Define the following terms.

adjusting entries	subsidiary ledger
closing entries	journal
ledger	remittance advice
general ledger	disbursement voucher

2. Describe an example of an organization structure for the financial management function in a typical business organization. What are the primary decision responsibilities and information requirements of the financial management function?

3. What accounting journal entries summarize the data processing activities involved in
   a) cash receipts,
   b) cash disbursements,
   c) recording of overhead costs,
   d) recording of expenses,
   e) maintenance of fixed assets records, and
   f) financial statement preparation at the end of a month?

4. Describe the data content and organization of the financial accounting data base.

5. Describe the basic format of all accounting ledger records.

6. What should be the relationship between a general ledger control account and its corresponding subsidiary ledger? List some examples of accounts for which subsidiary ledgers are commonly maintained.

7. Explain how the use of a data base management system may eliminate the need for a separate posting operation in an accounting system.

8. What departments in a business organization might typically be involved in the manual processing (a) of cash receipts, and (b) of cash disbursements? In both cases what documents might be used and what reports generated? What data or information would each document or report contain? In what department would each document or report originate, and where and for what purpose would each be distributed?

---

[2] For further discussion of financial planning models, see George W. Gershefski, The Development and Application of a Corporate Financial Model. Oxford, Ohio: The Planning Executives Institute, 1968.

9. What control procedures might be used in manual processing of receipts of payments on account? How is organizational independence achieved with respect to this process?

10. What procedures might be a retail organization establish to record and control cash sales?

11. What means of automating the recording of transactions are available to retail organizations?

12. What control procedures might be used in manual processing of cash disbursements in a typical business organization? How is organizational independence achieved with respect to this process?

13. Describe the imprest petty cash system. Indicate in your description the most significant control procedures in the system.

14. Describe procedures and controls in manual systems in a typical business organization for maintenance of (a) fixed asset records, and (b) the general ledger.

15. Describe the similarities and differences in data flows and departmental functions between manual systems and computerized systems for processing of receipts of payments on account.

16. Describe and illustrate, using a systems flowchart, a computer-based batch processing system for processing of cash receipts. Describe several control policies and procedures appropriate for such a system.

17. Describe the similarities and differences in data flows and departmental functions between manual systems and computerized systems for processing cash disbursements.

18. Describe and illustrate, using a systems flowchart, a computer-based batch processing system for processing of cash disbursements. Describe several control policies and procedures appropriate for such a system.

19. Describe and illustrate, using a systems flowchart, a computer-based batch processing system for maintaining fixed asset records. Describe several control policies and procedures appropriate for such a system.

20. Describe and illustrate, using a systems flowchart, a computer-based batch processing system for maintaining general ledger records.

21. In a fully integrated accounting information system in which the general ledger is maintained online at all times, what advantages may be realized?

22. Why is the processing of financial information not a common area for application of real-time computer systems?

23. Describe the nature and possible uses of real-time systems for processing of financial information in a typical business organization.

Discussion Questions

24. Discuss the similarities and differences between business organizations and nonprofit organizations with respect to the design of financial information systems.

25. Cite as many examples as you can of information processing interfaces (or interactions) between two or more of the marketing, logistics, personnel, and financial information subsystems of a typical business organization.

26. Discuss the similarities and differences in the functions of a Treasurer and a Controller. Is there a need for both of these functional specializations to exist within a typical business organization, or could one executive effectively fill both roles?

27. Discuss the usefulness of incorporating a real-time capability into a mathematical modeling system used for financial planning.

Problems and Cases

28. Describe appropriate controls in a procedure for processing receipts of payments on account which would provide the best protection against the following contingencies.
    a) Theft of checks received through the mail by personnel in the mail room.
    b) An undetected error in posting from remittance advices to the accounts receivable ledger.
    c) Theft of funds by a cashier who, instead of endorsing checks received for deposit, cashes them and keeps the cash without recording its receipt.
    d) Covering up of defalcations of checks received by adjustments of the accounts receivable ledger.
    e) Theft of cash by sales personnel in a retail organization, covered up by failure to record cash sales.

29. Describe appropriate controls in a procedure for maintaining fixed asset records that would provide the best protection against the following contingencies.
    a) Acquisition of a fixed asset for which no worthwhile use exists within the firm.
    b) A department supervisor reports that an asset in the factory has been scrapped, when actually the supervisor had removed it and taken it home.
    c) A large overstatement of the fixed asset control account after several errors are made in updating the account over a period of years.
    d) Inaccurate charging of depreciation to departments because several items of equipment are no longer located in the departments for which they were originally acquired.
    e) Unauthorized sale of a fixed asset by an employee who retains the proceeds.
    f) Unauthorized use of a fixed asset by an employee for personal reasons unrelated to employment.
    g) Payment of insurance and property taxes on assets no longer owned by the company.
    h) Continued ownership of obsolete or otherwise nonproductive assets.

30. Describe appropriate internal controls in a cash disbursements procedure that would protect against the following contingencies.
    a) An employee writing a check payable to the employee or to a fictitious company.
    b) A large overstatement of the accounts payable control account due to several errors made in posting to the account over a period of time.
    c) Payment of a fictitious invoice for goods that were never delivered.

    d) Issuance of two checks in payment of two copies of the same vendor invoice.

    e) Overpayment of a vendor due to errors in the calculation of extensions on the vendor's invoice.

    f) Overpayment of a vendor due to the use of inaccurate item prices on a vendor invoice.

    g) "Borrowing" of a portion of the petty cash fund for personal use by the fund custodian.

31. Cash receipts in the Whirlaway Company are processed in the following manner. The cashier opens all mail containing customer payments and prepares a batch control tape of the total amount received that is sent to the general ledger clerk to support the appropriate journal entry. The cashier prepares two copies of a deposit slip, deposits the cash receipts in the bank, and files the bank-validated copy of the deposit slip by date. The cashier also sends the remittance advices to the accounts receivable clerk, where they are posted to customer accounts.

Assume that no other operations or personnel are involved in the processing of cash receipts. Prepare a document flowchart of the processing described above. Then identify several (at least three) deficiencies in internal control of the process, and for each deficiency describe an error, manipulation, or inefficiency that could occur as a result.

32. Your company has just acquired a data base management system, and one of the first applications of it will be to accounts payable and cash disbursements processing. A disbursement voucher form identical to that in Fig. 20.6 is used, and in addition the account number or numbers of the general ledger accounts to which the payment is distributed are printed on the face of each voucher. Diagram the data structure of the disbursement voucher as a first step in the application design. Use a format similar to those in Figs. 16.7 and 17.2. Note that the data base will contain only the variable data on the disbursement voucher, not the constant data.

33. You are auditing the Alaska Branch of Far Distributing Co. This branch has substantial annual sales which are billed and collected locally. As a part of your audit, you find that the procedures for handling cash receipts are as follows:

Cash collections on over-the-counter sales and COD sales are received from the customer or delivery service by the cashier. Upon receipt of cash, the cashier stamps the sales ticket "paid" and files a copy for future reference. The only record of COD sales is a copy of the sales ticket which is given to the cashier to hold until the cash is received from the delivery service.

Mail is opened by the secretary to the credit manager and remittances are given to the credit manager for review. The credit manager then places the remittances in a tray on the cashier's desk. At the daily deposit cut-off time the cashier delivers the checks and cash on hand to the assistant credit manager who prepares remittance lists and makes up the bank deposit that the manager also takes to the bank. The assistant credit manager also posts remittances to the accounts receivable ledger cards and verifies the cash discount allowable.

You also ascertain that the credit manager obtains approval from the executive office at Far Distributing Co., located in Chicago, to write off uncollectible accounts, and that the manager has retained in custody as of the end of the fiscal year some remittances that were received on various days during the last month.

Required

   a) Describe the irregularities that might occur under the procedures now in effect for handling cash collections and remittances.

   b) Give procedures that you would recommend to strengthen internal control over cash collections and remittances.[3]

34. The collection functions of the Robinson Company, a small paint manufacturer, are attended to by a receptionist, an accounts receivable clerk, and a cashier who also serves as a secretary. The company's paint products are sold to wholesalers and retail stores. The following describes all of the procedures performed by the employees of the Robinson Company pertaining to collections.

Since the Robinson Company is short of cash, the deposit of receipts is expedited. The receptionist turns over all mail receipts and related correspondence to the accounts receivable clerk who examines the checks and determines that the accompanying vouchers or correspondence contains enough detail to permit posting of the accounts. The accounts receivable clerk then endorses the checks and gives them to the cashier who prepares the daily deposit. No currency is received in the mail and no paint is sold over the counter at the factory.

The accounts receivable clerk uses the vouchers or correspondence that accompanied the checks to post the accounts receivable ledger cards. The bookkeeping machine prepares a cash receipts register as a carbon copy of the postings. Monthly the general ledger clerk summarizes the cash receipts register for posting to the general ledger accounts. The accounts receivable clerk also corresponds with customers about unauthorized deductions for discounts, freight or advertising allowances, returns, etc., and prepares the appropriate credit memos. Disputed items of large amount are turned over to the sales manager for settlement. Each month the accounts receivable clerk prepares a trial balance of the open accounts receivable and compares the resultant total with the general ledger control account for accounts receivable.

Required

Discuss the internal control weaknesses in the Robinson Company's procedures related to customer remittances and the accounting for these transactions. In your discussion, in addition to identifying the weaknesses, explain what could happen as a result of each weakness.[4]

35. The Rock Island Brewery has recently acquired a new disk memory device. Previously all files maintained by the company's computerized data processing center had been on magnetic tape. You are involved in designing a computer appli-

---

[3] *Question 1,* Auditing Section, American Institute of Certified Public Accountants Examination, *November 1962. Copyright © 1962 by the American Institute of Certified Public Accountants and reprinted with permission.*

[4] *Adapted from Question 4, Auditing Section,* American Institute of Certified Public Accountants Examination, *May 1965. Copyright © 1965 by the American Institute of Certified Public Accountants and reprinted with permission.*

cation that will process disbursement vouchers approved for payment and keyed onto magnetic tape. Following keyverification, these voucher records are then sorted by vendor account number and processed to update an accounts payable master file (maintained on magnetic tape) and a general ledger file (maintained on magnetic disk). Output of this processing run will include the updated versions of the two master files, a printed report containing error transactions and summary information, and a disbursements tape listing all voucher records for which payment is due. The disbursements tape is processed to generate (1) a remittance advice and check in payment of each voucher on the tape, and (2) a disbursements register, which is simply a printed list of all checks paid.

Required

a) Prepare a systems flowchart of the operations described above.

b) What is the minimum hardware configuration required to perform the processes above? (Assume no spooling.)

c) What are the advantages of storing the general ledger file on the disk unit? What would be the advantages of storing the accounts payable file on the disk unit?

36. The Darwin Department Store maintains its customer accounts by computer. Once each day all receipts of payments on account are processed to update an accounts receivable master file maintained on a disk storage unit. All nonroutine file changes and other adjustments to the accounts receivable master are also processed at the same time. All of the input data records are keypunched, after which the punched cards are processed by a utility routine to transfer their contents to magnetic tape. The records on tape are then sorted and processed sequentially to update the accounts receivable master. The tape sort requires four tape drives. Output of the updating run includes (1) a printed report listing error transactions and summary information, and (2) a printed report listing the records of all past due accounts.

Required

a) What data should be included on each cash receipt input record?

b) Give two specific examples of the "nonroutine file changes and other adjustments" mentioned above.

c) Prepare a systems flowchart of all computer processes described above.

d) List the components of the hardware configuration necessary to accomplish all phases of the processing described in the case subsequent to keypunching. (Assume no spooling.)

e) Describe a comprehensive set of control policies and procedures for this accounts receivable application. For each policy or procedure, indicate the objective and exact method of operation. Be sure to relate each policy or procedure specifically to the accounts receivable processing system described above.

37. The Able Manufacturing Company maintains a master budget file on magnetic tape. At the end of each month this file is processed by computer together with a manufacturing overhead ledger, also maintained on magnetic tape, to generate performance reports for all production departments. The format of each such report is identical to that shown in Fig. 20.12, except that direct labor costs are not included in the report.

The budgeted amount of each cost element for the current month is computed as $(a + bx)$, where a is the fixed amount of that cost element per month, b is the variable rate of that cost element, and x is the value of the base to which the variable rate is applied. The rate base for each cost element is one of three different rate bases used, which are direct labor cost, direct labor hours, and machine hours. The value of each of these three bases for the current month is entered into the system at the beginning of processing.

Required   What specific data elements must be included in each overhead cost record of (a) the master budget, and (b) the manufacturing overhead ledger, in order for these files to be used as described above in generating performance reports for production departments?

38. Culp Electronics Company processes disbursement authorizations online as vendor invoices are matched with receiving reports, purchase orders, and other supporting documents in the accounting department. Each disbursement authorization is entered via a data terminal and processed to update the accounts payable master file. The debit portion of the entry is processed to update either (1) the inventory ledger, (2) the expense ledger, or (3) the fixed asset ledger, depending on what the disbursement is for.

For each disbursement authorization relating to an inventory purchase, the following data are entered: the vendor account number; amount due; discount rate; due date; and, for each item purchased, the part number, price, and quantity.

Required   Consider only disbursement authorizations relating to inventory purchases as described. Describe several means by which the system could be programmed to check the accuracy and validity of the input data. Relate your answer specifically to the data items mentioned above.

References   Bierman, Harold, Jr., and Seymour Smidt. *The Capital Budgeting Decision* (5th ed.). New York: Macmillan, 1980.

Hill, Dan J., and Garold L. Rutherford. "Computerized Financial Data Reporting System." *Management Accounting* (July 1976): 57–60.

Lubas, Daniel P. "Developing a Computerized General Ledger System." *Management Accounting* (May 1976): 53–56.

Morley, James E., Jr. "Cash Management–Working for the Extra 1% or 2%." *Management Accounting* (October 1978): 17–22.

Page, John R., and H. Paul Hooper. *Accounting and Information Systems.* Reston, Virginia: Reston Publishing, 1979.

Price Waterhouse & Co. *Guide to Accounting Controls—Financial Reporting.* New York: Price Waterhouse & Co., 1979.

_____. *Guide to Accounting Controls—Productive Assets.* New York: Price Waterhouse & Co., 1979.

_____. *Guide to Accounting Controls—Financial Management.* New York: Price Waterhouse & Co., 1979.

Schall, Lawrence D., and Charles W. Haley. *Introduction to Financial Management* (2nd ed.). New York: McGraw-Hill, 1980.

Volk, Douglas A. "Managing Accounts Receivables—Systematically." *Management Accounting* (July 1980): 46–51.

Welsch, Glenn A., and Robert N. Anthony. *Fundamentals of Financial Accounting* (Revised ed.). Homewood, Ill.: Irwin, 1977.

Index

Numerals in italics indicate references to illustrations.